JUDICIAL LAW-MAKING IN ENGLISH AND GERMAN COURTS

JUDICIAL LAW-MAKING IN ENGLISH AND GERMAN COURTS

Techniques and Limits of Statutory Interpretation

Martin Brenncke

Cambridge – Antwerp – Chicago

Intersentia Ltd
Sheraton House | Castle Park
Cambridge | CB3 0AX | United Kingdom
Tel.: +44 1223 370 170 | Fax: +44 1223 370 169
Email: mail@intersentia.co.uk
www.intersentia.com | www.intersentia.co.uk

Distribution for the UK and Ireland:
NBN International
Airport Business Centre, 10 Thornbury Road
Plymouth, PL6 7PP
United Kingdom
Tel.: +44 1752 202 301 | Fax: +44 1752 202 331
Email: orders@nbninternational.com

Distribution for Europe and all other countries:
Intersentia Publishing nv
Groenstraat 31
2640 Mortsel
Belgium
Tel.: +32 3 680 15 50 | Fax: +32 3 658 71 21
Email: mail@intersentia.be

Distribution for the USA and Canada:
Independent Publishers Group
Order Department
814 North Franklin Street
Chicago, IL 60610
USA
Tel.: +1 800 888 4741 (toll free) | Fax: +1 312 337 5985
Email: orders@ipgbook.com

Judicial Law-Making in English and German Courts. Techniques and Limits of Statutory Interpretation
© Martin Brenncke 2018

The author has asserted the right under the Copyright, Designs and Patents Act 1988, to be identified as author of this work.

No part of this book may be reproduced, stored in a retrieval system, or transmitted, in any form, or by any means, without prior written permission from Intersentia, or as expressly permitted by law or under the terms agreed with the appropriate reprographic rights organisation. Enquiries concerning reproduction which may not be covered by the above should be addressed to Intersentia at the address above.

Artwork on cover: © Praveetha Patalay, Flags

ISBN 978-1-78068-269-3
D/2018/7849/94
NUR 820

British Library Cataloguing in Publication Data. A catalogue record for this book is available from the British Library.

For Praveetha

FOREWORD

In Western democracies like Germany and the United Kingdom, the legal product of the democratic process is legislation. Legislation has to be read, understood and applied by a wide range of people. These include individual citizens, legal advisers, administrators and judges. When disputes arise, it is judges in courts who produce the authoritative final reading. But in doing that they have regard to how others are likely to have understood a statute. They also try to make sense of the legislation in the context of a range of other norms and values. Because legislation is everywhere and intrudes upon almost every legal relationship, statutory interpretation makes up a large part of what judges do and is one of the most important aspects of their work.

Working from the inside as a judge, the exercise of interpretation often feels more like an art than a science, even though one often feels a strong implicit sense of how to proceed. Yet the desirability of predictability in the application of law, which is inherent in the ideal of the rule of law, seems to demand that an objective science of interpretation be articulated and applied. Every legal system has to address the gap between the abstract statement of a law laid down in advance and its application to the facts of a particular case. There is no simple metric for weighing the relative normative force of different factors which may be relevant to giving determinate meaning to a statutory provision in its application to specific facts. Values of justice and reasonableness can operate as rather vague guides for how that gap is to be bridged. So can constitutional principles or a sense of hierarchy between norms bearing on the same subject matter as is addressed in the statute. Courts have to face up to the tension between positive statements of law in legislation and the pull of natural justice in spelling out the precise content of the legislative norm which they will identify as applicable to determine the dispute before them.

In the final analysis, it is the legal culture in a jurisdiction, generated within that jurisdiction's political and constitutional structures, which constrains judges in how far they feel able to go in imaginative interpretation of legislation. The ability of judges to give persuasive reasons for adopting one interpretation in preference to another is critical to the legitimacy of what they do. So some articulation of principle is required alongside the practice of interpretation, or as an inherent part of it. As Dr Brenncke explains, the use of determinate interpretative limits and techniques are important for reasons of legal certainty, upholding the proper separation of powers between judiciary and legislature and for the maintenance of public confidence in the judiciary. His book makes an important and sophisticated contribution to this endeavour, showing where lessons might be learned across the jurisdictional divide.

This book is a valuable study of how two jurisdictions approach the task of statutory interpretation in a complex and multivalent constitutional environment. It is the product of considerable scholarship across the two jurisdictions and a fine sensitivity to the various factors and different theoretical dimensions which inform the interpretative exercise. The exposition is clear. The argument is forceful. As with all the best works of comparative law, one reads this book and learns as much about one's own legal system as about the system with which it is compared.

As someone familiar with the English part of the comparison, I can attest that Dr Brenncke has a fine in-depth understanding of the processes of statutory interpretation used in the English courts. The detail of his exposition of the position in Germany shows that he has no lesser understanding of such processes in that jurisdiction. This makes him a guide to be listened to with attention.

Dr Brenncke's important theme is judicial law-making inherent in the process of statutory interpretation, and in particular the outer limits of what courts regard themselves as authorised to do in that regard. He rightly locates the practice of statutory interpretation in its constitutional setting in each jurisdiction. This important theoretical underpinning for what happens in judicial practice on the ground is sometimes obscured. The comparative approach reminds us of its importance and brings it to the fore. In Dr Brenncke's penetrating discussion, the practice of statutory interpretation becomes the basis for insights about the constitutional environment in both jurisdictions. Exploration of the outer boundaries of permissible judicial interpretations of legislation is a powerful way of tracing the practical implications of constitutional principles.

By comparing Germany and the United Kingdom (in particular, England & Wales) using his detailed methodology, Dr Brenncke moves beyond the abstract platitudes one often finds in works which compare and emphasise the contrasts between civilian and common law jurisdictions. He reveals that there is a considerable degree of similarity in the approach of English and German judges to the practice of statutory interpretation.

That is especially so where important norms exterior to a statute have to be brought into account when reading the statute, in relation to the production of rights-consistent interpretations which take due account of specified human rights and interpretations which are required to conform, so far as possible, with EU law under the *Marleasing*[1] principle. As Dr Brenncke points out, these interpretative obligations operate in tension with the desideratum of legal

---

[1] Case C-106/89, *Marleasing*, ECLI:EU:C:1990:395.

certainty in giving meaning to legislation; but if that value is given undue weight it would undermine the values which are served by those obligations and would reduce the effectiveness of human rights norms and of EU Directives. As he also observes, both approaches are likely to remain significant in English law after Brexit, notwithstanding the uncertainty as we write regarding the details of the post-Brexit settlement.

Rights-consistent statutory interpretation and interpretation in conformity with EU law are areas in which the constitutional settings in Germany and the United Kingdom have converged. The shift has been more marked for the United Kingdom, as a simple model of parliamentary sovereignty (with its own, relatively simple interpretative practice) has been replaced by a much more modulated model, which allows for the intrusion of different and competing constitutional values to a significant degree. Statutory interpretation in the United Kingdom has become more constitutionalised. The balance between will and reason, which is inherent in constitutional law and in the practice of statutory interpretation, has moved in the direction of reason. The simple statement of democratic will in the text of a statute has increasingly come to be read through the prism of constitutional reason. Nowadays, statutory meaning is derived less so by reference to simple textual analysis of what the legislating Parliament said, and increasingly by reference to an objective conception of meaning achieved through purposive interpretation and standards of reasonableness. Going still further beyond this, in relation to human rights and EU law the meaning of a statute is often the product of the judges' integration of the statutory text with human rights and EU norms. As Dr Brenncke says, the approach to interpretation becomes more result-driven (to identify what is the best rights- or EU law-compatible meaning which can be given to a statute) rather than process-driven (focusing on the process by which the statute came into existence). This is an intellectual process with which German courts have long been familiar through their own experience of the practice of statutory interpretation through integration with binding higher norms set out in Germany's constitutional Basic Law. It is fascinating to see how close interpretative practices have become in the two jurisdictions. Dr Brenncke's account bears out the impression I have obtained from discussion with German judges.

However, significant differences of approach remain, as Dr Brenncke is careful to acknowledge. Ordinary, conventional statutory interpretation is not so closely aligned in the two jurisdictions: see the discussion in Chapter 2. Again, I think he is right to trace the differences back to the respective constitutional contexts and the associated legal cultures in the two jurisdictions. The roots of the difference go back very far, reflecting the long parliamentary tradition in the United Kingdom. Franz Neumann, writing in the 1930s, observed that in the British doctrine of the Rule of Law associated with Dicey "the centre of gravity lies in the determination of the content of the laws by Parliament", while the German theory of the Rechtsstaat as developed in the 19th century "is uninterested in the genesis of the law, and is immediately concerned with the interpretation of a positive law, somehow and somewhere arisen"; "The German theory is liberal-constitutional; the English, democratic-constitutional."[2] No doubt the German approach has now become more interested in the democratic genesis of the law, as Dr Brenncke explains. But British statutory interpretation remains primarily concerned with identifying the meaning of legislation as intended by the enacting Parliament, while the German conception of "objectivised intention" looks more to giving sense to legislation as read in the light of the current function it is taken to fulfil and of values at the time of its application in the present. The British doctrine of treating a statute as "always speaking" is not the same. As Dr Brenncke observes, this doctrine operates to help identify the intention of the legislating Parliament; it does not justify a court in departing from that intention.

This book reveals how German and British judges in many ways think in similar legal categories and engage in similar interpretative practices, participating in a real sense in a common European legal culture. It also shows how the openness and flexibility of the English common law and parliamentary tradition, with both its positive and its negative aspects, still remains distinct from the civilian tradition and the German approach to legal science and interpretation in important respects.

Philip Sales
Lord Justice of Appeal,
England & Wales

---

[2] F. NEUMANN, *The Rule of Law: Political Theory and the Legal System in Modern Society*, [1935–], Berg, Leamington Spa 1986, p. 185.

PREFACE

Judicial Law-Making in English and German Courts addresses the often neglected relationship between statutory interpretation and constitutional law. The book is concerned with the limits of judicial power in a legal system. Judicial law-making occurs when judges restrict or extend the scope of application of a provision beyond or against the possible semantic meanings of the statutory language. How far do contemporary English and German judges go when they interpret national legislation? Where are the limits of statutory interpretation when judges venture outside the constraints of the text? Do these limits converge or diverge in both jurisdictions? The book critically analyses, reconstructs and compares judicial law-making in English and German courts from comparative, methodological and constitutional perspectives. It maps the differences and commonalities in both jurisdictions and then offers explanatory accounts for these differences and similarities based on constitutional, institutional, political, historical, cultural and international factors.

This book is addressed to a wide audience. It mainly appeals to an academic readership interested in the fields of statutory interpretation, legal methodology, constitutional law and comparative law. Practitioners in either jurisdiction will find it to be an accessible source of reference as this book reconstructs the fragmentary material on conventional, rights-consistent and EU-conforming judicial law-making in judicial opinions in English and German courts into a rational, coherent and systematic whole. Students of legal skills, constitutional law and comparative law will also find it a useful source of reference.

With regard to terminology, I use the term "case law" in a broad sense, meaning rulings of courts. The term "legislation" is solely used in this book to mean enacted law. "English courts" refers to the courts of England and Wales, and "English law" refers to the law applicable in England and Wales. The term "UK constitutional law" is used to refer to the constitutional law applicable in England. The term "provision" in this book refers to a specific section or part of a section either in primary or delegated legislation. "Construction" and "interpretation" are used interchangeably. All translations from German judgments are my own. Citations of German judgments do not link to the official reports as these are not available online, but rather to law journals where the judgments are published in full (these are available online via Beck-Online). Case law and literature are included up to 30 April 2018; Brexit-related legislation and legislative materials are included up to 1 August 2018.

Preface

I am immensely indebted to Rolf Sethe, Jens Scherpe and Matthias Lehmann, who have provided support and guidance since the initial stages of my career and of this book. My particular thanks go to colleagues who have read and provided helpful comments on full chapters of this book, Frances Burton, Ryan Murphy and Gayatri Patel, and to colleagues who have provided helpful feedback on specific parts of this book, James Brown, Andrea Dolcetti, Binesh Hass, Pieter Koornhof, Kristie Thomas and Stephen Weatherill. I owe a special debt to Binesh Hass and Pradeep Patalay. Both of them shouldered the arduous task of checking the language in the manuscript. I am very grateful to the team at Intersentia, especially Ann-Christin Maak-Scherpe for her help, encouragement and lots of patience and Rebecca Moffat for an excellent job in seeing the book through production.

I want to thank the universities where I was based while working on this book: the University of Zurich, the University of Oxford and Aston University. I am also grateful to the universities and institutes where I held visiting positions during this period: the British Institute of International and Comparative Law, the University of Cambridge, the Institute of Advanced Legal Studies and the Max Planck Institute for Comparative and International Private Law. Special thanks are due to the Fritz Thyssen Stiftung für Wissenschaftsförderung and the Deutsch-Britische Juristenvereinigung for funding my visiting fellowship at the British Institute of International and Comparative Law.

Last but not least, I would like to acknowledge the immense patience and support shown by my family and friends while I worked on this book.

Martin Brenncke
June 2018

CONTENTS

Foreword vii
Preface xi
List of Cases xvii
List of Abbreviations xxxi

Chapter 1. Introduction 1
1. The Neglected Comparative Constitutional Law Perspective 3
2. Key Findings 10
   2.1. Conventional Judicial Law-Making 12
   2.2. Rights-Consistent Judicial Law-Making 15
   2.3. The European Legal Duty of Conforming Interpretation 20
   2.4. The New Legal Duty of Conforming Interpretation after Brexit 26
   2.5. Trends and Convergence in Judicial Law-Making 26
3. (Ir)relevance of Limits and Techniques of Interpretation 28
4. Method and Scope of the Book 41

Chapter 2. Conventional Canons of Statutory Interpretation 49
1. Aim of Statutory Interpretation 49
2. The Interpretative Criteria and Their Weighing 54
   2.1. Interpretation in a Narrow Sense (*Auslegung*) ... 54
   2.2. Canons of Interpretation in England 58
   2.3. Comparative Analysis 66
3. Gap-Filling in Germany 68
   3.1. Judicial Law-Making *Praeter Legem* 72
   3.2. Judicial Law-Making *Extra Legem* 78
   3.3. Constitutionalising the Limits of Statutory Interpretation 86
      3.3.1. Common Limits, Different Application 87
      3.3.2. The Recognised Methods of Statutory Interpretation 91
      3.3.3. The Standard of Constitutional Review: Reasonableness 94
      3.3.4. Towards a Stricter Understanding of the Constitutional Limits of Interpretation 96
4. Reading In, Out or Down of Words in Legislation in England 102
   4.1. Literal Rule and the Doctrine of Parliamentary Sovereignty 103
   4.2. From Literalism to Purposivism 106

	4.3.	Saving Statutes from Absurdity 114
	4.4.	Correcting Obvious Drafting Errors 115
	4.5.	Updating Interpretation 119
5.	Comparative Analysis 125

Chapter 3. Rights-Consistent Interpretation 139

1. Introduction 142
   1.1. Constitution-Consistent Interpretation 142
   1.2. Section 3(1) Human Rights Act 144
2. Aim of Rights-Consistent Interpretation 151
3. Relationship with Conventional Canons of Interpretation 154
4. Interpretative Priority 158
5. Presumption of Compliance 159
6. Techniques of Judicial Law-Making 165
   6.1. Gap-Filling 165
   6.2. Reading In, Out or Down of Words in Legislation 166
   6.3. Comparative Analysis 173
7. Outer Interpretative Limits 179
   7.1. Constitution-Consistent Interpretation 179
   7.2. Section 3(1) Human Rights Act 188
        7.2.1. Statutory Language 189
        7.2.2. Intention of Parliament and Purpose of the Legislation 197
        7.2.3. Fundamental Features of the Legislation 208
        7.2.4. Scheme, Grain and Thrust of the Legislation 213
        7.2.5. Policy Choices and Issues Calling for Legislative
               Deliberation 216
   7.3. Comparative Analysis 223
        7.3.1. Wide Powers of Rights-Consistent Judicial Law-Making ... 225
        7.3.2. High Level of Congruence 228
        7.3.3. The Constitutional Law Perspective 234
        7.3.4. Formalism 235
        7.3.5. Evaluative Arguments 237
        7.3.6. Legal (Un)certainty 242
        7.3.7. Convergence of Judicial Reasoning 245
8. A Look into the Future: A UK Bill of Rights? 246

Chapter 4. The European Legal Duty of Conforming Interpretation 257

1. The European Dimension 260
   1.1. Scope of the EU Legal Duty of Conforming Interpretation 261
   1.2. Functions of Conforming Interpretation 265
   1.3. Principle of Equivalence 269

		1.4.	European Methodological Rules 270

- 1.4. European Methodological Rules 270
    - 1.4.1. Interpretative Priority of the Conforming Meaning 272
    - 1.4.2. Presumption of Compliance 272
    - 1.4.3. Relationship with National Legal Methodologies. 275
- 1.5. The *Contra Legem* Limit 277
2. Aim of Conforming Interpretation 279
3. Relationship with Other National Canons of Interpretation 288
    - 3.1. Interpretative Structure 288
    - 3.2. Conventional Limits of Judicial Law-Making 291
        - 3.2.1. Rejection of a "Europeanisation from the Inside" in Germany 292
        - 3.2.2. Endorsement of a "Europeanisation from the Inside" in England 295
        - 3.2.3. Comparative Analysis. 309
    - 3.3. Analogy to Rights-Consistent Interpretation. 311
        - 3.3.1. Constitution-Consistent Interpretation in Germany 311
        - 3.3.2. Section 3(1) Human Rights Act in England 313
        - 3.3.3. Comparative Analysis. 316
4. Interpretative Priority in National Courts. 318
5. Presumption of Compliance in National Courts 319
    - 5.1. The Presumption Rule in German Courts 319
    - 5.2. The Presumption Rule in English Courts 322
    - 5.3. Comparative Analysis 331
6. Techniques of Judicial Law-Making. 332
    - 6.1. Gap-Filling 332
        - 6.1.1. Legislation Adopted for the Purpose of Transposing a Directive 332
        - 6.1.2. Non-Implementing Legislation that Precedes a Directive 338
    - 6.2. Reading In, Out or Down of Words in Legislation 343
    - 6.3. Comparative Analysis 345
7. Outer Interpretative Limits 347
    - 7.1. Limits of Conforming Judicial Law-Making in Germany 348
    - 7.2. Limits of Conforming Judicial Law-Making in England 358
        - 7.2.1. Intention of the Enacting Parliament 359
        - 7.2.2. Statutory Language 368
        - 7.2.3. Scheme and Fundamental Features of the Legislation. 372
        - 7.2.4. Unsettled Outer Limits of Conforming Interpretation 374
    - 7.3. Comparative Analysis 380
        - 7.3.1. Development Towards Converging Outer Limits of Conforming Judicial Law-Making 381
        - 7.3.2. Evaluative Arguments and Judicial Discretion 385
        - 7.3.3. Judicial Attitudes and the Stretching of the Outer Interpretative Limits 387

		7.3.4. Adaptability of the Outer Interpretative Limits 392
		7.3.5. Legal (Un)certainty. 393
8.	A Look into the Future: Brexit 396
	8.1.	Retained EU Law 398
	8.2.	The Principle of the Supremacy of EU Law 401
	8.3.	The New Legal Duty of Conforming Interpretation 406
	8.4.	Interpretation of Retained EU Law 413
	8.5.	Transition Period 420

Chapter 5. Conclusion 423

Index. 433
About the Author. 437

LIST OF CASES

COURT OF JUSTICE OF THE EUROPEAN UNION*

Case 11/70, *Internationale Handelsgesellschaft*, ECLI:EU:C:1970:114 361
Case 43/75, *Defrenne v. Sabena*, ECLI:EU:C:1976:56 305
Case 33/76, *Rewe-Zentralfinanz eG and Rewe-Zentral AG
  v. Landwirtschaftskammer für das Saarland*, ECLI:EU:C:1976:188 311
Case 106/77, *Amministrazione delle Finanze dello Stato v. Simmenthal*,
  ECLI:EU:C:1978:49 361
Case 148/78, *Ratti*, ECLI:EU:C:1979:110 262
Case 61/81, *Commission v. United Kingdom*, ECLI:EU:C:1982:258 295
Case 14/83, *von Colson and Kamann v. Land Nordrhein-Westfalen*,
  ECLI:EU:C:1984:153 ....260, 263, 304
Case 79/83, *Harz v. Deutsche Tradax*, ECLI:EU:C:1984:155 ....263, 304
Case 143/83, *European Commission v. Denmark*, ECLI:EU:C:1985:34................ 395
Case 152/84, *Marshall v. Southampton and South West Hampshire AHA*,
  ECLI:EU:C:1986:84 ....262, 283, 312
Case C-106/89, *Marleasing v. La Comercial Internacional de Alimentación*,
  ECLI:EU:C:1990:395 .... 257, 261,
                                                                        277, 285, 303–304
Case C-91/92, *Faccini Dori v. Recreb Srl*, ECLI:EU:C:1994:292..............261–262, 313
Case C-334/92, *Wagner Miret v. Fondo de Garantía Salarial*,
  ECLI:EU:C:1993:945 .... 261, 272–274, 330
Case C-421/92, *Habermann-Beltermann v. Arbeiterwohlfahrt*, ECLI:EU:C:1994:187.... 263
Case C-31/93, *Webb v. EMO Air Cargo (UK) Ltd*, ECLI:EU:C:1994:300 284
Case C-63/93, *Duff v. Minister for Agriculture and Food and Attorney General*,
  ECLI:EU:C:1996:51 394
Case C-74/95, *Criminal proceedings against X*, ECLI:EU:C:1996:491..............264, 396
Case C-168/95, *Criminal proceedings against Arcaro*, ECLI:EU:C:1996:363.... 262, 264, 396
Case C-129/96, *Inter-Environnement Wallonie*, ECLI:EU:C:1997:628 265
Case C-197/96, *Commission v. France*, ECLI:EU:C:1997:155 267
Case C-111/97, *EvoBus Austria v. Niederösterreichische Verkehrsorganisations
  Gesellschaft mbH*, ECLI:EU:C:1998:434 260
Case C-78/98, *Preston v. Wolverhampton Healthcare NHS Trust*,
  ECLI:EU:C:2000:247 311
Case C-240/98, *Océano Grupo Editorial v. Roció Murciano Quintero*,
  ECLI:EU:C:2000:346 ....261, 263, 272
Case C-443/98, *Unilever Italia v. Central Food*, ECLI:EU:C:2000:496 262
Case C-456/98, *Centrosteel Srl v. Adipol GmbH*, ECLI:EU:C:2000:402................ 261

---

*   Cases arranged chronologically.

List of Cases

Case C-144/99, *Commission v. Netherlands*, ECLI:EU:C:2001:257 267
Case C-481/99, *Heininger v. Bayerische Hypo- und Vereinsbank AG*,
    ECLI:EU:C:2001:684 .... 294, 341
Case C-62/00, *Marks & Spencer plc. v. Commissioners of Customs and Excise*,
    ECLI:EU:C:2002:435 261
Case C-397/01, *Pfeiffer v. Deutsches Rotes Kreuz*, ECLI:EU:C:2004:584 ...... 257, 261–262,
                                                    266, 269, 272–273, 300, 386, 412
Case C-371/02, *Björnekulla Fruktindustrier v. Procordia Food*,
    ECLI:EU:C:2004:275 .... 257, 261, 274
Case C-235/03, *QDQ Media v. Alejandro Omedas Lecha*, ECLI:EU:C:2005:147 277
Case C-144/04, *Mangold v. Helm*, ECLI:EU:C:2005:709 .... 262, 265
Case C-212/04, *Adeneler et al. v. Ellinikos Organismos Galaktos*,
    ECLI:EU:C:2006:443 .... 257, 261–262, 264–266,
                                                                    272, 276–277, 300
Case C-268/06, *Impact v. Minister for Agriculture and Food and others*,
    ECLI:EU:C:2008:223 .... 262, 276–277, 394
Case C-308/06, *Intertanko v. Secretary of State for Transport*, ECLI:EU:C:2008:312 394
Case C-350/06, *Schultz-Hoff v. Deutsche Rentenversicherung Bund*,
    ECLI:EU:C:2009:18 341
Case C-404/06, *Quelle v. Bundesverband der Verbraucherzentralen und
    Verbraucherverbände*, ECLI:EU:C:2008:231 .... 293, 341–342
Case C-237/07, *Janecek v. Freistaat Bayern*, ECLI:EU:C:2008:447 .... 262, 268
Case C-378/07, *Angelidaki and Others v. Organismos Nomarkhiaki
    Aftodiikisi Rethimnis*, ECLI:EU:C:2009:250 .... 261, 264–265, 276–277
Case C-414/07, *Magoora v. Dyrektor Izby Skarbowej w Krakowie*,
    ECLI:EU:C:2008:766 .... 257, 272
Case C-555/07, *Kücükdeveci v. Swedex*, ECLI:EU:C:2010:21 257
Case C-12/08, *Mono Car Styling v. Dervis Odemis*, ECLI:EU:C:2009:466 .... 257, 262,
                                                                    269, 276–277, 394
Case C-63/08, *Pontin v. T-Comalux*, ECLI:EU:C:2009:666 311
Case C-201/08, *Planatol v. Hauptzollamt Darmstadt*, ECLI:EU:C:2009:539 394
Case C-305/08, *CoNISMa v. Regione Marche*, ECLI:EU:2009:807 .... 257, 272
Cases C-403/08 and C-429/08, *Football Association Premier League Ltd.
    et al. v. QC Leisure et al.*, ECLI:EU:C:2011:631 327
Opinion 1/09, *European Patent Court*, ECLI:EU:C:2011:123 386
Case C-65/09, *Gebr. Weber GmbH v. Wittmer*, ECLI:EU:C:2011:396 334
Case C-429/09, *Fuß v. Stadt Halle*, ECLI:EU:C:2010:717 312
Case C-53/10, *Land Hessen v. Franz Müksch OHG*, ECLI:EU:C:2011:585 264
Case C-214/10, *KHS AG v. Schulte*, ECLI:EU:C:2011:761 355
Case C-282/10, *Dominguez v. Centre informatique du Centre Ouest
    Atlantique*, ECLI:EU:C:2012:33 .... 262–263, 266–267
Case C-621/10, *Balkan and Sea Properties v. Direktor na Direktsia
    "Obzhalvane i upravlenie na izpalnenieto"*, ECLI:EU:C:2012:248 263
Case C-7/11, *Criminal proceedings against Caronna*, ECLI:EU:C:2012:396 257
Case C-61/11 PPU, *Hassen El Dridi*, ECLI:EU:C:2011:268 312
Case C-97/11, *Amia v. Provincia Regionale di Palermo*, ECLI:EU:C:2012:306 ..... 263, 266
Cases C-359/11 and C-400/11, *Schulz and Egbringhoff*, ECLI:EU:C:2014:2317 356
Case C-124/12, *AES-3C Maritza East 1 EOOD v. Direktor na Direktsia "Obzhalvane
    i upravlenie na izpalnenieto" pri Tsentralno upravlenie na Natsionalnata agentsia
    za prihodite, Plovdiv*, ECLI:EU:C:2013:488 263

Case C-142/12, *Marinov v. Direktor na Direktsia "Obzhalvane i upravlenie na izpalnenieto"*, ECLI:EU:C:2013:292 263
Case C-176/12, *Association de médiation sociale v. Union locale des syndicats CGT*, ECLI:EU:C:2014:2 278
Case C-209/12, *Endress v. Allianz*, ECLI:EU:C:2013:864 .... 321, 351
Case C-306/12, *Spedition Welter v. Avanssur*, ECLI:EU:C:2013:650 ..... 257, 263, 278, 393
Case C-539/12, *Lock v. British Gas Trading Ltd.*, ECLI:EU:C:2014:351 325
Case C-404/13, *ClientEarth v. Secretary of State for the Environment, Food and Rural Affairs*, ECLI:EU:C:2013:805 .... 262, 268
Case C-395/14, *Vodafone GmbH v. Bundesrepublik Deutschland*, ECLI:EU:C:2016:9. ... 337
Case C-441/14, *Dansk Industri (DI) v. Estate of Karsten Eigil Rasmussen*, ECLI:EU:C:2016:278 262
Case C-46/15, *Ambisig v. AICP*, ECLI:EU:C:2016:530 .... 263, 267
Case C-64/15, *BP Europa v. Hauptzollamt Hamburg-Stadt*, ECLI:EU:C:2016:62 .... 269, 358, 386
Case C-187/15, *Pöpperl v. Land Nordrhein-Westfalen*, ECLI:EU:C:2016:550 263
Case C-231/15, *Prezes Urzędu Komunikacji Elektronicznej and Petrotel v. Polkomtel*, ECLI:EU:C:2016:769 394

GERMANY

BAG, *EuZW* 2009, 465 (*Schultz-Hoff*) 54, 86, 262, 279, 289, 311, 319, 340–341, 348–349, 387
BAG, *NJW* 1970, 725 142
BAG, *NJW* 2003, 2473 .... 55, 72, 75
BAG, *NJW* 2006, 3161 .... 349, 353
BAG, *NJW* 2010, 557 352
BAG, *NJW* 2012, 3529 355
BAG, *NJW* 2014, 956 .... 72–73, 75, 354
BAG, *NZA* 2003, 742 .... 39, 261, 311, 318, 347, 352, 393
BAG, *NZA* 2004, 375 .... 342, 393
BAG, *NZA* 2005, 420 .... 54, 69, 75
BAG, *NZA* 2006, 862 .... 262, 289, 311, 318, 349, 352
BAG, *NZA* 2007, 751 72–73
BAG, *NZA* 2009, 378 262
BAG, *NZA* 2009, 1020 273
BAG, *NZA* 2010, 227 186
BAG, *NZA* 2010, 1020 (*Urlaubsentgelt*) 54–55, 174, 262, 268, 276, 280, 339–340, 342
BAG, *NZA* 2012, 514 355
BAG, *NZA-RR* 2013, 515 .... 54, 71

BGH, *BeckRS* 2012, 16505 230
BGH, *GRUR* 2002, 238 72
BGH, *NJW* 1952, 337 68
BGH, *NJW* 1953, 780 77–78
BGH, *NJW* 1954, 1153 68
BGH, *NJW* 1955, 1276 (*Tonband*) 58, 68, 73, 75, 92–93

List of Cases

BGH, *NJW* 1955, 1433 (*Fotokopie*) 58, 73–74, 92
BGH, *NJW* 1958, 827 (*Herrenreiter*) 80
BGH, *NJW* 1963, 902 (*Fernsehansagerin*) 58, 73, 79–81
BGH, *NJW* 1967, 343 .... 49, 51, 56–58
BGH, *NJW* 1969, 98 222
BGH, *NJW* 1970, 2017 222
BGH, *NJW* 1975, 213 .... 279, 319
BGH, *NJW* 1981, 1726 .... 55, 73
BGH, *NJW* 1988, 2109 .... 72, 78, 85
BGH, *NJW* 1994, 457 58
BGH, *NJW* 2000, 521 (*Heininger I*) 294, 341
BGH, *NJW* 2002, 1881 (*Heininger II*) 294, 341
BGH, *NJW* 2003, 1032 (*Macrotron*) 77
BGH, *NJW* 2006, 2997 75
BGH, *NJW* 2006, 3200 (*Quelle I*) 292, 341, 352
BGH, *NJW* 2007, 992 .... 78, 85
BGH, *NJW* 2007, 2419 (*Rügeverkümmerung*) 82
BGH, *NJW* 2008, 2257 .... 72, 75
BGH, *NJW* 2008, 3213 (*Dreiteilungsmethode*) 96
BGH, *NJW* 2009, 427 (*Quelle II*) 54, 57, 71, 261,
    279, 292–293, 310, 319, 332,
    334, 342, 347, 348–350, 353, 393
BGH, *NJW* 2009, 1962 (*Schiedsfähigkeit II*) 30, 188
BGH, *NJW* 2012, 1073 (*Weber II*) 71, 261, 279,
    292, 310, 319, 321,
    334–335, 349–350, 393
BGH, *NJW* 2012, 2422 265
BGH, *NJW* 2013, 2674 (*Interprofessionelle Sozietät*) 49, 51, 55–56,
    230, 273, 280, 289,
    292, 338, 342, 352
BGH, *NJW* 2014, 146 (*FRoSTA*) 77
BGH, *NJW* 2014, 2646 (*Lebensversicherung II*) 99, 238, 272, 279,
    290, 292, 321–322,
    327, 335–336, 349, 353
BGH, *NJW* 2015, 1023 (*Lebensversicherung im Antragsmodell*) 351
BGH, *NJW* 2015, 3511 (*Elektronische Leseplätze II*) 338
BGH, *NJW* 2016, 1718 (*Gasversorgung II*) 71, 99, 349, 356–357
BGH, *NJW* 2017, 1093 .... 57, 319, 349–350
BGH, *NJW* 2017, 2123 68
BGH, *NJW* 2017, 2842 238
BGH, *NJW* 2017, 3387 342
BGH, *NVwZ* 2014, 1111 .... 45, 87
BGH, *ZUM* 2010, 429 (*Bob Dylan (No. 2)*) 292, 338, 349

BVerfG, *BeckRS* 2016, 47202 .... 68, 231
BVerfG, *BeckRS* 2017, 136546 318
BVerfG, *BeckRS* 2018, 11032 57
BVerfG, decision of 16.2.2012, no. 1 BvR 127/10 94
BVerfG, *FamRZ* 2015, 1263 140
BVerfG, judgment of 31.20.2016, no. 1 BvR 871/13 46

BVerfG, *NJW* 1953, 1057. 143
BVerfG, *NJW* 1954, 65. 70
BVerfG, *NJW* 1958, 257 (*Lüth*). 161
BVerfG, *NJW* 1958, 1227. . . . . .87, 158, 180, 184
BVerfG, *NJW* 1958, 1388. 142
BVerfG, *NJW* 1958, 2059. . . . . 86, 183
BVerfG, *NJW* 1959, 1123. . . . . .158, 179–180
BVerfG, *NJW* 1960, 1563. . . . . 49, 51–53, 56, 58
BVerfG, *NJW* 1962, 1715. . . . . 55, 68
BVerfG, *NJW* 1964, 1563. 183
BVerfG, *NJW* 1965, 1427. . . . . .142, 158, 161
BVerfG, *NJW* 1966, 243. 166
BVerfG, *NJW* 1972, 25. 160
BVerfG, *NJW* 1972, 1123. 158
BVerfG, *NJW* 1972, 1934. 179
BVerfG, *NJW* 1973, 1221 (*Soraya*). 31, 58, 69, 73, 78–79,
81–82, 84, 86, 88, 222, 238
BVerfG, *NJW* 1973, 1491. . . . . 55–56, 68,
86–87, 142, 155, 158, 160
BVerfG, *NJW* 1975, 1355. . . . . 86, 158
BVerfG, *NJW* 1978, 2499. . . . . 86, 87
BVerfG, *NJW* 1979, 151. . . . . 35, 37, 143, 158, 180
BVerfG, *NJW* 1979, 305 (*Sachverständigenhaftung*) 36, 68, 87–88, 126
BVerfG, *NJW* 1979, 534. 161
BVerfG, *NJW* 1979, 1925. 37
BVerfG, *NJW* 1980, 2179. 143
BVerfG, *NJW* 1981, 39. . . . . .57, 87, 183
BVerfG, *NJW* 1982, 1375. 179–180
BVerfG, *NJW* 1982, 1509. 180
BVerfG, *NJW* 1983, 735. 52
BVerfG, *NJW* 1983, 2811. 158
BVerfG, *NJW* 1984, 475 (*Sozialplan*). 55, 69, 85, 101
BVerfG, *NJW* 1985, 1519. . . . . .143, 180
BVerfG, *NJW* 1985, 2315. . . . . .142, 179, 183
BVerfG, *NJW* 1985, 2395. 86
BVerfG, *NJW* 1985, 2939. 69
BVerfG, *NJW* 1986, 1672. 87
BVerfG, *NJW* 1987, 2427. 140
BVerfG, *NJW* 1988, 125. 142
BVerfG, *NJW* 1988, 1902. 87
BVerfG, *NJW* 1990, 1593. . . . . 3–4, 31, 35, 58,
69, 73–75, 81, 87, 90,
94–95, 126, 226, 238
BVerfG, *NJW* 1991, 1807. 143
BVerfG, *NJW* 1991, 2549. . . . . .41, 79, 89
BVerfG, *NJW* 1992, 890 (*Eilversammlungen*). 180–181, 184
BVerfG, *NJW* 1992, 1219. 92
BVerfG, *NJW* 1992, 2947. . . . . .143, 158
BVerfG, *NJW* 1993, 996. . . . . 79, 94
BVerfG, *NJW* 1993, 1379 (*Streikeinsatz von Beamten*) 89

BVerfG, *NJW* 1993, 2861... 55, 72–73, 75,
91, 142–143, 158, 165, 179
BVerfG, *NJW* 1994, 2475..87, 143, 183
BVerfG, *NJW* 1995, 1141.. 88
BVerfG, *NJW* 1997, 386... 30
BVerfG, *NJW* 1998, 519 (*Kind als Schaden*)............................. 6, 49, 58, 73,
81, 86–87, 91, 109, 383
BVerfG, *NJW* 1998, 1478...55, 142
BVerfG, *NJW* 1998, 1699.. 143
BVerfG, *NJW* 1998, 2269...71, 73, 88
BVerfG, *NJW* 1998, 3033.. 183
BVerfG, *NJW* 1999, 1853...183, 348
BVerfG, *NJW* 2000, 55.. 179
BVerfG, *NJW* 2000, 347.. 86, 98, 158, 179, 183
BVerfG, *NJW* 2000, 1175.. 179
BVerfG, *NJW* 2002, 1779...44, 51, 56, 68, 88
BVerfG, *NJW* 2003, 2520..88–89
BVerfG, *NJW* 2004, 750..57, 87, 126
BVerfG, *NJW* 2004, 1305 (*Geldwäsche durch Strafverteidiger*)................ 142–143,
160, 165, 179, 183
BVerfG, *NJW* 2004, 3407 (*Görgülü*)..140
BVerfG, *NJW* 2005, 126..35–37, 58
BVerfG, *NJW* 2005, 1923.. 158
BVerfG, *NJW* 2006, 3340..87, 126
BVerfG, *NJW* 2006, 3409 (*Marlene Dietrich*).............................. 31, 73–74,
86–87, 91–92, 101, 230, 238
BVerfG, *NJW* 2007, 2977 (*Strafzumessung durch Revisionsgerichte*)........87, 98, 143, 183
BVerfG, *NJW* 2008, 2409... 70
BVerfG, *NJW* 2009, 499.. 98
BVerfG, *NJW* 2009, 1469 (*Rügeverkümmerung*)...................... 6, 41, 58, 79, 83,
86–88, 90–91, 94, 96, 100, 136
BVerfG, *NJW* 2011, 819.. 96
BVerfG, *NJW* 2011, 842 (*Dreiteilungsmethode*).......................... 6, 57, 86–87,
91, 96–99, 101, 348
BVerfG, *NJW* 2011, 1723...73, 87, 94, 98
BVerfG, *NJW* 2012, 669... 35, 39, 45, 94, 294,
311, 318–319, 347–350, 393
BVerfG, *NJW* 2012, 2639..88–89
BVerfG, *NJW* 2012, 3081 (*Delisting*)............................. 49, 55, 57, 73, 77,
86–87, 91, 94–95, 98–99, 348
BVerfG, *NJW* 2013, 1058 (*Deal im Strafprozess*)................ 49, 51, 56, 58, 68, 87, 90
BVerfG, *NJW* 2014, 1874 (*Flashmob*)... 78
BVerfG, *NJW* 2015, 1294.. 342
BVerfG, *NJW* 2015, 1359 (*Kopftuch*)................... 58, 140, 155, 183, 185–186, 188
BVerfG, *NJW* 2015, 1506 (*Scheinvater*)...88–89
BVerfG, *NJW* 2015, 2549... 44
BVerfG, *NJW* 2015, 2949..94, 158, 160
BVerfG, *NJW-RR* 2016, 1366 .... 6, 35, 49, 86–87,
91, 94, 98–99, 101, 136, 261,
294, 319, 336, 347, 350, 393

BVerfG, *NVwZ* 1996, 574 ....91, 158, 180
BVerfG, *NVwZ* 2009, 1484 89
BVerfG, *NVwZ* 2010, 373 92
BVerfG, *NVwZ* 2015, 510 ....57–58, 142, 165, 179, 183–184
BVerfG, *NVwZ* 2017, 617 70
BVerfG, *NZA* 2015, 375...294
BVerfG, *NZA* 2015, 1117...79
BVerfG, *NZS* 2011, 18 ....94, 96
BVerfG, *NZS* 2011, 895 89
BVerfG, *NZS* 2015, 502 ....73, 89
BVerfG, *WM* 2017, 154, 155...86

BVerwG, *BeckRS* 2017, 103948.................................. 45, 322, 337–338, 353
BVerwG, *DVBl* 2004, 1379 45
BVerwG, judgment of 29.1.2004, no. 3 C 39.03 ....261, 291, 318
BVerwG, judgment of 10.08.2016, no. 1 B 82/16 (1 PKH 76.16)..................... 87
BVerwG, *NJW* 1964, 1586...142
BVerwG, *NJW* 2005, 1293... 73
BVerwG, *NVwZ* 1997, 384...142, 161
BVerwG, *NVwZ* 1998, 60... 184
BVerwG, *NVwZ* 2002, 858... 318
BVerwG, *NVwZ* 2003, 986... 88
BVerwG, *NVwZ* 2014, 1586...292, 337

LG Hamburg, decision of 1.2.1988, no. 11 S 398/87 74

UNITED KINGDOM

9 Cornwall Crescent London Ltd. v. Kensington and Chelsea RLBC
  [2005] EWCA Civ 324.. 60
A v. BBC [2014] UKSC 25... 156
Abley v. Dale (1851) 11 Common Bench Reports 378 106
Adler v. George [1964] 2 QB 7 (CA)...114
Advocate General for Scotland v. MacDonald [2003] UKHL 34...................... 53
Ahmed and others v. HM Treasury [2010] UKSC 2 .... 153, 190,
                                                                      201, 248, 250
Airtours Holidays Transport v. Revenue and Customs Commissioners
  [2016] UKSC 21 ....282, 348
Alderson v. Secretary of State for Trade and Industry [2003] EWCA Civ 1767......300, 318
Anisminic v. Foreign Compensation Commission [1969] 2 AC 147 (HL) 251, 255
AS (Somalia) v. Secretary of State for the Home Department [2009] UKHL 32 .....193, 196
Assange v. Swedish Prosecution Authority [2012] UKSC 22 .... 65, 299,
                                                                      314, 323, 372, 374
Associated Newspapers Ltd. v. Wilson [1995] 2 AC 454 (HL).....................62, 104
Attorney General's Reference (No. 4 of 2002) [2004] UKHL 43.................. 144, 153,
                                                                      169, 172, 197–198
Attorney-General v. Prince Ernest Augustus of Hanover [1957] AC 436 (HL) 52, 63, 273
Attorney-General v. Sillem (1864) 2 H & C 431 106

List of Cases

Austin v. Mayor and Burgesses of the London Borough of Southwark
  [2010] UKSC 28 417
AXA General Insurance Ltd. v. Lord Advocate [2011] UKSC 46 .... 110, 125, 248, 256
Axa UK Plc. v. Revenue and Customs Commissioners [2011] EWCA Civ 1607 322
B (a child) v. DPP [2000] 2 AC 428 (HL) 4
B (Algeria) v. Secretary of State for the Home Department [2018] UKSC 5 251
B v. Auckland District Law Society [2003] UKPC 38 200
Bear Scotland Ltd. v. Fulton [2015] ICR 221 322
Bearmans Ltd. v. Metropolitan Police District Receiver [1961] 1 WLR 634 (CA) 60
Bellinger v. Bellinger [2003] UKHL 21 .... 188, 218–219
Benkharbouche v. Embassy of Sudan [2014] ICR 169 223
Benkharbouche v. Embassy of Sudan [2015] EWCA Civ 33 .... 145, 210, 223, 373
Birmingham City Council v. Doherty [2008] UKHL 57 191
Birmingham Hippodrome Theatre Trust Ltd. v. Revenue and Customs
  Commissioners [2014] EWCA Civ 684 .... 285, 345
Black-Clawson International v. Papierwerke Waldhof-Aschaffenburg
  [1975] AC 591 (HL) 35, 51–52, 68,
                                                                 99, 103–104, 132, 134
Blackwood v. Birmingham and Solihull Mental Health NHS
  Foundation Trust [2016] EWCA Civ 607 .... 45, 290, 359, 373
Bloomsbury International Ltd. v. Sea Fish Industry Authority [2011] UKSC 25 ...... 60, 62
Bogdanic v. The Secretary of State for the Home Department
  [2014] EWHC 2872 (QB) 44, 102
Brent LBC v. Risk Management Partners Ltd. [2011] UKSC 7 323
British Airways plc. v. Williams [2012] UKSC 43 323
British Gas Trading Ltd. v. Lock [2016] EWCA Civ 983 .... 258, 261, 274,
                                                              290, 314, 323, 325–326, 344,
                                                                 348, 363–364, 374–375
Cachia v. Faluyi [2001] EWCA Civ 998 156
Carter v. Bradbeer [1975] 1 WLR 1204 (HL) 61, 63, 106
Cartier International AG v. British Sky Broadcasting Ltd. [2014] EWHC 3354 281
Cartier International AG v. British Sky Broadcasting Ltd.
  [2016] EWCA Civ 658 .... 290, 299
Cheng v. Governor of Pentonville Prison [1973] AC 931 (HL) 61–62
Churchill Insurance Co. Ltd. v. Fitzgerald & Wilkinson
  [2012] EWCA Civ 1166 .... 45, 189, 201, 215–216,
                                                                 285, 299, 314, 323,
                                                                 345, 368, 370, 372–374
Clark & Tokeley Ltd. (t/a Spellbrook) v. Oakes [1999] ICR 276 (CA) 60
Clarke v. Kato [1998] 1 WLR 1647 (HL) 102, 289, 308
Cooper v. HM Attorney General [2010] EWCA Civ 464 347
Crook v. Edmondson [1966] 2 QB 81 (CA) 128
Cutler v. Wandsworth Stadium Ltd. [1949] AC 398 (HL) 108
Dabas v. High Court of Justice in Madrid [2007] UKHL 6 314
Day v. Lewisham and Greenwich NHS Trust [2017] EWCA Civ 329 113
Digital Satellite Warranty Cover Ltd. v. The Financial Services Authority
  [2011] EWCA Civ 1413 .... 45, 314
Dingmar v. Dingmar [2006] EWCA Civ 942 .... 59, 108, 114
Director of the Serious Fraud Office v. B [2012] EWCA Crim 901 118
DPP of Jamaica v. Mollison [2003] UKPC 6 6

Duke v. GEC Reliance Ltd. [1988] AC 618 (HL).............. 52, 271, 307, 283, 347, 367
Duport Steels Ltd. v. Sirs [1980] 1 All ER 529 (HL) 6, 32, 51, 61, 104, 238–239
EB Central Services Ltd. v. Revenue and Customs Commissioners
    [2008] EWCA Civ 486... 322, 343, 373, 377
EBR Attridge Law LLP v. Coleman [2010] ICR 242............................265, 343
Ellen Street Estates v. Minister of Health [1934] 1 KB 590 (CA).................... 5, 204
EN (Serbia) v. Secretary of State for the Home Department
    [2009] EWCA Civ 630...280, 290, 323
English v. Thomas Sanderson Blinds Ltd. [2008] EWCA Civ 1421.................... 374
F Hoffmann-La Roche & Co. v. Secretary of State for Trade and Industry
    [1975] AC 295 (HL)... 306
Finnegan v. Clowney Youth Training Programme Ltd. [1990] 2 AC 407 (HL) 304
Fitzpatrick v. Sterling Housing Association Ltd. [2001] 1 AC 27 (HL)............. 2–3, 52,
                                                           120–122, 124, 126, 167, 190
Fleming (t/a Bodycraft) v. Customs and Excise Commissioners
    [2006] EWCA Civ 70.. 34, 177, 343, 345, 369
Fleming (t/a Bodycraft) v. Customs and Excise Commissioners [2008] UKHL 2 378
Football Association Premier League Ltd. v. QC Leisure
    [2012] EWCA Civ 1708...282, 327, 369
Football Association Premier League Ltd. v. QC Leisure
    [2012] EWHC 108 (Ch) 45, 327, 329
Fothergill v. Monarch Airlines Ltd. [1981] AC 251 (HL).........................108, 134
Garland v. British Rail Engineering Ltd. [1983] 2 AC 751 (HL)...........65, 106, 281, 367
Ghaidan v. Godin-Mendoza [2004] UKHL 30 ....3–4, 39, 144–147,
                                                           152–153, 155–156, 159, 162,
                                                           167–170, 172, 178, 181, 188–195,
                                                           197–198, 200, 202–203, 205, 208,
                                                           210–211, 213–217, 220–221, 227,
                                                           229, 299, 313, 343
Ghany v. Attorney General of Trinidad and Tobago [2015] UKPC 12.............117–118
Gladstone v. Bower [1960] 2 QB 384 (CA) 102–103, 134
Goode v. Martin [2001] EWCA Civ 1899 169
Google Inc. v. Vidal-Hall [2015] EWCA Civ 311 .... 45, 314, 343,
                                                           347, 372, 375–377
Greenweb Ltd. v. London Borough of Wandsworth [2008] EWCA Civ 910......113, 118, 128
H. v. Lord Advocate [2012] UKSC 24..110, 203
Hamnett v. Essex County Council [2017] EWCA Civ 6................................ 5
Hampshire v. Board of the Pension Protection Fund [2016] EWCA Civ 786..........45, 372
Hemming (t/a Simply Pleasure Ltd) v. Westminster City Council
    [2013] EWCA Civ 591...298–299
Hill v. East and West India Dock Co. (1884) 9 AC 448 (HL) 106
Holden & Co v. Crown Prosecution Service (No. 2) [1994] 1 AC 22 (HL)..........112, 128
Holmes v. Bradfield Rural District Council [1949] 2 KB 1......................... 61
Horton v. Sadler [2006] UKHL 27.. 65
Hounslow London Borough Council v. Powell [2011] UKSC 8 210
Howe v. Motor Insurers' Bureau [2017] EWCA Civ 932 ....258, 299, 374
In re S (Minors) [2001] EWCA Civ 757.. 209
In re S (Minors) [2002] UKHL 10..................................... 145, 147, 156,
                                                           169, 188, 194, 208–209, 218
Inco Europe Ltd. v. First Choice Distribution [2000] 1 WLR 586 (HL) ... 102, 115–116, 118

Inland Revenue Commissioners v. Hinchy [1960] AC 748 (HL) 53
Inland Revenue Commissioners v. McGuckian [1997] 1 WLR 991 (HL) 106
ITV Broadcasting Ltd. v. TV Catchup Ltd. (No. 2) [2011] EWHC 1874 .... 260, 299,
323, 343
ITV Broadcasting Ltd. v. TV Catchup Ltd. [2015] EWCA Civ 204 .... 45, 324,
343, 347, 372, 374, 384
Johnson v. Medical Defence Union Ltd. [2007] EWCA Civ 262 383
Johnson v. Moreton [1980] AC 37 (HL) 103, 106
Jones v. Director of Public Prosecutions [1962] AC 635 (HL) 103
Jones v. Secretary of State for Social Services [1972] AC 944 (HL) 61
Jones v. Wrotham Park Settled Estates [1980] AC 74 (HL) 103, 108, 116–117,
119, 123, 129
Kammins Ballrooms Co Ltd. v. Zenith Investments (Torquay) Ltd.
[1971] AC 850 (HL). 103, 117
Kay Green v. Twinsectra Ltd. [1996] 1 WLR 1587 (CA) 113
Kennedy v. The Charity Commission [2014] UKSC 20 .... 197, 210, 215, 249
Kirkness (Inspector of Taxes) v. John Hudson & Co. Ltd. [1955] AC 696 (HL) 63, 273
Lehman Brothers International (Europe) (In Administration), Re
[2012] UKSC 6. .... 285, 299, 343–344, 368
Leicester v. Pearson [1952] 2 QB 668 113
Litster v. Forth Dry Dock & Engineering Co Ltd. [1990] 1 AC 546 (HL). 261, 280,
282, 289–290, 296, 298,
300, 306, 322, 344, 387
Littlewoods Ltd. v. Revenue and Customs Commissioners [2015] EWCA Civ 515 374
Littlewoods Retail Ltd. v. Revenue and Customs Commissioners [2010] EWHC 1071 359
Macarthys Ltd. v. Smith [1979] ICR 785 (CA) 363
Macarthys Ltd. v. Smith [1981] QB 180 (CA). 63, 305
Madzimbamuto v. Lardner Burke [1969] 1 AC 645 (PC) 5
Magor and St Mellons Rural DC v. Newport Corporation
[1950] 2 All ER 1226 (CA) 129
Magor and St Mellons Rural DC v. Newport Corporation [1952] AC 189 (HL) 102–103,
106, 129, 175
Manchester City Council v. Pinnock [2010] UKSC 45 .... 155, 176, 198, 315
Maunsell v. Olins [1975] AC 373 (HL). 53, 60–62
McCartan Turkington Breen v. Times Newspapers Ltd. [2001] 2 AC 277 (HL) 52, 124
McDonald v. McDonald [2016] UKSC 28 .... 194, 214
McE v. Prison Service of Northern Ireland [2009] UKHL 15. 248
McMonagle v. Westminster City Council [1990] 2 AC 716 (HL) 114–115, 131
Monro v. Revenue and Customs Commissioners [2008] EWCA Civ 306. 105
Moohan v. Lord Advocate [2014] UKSC 67. 110
Moreno v. The Motor Insurers' Bureau [2016] UKSC 52 .... 282, 324
Nairn v. University of St Andrews [1909] AC 147 (HL) 249
NHS Leeds v. Larner [2012] EWCA Civ 1034. 343
O'Brien v. Ministry of Justice [2010] UKSC 34 378
O'Brien v. Ministry of Justice [2015] EWCA Civ 1000. .... 347, 368, 374
Oakley Inc. v. Animal Ltd. [2005] EWCA Civ 1191 .... 260, 323
Oliver Ashworth (Holdings) Ltd. v. Ballard (Kent) Ltd. [2000] Ch. 12 (CA) 58, 60, 62–63
Pepper v. Hart [1993] AC 593 (HL) 60, 62, 64
Perceval-Price v. Department of Economic Development [2000] IRLR 380 .... 378, 399
Percy v. Church of Scotland Board of National Mission [2005] UKHL 73 378

Pham v. Secretary of State for the Home Department [2015] UKSC 19 .... 4, 280
Pickstone v. Freemans Plc [1987] 3 WLR 811 (CA) 296, 298, 302, 323, 367
Pickstone v. Freemans Plc [1989] AC 66 (HL) 282, 285–286,
295–296, 301, 305, 322–323, 344–345
Pinner v. Everett [1969] 1 WLR 1266 (HL) 59
Pomiechowski v. District Court of Legnica [2012] UKSC 20 194
Poplar Housing and Regeneration Community Association Ltd.
 v. Donaghue [2001] EWCA Civ 595 .... 144, 152, 156–157, 188
Post Office v. Estuary Radio Ltd. [1968] 2 QB 740 (CA) 66
Principal Reporter v. K [2010] UKSC 56 .... 169, 176
Prudential Assurance Co Ltd. v. Revenue and Customs Commissioners
 [2013] EWHC 3249 .... 281, 370
Prudential Assurance Co. Ltd. v. Revenue and Customs Commissioners
 [2016] EWCA Civ 376 .... 345, 372, 374
R. v. A (No. 2) [2001] UKHL 25 .... 136, 145, 152–153,
155–156, 163, 169, 171–172,
187, 190, 194, 198, 200, 203
 R. v. D [2011] EWCA Crim 2082 116
 R. v. Holding [2005] EWCA Crim 3185 169
 R. v. Horncastle [2009] UKSC 14 315
 R. v. Ireland [1998] AC 147 (HL) 52
 R. v. Johnstone [2003] UKHL 28 .... 282, 322
 R. v. Kirkup [1993] 1 WLR 774 (CA) 128
 R. v. Lambert [2001] UKHL 37 .... 147, 169, 173, 194, 200
 R. v. Montila [2004] UKHL 50 65
 R. v. Moore [1995] QB 353 (CA) 102
 R. v. Registrar General ex p. Smith [1991] 2 QB 393 (CA) 62
 R. v. T [2009] UKHL 20 60
 R. v. Waya [2012] UKSC 51 .... 169, 215, 374
 R. (Allensway Recycling Ltd) v. Environment Agency [2015] EWCA Civ 1289 118
 R. (Anderson) v. Secretary of State for the Home Department
 [2002] UKHL 46 .... 4, 6, 188, 194, 200
 R. (Animal Defenders International) v. Secretary of State for culture,
 media and sport [2008] UKHL 15 147
 R. (Anufrijeva) v. Secretary of State for the Home Department [2003] UKHL 36 .... 37, 250
 R. (Brind) v. Secretary of State for the Home Department [1991] 1 AC 696 (HL) 66
 R. (Cart) v. Upper Tribunal [2011] UKSC 28 .... 37, 253
 R. (Chester) v. Secretary of State for Justice [2013] UKSC 63 326
 R. (Chief Constable of Staffordshire) v. Stafford Crown Court
 [1999] 1 WLR 398 (QB) 113
 R. (Confederation of Passenger Transport UK) v. Humber Bridge Board
 [2003] EWCA Civ 842 115
 R. (Countryside Alliance) v. Attorney General [2005] EWHC 1677 (Admin) 193
 R. (Doody) v. Secretary of State for the Home Department [1994] 1 AC 531 (HL) 239
 R. (Edison First Power Ltd.) v. Central Valuation Officer [2003] UKHL 20 32
 R. (Equal Opportunities) v. Secretary of State for Employment [1992] ICR 341 (CA) 363
 R. (Evans) v. Attorney General [2015] UKSC 21 .... 111, 248, 255
 R. (Factortame (No. 1)) v. Secretary of State for Transport [1990] 2 AC 85 (HL) 364, 367
 R. (Factortame (No. 2)) v. Secretary of State for Transport
 [1991] 1 AC 603 (HL) 301, 305, 361–362, 365

R. *(Fire Brigades Union)* v. *Secretary of State for the Home Department*
[1995] 2 AC 513 (HL) 5–6
R. *(Francis & Francis)* v. *Central Criminal Court* [1989] AC 346 (HL).........61, 102–103
R. *(GC)* v. *Commissioner of Police of the Metropolis* [2011] UKSC 21............ 163, 188,
202–203, 210–215, 221
R. *(Gillan)* v. *Commissioner of Police of the Metropolis* [2006] UKHL 12..............250
R. *(Gujra)* v. *Crown Prosecution Service* [2012] UKSC 52 251
R. *(Hammond)* v. *Secretary of State for the Home Department*
[2004] EWHC 2753 (Admin) 231
R. *(Hammond)* v. *Secretary of State for the Home Department* [2005] UKHL 69 148
R. *(Haw)* v. *Secretary of State for the Home Department* [2006] EWCA Civ 532....113–114
R. *(HS2 Action Alliance Ltd)* v. *Secretary of State for Transport*
[2014] UKSC 3.. 110, 139, 203, 361, 363
R. *(Hurst)* v. *Commissioner of Police of the Metropolis* [2007] UKHL 13 .... 155, 190,
290, 314
R. *(Irving)* v. *Secretary of State for Transport* [2008] EWHC 1200....................359
R. *(Jackson)* v. *Attorney General* [2005] UKHL 56....................4, 37, 59, 110–112,
125, 197, 204–205, 256, 362
R. *(JS)* v. *Secretary of State for Work and Pensions* [2015] UKSC 16.......65, 153, 204, 280
R. *(Kebilene)* v. *Director of Public Prosecutions* [2000] 2 AC 326 (HL)................146
R. *(Kelly)* v. *Secretary of State for Justice* [2008] EWCA Civ 177 .... 107, 112, 115, 118
R. *(M)* v. *Hackney London Borough Council* [2011] EWCA Civ 4....................169
R. *(M)* v. *Hammersmith and Fulham London Borough Council*
(1998) 30 HLR 10 (CA)..53
R. *(Miller)* v. *Secretary of State for Exiting the European Union*
[2016] EWHC 2768 (Admin) 4, 110–111, 204,
206, 249, 254, 362–363
R. *(Miller)* v. *Secretary of State for Exiting the European Union*
[2017] UKSC 51................................. 104, 110–111, 139, 203, 249, 254,
280, 361–363, 365–366, 406
R. *(Morgan Grenfell)* v. *Special Commissioners of Income Tax* [2002] UKHL 21....200, 249
R. *(Nicklinson)* v. *Ministry of Justice* [2013] EWCA Civ 961.....................249–252
R. *(Nicklinson)* v. *Ministry of Justice* [2014] UKSC 38.......... 11, 146, 189, 217, 220, 238
R. *(Noone)* v. *Governor of Drake Hall Prison* [2010] UKSC 30................115, 119, 123
R. *(Nutricia Ltd.)* v. *Secretary of State for Health* [2015] EWHC 2285 ....267, 300
R. *(Osborn)* v. *Parole Board* [2013] UKSC 61......................................249
R. *(Pierson)* v. *Secretary of State for the Home Department* [1998] AC 539 (HL) 31, 249
R. *(Plantagenet Alliance Ltd)* v. *Secretary of State for Justice*
[2014] EWHC 1662 (QB)..31, 109
R. *(Privacy International)* v. *Investigatory Powers Tribunal*
[2017] EWCA Civ 1868...249, 254
R. *(Public Law Project)* v. *Lord Chancellor* [2016] UKSC 39............ 110, 125, 305–306
R. *(Quintavalle)* v. *Secretary of State for Health* [2003] UKHL 13.............. 46, 51–52,
60, 62–63, 107, 119–122, 124
R. *(Reilly)* v. *Secretary of State for Work and Pensions* [2016] EWCA Civ 413..........193
R. *(Risk Management Partners Ltd.)* v. *Brent London Borough Council*
and Harrow London Borough Council [2011] UKSC 7.........................324
R. *(Roszkowski)* v. *Secretary of State for the Home Department*
[2017] EWCA Civ 1893..250
R. *(Shah)* v. *Barnet LBC* [1983] 2 AC 309 (HL) 126

R. (Simms) v. Secretary of State for the Home Department
    [2000] 2 AC 115 (HL) 149, 163, 201, 248–250, 315
*R. (Spath Holme) v. Secretary of State for the Environment, Transport
    and the Regions* [2001] 2 AC 349 (HL) 35, 37, 51–52,
    58–60, 62–65, 134, 198
R. (Unison) v. Lord Chancellor [2017] UKSC 51 35
R. (Westminster City Council) v. NASS [2002] UKHL 38 .... 63–64, 67–68
R. (Wilkinson) v. Inland Revenue Commissioners [2005] UKHL 30 .... 51, 162,
    193–194, 198, 208, 230
R. (Wright) v. Secretary of State for Health [2007] EWCA Civ 999 .... 152, 282
R. (Wright) v. Secretary of State for Health [2009] UKHL 3 214
R. (ZYN) v. Walsall Metropolitan Borough Council [2014] EWHC 1918 123
Revenue and Customs Commissioners v. IDT Card Services Ireland Ltd.
    [2006] EWCA Civ 29... 34–35, 39, 44, 261,
    278, 280–281, 285, 291, 299, 309,
    314, 343–345, 347–348, 359–360,
    363–364, 368, 370, 372–373, 393
Rhys-Harper v. Relaxion [2003] UKHL 33 299
River Wear Commissioners v. Adamson (1887) 2 App. Cas. 743 62
Robertson v. Swift [2014] UKSC 50 .... 45, 60, 261, 280, 314
Ropaigealach v. Barclays Bank plc. [2000] QB 263 (CA) 112
Rowstock Ltd. v. Jessemey [2014] EWCA Civ 185................. 115, 118, 170, 290, 299
*Royal College of Nursing of the United Kingdom v. Department
    of Health and Social Security* [1981] AC 800 (HL) 120–124
Russell v. TransOcean International Resources Ltd. [2011] UKSC 57 282
S v. L [2012] UKSC 30 .... 52, 152–153, 155–156, 197
Salomon v. Commissioners of Customs and Excise [1967] 2 QB 116 (CA) .... .60, 65–66, 280
Seaford Court Estates Ltd. v. Asher [1949] 2 KB 481 (CA) 129
Secretary of State for Defence v. Guardian Newspaper Ltd. [1985] AC 339 (HL)........ 128
Secretary of State for the Home Department v. AF [2009] UKHL 28..... 146, 148, 194, 196
Secretary of State for the Home Department v. GG [2009] EWCA Civ 786............. 248
Secretary of State for the Home Department v. JJ [2007] UKHL 45 146
Secretary of State for the Home Department v. MB [2007] UKHL 46 196
Secretary of State for Work and Pensions v. Hourigan [2002] EWCA Civ 1890 62
Serious Organised Crime Agency v. Gale [2010] EWCA Civ 759..................... 193
Shanning International Ltd. v. Lloyds TSB Bank plc [2001] UKHL 31 128
Sheldon v. RHM Outhwaite (Underwriting Agencies) Ltd. [1996] AC 102 (HL) 60
Simms v. Registrar of Probates [1900] AC 323 (PC)................................ 61
Steele Ford & Newton v. Crown Prosecution Service (No. 2) [1994] 1 AC 22 (HL) 128
Stevenson v. Rogers [1999] QB 1028 (CA).. 60
Stock v. Frank Jones (Tipton) Ltd. [1978] 1 WLR 231 (HL)..................... 35, 53,
    59–60, 102, 112, 134
*Test Claimants in the FII Group Litigation v. Revenue and Customs
    Commissioners* [2010] EWCA Civ 103 ....299, 326
*Test Claimants in the FII Group Litigation v. Revenue and Customs
    Commissioners* [2016] EWCA Civ 1180 ....299, 368
The United States of America v. Nolan [2014] EWCA Civ 71 336
The United States of America v. Nolan [2015] UKSC 63 374
Thoburn v. Sunderland City Council [2002] EWHC 195 (Admin) 5, 110,
    139, 203–205, 260, 363, 365–366

List of Cases

TV Broadcasting Ltd. v. TV Catchup Ltd. [2015] EWCA Civ 204 299
Unilin Beheer BV v. Berry Floor NV [2004] EWCA Civ 1021 282
Vacher & Sons v. London society of compositors [1913] AC 107 (HL) 59, 103
Victor Chandler International Ltd. v. Customs and Excise Commissioners
 [2000] 1 WLR 1296 (CA) 124
Vodafone 2 v. Revenue and Customs Commissioners [2008] EWHC 1569 ..... 359, 373–374
Vodafone 2 v. Revenue and Customs Commissioners [2009] EWCA Civ 446 .... 45, 189,
 201, 215–216, 285, 299, 314,
 316, 344–345, 368, 370–374
Watkins v. Secretary of State for the Home Department [2006] UKHL 17 .... 139, 249
Webb v. EMO Air Cargo (UK) Ltd. (No. 2) [1995] 4 All ER 577 (HL) 284
Webb v. EMO Air Cargo (UK) Ltd. [1992] 2 All ER 43 (CA) 284
Webb v. EMO Air Cargo (UK) Ltd. [1992] 4 All ER 929 (HL) 284
West Mercia Constabulary v. Wagener [1982] 1 WLR 127 113
White v. White [2001] UKHL 9 281
Wilson v. First County Trust Ltd. (No. 2) [2003] UKHL 40 .... 51, 53, 58, 63, 65,
 67–68, 145–146, 152, 163, 192
Yarl's Wood Immigration Ltd. v. Bedfordshire Police Authority
 [2009] EWCA Civ 1110 128
Yemshaw v. London Borough of Hounslow [2011] UKSC 3 .... 52, 122, 124–125
YL v. Birmingham City Council [2007] UKHL 27 .... 30, 61

LIST OF ABBREVIATIONS

AcP	Archiv für die civilistische Praxis
AG	Advocate General
AJCL	American Journal of Comparative Law
All ER	All England Law Reports
AöR	Archiv des öffentlichen Rechts
AP	Arbeitsrechtliche Praxis
art.	article
BAG	Bundesarbeitsgericht (German Federal Labour Court)
BeckRS	Beck online Rechtsprechung
BGB	Bürgerliches Gesetzbuch (German Civil Code)
BGH	Bundesgerichtshof (German Federal Court of Justice)
BSG	Bundessozialgericht (German Federal Social Court)
BVerfG	Bundesverfassungsgericht (German Federal Constitutional Court)
BVerfGG	Bundesverfassungsgerichtsgesetz (Act on the German Federal Constitutional Court)
BVerwG	Bundesverwaltungsgericht (German Federal Administrative Court)
CA	Court of Appeal of England and Wales
Cf.	Compare
CJEU	Court of Justice of the European Union
CLJ	Cambridge Law Journal
CMLR	Common Market Law Review
CUP	Cambridge University Press
Deb.	Debates
DöV	Die öffentliche Verwaltung
DVBl	Deutsches Verwaltungsblatt
EBLR	European Business Law Review
ECA	European Communities Act 1972
ECHR	European Convention on Human Rights
ECtHR	European Court of Human Rights
EEC	(Treaty establishing the) European Economic Community
EHRLR	European Human Rights Law Review
EHRR	European Human Rights Reports
EJIL	European Journal of International Law
ELJ	European Law Journal
ELR	European Law Review
EU	European Union

EuGRZ	Europäische Grundrechte-Zeitschrift
EuR	Europarecht
EU(W) Act	European Union (Withdrawal) Act 2018
EuZW	Europäische Zeitschrift für Wirtschaftsrecht
FamRZ	Zeitschrift für das gesamte Familienrecht
GG	Grundgesetz (German Basic Law)
GRUR	Gewerblicher Rechtsschutz und Urheberrecht
HC	House of Commons
HL	House of Lords
HRA	Human Rights Act 1998
ICLQ	International and Comparative Law Quarterly
I-CON	International Journal of Constitutional Law
IRLR	Industrial Relations Law Reports
JBl	Juristische Blätter
JR	Judicial Review
JuS	Juristische Schulung
JZ	JuristenZeitung
KG	Kammergericht (Berlin Appellate Court)
LG	Landgericht (German Regional Court)
LJ	Lady Justice of Appeal or Lord Justice of Appeal
LQR	Law Quarterly Review
MJ	Maastricht Journal of European and Comparative Law
MLR	Modern Law Review
MR	Master of the Rolls
n.	note
NJW	Neue Juristische Wochenschrift
NVwZ	Neue Zeitschrift für Verwaltungsrecht
NVwZ-RR	Neue Zeitschrift für Verwaltungsrecht, Rechtsprechungs-Report
NZA	Neue Zeitschrift für Arbeitsrecht
NZA-RR	Neue Zeitschrift für Arbeitsrecht, Rechtsprechungs-Report
NZS	Neue Zeitschrift für Sozialrecht
OJLS	Oxford Journal of Legal Studies
OLG	Oberlandesgericht (German Higher Regional Court)
OUP	Oxford University Press
QB	Queen's Bench Division of the High Court
PC	Privy Council of the United Kingdom
PL	Public Law
RabelsZ	Rabels Zeitschrift für ausländisches und internationales Privatrecht
RdA	Recht der Arbeit
RIW	Recht der internationalen Wirtschaft
s.	section
Sch.	Schedule
ss.	sections

SSRN	Social Science Research Network
StGB	Strafgesetzbuch (German Criminal Code)
TEU	Treaty on European Union
TFEU	Treaty on the Functioning of the European Union
UKSC	Supreme Court of the United Kingdom
Vol.	Volume
WLR	The Weekly Law Reports
WM	Wertpapier-Mitteilungen, Zeitschrift für Wirtschafts- und Bankrecht
ZaöRV	Zeitschrift für ausländisches öffentliches Recht und Völkerrecht
ZEuP	Zeitschrift für Europäisches Privatrecht
ZfPW	Zeitschrift für die gesamte Privatrechtswissenschaft
ZfRV	Zeitschrift für Europarecht, Internationales Privatrecht und Rechtsvergleichung
ZJS	Zeitschrift für das Juristische Studium
ZRP	Zeitschrift für Rechtspolitik
ZUM	Zeitschrift für Urheber- und Medienrecht

CHAPTER 1
INTRODUCTION

This book is concerned with the boundaries of what is possible as a matter of statutory interpretation for English and German courts. It is concerned with techniques and limits of statutory interpretation that English and German judges apply when they restrict or extend the scope of application of a provision beyond or against the possible semantic meanings of the statutory language, i.e. when they venture outside the constraints of the text (judicial law-making[1]). The book critically analyses how far English and German judges go in stretching what is possible under the guise of statutory interpretation when they construe national legislation. The interpretative criteria and the specific limits and techniques of judicial law-making as expressed in judicial opinions are ultimately judge-made law in both jurisdictions. The outer interpretative limits and techniques cannot be surpassed by judges without exceeding the judicial function. These limits and techniques aim to prevent courts from claiming powers that are constitutionally reserved to the legislature. They demarcate the border between permissible judicial law-making and impermissible judicial amendment of legislation. This border has often been described as unclear and nebulous in both jurisdictions.[2] The term "outer limits" of interpretation refers to all descriptions and methodological elements or items that are used in published written opinions in English and German courts in order to specify this border. For example, judicial law-making in Germany must not disregard the wording *and* the clearly identifiable intention of the legislature. An English court cannot adopt a meaning that is inconsistent with a fundamental feature of the legislation when interpreting a provision compatibly with Convention rights according to s. 3(1) Human Rights Act 1998 (HRA). In both jurisdictions, it is common for judges to emphasise that they would usurp the legislative function if they relied

---

[1] The term "judicial law-making" is used in this narrow sense throughout the book. It is not used in this book to refer to judge-made law as a separate source of law or to common law reasoning.

[2] R. CROSS, *Statutory interpretation*, 3rd ed., Butterworths, London 1995, p. 196; B. DICKSON, *Human rights and the United Kingdom Supreme Court*, OUP, Oxford 2013, p. 70 (regarding s. 3(1) HRA); M. JESTAEDT, Richterliche Rechtsetzung statt richterliche Rechtsfortbildung, in C. BUMKE (ed.), *Richterrecht zwischen Gesetzesrecht und Rechtsgestaltung*, Mohr Siebeck, Tübingen 2012, pp. 49, 51; S. VOGENAUER, *Die Auslegung von Gesetzen in England und auf dem Kontinent*, Mohr Siebeck, Tübingen 2001, pp. 1141, 1281.

on their own subjective ideas about policy when interpreting statutes according to conventional canons of construction.

Courts are sometimes accused of an inconsistent approach when determining or applying the outer limits of interpretation.[3] Indeed, judicial opinions in England and Germany that contain insights about the outer boundaries and techniques of judicial law-making are often fragmentary, ambiguous and sometimes inconsistent. That is why this book also aims to reconstruct this fragmentary material into a rational, coherent and systematic whole. The outer limits and techniques of judicial law-making concern the limits of the judicial function, the constitutional role of the courts and the separation of powers. This book thus addresses the often overlooked[4] relationship between statutory interpretation and constitutional law. In short, it critically analyses, reconstructs and compares judicial law-making in English and German courts from a comparative constitutional viewpoint. It maps the differences and commonalities in both jurisdictions and then offers explanatory accounts for these differences and similarities based on constitutional, institutional, political, historical, cultural and international factors.

The following two examples of statutory interpretation illustrate that the outer limits as well as the techniques of judicial law-making are not necessarily identical in both jurisdictions. This may reflect different understandings of the constitutional relationship between the judiciary and the legislature among English and German judges. The first example relates to the interpretation of the Rent Act 1977 in English courts, and the second example relates to the interpretation of the old s. 569a German Civil Code in German courts. Para. 2(1) of Sch. 1 to the Rent Act 1977 conferred the right of succession to a protected tenancy on the surviving "spouse" of the original tenant, and para. 2(2) stipulated that the word spouse includes a person who was living with the tenant "as his or her wife or husband". Can these latter words be interpreted so as to include cohabiting homosexual couples? The House of Lords ruled in *Fitzpatrick* in 1999 that para. 2(2) of Sch. 1 to the Rent Act 1977 cannot be construed under conventional canons of statutory interpretation to include persons in a same-sex relationship.[5] Such an interpretation would have exceeded the outer limits of permissible statutory interpretation according to

---

[3] R. EKINS, Legislative freedom in the United Kingdom, (2017) 133 *LQR* 582, 596; A. WAGNER and G. BARTH, Judicial interpretation or judicial vandalism? Section 3 of the Human Rights Act 1998, (2016) 21 *JR* 99, 100.

[4] For this assessment, see also: A. KAVANAGH, Choosing between sections 3 and 4 of the Human Rights Act 1998: judicial reasoning after Ghaidan v. Mendoza, in H. FENWICK, G. PHILIPSON and R. MASTERMAN (eds.), *Judicial reasoning under the UK Human Rights Act*, CUP, Cambridge 2007, pp. 114, 116; M. JESTAEDT, Rechtsprechung und Rechtsetzung – eine deutsche Perspektive, in W. ERBGUTH and J. MASING (eds.), *Die Bedeutung der Rechtsprechung im System der Rechtsquellen*, Richard Boorberg Verlag, Stuttgart 2005, pp. 25, 38; C. WALDHOFF, Gesetzesmaterialien aus verfassungserchtlicher Perspektive, in H. FLEISCHER (ed.), *Mysterium "Gesetzesmaterialien"*, Mohr Siebeck, Tübingen 2013, pp. 75, 85.

[5] *Fitzpatrick v. Sterling Housing Association Ltd.* [2001] 1 AC 27 (HL), 34 (Lord Slynn), 43 (Lord Nicholls), 47 (Lord Clyde), cf. 57 (Lord Hutton).

the House of Lords.[6] Less than five years later, the House of Lords faced the same question of statutory interpretation in *Ghaidan*.[7] This time, however, the Human Rights Act 1998 was applicable, and the House of Lords relied on its obligation to interpret legislation in a way which is compatible with Convention rights under s. 3(1) HRA. The court extended the scope of application of para. 2 of Sch. 1 to the Rent Act 1977 to the survivor of a couple of the same sex by reading additional words into the provision. This Convention-compatible reading of para. 2 was not inconsistent with a fundamental feature of the legislation or other outer limits of judicial law-making according to the majority of the judges in *Ghaidan*.[8]

The ambit of the statutory right of succession to a tenancy has also occupied German courts. The old s. 569a German Civil Code provided that surviving spouses and other family members succeed to a tenancy under certain conditions. Can this provision be construed as applying to the survivor of a relationship of unmarried partners who formed a common household? The clear wording of s. 569a German Civil Code did not cover cohabiting unmarried partners. The German Federal Constitutional Court (*Bundesverfassungsgericht*; BVerfG) declared in a judgment in 1990 that the wording of s. 569a German Civil Code contained a gap in the legislation.[9] That gap had arisen due to changing social circumstances. The BVerfG used an argument by analogy to close the gap. It extended the scope of application of s. 569a German Civil Code to cohabiting unmarried partners who had formed a common household with the deceased tenant.[10] The BVerfG argued that this interpretation of s. 569a German Civil Code did not exceed the outer limits of judicial law-making. For example, it did not breach the outer limit that a judge has to respect the fundamental decision of the legislature.

1. THE NEGLECTED COMPARATIVE CONSTITUTIONAL LAW PERSPECTIVE

Canons of interpretation (interpretative criteria, maxims of statutory interpretation)[11] are a central component of constitutional law.[12] They are

---

[6] Cf. ibid., 34 (Lord Slynn), 69 (Lord Hobhouse).
[7] *Ghaidan v. Godin-Mendoza* [2004] UKHL 30.
[8] Ibid., paras. 33, 35 (Lord Nicholls), para. 128 (Lord Rodger).
[9] BVerfG, *NJW* 1990, 1593, 1594.
[10] Ibid.
[11] The terms canons of interpretation (canons of construction), maxims of interpretation and interpretative criteria will be used interchangeably in this book. All terms are used in a wide sense and relate to the rules, principles, criteria and presumptions that judges employ when interpreting legislation.
[12] C. HILLGRUBER, Richterliche Rechtsfortbildung als Verfassungsproblem, *JZ* 1996, 118–125; J. IPSEN, *Richterrecht und Verfassung*, Duncker & Humblot, Berlin 1975, pp. 116–137; J. RÜCKERT and R. SEINECKE, Zwölf Methodenregeln für den Ernstfall, in J. RÜCKERT and R. SEINECKE (eds.), *Methodik des Zivilrechts – von Savigny bis Teubner*, 2nd ed., Nomos, Baden-Baden 2012, paras. 38–43.

linked with a specific legal system and in particular the system's allocation of competences between the judiciary and the legislature. Thus, different constitutional settings[13] ought to lead to different systems of interpretation.[14] Yet at least in England and Germany, constitutional law only sets a frame for legal methodology. It does not predetermine all of legal methodology and does not prescribe a specific legal methodology. The outer limits and techniques of statutory interpretation are, however, predetermined by constitutional law since these limits and techniques demarcate the constitutional boundary between the legislature and the judiciary. Judges in both jurisdictions link these limits with constitutional law and in particular with the allocation of competences between the legislature and the judiciary. The constitutional settings differ in both countries. The German Basic Law, Germany's constitution, is a source of law of the highest rank[15] in Germany and the BVerfG is its guardian. The legislature and the courts are bound by the German Basic Law as arts. 1(3) and 20(3) German Basic Law clarify. The BVerfG differs markedly from ordinary courts. It can review legislation and judicial decisions for their compliance with the German Basic Law. It has the power to invalidate non-complying statutes and quash judgments which contravene it (cf. art. 95(2), (3) Act on the German Federal Constitutional Court (*Bundesverfassungsgerichtsgesetz*; BVerfGG)), but does not have the power to substitute a non-complying statute with a complying one.

Constitutional judicial review of parliamentary legislation does not exist in the UK. The central principle of UK constitutional law is the doctrine of parliamentary sovereignty.[16] This doctrine has no equivalent in German constitutional law. According to the orthodox position of the doctrine as

---

[13] For a comparative introduction to German and UK constitutional law, see R. YOUNGS, *English, French & German comparative law*, 3rd ed., Routledge, London 2014, chapter 1. For an English introduction to the basic constitutional principles of the German Basic Law and the constitutional role of the BVerfG, see S. MICHALOWSKI and L. WOODS, *German constitutional law: the protection of civil liberties*, Dartmouth, Aldershot 1999, chapters 2 and 3.

[14] H. FLEISCHER, Rechtsvergleichende Beobachtungen zur Rolle der Gesetzesmaterialien bei der Gesetzesauslegung, (2011) 211 *AcP* 317, 318–319; M. HESSELINK, The Common Frame of Reference as a source of European private law, (2009) 83 *Tulane Law Review* 919, 936–937; C. HERRESTHAL, *Rechtsfortbildung im europarechtlichen Bezugsrahmen*, C.H. Beck, Munich 2006, p. 57; E.A. KRAMER, *Juristische Methodenlehre*, 4th ed., Stämpfli, Bern 2013, p. 44; G. WAGNER and R. ZIMMERMANN, Vorwort: Methoden des Privatrechts, (2014) 214 *AcP* 1, 5; cf. *Ghaidan v. Godin-Mendoza* [2004] UKHL 30, para. 120 (Lord Rodger); A. BARAK, *Purposive interpretation in law*, Princeton University Press, Princeton 2005, pp. 47, 234.

[15] For a short overview (in English) of the hierarchy of laws in Germany, see N. FOSTER and S. SULE, *German legal system and laws*, 4th ed., OUP, Oxford 2010, pp. 49–51, 164.

[16] *B (a child) v. DPP* [2000] 2 AC 428 (HL), 470 (Lord Steyn); *R. (Anderson) v. Secretary of State for the Home Department* [2002] UKHL 46, para. 39 (Lord Steyn); *R. (Jackson) v. Attorney General* [2005] UKHL 56, para. 9 (Lord Bingham, "bedrock of the British constitution"); *Pham v. Secretary of State for the Home Department* [2015] UKSC 19, para. 80 (Lord Mance); *R. (Miller) v. Secretary of State for Exiting the European Union* [2016] EWHC 2768 (Admin), para. 20 (Lord Thomas of Cwmgiedd CJ, Sir Terence Etherton MR, Sales LJ).

advanced by A.V. Dicey,[17] "Parliament ... has ... the right to make or unmake any law whatever; and further, that no person or body is recognised by the law of England as having a right to override or set aside the legislation of Parliament".[18] Under this orthodox position, Parliament possesses a *legally*[19] unlimited legislative authority in the UK,[20] with the limitation that it cannot bind future parliaments. Parliament can effect fundamental constitutional change and is at once a legislative and a constituent assembly. There is no formal distinction between ordinary and constitutional statutes. The law relating to constitutional matters has the same legal status as all other law, and Parliament can create and change constitutional law in the same way as "ordinary" law. This is the orthodox understanding of parliamentary sovereignty. It entails as a corollary a doctrine of implied repeal: in the event of conflict between two Acts of Parliament, the later Act will prevail and by implication repeal the earlier to the extent of the incompatibility, in accordance with the maxim *lex posterior derogat legi priori*.[21] We will discover later in this book that the doctrine of parliamentary sovereignty has evolved in recent times. UK constitutional law now recognises "ordinary" and "constitutional" statutes. Constitutional statutes like the Human Rights Act 1998 or the European Communities Act 1972 are not subject to implied repeal by later ordinary statutes. Notwithstanding this evolution of the doctrine of parliamentary sovereignty, Parliament can repeal constitutional

---

[17] For a historical overview of the development of parliamentary sovereignty in Britain, see N. DUXBURY, *Elements of legislation*, CUP, Cambridge 2013, pp. 31-35; I. MCLEOD, *Legal method*, 7th ed., Palgrave Macmillan, Basingstoke 2009, pp. 67-72.

[18] A.V. DICEY, *Introduction to the study of the law of the constitution*, 10th ed., Macmillan, Basingstoke 1967, pp. 39-40. See also LORD EVERSHED, The judicial process in twentieth century England, (1961) 61 *Columbia Law Review* 761, 765-766.

[19] This *legal* sovereignty is in practice restricted by *practical* and *political* restraints.

[20] *R. (Fire Brigades Union) v. Secretary of State for the Home Department* [1995] 2 AC 513 (HL), 567 (Lord Mustill); DICEY, above n. 18, p. 41; DUXBURY, above n. 17, pp. 32-33; M. ELLIOTT and R. THOMAS, *Public law*, 3rd ed., OUP, Oxford 2017, p. 12. See *Madzimbamuto v. Lardner Burke* [1969] 1 AC 645 (PC), 723 (Lord Reid, "It is often said that it would be unconstitutional for the United Kingdom Parliament to do certain things, meaning that the moral, political and other reasons against doing them are so strong that most people would regard it as highly improper if Parliament did these things. But that does not mean that it is beyond the power of Parliament to do such things. If Parliament chose to do any of them the courts could not hold the Act of Parliament invalid"). For a different view, see A. TUCKER, Uncertainty in the rule of recognition and in the doctrine of parliamentary sovereignty, (2011) 31 *OJLS* 61-88.

[21] *Ellen Street Estates v. Minister of Health* [1934] 1 KB 590 (CA), 595-596 (Scrutton LJ), 597 (Maugham LJ); *Thoburn v. Sunderland City Council* [2002] EWHC 195 (Admin), paras. 37-46 (Laws LJ); *Hamnett v. Essex County Council* [2017] EWCA Civ 6, para. 26 (Gross LJ); P. CRAIG, Constitutionalizing constitutional law: HS2, [2014] *PL* 373, 384-385; O. JONES and F.A.R. BENNION, *Bennion on Statutory Interpretation*, 6th ed., LexisNexis, London 2013, section 87; N. MACCORMICK, *Questioning sovereignty*, OUP, Oxford 1999, pp. 88-89. Different conceptions of implied repeal exist; for discussion, see N.W. BARBER and A. YOUNG, The rise of prospective Henry VIII clauses and their implications for sovereignty, [2003] *PL* 112, 115-116.

statutes by using express words. There is still no constitutional judicial review of parliamentary legislation and Parliament's absolute law-making power remains intact.

There are further obvious differences between UK and German constitutional law in relation to the separation of powers doctrine.[22] The UK constitution does not embrace a rigid doctrine of separation of powers.[23] The doctrine of parliamentary sovereignty allows little scope for the constitutional restraint of legislative power in the UK. Therefore, the extent to which the separation of powers doctrine exerts *normative* influence remains a point of uncertainty in UK constitutional law.[24] This can be contrasted with the understanding of the separation of powers laid down in art. 20(2) German Basic Law as a legal and judicially enforceable rule in Germany.[25] This understanding is informed by a comprehensive form of constitutional review under the German Basic Law, which sets legal limits to the political process. What is not uncertain but recognised in both jurisdictions is the following aspect of the separation of powers: judicial power is constrained vis-à-vis the legislature. The book will explore to what extent it is constrained. A separation of functions undoubtedly exists between the legislature's role in making law and the judiciary's role in applying and interpreting the law in both jurisdictions.[26] It is the doctrine of parliamentary sovereignty that influences this constitutional division of powers in England and constrains the English courts' interpretative function.[27] In Germany, it is art. 20(3) German Basic Law that binds the judiciary to "legislation and law" (*Gesetz und Recht*) and constrains the courts' powers to develop the law through judicial law-making.

We can see from this glimpse of UK and German constitutional law that the constitutional relationship between the judiciary and the legislature is different in both countries. A legalist would – leaving aside the controversy at what level of abstraction – expect different outer limits of interpretation that mirror

---

[22] For comparative insights, see C. MÖLLERS, *The three branches: a comparative model of separation of powers*, OUP, Oxford 2013, pp. 17–49.

[23] *R. (Anderson) v. Secretary of State for the Home Department* [2002] UKHL 46, para. 39 (Lord Steyn). For discussion, see P. LEYLAND, *The constitution of the United Kingdom: a contextual analysis*, 3rd ed., Hart, Oxford 2016, pp. 72–83.

[24] For discussion, see R. MASTERMAN and S. WHEATLE, Unpacking separation of powers: judicial independence, sovereignty and conceptual flexibility in the UK constitution, [2017] *PL* 469–487.

[25] MÖLLERS, above n. 22, pp. 36–37.

[26] *Duport Steels Ltd. v. Sirs* [1980] 1 All ER 529 (HL), 541 (Lord Diplock); *R. (Fire Brigades Union) v. Secretary of State for the Home Department* [1995] 2 AC 513 (HL), 567 (Lord Mustill); *R. (Anderson) v. Secretary of State for the Home Department* [2002] UKHL 46, para. 39 (Lord Steyn); *DPP of Jamaica v. Mollison* [2003] UKPC 6, para. 13; BVerfG, *NJW* 1998, 519–520 – *Kind als Schaden*; BVerfG, *NJW* 2009, 1469, para. 60 – *Rügeverkümmerung*; BVerfG, *NJW* 2011, 842 paras. 52–53 – *Dreiteilungsmethode*; BVerfG, *NJW-RR* 2016, 1366 paras. 34–37.

[27] MASTERMAN and WHEATLE, above n. 24, pp. 473–474.

the underlying constitutional differences. Yet S. Vogenauer finds that despite differences in terminology and classification, a fundamental unity of statutory interpretation in the judicial practice exists in England and Germany.[28] His analysis focuses on the interpretative criteria and their weighing and balancing where they conflict.[29] Other legal scholars have come to a similar conclusion.[30] The fundamental unity thesis is also supported by authors who assert that a gradual convergence of judicial views is taking place in Europe.[31] L.-P. Brandt argues that legal cultures in England and Germany are fundamentally similar.[32] The fundamental unity thesis is not uncontested, however. Other scholars have found substantial differences when comparing statutory interpretation in English and German courts.[33] This view is supported by authors who claim that legal cultures and legal mentalities in Europe are not converging.[34]

---

[28] S. Vogenauer, *Die Auslegung von Gesetzen in England und auf dem Kontinent*, Mohr Siebeck, Tübingen 2001, pp. 1295–1308.

[29] Ibid., pp. 17–18, 25.

[30] K.P. Berger, Auf dem Weg zu einem europäischen Gemeinrecht der Methode, ZEuP 2001, 4, 17; G. Hager, *Rechtsmethoden in Europa*, Mohr Siebeck, Tübingen 2009, pp. 71, 283.

[31] E. Kramer, Konvergenz und Internationalisierung der juristischen Methode, in H.-D. Assmann, G. Brüggemeier and R. Sethe (eds.), *Unterschiedliche Rechtskulturen – Konvergenz des Rechtsdenkens*, Nomos, Baden-Baden 2001, pp. 31, 34–39; B. Markesinis, Learning from Europe and learning in Europe, in B. Markesinis (ed.), *The gradual convergence: foreign ideas, foreign influences, and English law*, Clarendon Press, Oxford 1994, pp. 1, 30; R. Zimmermann, Europa und das römische Recht, (2002) 202 *AcP* 243, 311. More cautious, but also tending towards a convergence of judicial views: M.N. Marchenko, Convergence of Romano-Germanic and Anglo-Saxon law, in W. Butler, O. Kresin and I. Shemshuchenko (eds.), *Foundations of comparative law: methods and typologies*, Wildy, Simmonds & Hill, London 2011, pp. 276, 298–299.

[32] L.-P. Brandt, *Die Chancen für eine einheitliche Auslegung eines Europäischen Zivilgesetzbuches*, V&R unipress, Osnabrück 2009, pp. 144, 153–154. See also T. Henninger, *Europäisches Privatrecht und Methode*, Mohr Siebeck, Tübingen 2009, pp. 327–328.

[33] See, e.g. M. Gisewski, *Methodik der Auslegung im kontinentaleuropäischen und angelsächsischen Recht: Vergleich und Synthese juristischer Denkweisen vor dem Hintergrund der europäischen Privatrechtsvergleichung*, Kovač, Hamburg 2008, pp. 140, 277; J. Hellert, *Der Einfluss des EG-Rechts auf die Anwendung nationalen Rechts: Eine rechtsvergleichende Studie zum Recht in der Bundesrepublik Deutschland und im Vereinigten Königreich von Großbritannien und Nordirland*, Lang, Frankfurt am Main 2001, pp. 226–227 (for the EU legal duty of conforming interpretation); K. Krieger, *Die gemeinschaftsrechtskonforme Auslegung des deutschen Rechts*, LIT, Münster 2005, p. 328 (for the EU legal duty of conforming interpretation); T. Lundmark, *Charting the divide between common and civil law*, OUP, Oxford 2012, p. 341; M. Schillig, §25 Vereinigtes Königreich, in K. Riesenhuber (ed.), *Europäische Methodenlehre*, 3rd ed., C.H. Beck, Munich 2015, §25, para. 55; cf. Youngs, above n. 13, pp. 68, 73.

[34] P. Legrand, European legal systems are not converging, (1996) 45 *ICLQ* 52–81. See also C. Harlow, Voices of difference in a plural community, (2002) 50 *ACJL* 339, 347–348; G. Teubner, Legal irritants: good faith in British law or how unifying law ends up in new divergencies, (1998) 61 *MLR* 11, 12. For a criticism of Legrand's view, see A. Watson, Legal transplants and European private law, vol 4.4 *Electronic Journal of Comparative Law*, December 2000, available online at http://www.ejcl.org/44/art44-2.html.

Most legal scholarship comparing the methods of statutory interpretation in England and Germany does not include or only touches on a comparative constitutional perspective.[35] That is because this scholarship largely focuses on the interpretative criteria and their weighing where they conflict. These elements of legal methodology are to a significant extent not predetermined by constitutional law in England and Germany. In this book, in contrast to the prevailing approaches, I add a new perspective to the debate on converging/diverging statutory interpretation in England and Germany by focusing on judicial law-making and in particular on the outer limits and techniques of judicial law-making. This approach warrants the comparative constitutional analysis that I provide. This book's unique perspective is particularly justified due to changes in the UK's constitutional landscape with the adoption of the Human Rights Act 1998 and the European Communities Act 1972. This book therefore offers a comprehensive analysis of rights-consistent[36] and conforming[37] judicial law-making in both jurisdictions. I also aim to significantly reshape the debate about the changing meaning of the doctrine of parliamentary sovereignty in the UK by linking statutory interpretation and constitutional law. Existing comparative scholarship that touches on the outer limits and techniques of judicial law-making has failed to produce uniform results. Whereas some scholars claim that the scope of judicial law-making and the limits of the judicial role differ considerably in England and Germany,[38] others contend that both the scope and limits are fundamentally similar.[39] These differences justify a much closer look at the topic, and I will show that neither claim is correct. The reality is more nuanced. This book will evidence that a fundamental unity of statutory interpretation does not exist in English and German judicial

---

[35] This is also true of other comparative scholarship. P.S. ATIYAH and R.S. SUMMERS, *Form and substance in Anglo-American law*, Clarendon Press, Oxford 1987, chapter 4, compare statutory interpretation in England and the United States of America. Even though they explore the reasons for the differences in the methods of statutory interpretation employed in English and US courts, they place little emphasis on differences in constitutional law (ibid., pp. 104–105).

[36] "Rights-consistent interpretation" refers to the interpretative obligation of English courts under s. 3(1) HRA and the duty of German courts to interpret national legislation in conformity with the fundamental rights enshrined in the German Basic Law.

[37] "Conforming interpretation" refers to the EU legal duty to interpret national law in the light of the wording and the purpose of an EU directive in order to achieve the result sought by the directive.

[38] J. GOLDSWORTHY, *Parliamentary sovereignty: contemporary debates*, CUP, Cambridge 2010, pp. 228–230; HERRESTHAL, above n. 14, p. 319; J.M. HOFFMANN, *Die Europäische Menschenrechtskonvention und nationales Recht: ein Vergleich der Wirkungsweise in den Rechtsordnungen des Vereinigten Königreichs und der Bundesrepublik Deutschland*, Heymanns, Cologne 2010, pp. 128–129 (for rights-consistent interpretation); T. RADEMACHER, Reading up or down EU legislation: a plea for a principled approach to an extraordinary judicial power, (2017) 23 *European Public Law* 319, 321.

[39] VOGENAUER, above n. 28, pp. 1295–1308; K. RIESENHUBER, Methodendivergenzen ertragen!, *GPR* 2016, 158, 159 (for the EU legal duty of conforming interpretation).

practice in the sphere of conventional judicial law-making. This is different for rights-consistent and conforming judicial law-making, where it will be established that a very high level of convergence exists in the formulation and application of the outer interpretative limits in judicial practice.

UK constitutional law is facing an uncertain future with the looming Brexit. The European Union (Withdrawal) Act (EU(W) Act) intends to create a new body of law known as "retained EU law", a hierarchy of domestic laws and new provisions on statutory interpretation that will lead to a further fragmentation of statutory interpretation. One effect of the Act is to incorporate the maxims of statutory interpretation used by the Court of Justice of the European Union (CJEU) into UK law. The Act also empowers courts to disapply pre-exit legislation. It intends to "transfer" the modifications of the orthodox doctrine of parliamentary sovereignty that the supremacy of EU law entails to the body of retained EU law after Brexit. The Act entails changes in UK constitutional law, and I will demonstrate how these changes will impact on statutory interpretation after Brexit. The sections of the EU(W) Act relating to both the supremacy of retained EU law as well as the interpretation of retained EU law and other pre-exit legislation are riddled with ambiguity and vagueness. My analysis of the Act will solve these riddles. I will also show that the book's comparative findings will "survive" Brexit. That is because a purposive interpretation of the EU(W) Act ensures legal continuity after Brexit and because conforming interpretation will continue to apply and play a major role in the post-Brexit UK.

The wider debate this book feeds into is the debate about the proper degree and limits of judicial power in a legal system.[40] We will see in Chapter 3 and Chapter 4 that scholars in both jurisdictions have criticised the highest courts for exceeding the limits of the judicial function when establishing and applying the outer boundaries and techniques of rights-consistent and conforming judicial law-making. I will argue that this criticism is warranted for English judicial practice. The interpretation and application of s. 3(1) HRA, s. 2(4) European Communities Act 1972 (ECA) and the principle of legality in the highest English courts have redefined the judicial role and have altered the balance of power between the judiciary and the legislature as it is traditionally understood. This development is unconstitutional. Even though English courts formally preserve the absolute doctrine of parliamentary sovereignty, they undermine the constitutional doctrine in substance with tools of statutory interpretation. For German judicial practice, this book challenges scholarly claims that German courts have exceeded the limits of the judicial function.

---

[40] For recent contributions on this topic, see (2017) 36(2) *University of Queensland Law Journal*. See also M. ELLIOTT, Judicial power and the United Kingdom's changing constitution, SSRN 2017, available online at http://www.ssrn.com; J. FINNIS, Judicial power: past, present and future, October 2015, available online at http://judicialpowerproject.org.uk. See also the work of Policy Exchange's Judicial Power Project, http://judicialpowerproject.org.uk.

2. KEY FINDINGS

This book aims to answer four main questions. First, what are the outer interpretative limits and techniques that English and German judges apply to judicial law-making? Second, do these limits and techniques converge or diverge in England and Germany? Third, what factors can or cannot explain the converging or diverging limits and techniques of judicial law-making? The fourth question connects with a theme of the book that will be developed in the third section of this Chapter. I will argue that determinate interpretative limits and techniques are particularly important for judicial law-making for reasons of legal certainty and the separation of powers. The fourth question thus relates to how well the outer limits of statutory interpretation as expressed and applied in judicial practice fulfil their functions to (a) restrict the scope of possible meanings of a provision, (b) limit judicial power and thus address separation of powers concerns, (c) reduce the area of evaluative arguments and extra-legal considerations in statutory interpretation and (d) provide legal certainty. By investigating this question in English and German case law, the book aims to reshape and add substantially to the debate between realists and legalists about the (ir)relevance of outer limits and techniques for judicial law-making. The comparative analysis provided in this book also allows us to determine how the English and German legal systems balance the tension between legal certainty (formal justice) and substantive individual justice (material justice) in the realm of statutory interpretation. Further questions that are specific to Chapter 3 and Chapter 4 of the book will be mentioned at the beginning of these chapters. The reader who is interested in the main comparative insights of the book is guided to Section 5 of Chapter 2, Sections 6.3 and 7.3 of Chapter 3, Section 7.3 of Chapter 4 and the Conclusion.

I will demonstrate that widely assumed differences between common law and civil law jurisdictions do not exist in the context of rights-consistent and conforming judicial law-making in English and German courts. P. Legrand's claim that the deep structures of law, legal cultures and legal mentalities remain historically unique and cannot be bridged will be disproved in this book.[41] The extent to which the application of the outer limits of rights-consistent and conforming judicial law-making is governed by formal legal reasoning, evaluative arguments and judicial discretion appears almost identical in both jurisdictions. This commonality is based on a common understanding of the (constitutional) function of the judge vis-à-vis the legislature. Lord Mance, for example, has argued that differences between civil and common law jurisdictions in Europe are not simple differences of style but also of substance, including differences in the role which the judge is seen as occupying and in the values which judges put

---

[41] LEGRAND, above n. 34.

on legal certainty and pragmatic reasoning.[42] Analysing English and German case law on rights-consistent and conforming interpretation, I find that the opposite is true. A large legal cultural distinction or distinction in the style of legal reasoning does not exist. There is no dichotomy between an allegedly systematic and deductive style in Germany and an inductive and facts-centred style that is driven by the circumstances of the individual case in England. Context is equally important in both jurisdictions. R. Posner's claim[43] that continental European judges are more legalistic, less pragmatic and less creative than English ones is too unspecific and incorrect with regard to the formulation and application of outer limits of rights-consistent and conforming interpretation.

One of the theses I present in this book is that the level of predictability of the outcome of the judicial reasoning process can be enhanced by increasing the number of formal elements in statutory interpretation. I will also argue against the view[44] that the outer limits of judicial law-making cannot or should not be determined in abstract and general terms but should only be determined in the context of a particular case. It will be shown that judicial arguments can be categorised as formal legal reasoning, evaluative arguments and extra-legal considerations. These categories overlap in judicial practice. Formal legal reasoning in statutory interpretation is supported by constitutional law, particularly the rule of law and the separation of powers. Evaluative arguments open up the interpretative process to extra-legal considerations. Extra-legal considerations can be disguised in evaluative arguments. Since evaluative arguments are intertwined with formal legal reasoning in English and German judgments, it is possible for judges to disguise extra-legal considerations in formal legal reasoning. It will be asserted that legal certainty and public confidence in the judiciary can and ought to be improved by making judicial reasoning more determinate and objective, instead of concealing what the judiciary is actually doing. I will show that this can be achieved by either (a) specifying the applicable interpretative maxims to a greater extent, thereby reducing the area in which evaluative arguments can operate or (b) structuring permissible evaluative arguments such as justice and fairness in order to reduce the subjective element inherent in them.

It will also be demonstrated in this book that the outer limits and techniques of judicial law-making as expressed by the highest English and German courts do not differ according to whether the legislation at issue is private or public

---

[42] LORD MANCE, *The common law and Europe: differences of style or substance and do they matter?*, Haldsworth Club Presidential Address, November 2006, University of Birmingham 2007, p. 18.
[43] R. POSNER, *How judges think*, Harvard University Press, Cambridge, Mass. 2008, p. 263.
[44] See, e.g. A. KAVANAGH, *Constitutional review under the UK Human Rights Act*, CUP, Cambridge 2009, p. 406; cf. *R. (Nicklinson) v. Ministry of Justice* [2014] UKSC 38, para. 101 (Lord Neuberger); T. BINGHAM, The Human Rights Act, [2010] *EHRLR* 568, 572.

legislation, delegated or primary legislation. This finding also holds true for criminal legislation if a court engages in judicial law-making in favour of the defendant. The crux of this finding is that judges do not express but *apply* these outer limits and techniques more widely or more narrowly depending on the circumstances of the individual case.

2.1. CONVENTIONAL JUDICIAL LAW-MAKING

Chapter 2 critically analyses and compares judicial law-making in English and German courts in a purely domestic context without regard to European Union (EU) law or the European Convention on Human Rights (ECHR) (conventional judicial law-making). I will argue in Chapter 2 that it is inaccurate to characterise the contemporary English approach to statutory interpretation as predominantly literal and formal and the contemporary German approach as predominantly teleological. A trend is discernible in both jurisdictions that courts refer extensively to the legislative history of a provision when ascertaining its meaning. The growing use of legislative history goes hand in hand with the decline of the literal rule and the rise of purposivism in England. A greater reliance on legislative history also "compensates" for a loss of predictability of a provision's meaning that accompanied the change in drafting style of legislation in England.

This book establishes that the outer limits of conventional judicial law-making in Germany are not expressed in clear-cut terms in judicial practice. They are formulated in such vague words that a judge can take into account the context and the circumstances of the individual case. This leaves judges with a considerable amount of judicial discretion and allows judges to consider extra-legal factors. A discretionary element is built deliberately into the outer limits of judicial law-making by the BVerfG. As appears from judicial practice, it is the weighing of the interpretative criteria in an individual case that ultimately determines whether or not an outer interpretative limit is met. A comparison with judicial law-making in German judicial practice also illustrates that English judges do engage in gap-filling in exceptional cases under conventional canons of construction, including reasoning by analogy. English courts have used their interpretative powers to read in, out or down words in legislation in order to (a) save statutes from absurdity, (b) correct obvious drafting errors and (c) update legislation via interpretation. The book demonstrates that the outer interpretative limits in these three categories are characterised by a considerable degree of judicial discretion. Even though it is possible to categorise a good number of cases of conventional judicial law-making in England, these categories are not an exhaustive statement of permissible judicial law-making. Other cases do not seem to be categorisable but have been decided based on the circumstances of the particular case.

Despite existing parallels in the outer limits and techniques of judicial law-making in England and Germany, I will show that considerable differences remain. In contrast to their German counterparts, English judges have not expressly recognised a judicial power to contradict the intention of the enacting legislature. Neither have they expressly recognised a power to depart from the intention of the enacting parliament. A German court that deviates from the intention of the enacting legislature does not necessarily infringe the outer limits of the judicial function. Compared to an English court, a German court can therefore take more "objective" factors of interpretation into account, and that increases the scope of permissible policy considerations. The distinction in the outer limits of judicial law-making in England and Germany is due to different constitutional settings: art. 20(3) German Basic Law as interpreted by the BVerfG on the one hand and the UK constitutional doctrine of parliamentary sovereignty as understood in English courts on the other hand.

The default position in German courts in relation to judicial law-making is that it is a permissible function of the judge. That is not the case in England. Even in today's climate of purposivism, it will be submitted that the default position in England is that judicial law-making is generally impermissible and only available in exceptional cases. The filling of gaps remains an exceptional use of judicial powers under conventional methods of statutory interpretation in England due to concerns of legal certainty under the rule of law and due to the doctrine of parliamentary sovereignty as traditionally perceived by judges. English judges have (or at least traditionally had) a stricter understanding of the limits of the judicial function vis-à-vis the legislature compared to their German counterparts. It will be shown that the different default positions in England and Germany ultimately exist because of different constitutional doctrines that affect the outer limits of the judicial function. A consequence of the different default positions are different judicial attitudes towards judicial law-making. S. Vogenauer's thesis[45] that statutory interpretation in both countries is fundamentally uniform has to be qualified in the area of conventional judicial law-making.

The BVerfG has stipulated general techniques and boundaries of interpretation that apply to all cases of judicial law-making. No such general limits and techniques have been provided in English judgments. It follows that formal legal reasoning from abstract premises is more prevalent in German judgments than in English judgments on judicial law-making. If judicial law-making is impermissible as a general rule in England, there is no need to develop and stipulate general limits of interpretation that apply to all cases of judicial law-making. Stipulating such general limits would undermine the

---

[45] VOGENAUER, above n. 28, pp. 1295–1308.

default position and the constitutional principle of parliamentary sovereignty underlying it. This argument explains why approaches by individual judges to formulate general outer limits of conventional judicial law-making have failed in the past in English courts. This constitutional reasoning better explains the different approaches adopted by English and German judges when formulating limits of interpretation, rather than the more abstract claim that the English legal system is pragmatic and bound to facts whereas the German law legal system is systematic and bound to rules.

If the different default positions for judicial law-making are taken into account in both jurisdictions, the English system places a higher degree of importance on legal predictability than the German system as long as the default position stays intact and is not undermined by judicial practice. The book also demonstrates with regard to the outer limits of judicial law-making that the German legal system does not sacrifice individual justice and instead places a lower value on legal certainty and predictability than the English legal system. These findings refute or at least qualify the general claim that German law and judges place a high value on predictability and sacrifice individual justice by doing so. It is an incorrect over-generalisation to contend that the German legal system prefers legal predictability over individual justice and that the English legal system prefers individual justice over legal predictability. What is clear, however, is that the English legal system is drawing closer to the German system with regard to where the balance (a) between legal certainty and giving effect to the intention of Parliament and (b) between formal and material justice can be found. There are considerable incentives for the English judiciary to adopt the default position that conventional judicial law-making is a generally permissible function of the court. These incentives will continue to exist after Brexit.

This book will also highlight that judicial law-making in English courts deviates from German legal methodology in its focus on the change of the statutory language by reading statutory words in, out or down. German legal methodology concentrates on the change of the scope of application of a provision. The different emphases on substance and on the statutory language in both jurisdictions can be explained by distinctions in the underlying constitutional doctrines. The difference between substance and language also shows that reading in and reading down of words in legislation are not the same as or equivalent to argument by analogy and teleological reduction in Germany. This comparison illustrates how the use of terminology in courts can influence the scope of judicial law-making.

I will establish in Chapter 2 that the UK constitutional doctrine of parliamentary sovereignty does not require English courts to stay within the possible semantic meanings of the statutory words. Instead, parliamentary sovereignty demands that courts do not depart from the intention of the enacting parliament when they interpret legislation. It will be shown that the doctrine of parliamentary sovereignty is capable of supporting a system of interpretation according to which judicial law-making is generally permissible in order to give effect to the intention of the enacting legislature. The English courts' current limited approach to judicial law-making, particularly the reluctance of reading in additional words into legislation, is largely based on historical context and tradition, influenced by constitutional doctrine, rather than on constitutional requirements as such. In Germany, the core of the outer limits of judicial law-making is likewise based on judicial tradition and historical context, influenced by constitutional doctrine, rather than on rules deducible from the German Basic Law. These findings support the view that historical experiences, irrespective of constitutional theory, have a significant impact on shaping judicial practices like influencing the creativity of judges and their involvement in judicial law-making. Path dependence, historical factors and tradition can thus explain to a considerable degree the differences in judicial attitudes towards judicial law-making in both jurisdictions under conventional canons of construction.

2.2. RIGHTS-CONSISTENT JUDICIAL LAW-MAKING

Chapter 3 critically analyses and compares the interpretative obligation of English courts under s. 3(1) Human Rights Act 1998 (Convention-compatible interpretation) and the duty of German courts to construe national legislation in conformity with the fundamental rights enshrined in the German Basic Law (constitution-consistent interpretation). The term "rights-consistent interpretation" is used in this book to refer to both interpretative obligations. Chapter 3 shows that a court's power to strike down legislation or to issue a declaration of incompatibility is not necessarily the most intrusive tool in its bow of constitutional review. Instead, constitution-consistent interpretation in Germany and Convention-compatible interpretation under s. 3(1) HRA in England do the heavy lifting in rendering legislation compliant with rights. Scholars have criticised the highest English and German courts for exceeding the limits of the judicial function when establishing and applying the outer limits of rights-consistent judicial law-making.[46] I will argue that this criticism is warranted in relation to English, but not for German judicial practice. Other scholars have asserted that the outer limits of rights-consistent judicial

---

[46] J. ALLAN, The Victorian Charter of Human Rights and Responsibilities: exegesis and criticism, (2006) 30 *Melbourne University Law Review* 906, 910–911; M. HOWE, A UK Bill of Rights, in COMMISSION ON A BILL OF RIGHTS, *A UK Bill of Rights? The choice before us*, London 2012, pp. 192, 216, available online at http://www.justice.gov.uk/about/cbr; C.-W. CANARIS, Die verfassungskonforme Auslegung und Rechtsfortbildung im System der juristischen Methodenlehre, in H. HONSELL ET AL. (eds.), *Festschrift für E.A. Kramer*, Helbing & Lichtenhahn, Basel 2004, pp. 141, 151; L. KUHLEN, *Die verfassungskonforme Auslegung von Strafgesetzen*, C.F. Müller, Heidelberg 2006, p. 58.

law-making diverge significantly in both jurisdictions due to different underlying constitutional settings.⁴⁷ I will refute this thesis.

It will be established that rights-consistent interpretation is more result driven compared to the process-driven approach of ascertaining legislative intent according to conventional canons of statutory interpretation. That is because the rights-consistent meaning is predetermined by an external standard. The focus of rights-consistent interpretation in judicial practice shifts towards the question of whether the desired reading of the challenged legislation can be squared with the intention of the legislature. This brings the limits of rights-consistent interpretation to the fore. English and German courts apply an interpretative priority rule and a presumption of compliance for rights-consistent interpretation. The interpretative priority rule governs the choice between different possible meanings of a provision. The significant strength of the presumption of compliance will be highlighted. It is visible when an English court balances the intentions of two different parliaments and when a German court balances the identifiable and the presumed intention of the legislature. We will see that courts in both jurisdictions operate a "presumption of objective purpose" which is not necessarily linked to the purpose that the enacting legislature envisioned. It will be further argued that the presumption is rebutted if a court exceeds an outer limit of interpretation. The strength of the presumption thus ultimately depends on how narrowly or widely these limits are drawn.

Contrary to English conventional canons of construction, we will learn that the default position for rights-consistent judicial law-making under s. 3(1) HRA is that it is generally a permissible function of the judge. I will demonstrate that such a change in default position is not incompatible with the constitutional doctrine of parliamentary sovereignty so long as courts do not depart from the intention of the enacting parliament. English and German courts can expand or restrict the scope of application of a provision beyond its wording under rights-consistent judicial law-making. They do not focus on what adjustments to the statutory language are necessary in order to achieve the substantive result. The number or precise form of the words that are read into a provision are insignificant. English courts have held that the technique of judicial law-making used to achieve a Convention-compatible meaning does not matter. No German court has yet declared that the interpretative technique employed in order to reach a constitution-consistent meaning is insignificant. The opposite is true: interpretative technique matters and ought to constrain judicial law-making. Despite this difference, it will be submitted that English judges do not necessarily

---

47   J.M. HOFFMANN, *Die Europäische Menschnerechtskonvention und nationales Recht: ein Vergleich der Wirkungsweise in den Rechtsordnungen des Vereinigten Königreichts und der Bundesrepublik Deutschland*, Heymanns, Cologne 2010, pp. 128–129.

have greater powers than German judges to make law in the sphere of rights-consistent judicial law-making. One of the reasons for this is that the concept of a gap in the legislation as a requirement for legitimate judicial law-making in Germany hardly restricts judicial law-making in German judicial practice. I will show that the concept of gap can best be explained by historical context and tradition. Based on a comparison with English law, I will further argue that this concept is superfluous for judicial law-making as applied in German courts. The main result of the comparison of the techniques of rights-consistent judicial law-making in both jurisdictions is that differences in terminology and classification, firmly anchored in historical context and in legal practice, are readily apparent. If we turn the focus to substance, however, it becomes equally apparent that English and German courts proceed on converging lines. The extent of the commonalities is quite significant.

In Germany, the outer limits of constitution-consistent interpretation coincide with those of conventional canons of construction. English judges have also stipulated interpretative limits that serve as the outer boundaries of the judicial function for all cases of judicial law-making under s. 3(1) HRA. This can explain the perceived increase in formalism in Supreme Court judgments as general outer limits require a "formal" application to an individual case. It is asserted that the stipulation and application of general outer interpretative limits in the sphere of s. 3(1) HRA was necessitated by the change of the default position for rights-consistent judicial law-making. I will also establish that the change of the default position and the consequential change in judicial attitudes in English courts has led to a converging judicial mindset about the judicial role in both jurisdictions in the area of rights-consistent interpretation. The outer limits of rights-consistent interpretation in England and Germany are expressed in very similar terms, and a considerable congruence can be detected when comparing the application of these boundaries in English and German judicial practice. The differences in the interpretative powers of English and German courts that we will encounter in Chapter 2 have ceased to exist. The similar strength of rights-consistent judicial law-making in both countries also shows that the difference between a declaration of incompatibility (weak form of judicial review) and a strike-down power (strong form of judicial review) does not necessarily affect the interpretative power of the courts.

Multiple factors will be explored that incentivise English as well as German courts to adopt and apply wide outer limits of rights-consistent interpretation. In both countries, a court does not necessarily exceed the judicial function if it adopts a rights-consistent meaning that departs from a provision's unambiguous wording, a provision's underlying specific purpose and the intention of the enacting legislature. Rights-consistent judicial law-making cannot be described as "weak" in England and Germany. A court can restrict or complement the enacting legislature's intention, and policy choices can be taken by a court. It will be argued that German courts should therefore abandon the way they state the "policy considerations limit" of judicial law-making. The policy considerations limit mostly exists on paper and is often infringed in judicial practice. Even though courts in both jurisdictions can depart from unambiguous and specific statutory language, it does not follow that the statutory words are meaningless when determining the limits of judicial law-making. That is because the fundamental features of the legislation or of a provision, the thrust and grain of the legislation, a fundamental decision of the legislature, the fundamental normative content of a provision or the scheme of the legislation are all ultimately determined by a weighing of the interpretative criteria. Specific and clear statutory words can weigh heavily against the permissibility of rights-consistent judicial law-making in an individual case in both jurisdictions. The intention of the enacting legislature as manifested in the statutory wording can also weigh heavily against the permissibility of judicial law-making.

I will reject the thesis that s. 3(1) HRA merely expands or enhances methods of interpretation the courts have traditionally used.[48] Such a view downplays the new constitutional role of the courts under s. 3(1) HRA. Against this view, it is argued that English courts have exceeded their constitutional role by empowering themselves to depart from the intention of a post-HRA parliament when using s. 3(1) HRA. Such a power amounts to a fundamental constitutional change in the courts' law-making function. It will be demonstrated that this power cannot be reconciled with the doctrine of parliamentary sovereignty even if modifications and a weakening of the doctrine are taken into account. A comparison with German case law also shows that the way English courts have interpreted s. 3(1) HRA does not adhere to the constitutional doctrine of parliamentary sovereignty. That is another reason for the significant congruence of the outer limits of rights-consistent judicial law-making in England and Germany. I will argued that the HRA preserves the doctrine of parliamentary sovereignty in formal terms, but judicial practice applying s. 3(1) HRA undermines the constitutional doctrine in substantive terms. English courts have thus already made the transition from absolute parliamentary sovereignty to a qualified version of parliamentary sovereignty in the sphere of rights-consistent interpretation. It is shown in Chapter 2 of this book that the doctrine of parliamentary sovereignty is capable of supporting a system of interpretation according to which judicial law-making is generally permissible in order to give effect to the intention of the enacting legislature if that intention is insufficiently expressed in the statutory words. English courts did not but should have adopted such a system of interpretation under s. 3(1) HRA. Such a system would have looked convincing from an internal UK constitutional viewpoint and from a comparative constitutional viewpoint. The thesis[49] that s. 3(1) HRA would be

---

[48] For this view, see however KAVANAGH, above n. 44, pp. 108–109, 275, 404.
[49] Ibid., pp. 81, 114, 331.

rendered otiose if the courts were not empowered to go against the original intention of the enacting parliament will be rejected.

This book will establish that judges in both jurisdictions have deliberately chosen to express the outer limits of rights-consistent interpretation in vague terms, thus building an element of considerable evaluation and judicial discretion into these limits. As appears from judicial practice in England and Germany, it is mostly the weighing of the interpretative criteria in an individual case that ultimately determines whether or not the outer limits of interpretation are infringed. The weighing process is not governed by a priority ordering, rules, clear principled guidelines or a clear set of factors. It leaves considerable scope for evaluative arguments and judicial discretion. English and German judges possess an almost identical, considerable amount of flexibility and judicial discretion when applying the outer limits of rights-consistent interpretation in an individual case. This finding also demonstrates (a) that English and German judges share a very similar understanding of the value of legal certainty in rights-consistent interpretation and (b) that English and German judges adopt the same balance between formal justice and material justice. This is different under conventional canons of construction. Law is no more independent from values and policy arguments in German courts than in English courts when judges apply the outer limits of rights-consistent judicial law-making. For the outer limits of rights-consistent interpretation, these findings validate S. Vogenauer's thesis that statutory interpretation in England and Germany is fundamentally uniform. The style of rights-consistent judicial law-making in both jurisdictions appears formal and deductive on paper. In reality, however, I will demonstrate that English and German courts are significantly influenced by the facts of a case and policy arguments.

English and German courts have not provided patterns, regularities or generalised conclusions for evaluative arguments when applying the outer boundaries of rights-consistent interpretation. This result is not inevitable. I will show that the argument based on justice, for example, can be structured in a way that reduces the subjective element in evaluative arguments, makes the application of the outer limits of judicial law-making more determinate and increases the level of legal certainty in rights-consistent judicial law-making. It will also be argued that both English and German courts should provide a higher level of legal certainty in (rights-consistent) judicial law-making by adopting and honouring the outer limit that a judge cannot depart from the intention of the enacting legislature. This would remove some of the excesses of an overly objectivised approach to statutory interpretation. Judicial law-making would not be overly restrained and the legislature would not be overburdened if this outer boundary were adopted.

The principle of legality as applied in English courts will be critically analysed and compared with constitution-consistent judicial law-making in German courts at the end of Chapter 3 of this book. This is justified because of the uncertain future of the HRA and the growing use of the principle of legality in English courts. It will be established that an English court's interpretative powers under the principle of legality fall short of the interpretative powers available to judges under s. 3(1) HRA or under constitution-consistent judicial law-making in Germany. The view that the principle of legality departs from conventional canons of construction is nonetheless correct. One of the reasons for this is that the default position for judicial law-making by means of reading down general terms in legislation is that it is a permissible function of the judge under the principle of legality. Based on a comparative discussion with constitution-consistent interpretation in Germany, I will demonstrate that relying on constitutional background presumptions that Parliament must have had in mind when enacting the legislation at issue should only be handled carefully for the principle of legality. For example, these presumptions should be rebuttable by contrary indications in the text of the statute. English judicial practice demonstrates that there is a line that is too easily overstepped between using the principle of legality to ascertain the presumed intention of the enacting parliament and using the principle of legality to protect a right that Parliament ought to have had in mind. Clear outer limits of interpretation should guard this line. These limits do not exist in judicial practice. The reason for this lack goes back to the unclear relationship between the rule of law and the principle of parliamentary sovereignty. It will be contended that English judicial practice suffers from a lack of consistency when it (a) formally preserves the doctrine of absolute parliamentary sovereignty but (b) at the same time undermines the doctrine with tools of statutory interpretation. This inconsistency also undermines legal certainty.

2.3. THE EUROPEAN LEGAL DUTY OF CONFORMING INTERPRETATION

Chapter 4 critically analyses and compares the EU legal duty of conforming interpretation as applied in English and German courts, particularly conforming judicial law-making. The EU legal duty of conforming interpretation refers to the duty of national courts to construe national law in the light of the wording and the purpose of an EU directive in order to achieve the result sought by the directive. We will see that the strength of conforming interpretation has increased over time in both jurisdictions. This development has coincided with a widening of the outer limits of conforming interpretation over time. Whereas the rising strength of conforming interpretation has corresponded with a changing understanding of parliamentary sovereignty in England, a similar constitutional development has not occurred in Germany.

English and German scholars regularly accuse national courts of exceeding the limits of the judicial function when engaging in conforming judicial law-making.[50] I will argue that this criticism is warranted for English, but not for German judicial practice. Since the duty of conforming interpretation serves the interests of one party to the proceedings, the Member State and the EU, the book shows that there exist considerable incentives for a national court to find a conforming meaning. One way to make sure that this is possible is to adopt wide outer limits and techniques of conforming judicial law-making. English and German courts use the same outer limits and techniques of judicial law-making irrespective of whether the national legislation pre-dates or post-dates, implements or does not implement an applicable directive. Similarly to rights-consistent interpretation, conforming interpretation in judicial practice focuses on the question of whether a provision's desired conforming reading does not exceed the outer limits of the judicial function. The interpretative structure can be described as a "negative" approach in both jurisdictions. This applies to rights-consistent interpretation as well, but deviates from interpretation in a purely domestic context under conventional canons of construction.

Chapter 4 of this book eliminates the uncertainty about whether the outer limits of conforming interpretation stem from national law, EU law or a mix of both. It will be argued that the CJEU has developed European methodological rules that interact with national canons of statutory construction: the European interpretative priority rule and the presumption of compliance. I propose that the EU legal duty of conforming interpretation is a hybrid legal instrument according to its methodological design. The interpretative priority rule functions as a selection rule between different possible meanings of a provision. The EU presumption of compliance bears upon the range of possible meanings and interacts with national canons of construction. This illustrates the harmonising influence of European methodological rules on national legal methodologies. English and German courts operate a strong national as well as a European presumption of compliance when they interpret implementing legislation. The strength of the presumption of compliance is, however, not settled in English case law. The relationship between national legal methods and European methodological rules can be described with the following concepts: overlapping, intervention and "Europeanisation from the inside". The *contra legem* limit of conforming interpretation is principally but not fully determined by national legal methodology. For example, the CJEU has not yet decided

---

50   G. AIRS, Conforming construction, (2008) 956 *Tax Journal* 15; N. BALDAUF, *Richtlinienverstoß und Verschiebung der Contra-legem-Grenze im Privatrechtsverhältnis*, Mohr Siebeck, Tübingen 2013, pp. 179, 185, 191, 196; T. HERVEY and N. SHELDON, Judicial method of English courts and tribunals in EU law cases: a case study in employment law, in U. NEERGAARD, R. NIELSEN and L. ROSEBERRY (eds.), *European legal method – paradoxes and revitalisation*, DJØF Publishing, Copenhagen 2011, pp. 327, 370–371; L. MICHAEL and M. PAYANDEH, Richtlinienkonforme Rechtsfortbildung zwischen Unionsrecht und Verfassungsrecht, *NJW* 2015, 2392.

whether clear and unambiguous statutory language of national legislation marks or does not mark the *contra legem* limit as per European law. This question is governed by national law. National autonomy is however, confined by European methodological rules. The European presumption of compliance, in particular, has the ability to influence, to "stretch" or to shift the *contra legem* limit. For German law, I will show that the presumption of compliance has stretched, but not shifted the *contra legem* limit. The European presumption of compliance is thus a major factor that can explain the powerful operation of conforming judicial law-making in English and German courts for implementing legislation. Establishing this presumption comes close to harmonising the *contra legem* limit for conforming interpretation by stealth and without the likely backlash from national courts that an open and explicit harmonisation of the *contra legem* limit would have caused.

The default position for conforming judicial law-making in both jurisdictions is that it is a permissible function of the judge. I will demonstrate that Lord Oliver initiated this change in default position vis-à-vis English conventional canons of construction in *Pickstone*. This was a major converging move that brought the interpretative powers of English judges closer to the recognised interpretative powers of German judges. EU law did not require Lord Oliver to depart from a number of well-established canons of interpretation; neither did the Parliament of 1972. The significant modification of conforming interpretation initiated by Lord Oliver rather amounted to a (common law) evolution of statutory interpretation. This evolution was consistent with constitutional doctrine and it was motivated by constitutional developments. In the light of changes in the doctrine of parliamentary sovereignty, Lord Oliver redefined the constitutional role of the judiciary vis-à-vis the legislature in the field of conforming statutory interpretation. Whereas English courts can deviate from and surpass the limits and techniques of conventional judicial law-making for the EU legal duty of conforming interpretation, the BVerfG has clarified that the outer limits and techniques of conforming judicial law-making equal and may not exceed those of judicial law-making in a purely domestic context. Whereas the BVerfG has rejected a "Europeanisation from the inside" for German law, Lord Oliver's speech in *Pickstone* had the effect of establishing it for English law. These different approaches to extending judges' interpretative powers beyond those available under conventional canons of construction must be seen in the light that the default positions for conventional judicial law-making differ considerably in both jurisdictions.

English and German courts have drawn an analogy between conforming interpretation and rights-consistent interpretation. Judges in both countries would not only infringe this analogy but also their obligations under the EU legal duty of conforming interpretation if they fell short of adopting the outer limits and techniques of rights-consistent judicial law-making for conforming judicial law-making. The claim that "[n]othing in EU law … requires national courts to depart from the ordinary canons of statutory interpretation"[51] is therefore wrong. After the coming into force of the Human Rights Act 1998 and in particular after *Ghaidan*, the "Europeanisation from the inside" established by Lord Oliver in *Pickstone* has ceased to exist. This book proves that the EU principle of equivalence now requires English courts to apply the same outer limits and techniques of Convention-compatible interpretation for conforming construction. "Transferring" the outer boundaries of Convention-compatible interpretation to conforming interpretation further widened judicial powers, and this coincided with a further converging push towards the wide interpretative powers available to German judges.

From a UK constitutional viewpoint, however, this widening of the outer limits of conforming judicial law-making exceeds the judicial function. That is because the analogy with Convention-compatible interpretation empowers English courts to depart from what can reasonably be presumed to be the intention of the enacting parliament even if the challenged legislation post-dates the ECA. As for Convention-compatible interpretation, it will be shown that English courts have already made the transition from absolute parliamentary sovereignty to a qualified version of parliamentary sovereignty in the sphere of conforming interpretation. One reason for the significant congruence in the outer limits of conforming interpretation in England and Germany is that English judges have ventured outside their constitutional role. These domestic developments in the UK constitutional sphere are one of multiple factors that influence the move towards converging outer limits of conforming interpretation in England and Germany. A second factor is CJEU case law on conforming interpretation establishing the EU principle of equivalence and European methodological rules. A third factor is CJEU case law on the supremacy of EU law, which has triggered modifications in the doctrine of parliamentary sovereignty. It is also striking that, compared to the "high jumps" by English legal methodology, German legal methodology for conforming judicial law-making hardly deviates from what is otherwise accepted under conventional judicial law-making in Germany.

Courts in both jurisdictions follow the analogy between conforming and rights-consistent judicial law-making. Therefore, the key findings for Chapter 3 of this book also apply *mutatis mutandis* for the comparison of the techniques and outer limits of conforming judicial law-making in England and Germany. With regard to the outer limits of conforming interpretation, this book's findings validate S. Vogenauer's thesis that statutory interpretation in England and Germany is fundamentally uniform. There are no significant differences in the way the highest English and German courts express and apply the outer limits of

---

[51] T. HERVEY and N. SHELDON, Judicial method of English courts and tribunals in EU law cases: a case study in employment law, in U. NEERGAARD, R. NIELSEN and L. ROSEBERRY (eds.), *European Legal Method – Paradoxes and Revitalisation*, DJØF Publishing, Copenhagen 2011, pp. 327, 371.

conforming interpretation. Any remaining differences do not appear to have the potential to threaten the uniform effectiveness of directives in both countries.

This book will demonstrate that the outer limits and techniques of conforming judicial law-making are highly adaptable. They integrate European influences and safeguard the full effectiveness of directives in the national legal sphere. This can partly be explained by virtue of the indeterminate state of these limits and techniques. Examples of such adaptability include (a) the integration of the EU presumption of compliance into the judicial reasoning process in both jurisdictions, (b) the influence of the European presumption of compliance on the application of the double criterion and on the application of the concept of gap in Germany and (c) the change of the rules of interpretation for the EU legal duty of conforming interpretation in *Pickstone* in England. These examples strengthen the position of those who argue that legal cultures in Member States are not static and may evolve based on a European harmonisation programme.[52] Conversely, these examples weaken the position of those who suggest that legal cultures in Europe may not converge.[53]

It cannot be said that English or German methods of statutory interpretation are inapt for the interpretative tasks of domestic courts in a Europeanised environment. The aptness of directives as an instrument of European legal harmonisation is not challenged by national methods of conforming interpretation in England and Germany. The disclaimer is that the adaptability of national methods must be paired with a judicial attitude to do whatever lies in the court's jurisdiction in an individual case. The considerable latitude available to domestic judges under national canons of construction also explains why the cooperative relationship between the CJEU and national courts is a key element for the effectiveness of the EU legal duty of conforming interpretation. Whether or not English and German courts narrowly apply, liberally apply or stretch the outer limits of conforming judicial law-making depends on a multitude of legal and extra-legal factors that are weighed in an individual case. My analysis of the case law reveals that a preliminary reference ruling from the CJEU may de facto increase the willingness of a national court to find a conforming meaning. Even if the considerable amount of judicial discretion is taken into account, this book finds that the application of the outer limits of conforming judicial law-making converges in both jurisdictions. At least when construing implementing

---

[52] L.-P. BRANDT, Die Chancen für eine einheitliche Auslegung eines Europäischen Zivilgesetzbuches, V&R Unipress, Osnabrück 2009, pp 93, 145; M. GISEWSKI, *Methodik der Auslegung im kontinentaleuropäischen und angelsächsischen Recht: Vergleich und Synthese juristischer Denkweisen vor dem Hintergrund der europäischen Privatrechtsvergleichung*, Kovač, Hamburg 2008, p. 278; J. HAGE, Legal reasoning and legal integration, (2010) 10 *MJ* 67, 95; C. LYONS, Perspectives on convergence within the theatre of European integration, in P. BEAUMONT, C. LYONS and N. WALKER (eds.), *Convergence and divergence in European public law*, Hart, Oxford 2002, pp. 79, 84–85.

[53] See references in n. 34 above.

legislation, English and German judges use their discretion similarly to respond to existing incentives[54] by applying conforming interpretation in a powerful way. Overall, the book concludes that the highest English and German courts interpret national implementing legislation in conformity with directives "to the fullest extent possible". It follows that judges cannot be said to lack the will to interpret national law in conformity with EU directives in England or Germany. In contrast, it will be shown that a stretching of the outer limits of conforming judicial law-making has occurred in both jurisdictions. This stretching devalues the outer boundaries to a certain extent. That is, however, not an issue that is peculiar to conforming interpretation as a similar stretching of the outer limits of judicial law-making appears in the realm of rights-consistent interpretation in both jurisdictions. For example, the fundamental features of the legislation or the scheme of the legislation are highly indeterminate concepts. I will demonstrate that these limits are not fully settled in either jurisdiction. The case law is partly inconsistent and in need of clarification in both countries.

Compared with the interpretation of implementing legislation, a considerable restraint towards conforming judicial law-making can be discerned when the highest German courts construe non-implementing legislation that precedes an applicable directive. However, it will be established that there is no difference in the overall interpretative approach in such cases compared to cases where implementing legislation is at issue. The reluctance of the German Federal Court of Justice (*Bundesgerichtshof*; BGH) to adopt a highly objectivised approach to conforming interpretation fits in seamlessly with the emerging trend, driven by the BVerfG, towards a greater relevance of the intention of the enacting legislature in statutory construction.

I will also show that concerns of legal certainty that relate to the predictability of judicial law-making do not function as a further, independent limit for the possible conforming meanings of a provision outside the realm of legal methodology. From a national legal perspective, concerns of legal certainty are already exhaustively incorporated in the abstract stipulation and the specific application of the outer techniques and limits of judicial law-making. It will be argued that the EU principle of legal certainty requires that these techniques and limits must be sufficiently coherent and sufficiently determinate so that the interpretation and application of national legislation in conformity with an applicable directive is foreseeable by those subject to it. A powerful application of this EU safeguard has the potential to (a) demand narrow and determinate outer limits of conforming judicial law-making and (b) intervene in the national separation of powers. This potential has not been unlocked and is unlikely to

---

[54] One incentive is, for example, that the duty of conforming interpretation serves the interests of one party to the proceedings, the Member State and the EU. Another incentive is that the functions of conforming interpretation are fulfilled best if the outer limits of conforming interpretation are applied in a loose fashion.

be unlocked. One of the reasons for this is that a powerful application of the EU principle of legal certainty would weaken the functions of conforming interpretation and would undermine the effectiveness of EU directives.

2.4. THE NEW LEGAL DUTY OF CONFORMING INTERPRETATION AFTER BREXIT

It will be shown in Section 8 of Chapter 4 that the EU legal duty of conforming interpretation will continue to apply in the UK during the transition period as if the UK were still a Member State of the EU if the Withdrawal Agreement in its current draft form is finalised and incorporated into UK law.[55] I will also demonstrate that s. 5(2) of the EU(W) Act domesticates the EU legal duty of conforming interpretation. That means that conforming interpretation will continue to apply after exit day to UK legislation enacted prior to exit day at least for as long as that legislation remains unmodified after exit day. This analysis spells out that conforming interpretation will retain an important role in statutory interpretation in the UK after Brexit. It is further submitted that European methodological rules will continue to apply to conforming interpretation after exit day. There are, however, two modifications to the interpretative duty compared with the situation before Brexit: first, conforming interpretation under s. 5(2) of the EU(W) Act refers to the meaning of this interpretative obligation as construed by the CJEU prior to exit day. Second, the domesticated duty of conforming interpretation refers to EU directives in their interpretation by EU courts prior to exit day. I will argue that English courts should apply the same outer limits and techniques of conforming judicial law-making before and after exit day.[56] The main (comparative) findings of Chapter 4 will therefore continue to hold true after Brexit for a comparison between (a) the EU legal duty of conforming interpretation as applied in German courts and (b) the "new" duty of conforming interpretation under s. 5(2) of the EU(W) Act as applied in English courts.

2.5. TRENDS AND CONVERGENCE IN JUDICIAL LAW-MAKING

The critical analysis of English and German case law in this book reveals that the outer limits of judicial law-making in both jurisdictions perform poorly when

---

[55] Draft agreement on the withdrawal of the United Kingdom of Great Britain and Northern Ireland from the European Union and the European Atomic Energy Community, 19 March 2018. The draft withdrawal agreement is available online at https://www.gov.uk/government/publications/draft-withdrawal-agreement-19-march-2018.
[56] A qualification to this argument is that English courts should not depart from what can reasonably be presumed to be the enacting parliament's intent under the new legal duty of conforming interpretation after Brexit.

judged against their functions to (a) restrict the scope of possible meanings of a provision, (b) limit judicial power and thus address separation of powers concerns and (c) reduce the area of extra-legal considerations and subjective judicial evaluation in rights-consistent interpretation. The application of the outer limits of judicial law-making is to a considerable extent governed by evaluative arguments and judicial discretion. This finding undermines legal certainty, but it is not inevitable. First, it will be argued that courts could and should increase the level of specificity of the outer limits of judicial law-making by including more formal elements in judicial reasoning. Examples of such formal elements are priority rules, priority elements, a formal understanding of the "legislative deliberation limit" under s. 3(1) HRA etc. Second, courts should control and structure evaluative arguments, and I demonstrate how this is possible by structuring the argument based on justice.

It is possible to discern an increase in the weight given to legislative history in modern-day English and German courts. This is to be welcomed as it increases the level of legal certainty provided in statutory interpretation. It also reduces judicial reliance on a "reasonable" legislature and on presumed legislative intent. In parallel with this development, I detect a growing trend among contemporary BVerfG judges to place more emphasis on the intention of the enacting legislature in statutory interpretation. This change in judicial attitudes compared to case law in the second half of the 20th century affects the outer limits and techniques of judicial law-making. This change seems to be predominantly based on the way current judges understand their constitutional role vis-à-vis the legislature. I will propose that one underlying reason for this change is the failure of *Wertungsjurisprudenz*[57] to exert disciplining pressure on judicial law-making. English law is experiencing an opposite trend away from adhering to the intention of the enacting parliament and towards a more objectivised understanding of legislative intent. The key factor driving this development is a weakening of the doctrine of parliamentary sovereignty. Even though it is possible to recognise contrasting trends in statutory interpretation in English and German judicial practice, the book argues that both trends appear to bring the outer limits of judicial law-making in England and Germany closer to one another.

One conclusion of the book is that a fundamental unity of statutory interpretation exists in English and German judicial practice in the sphere of rights-consistent and conforming judicial law-making, but not in the area of conventional judicial law-making. A distinctive mode of legal thinking in England and Germany cannot be discerned in Chapters 3 and 4. This finding is surprising due to constitutional differences in both jurisdictions that ought to

---

[57] *Wertungsjurisprudenz* (the jurisprudence of values) was the predominant legal theory in Germany in the second half of the 20th century.

impact on judicial law-making. The explanation is that the constitutional settings have also converged. The UK constitutional framework has evolved, mainly due to modifications in the orthodox doctrine of parliamentary sovereignty. This change has been prompted by both domestic factors, in particular the introduction of the HRA, and European factors. These factors have triggered changes in judicial attitudes towards judicial law-making and in the institutional relationship between the judiciary and the legislature. The book establishes that these factors can explain to a considerable extent the converging outer limits and techniques of rights-consistent and conforming judicial law-making in both jurisdictions. Another reason for the high level of convergence in the sphere of rights-consistent and conforming judicial law-making is that English courts have exceeded their judicial powers and have stepped outside their constitutional role.

Compared to the significant developments in English legal methodology, German courts apply the same outer limits and techniques to all modes of judicial law-making. It will be argued that one of the reasons for this is that the interpretative powers under conventional judicial law-making are already extensive and highly malleable. These powers have proven flexible enough to accommodate the requirements of EU law and of the German Basic Law.

3. (IR)RELEVANCE OF LIMITS AND TECHNIQUES OF INTERPRETATION

This book aims to reshape the debate about the role of interpretative limits and techniques for judicial decision-making in the sphere of statute law. It is controversial whether and to what extent interpretative criteria determine the outcome of a judicial decision. Interwoven with this controversy is the question of whether interpretative criteria are used by judges in order to (a) discover the meaning of a statute or (b) solely to justify an interpretative decision that judges have reached based on other extra-legal factors of discovery. Such extra-legal factors can refer to intuition,[58] the personal or historic-societal pre-understanding[59] (*Vorverständnis*), emotions, personal values,[60] ideological

---

[58] A. WISTRICH and J. RACHLINSKI, Implicit bias in judicial decision making: how it affects judgment and what judges can do about it, in S.E. REDFIELD (ed.), *Enhancing justice: reducing bias*, ABA Book Publishing, Chicago 2018, pp. 87, 88.

[59] J. ESSER, *Vorverständnis und Methodenwahl in der Rechtsfindung*, 2nd ed., Athenäum Verlag, Frankfurt am Main 1972. For a further sub-categorisation of the concept of pre-understanding, see KRAMER, above n. 14, pp. 47–51, 328–330.

[60] R.J. CAHILL-O'CALLAGHAN, The influence of personal values on legal judgments, (2013) 40 *Journal of Law and Society* 596–623.

preferences and attitudes, pragmatic concerns or political persuasions.⁶¹ The debate about the role of legal methodology for judicial decision-making is ultimately concerned with the functions of legal methodology. A legalist would argue that in order to decide a case, a judge must know the facts and the law and then apply the law to the facts. Determining the applicable law necessitates interpretation of the law. The latter is governed by objective interpretative criteria that guide and limit the interpretation of legislation. These criteria are designed to provide courts with guidance in situations where the meaning of a provision is unclear. Furthermore, the rules of interpretation limit arbitrary judicial decisions. They ensure that judicial decisions are reached in a reasonable, replicable and predictable way.⁶² A realist would reply that the rules of interpretation are only used to construct justifications for an outcome of a case.⁶³ It is ultimately the facts of a case together with subconscious or unarticulated rules and extra-legal considerations, but not rules of interpretation, that guide the decision-making process of a judge.⁶⁴

A descriptive account of how judges reach decisions is most likely to be found somewhere in the middle between the legalist and realist extremes.⁶⁵ Assuming that an agreement exists about the applicable maxims of interpretation, formal

---

61   For an overview of the discussion, see G. BECK, *The legal reasoning of the Court of Justice of the EU*, Hart, Oxford 2012, pp. 17–51 (at pp. 46–47, Beck provides a categorisation of extra-legal factors of discovery); F. BYDLINSKI, *Juristische Methodenlehre und Rechtsbegriff*, 2nd ed., Springer-Verlag, Vienna 1991, pp. 140–175; KRAMER, above n. 14, pp. 47–51, 325–336; S.A.E. MARTENS, *Methodenlehre des Unionsrechts*, Mohr Siebeck, Tübingen 2013, pp. 34–49.

62   See e.g. HERRESTHAL, above n. 14, pp. 46–55; KRAMER, above n. 14, p. 50; S. VOGENAUER, Eine gemeineuropäische Methodenlehre des Rechts – Plädoyer und Programm, ZEuP 2005, 234, 235.

63   M. AMSTUTZ, In-between worlds: *Marleasing* and the emergence of interlegality in legal reasoning, (2005) 11 *ELJ* 766, 778; W. HASSEMER, Gesetzesbindung und Methodenlehre, *ZRP* 2007, 213, 218; cf. ESSER, above n. 59, pp. 122–124.

64   For an overview of realist accounts, see N.W. BARBER, Legal realism, pluralism, and their challengers, in ULLA NEERGAARD and RUTH NIELSEN (eds.), *European legal method: towards a new European legal realism?*, DJØF Publishing, Copenhagen 2013, pp. 189, 190–194; BYDLINSKI, above n. 61, pp. 141–162; F.B. CROSS, The new legal realism and statutory interpretation, (2013) 1 *The Theory and Practice of Legislation* 129–148.

65   For such an approach, see e.g. BECK, above n. 61, pp. 2–3; BYDLINSKI, above n. 61, pp. 173–175; J. KOMAREK, Legal reasoning in EU law, in A. ARNULL and D. CHALMERS (eds.), *The Oxford handbook of European Union law*, OUP, Oxford 2015, pp. 28, 34; KRAMER, above n. 14, pp. 50–51, 334–336; R. POSNER, *How judges think*, Harvard University Press, Cambridge, Mass. 2008, p. 43; B. RÜTHERS, *Die unbegrenzte Auslegung*, 7th ed., Mohr Siebeck, Tübingen 2012, pp. 505–506, 517–518; U. SCHROTH, Hermeneutik, Norminterpretatoin und richterliche Normanwendung, in A. KAUFMANN, W. HASSEMER and U. NEUMANN (eds.), *Einführung in Rechtsphilosophie und Rechtstheorie der Gegenwart*, 8th ed., C.F. Müller, Heidelberg 2011, pp. 270, 296. For an understanding of the interpretative criteria as a means to justify an interpretative result and as a means to limit the range of possible interpretative results (as opposed to a means to discover the meaning of a statute), see J. BRAUN, *Deduktion und Induktion*, Mohr Siebeck, Tübingen 2016, pp. 122–123.

legal reasoning does not fully determine the exact outcome of every case.[66] Formal legal reasoning refers to reasoning that proceeds deductively from legislation and according to formal features of a uniform interpretative methodology. There are multiple reasons why formal legal reasoning does not fully determine the outcome of every case. One is that legislation is of general application. It often uses general categorisations instead of exhaustive lists.[67] Legislative language is often not precise but rather vague and/or ambiguous, and it often does not prescribe with exactitude the limits of its own application in every case.[68] The legislature may also intend to grant judges a certain evaluative scope when they interpret a specific provision. The legislature can delegate law-making power to the courts, e.g. by consciously using vague terms in legislation, by deliberately not providing for any specific guidance to the judge or by not regulating a controversial matter at all and instead indicating in legislative materials that solving the issue is left to the judiciary.[69] The legislature may use vague terms in legislation in order to give judges the power to concretise the law to fit present social, economic and political circumstances. In these scenarios, even highly determinate and specific rules of interpretation are no panacea for subjectivity in interpretation.[70] If, for example, a specific subject matter is only incompletely regulated by statute, judges can only partially draw on existing statutory provisions and the legal values enshrined in them. They need to take into account evaluative arguments (policy arguments)[71] when deciding a case. If the statutory language is left deliberately indeterminate and if, therefore, the statutory words are open to multiple possible meanings, judges must choose between those meanings. Judges do make a policy choice[72] when deciding such a case.[73]

---

[66] For the building blocks of a well-designed (sufficiently prescriptive, complete, definite, general, internally structured and well-expressed) interpretative methodology, see R.S. SUMMERS, *Form and function in a legal system – a general study*, CUP, New York 2006, chapter 8. For the distinction between formalistic statutory interpretation and the overall form or formal features of an interpretative methodology, see ibid., pp. 275–281.

[67] *Del Rio Prada v. Spain* (2014) 58 EHRR 37, para. 92; D. GRIMM, Constitutional adjudication and constitutional interpretation: between law and politics, (2011) 4 *NUJS Law Review* 15, 22.

[68] J. LAWS, Judicial activism, ALBA papers on judicial activism, 12 December 2016, para. 5, available online at https://judicialpowerproject.org.uk/; R. ZIPPELIUS, Rechtsnorm und richterliche Entscheidungsfreiheit, (1970) 25 *JZ* 241–242.

[69] Cf. BVerfG, *NJW* 1997, 386, 388; BGH, *NJW* 2009, 1962, para. 13 – *Schiedsfähigkeit II*.

[70] Cf. MARTENS, above n. 61, p. 73.

[71] The terms "evaluative argument" and "policy argument" will be used synonymously in this book.

[72] Policy arguments can be defined as "substantive justifications for decisions to which judges appeal when the standards and rules of the legal system do not provide a clear resolution of a dispute. In contrast to authority reasons which appeal to clear rules and principles of the legal system, policy arguments appeal to the values which justify a choice of appropriate rule"; see J. BELL, Policy arguments in statutory interpretation, in R.S. SUMMERS, N. MACCORMICK and J. BELL (eds.), *Legal reasoning and statutory interpretation: Rotterdam lectures in jurisprudence*, Gouda Quint, Arnhem 1989, pp. 55, 58–59.

[73] J. BELL, *Policy arguments in judicial decisions*, Clarendon Press, Oxford 1983, pp. 244–245; BELL, above n. 72, pp. 59–60; D. LIEBWALD, Law's capacity for vagueness, (2013) 26 *International Journal for the Semiotics of Law* 391, 407; cf. *YL v. Birmingham City Council* [2007] UKHL 27, para. 128 (Lord Neuberger).

Apart from the text, system, history and purpose of the legislation under consideration, the interpretative process in English and German courts includes other (evaluative) criteria. These evaluative criteria, such as principles of justice, fairness and reasonableness, stand outside the specific statutory context, and they are independent of the statute itself (*außergesetzliche Wertungsmaßstäbe*).[74] Even though these suprapositive principles stand outside a specific statute, they may still be considered "law". A court does not necessarily exceed its judicial role if it takes them into account when interpreting legislation. In Germany, a judge is bound by "legislation and law" (*Gesetz und Recht*) according to art. 20(3) German Basic Law. The BVerfG has recognised that if a statute loosens its ability to provide a *just* solution for every case that falls within its scope of application due to changes in social values or political, technical or economic circumstances, a judge is entitled and obliged to examine what is *law* according to art. 20(3) German Basic Law.[75] Similarly, the BVerfG has recognised in its *Soraya* judgment that a judge may take into account evaluative assumptions such as justice that are immanent in the constitutional legal order when deciding a case.[76] In England, a judge can consider principles of justice, reasonableness and fairness as common law background assumptions when interpreting statutes.[77] That is because statutes are drafted on the basis that the ordinary rules and principles of the common law apply unless such rules and principles are expressly or impliedly excluded by the statute.[78] The common law principles of justice and fairness operate as constitutional principles.[79] When interpreting legislation, courts apply a presumption against implicit alteration of the common law. Evaluative arguments, such as those based on justice, fairness or reasonableness, are frequently consequentialist in character[80] as they are often based on the consequences a certain interpretation is likely to have. The difficulty

---

[74] Cf. LORD JUSTICE LAWS, The impact of the Human Rights Act 1998 on the interpretation of enactments in the UK, in R. BIGWOOD (ed.), *The statute: making and meaning*, LexisNexis NZ, Wellington 2003, p. 241.

[75] BVerfG, *NJW* 1990, 1593–1594; BVerfG, *NJW* 2006, 3409 – *Marlene Dietrich*.

[76] BVerfG, *NJW* 1973, 1221, 1225 – *Soraya*. For a more "direct" connection in the case law of the BVerfG between (a) the meaning of "law" in art. 20(3) German Basic Law and (b) the principle of justice, see BVerfG, *NJW* 2006, 3409 – *Marlene Dietrich*.

[77] *R. (Plantagenet Alliance Ltd) v. Secretary of State for Justice* [2014] EWHC 1662 (QB), paras. 90–91 (Hallett LJ); LAWS, above n. 68, paras. 5–7; T.R.S. ALLAN, *Law, liberty, and justice*, Clarendon Press, Oxford 1994, chapter 4.

[78] *R. (Pierson) v. Secretary of State for the Home Department* [1998] AC 539 (HL), 573 (Lord Browne-Wilkinson); *R. (Plantagenet Alliance Ltd) v. Secretary of State for Justice* [2014] EWHC 1662 (QB), paras. 91–92 (Hallett LJ).

[79] *R. (Pierson) v. Secretary of State for the Home Department* [1998] AC 539 (HL), 588–589 (Lord Steyn). See also ALLAN, above n. 77, chapter 4; T.R.S. ALLAN, Statutory interpretation: why complaints of judicial disobedience make no sense, University of Cambridge Faculty of Law Legal Studies Research Paper Series, no. 46/2015, September 2016, p. 23, available online at http://www.ssrn.com. For further discussion see below, Chapter 3, Section 8.

[80] Cf. N. MACCORMICK, *Legal reasoning and legal theory*, Hart, Oxford 1978, pp. 105–106.

lies in demarcating legitimate evaluative arguments from illegitimate evaluative arguments.[81] Whereas the former fall under "legislation and law" according to art. 20(3) German Basic Law, the latter belong to the realm of politics and, thus, the legislature. A judge who makes or justifies an interpretative choice on the basis of factors that lie outside legislation and law exceeds the judicial role in England and in Germany. That is why discovering or justifying the meaning of a provision based on extra-legal factors like emotions is outside the judicial function.

Evaluative arguments drawn from justice, fairness or reasonableness play a significant role when judges justify decisions in written judicial opinions in England and Germany. This corresponds with a presumption that the legislature did not intend to enact unjust, unfair and unreasonable legislation.[82] Rather than being a separate identifiable stage in legal reasoning, evaluative arguments are generally intertwined with formal legal reasoning in judicial practice. For example, the text, system and history of a provision can point in different directions and lead to rival possible meanings of a provision. Absent a clear hierarchy of maxims of interpretation or a clear system of weight attached to each maxim, an evaluative argument can be used to justify the choice between different meanings.[83] In other words, a judge can take into account the probable consequences of an interpretation when making a choice between multiple possible meanings. N. MacCormick refers to this process as second-order justification.[84] It is controversial whether and to what extent evaluative arguments can also be integrated into the teleological or purposive approach to statutory interpretation and thus form part of the first-order interpretative process. That depends on one's understanding of the teleological and the purposive criterion in statutory interpretation.[85] If we look at judicial practice in England and Germany, we can see that evaluative arguments not only function as second-order justification, but can also be intertwined with historical, systematic and particularly purposive or teleological reasoning.[86] Evaluative arguments thus co-determine the possible meanings of a provision. What is important for our purposes is that arguments such as justice, reasonableness or fairness

---

[81] For discussion, see W. HASSEMER, Politik aus Karlsruhe?, (2009) 63 JZ 1, 7–8.
[82] For examples, see VOGENAUER, above n. 28, pp. 44–48, 136–138, 999–1001, 1124–1129, 1234–1235; D. GREENBERG (ed.), *Craies on Legislation*, Sweet & Maxwell, London 2017, paras. 19.1.5–19.1.5.1 (for England). For an English case, see *R. (Edison First Power Ltd.) v. Central Valuation Officer* [2003] UKHL 20, paras. 116–117 (Lord Millett).
[83] Cf. *Duport Steels Ltd. v. Sirs* [1980] 1 All ER 529 (HL), 551 (Lord Scarman).
[84] MACCORMICK, above n. 80, p. 101.
[85] For discussion, see N. MACCORMICK, *Rhetoric and the rule of law*, OUP, Oxford 2005, pp. 132–137; F. REIMER, *Juristische Methodenlehre*, Nomos, Baden-Baden 2016, paras. 359–372.
[86] For discussion, see BELL, above n. 72, pp. 55, 58–61, 73–74; Z. BANKOWSKI and N. MACCORMICK, in N. MACCORMICK and R.S. SUMMERS (eds.), *Interpreting statutes*, Dartmouth, Aldershot 1991, pp. 359, 385; VOGENAUER, above n. 28, pp. 44–48, 136–138, 999–1001, 1124–1129, 1234–1235.

as applied in judicial practice are considerably indeterminate and evaluative, which is why they contain an element of subjectivity.[87] Evaluative arguments open up the interpretative process to extra-legal considerations. Extra-legal considerations can be disguised in evaluative arguments. Since evaluative arguments are intertwined with first-order judicial reasoning in English and German courts, it is possible for judges to disguise extra-legal considerations in first-order reasoning.

At least in a certain range of cases, let us call them hard cases,[88] judicial interpretation of legislation contains an element of choice and subjective evaluation. A judge uses discretion to decide the case.[89] The decision-making process is not fully determined by deductive reasoning and objective criteria. Instead, a frame exists within which different and competing interpretations are reasonable and tenable.[90] The choice between those meanings is an exercise in policy-making. Despite the subjective component in statutory interpretation, empirical evidence showing that formal legal reasoning is meaningless when judges reach judicial decisions in hard cases has not been provided yet. Legal arguments matter, and decisions are not necessarily result driven. Legal interpretation in hard cases is not simply the application of political criteria in a judicial setting. Experiments on formalistic legal context and formal legal language have shown that formality can function as a de-biasing mechanism for the judicial decision-making process. These experiments indicate the same effects for formal legal reasoning in written judicial opinions.[91] Even if formal legal reasoning does not determine the outcome of a case completely, it can still be an influential factor of discovery. To put it in a different way: judicial discretion is limited. The next question that arises is to what extent formal legal reasoning guides the interpretative process. That partly depends on which method (e.g. positivism, originalism or purposivism) is applied in courts.[92]

---

[87] Cf. H. KELSEN, *Was ist Gerechtigkeit?*, Reclam, Stuttgart 2016, p. 15; MACCORMICK, above n. 80, pp. 105–106, 251–254.

[88] For a discussion of the distinction between "easy" and "hard" cases, see J. BENGOETXEA, *The legal reasoning of the European Court of Justice*, Clarendon Press, Oxford 1993, pp. 181–217. For a definition of "hard case", see MACCORMICK, above n. 85, p. 50: "A hard case is now understood as a case where some difficulty of interpreting the law has arisen, where there are strong arguments for each of the rival understandings or interpretations of the law put forward by or on behalf of the parties".

[89] BARAK, above n. 14, pp. 39, 53, 60, 91–92, 207–217; BECK, above n. 61, p. 156; B. BIX, *Law, language, and legal determinacy*, Clarendon Press, Oxford 1993, p. 28; POSNER, above n. 65, p. 9; F. SCHAUER, *Thinking like a lawyer*, Harvard University Press, Cambridge, Mass. 2012, p. 175.

[90] BYDLINSKI, above n. 61, p. 174; KRAMER, above n. 14, pp. 334–336.

[91] Z. LIU, *Formalities and utilitarian decision: an experimental investigation of Chinese judges*, 2016, pp. 17–18, available online at http://www.ssrn.com.

[92] For discussion, see GRIMM, above n. 67, pp. 23–27.

We will discover in later chapters of this book that contemporary English and German judgments show a considerable engagement with matters of statutory interpretation and legal methodology when the meaning of a provision is difficult to reconcile with its wording. In this respect, the style of judgments is similar in both jurisdictions. These are hard cases, and in hard cases judges know that they operate at the border between permissible interpretation and impermissible judicial legislation.[93] An extensive explanation of a provision's meaning with formal legal reasoning in hard cases does not necessarily mean that the canons of statutory interpretation are a highly influential factor during the discovery process. It may only mean that judges (a) do not want to give the impression that they trespass into the sphere of the legislature, (b) want to increase the legitimacy of the interpretative result by giving extensive methodological arguments, (c) engage with legal doctrine as the appropriate discourse for the judicial decision, which is central to judges' professional identity, and/or (d) appeal to the public's belief that judicial decision-making should be determined by the law alone and not by judges' personal views. Yet, formal legal reasoning cannot be simply marginalised as a tool that disguises the real reasons why judges decide a case in a specific way.[94] Since judges are bound by statute, deriving decisions from provisions using formal legal reasoning is a constitutional necessity and expresses that judges recognise the binding force of statute. Formal legal reasoning and a formal application of the outer limits and techniques of judicial law-making aim to safeguard that a judge is bound by statute.

Providing formal legal reasoning in written judicial opinions, that is at the level of justification, fulfils important functions,[95] even if one accepts that evaluative arguments such as justice, fairness and reasonableness ought to influence the decision-making process of a judge and that subjective evaluations co-determine this process. This is true even if one is of the opinion that judges provide formal legal reasoning only to conceal their true motives and only to justify a decision that they have reached on other grounds. Formal legal reasoning can de-bias; it forces judges to reflect, and it serves as a controlling factor for the desired outcome of a case.[96] Not every desired outcome of a case can be justified by formal legal reasoning. Formal legal reasoning facilitates rational critique and, to a certain extent, predictability and controllability of judicial reasoning in an inter-subjective manner. Formal legal

---

[93] See, e.g. *Revenue and Customs Commissioners v. IDT Card Services Ireland Ltd.* [2006] EWCA Civ 29, para. 82 (Arden LJ); *Fleming (t/a Bodycraft) v. Customs and Excise Commissioners* [2006] EWCA Civ 70, para. 57 (per Arden LJ).
[94] H.L.A. HART, *The concept of law*, 2nd ed., OUP, Oxford 1994, pp. 140–141; U. KISCHEL, *Rechtsvergleichung*, C.H. Beck, Munich 2015, §6, para. 155.
[95] For a discussion of general justifications of formal reasoning in the law, see ATIYAH and SUMMERS, above n. 35, pp. 23–27.
[96] POSNER, above n. 65, p. 110.

reasoning increases legal certainty.[97] The principle of legal certainty is a constitutional principle in England and in Germany. The rule of law is a constitutional doctrine in the UK.[98] It incorporates the principle of legal certainty as a fundamental element.[99] An equivalent doctrine to the rule of law in England is the *Rechtsstaatsprinzip* in Germany,[100] which is enshrined in art. 20(2) and (3) German Basic Law.[101] The *Rechtsstaatsprinzip* also incorporates the principle of legal certainty as a fundamental element.[102] The term rule of law will be used in this book to refer to both the rule of law in the UK constitution and the *Rechtsstaatsprinzip* in Germany. A key difference between both constitutional doctrines is, however, that the requirements of the *Rechtsstaatsprinzip* do constrain the ordinary legislature, whereas the requirements of the rule of law in England do not ultimately limit the law-making power of Parliament according to the orthodox understanding of parliamentary sovereignty.

One dimension of the principle of legal certainty is predictability. Predictability implies an absence of arbitrariness. It generally demands that any actions of the state affecting an individual must be sufficiently foreseeable.[103] With regard to legislation, this means that citizens should be able to rely upon what they read in a statute so that they can regulate their conduct accordingly.[104] The application

---

[97] See H.P. AUST, A. RODILES and P. STAUBACH, Unity or uniformity? Domestic courts and treaty interpretation, [2014] *Leiden Journal of International Law* 75, 79; BARAK, above n. 14, pp. 40–41; KOMAREK, above n. 65, pp. 28–29; MARTENS, above n. 61, pp. 113, 121.

[98] *Black-Clawson International v. Papierwerke Waldhof-Aschaffenburg* [1975] AC 591 (HL), 638 (Lord Diplock); *R. (Unison) v. Lord Chancellor* [2017] UKSC 51, paras. 65–68 (Lord Reed, with whom Lord Neuberger, Lord Mance, Lord Kerr, Lord Wilson and Lord Hughes agreed).

[99] *R. (Spath Holme) v. Secretary of State for the Environment, Transport and the Regions* [2001] 2 AC 349 (HL), 397–398 (Lord Nicholls). See also T. BINGHAM, *The rule of law*, Penguin Books, London 2011, pp. 37–40.

[100] For an overview of the similarities and differences between the rule of law, as understood in UK constitutional law, and the German *Rechtsstaatsprinzip*, see: N. MACCORMICK, Der Rechtsstaat und die rule of law, *JZ* 1984, 65–70; K.-P. SOMMERMANN, in H. v. MANGOLDT, F. KLEIN and C. STARCK (eds.), *Kommentar zum Grundgesetz: Band 2, Artikel 20 bis 82*, 5th ed., Franz Vahlen, Munich 2005, Art. 20 Abs. 3, paras. 244–247.

[101] The case law of the BVerfG is inconsistent. The BVerfG sometimes refers to art. 20(3) German Basic Law as the legal basis for the *Rechtsstaatsprinzip*, and at other times the BVerfG refers to art. 20(2) and (3) German Basic law; for discussion, see SOMMERMANN, above n. 100, para. 227.

[102] BVerfG, *NJW* 1990, 1593; BVerfG, *NJW* 2005, 126; BVerfG, *NJW-RR* 2016, 1366, para. 57. See also FOSTER and SULE, above n. 15, p. 180.

[103] For Germany: BVerfG, *NJW* 1979, 151, 153; BVerfG, *NJW* 2012, 669, para. 61; BVerfG, *NJW-RR* 2016, 1366, para. 57; FOSTER and SULE, above n. 15, p. 180; E. SCHMIDT-ASSMANN, Der Rechtsstaat, in J. ISENSEE and P. KIRCHHOF (eds.), *Handbuch des Staatsrecht der Bundesrepublik Deutschland*, Band I, 2nd ed., C.F. Müller, Heidelberg 1995, §24, para. 81. For England: A. VON ARNAULD, *Rechtssicherheit*, Mohr Siebeck, Tübingen 2006, pp. 580–588.

[104] For Germany: BVerfG, *NJW* 1990, 1593. For England: *Stock v. Frank Jones (Tipton) Ltd.* [1978] ICR 347 (HL), 354 (Lord Simon); *Black-Clawson International v. Papierwerke Waldhof-Aschaffenburg* [1975] AC 591 (HL), 638 (Lord Diplock); *R. (Spath Holme) v. Secretary of State for the Environment, Transport and the Regions* [2001] 2 AC 349 (HL), 397–398 (Lord Nicholls); *Revenue and Customs Commissioners v. IDT Card Services Ireland Ltd.* [2006] EWCA Civ 29, para. 110 (Arden LJ).

of legislation to a specific situation must be sufficiently predictable. The binding force of statute thus safeguards legal certainty under the rule of law.[105] State action also includes judicial decision-making, which is why judicial interpretation must remain within the restraints set by the rule of law.[106] Where a statute is ambiguous or vague, the foreseeability of state action is reduced. Administrative bodies and institutions in particular may struggle with the implementation and application of vague law as they are not trained in legal methodology.[107] At the judicial level, uncertainties in statutory interpretation must be solved by applying methods of statutory interpretation and formal legal reasoning. At least in theory, the reduction in legal certainty due to vagueness or ambiguity in the statutory language can partly be compensated by a coherent and formal application of determinate interpretative criteria. Predictability of state action also presupposes that the interpretative maxims are sufficiently determinate. Strictly following determinate interpretative criteria promotes legal certainty and a high level of predictability of judicial decision-making in an individual case. Formal legal reasoning limits arbitrariness and discretion and thus increases the acceptability and legitimacy of the judgment and public confidence in the judiciary. "Law would lose its normative force if judicial decisions were widely perceived to be arbitrary, unpredictable, disconnected from the democratically legitimated legislative framework as well as simply incomprehensible in the very basic sense that there was no intelligible relation between what legal norms appear to say and what judges take them to mean".[108] A key task of formal legal reasoning is to reduce the scope of subjectivity in legal reasoning, to "objectify"[109] the activity of statutory interpretation and to make the application of law consistent with the rule of law.[110] That also guarantees the equal and just application of law (formal equality, formal justice).[111]

Analysing interpretative maxims against this background also shows how a legal system balances the tension between legal certainty (formal justice) and

---

[105] BVerfG, *NJW* 1979, 305, 306.
[106] BVerfG, *NJW* 2005, 126.
[107] LIEBWALD, above n. 73, pp. 391, 417.
[108] BECK, above n. 61, p. 150.
[109] This is not the place to enter into the debate about whether objectivity can exist in legal interpretation. For a good overview of the debate, see D.O. BRINK, Legal interpretation, objectivity, and morality, in B. LEITER (ed.), *Objectivity in law and morals*, CUP, Cambridge 2001, pp. 12–65; V. BREDA and L. RODAK (eds.), *Diverse narratives of legal objectivity*, Peter Lang, Frankfurt am Main 2016. See also K. GREENEWALT, *Law and objectivity*, OUP, New York 1992; J. HUSA and M. VAN HOECKE (eds.), *Objectivity in law and legal reasoning*, Hart, Oxford 2013.
[110] O.M. FISS, Objectivity and interpretation, (1981–1982) 34 *Stanford Law Review* 739, 744–745; GRIMM, above n. 67, pp. 15, 23; KRAMER, above n. 14, pp. 50–51; KOMAREK, above n. 65, pp. 28, 43; H. SCHULZE-FIELITZ, in DREIER (ed.), *Grundgesetz: Kommentar, Band II, Artikel 20–82*, Mohr Siebeck, Tübingen 2006, Art. 20 (Rechtsstaat), para. 176; SUMMERS, above n. 66, pp. 250, 269–270.
[111] BARAK, above n. 14, p. 40; B. RÜTHERS, C. FISCHER and A. BIRK, *Rechtstheorie*, 7th ed., C.H. Beck, Munich 2013, paras. 391, 396.

substantive individual justice and fairness (material justice). Lord Neuberger has referred to this tension as "the never ending tussle between certainty and fairness".[112] Neither of these values is absolute. According to case law in England and Germany, the rule of law contains both formal and substantive components: it protects legal certainty and material justice.[113] Interpretative maxims express to what degree a (constitutional) legal order values legal certainty. A legal system that places a strong emphasis on legal certainty could, for example, give significant weight to the wording of a provision or use the statutory wording as the outer limit of the judicial function. Such a strong emphasis on legal certainty carries the risk of legal fossilisation. It would also lead to charges of over- and under-inclusiveness in the application of legislation. A legal system that places a strong emphasis on material justice could, for example, give significant weight to purposive and teleological arguments in statutory interpretation since both canons of interpretation leave sufficient room for incorporating evaluative arguments. Such a system of interpretation would also make the law more responsive to an environment characterised by rapid economic, social and technological change. Such a system would, however, carry the risk of a lower predictability of the law. The comparative analysis provided in this book allows us to determine how the English and German legal systems balance this tension between formal and material justice. One caveat has to be added to this: preferring purposive over textual arguments also shows how a court solves the tension between legal certainty and giving effect to the intention of the legislature, which may be insufficiently expressed in the statutory words.[114] Maxims of interpretation thus also represent a compromise between legal certainty on the one hand and fidelity to the intention of the legislature on the other hand.[115]

The interpretative maxims must themselves be sufficiently determinate in order to achieve their functions. This proposition is backed by empirical evidence showing that rules constrain judges significantly more than do standards.[116] That brings us to the core of the realist critique. It is argued that

---

[112] LORD NEUBERGER, Tweaking the curial veil, November 2014, para. 48, available online at https://www.supremecourt.uk/news/speeches.html.

[113] For Germany: BVerfG, *NJW* 1979, 151, 153; BVerfG *NJW* 1979, 1925; BVerfG, *NJW* 2005, 126; for an overview of the discussion, see SOMMERMANN, above n. 100, paras. 227–241. For England: *R. (Spath Holme) v. Secretary of State for the Environment, Transport and the Regions* [2001] 2 AC 349 (HL), 398 (Lord Nicholls); *R. (Anufrijeva) v. Secretary of State for the Home Department* [2003] UKHL 36, para. 28 (Lord Steyn); *R. (Jackson) v. Attorney General* [2005] UKHL 56, para. 159 (Baroness Hale); *R. (Cart) v. Upper Tribunal* [2011] UKSC 28, para. 89 (Lord Phillips); for an overview of the discussion, see P. CRAIG, Formal and substantive conceptions of the rule of law: an analytical framework, [1997] *PL* 467–487.

[114] *R. (Spath Holme) v. Secretary of State for the Environment, Transport and the Regions* [2001] 2 AC 349 (HL), 397–398 (Lord Nicholls).

[115] CROSS, above n. 2, p. 153.

[116] B. SHEPPARD, Calculating the standard error: just how much should empirical studies curb our enthusiasm for legal standards?, (2011) 123 *Harvard Law Review Forum* 92, 97–105; B. SHEPPARD and A. MOSHIRNIA, For the sake of argument: a behavioral analysis of whether and how legal argument matters in decisionmaking, (2013) 40 *Florida State University Law Review* 537, 578.

current judicial practice shows that the function of interpretative maxims to limit judicial power remains utopian as these maxims tend to be expressed in indeterminate (vague)[117] terms and, thus, leave enough room for evaluative arguments and judicial discretion.[118] If the interpretative maxims are imprecise and vague, they grant a considerable area of interpretative latitude and choice to the judge. This loosens the binding force of statute under the rule of law. Vague interpretative maxims also undermine the transparency of the decision-making process as they can be used to present the outcome of a case as the only logical and legally conceivable option while concealing evaluative choices. There are two main ways to make judicial reasoning more determinate and objective. One way is to minimise the subjective element in statutory interpretation by specifying the applicable interpretative maxims to a greater extent, thereby reducing the area in which evaluative arguments can operate.[119] Increasing the precision of interpretative maxims by incorporating formal elements may not be able to eliminate uncertainties in statutory interpretation, but it can diminish these uncertainties. T. Endicott may be right in claiming that increasing precision in legal rules can increase arbitrariness if the higher degree of precision cannot be justified by the reasons underlying the legal rule.[120] Yet, there is also arbitrariness that comes with interpreting and applying vague standards. It will be shown in this book that the interpretative maxims as applied in judicial practice are far from operating as strict and clear rules. Raising the precision of interpretative maxims enhances the predictability of decision-making and adds consistency to judicial decision-making in all future cases (prior certainty); it thus reduces arbitrariness overall.

---

[117] The terms "indeterminate" and "vague" are used interchangeably in this book. A term is vague and indeterminate to the extent that it has borderline cases; see R. POSCHER, Ambiguity and vagueness in legal interpretation, in L.M. SOLAN and P.M. TIERSMA (eds.), *The Oxford handbook of language and law*, OUP, Oxford 2012, pp. 128, 129; R. SORENSEN, VAGUENESS, *The Stanford Encyclopedia of Philosophy* (Spring 2016 Edition), available online at http://plato.stanford.edu/archives/spr2016/entries/vagueness/.

[118] AMSTUTZ, above n. 63, pp. 766, 778; W. HASSEMER, Rechtssystem und Kodifikation: Die Bindung des Richters an das Gesetz, in A. KAUFMANN, W. HASSEMER and U. NEUMANN (eds.), *Einführung in Rechtsphilosophie und Rechtstheorie der Gegenwart*, 8th ed., C.F. Müller, Heidelberg 2011, pp. 251, 262–263; R. OGOREK, Gefährliche Nähe? Richterliche Rechtsfortbildung und Nationalsozialismus, in F. HERZOG and U. NEUMANN (eds.), *Festschrift für Winfried Hassemer*, C.F. Müller, Heidelberg 2010, pp. 159, 167–171; D. SIMON, *Die Unabhängigkeit des Richters*, Wissenschaftliche Buchgesellschaft Darmstadt, Darmstadt 1975, pp. 88–89.

[119] The claim that an increased strictness of formal legal reasoning in judicial practice will lead to a reduction of policy choices and value judgements by judges is controversial. In favour: RÜTHERS, above n. 65, pp. 505–511. Against: OGOREK, above n. 118, pp. 159, 169; HASSEMER, above n. 63, pp. 213, 214–215.

[120] T. ENDICOTT, *Vagueness in Law*, OUP, Oxford 2000, pp. 191–192. See also C. FORSYTH, "Blasphemy against Basics": doctrine, conceptual reasoning and certain decisions of the UK Supreme Court, in J. BELL, M. ELLIOTT, J. VARUHAS AND P. MURRAY (eds.) *Public law adjudication in common law systems: process and substance*, Hart, Oxford 2016, pp. 145, 147–148.

A second way to make judicial reasoning more determinate is to control, structure and provide common benchmarks for permissible evaluative arguments in order to reduce the subjective element inherent in them.[121] Judicial discretion is constrained and value pluralism is reduced.[122] For example, an argument based on justice is uncontrolled and unstructured if it only refers to what an individual judge thinks is best. Both ways to make judicial reasoning more objective complement each other. Both ways enhance the predictability of judicial decision-making, reduce subjectivity in legal interpretation and thus increase legal certainty. As a side note, it is not contradictory to be of the opinion that evaluative arguments like justice, fairness and reasonableness fulfil a valuable role in statutory interpretation and at the same time criticise judicial practice for leaving too large a role for these considerations and for not further specifying the interpretative maxims.

With regard to the outer limits of statutory interpretation, we can start with the premise that not every desired meaning of a provision can be brought within the framework set by them. This framework narrows the range of possible meanings. Meanings of a provision that surpass these limits cannot be justified. The outer limits of interpretation do not always determine which of the possible meanings of a provision a judge should choose. They mainly exclude meanings which he or she cannot choose. Judges in both jurisdictions have emphasised that they cannot go beyond these limits as that would be to intervene in the sphere of the legislature.[123] These judges also acknowledge the function of the outer limits of statutory interpretation in limiting judicial power. The outer limits of the judicial function demarcate legislation from adjudication. Altering these limits would thus affect the constitutional separation of powers between the judiciary and the legislature. A realist may reply to these considerations that outer limits of interpretation are neither expressly stipulated in the German Basic Law nor in (constitutional) statutes in England. They are ultimately judge-made inventions in both jurisdictions. Abstract constitutional principles of the separation of powers cannot be translated into determinate rules and limits of interpretation.[124]

---

[121] For such proposals, see, e.g. R. THIENEL, *Kritischer Rationalismus und Jurisprudenz*, Manz Verlag, Vienna 1991, pp. 216–220; A. RAFI, *Kriterien für ein gutes Urteil*, Duncker & Humblot, Berlin 2004, pp. 41–42, 79–148. Evaluating the likely economic consequences of possible interpretative choices (economic analysis of law) and obliging the judge to choose the economically superior meaning of the statute is one way that has been proposed, particularly in American legal scholarship, to structure the evaluative element in statutory interpretation; see POSNER, above n. 65, pp. 208–209, 212.

[122] See BECK, above n. 61, pp. 76–90 for an introduction to the concept of value pluralism and for its impact on judicial reasoning and legal certainty.

[123] BAG, *NZA* 2003, 742, 748; BVerfG, *NJW* 2012, 669, paras. 43–44, 55–56; *Ghaidan v. Godin-Mendoza* [2004] UKHL 30, para. 121 (Lord Rodger); *Revenue and Customs Commissioners v. IDT Card Services Ireland Ltd.* [2006] EWCA Civ 29, para. 82 (Arden LJ).

[124] Cf. A. VERMEULE, *Judging under uncertainty: an institutional theory of legal interpretation*, Harvard University Press, Cambridge, Mass. 2006, pp. 31, 71.

The principle of legal certainty, the rule of law and the constitutional separation of powers are affected to a significant degree when judges engage in judicial law-making. Judicial law-making thus provides a strong case for determinate limits and techniques of interpretation for two reasons. The first reason relates to legal certainty. When the statutory language is deliberately kept ambiguous or vague by the legislature, the judge is granted a certain evaluative scope in the decision-making process that is unguided by formal legal reasoning. It does not follow from this delegation of law-making power, however, that judges are empowered to venture outside the possible semantic meanings of (ambiguous or vague) statutory words and add language to the statutory text. If the statutory language is vague or ambiguous, a citizen ought to realise this indeterminacy and ought to realise that the text is open to different possible interpretations. A citizen cannot anticipate from the text of a statute, however, that judges may not follow the text. Surprise is an enemy of justice. A legislative drafting style that favours vague over precise statutory words is a factor militating against formalism and in favour of purposivism in statutory interpretation. A value-oriented and substance-oriented legal culture may thus be more inclined towards allowing judicial law-making. Yet, compared to statutory interpretation within the possible meanings of the statutory words, judicial law-making reduces the foreseeability of decision-making because citizens cannot rely upon what they read in a statute. The statutory language loses its guiding function. This is a strong argument that shifts the balance (a) between formal justice and material justice and (b) between legal certainty and giving effect to the intention of the legislature in favour of formal justice and legal certainty, compared to cases where statutory interpretation remains within the possible semantic meanings of the text. In other words, this argument demands that judicial law-making has determinate outer limits and techniques that restrict its scope. The second reason why judicial law-making requires determinate limits and techniques relates to the separation of powers. The danger that judges may venture outside the legislature's intention seems higher in a legal system where judges can engage in judicial law-making than in a legal system where they cannot add to, alter or ignore statutory words when interpreting legislation. In the latter system, the separation of powers can be controlled by policing the rather transparent border of the possible semantic meanings of the statutory words. In the former system, the level of transparency decreases and so does the level of controllability of the border between interpretation and amendment of legislation. The increased danger of exceeding the limits of the judicial role paired with the decrease in the level of transparency requires determinate limits and techniques of judicial law-making in order to safeguard the separation of powers between the judiciary and the legislature.

The bottom line is that English and German judges have extensively discussed the outer limits of interpretation in published judicial opinions.

Chapter 1. Introduction

It would be counterintuitive to deny them any role in the decision-making process. The analysis of the outer limits of interpretation in this book will enable us to assess their level of (in)determinacy. The analysis will allow us to assess how well these constraints fulfil their functions to (a) limit the scope of possible meanings of a provision, (b) limit judicial power and thus address separation of powers concerns, (c) reduce the area of extra-legal considerations and subjective judicial evaluation in statutory interpretation and (d) provide legal certainty. On the one hand, the more indeterminately these limits are expressed, (a) the bigger is the range of possible meanings that a judge can choose from, (b) the more room they leave for evaluative arguments and extra-legal considerations and (c) the less legal certainty they provide. On the other hand, the more determinate the manner in which the outer limits of interpretation are formulated, (a) the smaller is the range of possible meanings that a judge can choose from, (b) the less room the limits leave for evaluative arguments and extra-legal considerations, (c) the more the decision-making process can be contained by formal legal reasoning and (d) the higher is the level of legal certainty.

With regard to the legalist vs. realist debate, an extensive analysis of English and German case law stipulating and applying outer limits and techniques of judicial law-making is currently lacking. What is more common in the literature is bold claims not backed up with sufficient evidence. I will offer the necessary analysis. This book therefore substantially adds to the debate between realists and legalists about the (ir)relevance of outer limits and techniques for judicial law-making.

4. METHOD AND SCOPE OF THE BOOK

The scope of this book is limited to questions of statutory interpretation of national legislation in English and German judicial practice. The book focuses on the outer limits and techniques of statutory interpretation that English and German judges apply when they venture outside the possible semantic meanings of the statutory language (judicial law-making). These limits and techniques demarcate the outer boundary of the judicial function. The book is thus concerned with the separation of powers between the legislature and the judiciary and how this separation finds expression in limits and techniques of statutory interpretation.[125] It is concerned with the binding force of statute.

---

[125] Beyond the question of the competence of the judiciary vis-à-vis the legislature, judicial law-making in Germany must comply with the same substantive constitutional standards that bind the ordinary legislature, i.e. it must comply with the provisions of the German Basic Law (BVerfG, *NJW* 1991, 2549, 2551; BVerfG, *NJW* 2009, 1469, dissenting opinion by Judges Voßkuhle, Osterloh and Di Fabio, para. 104 – *Rügeverkümmerung*). This limit for judicial

The relationship between constitutional law and methods of interpretation is a key element of this book. The book will not discuss cases where courts have argued that the vague or ambiguous statutory words are capable of bearing a certain meaning, even though there may be disagreement in legal scholarship about whether such a meaning can be squared with the bounds of acceptable linguistic usage. The book will only analyse cases of judicial law-making under conventional canons of statutory interpretation (Chapter 2), s. 3(1) HRA in England and constitution-consistent interpretation in Germany (Chapter 3) and the EU legal duty to interpret national legislation in conformity with EU directives (Chapter 4). This selection was made for the following reasons.

First, a sufficient amount of case law is available in both jurisdictions. Second, the availability of case law mirrors the relevance of these modes of interpretation in judicial practice. Third, these modes of interpretation dominate the academic discussion in both countries about the proper limits of statutory interpretation. Fourth, a discussion of s. 3(1) HRA and conforming judicial law-making is particularly justified from an English perspective due to changes in the UK's constitutional landscape with the adoption of the HRA and the ECA. Fifth, conforming judicial law-making is affected by the EU legal order and by requirements stipulated by the CJEU. Discussing conforming judicial law-making thus allows us to assess how courts in both jurisdictions have coped with these influences, how responsive national legal methodology is to the plurality of legislators in Europe and to what extent an interlocking of both legal orders occurs in the realm of statutory interpretation. Furthermore, conforming interpretation as applied by English courts in more recent years remains under-explored in English scholarship when compared to the extensive literature that exists for Convention-compatible interpretation. Regarding Chapters 3 and 4, the interpretative exercise requires a two-stage test. The first stage involves interpreting the German Basic Law, an EU directive or a Convention right under the HRA. The second stage involves interpreting the national legislation at issue in the light of the meaning of the German Basic Law, the EU directive or the Convention right. Chapters 3 and 4 are only concerned with this second stage. Questions regarding how courts interpret and ought to interpret human rights provisions (including the contested nature of human rights questions and how best to decide them)[126] or provisions in EU directives fall outside the scope of this book.

Even though the book focuses on the link between statutory interpretation and constitutional law, it will not dwell on the theoretical depths of constitutional

---

law-making lies outside the scope of this book. An equivalent limit for judicial law-making does not exist in England due to the doctrine of parliamentary sovereignty.

[126] On this topic, see J. WALDRON, *Law and disagreement*, Clarendon Press, New York 1999; cf. G. WEBBER et al., *Legislated rights: securing human rights through legislation*, CUP, Cambridge 2018.

theory. It will explore in what way UK and German constitutional law, as understood and interpreted in the courts, affects or ought to affect the outer limits and techniques of judicial law-making that are expressed and applied in judicial reasoning. The book will not advocate for only one permissible interpretation, based on a specific constitutional theory, of the statutory words "possible" in s. 3(1) HRA, "construed" in s. 2(4) ECA or "legislation and law" in art. 20(3) German Basic Law. That would be incoherent with the approach to statutory interpretation adopted in this book. These vague terms can accommodate different possible interpretations, and they delegate to the judiciary the task to determine the interpretative maxims and outer limits and techniques of statutory interpretation. It is thus the task of the judges to work out a constitutionally appropriate division of labour between the courts and the legislature. This is a delegation of law-making power to the judiciary at the highest level. The book will explore how judges have understood these vague terms in relation to the outer techniques and limits of judicial law-making. It will aim to set out and illuminate the motives, incentives and reasons that led to a specific judicial interpretation of these terms. It will also highlight the consequences that flow from that interpretation for (a) the constitutional division of powers between the courts and the legislature and (b) the balance between formal justice and material justice and in particular for the principle of legal certainty. Section 3 thus presents (a) the theoretical framework within which and (b) the standard against which these judicial interpretations will be analysed and assessed.

This is a book on statutory interpretation, not on legal philosophy. The book critically analyses judicial reasoning in published written opinions of higher courts that justifies interpretative decisions and contains insights into the limits and techniques of statutory interpretation. For reasons given in the previous section, this book assesses the justificatory features and patterns of interpretative judicial practices in England and Germany. Extra-judicial speeches by judges on questions of statutory interpretation will be assessed as well. Academic literature will be used in order to highlight (a) the current academic debate on and (b) further implications for the limits and techniques of interpretation chosen by the courts. The discussion of the relevant case law is limited to decisions by the Federal Constitutional Court (BVerfG), the Federal Court of Justice (BGH), the Federal Labour Court (BAG) and the Federal Administrative Court (BVerwG) in Germany, and to decisions by the Supreme Court, the House of Lords[127] and the Court of Appeal in England. This limitation is justified as the limits and techniques of statutory interpretation have been laid down in detail by these courts, often in "leading cases", and their judgments carry considerable authority.

---

[127] The UK Supreme Court commenced its work in 2009. It replaced the appellate committee of the House of Lords and the judicial committee of the Privy Council.

In order to find German judgments on judicial law-making, I conducted searches on www.juris.de for *Rechtsfortbildung, Analogie* and *teleologische Reduktion* as a first step. I also looked at those judgments that did not contain any of these terms but were identified in legal scholarship as judicial law-making. As a second step, I examined whether the meaning adopted in those judgments goes beyond or against the possible semantic meanings of the statutory language. In England, no specific terms exist for statutory interpretation that goes beyond the possible meaning of the statutory words. I therefore searched for the terms conforming interpretation, conform interpretation, consistent interpretation, Marleasing, s. 3(1) HRA, s. 4 HRA, principle of legality, rights-consistent interpretation, updating interpretation, absurdity, drafting errors, reading in and reading down on www.westlaw.co.uk as a first step. I also used Westlaw's case analysis function in order to find cases citing key judgments that explore the limits and techniques of judicial law-making. As a second step, I analysed the search results and filtered out those judgments where the courts considered interpretation beyond or against the statutory words.

It will be demonstrated in this book that the limits and techniques of judicial law-making as developed by highest national courts do not differ according to whether the legislation at issue is private or public legislation, delegated or primary legislation. This statement also holds true for criminal legislation if a court engages in judicial law-making in favour of the defendant. The scope for judicial law-making of criminal legislation to the detriment of the defendant, for example by way of analogy, is, however, excluded in Germany[128] due to art. 103(2) German Basic Law. Even though judicial law-making of criminal legislation to the detriment of the defendant is not excluded in England, it is considered to be narrow[129] because criminal statutes are construed strictly against the Crown. For these reasons, cases of judicial law-making of criminal legislation to the detriment of the defendant generally fall outside the scope of this book. The EU legal duty of conforming interpretation as applied by English and German courts illustrates that common limits are used in private and public law cases. Arden LJ discussed the outer limits of conforming interpretation in *IDT Card Services* with regard to the interpretation of tax legislation. In that case, a duty to pay VAT was imposed upon an individual as a result of the conforming reading of the legislation. Arden LJ drew guidance from the House of Lords' decision in *Ghaidan*, a case that concerned the interpretation of a provision in the Rent Act 1977.[130] Her analysis has been adopted in later cases concerned

---

[128] BVerfG, *NJW* 2002, 1779, 1781; BVerfG, *NJW* 2015, 2549 paras. 60–61.
[129] *Bogdanic v. The Secretary of State for the Home Department* [2014] EWHC 2872 (QB), para. 52 (Sales J); for discussion, see GREENBERG, above n. 82, para. 15.1.7.1; VOGENAUER, above n. 28, pp. 1044–1057.
[130] *Revenue and Customs Commissioners v. IDT Card Services Ireland Ltd.* [2006] EWCA Civ 29, paras. 85–92 (Arden LJ).

with the interpretation of copyright legislation,[131] data protection legislation[132] and insurance legislation.[133] In *Vodafone 2*, Sir Andrew Morritt cited counsel for the appellant's summary of common principles for conforming interpretation. The counsel derived these principles from dicta coming from a wide variety of public and private law cases.[134] This summary has been endorsed in later cases concerning the conforming interpretation of consumer contract legislation,[135] anti-discrimination legislation,[136] copyright legislation,[137] pension legislation[138] and the interpretation of legislation relating to civil liability insurance cover.[139] In *Robertson v. Swift*, a unanimous Supreme Court held that the "breadth and importance of this principle [the EU legal duty of conforming interpretation] was authoritatively set out in *Vodafone 2*".[140] In Germany, the BGH's analysis of conforming judicial law-making in the private law case *Quelle II* has been adopted in cases concerning the conforming interpretation of public law legislation.[141] Furthermore, the BVerwG has applied conforming interpretation in cases between an individual and a public authority even if the conforming reading of the provision had the effect of denying an individual's claim against the public authority that would have existed if the provision had been interpreted exclusively according to national criteria.[142] That common outer limits of conforming interpretation apply to public and private law cases also follows from the jurisprudence of the BVerfG. This jurisprudence refers to the same outer limits of statutory interpretation in private and public law cases.[143]

---

[131] *ITV Broadcasting Ltd. v. TV Catchup Ltd.* [2015] EWCA Civ 204, para. 86 (Kitchin LJ); *Football Association Premier League Ltd. v. QC Leisure* [2012] EWHC 108 (Ch), paras. 24–25 (Kitchin LJ).

[132] *Google Inc. v. Vidal-Hall* [2015] EWCA Civ 311, para. 87 (Lord Dyson MR and Sharp LJ, with whom McFarlane LJ agreed).

[133] *Digital Satellite Warranty Cover Ltd. v. The Financial Services Authority* [2011] EWCA Civ 1413, para. 40 (Patten LJ).

[134] *Vodafone 2 v. Revenue and Customs Commissioners* [2009] EWCA Civ 446, paras. 37, 57 (Sir Andrew Morritt, C).

[135] *Robertson v. Swift* [2014] UKSC 50, para. 21 (Lord Kerr, with whom Lady Hale, Lord Wilson, Lord Carnwath and Lord Hodge agreed).

[136] *Blackwood v. Birmingham and Solihull Mental Health NHS Foundation Trust* [2016] EWCA Civ 607.

[137] *Football Association Premier League Ltd. v. QC Leisure* [2012] EWHC 108 (Ch), para. 26 (Kitchin LJ).

[138] *Hampshire v. Board of the Pension Protection Fund* [2016] EWCA Civ 786, para. 44 (Patten LJ).

[139] *Churchill Insurance Co Ltd. v. Fitzgerald & Wilkinson* [2012] EWCA Civ 1166, paras. 49–50 (Aikens LJ).

[140] *Robertson v. Swift* [2014] UKSC 50, para. 21 (Lord Kerr, with whom Lady Hale, Lord Wilson, Lord Carnwath and Lord Hodge agreed).

[141] BGH, *NVwZ* 2014, 1111 paras. 10–12; BVerfG, *BeckRS* 2017, 103948, para. 29.

[142] BVerwG, *DVBl* 2004, 1379–1380.

[143] It also demands that regular courts apply these common outer limits when they engage in conforming judicial law-making; see BVerfG, *NJW* 2012, 669 paras. 43–46.

Even though English and German courts stipulate the same outer limits and techniques for the interpretation of private and public legislation, that does not mean that the interpretative approaches within the framework set by these limits and techniques to do not differ. The book is not claiming that there are no differences when courts interpret tax legislation or social welfare legislation, for example.[144] What it does mean, however, is that the outer limits of the judicial function as expressed by interpretative maxims are the same in these cases irrespective of the branch of law the statute stems from. The book is not primarily concerned with a different application of these limits and techniques in different areas of law and according to the circumstances of the individual case. The book is also not primarily concerned with a different application of these limits and techniques in an individual case by different judges. Such differences in application are not predetermined by constitutional law. Constitutional law only sets a minimum standard, a framework for legal methodology. The book will compare the limits and techniques of judicial law-making in Germany and England at a macro level as opposed to a micro level. The book will also assess the (in)determinacy of these limits and techniques. This will allow us to determine to what extent these limits and techniques are open to such different applications.

The comparative methodology adopted in this book aims to omit at least some of the shortcomings of the traditional comparative method using country reports.[145] It does not follow the dialectical or reflexive method either, i.e. it does not look at the questions from the partial viewpoint of a single legal order as the starting point and later on in the comparative process distances itself from the original viewpoint. Instead, at a high level of abstraction, the individual chapters and non-country-specific headings within these chapters provide a common framework (typology) for the discussion.[146] That framework bridges terminological differences in both jurisdictions. It is informed by commonalities in statutory interpretation in England and Germany at a high level of abstraction. This framework is already a synthesis of initial comparative research. Within this framework, German and English case law will first be discussed according

---

[144] Judicial approaches to statutory interpretation vary from one branch of law to another. For example, different interpretative presumptions apply in different areas of law. For England: *R. (Quintavalle) v. Secretary of State for Health* [2003] UKHL 13, para. 21 (Lord Steyn); BANKOWSKI and MACCORMICK, above n. 86, pp. 359, 393–395. For Germany: BVerfG, judgment of 31.20.2016, no. 1 BvR 871/13, para. 21 (regarding tax legislation), available online at http://www.bundesverfassungsgericht.de; P.O. MÜLEERT, Einheit der Methodenlehre? – Allgemeines Zivilrecht und Gesellschaftsrecht im Vergleich, (2014) 214 *AcP* 188, 200–203. Generally for discussion, see H. FLEISCHER, Europäische Methodenlehre: Stand und Perspektiven, (2011) 75 *RabelsZ* 700, 721–722.

[145] For an overview of methods of constitutional comparison, see A. TSCHENTSCHER, Comparing constitutions and international constitutional law: a primer, February 2011, pp. 7–9, available online at http://www.ssrn.com.

[146] For the limitations of such an approach, see KISCHEL, above n. 94, §3, para. 240.

to their own terminology, methodology and legal culture. The focus will be on how each system works in its own terms. This first step will prevent a premature assumption of commonalities. That does not mean that comparative analyses will not be provided within this first step. Instead, the reader's attention will be directed to comparative insights whenever they appear valuable to illuminate the methodological choices made in one legal system. As a second step, a comparative analysis follows, with a particular focus on converging or diverging interpretative aspects and their possible explanation. This methodology provides broken-down country reports under (as far as possible) neutral topics. It aims to increase the scope for comparative analysis. It also aims to be faithful to the particularity of each individual legal system and, at the same time, allow for sufficient reflections on differences and similarities in both legal systems and their explanation.

CHAPTER 2
CONVENTIONAL CANONS OF STATUTORY INTERPRETATION

Chapter 2 explores the outer limits and techniques of judicial law-making applied by English and German courts under conventional modes of interpretation. The term "conventional" modes of interpretation refers to statutory interpretation in a purely domestic context without regard to EU law or the ECHR. It also excludes the interpretation of ordinary legislation in the light of a constitutional statute or constitutional principles. Chapter 2 is structured as follows: Section 1 discusses the aim of statutory interpretation. Section 2 explains the interpretative criteria and their weighing in both jurisdictions. These two sections provide some background to the main themes of this book. The next two sections introduce the reader to judicial law-making in Germany (Section 3) and England (Section 4). Both sections will focus on the outer limits and techniques of judicial law-making. Section 5 provides a concluding comparative analysis.

1. AIM OF STATUTORY INTERPRETATION

When German courts interpret statutory provisions, they aim to ascertain the intention of the legislature.[1] This presupposes that intentions can reasonably be ascribed to the legislature.[2] According to the BVerfG, the task of the judge is limited to applying as accurately as possible the sense and purpose of the provision as determined by the legislature to the facts of the particular case even if the circumstances have changed[3] or to fill an unintended (*planwidrige*) gap with the recognised methods of statutory interpretation.[4] The question of the appropriate aim of statutory interpretation is a highly controversial topic

---

[1] BVerfG, *NJW* 1960, 1563, 1564; BVerfG, *NJW* 2013, 1058, para. 66 – *Deal im Strafprozess*; BGH, *NJW* 1967, 343, 346; BGH, *NJW* 2013, 2674, para. 27.
[2] For a recent account of this contentious (philosophical) issue, see N. DUXBURY, *Elements of legislation*, CUP, Cambridge 2013, pp. 92–119.
[3] BVerfG, *NJW* 1998, 519, 520 – *Kind als Schaden*; BVerfG, *NJW* 2013, 1058, para. 66 – *Deal im Strafprozess*.
[4] BVerfG, *NJW* 2012, 3081, para. 75 – *Delisting*; BVerfG, *NJW-RR* 2016, 1366, para. 39.

in German legal scholarship.⁵ Existing theories can roughly be grouped into (a) subjective theories, (b) objective theories and (c) mixed theories. According to subjective theories, the notion of legislative intention and the aim of statutory interpretation to determine this intention refer to the original intention of the historical (or enacting) legislature at the time the statute was created (fixed or original meaning). This original intention is binding on the court. Objective theories argue that the aim of statutory interpretation is determined by the normative (or reasonable) sense and purpose inherent in the provision as understood at the time of its application (evolutionary or current meaning). Objective and subjective theories are not always that clear cut in legal scholarship; they can come in different shapes. Existing theories can be further clarified by distinguishing between whether judges should evaluate legislative intent as it existed at the time the statute was enacted (subjective) or at the time they interpret it (objective). Another distinction can be made between the intention of the author of the statute (subjective) and the intention of a reasonable legislature (objective). Particularly when authorial intent is unknown, it is also possible to distinguish between (a) the (hypothetical) intention that the historical legislature would have envisioned, had it been asked to resolve the legal question before the judge (imaginative reconstruction) and (b) the (hypothetical) intent that the legislature would have had as a reasonable person.⁶ A theory of interpretation could, for example, rely on the intention of a reasonable legislature (objective) at the time the statute was enacted (subjective). The use of the objective/subjective terminology in scholarship is a paradox⁷ because a "reasonable legislature" is a fiction. R. Posner has described the concept of a reasonable legislature as "a tool for maximizing the judge's discretion in statutory interpretation" as it is the judge who decides what is reasonable.⁸ In a similar vein, G. Beck has described the term "reasonable" as a "dummy standard which ... seeks to leave determination of individual cases to judicial discretion".⁹

---

[5] For an overview of the discussion, see N. BALDAUF, *Richtlinienverstoß und Verschiebung der Contra-legem-Grenze im Privatrechtsverhältnis*, Mohr Siebeck, Tübingen 2013, pp. 40–73; K. LARENZ and C.-W. CANARIS, *Methodenlehre der Rechtswissenschaft*, 3rd ed., Springer, Berlin 1995, pp. 137–141.

[6] For a more detailed account of subjective and objective systems of interpretation, see A. BARAK, *Purposive interpretation in law*, Princeton University Press, Princeton 2005, pp. 32–37, 150–151.

[7] On the irony of this use of the terminology in German legal scholarship, since the "objective" method often requires subjective judgement, see W. BRUGGER, Legal interpretation, schools of jurisprudence, and anthropology: Some remarks from a German point of view, (1994) 42 *AJCL* 395, 401. See also BARAK, above n. 6, pp. 282, 303 ("paying lip service to legislative intent but defining it as the intent of the reasonable legislature, which in turn becomes the intent of the court").

[8] R. POSNER, *How judges think*, Harvard University Press, Cambridge, Mass. 2008, p. 337.

[9] G. BECK, *The legal reasoning of the Court of Justice of the EU*, Hart, Oxford 2012, p. 96.

A discussion about which of these theories a court follows is not usually[10] found in German judgments. German judgments usually refer to an "objectivised intention" of the legislature as expressed in the provision and as determined by the provision's wording and its context.[11] This is a reference to a reasonable legislature. Critics argue that courts refer to an objectivised intention of the legislature because this concept allows them to deviate from the intention of the enacting legislature when they want to slip in their own subjective value judgements into the interpretative process.[12] We will discover later in this chapter that German judges recognise the need to adapt existing statutes to changing circumstances. They evaluate legislative intent at the time they interpret it. Nevertheless, we will also see in the next section that German courts frequently refer to legislative history,[13] in particular explanatory memoranda of a bill drafted by the relevant governmental department, as an aid to ascertaining the intention of the enacting legislature at the time the statute was enacted. Case law thus indicates that German courts follow a mixed approach, using objective as well as subjective criteria to ascertain the intention of the legislature.

When English courts interpret statutes, they aim to discern and give effect to the intention of Parliament, that is to say, they aim to ascertain the true meaning of the statutory words used by Parliament.[14] In the words of Lord Nicholls, the court is searching for the intention which "the court reasonably imputes to Parliament in respect of the language used".[15] Similarly, Lord Hoffmann stated in *Wilkinson* that a court is to discern the intention of Parliament in a way "which the *reasonable* reader would give to the statute read against its *background*".[16] It follows that discerning the intention of Parliament does not relate to ascertaining

---

10 For an exception see, however, BVerfG, *NJW* 1960, 1563, 1564.
11 BVerfG, *NJW* 1960, 1563, 1564; BVerfG, *NJW* 2002, 1779, 1781; BVerfG, *NJW* 2013, 1058, para. 66 – *Deal im Strafprozess*; BGH, *NJW* 1967, 343, 346; BGH, *NJW* 2013, 2674, para. 27.
12 B. RÜTHERS, C. FISCHER and A. BIRK, *Rechtstheorie*, 7th ed., C.H. Beck, Munich 2013, para. 800; B. RÜTHERS, Methodenfragen als Verfassungsfragen?, (2009) 40 *Rechtstheorie*, 253, 262–263.
13 The term "legislative history" is used in a wide sense in this book. It includes the government's statement of reasons for a bill, parliamentary materials and pre-parliamentary materials relating to the provision or statute.
14 *Black-Clawson International v. Papierwerke Waldhof-Aschaffenburg* [1975] AC 591 (HL), 613 (Lord Reid); *Duport Steels v. Sirs* [1980] 1 All ER 529 (HL), 541 (Lord Diplock); *R. (Spath Holme) v. Secretary of State for the Environment, Transport and the Regions* [2001] 2 AC 349 (HL), 396 (Lord Nicholls); *R. (Quintavalle) v. Secretary of State for Health* [2003] UKHL 13, para. 8 (Lord Bingham), para. 38 (Lord Millett); *Wilson v. First County Trust Ltd. (No. 2)* [2003] UKHL 40, para. 56 (Lord Nicholls). See also J. DYSON, The shifting sands of statutory interpretation, 2014, pp. 24–25, available online at http://www.statutelawsociety.co.uk/wp-content/uploads/2014/01/Sir_John_Dyson.pdf.
15 *R. (Spath Holme) v. Secretary of State for the Environment, Transport and the Regions* [2001] 2 AC 349 (HL), 396 (Lord Nicholls); *Wilson v. First County Trust Ltd. (No. 2)* [2003] UKHL 40, para. 56 (Lord Nicholls).
16 *R. (Wilkinson) v. Inland Revenue Commissioners* [2005] UKHL 30, para. 18 (Lord Hoffmann) – emphasis added.

the actual (subjective) intention of the author of the statute.[17] Neither does it relate to ascertaining the (hypothetical) intention that the historical legislature would have envisioned, had it been asked to resolve the legal question before the judge,[18] but rather to the intent that the legislature is presumed to have had as a reasonable person. That is an objectivised standard of interpretation and as such similar to the standard used in German judicial practice. Parliament's intention is to be derived from the terms of the statute as a whole, read in its context.[19]

As in Germany, it is assumed that general and specific intentions can be ascribed to the legislature. Lord Nicholls noted in *Spath Holme* that the intention of Parliament is an objective rather than subjective concept.[20] The intention of the legislature cannot be equated with subjective intentions of members of the executive or individual Members of Parliament. This is recognised by the BVerfG[21] and by proponents of subjective theories in Germany as well. As in Germany, a controversy exists about whether the notion of the intention of Parliament must be understood in a historical or contemporary sense.[22] With regard to the former, a court construes a statute as it would have been construed immediately after it became law, in which case the court searches for the historical meaning of a statute.[23] In relation to the latter, a court applies the current meaning of the statute to present-day conditions and in the light of the legal system as it exists today. Contemporary judges generally interpret statutes as "always speaking" statutes and look for the current meaning of the statute.[24] As Lord Woolf has said, a statute which is "always speaking" should be construed by continuously updating its wording to allow for changes since the

---

[17] BARAK, above n. 6, pp. 123–124, 346; J. STEYN, Interpretation: legal texts and their landscape, in B.S. MARKESINIS (ed.), *The coming together of the common law and the civil law*, Hart, Oxford 2000, pp. 79, 80–81.

[18] *R. (Quintavalle) v. Secretary of State for Health* [2003] UKHL 13, para. 15 (Lord Bingham), para. 36 (Lord Hoffmann), para. 39 (Lord Millett).

[19] *Black-Clawson International v. Papierwerke Waldhof-Aschaffenburg* [1975] AC 591 (HL), 613–614 (Lord Reid); *R. (Quintavalle) v. Secretary of State for Health* [2003] UKHL 13, para. 8 (Lord Bingham), para. 38 (Lord Millett); *S v. L* [2012] UKSC 30, para. 15 (Lord Reed, with whom all other members of the court agreed).

[20] *R. (Spath Holme) v. Secretary of State for the Environment, Transport and the Regions* [2001] 2 AC 349 (HL), 396 (Lord Nicholls).

[21] BVerfG, *NJW* 1960, 1563, 1564; BVerfG, *NJW* 1983, 735, 738.

[22] *R. v. Ireland* [1998] AC 147 (HL), 158 (Lord Steyn); R. CROSS, Statutory interpretation, 3rd ed., Butterworths, London 1995, pp. 51–52.

[23] See, e.g. *Attorney General v. HRH Prince Ernest August of Hanover* [1957] AC 436 (HL), 465 (Lord Normand); cf. *Duke v. GEC Reliance Ltd.* [1988] AC 618 (HL), 638 (Lord Templeman).

[24] *R. v. Ireland* [1998] AC 147 (HL), 158 (Lord Steyn); *Fitzpatrick v. Sterling Housing Association Ltd.* [2001] 1 AC 27 (HL), 49–50 (Lord Clyde); *McCartan Turkington Breen v. Times Newspapers Ltd.* [2001] 2 AC 277 (HL), 296 (Lord Steyn); *R. (Quintavalle) v. Secretary of State for Health* [2003] UKHL 13, para. 9 (Lord Bingham), para. 23 (Lord Steyn); cf. *Yemshaw v. London Borough of Hounslow* [2011] UKSC 3, paras. 25–28 (Lady Hale). See also O. JONES and F.A.R. BENNION, *Bennion on Statutory Interpretation*, 6th ed., LexisNexis, London 2013, sections 166, 288.

Act was initially framed.[25] That is an objectivised standard of interpretation.[26] As their German counterparts, English judges recognise the need to adapt existing statutes to changing circumstances (updating construction). They thus evaluate legislative intent at the time they interpret the legislation. We will discover in the next section that English judges also frequently refer to legislative history, particularly when identifying the purpose of the legislation. English courts thus use objective and subjective criteria to ascertain the intention of the legislature. Like their German counterparts, they follow a mixed approach. As in Germany, the contentious question about the aim of statutory interpretation is transferred into the weighing of the interpretative criteria. The approach to statutory interpretation adopted by the judiciary in England and in Germany ensures that adapting existing statutes to changing circumstances falls within the judicial function. It also firmly ensures that the power of statutory interpretation remains in the hands of the judges.

Despite these commonalities at this high level of abstraction, it does not follow that the same level of commonalities exists at lower levels of abstraction. For example, even though it is recognised that judges can update a provision's meaning in both jurisdictions, it does not follow from this that an English or German court can depart from the intention of the enacting legislature when updating the meaning of a provision. The limits of judicial law-making may be different in both jurisdictions. Compared to formulations of the aim of statutory interpretation in German judgments, more emphasis is put on the statutory language in English judgments.[27] This can be explained historically as will be shown later in Chapter 2 when the literal rule will be explored. Statutory interpretation in England has traditionally been preoccupied with "ascertain[ing] the meaning of the words used" and not with the question "whether the meaning thus identified of the statutory language is what the legislature meant to say".[28] From a practical viewpoint, differences in the abstract formulations of the aim of statutory interpretation in judgments seem far less important than the actual use and the weighing of the interpretative criteria as well as the aids to statutory interpretation that a court employs in order to identify the intention of the

---

[25] *R. (M) v. Hammersmith and Fulham London Borough Council* (1998) 30 HLR 10 (CA), 16 (Lord Woolf MR).
[26] N. MacCormick and R. Summers, Interpretation and justification, in N. MacCormick and R. Summers (eds.), *Interpreting statutes: a comparative study*, Dartmouth, Aldershot 1991, pp. 511, 524 characterise both England and Germany as wedded to an objective conception of interpretation.
[27] E.g. *Wilson v. First County Trust Ltd. (No. 2)* [2003] UKHL 40, para. 67 (Lord Nicholls, "In particular, it is a cardinal constitutional principle that the will of Parliament is expressed in the language used by it in its enactments"); *Advocate General for Scotland v. MacDonald* [2003] UKHL 34, para. 107 (Lord Hobhouse).
[28] *Maunsell v. Olins* [1975] AC 373 (HL), 391 (Lord Simon). See also *Inland Revenue Commissioners v. Hinchy* [1960] AC 748 (HL), 767 (Lord Reid); *Stock v. Frank Jones (Tipton) Ltd.* [1978] 1 WLR 231 (HL), 236 (Lord Simon); Duxbury, above n. 2, p. 129.

legislature. That means that the contentious question about the aim of statutory interpretation is transferred into the weighing of the interpretative criteria in both jurisdictions. This affects, for example, how much weight judges give to the legislative history of the provision compared to the weight they attribute to the provision's inherent objective purpose. It is this step of the interpretative process that elucidates how a judge understands the notion of the intention of Parliament.

2. THE INTERPRETATIVE CRITERIA AND THEIR WEIGHING

2.1. INTERPRETATION IN A NARROW SENSE (*AUSLEGUNG*)

German legal practice and dominant German legal theory differentiate between (a) statutory interpretation that remains within the possible semantic meanings of the statutory words (*Auslegung*; interpretation in a narrow sense) and (b) statutory interpretation that goes beyond or against the possible semantic meanings of the statutory words (*Rechtsfortbildung*;[29] judicial law-making, interpretation in a wide sense).[30] The latter kind of interpretation either extends or narrows the scope of application of a provision. Since the wording of the provision, as opposed to the historical intention of the enacting legislature, marks the boundary between *Auslegung* and *Rechtsfortbildung*, judicial practice in Germany recognises that the legislature's intention is primarily expressed by the provision's statutory language. The formal separation of the interpretative process in *Auslegung* and *Rechtsfortbildung* is a peculiarity of legal methodology

---

[29] Other English translations for *Rechtsfortbildung* used in scholarly writings include "interpretative law-making", "gap-filling", "judge-made law" or "further development of the law". The latter translation is used by the BVerfG.

[30] See, e.g. BGH, *NJW* 2009, 427, para. 21 – *Quelle II*; BAG, *NZA* 2005, 420, 422; BAG, *EuZW* 2009, 465, paras. 60, 64–65 – *Schultz-Hoff*; BAG, *NZA* 2010, 1020, paras. 28–29 – *Urlaubsentgelt*; BAG, *NZA-RR* 2013, 515, para. 20; F. BYDLINSKI, *Juristische Methodenlehre und Rechtsbegriff*, 2nd ed., Springer, Vienna 1991, pp. 467–468; M. KLATT, *Theorie der Wortlautgrenze*, Nomos, Baden-Baden 2004, pp. 19–20; LARENZ and CANARIS, above n. 5, pp. 143–144. For criticism of use of the possible semantic meanings of the statutory words as the decisive criterion to separate interpretation in a narrow sense from judicial law-making, see M. JESTAEDT, Richterliche Rechtsetzung statt richterliche Rechtsfortbildung, in C. BUMKE (ed.), *Richterrecht zwischen Gesetzesrecht und Rechtsgestaltung*, Mohr Siebeck, Tübingen 2012, pp. 49, 58–60; R. WANK, *Die juristische Begriffsbildung*, C.H. Beck, 1985, pp. 24–33. For criticism against the statutory wording as a methodological limit of interpretation in a narrow sense, see O. DEPENHEUER, *Der Wortlaut als Grenze*, R.v. Decker & C.F. Müller, Heidelberg 1988, pp. 17–18, 33–37, 41. For a criticism of the differentiation between *Rechtsfortbildung* and *Auslegung*, see U. LEMBKE, *Einheit aus Erkenntnis?*, Duncker & Humblot, Berlin 2009, pp. 182–183.

in German legal culture. Compared to Switzerland and Austria,[31] the constitutional permissibility of judicial law-making is not positively enacted but it is presupposed in a number of provisions in German procedural law.[32] Even though the distinction between both modes of interpretation can be expressed relatively clearly in theory, the boundaries between a restrictive *Auslegung* of a provision and judicial law-making by means of teleological reduction of a provision on the one hand and an extensive *Auslegung* and judicial law-making by means of argument by analogy on the other hand are blurred in practice. That is because the possible semantic meanings of the statutory words are themselves a vague boundary that demarcates *Auslegung* from *Rechtsfortbildung*. Furthermore, interpretation in a narrow sense and judicial law-making can be placed on a continuous spectrum of interpretation. They differ only gradually and not in principle in legal practice since courts have recourse to the interpretative criteria when they establish and fill a gap in a provision or statute.[33] The usage of terminology in legal practice does not always, some critics say rarely, uphold the distinction between *Auslegung* and *Rechtsfortbildung* either.[34] German legal scholars have also convincingly argued that a tendency in legal practice exists to conceal judicial law-making as restrictive or extensive interpretation in a narrow sense.[35]

In order to ascertain the intention of the legislature, a German court has recourse to the interpretative criteria. These criteria are not governed by statute

---

[31] S. 7 Austrian Civil Code (Austrian Allgemeines Bürgerliches Gesetzbuch); art. 1 Swiss Civil Code (Swiss Zivilgesetzbuch).
[32] See, e.g. s. 132(4) German Judicature Act (Gerichtsverfassungsgesetz), s. 11(4) German Administrative Procedure Code (Verwaltungsgerichtsordnung), s. 45(4) German Labour Court Act (Arbeitsgerichtsgesetz). The legitimacy of judicial law-making is controversial in German legal scholarship; for an overview of the discussion, see LEMBKE, above n. 30, pp. 250–268.
[33] See, e.g. BGH, *NJW* 1981, 1726, 1727; BAG, *NJW* 2003, 2473, 2475; BAG, *NZA* 2010, 1020 paras. 30–46 – *Urlaubsentgelt*; BVerfG, *NJW* 1973, 1491, 1494; BVerfG, *NJW* 1984, 475 – *Sozialplan*; BVerfG, *NJW* 1998, 1478, 1479; BVerfG, *NJW* 2012, 3081, para. 75 – *Delisting* ("to fill an unintended gap with the recognised methods of statutory interpretation"); LARENZ and CANARIS, above n. 5, p. 188; B. PIEROTH and T. AUBEL, Die Rechtsprechung des Bundesverfassungsgerichts zu den Grenzen richterlicher Entscheidungsfindung, *JZ* 2003, 504, 505. For criticism of this view, see RÜTHERS, FISCHER and BIRK, above n. 12, para. 831; JESTAEDT, above n. 30, pp. 49, 58–60; H. WIEDEMANN, Richterliche Rechtsfortbildung, *NJW* 2014, 2407–2408.
[34] See, e.g. BVerfG, *NJW* 1962, 1715; BVerfG, *NJW* 1973, 1491, 1494; BVerfG, *NJW* 1993, 2863; BVerfG, *NJW* 1998, 1478, 1479 ("restrictive interpretation in a narrow sense" and "via teleological reduction"); BVerfG, *NJW* 2001, 591, 592 – *Benetton*; BGH, *NJW* 2013, 2674, paras. 39, 43 – *Interprofessionelle Sozietät*. For discussion, see S. VOGENAUER, *Die Auslegung von Gesetzen in England und auf dem Kontinent*, Mohr Siebeck, Tübingen 2001, pp. 144–145.
[35] B. RÜTHERS, Rechtswissenschaft ohne Recht?, *NJW* 2011, 434; RÜTHERS, FISCHER and BIRK, above n. 12, paras. 825, 914; D. SCHMALZ, *Methodenlehre für das juristische Studium*, 4th ed., Nomos, Baden-Baden 1998, paras. 378, 403; VOGENAUER, above n. 34, pp. 60–61.

but are ultimately judge-made law. They comprise the wording of the provision (textual criterion), the relationship with other legal provisions (systematic criterion), the legislative history of the statute (historical criterion)[36] and the sense and purpose (*Sinn und Zweck*; *ratio legis*) of the provision (teleological criterion).[37] These criteria are complementary rather than exclusionary.[38] If, for example, the provision's wording is ambiguous or vague, a judge has recourse to the other interpretative criteria in order to determine the meaning of the provision. Among the interpretative criteria, none has absolute priority.[39] Neither has the judiciary created a complete or uniform ordering of priority for the interpretative criteria.[40] Their application often requires a weighing, particularly when the different criteria point to different interpretative results.[41] The relative weight given to each interpretative criterion is not determined by methodological criteria or meta-norms in judicial practice, but instead depends on the circumstances of the individual case.[42] This leaves considerable scope

---

[36] The historical criterion can be divided into (a) genetic interpretation, which requires an investigation into the enacting history of the statute and (b) historical interpretation, which requires an investigation into the pre-enacting history of the statute.

[37] BVerfG, *NJW* 1960, 1563, 1564; BVerfG, *NJW* 2013, 1058, para. 66 – *Deal im Strafprozess*; BGH, *NJW* 1967, 343, 346; BGH, *NJW* 2013, 2674, para. 27 – *Interprofessionelle Sozietät*; LARENZ and CANARIS, above n. 5, pp. 163–165; VOGENAUER, above n. 34, pp. 29–44. See A. BLECKMANN, Zu den Methoden der Gesetzesauslegung in der Rechtsprechung des BVerfG, *JuS* 2002, 942, 943–946 for an analysis of the case law of the BVerfG with regard to the four interpretative criteria.

[38] BVerfG, *NJW* 1960, 1563, 1564; BVerfG, *NJW* 1973, 1491, 1494; BVerfG, *NJW* 2013, 1058, para. 66 – *Deal im Strafprozess*; BGH, *NJW* 1967, 343, 346; BGH, *NJW* 2013, 2674, para. 27.

[39] BVerfG, *NJW* 2002, 1779, 1781; BVerfG, *NJW* 2013, 1058, para. 66 – *Deal im Strafprozess*; BGH, *NJW* 2013, 2674, para. 27.

[40] For exceptions to this general rule and a discussion of different kinds of priority ordering among conflicting arguments in different fields of the law, particularly criminal law, see R. ALEXY and R. DREIER, Statutory interpretation in the Federal Republic of Germany, in N. MACCORMICK and R. SUMMERS (eds.), *Interpreting statutes: a comparative study*, Dartmouth, Aldershot 1991, pp. 73, 92–99. For scholarly proposals for a hierarchy of the interpretative criteria, see BYDLINSKI, above n. 30, pp. 554–565; H.-J. KOCH and H. RÜSSMANN, *Juristische Begründungslehre*, C.H. Beck, Munich 1982, p. 182; J. NEUNER, *Die Rechtsfindung contra legem*, 2nd ed. 2005, C.H. Beck, Munich 2005, pp. 112–116. Other scholars argue against a hierarchy of the interpretative criteria: J. ESSER, *Vorverständnis und Methodenwahl in der Rechtsfindung*, 2nd ed., Athenäum Verlag, Frankfurt am Main 1972, pp. 122–124; A. RAFI, *Kriterien für ein gutes Urteil*, Duncker & Humblot, Berlin 2004, pp. 19–23; C.-W. CANARIS, Die verfassungskonforme Auslegung und Rechtsfortbildung im System der juristischen Methodenlehre, in H. HONSELL et al. (eds.), *Festschrift für E.A. Kramer*, Helbing & Lichtenhahn, Basel 2004, pp. 141, 144; K. LARENZ, *Methodenlehre der Rechtswissenschaft*, 6th ed., Springer, Berlin 1991, p. 340.

[41] BRUGGER, above n. 7, pp. 395, 402; G. HAGER, *Rechtsmethoden in Europa*, Mohr Siebeck, Tübingen 2009, pp. 41–42; VOGENAUER, above n. 34, p. 151.

[42] BYDLINSKI, above n. 30, pp. 555–556; LARENZ and CANARIS, above n. 5, pp. 140–141, 166; S.A.E. MARTENS, *Methodenlehre des Unionsrechts*, Mohr Siebeck, Tübingen 2013, pp. 40–41; VOGENAUER, above n. 34, p. 151. Arguing against a fixed weight (*Gewichtung*) of the interpretative criteria: M. KRIELE, *Theorie der Rechtsgewinnung*, 2nd ed., Duncker & Humblot, Berlin 1976, pp. 85–96; RAFI, above n. 40, pp. 23–24.

for considerations of reasonableness, justice and the consequences of the interpretative outcome as well as judicial discretion.[43]

Courts generally refer to a provision's legislative history if it contains relevant aspects for ascertaining the legislature's intention, e.g. aspects which point to the purpose of the provision as pursued and understood by the enacting legislature at the time when the law was made.[44] This is particularly true for more recent statutes.[45] It also shows that the notion of a provision's purpose is not used as a purely objective concept in case law. To the contrary, it can be significantly determined by the intention of the enacting legislature if a court primarily draws on the legislative materials when working out a provision's purpose. In Germany, draft legislation is mostly developed by government and then brought into Parliament. German courts assume that statements and reasons given in explanatory material to a bill which remain unchallenged in the course of the bill's legislative processing are indications of the actual intention of the enacting legislature.[46] They do not address but rather incidentally affirm the contentious issue whether explanatory memoranda of a bill drafted by the executive (*Regierungsbegründung*) can be used to ascertain the intention of the legislature, i.e. the German Bundestag.[47] In a 2004 judgment, the BVerfG stated that the objectivised intention of the legislature can be derived from the legislative history of a provision.[48] The BVerfG does not appear to apply any theory or any fixed criteria when using or when not using certain legislative materials for the interpretative process, and when determining the weight of legislative material for the interpretative process.[49]

German courts generally state that they aim to ascertain the objectivised intention of the legislature when they interpret legislation. Yet they often give significant weight to a provision's legislative history.[50] *Dicta* addressing the

---

[43] J. BRAUN, *Deduktion und Induktion*, Mohr Siebeck, Tübingen 2016, p. 81; RAFI, above n. 40, p. 24. Critically therefore: KRIELE, above n. 42, pp. 25–26, 314; RÜTHERS, FISCHER and BIRK, above n. 12, para. 815. C.-W. CANARIS, Das Rangverhältnis der "klassischen" Auslegungskriterien, demonstriert an Standardproblemen aus dem Zivilrecht, in V. BEUTHIEN et al. (eds.), *Festschrift für Dieter Medicus*, Carl Heymanns, Cologne 1999, pp. 25, 60–61 denies that the judicial discretion is considerable.

[44] BVerfG, *NJW* 2011, 842, paras. 68, 73–76 – *Dreiteilungsmethode*; BVerfG, *NVwZ* 2015, 510 paras. 93–96; BverfG, *BeckRS* 2018, 11032, paras. 74, 81–87; BGH, *NJW* 1967, 343, 348; BGH, *NJW* 2017, 1093 paras. 41–45.

[45] Cf. BVerfG, *NJW* 1981, 39, 42; ALEXY and DREIER, above n. 40, pp. 73, 97.

[46] BVerfG, *NJW* 2012, 3081, para. 86 – *Delisting*; BVerfG, *NVwZ* 2015, 510 paras. 93, 96; BGH, *NJW* 2009, 427, para. 31 – *Quelle II*.

[47] Cf. BGH, *NJW* 1967, 343, 348; BVerfG, *NVwZ* 2015, 510 paras. 93, 96.

[48] BVerfG, *NJW* 2004, 750, 755; cf. BGH, *NJW* 1967, 343, 348.

[49] For discussion, see T. WISCHMEYER, Der "Wille des Gesetzgebers", (2015) 70 JZ, 957, 964–966.

[50] RÜTHERS, FISCHER and BIRK, above n. 12, para. 800; P. MELIN, *Gesetzauslegung in den USA und in Deutschland*, Mohr Siebeck, Tübingen 2005, p. 280; cf. BGH, *NJW* 1967, 343, 348. This view is not uncontested. Other scholars (e.g. ALEXY and DREIER, above n. 40, p. 63) contend that contemporary judges ordinarily give greater weight to a provision's inherent objective purpose than the legislative materials encompassing the actual intention of the enacting legislature.

weight given to legislative history fail to show consistency, however. Even though the weight given to the legislative materials of a provision by the highest German courts seems to have increased in recent times,[51] *dicta* can still be found that claim that legislative materials are generally not a decisive factor for statutory interpretation.[52] The weight attributed to the historical criterion is generally reduced if a change in social, political, technical or economic conditions has occurred.[53] In such a case, an objectivised understanding of a provision's purpose at the time of application of the statute is likely to prevail in courts. The weight attributed to the identifiable intention of the enacting legislature also reduces with the ageing of the statute.[54] Again, this can only serve as a rough guideline since a powerful *dictum* by three dissenting judges in the BVerfG's *Rügeverkümmerung* decision states that the task of judicial law-making is to continuously enforce the intentions of the enacting (historical) legislature even if the law has evolved.[55]

2.2. CANONS OF INTERPRETATION IN ENGLAND

In order to identify the intention of Parliament, a contemporary English judge employs recognised canons of interpretation, including a variety of interpretative presumptions and aids.[56] The great majority of these interpretative criteria are based in the common law, that is to say, they are judge made.[57]

---

[51] Compare the weight attached to the legislative history in BVerfG, *NJW* 1960, 1563, 1564 ("only with a certain degree of caution, usually merely supportive") on the one hand and in BVerfG, *NJW* 2013, 1058, para. 66 – *Deal im Strafprozess* ("significant indicative effect") and BGH, *NJW* 1994, 457, 458 ("key significance") on the other hand. For a discussion of this development in the adjudication of the BVerfG, see B. RÜTHERS, Trendwende im BVerfG? Über die Grenzen des "Richterstaates", *NJW* 2009, 1461–1462; D. ULBER, Die Rechtsprechung des Bundesverfassungsgerichts zu Zulässigkeit und Grenzen richterlicher Rechtsfortbildung im Zivilrecht, *EuGRZ* 2012, 365, 375. See also (a) BVerfG, *NJW* 2009, 1469, dissenting opinion by Judges Voßkuhle, Osterloh, Di Fabio, paras. 107–120, 137–138, 142 – *Rügeverkümmerung*, and (b) BGH, *NJW* 1967, 343, 348 for a discussion of the relevance of legislative materials in statutory interpretation. For recent case law attaching significant weight to the legislative history of a provision when ascertaining the intention of the legislature, see BVerfG, *NVwZ* 2015, 510 paras. 93–96; BVerfG, *NJW* 2015, 1359 paras. 132–136 – *Kopftuch*.

[52] BVerfG, *NJW* 2005, 126, 129.

[53] See, e.g. BVerfG, *NJW* 1973, 1221, 1225 – *Soraya*; BVerfG, *NJW* 1990, 1593–1594; BVerfG, *NJW* 1998, 519, 520 – *Kind als Schaden*; BGH, *NJW* 1955, 1276, 1277–1278 – *Tonband*; BGH, *NJW* 1955, 1433 – *Fotokopie*; BGH, *NJW* 1963, 902, 903 – *Fernsehansagerin*.

[54] Cf. BVerfG, *NJW* 1973, 1221, 1225 – *Soraya*.

[55] BVerfG, *NJW* 2009, 1469, dissenting opinion by Judges Voßkuhle, Osterloh, Di Fabio, para. 142 – *Rügeverkümmerung*.

[56] *R. (Spath Holme) v. Secretary of State for the Environment, Transport and the Regions* [2001] 2 AC 349 (HL), 396–397 (Lord Nicholls); *Wilson v. First County Trust Ltd. (No. 2)* [2003] UKHL 40, para. 56 (Lord Nicholls). In detail: CROSS, above n. 22, chapters 3, 4 and 7; D. GREENBERG (ed.), *Craies on legislation*, Sweet & Maxwell, London 2017, Part 4.

[57] Cf. *Oliver Ashworth (Holdings) Ltd. v. Ballard (Kent) Ltd* [2000] Ch. 12 (CA), 34 (Laws LJ).

Chapter 2. Conventional Canons of Statutory Interpretation

The starting point for statutory interpretation is that language is taken to bear its ordinary meaning[58] in the light of its immediate and obvious context (plain meaning or literal rule).[59] If the ordinary meaning of the statute leads to an absurd result which Parliament could not have intended, however, a court is allowed to depart from this ordinary meaning.[60] This is the so-called golden rule. The proper scope of the golden rule is controversial and has changed over time.[61] Open issues concern (a) the threshold of absurdity, (b) the question of whether the intention of Parliament can only be discerned from the text of the statute or whether it is also possible to do so on the basis of presumptions or material outside the statutory language and (c) whether the golden rule can only be applied in order to give the statutory language a secondary meaning which the words are capable of bearing or whether it also allows judges to deviate from the statutory language by reading words into or out of a statute. Different formulations of the rule in different judgments can be found that support either of these positions. It is also possible to categorise the golden rule as an evaluative argument, because the standard of absurdity as applied by judges stands outside the specific statutory context and is inherently evaluative.[62]

Absurdity is not the only, and in modern times certainly not the most common, possible reason which allows judges to depart from the ordinary meaning of the statutory words. If the ordinary meaning leads to a result "which cannot reasonably be supposed to have been the intention of the legislature", then it is proper for a judge to apply another (secondary) meaning which the words are capable of bearing.[63] The reference to the notion of reasonableness in this quote refers to an objectivised standard of interpretation and also indicates that the process of

---

[58] The terms "ordinary meaning" and "literal meaning" are used synonymously in this book.
[59] *Pinner v. Everett* [1969] 1 WLR 1266 (HL), 1273 (Lord Reid); *British Concrete Pipe Association's Agreement, Re* [1983] 1 All ER 203 (CA), 205 (Donaldson MR); *R. (Spath Holme) v. Secretary of State for the Environment, Transport and the Regions* [2001] 2 AC 349 (HL), 397 (Lord Nicholls); Z. BANKOWSKI and N. MACCORMICK, in N. MACCORMICK and R.S. SUMMERS (eds.), *Interpreting statutes*, Dartmouth, Aldershot 1991, pp. 359, 382; DUXBURY, above n. 2, pp. 153–154; JONES and BENNION, above n. 24, section 285. For a scholarly argument that there is no plain meaning of rules, see A.C. HUTCHINSON, *Toward an informal account of legal interpretation*, CUP, New York 2016, chapter 3.
[60] *Vacher & Sons v. London society of compositors* [1913] AC 107 (HL), 117 (Lord Macnaghten); *Stock v. Frank Jones (Tipton) Ltd.* [1978] 1 WLR 231 (HL), 235–236 (Lord Simon); *Dingmar v. Dingmar* [2006] EWCA Civ 942, paras. 39–40 (Lloyd LJ).
[61] For an historical account of the development and the scope of the golden rule in courts, see DUXBURY, above n. 2, pp. 157–167.
[62] Cf. BANKOWSKI and MACCORMICK, above n. 59, p. 385; N. MACCORMICK, *Legal reasoning and legal theory*, Hart, Oxford 1978, p. 208. See also BARAK, above n. 6, p. 275. For an understanding of the meaning of absurdity that equates the term with an inconsistency with the purpose of a statute, see CROSS, above n. 22, p. 92.
[63] *Pinner v. Everett* [1969] 1 WLR 1266 (HL), 1273 (Lord Reid). See also *Maunsell v. Olins* [1975] AC 373 (HL), 391 (Lord Simon); *British Concrete Pipe Association's Agreement, Re* [1983] 1 All ER 203 (CA), 205 (Donaldson MR); *R. (Jackson) v. Attorney General* [2005] UKHL 56, para. 30 (Lord Bingham).

interpretation is not devoid of evaluative arguments. In order to determine what it is that the legislature intended, a judge may resort to the mischief rule or the purposive approach. Judges also resort to these two approaches[64] in order to determine the meaning of the words used if there is no plain meaning because the statutory language is ambiguous, i.e. capable of having more than one meaning in its context,[65] or because the statute contains vague or general terms. According to the mischief rule, courts take into account the mischief the statute is designed to remedy and construe it in a manner which suppresses the mischief and advances the remedy. The mischief rule has evolved into the modern purposive approach of interpretation.[66] Under the purposive approach, a court gives effect to the underlying purpose which the legislature intended to achieve when it enacted the statute.[67] The purposive approach goes beyond identifying the mischief and extends the context of a statute which a judge is allowed to consider when determining the meaning of the statute.[68] The degree of liberality permitted in using the purposive method of construction is affected by the context of the legislation.[69]

The canons of construction are complementary rather than exclusionary.[70] Among them, none has absolute priority. This is the same in Germany.

---

[64] Purposive approach: *Coltman v. Bibby Tankers Ltd.* [1986] AC 276 (HL), 300–301 (Lord Oliver); *Bloomsbury International Ltd. v. Sea Fish Industry Authority* [2011] UKSC 25, paras. 9–10 (Lord Mance, with whom Lord Walker, Lady Hale and Lord Collins agreed); *Bearmans Ltd. v. Metropolitan Police District Receiver* [1961] 1 WLR 634 (CA), 655 (Devlin LJ); *9 Cornwall Crescent London Ltd. v. Kensington and Chelsea RLBC* [2005] EWCA Civ 324, paras. 47–51 (Arden LJ); *Clark & Tokeley Ltd. (t/a Spellbrook) v. Oakes* [1999] ICR 276 (CA), 288–289 (Mummery LJ). Mischief rule: *Maunsell v. Olins* [1975] AC 373 (HL), 383 (Viscount Dilhorne), 395 (Lord Simon); *Sheldon v. RHM Outhwaite (Underwriting Agencies) Ltd.* [1996] AC 102 (HL), 153 (Lord Nicholls); *Stevenson v. Rogers* [1999] QB 1028 (CA), 1039–1040 (Potter LJ); *R. v. T* [2009] UKHL 20, para. 35 (Lord Phillips).

[65] *Maunsell v. Olins* [1975] AC 373 (HL), 382 (Lord Reid), 393 (Lord Simon); *R. (Spath Holme) v. Secretary of State for the Environment, Transport and the Regions* [2001] 2 AC 349 (HL), 400 (Lord Cooke); *Salomon v. Commissioners of Customs and Excise* [1967] 2 QB 116 (CA), 143 (Diplock LJ); *Clark & Tokeley Ltd. (t/a Spellbrook) v. Oakes* [1999] ICR 276 (CA), 288–289 (Mummery LJ).

[66] Cf. *Stock v. Frank Jones (Tipton) Ltd.* [1978] 1 WLR 231 (HL), 236 (Lord Simon). For an overview of this development, see C. MANCHESTER and D. SALTER, *Exploring the law: the dynamics of precedent and statutory interpretation*, Sweet & Maxwell, London 2006, para. 1-069; I. MCLEOD, *Legal method*, 7th ed., Palgrave Macmillan, Basingstoke 2009, p. 271; R. WARD and A. AKHTAR, *Walker & Walker's English Legal System*, 10th ed., OUP, Oxford 2008, pp. 47–53. Whether the purposive approach evolved from the mischief rule is controversial; for an overview of the discussion, see VOGENAUER, above n. 34, pp. 1110–1111.

[67] *Pepper v. Hart* [1993] AC 593 (HL), 617 (Lord Griffiths); *R. (Spath Holme) v. Secretary of State for the Environment, Transport and the Regions* [2001] 2 AC 349 (HL), 397 (Lord Nicholls); *R. (Quintavalle) v. Secretary of State for Health* [2003] UKHL 13, para. 8 (Lord Bingham); *Robertson v. Swift* [2014] UKSC 50, para. 30 (Lord Kerr).

[68] Law Commission (No. 21) and Scottish Law Commission (No. 11), *The interpretation of statutes*, London 1969, para. 46, para. 81 fn. 177.

[69] *R. (Quintavalle) v. Secretary of State for Health* [2003] UKHL 13, para. 21 (Lord Steyn).

[70] Cf. *Maunsell v. Olins* [1975] AC 373 (HL), 382 (Lord Reid); *Oliver Ashworth (Holdings) Ltd. v. Ballard (Kent) Ltd.* [2000] Ch. 12 (CA), 34 (Laws LJ).

Even though some canons of statutory construction are seen as primary[71] and others as secondary,[72] the judiciary has not created a complete or uniform hierarchy for the interpretative criteria.[73] A difficulty therefore arises when various canons point in different directions and return conflicting answers. As in Germany, applying the interpretative criteria in a case where they lead to rival interpretations often requires a weighing.[74] The relative weight given to each interpretative criterion is not determined by rules or guidelines, but depends on the circumstances of the individual case.[75] It thus leaves considerable scope for considerations of reasonableness, fairness, justice and the consequences of the interpretative outcome. In other words, evaluative arguments are used to justify the choice between different possible meanings.[76] In the words of Lord Reid: "[W]e ... decide *as a matter of judgment* what weight to attach to any particular 'rule'".[77] It is thus not surprising that different judges can form different opinions about the relative weight to be attached to the canons of construction in a specific case.[78] This deficiency of interpretative uniformity impairs values of the

---

[71] Plain meaning rule: *Cheng v. Governor of Pentonville Prison* [1973] AC 931 (HL), 951 (Lord Simon); *R. (Francis & Francis) v. Central Criminal Court* [1989] AC 346 (HL), 387 (Lord Oliver); cf. BANKOWSKI and MACCORMICK, above n. 59, pp. 359, 384–385.

[72] Presumption against absurdity: *Cheng v. Governor of Pentonville Prison* [1973] AC 931 (HL), 957 (Lord Simon).

[73] *Cheng v. Governor of Pentonville Prison* [1973] AC 931 (HL), 949 (Lord Simon); *Maunsell v. Olins* [1975] AC 373 (HL), 382 (Lord Reid), 394–395 (Lord Simon). See also BANKOWSKI and MACCORMICK, above n. 59, pp. 359, 385; MANCHESTER and SALTER, above n. 66, para. 1-065; VOGENAUER, above n. 34, pp. 1134, 1151–1152.

[74] Weighing is not the only possible way to settle the conflict between possible rival interpretations. Others include cancellation of arguments (one applicable argument wholly nullifies the justificatory force of another applicable argument) or overriding of arguments (an argument can be overridden when some other argument takes priority over it under a priority rule); for discussion see MACCORMICK and SUMMERS, above n. 26, pp. 511, 527–529.

[75] *Maunsell v. Olins* [1975] AC 373 (HL), 383 (Lord Reid), 395 (Lord Simon); *Carter v. Bradbeer* [1975] 1 WLR 1204 (HL), 1207 (Lord Diplock); BANKOWSKI and MACCORMICK, above n. 59, pp. 359, 385; LORD JUSTICE SALES, Modern statutory interpretation, (2017) 38 *Statute Law Review* 125, 130.

[76] See, e.g. *Simms v. Registrar of Probates* [1900] AC 323 (PC), 335 (Lord Hobhouse, "But where there are two meanings each adequately satisfying the language, and great harshness is produced by one of them, that has legitimate influence in inclining the mind to the other. ... It is more probable that the Legislature should have intended to use the word in that interpretation which least offends our sense of justice"); *Holmes v. Bradfield Rural District Council* [1949] 2 KB 1 (Divisional Court), 7–8 (Finnemore J).

[77] *Maunsell v. Olins* [1975] AC 373 (HL), 382 (Lord Reid) – emphasis added. Cf. also *Duport Steels Ltd. v. Sirs* [1980] 1 All ER 529 (HL), 551 (Lord Scarman); *YL v. Birmingham City Council* [2007] UKHL 27, para. 128 (Lord Neuberger).

[78] *Jones v. Secretary of State for Social Services* [1972] AC 944 (HL), 966 (Lord Reid); *Carter v. Bradbeer* [1975] 1 WLR 1204 (HL), 1207 (Lord Diplock with reference to *Maunsell v. Olins* [1975] AC 373 (HL)). See also JONES and BENNION, above n. 24, section 20(4); MACCORMICK, above n. 62, pp. 105, 210; D. ROBERTSON, *Judicial discretion in the House of Lords*, OUP, Oxford 1998, chapter 3.

rule of law, including consistent and equal application of the law, predictability and legal certainty. As in Germany, the indeterminacy runs through the whole of the interpretative process: from the aim of statutory interpretation, via the weighing of the interpretative criteria to the outer limits of judicial law-making.

English judges have traditionally attached great and decisive weight to the ordinary meaning: "[S]tatutory language must always be given presumptively the most natural and ordinary meaning".[79] Nowadays, the purposive approach is the predominant principle of statutory interpretation.[80] This change was and is influenced and accelerated by (a) the teleological approach to statutory interpretation as applied by the CJEU,[81] (b) the EU legal doctrine of conforming interpretation as it requires to give effect to the "purpose" of a directive, (c) the growing use of extraneous materials as an aid to construction[82] and (d) the interpretative obligation under s. 3(1) HRA. To what extent these factors can explain the rise of the purposive approach is debated in scholarship.[83] The weakening of the literal rule does not mean that it is not applied any longer in judicial practice.[84] It is still the starting point for statutory interpretation. Arguments from ordinary meaning can be and often are very decisive. The weakening of the literal rule is best understood if the distinction between the purposive and literal approach to interpretation is understood as one of degree only. The rise of the purposive approach only means that "the balance to be

---

[79] *Maunsell v. Olins* [1975] AC 373 (HL), 381 (Lord Simon). Cf. *River Wear Commissioners v. Adamson* (1887) 2 App. Cas. 743, 764–765 (Lord Blackburn); *Cheng v. Governor of Pentonville Prison* [1973] AC 931 (HL), 950–951 (Lord Simon). See also Law Commission (No. 21) and Scottish Law Commission (No. 11), *The interpretation of statutes*, London 1969, para. 80(c); BANKOWSKI and MACCORMICK, above n. 59, pp. 359, 384.

[80] *Pepper v. Hart* [1993] AC 593 (HL), 617 (Lord Griffiths); *R. (Spath Holme) v. Secretary of State for the Environment, Transport and the Regions* [2001] 2 AC 349 (HL), 400 (Lord Cooke); *R. (Quintavalle) v. Secretary of State for Health* [2003] UKHL 13, para. 21 (Lord Steyn); *Bloomsbury International Ltd. v. Sea Fish Industry Authority* [2011] UKSC 25, para. 10 (Lord Mance, with whom Lord Walker, Lady Hale and Lord Collins agreed); *Oliver Ashworth (Holdings) Ltd. v. Ballard (Kent) Ltd.* [2000] Ch 12 (CA), 34 (Laws LJ); VOGENAUER, above n. 34, pp. 1150–1151. Laws LJ has noted two reasons for this development: (1) the interpretation of legislative measures of the EU by the CJEU and (2) the House of Lords' decision in *Pepper v. Hart* [1993] AC 593; *Oliver Ashworth (Holdings) Ltd. v. Ballard (Kent) Ltd.* [2000] Ch 12 (CA), 34 (Laws LJ).

[81] *R. (Quintavalle) v. Secretary of State for Health* [2003] UKHL 13, para. 21 (Lord Steyn); *Oliver Ashworth (Holdings) Ltd. v. Ballard (Kent) Ltd.* [2000] Ch 12 (CA), 34 (Laws LJ); cf. *R. v. Registrar General ex p. Smith* [1991] 2 QB 393 (CA), 404 (Staughton LJ).

[82] *Oliver Ashworth (Holdings) Ltd. v. Ballard (Kent) Ltd.* [2000] Ch 12 (CA), 34 (Laws LJ).

[83] See, e.g. A. JOHNSTON, "Spillovers" from EU law into national law: (un)intended consequences for private law relationships, in D. LECZYKIEWICZ and S. WEATHERILL (eds.), *The involvement of EU law in private law relationships*, Hart, Oxford 2013, pp. 357, 385–387; VOGENAUER, above n. 34, pp. 1317–1323.

[84] See, e.g. *Associated Newspapers Ltd. v. Wilson* [1995] 2 AC 454 (HL), 475 (Lord Bridge); *Secretary of State for Work and Pensions v. Hourigan* [2002] EWCA Civ 1890, para. 33 (Auld LJ). For a discussion of the various functions of the plain meaning rule, see DUXBURY, above n. 2, pp. 150–155.

struck, in the particular case, between the literal meaning of the words on the one hand and the context and purpose of the measure in which they appear on the other" tilts more towards the latter in contemporary English judgments if there is a potential clash between both meanings.[85] What is important for our purposes is that the ordinary meaning of the statutory words does not function as an outer limit of statutory interpretation.

Courts take account of internal and external aids to construction when seeking the intention of Parliament.[86] Other provisions in the same statute serve as an internal aid, for example, whereas other provisions in other statutes or the legislative history of the statute is extraneous material. According to older case law, English canons of construction did not permit a judge to look outside the statute to external aids to construction if the wording of a statute is unambiguous.[87] This has changed with the weakening of the literal rule. Lord Nicholls declared in *Spath Holme* that a judge can use external aids to construction when deciding whether statutory language is clear and unambiguous and not productive of absurdity.[88] Whether the statutory language is ambiguous or not is determined by looking at not just the words alone, but also at the provision's context, including its legislative history.[89]

---

[85] *Oliver Ashworth (Holdings) Ltd. v. Ballard (Kent) Ltd.* [2000] Ch. 12 (CA), 34 (Laws LJ). See also *Carter v. Bradbeer* [1975] 1 WLR 1204 (HL), 1206–1207 (Lord Diplock); *R. (Quintavalle) v. Secretary of State for Health* [2003] UKHL 13, para. 21 (Lord Steyn, "The pendulum has swung towards purposive methods of construction"); GREENBERG, above n. 56, para. 18.1.7. For a seemingly different assessment, see JONES and BENNION, above n. 24, section 285 ("In general, the weight to be attached to the literal meaning is far greater than applies to any other interpretative criterion"); R. SUMMERS and M. TARUFFO, Interpretation and comparative analysis, in N. MACCORMICK and R. SUMMERS (eds.), *Interpreting statutes: a comparative study*, Dartmouth, Aldershot 1991, pp. 461, 481–482.

[86] *R. (Spath Holme) v. Secretary of State for the Environment, Transport and the Regions* [2001] 2 AC 349 (HL), 397 (Lord Nicholls); *Wilson v. First County Trust Ltd. (No. 2)* [2003] UKHL 40, para. 56 (Lord Nicholls). In detail CROSS, above n. 22, chapters 5 and 6.

[87] See, e.g. *Macarthys v. Smith* [1981] QB 180 (CA), 201–201 (Cumming-Bruce LJ).

[88] *R. (Spath Holme) v. Secretary of State for the Environment, Transport and the Regions* [2001] 2 AC 349 (HL), 398 (Lord Nicholls).

[89] *R. (Westminster City Council) v. NASS* [2002] UKHL 38, para. 5 (Lord Steyn, with reference to explanatory notes); *R. (Spath Holme) v. Secretary of State for the Environment, Transport and the Regions* [2001] 2 AC 349 (HL), 397 (Lord Nicholls). See also *Kirkness (Inspector of Taxes) v. John Hudson & Co. Ltd.* [1955] AC 696 (HL), 735–736 (Lord Reid, "A provision is not ambiguous merely because it contains a word which in different contexts is capable of different meanings"); *Attorney-General v. Prince Ernest Augustus of Hanover* [1957] AC 436 (HL), 461 (Viscount Simonds, "… words, and particularly general words, cannot be read in isolation: their colour and content are derived from their context"), 473 (Lord Somervell); Law Commission (No. 21) and Scottish Law Commission (No. 11), *The interpretation of statutes*, London 1969, para. 31; BARAK, above n. 6, pp. 138, 274. See DEPENHEUER, above n. 30, pp. 38–43 for the argument, informed by language theory, that the possible semantic meanings of a provision cannot be determined without taking the contextual scene into account.

Until the House of Lords' decision in *Pepper v. Hart*,[90] references to parliamentary materials (particularly Hansard)[91] as an aid to statutory construction were generally not permissible. This exclusionary rule has been relaxed, and referring to such materials is permissible where (a) legislation is ambiguous or obscure or leads to absurdity; (b) the material relied on consists of one or more statements by a minister or another advocate of the bill, together, if necessary, with such other parliamentary material as might be necessary to understand such statements and their effect; and (c) the effect of such statements is clear.[92] Another part of the legislative history of a statute are the explanatory notes which accompany a bill on introduction. They are usually prepared by the government department responsible for the legislation if a government minister proposes a public bill. The explanatory notes are updated in the light of changes to a bill made in the parliamentary process. They do not form part of the bill, do not receive Parliament's approval and cannot be amended by Parliament. They are intended to aid the understanding of members of the legislature. The explanatory notes are a relatively new development in England. They debuted in the 1998–1999 parliamentary session, and they now accompany every public bill laid before Parliament. A court can always have recourse to these materials in order to explain the purpose of the legislation or the mischief Parliament intended to remedy by the provision. According to Lord Steyn, the conditions of *Pepper v. Hart* do not apply to explanatory notes.[93] When contemporary courts refer to legislative history, they most often refer to the explanatory notes. That resembles the situation in Germany, where courts most often refer to the government's explanatory memorandum. This similarity mirrors a structural similarity in the legislative process in both jurisdictions since it is primarily the executive that brings draft legislation into Parliament/the German Bundestag and prepares the explanatory material.

The use of extraneous materials as an aid to construction has become more liberal in courts in line with the strengthening of the purposive approach.[94] Courts refer to these materials in order to clarify ambiguous statutory words, add greater or less weight to different possible semantic meanings, explain

---

[90] *Pepper v. Hart* [1993] AC 593 (HL).
[91] Hansard refers to the official record of parliamentary debates, including ministerial statements to Parliament.
[92] *Pepper v. Hart* [1993] AC 593 (HL), 631, 634, 640 (Lord Browne-Wilkinson); *R. (Spath Holme) v. Secretary of State for the Environment, Transport and the Regions* [2001] 2 AC 349 (HL), 391 (Lord Bingham). For academic commentary, see LORD STEYN, Pepper v. Hart; a re-examination, (2001) 21 *OJLS* 59–72 and S. VOGENAUER, A retreat from Pepper v. Hart? A reply to Lord Steyn, (2005) 25 *OJLS* 629–674. For recent discussion, see GREENBERG, above n. 56, chapter 28.
[93] *R. (Westminster City Council) v. NASS* [2002] UKHL 38, para. 5 (Lord Steyn).
[94] Cf. *Pepper v. Hart* [1993] AC 593 (HL), 617 (Lord Griffiths).

the purpose of a statute, identify the mischief at which it is directed or set the legislation into its social and practical context.[95] Lord Nicholls expressed the opinion in *Spath Holme* in 2000 that courts should approach the use of extraneous material with caution due to arguments of legal certainty.[96] Based on current court practice, however, it is possible to describe the use of legislative history in statutory interpretation as widespread.[97] Lord Hope said in 2004 that it "has become common practice for their Lordships to ask to be shown the Explanatory Notes when issues are raised about the meaning of words used in an enactment".[98] As is the case in Germany, English courts do not appear to apply any theory or fixed criteria when determining whether to use certain legislative materials for the interpretative process or when determining the weight of the legislative material in the interpretative process.

The recognised maxims of interpretation also include a variety of interpretative presumptions. Of particular relevance for Chapters 3 and 4 of this book is the strong common law presumption that Parliament intends to give effect to the UK's international obligations fully and consistently.[99] This entails a strong presumption "in favour of interpreting an English statute in a way which does not place the United Kingdom in breach of its international obligations".[100] This presumption of compatibility can be traced back to the rule of law which requires compliance by the state with its obligations in international as in national law.[101] The English presumption of compatibility yields to contrary parliamentary intent and does not exclude other canons of construction.[102] That is to say, it may be outweighed in an individual case by another canon of construction or another aid to interpretation pointing in a different direction. What is more important is that the presumption of compatibility is only used to resolve ambiguities, i.e. it requires ambiguous statutory words to apply. It cannot be used to read down unambiguous legislation or to read in additional words into unambiguous legislation for the purpose of consonance with

---

[95] See, e.g. *Wilson v. First County Trust Ltd. (No. 2)* [2003] UKHL 40, para. 56 (Lord Nicholls); *Horton v. Sadler* [2006] UKHL 27, para. 27 (Lord Bingham).
[96] *R. (Spath Holme) v. Secretary of State for the Environment, Transport and the Regions* [2001] 2 AC 349 (HL), 397–398 (Lord Nicholls).
[97] NN, Editorial: The new golden rule, (2014) 35 *Statute Law Review* v–vii.
[98] *R v. Montila* [2004] UKHL 50, para. 35 (Lord Hope).
[99] *Garland v. British Rail Engineering Ltd.* [1983] 2 AC 751 (HL), 771 (Lord Diplock); *Assange v. Swedish Prosecution Authority* [2012] UKSC 22, para. 122 (Lord Dyson), para. 201 (Lord Mance); *R. (JS) v. Secretary of State for Work and Pensions* [2015] UKSC 16, para. 239 (Lord Kerr); *Salomon v. Commissioners of Customs and Excise* [1967] 2 QB 116 (CA), 143 (Diplock LJ).
[100] *Assange v. Swedish Prosecution Authority* [2012] UKSC 22, para. 122 (Lord Dyson).
[101] Cf. T. BINGHAM, *The rule of law*, Penguin Books, London 2011, p. 110.
[102] *Assange v. Swedish Prosecution Authority* [2012] UKSC 22, para. 201 (Lord Mance).

international treaties.[103] This limitation of the presumption illustrates the reign of the theory of absolute parliamentary sovereignty as applied in judicial practice over the rule of law. In the words of Diplock LJ, as he then was: "If the terms of the legislation are clear and unambiguous, they must be given effect to, whether or not they carry out Her Majesty's treaty obligations, for the sovereign power of the Queen in Parliament extends to breaking treaties".[104]

2.3. COMPARATIVE ANALYSIS

A certain method of interpretation is not prescribed by legislation in England or Germany. Legal method is thus to a large extent a matter of judicial choice in both jurisdictions. English and German courts have not created a uniform priority ordering for the interpretative criteria. Their application requires a weighing, and the relative weight given to each criterion depends on the circumstances of the individual case. That also means that the contentious question about the aim of statutory interpretation is not decided on a principled but on a case-by-case basis. Contemporary judges in both jurisdictions apply a mix of objective and subjective criteria when they ascertain the intention of the legislature.[105] This grants a considerable flexibility to judges and leaves considerable scope for considerations of reasonableness, justice and the consequences of the interpretative outcome. Other studies have shown that the types of arguments for resolving interpretative issues that figure in judicial opinions in England and Germany are similar.[106] This book confirms the finding. A characterisation of the contemporary English approach to statutory interpretation as predominantly literal and formal and the contemporary German approach as predominantly teleological is not accurate.[107]

In both jurisdictions, a trend is discernible that contemporary courts refer extensively to the legislative history of a provision when ascertaining its meaning. Multiple reasons may explain this trend. In England, explanatory notes only

---

[103] See the case law cited by Lord Kerr in *R. (JS) v. Secretary of State for Work and Pensions* [2015] UKSC 16, para. 239; cf. *R. (Brind) v. Secretary of State for the Home Department* [1991] 1 AC 696 (HL), 748 (Lord Bridge), 761–762 (Lord Ackner); *Post Office v. Estuary Radio Ltd.* [1968] 2 QB 740 (CA), 757 (Diplock LJ); *Salomon v. Commissioners of Customs and Excise* [1967] 2 QB 116 (CA), 143 (Diplock LJ). See also G. DE BÚRCA, Giving effect to European Community Directives, (1992) 55 *MLR* 215, 219–220.
[104] *Salomon v. Commissioners of Customs and Excise* [1967] 2 QB 116 (CA), 143 (Diplock LJ).
[105] VOGENAUER, above n. 34, p. 1254.
[106] SUMMERS and TARUFFO, above n. 85, pp. 461, 462; VOGENAUER, above n. 34, pp. 1254–1255. For a different view, see T. LUNDMARK, *Charting the divide between common and civil law*, OUP, Oxford 2012, p. 426.
[107] For a different view, see LUNDMARK, above n. 106, pp. 432–433.

debuted in the 1998-1999 parliamentary session, and nowadays they are readily available and accompany every public bill laid before Parliament. It is plausible to assume that this change in the making of legislation also affected the use of legislative history in courts. This is just one example of the interrelationship between the making of legislation and its judicial interpretation. In Section 4.2, for example, I will explore the interrelationship between legislative drafting and the interpretative criteria. I will show that a change in drafting style of legislation from detailed statutory language to general terms and ambiguous words has occurred in England. This change in drafting technique undermines a strict literal rule. The growing use of legislative history thus also goes hand in hand with the decline of the literal rule and the rise of purposivism. Courts refer to legislative history when clarifying ambiguous statutory words or when explaining the purpose of a statute. This contributes to predictability and legal certainty, which were previously achieved through detailed statutory language and the application of the literal rule. A greater reliance on legislative history therefore "compensates" for a loss of predictability that accompanied the change in drafting style of legislation. In Germany there appears to be a growing trend among contemporary BVerfG judges to place more emphasis on the intention of the enacting legislature in statutory interpretation. This change in judicial attitudes seems to be predominantly based on the way current judges understand their constitutional role vis-à-vis the legislature. The trend in both countries to refer to the legislative history of a provision is to be welcomed, at least in relation to explanatory notes and memoranda. The scope for evaluative arguments increases when there is no plain meaning due to ambiguous or vague statutory language or when a court eschews a literal interpretation in favour of giving effect to the provision's underlying purpose. That is because a judge can use policy arguments to determine a provision's purpose. One possibility to counteract the increased scope for evaluative arguments in judicial reasoning is to allow judges to have recourse to legislative history when determining a provision's purpose. Reference to legislative history reduces judicial reliance on a reasonable legislature and on presumed legislative intent. The latter two concepts leave the determination of individual cases to a considerable extent to judicial discretion.

When assessing the weight that a court attaches to a provision's legislative history, at least some English judges use more cautious language than their German counterparts. Whereas statements and reasons in explanatory memoranda of a bill are treated as direct evidence of the actual intention of the legislature in Germany, Lord Steyn[108] has argued that the aims of the executive as revealed in the explanatory notes accompanying a bill cannot be attributed to Parliament. The same is true of ministerial statements made in Parliament.[109]

---

[108] *R. (Westminster City Council) v. NASS* [2002] UKHL 38, para. 6 (Lord Steyn).
[109] *Wilson v. First County Trust Ltd. (No. 2)* [2003] UKHL 40, paras. 58–59 (Lord Nicholls).

Therefore, a provision's legislative history may be used to discern the purpose of the provision or the mischief the provision targets, but not as direct evidence to find the intention of Parliament as expressed by the enacted words.[110] How much this distinction between English and German practice affects the outcome of cases seems questionable, however. That is because an English court can adopt the meaning suggested by an external aid (such as legislative history) as the intention to be imputed to Parliament in using the words in question.

3. GAP-FILLING IN GERMANY

This section and Section 4 will examine the outer limits and techniques of conventional judicial law-making in Germany and England. The formal separation of the interpretative process in *Auslegung* and *Rechtsfortbildung* shows that a provision's wording does not function as an outer limit of statutory interpretation in Germany. A German judge can go beyond statutory interpretation in a narrow sense, i.e. beyond the possible semantic meanings of the statutory words, if the conditions for judicial law-making are satisfied.[111] In the words of the BVerfG: "The statutory words do not always sufficiently indicate the intention of the legislature".[112] "Even an interpretation against the wording of a provision may be possible if other indications clearly show that the provision's purpose has been insufficiently expressed in the text of the statute".[113] The power of German judges to engage in *Rechtsfortbildung* is thus aligned with the aim of statutory interpretation to ascertain the intention of the legislature. *Rechtsfortbildung* may be possible even against the clear and unambiguous wording of a provision.[114] Since *Rechtsfortbildung* departs from the statutory words, it raises issues of the binding nature of the statute, the separation of powers and legal certainty to a significant degree. This necessitates stricter requirements for its admissibility according to German legal practice

---

[110] *R. (Westminster City Council) v. NASS* [2002] UKHL 38, para. 6 (Lord Steyn). See also *Black-Clawson International v. Papierwerke Waldhof-Aschaffenburg* [1975] AC 591 (HL), 614–615 (Lord Reid); *Wilson v. First County Trust Ltd. (No. 2)* [2003] UKHL 40, paras. 58, 66 (Lord Nicholls); LORD STEYN, above n. 92, pp. 59, 68.

[111] One exception to this rule applies for an interpretation of national legislation determining or aggravating a defendant's liability in criminal law. In these cases, permissible statutory interpretation cannot go beyond the possible semantic meanings of the enacted words due to the principle *nulla poena sine lege* enshrined in art. 103(2) GG (BVerfG, *NJW* 2002, 1779, 1781).

[112] BVerfG, *NJW* 2013, 1058, para. 66 – *Deal im Strafprozess*.

[113] BVerfG, *BeckRS* 2016, 47202, para. 7; BGH, *NJW* 2017, 2123, para. 13.

[114] See BVerfG, *NJW* 1979, 305, 306; BVerfG, *BeckRS* 2016, 47202, para. 7; BGH, *NJW* 1952, 337, 338 ("Against the clear wording of section 400 German Civil Code ..."); BGH, *NJW* 1954, 1153, 1154; BGH, *NJW* 1955, 1276, 1277–1278 – *Tonband*; cf. BVerfG, *NJW* 1962, 1715; BVerfG, *NJW* 1973, 1491, 1494.

and scholarship.¹¹⁵ This may also explain why a tendency is detectable in German judgments to declare apparently clear statutory wording ambiguous or vague¹¹⁶ so that the interpretative result adopted by the court still falls within the scope of interpretation in a narrow sense instead of judicial law-making. Interpretation in a narrow sense gives the impression of a higher level of fidelity to legislation than does judicial law-making. German legal scholars have convincingly shown that a tendency in judicial practice exists to conceal judicial law-making as restrictive or extensive interpretation in a narrow sense.¹¹⁷

The BVerfG has advanced two explanations that justify the power of judges to engage in judicial law-making under the rule of the German Basic Law (Grundgesetz; GG). Both justifications have been criticised in the literature.¹¹⁸ The first is a historical argument: "Judicial law-making has always been a recognised function of the courts in German legal history; it is virtually indispensable in the modern state".¹¹⁹ The second is a textual argument: the judiciary is bound by legislation and law according to art. 20(3) GG. Since art. 20(3) incorporates the wider notion of law, the binding force of statute is loosened and permissible statutory interpretation includes not only interpretation in a narrow sense, but also judicial law-making.¹²⁰ The BVerfG understands art. 20(3) GG as rejecting a narrow legal positivism. Legislation and law usually coincide, but this is not necessary and does not happen all the time.¹²¹ The BVerfG may be right to say that the binding force of statute is loosened under art. 20(3) GG but the wording of this provision does not elucidate the relationship between legislation and law.¹²² It does not follow inevitably from the words of art. 20(3) GG that judges are empowered to go beyond or against the statutory words when interpreting a statute. There is ample scope for evaluative considerations that stand outside the specific statutory context. "Law" in art. 20(3) GG could also mean that these considerations can influence the decision-making process of a judge when the statutory language is ambiguous or vague. Other scholars contend that "law"

---

[115] BAG, *NZA* 2005, 420, 422; KLATT, above n. 30, pp. 20, 22–23; J. SCHÜRNBRAND, Die Grenzen richtlinienkonformer Rechtsfortbildung im Privatrecht, *JZ* 2007, 910, 911.
[116] VOGENAUER, above n. 34, pp. 60–61.
[117] RÜTHERS, above n. 35, p. 434; RÜTHERS, FISCHER and BIRK, above n. 12, paras. 825, 914; SCHMALZ, above n. 35, paras. 378, 403; VOGENAUER, above n. 34, pp. 60–61.
[118] See, e.g. C. HILLGRUBER, "Neue Methodik" – ein Beitrag zur Geschichte der richterlichen Rechtsfortbildung in Deutschland, *JZ* 2008, 745, 746–755; C. HILLGRUBER, in T. MAUNZ and G. DÜRIG (founders), *Grundgesetz-Kommentar*, C.H. Beck, Munich 2017, Art. 97 GG, paras. 37, 64–68.
[119] BVerfG, *NJW* 1984, 475 – *Sozialplan*; BVerfG, *NJW* 1985, 2939.
[120] Cf. BVerfG, *NJW* 1990, 1593–1594; BVerfG, *NJW* 1973, 1221 1225 – *Soraya*.
[121] BVerfG, *NJW* 1973, 1221, 1225 – *Soraya*.
[122] The relationship between legislation and law is highly controversial in German legal scholarship. For an overview of the discussion, see M. SCHRÖDER, *Gesetzesbindung des Richters und Rechtsweggarantie im Mehrebenensystem*, Mohr Siebeck, Tübingen 2010, pp. 60–64.

in art. 20(3) GG refers to constitutional law.[123] This reading of art. 20(3) GG appears capable of allowing constitution-consistent judicial law-making of ordinary legislation. Moreover, this reading of art. 20(3) GG does not necessarily rule out or significantly limit conventional judicial law-making and conforming judicial law-making. That is because the scope of constitution-consistent judicial law-making could be understood broadly, based on a wide interpretation of art. 3(1) GG. A premise of art. 3(1) GG is that like cases must be treated alike, different cases differently (equal treatment before the law).[124] We will see in the next section that the justification for the most common techniques of judicial law-making goes back to these principles. The proper scope of judicial law-making would thus depend on how widely or narrowly art. 3(1) GG is interpreted.[125]

Even if one reads art. 20(3) GG as allowing judicial law-making in certain circumstances, it is possible to understand the provision in its historical context, i.e. in the light of the injustices of the Nazi regime. It has been argued that "law" was included in art. 20(3) GG in order to emphasise that legislation and law may not coincide if a statute fails to meet the demands of fundamental principles of justice.[126] The BVerfG stated in a 1953 judgment that the German legislature created injustices during the Nazi regime. Therefore, "it must be possible in extreme cases to value the principle of material justice higher than the principle of legal certainty", the latter being expressed in the application of the positive law to the facts of the case.[127] Against this background, it is possible to interpret art. 20(3) GG as empowering judges to venture outside the statutory words only if this is necessary to reject a fundamentally unjust statute.[128] According to G. Radbruch, "preference is given to the positive law … unless its conflict with justice reaches so intolerable a level that the statute becomes in effect, 'false' law [*unrichtiges Recht*] and must therefore yield to justice".[129] Such a narrow understanding of "law" and such a limitation of judicial law-making powers to

---

[123] C. HILLGRUBER, in T. MAUNZ and G. DÜRIG (founders), *Grundgesetz-Kommentar*, C.H. Beck, Munich 2017, Art. 97 GG, para. 38.
[124] BVerfG, *NJW* 2008, 2409, para. 150; BVerfG, *NVwZ* 2017, 617, para. 38.
[125] According to the BVerfG, the content and limits of art. 3(1) GG cannot be determined in an abstract formula but depend on the circumstances of the individual case (BVerfG, *NVwZ* 2017, 617, paras. 38–39). For an overview of the debate about the correct interpretation of art. 3(1) GG, see U. KISCHEL, in V. EPPING and C. HILLGRUBER (eds.), *Beck'scher Online-Kommentar GG*, C.H. Beck, Munich 2015, Art. 3 GG, paras. 15–33.1; P. KIRCHHOF, in T. MAUNZ and G. DÜRIG (founders), *Grundgesetz-Kommentar*, C.H. Beck, Munich 2017, Art. 3 GG, paras. 264–268.
[126] B. GRZESZICK, in T. MAUNZ and G. DÜRIG (founders), *Grundgesetz-Kommentar*, C.H. Beck, Munich 2017, Art. 20 Abs. 3 GG, para. 63.
[127] BVerfG, *NJW* 1954, 65–66.
[128] This is just one way to interpret the term "law" in art. 20(3) GG. For an overview of the discussion in legal scholarship, see GRZESZICK, above n. 126, Art. 20 Abs. 3 GG, para. 65.
[129] G. RADBRUCH, Gesetzliches Unrecht und übergesetzliches Recht, (1946) 1 *Süddeutsche Juristen-Zeitung* 105, 107.

extreme cases of injustice have, however, not been adopted by German judicial practice. In the face of these controversies it is evident that the outer limits of statutory interpretation are not *clearly* set by the German Basic Law. Instead, the authors of art. 20(3) GG have delegated to the courts the power to determine the extent of judicial law-making. This also means that different interpretations of art. 20(3) GG are possible and permissible as long as they remain within the loose boundaries set by art. 20(3) GG read in context with other provisions of the German Basic Law.

All forms of judicial law-making require a gap in the legislation or the law according to German judicial practice.[130] The term gap-filling is thus often used as a synonym for judicial law-making in Germany. The process of gap-filling can be divided into (a) establishing a gap and (b) filling a gap in legislation. As a third step, a judge examines whether adopting the interpretative meaning remains within the framework set by the outer limits of judicial law-making. All of these steps include evaluative elements.[131] It is possible that a gap exists but that a court cannot close it as this would exceed the outer limits of its judicial function.[132] The concept of gap is the holy grail of judicial law-making in German legal methodology. One function of the concept of gap is to demarcate judicial law-making from interpretation in a narrow sense. The legal concept of gap goes back to the ideal that the law, either the whole of the law or the whole of the law in a certain area, is embodied in enacted law. Attempts to further define the concept of gap and classify gaps have been made by scholars in order to limit the amount of discretion available to a judge when establishing and filling a gap.[133] These attempts have by and large not been picked up in judicial practice.

A gap is commonly defined as an unintended incompleteness (*planwidrige Unvollständigkeit*) in an individual provision, in a statute or in the whole legislation.[134] A gap in a provision, for example, can occur when there is a mismatch between the provision's wording and the provision's intended plan and purpose. Whether the incompleteness is unintended (*planwidrig*) or intended (*planmäßig*) is determined by the intention of the legislature. The intention of

---

[130] We will see that this view results in a rather wide understanding and application of the notion of gap by German courts. This view is not uncontested in German legal scholarship; see, e.g. W.-H. ROTH and C. JOPEN, §13 Die richtlinienkonforme Auslegung, in K. RIESENHUBER (ed.), *Europäische Methodenlehre*, 3rd ed., De Gruyter, Munich 2015, §13, para. 51.

[131] R. ZIPPELIUS, Rechtsnorm und richterliche Entscheidungsfreiheit, (1970) 25 *JZ* 241, 243–245.

[132] Cf. BVerfG, *NJW* 1998, 2269, 2270; BGH, *NJW* 2012, 1073 para. 37 – *Weber II*; C.-W. CANARIS, *Die Feststellung von Lücken im Gesetz*, 2nd ed., Duncker & Humblot, Berlin 1983, pp. 172–177, 194; LARENZ and CANARIS, above n. 5, p. 221.

[133] RÜTHERS, FISCHER and BIRK, above n. 12, paras. 841–863; CANARIS, above n. 132, pp. 134–138; LARENZ, above n. 40, pp. 370–381.

[134] See, e.g. BGH, *NJW* 2009, 427, para. 22 – *Quelle II*; BGH, *NJW* 2016, 1718, para. 37 – *Gasversorgung II*; BAG, *NZA* 2013, 515, para. 37.

the legislature can refer to the plan and purpose (*Regelungsplan*) of the provision, the statute or the whole of the law.[135] In order to determine the intended plan and purpose of a provision, a court has recourse to the interpretative criteria.[136] The "unintendedness criterion" demarcates permissible judicial law-making from an impermissible amendment of the legislation contrary to art. 20(2), (3) GG and in particular from policy considerations by the judge.[137] This function of the criterion is the weaker the more evaluative arguments affect the criterion's determination. The influence of evaluative arguments is the larger the more the notion of purpose is removed from the purpose intended by the enacting legislature into apparently more "objectivised" waters and the more the purpose of the whole of the law (as opposed to the purpose of the specific provision under consideration) is taken into account.

Legal practice and doctrine sometimes differentiate between judicial law-making *praeter legem* (*gesetzesimmanente Rechtsfortbildung*) and judicial law-making *extra legem* (*gesetzesüberschreitende Rechtsfortbildung*).[138] The transitions between both concepts are fuzzy. What is important is that judicial law-making is permissible under both categories and that the same outer interpretative limits apply.

3.1. JUDICIAL LAW-MAKING *PRAETER LEGEM*

Whether a gap exists in a provision or statute is determined by its intended plan and purpose for judicial law-making *praeter legem*. The individual provision or statute must be incomplete according to its own plan and purpose.[139] German legal practice and doctrine differentiate between open and covert gaps. An open gap exists if the wording of a provision or statute does not cover a certain case even though the case is covered by the intended plan and purpose of the provision or statute.[140] An open gap does not exist if the provision in question or

---

[135] It is controversial in German legal scholarship whether the "unintendedness criterion" can be determined by the intended plan and purpose of the whole of the law. See M. WEBER, *Grenzen EU-rechtskonformer Auslegung und Rechtsfortbildung*, Nomos, Baden-Baden 2010, pp. 37–38 for an overview of the discussion.
[136] See, e.g. BAG, NZA 2007, 751 paras. 14–18; BAG, NJW 2014, 956 paras. 24–28.
[137] C.-W. CANARIS, Die richtlinienkonforme Auslegung und Rechtsfortbildung im System der juristischen Methodenlehre, in H. KOZIOL and P. RUMMEL (eds.), *Festschrift für Franz Bydlinski*, Springer, Vienna 2002, pp. 47, 83; CANARIS, above n. 132, pp. 17–18, 21; LARENZ and CANARIS, above n. 5, p. 195.
[138] BGH, NJW 1988, 2109, 2110; cf. BVerfG, NJW 1993, 2861, 2863; LARENZ and CANARIS, above n. 5, pp. 187–189. This terminology is not always used consistently in case law and in legal scholarship.
[139] BGH, GRUR 2002, 238, 241; BGH, NJW 2008, 2257, 2258, para. 7; BAG, NJW 2003, 2473, 2474–2475.
[140] Cf. BAG, NJW 2003, 2473, 2474–2475.

the statutory scheme is exhaustive, i.e. if the legislature intended not to apply the provision's legal rule to a certain set of facts and therefore did not cover this case under the provision's wording (conscious silence).[141] Whether or not a provision is exhaustive is determined by the interpretative criteria.[142] A covert gap exists if a provision's wording covers a certain case even though the case falls outside the provision's plan and purpose.[143] It is important to note in this context that it is possible to restrict a provision's purpose and scope of application in order to reach the purpose of another statutory provision.[144]

Gaps can exist from the time a provision or statute comes into force, for example if the legislature has inadvertently failed to consider a particular case.[145] They can also arise subsequently due to changing legal conditions, for example due to legislative activity in related areas of law.[146] Gaps can also emerge subsequently due to changes in social values or political, technical or economic circumstances over time if the enacting legislature did not foresee or could not have possibly foreseen the changing circumstances.[147] For subsequent gaps the key question is this: who should carry out the necessary adaptation of the law, the court or the legislature? The BVerfG has answered this question as follows: "In view of the accelerated change in social conditions and the limited possibilities of the legislature reacting to this change, as well as the open formulation of numerous provisions, the adaptation of existing law to changing circumstances is a task of the judiciary".[148]

> A clear and complete provision can become incomplete and in need of adaptation due to actual or legal developments. Establishing and filling gaps in legislation is justified under the German constitution because statutes are subject to an ageing process. Statutes exist in the context of certain social conditions and socio-political perceptions. If this context changes, the content of the statute may change as well.[149]

Both excerpts show that according to the BVerfG the role of the judge is to help bridge the gap between legislation and society's changing needs. If a court fills a subsequent gap, judicial law-making surpasses the wording of the provision

---

[141] Cf. BVerfG, *NJW* 1990, 1593, 1594; BVerfG, *NJW* 2012, 3081, para. 79 – *Delisting*; BAG, *NZA* 2007, 751 paras. 14–18; BAG, *NJW* 2014, 956 paras. 23–24.
[142] See, e.g. BAG, *NJW* 2014, 956 paras. 24–28; BVerfG, *NZS* 2015, 502 paras. 22–25.
[143] Cf. BVerfG, *NJW* 1993, 2861, 2863.
[144] See LARENZ and CANARIS, above n. 5, pp. 214–215 for examples.
[145] See BVerfG, *NJW* 2011, 1723 paras. 19, 24.
[146] BVerwG, *NJW* 2005, 1293, 1294; cf. BGH, *NJW* 1981, 1726, 1727.
[147] See BVerfG, *NJW* 1973, 1221, 1225 – *Soraya*; BVerfG, *NJW* 1990, 1593–1594; BVerfG, *NJW* 1993, 2861, 2863; BVerfG, *NJW* 1998, 2269, 2270 – *Sozietätsverbot*; BVerfG, *NJW* 2006, 3409, 3410 – *Marlene Dietrich*; BGH, *NJW* 1955, 1276, 1277–1278 – *Tonband*; BGH, *NJW* 1955, 1433–1434 – *Fotokopie*; BGH, *NJW* 1963, 902, 903.
[148] BVerfG, *NJW* 1998, 519, 520 – *Kind als Schaden*.
[149] BVerfG, *NJW* 1990, 1593–1594. For criticism, see C. HILLGRUBER, Richterliche Rechtsfortbildung als Verfassungsproblem, *JZ* 1996, 118, 121–122.

and can also depart from or even contradict¹⁵⁰ the intention of the enacting legislature. These controversial cases may be described as the adaptation and reinterpretation of ageing legislation due to new realities.¹⁵¹ When a court departs from the historical intention of the enacting legislature, it is guided by the (objective) sense and purpose of the legislation as understood at the time of its application. According to the BVerfG, the vague words of art. 20(3) GG can be construed so as to permit courts to take objective factors of interpretation into account and to depart from the intention of the enacting Parliament.¹⁵² Thus, the BVerfG advocates a "partnership model"¹⁵³ between the judge and the legislature. It derives the constitutional legitimacy of this model from art. 20(3) GG. The problem is, however, that an objective standard that informs a judge when a relevant change in social, political, technical or economic circumstances has happened does not exist. It is difficult to demarcate (a) a legitimate modification of the meaning of a provision over time due to changing conditions from (b) illegitimate policy decisions by judges. Critics therefore disagree with the partnership model and argue that it is the task of the legislature to adjust legislation to changes in social and societal conditions.¹⁵⁴

One example of a gap arising due to changes in social circumstances is illustrated by judgments interpreting the old s. 569a German Civil Code. The provision provided that surviving spouses and other family members succeed to a tenancy under certain conditions. The claimant in the case was the surviving unmarried partner of a tenant and both had lived in the flat for about 18 years. The clear wording of s. 569a German Civil Code did not cover cohabiting unmarried partners. According to the regional court, cohabitations only became a rising social phenomenon in the 1970s, which the legislature did not foresee at the time of enacting s. 569a German Civil Code in 1964. The legislature had explicitly taken cohabitations into account in more recent legislation and had covered them in the wording of statutory provisions, thus recognising the legal relevance of cohabitations. The regional court further stated that s. 569a German Civil Code had a social function and protected members of the common household of the deceased tenant. This wide purpose covered surviving unmarried partners who formed a common household with the deceased tenant.¹⁵⁵ When the case came to the BVerfG, it approved the regional court's

---

[150] See, e.g. BVerfG, *NJW* 2006, 3409, 3410 – *Marlene Dietrich* (the judicial law-making by the BGH "may contradict the actual intention of the historical legislation in 1907 …. It does not, however, infringe constitutional law …"); BGH, *NJW* 1955, 1433–1434 – *Fotokopie*.
[151] For arguments against the permissibility of judicial law-making in these cases, see HILLGRUBER, above n. 149, p. 121; WEBER, above n. 135, pp. 53–54.
[152] BVerfG, *NJW* 1990, 1593–1594.
[153] BARAK, above n. 6, pp. 249–250.
[154] HILLGRUBER, above n. 149, p. 122.
[155] See the reasoning by the lower court: LG Hamburg, decision of 1.2.1988, no. 11 S 398/87, paras. 5–7, available online at http://www.juris.de.

reasoning and clarified that the wording of s. 569a German Civil Code contained a gap since it did not cover cohabiting unmarried partners.[156] This case illustrates that ascribing a wide as opposed to a specific purpose to the provision at issue increases the scope of judicial law-making.

Gaps in the legislation can be filled by certain interpretative techniques of which the most widely used are argument by analogy and teleological reduction.[157] Both techniques change the scope of a statutory provision in order to accomplish the plan and purpose of the provision or the statute. Teleological reduction is used to fill covert gaps by restricting the scope of application of a provision, i.e. by excluding a case from its scope against its wording.[158] In effect, the provision is extended by an unwritten exception in a general and abstract manner. The justification of gap-filling by teleological reduction goes back to the principle that different cases ought to be treated differently. They ought to be governed differently by the law.

Argument by analogy is used to close open gaps by extending the scope of application of a provision to a case not explicitly governed by the statutory words. The provision's rule or legal consequence is extended to cover the novel case. Gap-filling by analogy goes back to the premise that like cases ought to be treated alike. They ought to be governed by the law in the same way. Gap-filling by analogy requires that the novel case and the case covered by the provision's wording are fundamentally similar judged against the standard of the provision's intended plan and purpose.[159] Even though the standard of comparison and the characteristics that determine the necessary degree of similarity are derived from the provision, an argument by analogy includes evaluative elements.[160]

---

[156] BVerfG, *NJW* 1990, 1593, 1594. For criticism of the BVerfG's reasoning, see RÜTHERS, FISCHER and BIRK, above n. 12, para. 875; G. ROELLECKE, Anmerkung, *JZ* 1990, 813–814.

[157] For an overview of interpretative techniques to fill gaps, see RÜTHERS, FISCHER and BIRK, above n. 12, paras. 888–912. Interpretation of general terms and ambiguous statutory language is sometimes also considered as a technique of gap-filling in legal doctrine, but generally not by courts; see, e.g., J. IPSEN, *Richterrecht und Verfassung*, Duncker & Humblot, Berlin 1975, p. 61; J. RAZ, *The authority of law*, Clarendon Press, Oxford 1979, pp. 194–195; C.P. MCGRATH and H. KOZIOL, Is style of reasoning a fundamental difference between the common law and the civil law, (2014) 78 *RabelsZ* 709, 716 f.; R. WANK, *Grenzen richterlicher Rechtsfortbildung*, Duncker & Humblot, Berlin 1978, pp. 145–146. For arguments against categorising the interpretation of general terms as judicial law-making, see CANARIS, above n. 132, pp. 26–29; S. EMMENEGGER and A. TSCHENTSCHER, in H. HAUSHEER and H.P. WALTER (eds.), *Berner Kommentar – Kommentar zum schweizerischen Privatrecht*, Bd. I/1, Stämpfli, Bern 2012, Art. 1 ZGB, para. 370.

[158] Cf. BVerfG, *NJW* 1993, 2861, 2863; BGH, *NJW* 1955, 1276, 1278–1279 – *Tonband*; LARENZ and CANARIS, above n. 5, pp. 210–211.

[159] See BVerfG, *NJW* 1990, 1593, 1594; BGH, *NJW* 2008, 2257, 2258, paras. 7, 9; BGH, *NJW* 2006, 2997, paras. 18, 25; BAG, *NJW* 2003, 2473, 2474–2475; BAG, *NZA* 2005, 420, 422; BAG, *NJW* 2014, 956, paras. 23–24.

[160] CANARIS, above n. 132, p. 17; RÜTHERS, FISCHER and BIRK, above n. 12, paras. 834, 896; cf. MACCORMICK, above n. 62, pp. 183, 185, 192.

That is specifically true for the assessment whether the similarity between both cases is sufficiently fundamental. Furthermore, a provision's intended plan and purpose can refer to the actual or inferred intent of the enacting legislature or to the provision's underlying objective purpose and sense. In German legal scholarship, the gap-filling technique of "teleological extension" is often distinguished from argument by analogy.[161] Teleological extension means that the scope of a provision is extended in order to cover a new case which the enacting legislature intended to provide for, but inadvertently failed to cover under the provision's wording. For an argument by analogy, a provision's legal consequence is applied to a new case because both cases are so similar that the legislature, had it seen the gap, would have chosen the same legal consequence for the new case.[162] Argument by analogy and teleological extension both require that the novel case is covered by the provision's intended plan and purpose. Whereas for a teleological extension that purpose can be expressed in quite specific terms, a more general assessment of the intention of the legislature is required for argument by analogy.[163] Teleological extension is thus a special case of argument by analogy.[164] That may explain why the BGH and the BVerfG do not differentiate between both categories, but only refer to argument by analogy when they extend the scope of a provision beyond its wording.[165] In the above-mentioned case concerning the interpretation of s. 569a German Civil Code, a gap arose due to changing social circumstances. The court closed the gap by extending the scope of s. 569a German Civil Code to cohabiting unmarried partners who had formed a common household with the deceased tenant. According to the BVerfG, the issue at hand was similar to the cases covered by the provision's wording since s. 569a German Civil Code already provided that surviving spouses and other family members could succeed to the tenancy if they had formed a common household with the deceased tenant.[166]

---

[161] See, e.g. C. HERRESTHAL, *Rechtsfortbildung im europarechtlichen Bezugsrahmen*, C.H. Beck, Munich 2006, pp. 243–244; LARENZ and CANARIS, above n. 5, pp. 216–218; D. LOOSCHELDERS and W. ROTH, *Juristische Methodik im Prozeß der Rechsanwendung*, Duncker & Humblot, Berlin 1996, pp. 267–271.

[162] RÜTHERS, FISCHER and BIRK, above n. 12, para. 889.

[163] LOOSCHELDERS and ROTH, above n. 161, pp. 270–271.

[164] B.P. PAAL, Methoden der Lückenfüllung: UN-Kaufrecht und BGB im Vergleich, *Zeitschrift für vergleichende Rechtswissenschaft* 2011, 64, 76; RÜTHERS, FISCHER and BIRK, above n. 12, para. 904. This assessment of the difference between argument by analogy and teleological extension is controversial in legal scholarship; for an overview of the discussion, see P. MEIER and F. JOCHAM, Rechtsfortbildung – Methodischer Balanceakt zwischen Gewaltenteilung und materialler Gerechtigkeit, *JuS* 2016, 392, 394.

[165] Cf. also M. KLATT, *Making the law explicit*, Hart 2008, p. 5, who states that any application of a statute beyond the scope of the possible meaning of its wording is a development of the law, which is either an analogy or a teleological reduction.

[166] Cf. BVerfG, *NJW* 1990, 1593, 1594. For a different view see ROELLECKE, above n. 156, pp. 813–814.

Gap-filling by analogy can also be used to transfer the underlying common reason(s) of not just one individual provision but of several, related statutory provisions to a case not explicitly governed by the statutory words (*Gesamtanalogie* or *Rechtsanalogie*). In this scenario, a judge extracts (through induction) a general legal principle common to several provisions or statutes that provide for the same rule or legal consequence for different cases. The judge then (through deduction) applies this general legal principle to the fundamentally similar case not explicitly covered by the statutory words and applies the rule or legal consequence of the statutory provisions to this novel case.[167]

One example of a *Gesamtanalogie* is the BGH's judgment establishing that a shareholder of a German limited liability company (GmbH) can be excluded on serious grounds,[168] even if the articles of association of the company do not provide for such a possibility.[169] The plaintiff was a shareholder of a German limited liability company. He was excluded from the company on serious grounds by a resolution of the remaining shareholders. The plaintiff argued that the articles of association of the company contained no provision governing the exclusion of a shareholder. The German Limited Liability Companies Act lacked a provision governing the exclusion of a shareholder on serious grounds. The BGH argued that strong and pressing considerations of legal practicality demand that a shareholder can be excluded from a German limited liability company if a serious ground exists. The court established in effect that a gap existed in the German Limited Liability Companies Act. German statutory law recognised the right to exclude a shareholder on serious grounds for two other types of companies. Yet, the BGH rejected an argument by analogy based on these statutory provisions because of differences between these two types of companies and the limited liability company. Instead, the court went on to show that a general legal principle can be extracted from a wide range of provisions in the German Civil Code and the German Commercial Code that a long-term legal relationship can be terminated prematurely on serious grounds. This is the

---

[167] Cf. BGH, *NJW* 1953, 780, 781; BGH, *NJW* 2003, 1032, 1035 – *Macrotron*; BVerfG, *NJW* 2012, 3081, paras. 80–85 – *Delisting*.

[168] For a discussion of further case law, see RÜTHERS, FISCHER and BIRK, above n. 12, para. 892. For a more recent example, see (a) BGH, *NJW* 2003, 1032, 1035 – *Macrotron*, (b) KG, *WM* 2008, 125, 126–127 and (c) BVerfG, *NJW* 2012, 3081, paras. 78–84 – *Delisting*: German statutory law does not require a mandatory offer by a company or its main shareholder to the other shareholders if the company decides to remove a stock from a stock exchange (delisting). Statutory provisions in the German Stock Corporation Act (*Aktiengesetz*) and the German Act of Company Transformation and Reorganisation (*Umwandlungsgesetz*) provide for such an offer for other forms of company reorganisation. The German courts argued that due to the similarity between (a) the governed cases of company reorganisation requiring a mandatory offer and (b) delisting, a mandatory offer is required for delisting as well. In a later decision, the BGH argued against this similarity and held that a mandatory offer is not required for delisting (BGH, *NJW* 2014, 146, paras. 10–12 – *FRoSTA*).

[169] BGH, *NJW* 1953, 780.

case if the relationship strongly interacts with the life activities of those involved or entails a special mutual interlocking of interests and requires collaboration at a personal level, harmonious relations or undisturbed mutual trust between the parties involved.[170] Since the relationship between the shareholders and their limited liability company is such a legal relationship, the BGH closed the gap by applying the general legal principle to the law governing a limited liability company. The court held that it is possible to exclude a shareholder of a limited liability company on serious grounds.[171] This decision by the BGH arguably goes beyond the ambit of judicial law-making *praeter legem* and can be better characterised as judicial law-making *extra legem*, to which we will turn now.

3.2. JUDICIAL LAW-MAKING *EXTRA LEGEM*

For judicial law-making *extra legem*, a gap is determined not only by the plan and purpose of an individual provision or statute, but also by the needs and guiding principles of the whole of the law.[172] Particular importance is attached to the requirements of the constitution and the considerations of legal practicality (*Bedürfnisse des Rechtsverkehrs*).[173] Famous examples of judicial law-making *extra legem* include the introduction of *culpa in contrahendo* and positive violation of a claim (*positive Forderungsverletzung*), even though both institutions lacked express provisions in the law. Cases of judicial law-making *extra legem* may appear in areas that require legal rules, but which are hardly governed by legislation, like the right to industrial dispute[174] in Germany.[175] Judicial law-making *extra legem* often surpasses the plan and purpose of an individual statute because there is an insufficient amount of legislation regulating a certain area of law. In other words, there is no plan or purpose of an individual statute that can bind a judge. The judge is bound by more general legal principles governing or underlying a specific area of law instead. This also means that the notion of gap is objectivised as it extends beyond the intention of the enacting legislature

---

[170] Ibid., 780–781.
[171] Ibid., 781.
[172] BGH, *NJW* 2007, 992, para. 20.
[173] BGH, *NJW* 1988, 2109, 2110; BGH, *NJW* 2007, 992, para. 20; cf. BVerfG, *NJW* 1973, 1221, 1226 – *Soraya*. For scholarly attempts to structure judicial law-making *extra legem*, see LARENZ and CANARIS, above n. 5, pp. 233–245. Judicial law-making *extra legem* that is based on the requirements of the German Basic Law is generally endorsed in German legal scholarship. Judicial law-making *extra legem* that goes beyond that category is opposed by some scholars; see, e.g. HILLGRUBER, above n. 149, pp. 118, 122.
[174] BVerfG, *NJW* 2014, 1874, 1877 – *Flashmob* ("insufficient amount of statutory requirements").
[175] For an analysis of judicial law-making *extra legem* in German company law, see P.O. MÜLBERT, Einheit der Methodenlehre? – Allgemeines Zivilrecht und Gesellschaftsrecht im Vergleich, (2014) 214 *AcP* 188, 284–288.

Chapter 2. Conventional Canons of Statutory Interpretation

of a specific provision or statute at issue.[176] Judicial law-making *extra legem* occurs *intra ius*. Compared to its *praeter legem* counterpart, judicial law-making *extra legem* gives judges greater interpretative freedom since directly applicable statutory rules are often missing.[177] From the perspective of a common law lawyer, judicial law-making *extra legem* has more in common with common law (judge-made law) than with statute law and statutory interpretation, even though judge-made law is not officially recognised as a binding source of law by German judicial practice.[178] That is also why cases of judicial law-making *extra legem* will not be discussed in this book, as the book only deals with the interpretation of legislation. One exception to this is a line of cases leading to the BVerfG's decision in *Soraya*. The *Soraya* judgment contains an important discussion of the outer limits of judicial law-making.

This line of cases concerns the question of whether civil courts are able to grant compensation for non-pecuniary damage in a case of substantial violation of the general right of personality. The BGH had granted such compensation to Princess Soraya due to an interview about her private life that was totally fabricated by a journalist and published in a tabloid. Section 253 German Civil Code allowed compensation for non-pecuniary damage "only" in cases determined by the law, which was not the case for a violation of the general right of personality. This right is derived from arts. 1 and 2 GG. Before the German Basic Law came into force, the enacting legislature of the German Civil Code in 1900 had explicitly, as evidenced by the legislative materials, denied a general claim to monetary compensation for non-pecuniary damages.[179] The enacting legislature intended to allow such a claim only in cases where legislation expressly recognised it. In its *Herrenreiter* judgment in 1958, the BGH had argued that

---

[176] It is controversial in legal scholarship whether there exists a common plan of the whole of the national legal system (*Plan der Gesamtrechtsordnung*). It is less controversial that legal rules or principles standing outside a specific provision or statute can affect the provision's or statute's plan and purpose. For discussion, see L. MICHAEL, Verfassungsrechtliche Grenzen richtlinienkonformer Rechtsfortbildung, (2015) 54 *Der Staat* 349, 354–355.

[177] IPSEN, above n. 157, p. 83; MÜLBERT, above n. 175, 203; RÜTHERS, FISCHER and BIRK, above n. 12, paras. 906–912.

[178] BVerfG, *NJW* 1991, 2549, 2550; BVerfG, *NJW* 1993, 996; BVerfG, *NJW* 2009, 1469, para. 57; BVerfG, *NZA* 2015, 1117, para. 72. See also H.E. MEISTER, *Europäische Rechtslehre*, Band 1, Pro Business Verlag, Berlin 2015, p. 803. For an overview of the exceptions to the general rule, see N. FOSTER and S. SULE, *German legal system and laws*, 4th ed., OUP, Oxford 2010, p. 54. It is controversial in legal scholarship whether judge-made law is a binding source of law in Germany; for an overview of the discussion, see RÜTHERS, FISCHER and BIRK, above n. 12, paras. 235–256. Even if judge-made law is not regarded as a binding source of law, the relevance of judgments by the highest German courts for legal practice can be described as similar to the relevance of statutes for legal practice; see U. KISCHEL, *Rechtsvergleichung*, C.H. Beck, Munich 2015, §6 paras. 28–35; RÜTHERS, FISCHER and BIRK, above n. 12, para. 244. For a comparative analysis, arguing that judge-made law is of similar significance in legal practice in the UK and in Germany, see SUMMERS and TARUFFO, above n. 85, pp. 461, 487–488.

[179] See BVerfG, *NJW* 1973, 1221 – *Soraya*; BGH, *NJW* 1963, 902, 903 – *Fernsehansagerin*.

granting compensation for non-pecuniary damage in a case of violation of the general right of personality is required by the German Basic Law and can be justified by an analogy to the old s. 847 German Civil Code.[180] Section 847 allowed for compensation for non-pecuniary damage in a case of deprivation of physical freedom. The BGH effectively used judicial law-making *praeter legem* to fill a gap in the German Civil Code. This judgment was criticised on the grounds that the use of the word "only" in s. 253 German Civil Code meant that the legislature explicitly wanted to allow for compensation for non-pecuniary damage only in cases stipulated by legislation.[181] Such a reading of s. 253 German Civil Code excludes a gap in the German Civil Code and consequently an analogy to its s. 847. If this understanding of s. 253 as an exhaustive provision is adopted, it is also not possible to extract a general legal principle of compensation for non-pecuniary damage out of the several statutory provisions in the German law that explicitly recognise such compensation.

The BGH stopped using the analogy to s. 847 German Civil Code in later decisions and, instead, directly based its reasoning on arts. 1 and 2 GG. It argued in its *Fernsehansagerin* judgment that the enacting legislature of the German Civil Code in 1900 could not have foreseen the coming into force of the German Basic Law 50 years later and the development of a general right of personality leading to a changing perception of the protection of non-material values through private law. The BGH explicitly stated that a judge cannot be bound any longer by the intention of the enacting legislature of 1900 to deny compensation for non-pecuniary damage in a case of substantial violation of the general right of personality.[182] This is a clear statement that judicial law-making can be permissible even against the explicit and plain intention of the enacting legislature. The BGH affirmed in effect a gap in the law that was not determined by the plan and purpose of the German Civil Code, but by guiding principles of the whole of the law, *in concreto* by arts. 1 and 2 GG. A further argument relied on by the BGH in order to justify the gap was the changing social and technical developments after the coming into force of the German Civil Code, which the enacting legislature could not possibly have foreseen. These developments created the need for a strengthened protection of personality rights through possible claims for compensation for non-pecuniary damage.

The BVerfG held that this reasoning of the BGH complies with the German Basic Law in its *Soraya* judgment in 1973. The BVerfG agreed that a gap in the law existed since the German civil law did not provide for compensation for non-pecuniary damage in a case of substantial violation of the general right of

---

[180] BGH, *NJW* 1958, 827, 830 – *Herrenreiter*. For an endorsement of the analogy to s. 847 German Civil Code, see LARENZ and CANARIS, above n. 5, pp. 249–250. For criticism of the reasoning of the BGH, see IPSEN, above n. 157, pp. 94–95.
[181] K. LARENZ, Anmerkung zu BGH, Urteil vom 14.2.1958 – I ZR 151/56, *NJW* 1958, 830.
[182] BGH, *NJW* 1963, 902, 903 – *Fernsehansagerin*.

personality. According to the BVerfG, this gap arose due to a "change of legal awareness" and "the values of a new constitution", in particular the recognition of a general right of personality under the remit of the German Basic Law. The enacting legislature of the German Civil Code could not have foreseen these changing circumstances.[183] The German civil courts were right in closing the gap by granting compensation for non-pecuniary damage in a case of substantial violation of the general right of personality. The BVerfG's reasoning exemplifies that the arguments used to establish and fill a gap in the law can hardly be separated for judicial law-making *extra legem*. A certain technique to fill the gap in the law is also not discernible.

Regarding the limits of judicial law-making, the BVerfG went on to say the following in *Soraya*:

> Under the rule of the German constitution, the task and competence of the judge to engage in creative law-finding (*schöpferische Rechtsfindung*) has never been questioned. ... The highest German courts have undertaken this task from the beginning. ... The BVerfG has always recognised it. .... Only the limits of such a creative law-finding can be debatable.[184]

The BVerfG argued that the interpretation of a provision is not always limited by its purpose as understood at the time of its passing. What has to be considered instead is what reasonable function a provision fulfils at the time of its application in the context of the relevant social conditions and socio-political beliefs. A provision's content can and sometimes must change due to changes in these conditions.[185] The older a provision becomes, the greater is the freedom of the judge to engage in creative law-finding, particularly if a substantial change in the social conditions, legal opinion and ideas of justice in society has occurred.[186] This was the case in the situation at hand according to the BVerfG. It is implicit in this reasoning that the BVerfG's interpretation of s. 253 German Civil Code was guided by the objective purpose of the provision at the time of its application. The BVerfG also implicitly approved of the BGH's reasoning that judicial law-making may be permissible even against the explicit and unambiguous intention of the enacting legislature.

Furthermore, the BVerfG emphasised that the German civil law already contained cases of compensation for non-pecuniary damage. The German civil courts had only extended these by one further case. Therefore, the German civil courts had not applied their own policy considerations,

---

[183] BVerfG, *NJW* 1973, 1221, 1225 – *Soraya*.
[184] Ibid.
[185] Affirmed in BVerfG, *NJW* 1990, 1593–1594.
[186] BVerfG, *NJW* 1973, 1221, 1225 – *Soraya*; confirmed in BVerfG, *NJW* 1998, 519, 520 – *Kind als Schaden*. For criticism, see HILLGRUBER, above n. 149, pp. 118, 121–122; F. REIMER, *Juristische Methodenlehre*, Nomos, Baden-Baden 2016, para. 259.

but had solely developed basic principles of the legal order. These principles are themselves informed by the German constitution.[187] In this passage of its reasoning, the BVerfG suggests that judges exceed the outer limits of judicial law-making if they base their legal reasoning on their own policy considerations. This is a highly vague constraint, however. We have already seen in Chapter 1 that judges do make policy choices when interpreting legislation. Furthermore, it has been asserted that it is a policy argument but not a legal argument when judges claim that the civil law protection of the general right of personality remains incomplete if it does not provide for compensation for non-pecuniary damages in a case of substantial violation of this right. It should be the task of the legislature and not the courts to determine the consequences of an infringement of a right.[188] The BVerfG also argued in *Soraya* that the government intended to reform the law relating to the protection of the general right of personality twice after the German Civil Code came into force. Both times, however, the bills "failed early in the legislative process even though there was no indication of any legislative intention to perpetuate the status quo".[189] This argument is not compelling.[190] One might argue equally well that the judicial law-making approved by the BVerfG in *Soraya* amounts to a policy decision since an agreement on how to protect the general right of personality could not be reached in the German Bundestag.

The reasoning of the BVerfG in *Soraya* can also be contrasted with the dissenting opinion of three judges in a more recent BVerfG case. *Rügeverkümmerung* concerned the interpretation of s. 274 German Code of Criminal Procedure. The provision provides that compliance with the formalities required for the main hearing can only be proved by the content of the minutes of the main hearing. The provision also provides for the possibility of alleging the falsity of the minutes with regard to the formalities of the main hearing only in the case of forgery. If the minutes do not contain an essential procedural formality of the main hearing, an appeal on law (*Revision*) may be filed. The criminal courts had argued in the past that the German Code of Criminal Procedure contains an unintended gap since it does not explicitly govern whether subsequent corrections of the minutes are permissible and relevant for appeal proceedings. In a 2007 judgment, the BGH extended this case law and held that appellate proceedings that are based on a procedural irregularity as evidenced by the minutes can be deprived of their basis, even to the disadvantage of the appellant, through a subsequent correction of the minutes.[191] In *Rügeverkümmerung*, the

---

[187] BVerfG, *NJW* 1973, 1221, 1226 – *Soraya*. Cf. the criticism by WANK, above n. 157, p. 86 in relation to the BVerfG's assertion that the BGH did not rely on its own policy considerations: "The opposite is obvious".
[188] LARENZ, above n. 181, p. 830.
[189] BVerfG, *NJW* 1973, 1221, 1226 – *Soraya*.
[190] See also IPSEN, above n. 157, p. 194.
[191] BGH, *NJW* 2007, 2419 – *Rügeverkümmerung*.

reading out of the bill of indictment did not appear in the minutes. The defendant raised this during the appellate proceedings. The minutes were corrected by the court after hearing the participants in the case. This deprived the appellate proceedings of their basis. When the case arrived at the BVerfG, the majority of the court approved of the BGH's reasoning. Similar to the facts in *Soraya*, s. 274 German Code of Criminal Procedure came into force before 1900. The enacting legislature's decision had been heavily criticised by legal doctrine and practice almost since the birth of the legislation. Despite legislative efforts to reform the provision, it remained unamended. The dissenting judges in the BVerfG argued that the BGH had replaced the legislature's fundamental decision with its own policy considerations.[192] In the BVerfG's reasoning in *Soraya*, one factor militating in favour of judicial law-making was that later bills had not revealed any intention of the legislature to keep the law unchanged. The dissenting judges in *Rügeverkümmerung* stressed the opposite. They argued that the fact that later bills did not reveal any such intention on the part of the legislature indicated that the legislature did not intend to renounce but to retain the law as understood at the time of its coming into force.[193] The legislature is not obliged to confirm its intentions in respect of a provision with the passing of time.[194] An important factor distinguishing *Rügeverkümmerung* from *Soraya* was, however, that the judicial law-making in *Soraya* served to protect a legal interest that was protected under the German Basic Law. The outer limits of judicial law-making are often applied rather leniently in these cases.[195]

The reasoning of the BVerfG in *Soraya* also includes one of the boldest, most controversial and certainly exceptional statements on the legitimacy of judicial law-making in a written judicial opinion.[196] J. Goldsworthy has said that such a statement would never be found in an English judgment as English judges rarely openly acknowledge doing surgery on statutes.[197] Due to art. 20(3) GG, a judge is not only bound by legislation, but also by law. The BVerfG used the latter notion in *Soraya* to loosen the binding force of statute as follows:[198]

> The law is not identical with the aggregate of the written statutes. Beyond the positive norms enacted by the state there can be a surplus of law (*ein Mehr an Recht*) which has

---

[192] BVerfG, *NJW* 2009, 1469, dissenting opinion by Judges Voßkuhle, Osterloh, Di Fabio, paras. 129–142 – *Rügeverkümmerung*.
[193] Ibid., para. 142.
[194] Ibid., para. 101.
[195] This issue will be explored in Chapter 3 of this book.
[196] For criticism, see F. MÜLLER, Richterrecht – rechtstheoretisch formuliert, in *Richterliche Rechtsfortbildung: Erscheinungsformen, Auftrag und Grenzen*, C.F. Müller, Heidelberg 1986, pp. 65, 75–76; WANK, above n. 157, pp. 83–87.
[197] J. GOLDSWORTHY, *Parliamentary sovereignty: contemporary debates*, CUP, Cambridge 2010, p. 229.
[198] See also G. HIRSCH, Zwischenruf: Der Richter wird's schon richten, *ZRP* 2006, 161. This interpretation of art. 20(3) GG by the BVerfG has not remained uncontested; see HILLGRUBER, above n. 149, pp. 118, 121–125.

its source in the constitutional legal order as an all-embracing system and which can function as a corrective to the written law; to find it and to deliver it in decisions is the task of the courts. The German Basic Law does not limit the judge to apply instructions of the legislature to a particular case and to stay within the possible semantic meanings of the statutory words. ... The task of a judge is not limited to ascertaining and implementing legislative decisions. The task of adjudication can demand especially that evaluative assumptions – which are immanent in the constitutional legal order, but are not, or are only incompletely, expressed in the texts of the written statutes – be brought to light and implemented in decisions by an act of evaluative cognition which, admittedly, does not lack volitional elements. In performing this task, the judge must avoid arbitrariness; his decision must be based upon rational arguments (*rationaler Argumentation*). The judge must make it clear that the written statute fails to fulfil its function of providing a just solution for the legal problem at hand. The judicial decision then fills this gap by relying on the standards of practical reason (*den Maßstäben der praktischen Vernunft*) and the community's well-founded general ideas of justice (*fundierten allgemeinen Gerechtigkeitsvorstellungen der Gemeinschaft*).[199]

The last two sentences of the BVerfG's reasoning refer to establishing and filling a gap for judicial law-making *extra legem*. The BVerfG explicitly recognises that this process is not only guided by legal methodology or objective factors, but involves subjective evaluations. Such explicit recognition of judicial discretion in the realm of statutory interpretation can rarely be found in published judicial opinions in Germany. Despite recognising the subjective element, the decision of the judge must be guided by rational argumentation, practical reason and the community's well-founded general ideas of justice. These criteria stand outside the specific statutory context. The BVerfG refers to them in order to establish and fill a gap in the law. Even though rational argumentation, practical reason and the community's well-founded general ideas of justice are on the face of it objective, albeit non-positivistic criteria, they hardly provide control, structure or limits to the scope of permissible evaluative arguments. They leave a considerable role for personal evaluations.[200] That is because the demarcation between these highly indeterminate criteria and the outer limit of interpretation that judges cannot apply their own policy considerations is hardly feasible. It follows that the controllability of the policy considerations limit of interpretation is undermined. This is true all the more if the standard of practical reason is understood as an "essentially contestable concept".[201] This conclusion does not change even when

---

[199] BVerfG, *NJW* 1973, 1221, 1225 – *Soraya*.
[200] Cf. Bydlinski, above n. 30, pp. 154–158; Rüthers, Fischer and Birk, above n. 12, paras. 916–918. For a criticism of the notion of consent as a standard to justify an interpretative result, see Rafi, above n. 40, pp. 29–36. In favour of applying these criteria, see, however, Esser, above n. 40, pp. 9, 12, 151–168.
[201] On essentially contestable concepts, see Beck, above n. 9, pp. 61–71.

an attempt is made to contextualise both concepts in the sphere of gap-filling. A concept related to rational argumentation and practical reason is the concept of reasonableness, which refers to identifying the relevant considerations and balancing them according to their weight. A decision is reasonable if it is reached after the proper weight is given to the different considerations that need to be taken into account.[202] Even if this understanding of reasonableness is applied to the concepts of rational argumentation and practical reason, they remain highly indeterminate. That is because the BVerfG did not (a) give guidance on what distinguishes relevant from irrelevant considerations, (b) provide an order of priority among competing considerations and (c) explain any further the distinction between giving proper or improper weight to these considerations. The legitimate scope of gap-filling *extra legem* is seemingly unconstrained by specific legal limitations. The community's well-founded general ideas of justice, for example, are a nebulous concept.[203] Such ideas of justice are diminishing in a pluralistic society. There does not seem to be a clear way of ascertaining what the community (the majority of people?) believe to be right or acceptable with any degree of accuracy.[204] Historically, German judges have invoked the notion of justice as a teleological criterion in order to give a new interpretation to existing statutes in the light of a new political value system.[205]

Compared to judicial law-making *praeter legem*, the criteria for establishing a gap in the law due to the needs and guiding principles of the whole of the law have remained open and unclear in case law until today.[206] For example, written judicial opinions have suggested that a gap in the law can arise due to "an irrefutable requirement of legal relations" (*ein unabweisbares Bedürfnis des Rechtsverkehrs*).[207] The problem with this vagueness is that the concept of gap has a limiting function for permissible judicial law-making, since a judge is only allowed to engage in judicial law-making after establishing a gap in the legislation or the law.[208] This function is compromised with the open and wide understanding of this concept in *Soraya*. Having said that, more recent judgments by the BVerfG are framed in more restrictive terms. The dissenting opinion of three judges in *Rügeverkümmerung*, for example, denies that judicial law-making

---

[202] BARAK, above n. 6, p. 199.
[203] Cf. M. GORDON, *Parliamentary sovereignty in the UK constitution*, Hart, Oxford 2015, p. 144 (with further references).
[204] For criticism in this direction, see also ROBERTSON, above n. 78, pp. 400–401.
[205] In detail B. RÜTHERS, *Die unbegrenzte Auslegung*, 7th ed., Mohr Siebeck, Tübingen 2012, pp. 117–120, 178–180, 322–335.
[206] Cf. WIEDEMANN, above n. 33, pp. 2407, 2412. For criticism of the BVerfG's case law in this respect, see J.-H. BAUER and C. MOENCH, Sozialplanabfindungen im Konkurs, *NJW* 1984, 468, 469. See LARENZ and CANARIS, above n. 5, pp. 233–245 for an attempt to categorise different cases of judicial law-making *extra legem*.
[207] BGH, *NJW* 1988, 2109, 2110. Cf. BGH, *NJW* 2007, 992, para. 20.
[208] BVerfG, *NJW* 1992, 1219; cf. BVerfG, *NJW* 1984, 475 – *Sozialplan*.

can depart from the fundamental decision of the legislature and replace it with general principles of material justice.[209] This view can be contrasted with the older *Soraya* decision, where the BVerfG said that a judge is "forced to a more liberal handling of legal provisions" if the provision conflicts with the "material conceptions of justice of a transformed society".[210]

3.3. CONSTITUTIONALISING THE LIMITS OF STATUTORY INTERPRETATION

Article 20(2) GG expresses the doctrine of separation of powers between the judiciary and legislature, and art. 20(3) GG enshrines the binding nature of statute. Since the methods of statutory interpretation can affect both constitutional doctrines, they have a constitutional dimension according to the BVerfG and dominant legal doctrine.[211] Based on art. 20(2), (3) GG, the BVerfG has established outer limits of statutory interpretation that judges are not allowed to surpass.[212] These limits are binding on all courts.[213] They apply to primary as well as delegated legislation,[214] and they separate the power of judges to develop the law through judicial law-making from the power of the legislature to amend legislation.[215] The outer methodological limits of permissible statutory interpretation correspond with the constitutional border between the function of the judge and the function of the legislature. This border is thus determined by constitutional law. Amendment of legislation is reserved for the legislature. If a judge exceeds the constitutional limits of statutory interpretation, he or she engages in impermissible *contra legem* interpretation.[216]

---

[209] BVerfG, *NJW* 2009, 1469, dissenting opinion by Judges Voßkuhle, Osterloh, Di Fabio, para. 142 – *Rügeverkümmerung*.
[210] BVerfG, *NJW* 1973, 1221, 1225 – *Soraya*.
[211] See BVerfG, *NJW* 2009, 1469, dissenting opinion by Judges Voßkuhle, Osterloh, Di Fabio, para. 103 – *Rügeverkümmerung*.
[212] See, e.g. BVerfG, *NJW* 1998, 519–520 – *Kind als Schaden*; BVerfG, *NJW* 2009, 1469, para. 60 – *Rügeverkümmerung*; BVerfG, *NJW* 2011, 842 paras. 52–53 – *Dreiteilungsmethode*; BVerfG, *NJW-RR* 2016, 1366 paras. 34–37. The BVerfG does not explicitly refer to the requirement of democratic legitimacy for law-making institutions, enshrined in art. 20(2) GG, as another constitutional base for establishing outer methodological limits of judicial law-making; for a discussion in scholarship, see IPSEN, above n. 157, pp. 196–206.
[213] BVerfG, *NJW* 1975, 1355, 1356.
[214] See BVerfG, *NJW* 2000, 347, 349; BVerfG, *WM* 2017, 154, 155.
[215] See, e.g. BVerfG, *NJW* 2009, 1469, dissenting opinion by Judges Voßkuhle, Osterloh, Di Fabio, para. 103 – *Rügeverkümmerung*; BVerfG, *NJW* 2012, 3081, para. 75 – *Delisting*; BVerfG, *NJW-RR* 2016, 1366 paras. 35–36.
[216] See BVerfG, *NJW* 1958, 2059, 2060–2061; BVerfG, *NJW* 1973, 1491, 1494; BVerfG, *NJW* 1978, 2499, 2500; BVerfG, *NJW* 1985, 2395, 2402; BVerfG, *NJW* 2006, 3409, 3410; BAG, *EuZW* 2009, 465, para. 65. The term *contra legem* interpretation is not used consistently in German legal scholarship; see LARENZ and CANARIS, above n. 5, pp. 251–252. Some scholars contend

3.3.1. Common Limits, Different Application

The case law of the BVerfG contains recurring methodological limits for permissible statutory interpretation. The court applies these limits irrespective of the facts and the surrounding context of the case when it reviews the constitutionality of judicial decisions that interpret private, criminal or public legislation. These limits also apply irrespective of whether a regular court engages in interpretation in a narrow sense or judicial law-making *praeter* or *extra legem*.[217] Common outer limits of interpretation do exist. That can be derived from art. 20(3) GG, since the binding nature of statute does not differentiate between different kinds of statutory interpretation.[218] These limits include, for example,

- that a judge has to respect the fundamental decision of the legislature (*gesetzgeberische Grundentscheidung*);[219]
- that a judge cannot alter or replace a clear decision of the legislature with his or her own policy ideas;[220]
- that a judge cannot fundamentally redefine the normative content of a provision;[221]
- that a judge cannot distort or neglect a fundamental feature of a provision's objective;[222] and
- that a teleological reduction cannot reduce the scope of application of a provision to zero,[223] i.e. that a teleological reduction cannot bring about a de facto repeal of a provision.

---

[217] that a *contra legem* interpretation is permissible under certain exceptional circumstances. According to the usage of the term by German courts, however, a *contra legem* interpretation always infringes art. 20(2), (3) GG; cf. MÜLBERT, above n. 175, *AcP* 214 (2014), 188, 197.
PIEROTH and AUBEL, above n. 33, pp. 505–506, 509. The BVerfG applies these limits with regard to interpretation in a narrow sense and judicial law-making. See also BGH, *NVwZ* 2014, 1111, para. 10.
[218] Ibid., pp. 505–509.
[219] BVerfG, *NJW* 1998, 519, 520 – *Kind als Schaden*; BVerfG, *NJW* 2006, 3409 – *Marlene Dietrich*; BVerfG, *NJW* 2009, 1469, para. 37 – *Rügeverkümmerung*; BVerfG, *NJW* 2011, 842, para. 53 – *Dreiteilungsmethode*; BVerfG, *NJW* 2011, 1723, para. 15; BVerfG, *NJW* 2012, 3081, para. 76 – *Delisting*; BVerfG, *NJW-RR* 2016, 1366 paras. 35, 40.
[220] BVerfG, *NJW* 1979, 305, 306 – *Sachverständigenhaftung*; BVerfG, *NJW* 1990, 1593; BVerfG, *NJW* 2004, 750, 761; BVerfG, *NJW* 2006, 3340, 3341.
[221] BVerfG, *NJW* 1981, 39, 43; BVerfG, *NJW* 1994, 2475, 2476; BVerfG, *NJW* 2007, 2977, para. 91 – *Strafzumessung durch Revisionsgerichte*.
[222] BVerfG, *NJW* 1958, 1227; BVerfG, *NJW* 1973, 1491, 1494; BVerfG, *NJW* 1978, 2499, 2500; BVerfG, *NJW* 1981, 39, 43; BVerfG, *NJW* 1988, 1902; BVerfG, *NJW* 2013, 1058, para. 66 – *Deal im Strafprozess*.
[223] BVerwG, judgment of 10.08.2016, no. 1 B 82/16 (1 PKH 76.16), para. 8, available online at http://www.bverwg.de.

In *Soraya*, the BVerfG stated that the outer limits of judicial law-making cannot be captured in a single formula that applies equally to all areas of law and all legal relationships.[224] The clearest example of the merit of this statement refers to the interpretation of criminal legislation determining or aggravating a defendant's liability in criminal law. In these cases, permissible statutory interpretation cannot go beyond the possible semantic meanings of the enacted words due to the principle *nulla poena sine lege* enshrined in art. 103(2) GG.[225] The latter constitutional principle intensifies the binding nature of the statute. Moreover, case law shows that the outer limits of judicial law-making are applied liberally if the law-making serves to protect a legal interest (*Rechtsgut*) that is itself enshrined in and protected under the constitution, as was the case in *Soraya*.[226] In contrast, these limits are applied narrowly if a court engages in judicial law-making in order to limit a legal right or claim of an individual that the legislature granted to the individual based on constitutional considerations.[227]

Even though the BVerfG has derived from art. 20(3) GG that any limitation of fundamental human rights by the state requires an explicit legislative basis (*Gesetzesvorbehalt*), gap-filling to the detriment of the individual remains possible in public law cases.[228] Judicial law-making can thus have the effect of limiting an individual's fundamental right guaranteed by the German Basic Law and favouring the legal position of the state (as opposed to the legal position of another individual). The requirement of an explicit legal basis has only a restricted autonomous function for judicial law-making since the limits of permissible judicial law-making coincide with the binding force of legislation

---

[224] BVerfG, *NJW* 1973, 1221, 1225 – *Soraya*. Cf. BVerfG, *NJW* 2015, 1506, para. 40 – *Scheinvater* ("The limits of permissible judicial law-making must be determined on a case-by-case basis").

[225] BVerfG *NJW* 1986, 1672; BVerfG, *NJW* 1995, 1141; BVerfG, *NJW* 2002, 1779, 1781.

[226] BVerfG, *NJW* 2009, 1469, para. 60 and dissenting opinion by Judges Voßkuhle, Osterloh, Di Fabio, para. 105 – *Rügeverkümmerung*; cf. BVerfG, *NJW* 1979, 305, 306–307 – *Sachverständigenhaftung*; BVerfG, *NJW* 2015, 1506, para. 41 – *Scheinvater*.

[227] BVerfG, *NJW* 1985, 2395, 2402; BVerfG, *NJW* 2009, 1469, dissenting opinion by Judges Voßkuhle, Osterloh, Di Fabio, para. 105 – *Rügeverkümmerung*; cf. BVerfG, *NJW* 1979, 305, 306–307 – *Sachverständigenhaftung*; BVerfG, *NJW* 2015, 1506, para. 41 – *Scheinvater*.

[228] See, e.g. BVerfG, *NJW* 1998, 2269, 2270; BVerfG, *NJW* 2003, 2520; BVerfG, *NJW* 2012, 2639, para. 62; BVerwG, *NVwZ* 2003, 986, 988. It is controversial in German legal scholarship whether the relationship between the constitutional requirement of *Gesetzesvorbehalt* and judicial law-making entails that judicial gap-filling in public law cases, particularly tax law cases, to the detriment of the individual is impermissible or not; for an overview of the discussion, see GRZESZICK, above n. 126, Art. 20 Abs. 3 GG, paras. 88–90; T. RADEMACHER, Reading up or down EU legislation: a plea for a principled approach to an extraordinary judicial power, (2017) 23 *European Public Law* 319, 332–333; S. WILKE, *Grenzen einheitlicher Rechtsanwendung von Ver- und Geboten des Wertpapierhandelsgesetzes*, Kovač, Hamburg 2010, pp. 263–295. Some assert that the wording of the statutory provision has strict priority in these cases (ALEXY and DREIER, above n. 40, pp. 73, 95; K. LANGENBUCHER, Argument by analogy in European law, (1998) 57 *CLJ* 481, 486). This view is not supported by recent case law, however.

and law under art. 20(3) GG.[229] Yet, the limitation of the fundamental right brought about by judicial law-making must comply with the same standards applicable to the ordinary legislature when it enacts legislation limiting fundamental rights.[230] In other words, fundamental rights are binding on the legislature and the judiciary (cf. art. 1(3) GG). Judicial law-making infringes the German Basic Law if a court reaches an interpretative result that the legislature could not have enacted without infringing a fundamental right enshrined in the German Basic Law.[231] Furthermore, the more judicial law-making interferes with fundamental rights guaranteed by the German Basic Law,[232] the more prominently the intentions of the legislature must be expressed in the legislation in order to justify the permissibility of the judicial law-making, since severe restrictions of fundamental rights ultimately lie outside the judicial function and are a power that belongs to the legislative domain.[233] It follows that a certain meaning of a provision may not be adopted by judicial law-making even though it could be enacted by the ordinary legislature.[234] This result can also be traced back to the principle of legal certainty under the rule of law, which requires inter alia that provisions must be sufficiently clear and precise. The more a provision affects individual rights, the clearer and more precise it must be.[235] If judicial law-making in a horizontal scenario limits an individual's constitutional right and at the same time benefits another individual's constitutional right, the BVerfG indicated in its *Scheinvater* judgment in 2015 that the scope of the competences of a court to engage in judicial law-making needs to be determined by balancing the opposing constitutional legal positions in the individual case.[236] The upshot

---

[229] GRZESZICK, above n. 126, Art. 20 Abs. 3 GG, para. 90 argues that the requirement of an explicit legal basis has no autonomous function for judicial law-making.
[230] BVerfG, *NJW* 1991, 2549, 2551; BVerfG, *NJW* 2003, 2520; BVerfG, *NJW* 2012, 2639, para. 62.
[231] See, e.g. BVerfG, *NJW* 1991, 2549, 2551; BVerfG, *NVwZ* 2009, 1484, 1485; BVerfG, *NZS* 2011, 895, para. 32; BVerfG, *NZS* 2015, 502 paras. 28–29.
[232] Judicial law-making must comply not only with the outer limits of the judicial function vis-à-vis the legislature as expressed in methodological terms in the outer limits of interpretation, but also with the substantive requirements arising from the provisions of the German Basic Law.
[233] Cf. BVerfG, *NJW* 2015, 1506, paras. 41–42, 48 ("specific connecting factors in the legislation"), 52 – *Scheinvater*. For a further development of this argument and a development of the constitutional limits of judicial law-making in parallel to the constitutional requirements for permissible legislative activity, in particular the constitutional requirement that any limitation of fundamental human rights by the state requires an explicit legislative basis (*Gesetzesvorbehalt*) and a certain level of determinacy of a provision, see CH. MÖLLERS, Nachvollzug ohne Maßstabsbildung: richterliche Rechtsfortbildung in der Rechtsprechung des Bundesverfassungsgerichts, *JZ* 2009, 668, 672. The BVerfG has not explicitly adopted such restrictions for judicial law-making when the case concerns the relationship between private individuals; see BVerfG, *NJW* 1991, 2549, 2550; BVerfG, *NJW* 1993, 1379, 1380 – *Streikeinsatz von Beamten*.
[234] BVerfG, *NJW* 2015, 1506, para. 52 – *Scheinvater*.
[235] FOSTER and SULE, above n. 178, p. 181.
[236] BVerfG, *NJW* 2015, 1506, paras. 40–42 – *Scheinvater*. For criticism, see J. NEUNER, Die Kontrolle zivilrechtlicher Entscheidungen durch das Bundesverfassungsgericht, *JZ* 2016, 435, 438.

of this balancing exercise is that the outer limits of judicial law-making remain considerably indeterminate. I will show that this is a theme that runs throughout the German case law on judicial law-making.

A BVerfG judgment in 2009, *Rügeverkümmerung*, explains the seeming contradiction between common interpretative limits and their narrow or liberal application as follows.[237] The outer interpretative limits arising out of art. 20(2) and (3) GG cannot in principle be defined more narrowly or more widely depending on whether a provision's interpretation is burdensome on an individual or benefits an individual. The binding nature of the statute, the separation of powers doctrine and the decisions of the legislature do not differ in this respect. However, these limits as expressed in judicial practice contain sufficient scope for "interpretation". They can be applied in a narrower or more liberal fashion depending on the circumstances of the individual case. The BVerfG thus admits what was already demonstrated in relation to the policy considerations limit: the outer interpretative limits are not expressed in clear-cut terms, but in such vague words that they leave a substantial amount of discretion to a judge to take into account the context and the circumstances of the individual case. A discretionary element is deliberately built into the outer limits of interpretation by the BVerfG. These limits also leave substantial freedom for the BVerfG to tighten or loosen its judicial review according to the circumstances of the individual case.

With regard to the fundamental feature limit,[238] for example, the BVerfG has not further specified when a feature of a provision or a statute amounts to being fundamental. Case law is devoid of factors or principled guidelines. The same applies to the question of when a decision of a legislature has to be regarded as fundamental.[239] Furthermore, the policy ideas limit as expressed by the BVerfG requires a clear decision from the legislature.[240] Whether a legislature's decision is clear can only be determined by applying the recognised interpretative criteria.[241] The same is true when establishing whether a feature of the legislation is fundamental or whether a decision by the legislature is fundamental.[242] Thus, the interpretative criteria fulfil a crucial function when judges determine whether or not the outer limits of judicial law-making are exceeded. The weighing of the interpretative criteria is not governed by a priority ordering and is

---

[237] BVerfG, *NJW* 2009, 1469, para. 60 – *Rügeverkümmerung*. For criticism, see MÖLLERS, above n. 233, pp. 668, 671.
[238] A judge cannot distort or neglect a fundamental feature of a provision's objective.
[239] A judge has to respect the fundamental decision of the legislature.
[240] A judge cannot alter or replace a clear decision of the legislature with his or her own policy ideas.
[241] BVerfG, *NJW* 2009, 1469, dissenting opinion by Judges Voßkuhle, Osterloh, Di Fabio, para. 97 – *Rügeverkümmerung*; BVerfG, *NJW* 2013, 1058, para. 66 – *Deal im Strafprozess*.
[242] See ULBER, above n. 51, pp. 365, 371–375 with a discussion of case law. Cf. BVerfG, *NJW* 2013, 1058, para. 66 – *Deal im Strafprozess*.

affected by the circumstances of the individual case. The weighing process leaves considerable scope for judicial discretion, which directly impacts on the outer limits of statutory interpretation. The framework set by the outer interpretative limits as expressed in judicial practice thus hardly limits the decision-making process of a judge. A judge can to a large extent determine the content and effectiveness of the outer limits of interpretation. In *Rügeverkümmerung* itself, there was disagreement between the majority and three dissenting judges on whether s. 274 German Code of Criminal Procedure contains an *unambiguous* decision of the legislature in relation to the irrelevance of subsequent corrections of the minutes for appeal proceedings.[243] The disagreement on this point led directly to a disagreement among the judges on whether the BGH's adjudication had exceeded the constitutional limits of the judicial function.

3.3.2. The Recognised Methods of Statutory Interpretation

The BVerfG stipulates that art. 20 GG does not oblige a judge to follow a specific methodology or theory of statutory interpretation.[244] One consequence of this viewpoint is that legal methodology is partly a matter of judicial choice. However, the BVerfG consistently holds that a judge surpasses the constitutional limits of permissible statutory interpretation if he or she does not follow the recognised methods of statutory interpretation.[245] These recognised methods refer to the interpretative criteria and the techniques of judicial law-making.[246] What the BVerfG has not clarified is by whom the methods of statutory interpretation have to be recognised. The right answer would be by the German

---

[243] BVerfG, *NJW* 2009, 1469, paras. 40, 45, 48, 53, 61 and dissenting opinion by Judges Voßkuhle, Osterloh, Di Fabio paras. 106–107, 120–121 – *Rügeverkümmerung*.

[244] BVerfG, *NJW* 1990, 1593; BVerfG, *NJW* 1993, 2861, 2863; BVerfG, *NJW* 1998, 519 – *Kind als Schaden*. In favour: U. BABUSIAUX, *Die richtlinienkonforme Auslegung im deutschen und französischen Zivilrecht*, Nomos, Baden-Baden 2007, pp. 135–136; W. DURNER, Verfassungsrechtliche Grenzen richtlinienkonformer Rechtsfortbildung, *Schriftenreihe des Zentrums für Europäisches Wirtschaftsrecht* Nr. 180, Bonn 2010, pp. 25, 35; W. HASSEMER, Rechtssystem und Kodifikation: Die Bindung des Richters an das Gesetz, in A. KAUFMANN, W. HASSEMER and U. NEUMANN (eds.), *Einführung in Rechtsphilosophie und Rechtstheorie der Gegenwart*, 8th ed., C.F. Müller, Heidelberg 2011, pp. 251, 263; HERRESTHAL, above n. 161, pp. 8–9, 118, 120; ULBER, above n. 51, pp. 365, 369. For criticism, see C. HILLGRUBER, Richterliche Rechtsfortbildung – Demokratische und rechtsstaatliche Bedenken gegen eine scheinbare Selbstverständlichkeit, (2001) 9 *Journal für Rechtspolitik* 281, 284; B. RÜTHERS, Klartext zu den Grenzen des Richterrechts, *NJW* 2011, 1856, 1857; RÜTHERS, above n. 12, pp. 276–277. For an argument deducing specific techniques of statutory interpretation from the German Basic Law, see H. SCHLEHOFER, Juristische Methodologie und Methodik der Fallbearbeitung, *JuS* 1992, 572, 573–578.

[245] BVerfG, *NJW* 1998, 519, 520 – *Kind als Schaden*; BVerfG, *NJW* 2006, 3409 – *Marlene Dietrich*; BVerfG, *NJW* 2009, 1469, para. 37 – *Rügeverkümmerung*; BVerfG, *NJW* 2011, 842, para. 53 – *Dreiteilungsmethode*; BVerfG, *NJW* 2012, 3081, para. 76 – *Delisting*.

[246] See BVerfG, *NVwZ* 1996, 574, 578; BVerfG, *NJW* 1993, 2861, 2863; BVerfG, *NJW* 2011, 842, para. 68 – *Dreiteilungsmethode*; BVerfG, *NJW-RR* 2016, 1366, para. 40.

Basic Law, but no provision in the German Basic Law expressly governs statutory interpretation. What the BVerfG regards as *recognised* methods of interpretation is thus an amalgam of historical development, preceding the German Basic Law and having its roots in the civil law method of the 19th century,[247] and the common use of methods of interpretation in legal practice, courts and legal scholarship. It is a highly indeterminate standard, which the BVerfG has elevated to a constitutional standard that demarcates the competences of the judiciary and the legislature.[248] Regarding the techniques of judicial law-making, the BVerfG derives the limiting function of the concept of gap from art. 20 GG: without establishing a gap, judicial law-making breaches the constitutional boundary between the competences of a court and the competence of the legislature to amend legislation.[249] The BVerfG has not, however, developed a complete or uniform priority ordering of the interpretative criteria out of art. 20 GG. This adjudication of the BVerfG is not contradictory since it is possible to differentiate between outer limits for statutory interpretation and a specific method of statutory interpretation. If a judge keeps within the framework set by the outer limits, he or she is not bound to follow a specific methodology.[250]

We have already explored why the concept of gap is a highly vague interpretative limit for judicial law-making *extra legem*. For judicial law-making *praeter legem*, a provision or a statute must be incomplete, judged by its own plan and purpose. The BVerfG has not defined the concept of gap further. The plan and purpose of a provision is determined by the interpretative criteria to which a court has recourse when considering whether there is a gap. The provision's plan and purpose can be understood more objectively or more subjectively based on the circumstances of the individual case. The weighing of the subjective and objective criteria in the case at issue thus directly impacts on the concept of gap as an outer limit of interpretation.

One example that illustrates this point is the BGH's *Fotokopie* judgment in 1955.[251] The BGH had to decide the question of whether s. 15(2) of the old German Copyright Law (LitUrhG) applies to photocopies. Section 15(2)

---

[247] R. GROTE, Internationalization of the German legal method, in I. HELLAND and S. KOCH (eds.), *Nordic and Germanic legal methods*, Mohr Siebeck, Tübingen 2015, pp. 325, 326–327.

[248] Very critical of the BVerfG: M. JESTAEDT, Rechtsprechung und Rechtsetzung – eine deutsche Perspektive, in W. ERBGUTH and J. MASING (eds.), *Die Bedeutung der Rechtsprechung im System der Rechtsquellen*, Richard Boorberg Verlag, Stuttgart 2005, pp. 25, 36.

[249] BVerfG, *NJW* 1992, 1219. This view is not uncontested. Some legal scholars assert that judicial law-making is not restricted to the filling of gaps; see, e.g. RÜTHERS, FISCHER and BIRK, above n. 12, para. 854. This controversy is intertwined with the controversy about the proper scope of gap-filling; cf. LARENZ, above n. 40, p. 368.

[250] See BVerfG, *NJW* 2006, 3409 – *Marlene Dietrich*; BVerfG, *NVwZ* 2010, 373, paras. 25–28; BVerfG, *NZS* 2011, 18, para. 20; ULBER, above n. 51, p. 369. For criticism, see RÜTHERS, FISCHER and BIRK, above n. 12, para. 812.

[251] BGH, *NJW* 1955, 1433 – *Fotokopie*.

contained an exception to copyright infringement. It allowed copying for personal use without requiring permission from the rights holder. Notwithstanding that the BGH expressly stated that the plain wording of the provision applied to photocopies, the court excluded photocopies from the provision's scope by interpreting s. 15(2) in the light of its sense and purpose.[252] The BGH effectively engaged in judicial law-making by means of teleological reduction even though the court spoke of a restrictive interpretation in a narrow sense. Section 15(2) LitUrhG incorporated the result of a balancing process between the copyright holder's rights and the public interest in the dissemination of the work. At the time of its enactment in 1901 and its amendment in 1910, the enacting legislature could not have foreseen the new technical development of photocopies. The BGH argued that the balancing of interests with regard to photocopies differs from the balancing of interests carried out by the enacting legislature. Even though the BGH tried to align its restrictive interpretation of s. 15(2) LitUrhG with the purpose of the provision as pursued and understood by the enacting legislature, the BGH also stated that the enacting legislature did not address and could not have addressed the new conflict of interest with regard to photocopies. It is clear from the BGH's reasoning that the court itself carried out the balancing of interest with regard to photocopies and decided that the result of the balancing does not correspond with the result of the balancing process enacted in s. 15(2) by the legislature. Therefore, the BGH went against not only the plain wording of s. 15(2) LitUrhG, but also beyond the intention of the enacting legislature and the provision's purpose as understood by the enacting legislature. The BGH's reasoning may be described as a teleological interpretation of s. 15(2) in the light of the provision's objective sense and purpose at the time of the provision's application to the facts of the case. This terminology disguises the fact that the court's interpretation and the establishing of a gap in s. 15(2), in particular the balancing of interests, was guided by subjective value judgements and policy considerations. The BGH's *Fotokopie* judgment thus illustrates that the more a court is able to determine the plan and purpose of a provision detached from its wording and from the intention of the historical legislature, the greater the margin for the judge to include personal valuations and policy considerations into establishing and filling a gap.[253] The *Fotokopie* judgment highlights that the policy considerations limit as expressed by the BVerfG in *Soraya* is a highly tame constraint of judicial law-making. From a comparative angle, the *Fotokopie* judgment also illustrates

---

[252] For a similar case and reasoning of the BGH with regard to magnetic tape recordings, see BGH, *NJW* 1955, 1276, 1277–1278 – *Tonband*. Even though the BGH spoke of a restrictive interpretation in a narrow sense of s. 15(2) LitUhrG, the case concerned judicial law-making by means of teleological reduction since the BGH's interpretation went against the plain wording of s. 15(2) LitUhrG.

[253] For a critical discussion of further case law, see RÜTHERS, FISCHER and BIRK, above n. 12, paras. 873–877.

why Lady Hale's opinion in *Yemshaw*, discussed in Section 4 below, has rightly been criticised.

3.3.3. *The Standard of Constitutional Review: Reasonableness*

According to the BVerfG, a court does not breach constitutional law simply because a decision is incorrect if judged against the benchmark of ordinary statutory law *(am einfachen Recht gemessen)*. The interpretation of ordinary statutory law, including judicial law-making, and a court's choice of the method of interpretation is not comprehensively reviewed by the BVerfG. It is only subject to a limited constitutional review *(Vertretbarkeitskontrolle)*.[254] For example, the BVerfG does not second-guess the particular weight a court applies to an interpretative criterion when construing a provision as long as that decision is not unreasonable *(unvertretbar)*.[255] Two reasons justify this limited review. First, the German Basic Law does not require a court to follow a specific methodology. Legal methodology is not specified constitutional law only,[256] i.e. the whole of legal methodology cannot be derived from constitutional law. Second, statutory interpretation involves an element of judicial discretion and policy choices. When the BVerfG polices the outer limits of the judicial function enshrined in art. 20(2) and (3) GG for statutory interpretation, the court examines whether a regular court applies the recognised methods of statutory interpretation in a reasonable manner.[257] Regarding the interpretative techniques of judicial law-making, the BVerfG has held that the constitutional review of a court's decision is limited to whether the court has established and filled a gap on reasonable grounds.[258] The constitutional limit that a judge must follow the recognised methods of statutory interpretation can thus be specified in the following way for judicial law-making: judicial law-making exceeds the judicial function if it cannot be based on a *reasonable* application of the techniques of judicial law-making, i.e. establishing the existence of a gap and filling of a gap.[259]

---

[254] BVerfG, *NJW* 1990, 1593; BVerfG, *NJW* 2009, 1469, para. 37 – *Rügeverkümmerung*; BVerfG, *NJW* 2011, 1723, para. 16; BVerfG, *NJW* 2012, 669, para. 43; BVerfG, decision of 16.2.2012, 1 BvR 127/10, para. 20. For a detailed discussion of the case law, see ULBER, above n. 51, pp. 368–375. The standard of constitutional review is not limited but comprehensive when the BVerfG assesses whether a provision's interpretation by regular courts complies with the requirements of art. 103(2) GG; BVerfG, *NJW* 2015, 2949, para. 65.

[255] Cf. BVerfG, *NJW* 1993, 996, 997.

[256] Cf. A. VOSSKUHLE, Zur Einwirkung der Verfassung auf das Zivilrecht, in A. BRUNS et al. (eds.), *Festschrift für Rolf Stürner*, Volume I, Mohr Siebeck, Tübingen 2013, pp. 79, 91.

[257] BVerfG, *NJW* 2009, 1469, para. 37 – *Rügeverkümmerung*; BVerfG, *NZS* 2011, 18, para. 20; BVerfG, *NJW* 2012, 669, para. 43; BVerfG, *NJW-RR* 2016, 1366, para. 35.

[258] BVerfG, *NJW* 1990, 1593, 1594 (for argument by analogy); BVerfG, *NJW* 2011, 1723, para. 16 (for argument by analogy); cf. BVerfG, *NJW* 2012, 3081 paras. 76, 82–83 – *Delisting* (for argument by analogy).

[259] See BVerfG, *NZS* 2011, 18, para. 20.

The standard of reasonableness is anything but determinate. It is not further defined in the case law of the BVerfG. It leaves considerable room for the BVerfG to tighten or loosen its judicial review according to the circumstances of the individual case. Depending on how loosely or tightly this standard is applied, the function of the outer limits of interpretation to exclude impossible meanings is more or less effective. The vague outer limits of interpretation together with a loose standard of constitutional review lead to the result that the limits do not bite.[260] As long as the reasoning used by a court in order to establish the existence of a gap is deemed reasonable by the BVerfG, it is irrelevant that another reasoning militating against the existence of a gap in the legislation would have been possible and reasonable as well.[261] As this example shows, out of two opposing interpretative results, each may be reasonable and therefore within the framework set by the outer limits of interpretation. The BVerfG is more inclined to regard a regular court's reasoning as reasonable if the court has openly dealt with the various possible ways to solve an interpretative problem.[262] The BVerfG effectively reviews a regular court's reasoning, but not the interpretative result itself (*Begründungskontrolle, keine Ergebniskontrolle*).[263] This incentivises regular courts to comprehensively disclose their interpretative reasoning in written judicial opinions.[264]

The standard of reasonableness applies to all limits of interpretation.[265] That is because these limits are necessarily linked to the interpretation of ordinary statutory law by regular courts. The interpretation of ordinary statutory law is only subject to a limited constitutional judicial review by the BVerfG. Since the BVerfG has not developed a priority ordering for the interpretative criteria, it would be inconsistent if the BVerfG fully reviewed whether a regular court has correctly assessed whether a decision by the legislature is fundamental or unambiguous, for example. These are questions of interpretation of ordinary statutory law, so that the standard of review ought to be whether a regular court has reasonably demonstrated that a legislative decision is fundamental or unambiguous. The distinction between a full and a reasonable standard of review may sound clear in theory, but if one looks at the judicial practice of the

---

[260] Cf. the discussion of judicial law-making in German company law by MÜLBERT, above n. 175, 214 *AcP* 188, 285–291.
[261] Cf. BVerfG, *NJW* 2012, 3081, para. 81 – *Delisting*; BVerfG, judgment of 28.6.2014, ECLI:DE:BVerfG:2014:rk20140628.1bvr115712, para. 8, available online at http://www.bundesverfassungsgericht.de. See ULBER, above n. 51, p. 375 with a discussion of case law.
[262] Cf. BVerfG, *NJW* 2012, 669, para. 59.
[263] MÖLLERS, above n. 233, pp. 668, 669; ULBER, above n. 51, pp. 366, 377.
[264] See ULBER, above n. 51, pp. 366, 370.
[265] PIEROTH and AUBEL, above n. 33, pp. 504, 507; ULBER, above n. 51, pp. 371–372, 375; cf. BVerfG, *NJW* 1990, 1593, 1594.

BVerfG the picture that emerges is unclear. This may be due to a disagreement among the judges of the BVerfG about whether at all and if so how strong a test of reasonableness should apply when the BVerfG polices the outer constitutional limits of statutory interpretation.[266]

Even though the standard of constitutional review and the limits of the judicial function can be heavily intertwined in written judicial opinions by the BVerfG,[267] it is necessary to differentiate between both. The standard of constitutional review of regular courts' judgments by the BVerfG is a peculiarity of German constitutional law. When regular courts apply the outer limits of statutory interpretation, they do not refer to or apply this standard of reasonableness. Therefore, it is less relevant for the purposes of this book. The standard of constitutional review must be kept in mind, however, when reading and evaluating BVerfG judgments about the outer limits of statutory interpretation.

3.3.4. Towards a Stricter Understanding of the Constitutional Limits of Interpretation

The disagreement among BVerfG judges about the standard of judicial review for the outer constitutional limits of statutory interpretation appears to be part of a wider debate about the proper separation of powers between the legislature and the courts. A more recent case by the BVerfG, *Dreiteilungsmethode*,[268] has been interpreted by legal scholars as following in the footsteps of the dissenting opinion in *Rügeverkümmerung*. *Dreiteilungsmethode* has been described as illustrating a stricter understanding of the constitutional limits of statutory interpretation as well as a stricter judicial review of the limits of interpretation by the BVerfG.[269] The case dealt with the interpretation of s. 1578(1) German Civil Code by the German Federal Court of Justice (BGH). Section 1578(1) stipulates that the level of maintenance of a divorced spouse is determined by the "marital living conditions". Older BGH case law had established that marital living conditions had to be assessed at the time of a divorce's legal force. In a 2008 decision, however, the BGH changed its interpretation of s. 1578(1) German Civil Code and applied a new method to calculate the maintenance requirement of the divorced spouse.[270] The BGH in effect did not assess the maintenance requirement at the time of a divorce's legal force, but according to the actual living conditions at the time of the assertion of the maintenance

---

[266] See BVerfG, *NJW* 2009, 1469, dissenting opinion by Judges Voßkuhle, Osterloh, Di Fabio, para. 103 – *Rügeverkümmerung*.
[267] See, e.g. BVerfG, *NZS* 2011, 18, para. 20.
[268] BVerfG, *NJW* 2011, 842 – *Dreiteilungsmethode*.
[269] RÜTHERS, above n. 244, pp. 1856, 1857. For a more cautious assessment, see V. RIEBLE, Richterliche Gesetzesbindung und BVerfG, *NJW* 2011, 819.
[270] BGH, *NJW* 2008, 3213, paras. 31, 48 – *Dreiteilungsmethode*.

claim. It held that the maintenance requirement of a new spouse could reduce the maintenance requirement of the divorced spouse and that the latter's maintenance requirement is to be dependent on the financial situation of the new spouse. Based on the BGH's new calculation method, the county court reduced the claimant's level of maintenance in the case at issue after her husband married again and had a maintenance obligation towards his new spouse. The higher regional court upheld the county court's judgment. The claimant argued that the new interpretation of s. 1578(1) breaches the constitutional limits of permissible statutory interpretation.

When the case came to the BVerfG, the court relied on the legislative materials and explained that the enacting legislature in 1977 intended that the income conditions of divorced spouses shall be assessed at the time of a divorce's legal force. The *purpose* of s. 1578(1) German Civil Code behind this intention was to grant to the dependent spouse equal participation in the status reached at the time of the divorce's legal force in order to prevent a decline in the divorcee's social circumstances. The German legislature reformed the law of maintenance in the German Civil Code in 2007 in order to adapt the law to changing social situations[271] and to strengthen the principle of economic autonomy after divorce in s. 1569 German Civil Code. Despite these changes in the law of maintenance, the legislature did not alter s. 1578(1), but explicitly expressed its intention in the legislative materials to leave unchanged the criterion of "marital living conditions". Furthermore, the legislature used the same criterion in the new s. 1578b German Civil Code, which provided for the possibility of reducing the maintenance requirement under certain circumstances. This was evidence enough for the BVerfG that the legislature of the 2007 amending Act had confirmed the historical intention and purpose of s. 1578(1) German Civil Code. The BVerfG concluded that the legislature in 2007 also intended to calculate the maintenance requirement based on marital living conditions at the time of a divorce's legal force. The full reasoning of the BVerfG includes a detailed analysis of the legislative materials.[272] It exhibits a rather exhaustive analysis of the fundamental decision of the legislature in respect of s. 1578(1) German Civil Code, even though this is a question of ordinary statute law. *Dreiteilungsmethode* illustrates a rather strict constitutional review of the BGH's reasoning under the standard of reasonableness. The more strictly this review is applied, the more it moves from a review of the process of judicial reasoning by a regular court to a review of whether the interpretative result itself is correct.

---

[271] Rising divorce figures, changing marital arrangements, improved education and working conditions for women and a rise in second marriages (cf. BVerfG, *NJW* 2011, 842, para. 59 – *Dreiteilungsmethode*).

[272] BVerfG, *NJW* 2011, 842 paras. 56–61, 65, 76 – *Dreiteilungsmethode*.

With regard to the constitutional limits of judicial law-making, the BVerfG stated the following:

> A judge is not allowed to depart from the sense and purpose of the provision as determined by the legislature. He has to respect the fundamental decision of the legislature and he has to apply as accurately as possible the intention of the legislature even if the conditions have changed. He must follow the recognised methods of statutory interpretation. ... An interpretation in the form of judicial law-making impermissibly violates the competences of the legislature possessing democratic legitimacy if the interpretation goes beyond the plain wording of the statute, is not reflected in the statute *and* is not approved by the legislature either explicitly or, in the case of an identifiable unintended gap, implicitly.[273]

It is worth noting that the BVerfG links the conditions of impermissible judicial law-making in the last sentence of this quote with a conjunction: the word "and". That means that the plain wording of the statute is not an outer limit of judicial law-making in itself. This is self-evident since judicial law-making by definition derogates from the possible semantic meanings of statutory words. The statutory wording is, however, not at all meaningless for the limits of judicial law-making. The wording of a provision is one of the interpretative criteria that also affects the constitutional limits of judicial law-making.[274] An unambiguous wording may not be an outer limit of judicial law-making in itself, but it can weigh heavily against the permissibility of judicial law-making in an individual case.[275]

By a majority of 5:3, the BVerfG held in *Dreiteilungsmethode* that the BGH's new method to calculate the maintenance requirement of the divorced spouse breaches the constitutional limits of judicial law-making. According to the BVerfG, the BGH's interpretation departs from the scheme of the maintenance law and the understanding of s. 1578(1) German Civil Code, which the historical legislation prescribed in 1977 and which the amending legislation retained in 2007. The BGH's judgment introduces a new standard and a system change by replacing the fundamental decision of the legislature with a new scheme and with the court's own ideas of justice.[276] This reasoning of the BVerfG contains further clarifications for the outer limits of judicial law-making: (a) a judge is not allowed to introduce a new scheme into the legislation, and (b) a court cannot substitute the legislature's ideas of justice with its own.[277]

---

[273] Ibid., para. 53 – emphasis added. See also BVerfG, *NJW* 2007, 2977, para. 121; BVerfG, *NJW* 2011, 1723, para. 15.
[274] See, e.g. BVerfG, *NJW* 2000, 347, 349.
[275] Cf. BVerfG, *NJW* 2011, 842 paras. 68–70 – *Dreiteilungsmethode*.
[276] Ibid., paras. 55, 62, 65.
[277] Ibid., para. 52. See also BVerfG, *NJW* 2009, 499, 500; BVerfG, *NJW* 2012, 3081, para. 75 – *Delisting*; BVerfG, *NJW-RR* 2016, 1366, para. 39.

Chapter 2. Conventional Canons of Statutory Interpretation

The BVerfG also referred to the legislature's intention as a limit of statutory interpretation in *Dreiteilungsmethode*.[278] This notion is reflected in the aim of statutory interpretation. If the aim of statutory interpretation is to ascertain the intention of the legislature, going beyond this intention would not be justified by its aim. Using legislative intent to describe the aim as well as the limit of statutory interpretation is thus expressing two sides of the same coin. The limiting function of the legislature's intention[279] is usually expressed in the case law in the so-called double criterion: a court surpasses the outer limits of the judicial function if its interpretation disregards the wording *and* the clearly identifiable intention of the legislature.[280] This formulation of the double criterion is ambiguous as it combines an interpretative criterion (textual criterion) with the aim of statutory interpretation (intention of the legislature). Disregarding the latter on its own always exceeds the limits of judicial interpretation. The ambiguity can be clarified if one considers that the notions of legislative intent and purpose are often used interchangeably in German judgments.[281] If intention is used to denote purpose,[282] the double criterion indeed combines two interpretative criteria. In that form it corresponds with the view of legal scholars who contend that the *contra legem* limit is infringed if an interpretation contravenes the wording *and* the purpose of the provision.[283] Yet, even this reading of the double criterion does not resolve the ambiguity.

If a court engages in judicial law-making, it goes beyond the possible semantic meanings of the statutory words. It disregards the first element of the double criterion. The double criterion is only infringed if a court also disregards "the clearly identifiable intention of the legislature". Even though a provision's purpose plays a significant role in determining the second element of the double criterion, this element integrates all interpretative criteria in judicial practice. For example, a (clear and unambiguous) wording of a provision can influence whether or not the intention of the legislature is clearly identifiable. The double criterion serves as an example of the prominent role that the textual criterion can play in statutory interpretation as it affects both elements of the

---

[278] BVerfG, *NJW* 2011, 842, para. 53 – *Dreiteilungsmethode*.
[279] BGH, *NJW* 2016, 1718, para. 38 – *Gasversorgung II*.
[280] BVerfG, *NJW* 2012, 3081, para. 75 – *Delisting*; BVerfG, *NJW-RR* 2016, 1366, para. 39.
[281] See, e.g. BGH, *NJW* 2014, 2646, para. 23 – *Lebensversicherung II*. The same appears in English judgments; see *Black-Clawson International Ltd. v. Papierwerke Waldhof-Aschaffenburg A.G.* [1975] AC 591 (HL), 622 (Viscount Dilhorne).
[282] Cf. R. EKINS, The intention of Parliament [2010] *Public Law* 709, 726 ("One's purpose is an aspect of one's intention …").
[283] F. BYDLINSKI, Über die lex-lata-Grenze der Rechtsfindung, in I. KOLLER et al. (eds.), *Einheit und Folgerichtigkeit im juristischen Denken*, C.H. Beck, Munich 1998, pp. 27, 47; CANARIS, above n. 137, pp. 47, 92.

double criterion.²⁸⁴ This may be welcomed from the perspective of legal certainty but the problem is that the case law is incoherent and fails to provide legal certainty. On the one hand, there is case law that highlights the prominent role of the statutory language, particularly when judicial law-making is deemed to exceed the outer limits of interpretation. On the other hand, there are other cases in which courts go beyond a provision's clear wording. As appears from judicial practice, it is the weighing of the interpretative criteria in an individual case that ultimately determines whether or not the double criterion is met.²⁸⁵ Other limits of interpretation derived from art. 20(3) and (3) GG by the BVerfG can be characterised in the same way.²⁸⁶ German judicial practice also gives the impression that the weight attached to different interpretative criteria is outcome driven. How this practice can be reconciled with the abstract formulation of the double criterion, for example through the adjective "clearly" or through relying on the wording, the systemic criterion and the history of a provision to determine its purpose,²⁸⁷ is of marginal importance.

Furthermore, the notion of the "identifiable intention of the legislature" in the double criterion does not necessarily refer to the actual or inferred intent of the enacting legislature. It can also refer to the underlying objective purpose and sense of the statutory provision.²⁸⁸ The term "legislature" in the double criterion is ambiguous. This is no surprise since this indeterminacy runs through the whole of the interpretative process, from the aim of statutory interpretation via the weighing of the interpretative criteria and all the way to the establishing of a gap and the outer limits of judicial law-making. German courts use objective as well as subjective criteria to ascertain the intention of the legislature. The meaning of legislative intent as a limit of interpretation cannot therefore be derived from (a) the actual intention of the enacting legislature or (b) the provision's underlying objective sense and purpose alone. In *Dreiteilungsmethode*, the BVerfG relied heavily on neighbouring provisions in the law of maintenance of the German Civil Code, legislative materials of the enacting legislature and legislative materials of an Act amending the law of maintenance. The court's reasoning attaches a strong weight to the historical criterion of interpretation and, consequently, the BVerfG adopted an understanding of the purpose of s. 1578(1) that is mainly determined by the identifiable intention of the enacting

---

[284] But see BYDLINSKI, above n. 283, pp. 27, 47, who argues that the *contra legem* limit is infringed if judicial law-making infringes the clear wording of a provision and the corresponding intention of the legislature (purpose of the legislation), the latter being derived from interpretative criteria other than the statutory wording. This is methodologically sound, but not the case law of the BVerfG.

[285] Cf. CANARIS, above n. 137, pp. 47, 92–93.

[286] See Section 3.3.1 above.

[287] The interpretative criteria (textual, systemic and historical) play a central role in determining a provision's purpose. See CANARIS, above n. 137, pp. 47, 93.

[288] Cf. BVerfG, *NJW* 2009, 1469, dissenting opinion by Judges Voßkuhle, Osterloh, Di Fabio, para. 98 ("the (subjective or objectivised) intention of the legislature") – *Rügeverkümmerung*.

legislature. *Soraya*, on the other hand, illustrates that the function of the intention of the enacting legislature to guide and limit the interpretative process decreases with the ageing of a statute if a change in social, political, technical or economic conditions has occurred which the historical legislature could not have foreseen. Another differentiating factor between *Dreiteilungsmethode* and *Soraya* was that in *Dreiteilungsmethode* the legislature had recently amended neighbouring provisions in the legislation. It appears from case law that recent legislative amendments to the relevant statute or legislative activity in neighbouring areas of law militate against the permissibility of judicial law-making if they indicate the legislature's intention to leave the statutory provision under discussion unchanged.[289]

The meaning of the legislature's intention as a limit of interpretation very much depends on the circumstances of the individual case. These circumstances are not defined exhaustively in the case law. I have argued in the preceding paragraph that case law contains a few principled guidelines, but it is devoid of concrete factors. The criterion of rational argument without arbitrariness, as expressed in *Soraya*, hardly functions as a limiting factor. What is important for our purposes is that *Soraya* shows that the intention of the legislature as an outer limit of interpretation can shift so far towards an objective understanding in an individual case that judicial law-making does not infringe art. 20(2) and (3) GG even if it goes against the explicit and plain intention of the enacting legislature.[290] Whether the BVerfG's reasoning in *Dreiteilungsmethode* has paved the way for a stricter understanding of the binding force of statute, a stricter review of the constitutional limits of judicial law-making by the BVerfG and a strengthened relevance of the actual intention of the enacting legislature in the interpretative process – as proclaimed in the literature[291] – remains to be seen. I will show in Chapters 3 and 4 that further indicators indeed exist that point in this direction. A heightened role for the intention of the enacting legislature in statutory interpretation can, for example, be seen in a 2016 chamber decision by the BVerfG, where the BVerfG said with regard to the constitutional limits of judicial law-making that a court cannot disregard the identifiable original (*ursprünglich*) intention of the legislature.[292]

---

[289] Cf. BVerfG, *NJW* 1984, 475–476 – *Sozialplan*; BVerfG, *NJW* 2011, 842 paras. 58–60 – *Dreiteilungsmethode*. See with a discussion of the case law ULBER, above n. 51, pp. 373–375.

[290] See also BVerfG, *NJW* 2006, 3409, 3410 – *Marlene Dietrich* (The BGH's judicial law-making "may contradict the actual intention of the historical legislation in 1907 .... It does not, however, infringe constitutional law ..."). For a discussion of further case law where courts have departed from the plain intention of the enacting legislature in order to adapt the legislation at issue to changing political, economic or social circumstances, see RÜTHERS, FISCHER and BIRK, above n. 12, paras. 940–943.

[291] RÜTHERS, above n. 244, pp. 1856, 1858.

[292] BVerfG, *NJW-RR* 2016, 1366, para. 42. That is difficult to reconcile with other case law (BVerfG, *NJW* 2006, 3409, 3410 – *Marlene Dietrich*) stipulating that judicial law-making that contradicts the intention of the enacting legislature does not necessarily infringe art. 20(2) and (3) GG.

All in all, it is clear that the BVerfG has not devised clear-cut constraints for judicial law-making. The circumstances of the individual case heavily impact on the application of the outer interpretative limits. This leaves judges with a considerable scope for judicial discretion and allows judges to consider extra-legal factors. This case law performs rather poorly when judged against the functions of the outer limits of interpretation to (a) limit the scope of possible meanings of a provision, (b) limit judicial power and thus address separation of powers concerns, (c) reduce the area of extra-legal considerations and subjective judicial evaluation in statutory interpretation and (d) provide legal certainty.

4. READING IN, OUT OR DOWN OF WORDS IN LEGISLATION IN ENGLAND

English legal methodology does not formally distinguish between interpretation in a narrow sense, i.e. interpretation which remains within the possible semantic meanings of the statutory words, and judicial law-making, i.e. interpretation which goes beyond or against the range of possible semantic meanings of the statutory words, in the way that German legal methodology does.[293] "Alterations" to the statutory language by means of judicial interpretation are considered under the conventional canons of construction, particularly the golden rule, the mischief approach and the purposive approach. Reading in, out or down of words in legislation is not separated from interpretation. Judicial law-making is sometimes referred to as a "strained construction"[294] or "rectifying interpretation",[295] but neither of those terms is used uniformly. A court contemplates judicial law-making if it is satisfied that any of the possible semantic meanings of the statutory words cannot reasonably be supposed to have been the intention of Parliament. That also means that even when reading in, out or down words in legislation, a court aims to give effect to legislative intent. As in Germany, the limits of statutory interpretation have a constitutional dimension[296] since they demarcate the boundary between interpretation and impermissible judicial legislation.[297] If a court exceeds these limits, it trespasses on powers that belong to Parliament.

---

[293] VOGENAUER, above n. 34, p. 1280; cf. BANKOWSKI and MACCORMICK, above n. 59, pp. 359, 362.
[294] *Clarke v. Kato* [1998] 1 WLR 1647 (HL), 1656 (Lord Clyde); JONES and BENNION, above n. 24, section 157.
[295] *Bogdanic v. The Secretary of State for the Home Department* [2014] EWHC 2872 (QB), para. 43 (Sales J); *R. v. Moore* [1995] QB 353 (CA), 362 (Sedley LJ, "rectifying construction").
[296] Cf. MCLEOD, above n. 66, p. 75 ("Legal method is an aspect of constitutional law").
[297] *Magor and St Mellons Rural DC v. Newport Corp* [1952] AC 189 (HL), 191 (Lord Simonds), 192 (Lord Morton); *Stock v. Frank Jones (Tipton) Ltd.* [1978] 1 WLR 231 (HL), 236–237 (Lord Simon); *R. (Francis & Francis) v. Central Criminal Court* [1989] AC 346 (HL), 387, 389–390 (Lord Oliver); *Inco Europe Ltd. v. First Choice Distribution* [2000] 1 WLR 586 (HL), 592 (Lord Nicholls); *Gladstone v. Bower* [1960] 2 QB 384 (CA), 395–396 (Devlin LJ).

4.1. LITERAL RULE AND THE DOCTRINE OF PARLIAMENTARY SOVEREIGNTY

The question of whether a court can adopt a meaning that the statutory words cannot reasonably bear has traditionally, at least from the 19th century, been answered in the negative in English case law. Lord Salmon expressed this position in the following two principles of construction in *Johnson v. Moreton* in 1978:[298]

> 1. 'If the language of a statute be plain, admitting of only one meaning, the legislature must be taken to have meant and intended what it has plainly expressed, and whatever it has in clear terms enacted must be enforced though it should lead to absurd or mischievous result.'[299] ...
>
> 2. The courts have no power to fill in a gap in a statute, even if satisfied that it had been overlooked by the legislature and that if the legislature had been aware of the gap, the legislature would have filled it in.[300]

These two principles can be supplemented by a third rule of construction that was expressed by Lord Reid in *Jones v. Director of Public Prosecutions*:

> It is a cardinal principle applicable to all kinds of statutes that you may not for any reason attach to a statutory provision a meaning which the words of that provision cannot reasonably bear. If they are capable of more than one meaning, then you can choose between those meanings, but beyond that you must not go. If certain authorities have adopted some other method which produces a meaning which the words of the statute cannot reasonably bear, then in my judgment this House ought not to approve of them.[301]

According to these restrictive *dicta*, which can be found in judicial opinions until the 1980s, judges must not add to, alter or ignore statutory words when interpreting legislation. If this rule were to be relaxed, as Lord Justice Devlin explained, "sooner or later the court would be saying what Parliament meant and would get it wrong and thus usurp the law-making function".[302]

---

[298] *Johnson v. Moreton* [1980] AC 37 (HL), 50 (Lord Salmon).
[299] See also *Kammins Ballrooms Co Ltd. v. Zenith Investments (Torquay) Ltd.* [1971] AC 850 (HL), 859 (Lord Reid); *Black-Clawson International Ltd. v. Papierwerke Waldhof-Aschaffenburg A.G.* [1975] AC 591 (HL), 613 (Lord Reid); *Vacher & Sons Ltd. v. London Society of Compositors* [1913] AC 107 (HL), 121–122 (Lord Atkinson).
[300] See also *Magor and St Mellons Rural DC v. Newport Corp* [1952] AC 189 (HL), 191 (Lord Simonds), 192 (Lord Morton); *Jones v. Wrotham Park Settled Estates* [1980] AC 74 (HL), 107 (Lord Salmon); *R. (Francis & Francis) v. Central Criminal Court* [1989] AC 346 (HL), 387–388, 389–390 (Lord Oliver); *Gladstone v. Bower* [1960] 2 QB 384 (CA), 395–396 (Devlin LJ).
[301] *Jones v. Director of Public Prosecutions* [1962] AC 635 (HL), 662 (Lord Reid).
[302] *Gladstone v. Bower* [1960] 2 QB 384 (CA), 395–396 (Devlin LJ).

This explanation links with the relationship between the courts and Parliament, which is based on the separation of powers. In the words of Lord Diplock, "the British constitution, though largely unwritten, is firmly based upon the separation of powers; Parliament makes the laws, the judiciary interpret them".[303] Devlin LJ's explanation also indicates that English judges have (or at least traditionally had) a stricter understanding of the limits of the judicial function vis-à-vis the legislature than their German counterparts. The key factor supporting this view is the constitutional doctrine of parliamentary sovereignty, which has no equivalent in German constitutional law. The doctrine of parliamentary sovereignty establishes the legal supremacy of statute.[304] Courts are bound by the parliament that passed the statute. As Lord Diplock put it: "Parliament ... is sovereign only in respect of what it expresses by the words used in the legislation it has passed".[305] It flows from the doctrine of parliamentary sovereignty that courts are bound by the intention of the parliament that enacted the legislation.[306] The courts adhered to the intention of the enacting parliament by following the statutory words, that is Parliament's enacted intentions, as the statutory words best declared this intention.[307] The judge's adherence to the literal meaning of the statutory words thus developed as a consequence of the powerful doctrine of parliamentary sovereignty.[308] Another factor that explains the English judges' fidelity to the statutory language was the drafting style of English legislation. Since the statutory language was technical, detailed and precise, English judges took the approach that Parliament intended to express its intentions precisely.[309]

---

[303] *Duport Steels Ltd. v. Sirs* [1980] 1 All ER 529 (HL), 541 (Lord Diplock).

[304] *R. (Miller) v. Secretary of State for Exiting the European Union* [2017] UKSC 51, para. 226 (Lord Reed, "primacy of statute"); GORDON, above n. 203, p. 132; C. TURPIN and A. TOMKINS, *British government and the constitution*, 7th ed., CUP, Cambridge 2011, p. 59.

[305] *Black-Clawson International v. Papierwerke Waldhof-Aschaffenburg* [1975] AC 591 (HL), 638 (Lord Diplock).

[306] R. EKINS, Legislative freedom in the United Kingdom, (2017) 133 *LQR* 582, 595; R. EKINS and C. FORSYTH, *Judging the public interest: the rule of law vs. the rule of courts*, Policy Exchange, London 2015, p. 14; M. ELLIOTT, Ekins and Forsyth on Evans: A brief response, 03.12.2015, available online at http://publiclawforeveryone.com/2015/12/03/ekins-and-forsyth-on-evans-a-brief-response/; cf. DUXBURY, above n. 2, p. 229; GOLDSWORTHY, above n. 197, pp. 253–254; JONES and BENNION, above n. 24, sections 163, 403.

[307] *The Sussex Peerage* (1844) 11 Clark & Finnelly 85, 143 (Tindal CJ; "My Lords, the only rule for the construction of Acts of Parliament is, that they should be construed according to the intent of the Parliament which passed the Act. If the words of the statute are of themselves precise and unambiguous, then no more can be necessary than to expound those words in their natural and ordinary sense. The words themselves do, in such case, best declare the intention of the legislature"); cf. *Associated Newspapers Ltd. v. Wilson* [1995] 2 AC 454 (HL), 475 (Lord Bridge). See GREENBERG, above n. 56, para. 17.1.1; DUXBURY, above n. 2, p. 224.

[308] DUXBURY, above n. 2, p. 150; R. MASTERMAN and S. WHEATLE, Unpacking separation of powers: judicial independence, sovereignty and conceptual flexibility in the UK constitution, [2017] *PL* 469, 474; MCLEOD, above n. 66, p. 268; VOGENAUER, above n. 34, p. 886; cf. *Black-Clawson International v. Papierwerke Waldhof-Aschaffenburg* [1975] AC 591 (HL), 638 (Lord Diplock).

[309] DUXBURY, above n. 2, pp. 155–156, 207.

Chapter 2. Conventional Canons of Statutory Interpretation

It is important to note that the doctrine of parliamentary sovereignty does not force judges to invariably give effect to nothing other than the literal meaning of the words used by Parliament.[310] The strict literal rule was a creation of the courts, rather than Parliament. It has been described as a form of self-imposed judicial restraint.[311] The absence of constitutional judicial review of parliamentary legislation also encouraged the development of a strict literal rule of construction in England.[312] Furthermore, if common law is viewed as a framework into which legislation has to be fitted,[313] and if statute law is viewed as an intrusion into common law,[314] applying a strict literal rule as opposed to a wider purposive approach entails that greater areas of judge-made law are left untouched by legislation.[315] This provides another incentive for judges to adopt a strict literal rule and to apply a presumption against implicit alteration of the common law.[316] From this perspective, the courts' reluctance to become involved in the development of legislation appears as judicial deference to Parliament, but has the effect of preserving pre-existing judge-made law (if such common law principles existed). It also follows from this conception of the relationship between common law and statute that it is the common law that is capable of

---

[310] A. LESTER, English judges as law makers, [1993] *PL* 269, 272; J. GOLDSWORTHY, Parliamentary sovereignty and statutory interpretation, in R. BIGWOOD (ed.), *The statute: making and meaning*, LexisNexis, Wellington 2004, pp. 187, 191, 193; M. ELLIOTT, A tangled constitutional web: the black-spider memos and the British constitution's relational architecture, [2015] *PL* 539, 548.

[311] MACCORMICK, above n. 62, p. 211 ("measure of deference to the sovereignty of Parliament"); VOGENAUER, above n. 34, pp. 890, 900. Vogenauer gives reasons for this judicial restraint and the judges' adherence to the strict literal rule, for example the democratic legitimacy of Parliament, the professionalisation of legislative drafting, the detailed drafting style and the increased efficiency of the legislative process (pp. 890–901).

[312] LORD EVERSHED, The judicial process in twentieth century England, (1961) 61 *Columbia Law Review* 761, 766; VOGENAUER, above n. 34, p. 889.

[313] Against this view, Lord Steyn rightly opined that nowadays "the common law has an important but nevertheless residual role to play"; LORD STEYN, Dynamic interpretation amidst an orgy of statutes, [2004] *EHRLR* 245, 246.

[314] *Re F (mental patient sterilisation)* [1990] 2 AC 1 (HL), 13 (Lord Donaldson MR); T.R.S. ALLAN, *Law, liberty, and justice*, Clarendon Press, Oxford 1994, chapter 4; BANKOWSKI and MACCORMICK, above n. 59, pp. 359, 363.

[315] A common law rule yields to a contrary provision of statute; BINGHAM, above n. 101, p. 167. On the (controversial) relationship between common law and statute law (leaving aside the claims of common law constitutionalism), see *Monro v. Revenue and Customs Commissioners* [2008] EWCA Civ 306, paras. 3–9, 20–23 (Arden LJ); J. BEATSON, The role of statue in the development of common law doctrine, (2001) 117 *LQR* 247–272; VOGENAUER, above n. 34, pp. 1309–1311.

[316] DUXBURY, above n. 2, pp. 36–39; L. SCARMAN, *The approach of British courts to legislation*, UGA, Heule 1974, pp. 5–7; cf. MACCORMICK, above n. 62, p. 211; M. SCHILLIG, §25 Vereinigtes Königreich, in K. RIESENHUBER (ed.), *Europäische Methodenlehre*, 2nd ed., C.H. Beck, Munich 2010, §25, para. 54; sceptically, however, VOGENAUER, above n. 34, p. 1313. For a discussion of the rebuttable presumption against legislative interference with common law, see GREENBERG, above n. 56, paras. 14.1.7–14.1.18.

filling the gaps left by statute law.[317] It does not follow from this, however, that the common law is actually developed further in cases where judges refuse to fill in a gap in a statute. S. Vogenauer has shown that in practice, judges almost never developed further the common law in these cases.[318]

Another consequence of the powerful doctrine of parliamentary supremacy and the strict literal rule of construction was that English courts rejected a judicial power to fill in gaps by statutory interpretation.[319] Departing from the ordinary meaning of the precise words used was equated with an assumption of the functions of the legislature.[320] Based on these constitutional arguments, judges rejected (a) restricting the scope of application of a provision by excluding a case that was covered by its wording[321] or (b) extending the scope of application of a provision to cases that were not covered by its wording.[322] Remedying gaps in legislation amounted to "a naked usurpation of the legislative function under the thin disguise of interpretation. ... If a gap is disclosed, the remedy lies in an amending Act".[323]

4.2. FROM LITERALISM TO PURPOSIVISM

Statutory interpretation in the English courts has undergone a change in judicial attitude from a sometimes excessively narrow literal approach to a wider purposive approach since the second half of the 20th century.[324] This process originated before the UK acceded to the European Communities in 1973.[325] In 1969 the Law Commission proposed that judges should adopt a purposive approach to statutory interpretation instead of over-emphasising a literal meaning of a provision.[326] That was at a time when the orthodox doctrine

---

[317] *Re F (mental patient sterilisation)* [1990] 2 AC 1 (HL), 13 (Lord Donaldson MR); SUMMERS and TARUFFO, above n. 85, pp. 461, 471–472.
[318] VOGENAUER, above n. 34, p. 1310.
[319] DUXBURY, above n. 2, pp. 34–35; SCARMAN, above n. 316, pp. 6–7. See, e.g., *Johnson v. Moreton* [1980] AC 37 (HL), 50 (Lord Salmon); *Magor and St Mellons Rural DC v. Newport Corp* [1952] AC 189 (HL), 191 (Lord Simonds), 192 (Lord Morton). ALLAN, above n. 314, chapter 4 argues that extending the scope of application of a provision by argument by analogy is an impermissible inroad into the common law.
[320] *Abley v. Dale* (1851) 11 Common Bench Reports 378, 391 (Jervis CJ); cf. *Hill v. East and West India Dock Co.* (1884) 9 AC 448 (HL), 465 (Lord Bramwell).
[321] *Garland v. Carlisle* (1837) 4 Clark & Finnelly 693, 726 (Williams J).
[322] *Attorney-General v. Sillem* (1864) 2 H & C 431, 567 (Channell B).
[323] *Magor and St Mellons Rural DC v. Newport Corp* [1952] AC 189 (HL), 191 (Lord Simonds).
[324] *Inland Revenue Commissioners v. McGuckian* [1997] 1 WLR 991 (HL), 999 (Lord Steyn); A. KING, *The British constitution*, OUP, Oxford 2007, chapter 6; SCARMAN, above n. 316, pp. 8–9; MCLEOD, above n. 66, p. 268. In detail VOGENAUER, above n. 34, pp. 963–1253.
[325] See, e.g. *Carter v. Bradbeer* [1975] 1 WLR 1204 (HL), 1206–1207 (Lord Diplock); *Hansard*, HL Deb. 9 March 1981, vol. 418 cc 74–75 (Lord Wilberforce); SCARMAN, above n. 316, p. 9; CROSS, above n. 22, pp. 17–18.
[326] Law Commission (No. 21) and Scottish Law Commission (No. 11), *The interpretation of statutes*, London 1969, para. 80(c) and Appendix A, draft bill, clause 2(a).

Chapter 2. Conventional Canons of Statutory Interpretation

of parliamentary sovereignty was accepted "without equivocation" by English judges.[327] Expounding the factors that drove the development from literalism to purposivism in detail is beyond the scope of this book.[328] These factors include, inter alia, (a) a trend in legislative drafting style away from detailed statutory language towards more general language, (b) growing concerns about democratic deficiencies in Parliament's law-making processes and (c) the negative effect of the growing quantity of legislation on its clarity and quality. In parallel with these developments, judges showed less deference to Parliament.[329] Yet, English judges continued to adhere to the will of Parliament by seeking to interpret legislation in accordance with its true purpose.[330] Lord Bingham explained that a purely literal approach to statutory interpretation "may also (under the banner of loyalty to the will of Parliament) lead to the frustration of that will, because undue concentration on the minutiae of the provision may lead the court to neglect the purpose which Parliament intended to achieve when it enacted the statute".[331] Laws LJ pointed out, however, that purposive constructions

> have their dangers; there is a price to be paid in the coin of legal certainty, and in a debasement, however marginal, of the constitutional truth that it is the legislature's will, found from the words of the Act, and not the executive's will, found from the promoter's intentions, that drives the meaning of statute law.[332]

The change from literalism to purposivism in judicial practice also illustrates that clear-cut methodological requirements do not follow from the abstract constitutional doctrine of parliamentary sovereignty.

Another consequence of the rise of the purposive approach to interpretation is that exceptions to the general rule that judges cannot fill in gaps in legislation have been created.[333] Whether or not and how far judicial law-making is permissible is not a static issue in English case law, but an evolutionary process that is similar to the ongoing shift from the literal rule to the purposive approach. That also means that it is still an unsettled issue when and to what extent judges are authorised to fill gaps in legislation. This issue can be expressed in terms of how much weight a judge attaches to the statutory words on the one hand and the purpose of the legislation on the other hand. Since individual judges may

---

[327] EVERSHED, above n. 312, pp. 761, 765.
[328] For a detailed discussion, see VOGENAUER, above n. 34, pp. 1163–1197. See also EVERSHED, above n. 312, pp. 761, 790; SCARMAN, above n. 316, pp. 8–9.
[329] KING, above n. 324, chapter 6 and p. 357.
[330] LESTER, above n. 310, pp. 269, 273. See, e.g. *R. (Quintavalle) v. Secretary of State for Health* [2003] UKHL 13, para. 8 (Lord Bingham).
[331] *R. (Quintavalle) v. Secretary of State for Health* [2003] UKHL 13, para. 8 (Lord Bingham).
[332] *R. (Kelly) v. Secretary of State for Justice* [2008] EWCA Civ 177, para. 24 (Laws LJ).
[333] Ibid. For an overview, see GREENBERG, above n. 56, paras. 20.1.9–20.1.16; CROSS, above n. 22, pp. 93–105.

differ about the relative weight they give to canons of construction in a specific case, it is not surprising that they may disagree on whether or not a court can deviate from the statutory words used by Parliament in a specific case under the guise of statutory interpretation.[334] That means, for example, that even though the literal meaning appears to produce an absurd result, the absurdity may not be significant enough in an individual case to convince a judge to depart from the literal meaning. As in Germany, the balancing of the interpretative criteria directly affects the limits of statutory construction. The indeterminacy inherent in the judicial balancing exercise is transported into the limits of statutory interpretation, creating room for evaluative arguments.

Two factors that influence the development from literalism to purposivism merit further elaboration. The first factor is a change in drafting style of legislation. Legal scholarship often differentiates between general terms that give wide interpretative power to the judges (as is often the case in continental civil law systems like Germany) and detailed legislation that seeks to cover every foreseeable situation (a general feature of the English legal system).[335] This classical characterisation of the different drafting styles in common and civil law countries has come under attack. H. Xanthaki finds a noted convergence between common and civil law legislative drafting extending from conceptual approaches to actual drafting conventions.[336] Others have argued that the drafting technique of legislation in England has seen a continuing trend away from technical, detailed and precise statutory language to general terms and deliberately vague language.[337] "There is an inevitable interaction between the methods of parliamentary drafting and the principles of judicial interpretation".[338] An extremely detailed legislative drafting style favours the assumption that the statute regulates everything that the legislature intended to regulate. The drafting style thus promotes a method of interpretation that is

---

[334] Compare, e.g. (1) the reasoning of Lord Diplock in *Jones v. Wrotham Park Settled Estates* [1980] AC 74 (HL), 105–106 with that of Lord Salmon (p. 107) in the same case and (2) the reasoning of Lloyd LJ in *Dingmar v. Dingmar* [2006] EWCA Civ 942, para. 43 with the reasoning of Jacob LJ (paras. 63–65) in the same case. See also GREENBERG, above n. 56, para. 18.1.2 ("the principal point of disagreement over the years"); MCLEOD, above n. 66, pp. 268–269; VOGENAUER, above n. 34, pp. 1123–1124, 1141.

[335] E.C. RITAINE, Mixed and hybrid jurisdictions: comparative and methodological considerations, in E.C. RITAINE, S.P. DONLAN and M. SYCHOLD (eds.), *Comparative law and hybrid legal traditions*, Schulthess, Zurich 2010, pp. 141, 147. For an overview of the literature, see H. XANTHAKI, Editorial: burying the hatchet between common and civil law drafting styles in Europe, (2012) 6 *Legisprudence* 133, 135.

[336] XANTHAKI, above n. 335, p. 147.

[337] VOGENAUER, above n. 34, pp. 1188–1193; cf. GREENBERG, above n. 56, para. 18.1.13.A1.

[338] *Cutler v. Wandsworth Stadium Ltd.* [1949] AC 398 (HL), 411 (Lord du Parcq); cf. *Fothergill v. Monarch Airlines Ltd.* [1981] AC 251 (HL), 279–280 (Lord Diplock). For further discussion of this relationship, see P.S. ATIYAH and R.S. SUMMERS, *Form and substance in Anglo-American law*, Clarendon Press, Oxford 1987, pp. 315–318; CROSS, above n. 22, pp. 199–203; VOGENAUER, above n. 34, p. 1314.

as far as possible faithful to the statutory wording. This in turn incentivises the legislature to enact more and more detailed provisions. In a legal system that prefers detailed statutory language over vague terms, following a strict literal rule is a more feasible option than in a legal system that prefers vague terms over detailed statutory language. The BVerfG has argued that the power of German judges to develop the law further is partly justified due to the "open formulation of numerous provisions".[339] This open formulation echoes to a certain extent the fact that bills often reflect political compromise that had to be reached due to the prevalence of coalition governments in Germany. Since imprecise language does not have plain meanings, judges must resort to other principles of statutory construction like the purposive approach in order to determine the meaning of a statute. The higher the imprecision of the statutory words, the wider the interpretative latitude available to judges.

Reliance on the purposive approach to interpretation also increases the role of judges as a driver of legal development because the purpose of a provision may not be clear, there may be multiple purposes that have to be aligned or there is freedom for the judge to express the purpose in narrow or wide terms. Furthermore, it has been argued that statutory language is often over-inclusive in order to plug loopholes.[340] To avoid the application of the statute outside its purpose, it may be necessary to read down general or vague terms in a provision. This relationship between general or vague terms in legislation and a strong purposive approach is also illustrated by the extremely concise drafting style of statutes enacted before the 18th century in England and the then extensive power of the courts to add words to the statutory language or vary the words of the statutory language by means of judicial interpretation.[341] The change in drafting style of legislation in England means that Parliament itself delegates to the judges considerable power to develop the law and undermines a strict literal rule under which the legislature's will is to be derived from the words of the statute alone.[342] The weight attached to the statutory words thus decreases compared to other considerations like the purpose of the legislation. The legislature itself places the judges in positions where they are required to make policy choices. This is of course not a one-way street. A practical result of the courts adopting a purposive approach to the interpretation of legislation is that the draftsman of legislation assumes a purposive approach to construction. This encourages brevity in legislative drafting.[343]

---

[339] BVerfG, *NJW* 1998, 519, 520 – *Kind als Schaden*.
[340] POSNER, above n. 8, p. 215.
[341] *R. (Plantagenet Alliance Ltd) v. Secretary of State for Justice* [2014] EWHC 1662 (QB), para. 89 (Hallett LJ); DUXBURY, above n. 2, pp. 155–156.
[342] VOGENAUER, above n. 34, pp. 1192.
[343] GREENBERG, above n. 56, paras. 18.1.10–18.1.11.2.

The second factor in the ongoing development from literalism to purposivism in England, which merits particular attention, is that cracks appear in the facade of the doctrine of parliamentary sovereignty.[344] The reasons explaining why parliamentary sovereignty has come under attack include (a) membership of the EU and the doctrine of supremacy of EU law over national law,[345] (b) the coming into force of the Human Rights Act 1998 with its wide interpretative powers for judges and the possibility of a declaration of incompatibility,[346] (c) the judicial development of constitutional statutes, which are immune from implied repeal by later ordinary statutes,[347] (d) the use of the principle of legality in the highest English courts[348] and (e) judicial *dicta*[349] declaring that

---

[344] For an overview of the discussion, see M. ELLIOTT, United Kingdom: parliamentary sovereignty under pressure, (2004) 2 *I-CON* 2004, 545, 547–554. For a scholarly argument that the doctrine of parliamentary sovereignty is no longer the principal basis of the British constitution, see B. MALKANI, Human rights treaties in the English legal system, [2011] *PL* 554–576.

[345] See *R. (Jackson) v. Attorney General* [2005] UKHL 56, para. 105 (Lord Hope); LORD PHILLIPS, The art of the possible: statutory interpretation and human rights, First Lord Alexander of Weedon lecture, April 2010, p. 41, available online at https://www.supremecourt.uk/news/speeches.html. There are multiple theories for the supremacy of EU law at national level and for the implications of this position for parliamentary sovereignty. For a summary of these accounts, see N. BAMFORTH, Courts in a multi-layered constitution, in N. BAMFORTH and P. LEYLAND (eds.), *Public law in a multi-layered constitution*, Hart, Oxford 2003, pp. 277, 279–289; M. ELLIOTT and R. THOMAS, *Public law*, 3rd ed., OUP, Oxford 2017, pp. 365–370.

[346] *R. (Jackson) v. Attorney General* [2005] UKHL 56, paras. 105, 107 (Lord Hope). This will be discussed in Chapter 3 of this book.

[347] *Thoburn v. Sunderland City Council* [2002] EWHC 195 (Admin), paras. 60–67 (Laws LJ); *H. v. Lord Advocate* [2012] UKSC 24, para. 30 (Lord Hope); *R. (HS2 Action Alliance Ltd) v. Secretary of State for Transport* [2014] UKSC 3, paras. 207, 208 (Lord Neuberger and Lord Mance (with whom Lady Hale, Lord Kerr, Lord Sumption, Lord Reed and Lord Carnwath agreed)); *R. (Miller) v. Secretary of State for Exiting the European Union* [2017] UKSC 51, para. 66 (Lord Neuberger, Lady Hale, Lord Mance, Lord Kerr, Lord Clarke, Lord Wilson, Lord Sumption, Lord Hodge); *R. (Miller) v. Secretary of State for Exiting the European Union* [2016] EWHC 2768 (Admin), paras. 43, 88 (Lord Thomas of Cwmgiedd CJ, Sir Terence Etherton MR, Sales LJ). See also PHILLIPS, above n. 345, pp. 41–43. The case law is unclear about whether the recognition of constitutional statutes leaves any room for implied repeal, and if so how much. For discussion, see P. CRAIG, Constitutionalizing constitutional law: HS2, [2014] *PL* 373, 382–393. For an argument that constitutional statutes are not immune from implied repeal, see F. AHMED and A. PERRY, The quasi-entrenchment of constitutional statutes, (2014) 73 *CLJ* 514, 527.

[348] The principle of legality will be discussed in Chapter 3, Section 8.

[349] *R. (Jackson) v. Attorney General* [2005] UKHL 56, para. 102 (Lord Steyn), paras. 104, 107 (Lord Hope); *Axa Insurance v. Lord Advocate* [2011] UKSC 46, paras. 50–51 (Lord Hope); *Moohan v. Lord Advocate* [2014] UKSC 67, para. 35 (Lord Hodge); *R. (Public Law Project) v. Lord Chancellor* [2016] UKSC 39, para. 20 (Lord Neuberger, with whom all other members of the Supreme Court agreed, "In our system of parliamentary supremacy (subject to arguable extreme exceptions, which I hope and expect will never have to be tested in practice), it is not open to a court to challenge or refuse to apply a statute …"). For discussion, see J. LAWS, Law and democracy, [1995] *PL* 72–93; DUXBURY, above n. 2, pp. 42–53; M. ELLIOTT, The principle of parliamentary sovereignty in legal, constitutional, and political perspective, in J. JOWELL, D. OLIVER and C. O'CINNEIDE (eds.), *The changing constitution*, 5th ed., OUP, Oxford 2015, pp. 38, 54–63. Very critically R. EKINS, Acts of Parliament and the Parliament Acts, (2007) 123 *LQR* 91, 103.

parliamentary sovereignty is not absolute, but qualified and that it may have to yield to other fundamental constitutional principles like the rule of law or human rights in exceptional circumstances (common law constitutionalism). These constitutional developments have put into doubt the Diceyan orthodoxy that Parliament possesses unlimited legislative authority, even though it is certainly not undisputed[350] among the judiciary that parliamentary sovereignty has developed from an absolute to a limited doctrine. The bottom line, however, is that no judgment of an English court has yet rejected the doctrine of absolute parliamentary sovereignty. There is no precedent for the courts striking down an Act of Parliament as being contrary to the common law, refusing to apply a statute or openly imposing substantive limits upon parliamentary sovereignty.[351] Dicey's understanding of parliamentary sovereignty is frequently quoted and relied on in courts even nowadays.[352] The absolute doctrine advanced by Dicey remains formally intact, and it was recently referred to as a fundamental principle of the UK constitution in the High Court and the Supreme Court in *Miller*.[353] That is why the absolute doctrine is adopted in this book as the constitutional benchmark against which judicial law-making is judged. One caveat must be added to this: I will demonstrate in Chapters 3 and 4 that the UK constitution has evolved from Dicey's conception of parliamentary sovereignty as it distinguishes between ordinary and constitutional statutes. Despite this evolution, the doctrine of absolute parliamentary sovereignty is still intact. Parliament can expressly change or repeal a constitutional statute just like any other statute.

Notwithstanding the benchmark of absolute parliamentary sovereignty, there are increasing, albeit tentative, signs that the courts are developing the idea that there are substantive limits on Parliament's authority to make law. For example, Lord Steyn said in *Jackson* that the Diceyan doctrine of absolute supremacy of Parliament is out of place in the modern UK. He added that the "supremacy of Parliament is still the general principle of our constitution" and continued, but without exploring it any further, that the Supreme Court

---

[350] In favour of an absolute doctrine of parliamentary sovereignty: *R. (Jackson) v. Attorney General* [2005] UKHL 56, para. 9 (Lord Bingham); LORD NEUBERGER, Who are the masters now? Second Lord Alexander of Weedon Lecture, 6 April 2011, paras. 73–74, available online at http://webarchive.nationalarchives.gov.uk/20131202164909/http://judiciary.gov.uk/Resources/JCO/Documents/Speeches/mr-speech-weedon-lecture-110406.pdf. See also *R. (Evans) v. Attorney General* [2015] UKSC 21, para. 154 (Lord Hughes), para. 168 (Lord Wilson).

[351] For a discussion of case law, see GORDON, above n. 203, pp. 132–136.

[352] See the case law cited by VOGENAUER, above n. 34, p. 887.

[353] *R. (Miller) v. Secretary of State for Exiting the European Union* [2017] UKSC 51, para. 43 (Lord Neuberger, Lady Hale, Lord Mance, Lord Kerr, Lord Clarke, Lord Wilson, Lord Sumption, Lord Hodge); *R. (Miller) v. Secretary of State for Exiting the European Union* [2016] EWHC 2768 (Admin), paras. 20–23 (Lord Thomas of Cwmgiedd CJ, Sir Terence Etherton MR, Sales LJ).

"may have to consider" whether there are "constitutional fundamental[s] which even a sovereign Parliament … cannot abolish".[354] It is clear that this non-binding *obiter* statement, riddled with vagueness,[355] cannot function as a benchmark against which the limits of the judicial function are judged. According to Lord Steyn, there is a line that Parliament is not allowed to cross, albeit it is not at all clear from Lord Steyn's *dictum* in *Jackson* where this line is to be drawn. I will consider in this book whether developments in statutory interpretation are compatible with or go beyond the absolute doctrine of parliamentary sovereignty. It may well be that the courts have already taken the step of undermining parliamentary sovereignty by means of adventurous reinterpretation of legislation, while avoiding declaring openly that they are refusing to apply a statute.

The cracks in the facade of the orthodox doctrine of parliamentary sovereignty arguably accelerate the development from literalism to purposivism in statutory interpretation.[356] If we keep in mind that the outer limits of statutory interpretation are affected by the doctrine of parliamentary sovereignty, it is plausible to assume that a weakening of the constitutional doctrine has effects on legal methodology. Moreover, the wide interpretative powers that courts enjoy under the EU legal duty of conforming interpretation and under s. 3(1) HRA can also incentivise courts to adopt a liberal view of the extent of their law-making powers under conventional canons of statutory interpretation. The leading cases on updating interpretation and on correcting obvious drafting errors have extended the scope of permissible judicial law-making under conventional canons of interpretation. It may not be a coincidence that these cases were decided after the Human Rights Act 1998 had received royal assent and after *Pickstone* and *Litster* had established[357] that a court can exceed the outer limits of conventional canons of statutory interpretation for the EU legal duty of conforming interpretation.

Despite these developments from literalism to purposivism, it is important to note that even today, it is submitted, the filling of gaps remains an exceptional use of judicial powers under conventional methods of statutory interpretation in England due to concerns about legal certainty under the rule of law and due to the doctrine of parliamentary sovereignty as traditionally perceived by judges.[358]

---

[354] R. *(Jackson) v. Attorney General* [2005] UKHL 56, para. 102 (Lord Steyn).
[355] Lord Steyn did not say that the Supreme Court "will" consider this question. Furthermore, if Parliament can abolish constitutional law but not constitutional fundamentals, what are such constitutional fundamentals?
[356] See DUXBURY, above n. 2, p. 35 with regard to the Human Rights Act 1998 and the UK's accession to the European Communities.
[357] In detail, see Chapter 4, Section 3.
[358] *Stock v. Frank Jones (Tipton) Ltd.* [1978] 1 WLR 231 (HL), 236–237 (Lord Simon); *Holden & Co v. Crown Prosecution Service (No. 2)* [1994] 1 AC 22 (HL), 33 (Lord Bridge); *Ropaigealach v. Barclays Bank plc.* [2000] QB 263 (CA), 282 (Chadwick LJ); *R. (Kelly) v. Secretary of State*

Chapter 2. Conventional Canons of Statutory Interpretation

This may explain why a tendency is detectable in English judgments to declare apparently clear statutory wording as ambiguous or vague,[359] so that the interpretative result adopted will be a meaning which the words are capable of bearing. As in Germany, a tendency can be detected in judicial practice to conceal judicial law-making as a restrictive or extensive interpretation of the statutory words. In the following three sections, three categories of case law will be presented in which English courts have used their limited interpretative powers to read in, out or down words in legislation: (a) saving statutes from absurdity, (b) correction of obvious drafting errors and (c) updating interpretation. These categories are not an exhaustive statement of permissible judicial law-making in England. Other cases of judicial law-making[360] do not seem to be categorisable but have been decided based on the circumstances of the particular case.[361] The area of judicial law-making has been described as a "no-man's land",[362] and different judges may take different views about the exercise of the exceptional power of adding to, ignoring or altering statutory words. This conflict of views among judges reflects broader debates about the constitutional role of judges in society and about balancing the tension between formal justice and material justice. The answers to these debates are influenced by a number of variables such as "historically received ideas, external views of the political, social and legal communities, and internally generated ideas within the judiciary itself".[363] These variables can change over time and so can the views of judges about the extent of their law-making powers. In order to illustrate further that English judges do engage in gap-filling in exceptional cases under conventional canons of interpretation, including reasoning by analogy,[364] the cases discussed in

---

for Justice [2008] EWCA Civ 177, para. 24 (Laws LJ); *Greenweb Ltd. v. London Borough of Wandsworth* [2008] EWCA Civ 910, paras. 28–32 (Stanley Burnton LJ, with whom Thomas and Buxton LJJ agreed). See also M. ARDEN, The changing judicial role: human rights, Community law and the intention of Parliament, (2008) 67 *CLJ* 487, 489–490 ("the courts cannot fill gaps in legislation"); GREENBERG, above n. 56, paras. 20.1.10, 20.1.14; A. KAVANAGH, *Constitutional review under the UK Human Rights Act*, CUP, Cambridge 2009, pp. 102–103; CROSS, above n. 22, p. 99.

[359] VOGENAUER, above n. 34, pp. 1009–1044, 1125.
[360] See, e.g. *Leicester v. Pearson* [1952] 2 QB 668 (High Court), 672 (Hilbery J); *West Mercia Constabulary v. Wagener* [1982] 1 WLR 127 (High Court), 131 (Forbes J); *R. (Chief Constable of Staffordshire) v. Stafford Crown Court* [1999] 1 WLR 398 (QB), 404 (Laws J); *Kay Green v. Twinsectra Ltd.* [1996] 1 WLR 1587 (CA), 1597 (Aldous LJ), 1603 (Staughton LJ); *Day v. Lewisham and Greenwich NHS Trust* [2017] EWCA Civ 329, para. 18 (Elias LJ, with whom Moylan LJ and Gloster LJ agreed).
[361] Cf. *R. (Haw) v. Secretary of State for the Home Department* [2006] EWCA Civ 532, para. 22 (Sir Anthony Clarke MR, "Thus all depends upon the circumstances of the particular case, even if the case involves the construction of a statute which contains penal provisions").
[362] CROSS, above n. 22, p. 66.
[363] J. BELL, *Judiciaries within Europe: a comparative review*, CUP, Cambridge 2006, pp. 372, 374, 382.
[364] VOGENAUER, above n. 34, p. 1304. For a different view, see LUNDMARK, above n. 106, pp. 424, 433.

the following sections will also be "transplanted" into German law and solved according to German conventional canons of interpretation.

4.3. SAVING STATUTES FROM ABSURDITY

One exception to the general rule that judges cannot fill in gaps in legislation is that judges have been willing to depart from the possible meanings of statutory words according to their linguistic usage in order to save a statute from an absurd interpretation.[365] This exception, even though it is rarely used,[366] leaves a considerable scope of discretion to a judge because the threshold of absurdity is not set, and case law has not clarified the necessary quality or extent of absurdity. Whether or not an interpretative outcome is deemed absurd by a judge is a highly evaluative decision comprising considerations of justice, fairness and reasonableness. This criticism was clearly expressed by the English and Scottish Law Commissions in 1969.[367] At the core of the exception lies a hypothesis about what Parliament cannot possibly have intended. In *McMonagle v. Westminster City Council*, for example, the defendant appealed against his conviction for using premises as a sex encounter establishment without a licence contrary to the Local Government (Miscellaneous Provisions) Act 1982.[368] According to paragraph 3A of Schedule 3 to that Act, a sex encounter establishment was defined as providing entertainments "which are not unlawful". It required a licence granted by the local authority. The defendant argued that in order for this paragraph to apply, it must be shown that the entertainment provided at the premises did not amount to a criminal offence The defendant argued that the entertainment which took place at his premises was indeed unlawful and therefore did not require a licence. The defendant effectively argued that the activity on which his conviction was founded did not fall under the terms of the Act as the activity proved him guilty of another much graver indictable offence. Lord Bridge, with whom the rest of their Lordships agreed, said that reading the statutory words in their literal sense would substantially frustrate the primary purpose of the statutory provisions relating to sex encounter establishments. It seemed to him manifestly absurd to suppose that the legislature intended to provide for the licensing control of just those sex encounter establishments

---

[365] See, e.g. *Adler v. George* [1964] 2 QB 7 (CA), 10 (Lord Parker CJ); *R. (Haw) v. Secretary of State for the Home Department* [2006] EWCA Civ 532, para. 22 (Sir Anthony Clarke MR); *Dingmar v. Dingmar* [2006] EWCA Civ 942 paras. 69–70 (Jacob LJ), paras. 98–99 (Ward LJ).

[366] Courts apply a presumption against absurdity when interpreting statutes; for discussion, see GREENBERG, above n. 56, para. 19.1.12.

[367] Law Commission (No. 21) and Scottish Law Commission (No. 11), *The interpretation of statutes*, London 1969, para. 32.

[368] *McMonagle v. Westminster City Council* [1990] 2 AC 716 (HL).

conducted in the least offensive way. He avoided the absurdity by disregarding the phrase "which are not unlawful", i.e. by treating them as mere surplusage.[369]

Under German law, determining or aggravating a defendant's liability in criminal law by means of an interpretation that goes beyond the possible meanings of the enacted words according to their linguistic usage is excluded by art. 103(2) GG. It seems likely that this barrier to judicial law-making would have been breached if *McMonagle v. Westminster City Council* had been considered according to German law. Assuming that this barrier would not have been surpassed, this case could have been solved by gap-filling via argument by analogy. An open gap existed as the wording of the 1982 Act did not cover unlawful sex encounter establishments even though they were covered by the purpose of the Act. The gap had existed since the coming into force of the 1982 Act. The gap could have been closed by extending the scope of paragraph 3A of Schedule 3 to the 1982 Act to unlawful sex encounter establishments. Judged by the purpose of the Act, lawful and unlawful sex encounter establishments are fundamentally similar. The legal consequence (licensing control) could have been applied analogously to unlawful sex encounter establishments.

4.4. CORRECTING OBVIOUS DRAFTING ERRORS

Another exception to the general rule, that courts cannot add, omit or substitute words under conventional methods of English statutory construction is the correction of obvious drafting errors by means of statutory interpretation.[370] The leading case is *Inco Europe*. It was decided by the House of Lords in March 2000. The court interpreted s. 18(1)(g) of the Supreme Court Act 1981, which originally referred to the Arbitration Act 1979 and which was concerned with restrictions on appeals to the Court of Appeal from the High Court. The Arbitration Act 1996 replaced the Arbitration Act 1979 and also amended s. 18(1)(g) of the 1981 Act. The sole and "abundantly plain" aim of this amendment was to substitute "a new paragraph (g) that would serve the same purpose regarding the Act of 1996 as the original paragraph (g) had served regarding the Act of 1979".[371] On a literal reading, however, the new s. 18(1)(g) made a major legislative change and was not apt to achieve the intended result. Lord Nicholls, with whom the other members of the House agreed, was "left in no doubt that, for once, the draftsman

---

[369] Ibid., 725–727 (Lord Bridge).
[370] See, e.g. *R. (Noone) v. Governor of Drake Hall Prison* [2010] UKSC 30, paras. 43, 47 (Lord Brown), paras. 71–75 (Lord Mance); *Rowstock Ltd. v. Jessemey* [2014] EWCA Civ 185 paras. 50–54 (Underhill LJ); *R. (Confederation of Passenger Transport UK) v. Humber Bridge Board* [2003] EWCA Civ 842, paras. 19–20, 36, 53 (Clarke LJ, with whom Auld LJ and Jonathan Parker LJ agreed); *R. (Kelly) v. Secretary of State for Justice* [2008] EWCA Civ 177 paras. 12–13, 23, 25 (Laws LJ). See also JONES and BENNION, above n. 24, section 287.
[371] *Inco Europe Ltd. v. First Choice Distribution* [2000] 1 WLR 586 (HL), 589, 592 (Lord Nicholls).

slipped up". He restricted the scope of s. 18(1)(g) in order to give effect to the parliamentary intention by reading the phrase "from any decision of the High Court under that Part" as "from any decision of the High Court under a section in that Part which provides an appeal from such decision".[372]

Lord Nicholls freely acknowledged that this interpretation of s. 18(1)(g) involves reading words into the provision. He noted that the power of a court to add, omit or substitute words is confined to correcting obvious drafting mistakes. The court must be

> abundantly sure of three matters: (1) the intended purpose of the statute or provision in question; (2) that by inadvertence the draftsman and Parliament failed to give effect to that purpose in the provision in question; and (3) the substance of the provision Parliament would have made, although not necessarily the precise words Parliament would have used, had the error in the Bill been noticed.[373]

Even when these conditions are met, a court may still decline to correct an obvious drafting error on the ground that the "alteration in language may be too far-reaching. ... [T]he insertion must not be too big, or too much at variance with the language used by the legislature. Or the subject matter may call for a strict interpretation of the statutory language, as in penal legislation".[374]

The condition that the insertion must not be too big illustrates the heritage of the literal rule. It seems to be aimed at those judges who attach stronger weight to the statutory words than to the purpose of the legislation. In contrast to this restriction, the third criterion from Lord Nicholls's test focuses on the substance and not on the precise words when a court corrects a drafting mistake. Lord Nicholls highlighted that this third criterion "is of crucial importance. Otherwise any attempt to determine the meaning of the enactment would cross the boundary between construction and legislation: see *per* Lord Diplock in Jones v. Wrotham".[375] Lord Diplock, however, seemed to have given more weight to the statutory words in his 1978 judgment in *Jones v. Wrotham* when he said *obiter* that it must be "possible to state with certainty what were the additional words that would have been inserted by the draftsman and approved by Parliament had their attention been drawn to the omission before the Bill passed into law".[376] If this condition were not fulfilled, Lord Diplock continued, any attempt by a court to repair the drafting error would cross the constitutional boundary between construction and legislation.[377] When *Inco Europe* was decided

---

[372] Ibid., 592 (Lord Nicholls).
[373] Ibid., 592 (Lord Nicholls).
[374] Ibid., 592 (Lord Nicholls). The sectoral exclusion of penal legislation has in recent judgments not been accepted as a strict boundary; see *R. v. D* [2011] EWCA Crim 2082, para. 66 (Thomas LJ).
[375] Ibid., 592 (Lord Nicholls).
[376] *Jones v. Wrotham Park Settled Estates* [1980] AC 74 (HL), 105 (Lord Diplock).
[377] Ibid., 105–106 (Lord Diplock).

in 2000, the purposive approach to interpretation was already well recognised and Lord Nicholls gave greater weight to the substance of the judicial law-making rather than the specific wording of the altered statutory language.

The outer interpretative limits for correcting obvious drafting mistakes incorporate a considerable degree of judicial discretion. First, whether or not an insertion is too big is a highly vague standard. It depends on the circumstances of the individual case[378] and leaves ample scope for judicial discretion. Second, a judge must be "abundantly" sure that the three conditions expounded by Lord Nicholls are met. This is a high and very vague standard of proof that was not further elucidated in *Inco Europe*. Arguably, a court cannot be abundantly sure of the substance of the provision Parliament would have made if Parliament could correct the drafting mistake in multiple possible ways. Third, it is not clear in Lord Nicholls's speech whether a court must establish an obvious drafting error as a first step and then proceed to the *Inco Europe* conditions in order to gauge whether the error can be corrected by means of statutory interpretation. If this first reading of the case is adopted, then questions arise about (a) what counts as a drafting error and (b) when a drafting error becomes obvious. Answering these questions leaves ample scope for judicial discretion. Alternatively, the *Inco Europe* conditions could be applicable in all cases where the literal meaning of the language used leads to a result that clearly defeats the underlying purpose of the statute as intended by the enacting Parliament. If this second reading is applied, fulfilling the first two of the *Inco Europe* conditions would automatically establish an obvious drafting error. This reading of *Inco Europe* would arguably be more in line with Lord Diplock's *dictum* in *Jones v. Wrotham*.[379]

---

[378] *Ghany v. Attorney General of Trinidad and Tobago* [2015] UKPC 12, para. 35 (Sir David Lloyd Jones).

[379] Lord Diplock enumerated three conditions in *Jones v. Wrotham Park Settled Estates* [1980] AC 74 (HL), 105–106 which must be established by a court in order for the court to be able to read words into a statute which are not expressly included in it. The first two of these conditions are very similar to the first two conditions stated by Lord Nicholls in *Inco Europe*. In *Jones v. Wrotham*, Lord Diplock referred to his speech in *Kammins Ballrooms Co. Ltd. v. Zenith Investments (Torquay) Ltd.* [1971] AC 850 (HL), 880, 881 as an example of an application of this test. A question that arose in *Kammins Ballrooms* was whether a court has jurisdiction to entertain an application for a new tenancy made less than two months after the making of a tenant's request for a new tenancy under s. 26 of the Landlord and Tenant Act 1954, notwithstanding the provision of section 29(3) of the Act which stated that "no application … shall be entertained unless" it is made not less than two nor more than four months after the making of such a request. Lord Diplock read an exception into s. 29(3) of the Landlord and Tenant Act 1954 in order to reduce its scope of application even though the statute used unqualified und unequivocal words. In both *Jones v. Wrotham* and *Kammins Ballrooms*, Lord Diplock did not seem to have restricted this judicial law-making power to plain cases of drafting mistakes, but seemed to have regarded it as applicable in all cases where the literal meaning of the language used would lead to results that would clearly defeat a statute's purpose. In both cases, however, none of the other members of the House of Lords agreed with Lord Diplock's analysis. For a discussion of both cases, see VOGENAUER, above n. 34, pp. 1114–1116, 1142–1143.

Later case law is not clear which reading ought to prevail. On the one hand, case law advocating for the first reading exists.[380] Further judicial opinions in other cases point in the same direction.[381] On the other hand, case law advocating for the second reading exists as well.[382] Underhill LJ's definition of an obvious drafting error in *Rowstock Ltd v. Jessemey* advocates against the first reading, for example. He said that an obvious drafting error "occurs if the draftsman positively intended to include a provision which in fact he omitted".[383] The second reading of *Inco Europe* also has the potential to virtually match the powers of German judges to close gaps in legislation that have existed since the coming into force of a provision. Such a wide understanding of *Inco Europe* would, however, modify the default position for judicial law-making under conventional methods of interpretation, namely that judicial law-making is generally not possible unless exceptional circumstances are met.[384] Judicial *dicta* highlighting that the scope of *Inco Europe* is tightly confined also speak against the second reading.[385] Even if one is of the opinion that an obvious drafting error is not a separate criterion distinguishable from the other three *Inco Europe* conditions, it does not necessarily follow that *Inco Europe* changed the default position for judicial law-making. That is because Lord Nicholls also highlighted that a court must be "abundantly sure" of the three *Inco Europe* conditions. This high standard of proof is in line with the view that the scope of *Inco Europe* is tightly confined. Applying this highly indeterminate standard of proof reaches a middle ground between the two readings of *Inco Europe*.

Since the *Inco Europe* conditions leave considerable judicial discretion, they can be applied restrictively or widely in individual cases. The judicial discretion inherent in the formulation of the *Inco Europe* conditions allows judges to take the context and the circumstances of the individual case into account.[386]

---

[380] See, e.g. *R. (Kelly) v. Secretary of State for Justice* [2008] EWCA Civ 177, paras. 23–25 (Laws LJ).
[381] *Greenweb Ltd. v. London Borough of Wandsworth* [2008] EWCA Civ 910, paras. 20, 28–32, 36 (Stanley Burnton LJ, with whom Thomas and Buxton LJJ agreed).
[382] *Director of the Serious Fraud Office v. B* [2012] EWCA Crim 901, paras. 24–30 (Gross LJ).
[383] *Rowstock Ltd. v. Jessemey* [2014] EWCA Civ 185, paras. 52–53 (Underhill LJ).
[384] In detail, see Section 5 below.
[385] See, e.g. *R. (Kelly) v. Secretary of State for Justice* [2008] EWCA Civ 177, para. 24 (Laws LJ).
[386] For the interaction between the *Inco Europe* conditions and the individual case, see *Ghany v. Attorney General of Trinidad and Tobago* [2015] UKPC 12, paras. 15, 35 (Sir David Lloyd Jones); *R. (Kelly) v. Secretary of State for Justice* [2008] EWCA Civ 177, paras. 26–28 (Laws LJ); *R. (Allensway Recycling Ltd) v. Environment Agency* [2015] EWCA Civ 1289, para. 28 (Richards LJ); cf. *Inco Europe Ltd. v. First Choice Distribution* [2000] 1 WLR 586 (HL), 592 (Lord Nicholls, "Sometimes, even when these conditions are met, the court may find itself inhibited from interpreting the statutory provision in accordance with the language used by the legislature. ... Or the subject matter may call for a strict interpretation of the statutory language, as in penal legislation").

In *R. (Noone) v. Governor of Drake Hall Prison*, Lord Mance remarked that the *Inco Europe* approach is more readily available for the interpretation of delegated legislation made by executive action.[387] That also means that Lord Mance applied the same outer interpretative limits (here the *Inco Europe* conditions) that are applicable to the interpretation of Acts of Parliament to the interpretation of delegated legislation. That in itself is not surprising as courts apply the same canons of interpretation for Acts of Parliament and for delegated legislation.[388] As under German legal methodology, it is not the limits themselves but their application in individual cases that can vary due to their inherent discretional element. If *Inco Europe* were considered under German legal methodology, it would be a case of gap-filling by means of teleological reduction. A covert gap existed since the wording of s. 18(1)(g) of the Supreme Court Act 1981 covered cases that fell outside the provision's plan and purpose. This gap had existed since the coming into force of the legislative amendment. The gap could be closed by excluding from the scope of s. 18(1)(g) and against its wording the cases that fell outside the provision's purpose.

4.5. UPDATING INTERPRETATION

Even though Lord Nicholls confined the power of courts to alter statutory language to cases of obvious drafting errors in *Inco Europe*, his opinion is not an exhaustive statement of judicial law-making in England as the cases on updating construction show. In *Quintavalle*, Lord Bingham and Lord Steyn limited the precedential value of *Inco Europe* and *Jones v. Wrotham* to cases that deal with the circumstances in which a court may correct a clear drafting mistake.[389] There was no such mistake in *Quintavalle*. The House of Lords had to answer the question of whether a statute can be held to cover a new scientific development not known by Parliament when the statute was passed. The relevant legislation was s. 1(1)(a) of the Human Fertilisation and Embryology Act 1990: "(1) In this Act, except where otherwise stated – (a) embryo means a live human embryo where fertilisation is complete". One issue in this appeal was whether embryos created by cell nuclear replacement fall outside the scope of s. 1(1)(a) of the 1990 Act. Cell nuclear replacement is a form of cloning and involves the creation of live human embryos without fertilisation. In 1990, at the time of the passing of the Act, this technology was unknown to Parliament. Embryos created through cell nuclear replacement did not fall under s. 1(1)(a) of the 1990 Act on a literal

---

[387] *R. (Noone) v. Governor of Drake Hall Prison* [2010] UKSC 30, para. 75 (Lord Mance).
[388] Law Commission (No. 21) and Scottish Law Commission (No. 11), *The interpretation of statutes*, London 1969, para. 77; JONES and BENNION, above n. 24, section 60.
[389] *R. (Quintavalle) v. Secretary of State for Health* [2003] UKHL 13, para. 10 (Lord Bingham), para. 25 (Lord Steyn).

reading as they were not created by fertilisation. Lord Bingham, Lord Steyn and Lord Hoffmann applied the guidance given by Lord Wilberforce in his dissenting judgment in *Royal College of Nursing of the United Kingdom*. They held that s. 1(1)(a) applies to embryos created by cell nuclear replacement since the new scientific technique is covered by the parliamentary intent.[390] *Royal College of Nursing of the United Kingdom* dealt with the interpretation of the Abortion Act 1967 and in particular the issue of whether nurses could lawfully take part in a termination procedure not known when the Act was passed. Lord Wilberforce's analysis was approved in *Fitzpatrick*[391] and was regarded as authoritatively settling the limits of updating construction by Lord Bingham and Lord Steyn in *Quintavalle*.[392] It reads as follows:

> In interpreting an Act of Parliament it is proper, and indeed necessary, to have regard to the state of affairs existing, and known by Parliament to be existing, at the time. It is a fair presumption that Parliament's policy or intention is directed to that state of affairs. ... when a new state of affairs, or a fresh set of facts bearing on policy, comes into existence, the courts have to consider whether they fall within the Parliamentary intention. They may be held to do so, if they fall within the same genus of facts as those to which the expressed policy has been formulated. They may also be held to do so if there can be detected a clear purpose in the legislation which can only be fulfilled if the extension is made. How liberally these principles may be applied must depend upon the nature of the enactment, and the strictness or otherwise of the words in which it has been expressed. The courts should be less willing to extend expressed meanings if it is clear that the Act in question was designed to be restrictive or circumscribed in its operation rather than liberal or permissive. They will be much less willing to do so where the subject matter is different in kind or dimension from that for which the legislation was passed. In any event there is one course which the courts cannot take, under the law of this country; they cannot fill gaps; they cannot by asking the question "What would Parliament have done in this current case – not being one in contemplation – if the facts had been before it?" attempt themselves to supply the answer, if the answer is not to be found in the terms of the Act itself.[393]

Lord Wilberforce speaks of the willingness of the courts and of the judicial decision for or against a liberal application of the above-mentioned principles. His analysis leaves ample scope for a judge to consider the circumstances of the individual case when deciding for or against an updated meaning. It is obvious that a discretionary element is inherent in such a formulation of the outer limits

---

[390] Ibid., paras. 10, 15 (Lord Bingham), paras. 24–26 (Lord Steyn), paras. 32, 36 (Lord Hoffmann).
[391] *Fitzpatrick v. Sterling Housing Association Ltd.* [2001] 1 AC 27 (HL), 33 (Lord Slynn), 45 (Lord Nicholls), 68 (Lord Hobhouse).
[392] *R. (Quintavalle) v. Secretary of State for Health* [2003] UKHL 13, para. 10 (Lord Bingham), para. 24 (Lord Steyn).
[393] *Royal College of Nursing of the United Kingdom v. Department of Health and Social Security* [1981] AC 800 (HL), 822 (Lord Wilberforce, dissenting).

of interpretation. An updating construction of a statutory provision that is guided by this analysis leaves room for taking into account not only the circumstances of the individual case, but also personal valuations. In *Royal College of Nursing of the United Kingdom*, the new state of affairs was a new medical method used to carry out abortions that was unknown to Parliament at the time of the passing of the Abortion Act 1967. In *Quintavalle*, the new state of affairs was a scientific development that was unknown to Parliament at the time of the passing of the Human Fertilisation and Embryology Act 1990. In the earlier case of *Fitzpatrick*, the new state of affairs was a change in social conditions between 1920, the time when the first Rent Act legislation came into existence, and 1999, the time of the judgment. The new state of affairs led the majority of the House of Lords in *Fitzpatrick* to interpret the concept of "tenant's family" in paragraph 3(1) of Schedule 1 to the Rent Act 1977 to include a cohabiting homosexual partner in a committed relationship. The court gave the term "family" in the Rent Act legislation a different and wider meaning than when it was first enacted in 1920.[394]

Quintavalle further illustrates that there is a thin line between updating construction and what Lord Wilberforce considered as inadmissible judicial gap-filling. The House of Lords in *Quintavalle* applied Lord Wilberforce's principles and held that the evident purpose of the Human Fertilisation and Embryology Act 1990 was to make comprehensive provision for the protection of human embryos however created.[395] Lord Steyn pointed out that ambiguous statutory language is not a precondition for updating construction. He considered it possible to imply a phrase into s. 1(1)(a) "so that it defines embryo as 'a live human embryo where [if it is produced by fertilisation] fertilisation is complete'",[396] but preferred to read the phrase "where fertilisation is complete" as merely illustrative of the legislative purpose.[397] The latter interpretation confines the application of the statutory words "where fertilisation is complete" to fertilised embryos.[398] In other words, the scope of application of s. 1(1) of the 1990 Act was extended and the statutory language was read down in relation to cloned embryos, a new scientific development not known to Parliament at the time of the passing of the Act. As a result, the scope of s. 1(1) of the 1990 Act was altered in order to give effect to the provision's legislative purpose. Even though an updating construction will often be possible within the statutory language, *Quintavalle* illustrates that judges may also venture outside the constraints of the text when they update a provision's meaning.

---

[394] *Fitzpatrick v. Sterling Housing Association Ltd.* [2001] 1 AC 27 (HL), 39 (Lord Slynn), 45 (Lord Nicholls), 52–53, 55 (Lord Clyde).
[395] *R. (Quintavalle) v. Secretary of State for Health* [2003] UKHL 13, paras. 44, 49 (Lord Millett), para. 14 (Lord Bingham), para. 26 (Lord Steyn).
[396] Lord Millett (ibid., para. 49) was more dismissive of such a course of action.
[397] Ibid., paras. 25–26 (Lord Steyn).
[398] Ibid., para. 32 (Lord Hoffmann), para. 49 (Lord Millett).

Echoing Lord Wilberforce's guidance, their Lordships in *Quintavalle* agreed that it is impermissible to ask what Parliament would have done if the unforeseen circumstances had been before it.[399] According to Lord Bingham, it is a different, and permissible, question to ask "whether Parliament ... could rationally have intended to leave live human embryos created by CNR outside the scope of regulation had it known of them as a scientific possibility".[400] The latter question refers to Parliament's reasonable intention had it foreseen the later scientific technology. Lord Millett's speech also shed some light on Lord Wilberforce's distinction between updating interpretation and gap-filling. Lord Millett emphasised that the search must be for what Parliament "did intend". The right question to ask was thus "whether Parliament intended to legislate only for embryos created by a process which does involve the use of a fertilised egg or whether it intended to legislate for embryos by whatever process they are created".[401] This is consonant with the beginning of the passage from Lord Wilberforce's opinion in *Royal College of Nursing of the United Kingdom*, which reveals that an updated meaning must be reconcilable with the intention of the enacting parliament. The search for this intention will often mean that a court discerns what can reasonably be supposed to have been the intention of the enacting legislature. Lord Millett's test and Lord Bingham's test therefore overlap to a considerable extent. A distinction remains between both tests as Lord Millett's test seems to rely on inferred intent, whereas Lord Bingham's test seems to rely on imputed intent.[402] The House of Lords attributed a wide purpose to the Human Fertilisation and Embryology Act 1990 in *Quintavalle*. This enabled the court to bring the updated meaning of s. 1(1) of the 1990 Act within the provision's underlying legislative purpose. *Quintavalle* thus illustrates the significance of ascribing a wide or narrow purpose to Parliament.[403] *Fitzpatrick* is another example in this respect.[404] We have already seen that attaching a wide or narrow purpose to Parliament entails an element of judicial discretion. In *Quintavalle*, it was this element that gave rise to academic criticism that the House of Lords' purposive interpretation bears the hallmarks of its own

---

[399] Ibid., para. 15 (Lord Bingham), para. 36 (Lord Hoffmann), para. 39 (Lord Millett).
[400] Ibid., para. 15 (Lord Bingham).
[401] Ibid., para. 39 (Lord Millett).
[402] Imputation involves concluding what the legislature would have intended whereas inference involves concluding what the legislature did intend.
[403] For another illustration, see *Yemshaw v. London Borough of Hounslow* [2011] UKSC 3 and the critical comments by C. BEVAN, Interpreting statutory purpose – lessons from Yemshaw v. Hounslow London Borough Council, (2013) 76 *MLR* 742, 753 ("overly broad and illegitimate interpretation of the statute's purpose") and R. EKINS, Updating the meaning of violence, 2013 (129) *LQR* 17, 19.
[404] *Fitzpatrick v. Sterling Housing Association Ltd.* [2001] 1 AC 27 (HL), 45 (Lord Nicholls), 52 (Lord Clyde).

moral views and value judgements rather than being a discovery of the true parliamentary intent.[405] I have evidenced above in Section 3 that ascribing a wide as opposed to a narrow purpose to legislation is also undertaken by German courts and increases their scope for updating construction.

If s. 1(1)(a) of the Human Fertilisation and Embryology Act 1990 and the facts in *Quintavalle* were considered under German canons of interpretation, the provision could be given the same updated meaning by means of gap-filling. The gap arose subsequently due to changes in technical circumstances which the enacting legislature could not possibly have foreseen. The gap was open as the wording of s. 1(1)(a) did not cover embryos created by cell nuclear replacement without fertilisation even though these embryos were covered by the provision's wide purpose. The gap would have been closed via an argument by analogy by extending the scope of s. 1(1)(a) to cover embryos created by cell nuclear replacement. In the light of the wide purpose of the Human Fertilisation and Embryology Act 1990, the creation of human embryos with fertilisation or by cell nuclear replacement was fundamentally similar. Despite Lord Wilberforce's explicit *dictum* to the contrary in *Royal College of Nursing of the United Kingdom*, the comparison with German legal method shows that gap-filling can be permissible under conventional canons of statutory interpretation in England.[406] This conclusion needs a disclaimer, however, as it presupposes at least a common core of the meaning of the concept of gap in English and German legal terminology. It is, however, not possible to derive a reliable definition of the term gap from written judicial opinions in England. Furthermore, not all judges exhibit the same reluctance as Lord Wilberforce did in using the term gap-filling. Some refer to gap-filling when considering statutory interpretation that goes beyond or against the statutory words.[407]

It is submitted here that the limits of judicial law-making in Germany go beyond the limits of the judicial function in England, when courts are faced with a subsequent gap that arose due to changes in social values or political, technical or economic circumstances. Like German judges, English judges recognise that it is generally within the judicial function, as opposed to the legislative function, to update legislation in respect of changes in technology, society or in other conditions over time.[408] As in Germany, the role of the judge encompasses bridging the gap between legislation and society's changing needs. In contrast to their German counterparts, however, English judges have not expressly

---

[405] K. LIDDELL, Purposive interpretation and the march of genetic technology, (2003) 62 *CLJ* 563, 565–566.
[406] In a similar vein, from a domestic point of view, see CROSS, above n. 22, p. 196.
[407] See, e.g. *Jones v. Wrotham Park Settled Estates* [1980] AC 74 (HL), 106 (Lord Diplock); *R. (Noone) v. Governor of Drake Hall Prison* [2010] UKSC 30, para. 71 (Lord Mance).
[408] *R. (ZYN) v. Walsall Metropolitan Borough Council* [2014] EWHC 1918 (Admin), para. 45 (Leggatt J).

recognised a judicial power to contradict the intention of the enacting legislature when they engage in updating construction. Neither have they expressly recognised a power to depart from the intention of the enacting parliament. An updated meaning must be reconcilable with and must not depart from the intention of the enacting parliament under conventional methods of English statutory interpretation.[409] The distinction in the outer limits of interpretation in England and Germany is due to different constitutional settings: art. 20(3) GG as interpreted by the BVerfG on the one hand and the doctrine of parliamentary sovereignty in England on the other hand. Constitutional law thus helps to elucidate the relationship between the historical legislature and objective intent when a judge determines ultimate legislative intent.[410]

This difference in the outer interpretative limits is softened when judicial practice is taken into account. That is because the outer interpretative limit in England, that a court cannot derogate from the intention of the enacting parliament, leaves sufficient room for updating construction as evidenced by *Quintavalle*.[411] Traditionally, that intention was derived first and foremost from the statutory language. With the rise of purposivism, courts have taken other interpretative criteria and more context into account when discerning that intention. They feel more comfortable to venture outside the statutory words if they are satisfied that any of the possible semantic meanings of the statutory words cannot reasonably be supposed to have been intended by the enacting parliament. When English judges are faced with changes in social values or political, technical or economic circumstances unforeseen by the enacting parliament, they may be able to ascribe a wide purpose to the legislation which covers the new state of affairs.[412] The answer to the question of whether a statute can be updated in the wake of a new state of affairs affords judges a reasonable degree of judicial discretion as it depends on how narrow or broad a purpose can be ascribed to the enacting legislature.[413] Furthermore, what can reasonably be supposed to have been the intention of the enacting parliament is an intention that a judge supposes to be attributable to the enacting parliament. The standard

---

[409] See to that effect: *Royal College of Nursing of the United Kingdom v. Department of Health and Social Security* [1981] AC 800, 822 (Lord Wilberforce) *Fitzpatrick v. Sterling Housing Association Ltd.* [2001] 1 AC 27, 34 (Lord Slynn), 45 (Lord Nicholls); *Victor Chandler International Ltd. v. Customs and Excise Commissioners* [2000] 1 WLR 1296 (CA), 1306–1309 (Chadwick LJ); cf. *R. (Quintavalle) v. Secretary of State for Health* [2003] UKHL 13, para. 36 (Lord Hoffmann), para. 39 (Lord Millett).

[410] BARAK, above n. 6, pp. 224, 232.

[411] For criticism of the approach of English judges to updating construction, see DUXBURY, above n. 2, p. 228–231.

[412] E.g. *Fitzpatrick v. Sterling Housing Association Ltd.* [2001] 1 AC 27, 45 (Lord Nicholls); *R. (Quintavalle) v. Secretary of State for Health* [2003] UKHL 13, para. 26 (Lord Steyn); *Yemshaw v. London Borough of Hounslow* [2011] UKSC 3, para. 46 (Lord Rodger).

[413] Compare Lord Rodger's speech in *Yemshaw v. London Borough of Hounslow* [2011] UKSC 3, paras. 45–46 with Lord Brown's speech in that case (paras. 48–49, 51).

of reasonableness is an inherently malleable concept that leaves sufficient room for judicial discretion. The objectivised notion of legislative intent is also affected by common law background assumptions. This book will further explore how far English judges have stretched the concept of the reasonably presumed intention of the enacting legislature in Section 8 of Chapter 3 when analysing the principle of legality.

The outer limits of the judicial function are not static. Modern English statutory interpretation is arguably moving closer towards the interpretative power available to German judges as a speech by Lady Hale in *Yemshaw* indicates. The case concerned the issue of whether the term "domestic violence" in s. 177(1) Housing Act 1996 is confined to physical violence or is capable of being extended to abusive psychological behaviour. Lady Hale, with whom the majority of the judges agreed, argued that the concept of domestic violence in 1996 had developed beyond physical contact and included abusive psychological behaviour. The latter thus fell within the purpose of s. 177(1) as understood by the enacting legislature. Lady Hale's construction arguably remained within the possible semantic meanings of the statutory words "domestic violence". Lady Hale did not stop there, however. She argued that if she were wrong about that, there was no doubt that the concept of domestic violence had moved on and, at the time of its application to the facts in *Yemshaw*, included psychological abuse.[414] This *dictum* has rightly evoked academic criticism[415] as it is at least inattentive to what Parliament did intend. The *dictum* seems to expand the concept of domestic violence beyond the intention of the enacting legislature. Lady Hale's speech in *Yemshaw* can also be read in the light of common law constitutionalism. From that perspective, her *dictum* may show a judicial willingness to develop the outer limits of statutory interpretation beyond the constraints of the doctrine of parliamentary sovereignty. Such a development in the realm of conventional canons of interpretation would run parallel with an explicit questioning of the absolute nature of parliamentary sovereignty in other judicial *dicta* since the early 2000s.[416]

5. COMPARATIVE ANALYSIS

On the face of it, the outer limits and techniques of judicial law-making in England and Germany deviate from each other considerably in relation to

---

[414] *Yemshaw v. London Borough of Hounslow* [2011] UKSC 3, para. 24 (Lady Hale).
[415] EKINS, above n. 403, p. 19.
[416] *R. (Jackson) v. Attorney General* [2005] UKHL 56, para. 102 (Lord Steyn), paras. 104, 107 (Lord Hope); *Axa Insurance v. Lord Advocate* [2011] UKSC 46, paras. 50–51 (Lord Hope); *Moohan v. Lord Advocate* [2014] UKSC 67, para. 35 (Lord Hodge); *R. (Public Law Project) v. Lord Chancellor* [2016] UKSC 39, para. 20 (Lord Neuberger, with whom all other members of the Supreme Court agreed).

the terminology used, but not so much in substance. There seem to exist clear parallels between correcting obvious drafting errors in England and filling a gap that has existed since the coming into force of a statute in Germany. Further clear parallels seem to exist between updating interpretation in England and filling a subsequent gap in Germany. In both jurisdictions it is common for judges to emphasise that they would usurp the legislative function if they relied on their own subjective ideas about policy when interpreting statutes.[417] Policy decisions carry the stigma that they belong exclusively to the realm of the legislature and that judges lack the democratic legitimacy to make policy decisions. In reality, however, both English and German judges frequently make policy choices when they engage in judicial law-making. We have also seen in Chapter 1 in this book that policy choices cannot be avoided in hard cases. In question can only be the level of policy choices that judges are allowed to make without trespassing into territory occupied by the legislature. Individual judges can have different understandings about where this border between the judiciary and the legislature should be drawn. The German judiciary has been described as fundamentally apolitical when compared with the English judiciary[418] but the level of non-transparency regarding judicial policy choices is similarly high in both jurisdictions when courts apply the outer limits of statutory interpretation.[419] The BVerfG's *Soraya* decision has remained an exception in Germany. Deference to the legislature may be one reason why the level of transparency regarding judicial policy choices in statutory interpretation is low in both jurisdictions.[420]

With regard to the weighing and balancing of the interpretative criteria, English judges appear to be more transparent than their German counterparts about the element of choice and evaluation inherent in this process. One possible reason for this finding may be that English judges are used to making policy choices when developing the common law. Another reason may simply be that opinions given by individual judges are common in English judgments but absent in the highest German courts, with the exception of dissenting speeches by individual judges in the BVerfG. In the highest German courts the judgment is given as a single majority opinion of the entire court. Such a judgment often involves compromise formulations that cover up disagreements between individual

---

[417] For England: *R. (Shah) v. Barnet LBC* [1983] 2 AC 309 (HL), 346 (Lord Scarman); *Fitzpatrick v. Sterling Housing Association Ltd.* [2001] 1 AC 27 (HL), 67 (Lord Hobhouse). For Germany: BVerfG, *NJW* 1979, 305, 306 – *Sachverständigenhaftung*; BVerfG, *NJW* 1990, 1593; BVerfG, *NJW* 2004, 750, 761; BVerfG, *NJW* 2006, 3340, 3341.

[418] BELL, above n. 363, pp. 171–172.

[419] For England, see also J. BELL, Policy arguments in statutory interpretation, in R.S. SUMMERS, N. MACCORMICK and J. BELL (eds.), *Legal reasoning and statutory interpretation: Rotterdam lectures in jurisprudence*, Gouda Quint, Arnhem 1989. pp. 55, 58–59. For Germany, see LUNDMARK, above n. 106, pp. 132, 433; T. LUNDMARK, Legal science and European harmonisation, (2014) 130 *LQR* 68, 77–79, 82.

[420] BELL, above n. 419, pp. 55, 60–62.

judges. The absence of dissenting opinions in German courts also represents an impersonal approach that emphasises the rational and impartial authority, rather than the personality, of the judge.[421] Non-transparency regarding judicial discretion in statutory interpretation concords with such a rational, impersonal approach. It has further been contended in England and in Germany that there are good reasons to conceal the fact that judges are empowered to make policy choices in the area of statutory interpretation.[422] J. Bell has described this view as being prevalent among the English judiciary.[423] The non-transparency aims to create a feeling of legal certainty and public confidence in the law as well as a perception of a strong binding force of statute. This non-transparency has been attacked on democratic grounds.[424] A key thesis of this book is that the level of predictability in cases of judicial law-making can be enhanced by increasing the number of formal elements in judicial reasoning. These formal elements constrain evaluative arguments, policy choices and judicial discretion. Instead of concealing what the judiciary is really doing, legal certainty and public confidence in the judiciary can and ought to be achieved by either reducing the level of evaluative arguments and policy choices or structuring these arguments. That can be achieved by including more formal elements into the judicial decision-making process, as I have argued in Chapter 1. That also clearly links with the functions of formal legal reasoning to increase legal certainty and public confidence in the judiciary.

Despite existing parallels in the outer limits and techniques of judicial law-making in England and Germany, a clear difference is recognisable as well. Judicial law-making is certainly an exceptional occurrence in both countries when compared to interpretation in a narrow sense and, in particular, when compared to the interpretation of vague or ambiguous statutory language. Nonetheless, it is settled case law in Germany that judicial law-making is part of the competence of the judge under the German constitution. Only its limits can be debatable. The BVerfG is therefore preoccupied with developing general interpretative maxims that limit judicial power. The default position in Germany in relation to judicial law-making is that it is a permissible function of the judge. That is not the case in England. Even in today's climate of purposivism, the default position in England is that judicial law-making is generally impermissible and only available in exceptional cases. That means that the possible semantic meanings of the statutory words generally demarcate the outer limit of statutory

---

[421] Ibid.
[422] H. KELSEN, Juristischer Formalismus und Reine Rechtslehre, (1929) 58 *Juristische Wochenschrift* 1723, 1726; LORD RADCLIFFE, The lawyer and his times, in A.E. SUTHERLAND (ed.), *The path of law from 1967*, Harvard University Press, Cambridge, Mass. 1969, p. 16.
[423] For discussion, see J. BELL, *Policy arguments in judicial decisions*, Clarendon Press, Oxford 1983, pp. 268–270.
[424] Ibid., pp. 268–270.

interpretation in England.[425] It is therefore correct when scholars argue that the wording of a provision is generally given greater weight in statutory interpretation in England than in Germany.[426] The different default positions explain why English judges emphasise their limited powers to fill in gaps in legislation. In the words of Lord Bridge: "The rule of general application which limits the court's power to read into legislation words which the draftsman has not used is, even in today's climate of purposive construction, still an important rule which cannot be disregarded".[427] Even if a court is convinced that Parliament could not have intended the interpretative result that arises as a consequence of the application of clear and unambiguous statutory words, a court will only exceptionally derogate from this interpretative result.[428] This is different in Germany, where a provision's clear wording is only one element of the double criterion. Compared to the reading down of general statutory language in accordance with the statute's purpose,[429] the reading of additional words into a statute is permitted in very limited cases in England. That is because

> within the constitution as it has developed based on the sovereignty of Parliament, legislative intent is taken to be derived from the actual language used by Parliament, and for a court to read in additional words to extend the application of a statute

---

[425] A strained construction is permitted only in comparatively rare cases: *Shanning International Ltd. v. Lloyds TSB Bank plc* [2001] UKHL 31, para. 24 (Lord Steyn); *Holden & Co v. Crown Prosecution Service (No. 2)* [1994] 1 AC 22 (HL), 33 (Lord Bridge); JONES and BENNION, above n. 24, section 311. Cf. *Secretary of State for Defence v. Guardian Newspaper Ltd.* [1985] AC 339 (HL), 369 (Lord Roskill, "The language of the relevant statute is subject to the ordinary rules of statutory construction, always remembering first that neither additions nor subtractions should be made to the natural meaning of the words used unless they are essential in order to give an intelligible meaning to the statutory language ..."); *Greenweb Ltd. v. London Borough of Wandsworth* [2008] EWCA Civ 910, paras. 28–32 (Stanley Burnton LJ, with whom Thomas and Buxton LJJ agreed); *Yarl's Wood Immigration Ltd. v. Bedfordshire Police Authority* [2009] EWCA Civ 1110, paras. 68–69 (Rix LJ); ARDEN, above n. 358, pp. 487, 489–490 ("the courts cannot fill gaps in legislation"); ALLAN, above n. 314, p. 84; BANKOWSKI and MACCORMICK, above n. 59, pp. 359, 365. For a different view, see SCARMAN, above n. 316, p. 11 ("judges are having no difficulty of ... adapting the techniques of analogy and extension ...").

[426] HAGER, above n. 41, p. 60.

[427] *Steele Ford & Newton v. Crown Prosecution Service (No. 2)* [1994] 1 AC 22 (HL), 33 (Lord Bridge).

[428] *Greenweb Ltd. v. London Borough of Wandsworth* [2008] EWCA Civ 910, paras. 20, 28–32, 36 (Stanley Burnton LJ, with whom Thomas and Buxton LJJ agreed).

[429] For an example of a reading down of general statutory words, see *Crook v. Edmondson* [1966] 2 QB 81 (CA), 90–91 (Winn LJ, with whom Lord Parker CJ agreed). Section 32 of the Sexual Offences Act 1956 made it an offence "for a man persistently to solicit or importune in a public place for immoral purposes". Winn LJ did not read the words "immoral purposes" in their ordinary wide meaning but imposed a limit on the meaning of immoral purposes to immoral purposes of a sexual nature in accordance with the underlying purpose of the statute which related solely to sexual offences. He thus restricted the scope of application of s. 32 of the Sexual Offences Act 1956. This reasoning was confirmed in *R. v. Kirkup* [1993] 1 WLR 774 (CA), 778 (Staughton LJ).

(as distinct from modifying its application within its ostensible field of application, by "reading down") will usually appear to conflict with the limited interpretative role which the courts enjoy outside the EU and HRA contexts.[430]

Individual judges in England, most notably Lord Denning, have attempted to change the default position such that judges have a general (as opposed to exceptional) power to fill in gaps in legislation.[431] Yet these attempts have not met with success.[432]

A consequence of the different default positions are different judicial attitudes towards judicial law-making in England and Germany. The different default positions also affect judges' reasoning because English and German judges start from opposite sides of a spectrum that stretches from permissibility to impermissibility of judicial law-making when they assess judicial law-making in an individual case. Therefore, S. Vogenauer's thesis that statutory interpretation in England and Germany is fundamentally uniform has to be qualified in the area of judicial law-making.[433] The different default positions in England and Germany ultimately exist because of different constitutional doctrines that affect the outer limits of the judicial function. In other words, the different conceptions of the judicial role are informed by constitutional context. This shows that differences in the separation of powers doctrine can translate into different outer limits of interpretation at least at a high level of abstraction. A clear example can be seen in the area of updating construction, where an English court cannot depart from the intention of the enacting parliament. A German court that deviates from the intention of the enacting parliament does not necessarily infringe the outer limits of the judicial function. Compared to an English court, a German court can thus take more "objective" factors of interpretation into account, and that increases the scope of permissible policy considerations by judges, as shown by the BGH's *Fotokopie* judgment. It may be more accurate to say, however, that the different default positions in both jurisdictions can be attributed to different

---

[430] P. SALES, A comparison of the principle of legality and section 3 of the Human Rights Act 1998, (2009) 125 *LQR* 598, 611. But see CROSS, above n. 22, pp. 195–196, where the distinction between the reading in of words and the ignoring of statutory words is described as being of "doubtful validity".

[431] *Seaford Court Estates Ltd. v. Asher* [1949] 2 KB 481 (CA), 499 (Denning LJ); *Magor and St Mellons Rural DC v. Newport Corporation* [1950] 2 All ER 1226 (CA), 1236 (Denning LJ); *Jones v. Wrotham Park Settled Estates* [1980] AC 74 (HL), 105–106 (Lord Diplock).

[432] *Magor and St Mellons Rural DC v. Newport Corporation* [1952] AC 189 (HL), 191 (Lord Simons); *Jones v. Wrotham Park Settled Estates* [1980] AC 74 (HL), 107 (Lord Salmon).

[433] VOGENAUER, above n. 34, pp. 1281, 1295–1308 extends his fundamental unity thesis to the area of judicial law-making. See P. LEGRAND, The same and the different, in P. LEGRAND and R. MUNDAY (eds.), *Comparative legal studies: traditions and transitions*, CUP, Cambridge 2003, pp. 240, 296–297 for a general criticism of a unifying, monistic model of the civil-law and common-law worlds.

constitutional doctrines as understood and interpreted by judges. The BVerfG has relied on art. 20(3) GG to loosen the binding nature of the statute and to justify the law-making power of a judge. A similar constitutional principle that loosens the binding force of statute does not exist in England, where the doctrine of parliamentary sovereignty is the central feature of the UK constitution.

In Germany, where judicial law-making is generally a permissible function of the judge, the BVerfG has stipulated general techniques and limits of interpretation that apply to all cases of judicial law-making. No such general limits and techniques have been stipulated in England. It follows that formal legal reasoning from abstract premises is more prevalent in German judgments than in English judgments on judicial law-making. An approach that may have worked in England would have been to (a) state that judicial law-making is possible under exceptional circumstances and (b) then exhaustively categorise these exceptions and the outer interpretative limits for these categories. Yet that is not the approach taken by English courts. Even though it is possible to "fit" a good number of cases into three categories of permissible judicial law-making in England, these categories are not an exhaustive statement of judicial law-making. Clear guidance on where to find the demarcation line between judicial interpretation and amendment of legislation has not been provided by the English judiciary. This seems to be an unattractive approach from the perspective of legal certainty.[434] This description of judicial law-making in England is an illustration of inductive reasoning, which moves from specific instances to patterns, regularities and generalised conclusions. The three categories of judicial law-making in England represent such patterns and regularities without capturing all cases of judicial law-making. There is thus a distinction in style between the more deductive approach of German courts and the more inductive approach of English courts to judicial law-making. This distinction should not be overstated, however, because the general outer limits of interpretation formulated by the highest German courts leave ample scope for pragmatist concerns and for taking the circumstances of the individual case into account.[435]

It may be said that the pragmatic approach to judicial law-making in England is filled by a desire to retain maximum flexibility but this is certainly not the full picture as it is also this approach that most clearly shows the different default positions in Germany and England. If judicial law-making is impermissible as a general rule, there is no need to develop and stipulate general limits of interpretation that apply to all cases of judicial law-making. Stipulating such

---

[434] Very critically KLATT, above n. 165, p. 9 ("the issue is totally unresolved as to which criteria determine whether there is 'appropriate occasion' to depart from the words ... Overall, the inconsistent practice of the courts nowadays shows a serious lack of both orientation and legal certainty").

[435] I will explore this further in Chapter 3, Section 7.

general limits would undermine the default position and the constitutional principle of parliamentary sovereignty underlying it. This demonstrates why approaches by individual judges to formulate general outer limits of judicial law-making have failed in the past in England. This constitutional reasoning thus better explains the different approaches of English and German judges when formulating limits of interpretation, rather than the more abstract claim[436] that the English legal system is pragmatic and bound to facts whereas the German law legal system is systematic and bound to rules.

What English cases like *McMonagle v. Westminster City Council*, *Inco Europe* and *Quintavalle* have in common with German legal methodology is that the need for judicial law-making is determined by the purpose of the legislation. The purpose determines whether the field of application of a provision needs to be limited or expanded beyond its wording. Where the English cases differ from German legal methodology is in their focus on the change of the statutory language by reading statutory words in, out or down. The different emphasis on substance and the statutory language in judicial law-making in England and Germany can be explained by differences in the underlying constitutional doctrines. For judicial law-making in Germany, it does not matter whether an interpretative result is achieved by means of a reading in, out or down of words in legislation. Comparatively little attention is given in judicial practice to how the existing statutory language must be altered in order to reach the interpretative result. It is not the alteration of the statutory language but the substantive effect that matters, i.e. whether the scope of application of a provision is limited (teleological reduction) or extended (argument by analogy). A teleological reduction, for example, can involve either the reading in of additional words or the reading down of existing statutory language, depending on the specific wording of the provision under consideration. For English courts, on the other hand, alterations of the statutory language by way of interpretation matter. This is because under the orthodox doctrine of parliamentary sovereignty as it has developed in courts, legislative intent is taken to be derived from the actual language used by Parliament. A reading in of additional words into legislation carries with it a greater perception of impermissible judicial legislation than a reading down of general words in legislation. Both reading in and reading down can limit or extend the scope of application of a provision. The difference between substance and language also shows that reading in and reading down of words in legislation are not the same as or equivalent to argument by analogy and teleological reduction in Germany. Furthermore, a court that emphasises a change in statutory language when engaging in judicial law-making creates

---

[436] Cf. also SUMMERS and TARUFFO, above n. 85, pp. 461, 471 ("The casuistic nature of the common law tradition is probably a major factor accounting for the less abstract and non-generalizing approach to statute law in Britain …").

a greater perception of trespassing into the territory of the legislature than a court that focuses on the less transparent substantive change of the scope of application of a provision. That is because the addition of words, the removal of words and the substitution of some words for other words are all forms of amending legislation. Teleological reduction and argument by analogy are not forms of amending legislation; both appear to be different to legislative activity. This comparison also shows how the use of terminology in courts can influence the scope of judicial law-making.

There is one caveat to all this. The constitutional doctrine of parliamentary sovereignty as expressed in the Diceyan orthodoxy does not require English courts to stay within the possible semantic meanings of the statutory words.[437] Instead, parliamentary sovereignty requires that courts do not depart from the intention of the enacting parliament when they interpret legislation. The statutory text is only one interpretative criterion to ascertain Parliament's intention. Another source to determine the intention of the enacting parliament is the purpose of the legislation. The doctrine of parliamentary sovereignty certainly does not rule out that a court can take this source into account. The reading down of general words and the reading in of words into legislation in order to fulfil the identifiable intention of the enacting legislature that is insufficiently expressed in the statutory words is reconcilable with constitutional doctrine. If English judges had adopted such an understanding of legitimate judicial law-making, one may be tempted to argue that this could have inserted a greater degree of "honesty" into statutory interpretation in England. There would certainly have been less need to force contrived interpretations into what statutory words can possibly mean based on their linguistic usage. The counter-argument to this hypothesis from a comparative perspective is, however, that German judicial practice has a very similar tendency to conceal judicial law-making as restrictive or extensive interpretation within the possible semantic meanings of the statutory words. One reason for this is that judicial fidelity to the statutory text shows a high fidelity to the binding force of statute under the rule of law. It gives the impression of a higher level of fidelity to the will of the legislature when compared to judicial law-making. Moreover, it is certainly true that there is a danger that the courts can get Parliament's intention wrong when they deviate from the statutory words and decide to add to, alter or ignore statutory words. Avoiding this danger favours a restrictive approach to judicial law-making. Ultimately though, literalism as it developed in England was a judicial choice. Lord Lester has rightly pointed out that there was nothing in the UK constitution

---

[437] For a more restrictive approach, see, however, *Black-Clawson International v. Papierwerke Waldhof-Aschaffenburg* [1975] AC 591 (HL), 638 (Lord Diplock, "Parliament, under our constitution, is sovereign only in respect of what it expresses by the words used in the legislation it has passed"); ALLAN, above n. 314, p. 82.

which compelled English judges to limit their powers by adopting literal rules for the interpretation of Acts of Parliament.[438] The doctrine of parliamentary sovereignty could likewise support a system of interpretation according to which judicial law-making is generally permissible in order to give effect to the intention of the enacting legislature. Concerns of legal certainty under the rule of law would have to yield to parliamentary sovereignty. This alternative scenario also illustrates that determinate outer limits of interpretation cannot be deduced from the abstract doctrine of parliamentary sovereignty alone.

It follows that the English courts' current limited approach to judicial law-making, particularly the reluctance to read additional words into legislation, is largely based on historical context and tradition, influenced by constitutional doctrine, rather than on constitutional requirements as such. English courts have not yet drawn the full consequences from the purposive approach to interpretation since the default position that judicial law-making is generally not permissible is still intact under conventional English canons of interpretation. If the English courts' limited approach to judicial law-making is largely based on path dependence,[439] the outer limits of interpretation are determined to a large extent by (judicial) tradition and historical context. I have shown that a very similar picture exists in Germany. The outer limits of judicial law-making in Germany are largely determined by the interpretative criteria. The recognised methods of statutory interpretation in Germany are based on an amalgam of historical development and the common use of methods of interpretation in legal practice. The core of the outer limits of interpretation is therefore based on judicial tradition and historical context, influenced by constitutional doctrine, rather than on rules deducible from the German Basic Law. These findings support the view that historical experiences, irrespective of constitutional theory, have a significant impact on shaping judicial practices such as influencing the creativity of judges and their involvement in judicial law-making.[440] Path dependence, historical factors and tradition can thus explain to a considerable degree the differences in judicial attitudes towards judicial law-making in both jurisdictions.

In the German legal system, where judicial law-making is a permissible function of the judge, the guiding function of the wording of a statute is limited. Furthermore, the danger that judges may get the legislature's intention wrong or venture outside the legislature's intention appears higher than in a legal system

---

[438] LESTER, above n. 310, pp. 269, 272. For a seemingly different view, see MASTERMAN and WHEATLE, above n. 308, pp. 469, 473–475.

[439] For an explanation of the term path dependence, see J. MAHONEY and D. SCHENSUL, Historical context and path dependence, in R.E. GOODIN and C. TILLY (eds.), *The Oxford handbook of contextual political analysis*, OUP, Oxford 2006, pp. 454–471.

[440] BELL, above n. 363, pp. 351–352; P.E. GELLER, Staffing the judiciary and "tastes" in justice, (1989) 61 *Southern California Law Review* 1849, 1854.

where judges cannot add to, alter or ignore statutory words when interpreting legislation.[441] Both concerns are addressed by German courts formulating general limits of interpretation that apply in every case and aim to (a) provide for a higher level of legal certainty and predictability than a pure case-by-case approach of judicial law-making and (b) ensure that judges stay within the bounds of their constitutional role. These general limits of interpretation are meant to be objective criteria. They also aim to ensure that judges cannot, without any democratic endorsement, rely on their own personal values and ideas about policy when interpreting legislation. Without these general limits, the balance between legal certainty and material justice would tilt heavily towards the latter, and the policing of the outer limits of the judicial function would appear elusive. The outer methodological limits of judicial law-making in Germany, at least in theory, replace the guiding function of the wording of a statute from the viewpoint of legal certainty. It will be demonstrated in Section 7 of Chapter 3 that the general outer limits of judicial law-making do poorly in fulfilling this function.

In the English legal system, where judicial law-making is generally an impermissible function of the judge, the guiding function of the wording tends to be stronger than in Germany. R.S. Summers has correctly pointed out that a language-oriented criterion is relatively more constraining on judicial powers than any of the other interpretative criteria.[442] Particularly in the heyday of the literal rule, the level of legal certainty and predictability provided in the realm of statutory interpretation in England thus outweighed the level of legal certainty provided in the current German legal system (given that the outer limits of judicial law-making in Germany are expressed in vague terms). In the area of statutory interpretation, the balance between formal justice and material justice in England tilted more towards the former when compared to the German legal system. So did the balance between legal certainty and giving effect to the intention of Parliament (from whatever source that intention can be gleaned), albeit English judges have not necessarily seen this tension through this lens. Even though the link between the pre-eminence of the statutory text and legal certainty is recognised in English judgments,[443] English judges have justified a strict literal rule predominantly on the basis of the doctrine of parliamentary sovereignty, with the argument from legal certainty remaining in its shadow. As Tindall CJ said in *The Sussex Peerage*: "The [statutory] words best declare the

---

[441] Cf. *Gladstone v. Bower* [1960] 2 QB 384 (CA), 395–396 (Devlin LJ).
[442] R.S. SUMMERS, *Form and function in a legal system – a general study*, CUP, New York 2006, p. 257. See also ATIYAH and SUMMERS, above n. 338, pp. 108–109.
[443] *Black-Clawson International v. Papierwerke Waldhof-Aschaffenburg* [1975] AC 591 (HL), 638 (Lord Diplock); *Stock v. Frank Jones (Tipton) Ltd.* [1978] 1 WLR 231 (HL), 237 (Lord Simon); *Fothergill v. Monarch Airlines Ltd.* [1981] AC 251 (HL), 279–280 (Lord Diplock); cf. *R. (Spath Holme) v. Secretary of State for the Environment, Transport and the Regions* [2001] 2 AC 349 (HL), 397–398 (Lord Nicholls). For criticism, see BARAK, above n. 6, pp. 274–275.

intention of the legislature".[444] Thus, it appears that legal certainty was provided as a byproduct of paying heed to parliamentary sovereignty. One reason for this may be that the principle of legal certainty under the rule of law cannot limit and has to yield to the absolute understanding of parliamentary sovereignty. In Germany, legal certainty is hardly used as an argument in written judicial opinions when courts justify the setting of general outer limits of judicial law-making. German judges refer to the separation of powers and the binding force of statute instead. The reason why courts do not rely on legal certainty may be that the separation of powers and the binding force of statute are explicitly mentioned in art. 20 GG, whereas the rule of law and legal certainty are not.

With the rise of the purposive approach to statutory interpretation in England, the balance between (a) legal certainty and giving effect to the intention of Parliament and (b) formal and material justice has shifted more towards giving effect to legislative intent and to material justice. English judges appear more and more often willing to expressly engage in judicial law-making in order to give full effect to the purpose of the legislation. From a viewpoint of legal certainty and the separation of powers, the need for general limits of interpretation that apply in every case of judicial law-making is still less than in Germany as long as the default position remains intact and is not undermined by judicial practice. Thus, much depends on how often and to what extent courts deviate from the default position and undermine the guiding function of the statutory words.[445] What is clear, however, is that the English legal system is drawing closer to the German system with regard to where the balance (a) between legal certainty and giving effect to the intention of Parliament and (b) between formal and material justice can be found. Even though the current English approach to the limits of judicial law-making under conventional canons of interpretation was described above as an unattractive approach, this has to be seen in perspective when compared to the German approach, where the default position is that judicial law-making is permissible and where the outer limits of interpretation are expressed in indeterminate terms. The English position thus seems to be the lesser of the two evils from the perspective of legal certainty, at least for the time being.

These findings refute or at least qualify the general claim that German law and judges place a high value on predictability and sacrifice individual justice by doing so.[446] It is an incorrect over-generalisation to contend that the German legal system prefers legal predictability over individual justice and that the

---

[444] *The Sussex Peerage* (1844) 11 Clark & Finnelly 85, 143 (Tindal CJ).
[445] For a critical discussion of English judicial practice in this respect, see VOGENAUER, above n. 34, pp. 1009–1044, who does not appear to agree with the view that the default position in England is that judicial law-making is generally impermissible and only available in exceptional cases.
[446] LUNDMARK, above n. 106, p. 77; cf. I. HELLAND, Introduction to German legal method, in I. HELLAND and S. KOCH (eds.), *Nordic and Germanic legal methods*, Mohr Siebeck, Tübingen 2015, pp. 188, 219.

English legal system prefers individual justice over legal predictability.[447] If the different default positions for judicial law-making are taken into account in both jurisdictions, the English system places a higher degree of importance on legal predictability than the German system as long as the default position stays intact and is not undermined by judicial practice. With regard to the outer limits of judicial law-making, the German legal system does not sacrifice individual justice and instead places a lower value on predictability than the English legal system. How long this assessment of the English judicial practice will remain valid seems rather uncertain. There are considerable incentives for the English judiciary to adopt a system of interpretation according to which judicial law-making is generally permissible in order to give effect to the intention of the legislature. These incentives include the growing use of legislative history in statutory interpretation and possible spillover effects from (a) interpreting EU legislation based on EU legal methods employed by the CJEU,[448] (b) judicial law-making under s. 3(1) HRA and (c) conforming judicial law-making. I will show in Chapters 3 and 4 of this book that the default position for Convention-compatible and conforming judicial law-making in England is that judicial law-making is generally a permissible function of the court.

In Germany, the outer limits of the judicial function are not static either.[449] There are signs in recent German case law that strengthen the relevance of the intention of the enacting legislature in statutory interpretation. There is even tentative support in recent case law for the position that a court cannot depart from the intention of the enacting legislature.[450] This development in German case law, if one is willing to see it as a development, brings German

---

[447] For these findings based on a survey among lawyers, see however LUNDMARK, above n. 106, pp. 124–125. M. SIEMS, Comparative legal certainty: legal families and forms of measurement, SSRN, May 2017, pp. 10, 22, available online at http://www.ssrn.com, on the other hand, correctly argues that general statements about a civil–common law divide in legal certainty do not hold up to scrutiny.

[448] It is controversial in legal scholarship whether and how much English statutory interpretation in the sphere of conventional canons of construction has evolved due to the legal methods employed by the CJEU. For a discussion of the various academic opinions, see VOGENAUER, above n. 34, pp. 1317–1323. Some scholars argue that (a) English judges have slowly adopted the interpretative methods used by the CJEU and that (b) this process has accelerated the convergence of legal methodologies in England and continental Europe; see M. GISEWSKI, *Methodik der Auslegung im kontinentaleuropäischen und angelsächsischen Recht: Vergleich und Synthese juristischer Denkweisen vor dem Hintergrund der europäischen Privatrechtsvergleichung*, Kovač, Hamburg 2008, pp. 213–219, 278; M. REINHARDT, *Konsistente Jurisdiktion: Grundlegung einer verfassungsrechtlichen Theorie der rechtsgestaltenden Rechtsprechung*, Mohr Siebeck, Tübingen 1997, p. 287; cf. B. MARKESINIS, Learning from Europe and learning in Europe, in B. MARKESINIS (ed.), *The gradual convergence: foreign ideas, foreign influences, and English Law*, Clarendon Press, Oxford 1994, pp. 1, 30; for a different view, see VOGENAUER, above n. 34, pp. 1317–1323.

[449] See Section 3.3.4 above.

[450] See BVerfG, *NJW-RR* 2016, 1366, para. 42; BVerfG, *NJW* 2009, 1469, dissenting opinion by Judges Voßkuhle, Osterloh, Di Fabio, para. 142 – *Rügeverkümmerung*.

law closer to the power of English courts to update legislation via judicial law-making. If German courts were to adopt the position that they cannot diverge from the intention of the enacting legislature, they would also adopt a stricter understanding of the binding force of statute than the understanding that prevailed in *Soraya*. This would be a possible interpretation of art. 20(2), (3) GG, thanks to the vague terms of art. 20(3) GG ("legislation and law"). Such a development can be described as an increased deference to the legislature. What is unclear is why this development is occurring as it cannot be explained by changes in constitutional law. One possible answer is that the outer limits of judicial law-making sit at the junction between interpretation and legislation. They are affected by judges' understanding of their constitutional role, and each generation of judges may understand this role differently.

CHAPTER 3
RIGHTS-CONSISTENT INTERPRETATION

Chapter 3 compares the interpretative obligation under s. 3(1) Human Rights Act 1998[1] in England and the duty of German courts to interpret national legislation in conformity with the fundamental rights enshrined in the German Basic Law (*grundrechtskonforme Interpretation*). The term rights-consistent interpretation will be used in this book to cover both interpretative obligations. Interpretation in conformity with the fundamental rights enshrined in the German Basic Law is a significant subgroup of constitution-consistent interpretation (*verfassungskonforme Interpretation*)[2] in Germany. I will argue in this chapter that rights-consistent interpretation in English and German courts exhibits striking similarities. Lord Rodger opined in *Watkins* that the Convention rights protected under the HRA "form part of our law and provide a rough equivalent of a written code of constitutional rights".[3] Lord Steyn has remarked extrajudicially that since 2001 the ECHR has "effectively [been] our constitutional Bill of Rights".[4] Despite existing similarities, the HRA is not the UK equivalent of the German Basic Law even though the HRA has been characterised as a "constitutional statute" in English courts.[5] Nevertheless, the HRA has aptly been described as a "Bill of Rights", incorporating "constitutional rights".[6] Therefore, interpretation of legislation in conformity

---

[1] The terms "Convention-compatible" and "Convention-compliant" interpretation will be used as synonyms for the interpretative obligation under s. 3(1) HRA.
[2] The term "constitution-consistent" interpretation will only be used in this book to refer to *verfassungskonforme* interpretation in Germany. Since German courts predominantly use the term constitution-consistent interpretation when they interpret legislation in conformity with the fundamentals rights enshrined in the German Basic Law, this book will also predominantly use this term.
[3] *Watkins v. Secretary of State for the Home Department* [2006] UKHL 17, para. 61 (Lord Rodger).
[4] LORD STEYN, The case for a Supreme Court, (2002) 118 *LQR* 382, 385.
[5] *Thoburn v. Sunderland City Council* [2002] EWHC 195 (Admin), para. 62 (Laws LJ); *R. (HS2 Action Alliance Ltd) v. Secretary of State for Transport* [2014] UKSC 3, paras. 207, 208 (Lord Neuberger and Lord Mance (with whom Lady Hale, Lord Kerr, Lord Sumption, Lord Reed and Lord Carnwath agreed)); cf. *R. (Miller) v. Secretary of State for Exiting the European Union* [2017] UKSC 51, para. 66 (Lord Neuberger, Lady Hale, Lord Mance, Lord Kerr, Lord Clarke, Lord Wilson, Lord Sumption, Lord Hodge).
[6] A. KAVANAGH, *Constitutional review under the UK Human Rights Act*, CUP, Cambridge 2009, pp. 307–309.

with the fundamental rights enshrined in the German Basic Law appears to be the best German comparator to Convention-compatible interpretation under s. 3(1) HRA.

Another possible comparator to s. 3(1) HRA would be the principle of interpretation in harmony with public international law (*völkerrechtskonforme Interpretation*) in the shape of interpretation in harmony with the ECHR. The BVerfG has recognised that statutes must be interpreted in accordance with the obligations of international law under the ECHR.[7] That is because it cannot be assumed that the German legislature would deviate from Germany's obligations under international law or would allow the violation of such obligations unless it had clearly expressed its contrary intention.[8] The practical significance of this obligation to construe legislation in conformity with the ECHR is, however, lower compared to the interpretation of legislation in conformity with the fundamental rights enshrined in the German Basic Law. The reason for this is that the ECHR has the status of a federal statute in Germany. It ranks below the German Basic Law in the hierarchy of norms. It follows that the ECHR does not constitute a directly applicable standard for constitutional review. In a constitutional complaint to the BVerfG, a complainant cannot directly assert a violation of human rights contained in the ECHR.[9] The BVerfG does, however, recognise that the German Basic Law is committed to international law (*Völkerrechtsfreundlichkeit*). It interprets the Basic Law's fundamental rights in the light of the ECHR, taking into account the jurisprudence of the European Court of Human Rights (ECtHR).[10] This reasoning is remarkable as a lower-ranking rule informs the interpretation of a higher-ranking rule. The BVerfG nonetheless retains the final say about the scope of fundamental rights protection under the German Basic Law. Its case law also has the effect that the directly decisive provision in a legal dispute is usually not the Convention right but the corresponding Basic Law's fundamental right. This is another reason why the "visibility" of interpreting federal statutes in harmony with the ECHR is reduced.

Beyond the questions set out in Chapter 1, Chapter 3 will address additional issues: do the outer limits and techniques of rights-consistent interpretation deviate from conventional canons of statutory interpretation? Do they surpass these canons and widen the limits of the judicial function? Scholars in both jurisdictions have criticised the highest English and German courts for exceeding the limits of the judicial function when establishing and applying

---

[7] BVerfG, *NJW* 2015, 1359, para. 149; BVerfG, *FamRZ* 2015, 1263, para. 47.
[8] BVerfG, NJW 1987, 2427.
[9] BVerfG, *NJW* 2015, 1359, para. 149.
[10] BVerfG, *NJW* 1987, 2427; BVerfG, *NJW* 2004, 3407, 3408, 3411 – *Görgülü*; BVerfG, *FamRZ* 2015, 1263, para. 47.

Chapter 3. Rights-Consistent Interpretation

the outer limits of rights-consistent judicial law-making.[11] I will show that this criticism is justified in relation to English, but not for German judicial practice. Other scholars have argued that the outer limits of rights-consistent judicial law-making diverge significantly in both jurisdictions due to different underlying constitutional settings.[12] I will refute this thesis in Chapter 3. Chapter 3 will assess how the application of rights-consistent interpretation in judicial practice affects the constitutional relationship between the courts and the legislature. Chapter 3 will also analyse whether the outer limits of rights-consistent interpretation are influenced by the presence or absence of a court's power to strike down unconstitutional legislation (strong form of judicial review). The power of constitutional courts to strike down legislation has been at the forefront of constitutional legal scholarship that deals with the power of courts to review legislation for compliance with rights. Yet, as A. Kavanagh has pointed out, if rights-consistent interpretation allows courts to modify the meaning of a statute, then this practice warrants serious scholarly attention.[13] I will argue that the courts' power to strike down legislation or to issue a declaration of incompatibility is not necessarily the most intrusive tool in their bow of constitutional review. Instead, rights-consistent interpretation has an immense constitutional significance and does the heavy lifting in rendering legislation compliant with rights.

Chapter 3 is structured as follows. Section 1 provides an introduction to constitution-consistent interpretation in Germany and to s. 3(1) HRA in England. Section 2 discusses the aim of rights-consistent interpretation, and Section 3 explores the relationship between rights-consistent interpretation and conventional canons of construction in both jurisdictions. The next two sections examine two characteristics of rights-consistent interpretation: the interpretative priority rule and the presumption of compliance. Section 6 analyses the techniques of rights-consistent judicial law-making and Section 7 its outer interpretative limits. The last section critically evaluates the principle of legality against the background of a possible post-HRA UK human rights framework.

---

[11] J. ALLAN, The Victorian Charter of Human Rights and Responsibilities: exegesis and criticism, (2006) 30 *Melbourne University Law Review* 906, 910–911; M. HOWE, A UK Bill of Rights, in Commission on a Bill of Rights, *A UK Bill of Rights? The choice before us*, Vol. 1, London 2012, pp. 192, 216, available online at http://webarchive.nationalarchives.gov.uk/20130206021312/ http://www.justice.gov.uk/about/cbr/; C.-W. CANARIS, Die verfassungskonforme Auslegung und Rechtsfortbildung im System der juristischen Methodenlehre, in H. HONSELL ET AL. (eds.), *Festschrift für E.A. Kramer*, Helbing & Lichtenhahn, Basel 2004, pp. 141, 151; L. KUHLEN, *Die verfassungskonforme Auslegung von Strafgesetzen*, C.F. Müller, Heidelberg 2006, p. 58.
[12] J.M. HOFFMANN, *Die Europäische Menschnerechtskonvention und nationales Recht: ein Vergleich der Wirkungsweise in den Rechtsordnungen des Vereinigten Königreichs und der Bundesrepublik Deutschland*, Heymanns, Cologne 2010, pp. 128–129.
[13] A. KAVANAGH, Situating the strike-down power, draft paper 2017 (on file with author); see also R. LECKEY, *Bills of rights in the common law world*, CUP, Cambridge 2016, p. 10.

1. INTRODUCTION

1.1. CONSTITUTION-CONSISTENT INTERPRETATION

Every German court is obliged to construe ordinary national legislation in conformity with the rights and principles enshrined in the German Basic Law. This obligation requires national courts to engage in constitution-consistent interpretation not only in a narrow sense (*verfassungskonforme Auslegung*), but also, if necessary, in constitution-consistent judicial law-making (*verfassungskonforme Rechtsfortbildung*).[14] By definition, constitution-consistent judicial law-making departs from the possible semantic meanings of the statutory words. The doctrine of constitution-consistent interpretation is not positively enacted. It is judge-made law. It applies to all legislation pre-dating or post-dating the German Basic Law.[15] The Basic Law is part of the background against which ordinary legislation is being enacted and thus influences the interpretation of ordinary legislation. It carries great weight when courts balance the interpretative criteria. This is not surprising because the German Basic Law is a source of law of the highest rank in Germany and takes precedence over incompatible ordinary legislation. It follows from the hierarchy of norms[16] that a statutory provision of a lower rank (here: ordinary legislation) must be interpreted in such a way that it does not conflict with statutory provisions of a higher rank (here: German Basic Law).[17] This reasoning cannot, however, fully explain the principle of constitution-consistent interpretation as applied

---

[14] See BVerfG, *NJW* 1973, 1491, 1494; BVerfG, *NJW* 1985, 2315, 2318 (dissenting opinion of Judge Steinberger); BVerfG, *NJW* 1988, 125, 126; BVerfG, *NJW* 1993, 2861, 2863; BVerfG, *NJW* 1998, 1478, 1479; BVerfG, *NJW* 2004, 1305, 1310–1311 – *Geldwäsche durch Strafverteidiger*; BVerfG, *NVwZ* 2015, 510, para. 93. It is controversial in German legal scholarship whether the BVerfG can apply constitution-consistent judicial law-making itself or whether this interpretative power rests solely with regular courts; see, e.g. O. Sauer, Wortlautgrenze der verfassungskonformen Auslegung?, August 2006, pp. 9–12, available online at http://www.jura.uni-freiburg.de/institute/ioeffr3/forschung/papers.php; A. Voßkuhle, Theorie und Praxis der verfassungskonformen Auslegung von Gesetzen durch Fachgerichte, *AöR* 125 (2000), 177, 197–198.

[15] For legislation pre-dating the German Basic Law, see BVerfG, *NJW* 1958, 1388–1389; BVerfG, *NJW* 1965, 1427, 1430; BVerwG, *NJW* 1964, 1586–1587; BVerwG, *NVwZ* 1997, 384, 385–386; BAG, *NJW* 1970, 725.

[16] F. Ossenbühl, Vorrang und Vorbehalt des Gesetzes, in J. Isensee and P. Kirchhof (eds.), *Handbuch des Staatsrechts der Bundesrepublik Deutschland*, Volume V, 3rd ed., C.F. Müller, Heidelberg 2007, §101 para. 2.

[17] This is not uncontroversial in German scholarship. Proponents of this view include: Canaris, above n. 11, pp. 141, 148; F. Bydlinski, *Juristische Methodenlehre und Rechtsbegriff*, 2nd ed., Springer, Vienna 1991, p. 456; B. Rüthers, C. Fischer and A. Birk, *Rechtstheorie*, 7th ed., C.H. Beck, Munich 2013, para. 763; cf. BVerfG, *NJW* 1985, 2315, 2318 (dissenting opinion of Judge Steinberger). For an overview of the discussion, see U. Lembke, Einheit aus Erkenntnis?, Duncker & Humblot, Berlin 2009, pp. 88–90.

by the BVerfG. First, it cannot explain why German courts, as we will see, apply an interpretative priority rule.[18] Second, the supremacy of the German Basic Law could also be safeguarded by invalidating inconsistent ordinary legislation.

In its earlier case law, the BVerfG derived the obligation of constitution-consistent interpretation from a presumption that a provision is constitution consistent: the principle underlying this presumption entails that provisions have to be interpreted in conformity with the German Basic Law.[19] Newer case law rightly stresses the interest in preserving a legal provision (*favor legis*) and the respect for the ordinary legislature as the underlying reasons for the doctrine of constitution-consistent interpretation.[20] Since the BVerfG has the power to invalidate unconstitutional legislation (cf. ss. 78, 95(3) BVerfGG),[21] ensuring the validity of ordinary legislation through constitution-consistent interpretation respects and shows deference to the legislature's authority. In other words, the doctrine of constitution-consistent interpretation contains a form of judicial restraint vis-à-vis the legislature,[22] at least from a theoretical viewpoint. The BVerfG can only use its power to declare void unconstitutional legislation if it is not possible to construe a provision in conformity with the German Basic Law.[23] The interpretative obligation is the solution of first resort for resolving inconsistencies between ordinary national legislation and the German Basic Law.[24] Regular courts also have the power to examine the constitutionality of legislation. If a regular court is of the opinion that the ordinary legislation at issue cannot be construed in conformity with the German Basic Law and is thus unconstitutional, it must stay the proceedings and refer the question to the BVerfG (art. 100(1) GG). It has been argued in legal scholarship that the BVerfG would exceed its competences if it engaged in constitution-consistent

---

[18] See C.-W. CANARIS, Gemeinsamkeiten zwischen verfassungs- und richtlinienkonformer Rechtsfindung, in H. BAUER et al. (eds.), *Festschrift für Reiner Schmidt*, C.H. Beck, Munich 2006, pp. 41, 42.

[19] BVerfG, *NJW* 1953, 1057, 1059. For a criticism of this reasoning, see VOSSKUHLE, above n. 14, pp. 177, 182–183; LEMBKE, above n. 17, pp. 73–77.

[20] BVerfG, *NJW* 1979, 151; BVerfG, *NJW* 1985, 1519, 1528; BVerfG, *NJW* 1994, 2475, 2476; BVerfG, *NJW* 2004, 1305, 1311 – *Geldwäsche durch Strafverteidiger*; BVerfG, *NJW* 2007, 2977, para. 91 – *Strafzumessung durch Revisionsgerichte*. See also CANARIS, above n. 18, pp. 41, 42–43.

[21] For ordinary federal legislation post-dating the German Basic Law, this power rests exclusively with the BVerfG; see art. 100(1) GG. For unconstitutional legislation pre-dating the German Basic Law, however, art. 100(1) GG is not applicable. Regular courts have the power not to apply this legislation; see BVerfG, *NJW* 1998, 1699.

[22] S. KORIOTH, in S. KORIOTH and K. SCHLAICH (eds.), *Das Bundesverfassungsgericht*, 9th ed., C.H. Beck, Munich 2012, para. 449; LEMBKE, above n. 17, pp. 78–79.

[23] BVerfG, *NJW* 1979, 151; BVerfG, *NJW* 1980, 2179, 2181; BVerfG, *NJW* 1991, 1807, 1809; BVerfG, *NJW* 1992, 2947, 2950; BVerfG, *NJW* 1993, 2861, 2863.

[24] For the advantages of constitution-consistent interpretation from the perspective of legal practice, which explain why this method is preferred in regular courts over a judicial review proceeding according to art. 100 GG, see J. IPSEN, *Richterrecht und Verfassung*, Duncker & Humblot, Berlin 1975, p. 172.

judicial law-making,[25] but in judicial practice the BVerfG does not restrict its interpretative powers to constitution-consistent interpretation in a narrow sense.

1.2. SECTION 3(1) HUMAN RIGHTS ACT

English courts are obliged to interpret national legislation compatibly with Convention rights[26] "so far as it is possible to do so" (s. 3(1) HRA). In contrast to the doctrine of constitution-consistent interpretation in Germany, this interpretative obligation is a statutory rule of construction. It applies to all legislation, past, present and future.[27] The aim of the HRA is to enable people in the UK to enforce their rights under the ECHR against public authorities before domestic courts rather than having to take their case to the ECtHR.[28] One effect of the HRA was to broaden the scope of rights protected by English courts. Section 3(1) HRA is intended to secure that rights are "effectively brought home", which is why s. 3(1) HRA is the prime remedial measure, and a declaration of incompatibility under s. 4 HRA a measure of last resort.[29] Similarly, but for different underlying reasons, constitution-consistent interpretation in Germany trumps an invalidation of legislation by the BVerfG. In order to fulfil its function, s. 3(1) HRA "imposes a stronger and more radical obligation than to adopt a purposive interpretation in the light of the ECHR".[30] When the Human Rights Bill was debated in Parliament, the then Lord Chancellor, Lord Irvine, expressed the opinion that "in 99 per cent of the cases that will arise, there will be no need for judicial declarations of incompatibility"[31] as the matter can be resolved by statutory construction. This statement was echoed by the Home Secretary, who opined that "in almost all cases, the courts will be able to interpret legislation compatibly with the convention".[32] "Possible" in s. 3(1) HRA also means more

---

[25] Voßkuhle, above n. 14, pp. 177, 197–198.
[26] As defined in ss. 1 and 21(1) HRA.
[27] *Hansard*, HL Deb 5 February 1998, vol 585 col 840 (Lord Irvine); White Paper, Rights brought home: the Human Rights Bill, October 1997 (CM 3782), para. 2.8; *Poplar Housing and Regeneration Community Association Ltd. v. Donaghue* [2001] EWCA Civ 595, para. 75 (Lord Woolf CJ).
[28] *Hansard*, HL Deb 5 February 1998, vol 585 cols 755, 839 (Lord Irvine); *Hansard*, HC Deb 16 February 1998, vol 306 cols 767–768, 769–770 (Home Secretary).
[29] *Ghaidan v. Godin-Mendoza* [2004] UKHL 30, para. 46 (Lord Steyn); cf. *Attorney-General's Reference (No. 4 of 2002)* [2005] 1 AC 264 (HL), 303 (Lord Bingham). An analysis of case law shows that a declaration of incompatibility is a measure of last resort in judicial practice; see C. Crawford, Dialogue and rights-compatible interpretations under section 3 of the Human Rights Act 1998, (2014) 25 *King's Law Journal* 34, 45–46.
[30] *Ghaidan v. Godin-Mendoza* [2004] UKHL 30, para. 44 (Lord Steyn).
[31] *Hansard*, HL Deb 5 February 1998, vol 585 col 840 (Lord Irvine).
[32] *Hansard*, HC Deb 16 February 1998, vol 306 col 778 (Home Secretary).

than "reasonably possible" because an amendment to that effect was rejected in the House of Commons.[33] There is support in *Hansard* that s. 3(1) HRA empowers courts to depart from conventional canons of construction.[34] The ministerial statements in *Hansard* are not clear, however,[35] since Lord Cooke expressed the view that a "strained interpretation" would not be possible under s. 3(1) HRA.[36] The White Paper *Rights Brought Home* had articulated the view that the clause which later became s. 3(1) HRA "goes far beyond the present rule which enables the courts to take the Convention into account in resolving any ambiguity in a legislative provision".[37]

The existence of s. 3(2) and s. 4 HRA shows that the interpretative power under s. 3(1) HRA is limited.[38] The word "possible" in s. 3(1) HRA also indicates that instances exist where a constitution-consistent interpretation will not be possible.[39] Section 3(1) HRA confines courts to an interpretative, as distinct from a legislative, role. If primary legislation cannot be rendered Convention-compliant by means of interpretation, certain courts[40] "may" make a declaration of incompatibility under s. 4 HRA. As long as a Convention-compatible interpretation is possible, however, a court cannot be satisfied that the contested provision is incompatible with a Convention right and, therefore, cannot make a declaration of incompatibility (cf. ss. 3(1) and 4(2) HRA).[41] A court must exhaust its interpretative power under s. 3(1) HRA before recourse to s. 4 HRA is possible. That is why it is ultimately the outer interpretative limits that govern the choice between s. 3(1) and s. 4 HRA. In contrast to the powers of the BVerfG, incompatible primary legislation continues to operate and English courts have no power to set aside or declare void primary legislation under the HRA (cf. s. 4(6) HRA). "The declaration acts primarily as a signal to Parliament that it needs to consider amending that legislation".[42] A declaration of incompatibility does not require Parliament (or the government) to do anything by way of response, and one of its key characteristics is that it is not binding on the parties.

---

[33] *Hansard*, HC Deb 3 June 1998, vol 313 cols 415–437.
[34] For discussion, see J. BEATSON et al. (eds.), *Human rights: judicial protection in the United Kingdom*, Sweet & Maxwell, London 2008, paras. 5-72–5-75.
[35] For discussion, see G. MARSHALL, The lynchpin of parliamentary intention: lost, stolen or strained?, [2003] *PL* 236, 238–239.
[36] *Hansard*, HL Deb 18 November 1997, vol 583 col 533 (Lord Cooke).
[37] White Paper, Rights brought home: the Human Rights Bill, October 1997 (CM 3782), para. 2.7.
[38] *R. v. A (No. 2)* [2001] UKHL 25, para. 108 (Lord Hope); *In re S (Minors)* [2002] UKHL 10, para. 38 (Lord Nicholls); *Ghaidan v. Godin-Mendoza* [2004] UKHL 30, para. 27 (Lord Nicholls), para. 62 (Lord Millett), para. 104 (Lord Rodger).
[39] *Ghaidan v. Godin-Mendoza* [2004] UKHL 30, para. 27 (Lord Nicholls), para. 49 (Lord Steyn).
[40] See s. 4(5) HRA.
[41] *Wilson v. First County Trust Ltd. (No. 2)* [2003] UKHL 40, para. 14 (Lord Nicholls).
[42] *Benkharbouche and Janah v. Embassy of Sudan and others* [2015] EWCA Civ 33, para. 72 (Lord Dyson MR).

It offers litigants no remedy. This can incentivise courts to adopt a strained Convention-compatible interpretation, and this further explains why s. 3(1) HRA is regarded as the prime remedial measure in judicial practice. With regard to delegated legislation, the HRA permits courts to declare such legislation invalid if it is incompatible with Convention rights, so long as primary legislation does not prevent removal of the incompatibility (cf. s. 3(2)(c)).

A declaration of incompatibility does not affect the continuing validity of primary legislation.[43] Both the Lord Chancellor and the Home Secretary therefore expressed the view during the parliamentary debates of the Human Rights Bill that the Bill and in particular its clause 4 (now s. 4 HRA) is consistent with the principle of parliamentary sovereignty.[44] The Bill does not affect Parliament's competence to enact any legislation on any matter of its choosing.[45] "Parliament has retained the right to enact legislation in terms which are not Convention-compliant".[46] Section 6(3) HRA confirms this position as it exempts Parliament from the general duty of public authorities, contained in s. 6(1) HRA, to act in a way which is compatible with Convention rights. This is the formal legal position. In practice, however, a declaration of incompatibility has almost always led to reform of the law through the making of legislation.[47] That is because a declaration of incompatibility exerts considerable political pressure on the

---

[43] Its only legal effect is that it triggers the power of the government to issue a remedial order under s. 10 HRA.

[44] *Hansard*, HL Deb 5 February 1998, vol 585 col 839 (Lord Irvine); *Hansard*, HC Deb 16 February 1998, vol 306 col 778, 769–770 (Home Secretary). See also White Paper, Rights brought home: the Human Rights Bill, October 1997 (CM 3782), para. 2.13; *R. (Kebilene) v. Director of Public Prosecutions* [2000] 2 AC 326 (HL), 367 (Lord Steyn). Regarding s. 4 HRA, see also *Wilson v. First County Trust Ltd. (No. 2)* [2003] UKHL 40, para. 127 (Lord Hobhouse); *R. (Nicklinson) v. Ministry of Justice* [2014] UKSC 38, para. 343 (Lord Kerr); LORD NEUBERGER, The role of judges in human rights jurisprudence: a comparison of the Australian and UK experience, speech at a conference at the Supreme Court of Victoria, Melbourne, 2014, p. 5, para. 11, available online at https://www.supremecourt.uk/news/speeches.html.

[45] But see *Secretary of State for the Home Department v. JJ* [2007] UKHL 45, para. 65 (Lord Carswell, "Parliament is not free to legislate as it chooses in this sphere: its ability to do so is limited by the provisions of the Human Rights Act 1998 …").

[46] *Ghaidan v. Godin-Mendoza* [2004] UKHL 30, para. 33 (Lord Nicholls). See also ibid., para. 43 (Lord Steyn); *Secretary of State for the Home Department v. AF* [2009] UKHL 28, para. 97 (Lord Scott).

[47] Ministry of Justice, Responding to human rights judgments, Cm 9360, November 2016, p. 45, available online at http://www.gov.uk/government/collections/human-rights-the-governments-response-to-human-rights-judgments. The one exceptions relates to the ban on prisoner voting; for discussion, see S. GARDBAUM, What's so weak about "weak-form review"? A reply to Aileen Kavanagh, (2015) 13 *I-CON* 1040, 1043–1044. For discussion of whether and how Parliament has responded to declarations of incompatibility by the courts in the past, see Joint Committee on Human Rights, Human rights judgments, HL Paper 130, HC 1088, 2014–15, particularly para. 4.13.

government and Parliament to change the law.[48] One underlying reason is that a declaration of incompatibility usually carries the implication that the UK is in breach of its obligation in international law to secure Convention rights under art. 1 ECHR. For Baroness Hale, the purpose of a declaration of incompatibility is, therefore, "to warn Government and Parliament that, in [the court's] view, the United Kingdom is in breach of its international obligations".[49] The practical effect of a declaration of incompatibility comes close to a power to strike down legislation.[50] It follows from this contextualised analysis that the distinction between strong-form judicial review in Germany and weak-form judicial review under the HRA seems, at least for the time being, negligible.[51]

Judges have also declared that s. 3(1) HRA respects the sovereignty of Parliament as it only allows a Convention-compatible interpretation of legislation "so far as it is possible to do so".[52] Furthermore, "[i]f Parliament disagrees with an interpretation by the courts under section 3(1), it is free to override it by amending the legislation and expressly reinstating the incompatibility".[53] This aspect of the relationship between the courts and the legislature under the HRA may be understood as fostering inter-institutional dialogue between the two branches of the state about how human rights should be applied.[54] Yet, Parliament rarely "overrules" a court's Convention-compatible

---

[48] For a discussion of the reasons for this, see C. CHANDRACHUD and A. KAVANAGH, The United Kingdom: rights-based constitutional review in the UK: from form to function, in J. BELL and M.-L. PARIS (eds.), *Rights-based constitutional review: constitutional courts in a changing landscape*, Edward Elgar, Cheltenham 2016, pp. 63, 82–91; M. ELLIOTT and R. THOMAS, *Public law*, 3rd ed., OUP, Oxford 2017, pp. 793–795.

[49] *R. (Animal Defenders International) v. Secretary of State for culture, media and sport* [2008] UKHL 15, para. 53 (Baroness Hale).

[50] A. KAVANAGH, *Constitutional review under the UK Human Rights Act*, CUP, Cambridge 2009, pp. 281–292, 308, 320–322; P. SALES and R. EKINS, Rights-consistent interpretation and the Human Rights Act 1998, (2011) 127 *LQR* 217, 230.

[51] A. KAVANAGH, What's so weak about weak-form review?, (2015) 13 *I-CON* 1008, 1030 describes the HRA as "'effectively strong-form' [review] within a nominally 'weak-form system'"; cf. LORD HOFFMANN, Human rights and the House of Lords, (1999) 62 *MLR* 159–160 ("technical distinction"). Rather sceptical about this assessment: GARDBAUM, above n. 47, pp. 1046–1047.

[52] *R. v. Lambert* [2001] UKHL 37, para. 79 (Lord Hope); *In re S (Minors)* [2002] UKHL 10, para. 39 (Lord Nicholls); *Ghaidan v. Godin-Mendoza* [2004] UKHL 30, para. 57 (Lord Millett), para. 120 (Lord Rodger). But see Hansard, HL Deb 18 November 1997, vol 583 col 509 (Lord Irvine, "That might give rise to the doctrine of implied repeal. That is a doctrine that can have no application because of the express terms of Clause 3").

[53] *Ghaidan v. Godin-Mendoza* [2004] UKHL 30, para. 43 (Lord Steyn).

[54] R. CLAYTON, Judicial deference and "democratic dialogue": the legitimacy of judicial intervention under the Human Rights Act 1998, [2004] *PL* 33, 46. Whereas s. 4 HRA is seen in legal scholarship as an engine for dialogue between the judiciary and the legislature, some scholars argue that Convention-compatible interpretations under s. 3(1) HRA do not have a dialogic character; for discussion, see T. HICKMAN, Constitutional theories, constitutional dialogue and the Human Rights Act 1998, [2005] *PL* 306–335. For criticism of the so-called "dialogue theory", see A. KAVANAGH, The lure and the limits of dialogue, (2016) 66 *University of Toronto Law Journal* 83–120; CRAWFORD, above n. 29, pp. 34–46.

interpretation by expressly reinstating the incompatibility.[55] If Parliament were regularly not to react to declarations of incompatibility, courts would have an incentive to prefer strained Convention-compatible interpretations over declarations of incompatibility.[56] That would necessitate wide limits of interpretation. The current legislative practice is, however, that Parliament almost always reacts to and follows a declaration of incompatibility. Parliament's practice therefore appears as a negligible factor when a court determines whether it should adopt a strained Convention-compatible interpretation or make a declaration of incompatibility. There are nevertheless two different factors incentivising courts to hold that a rights-consistent interpretation is possible and to adopt wide outer limits of Convention-compatible interpretation. First, a declaration of incompatibility offers litigants no remedy. Second, s. 4 HRA puts considerable political pressure on the government and Parliament, whereas s. 3(1) HRA does not. A declaration of incompatibility carries with it the notion that the government failed to protect human rights, and the government rarely wants to be exposed to political criticism from the general British public that it does not respect human rights.[57] This also explains why the government often prefers a strained rights-consistent interpretation when it joins as a party to the proceedings in cases where a court is considering whether to make a declaration of incompatibility (cf. s. 5 HRA). There is case law suggesting that the government's submission in favour of using s. 3(1) HRA rather than s. 4 HRA can affect judges' willingness to adopt a strained interpretation under s. 3(1) HRA.[58] It has rightly been pointed out, however, that a tactical decision by the government in the course of litigation should not be capable of affecting the meaning of legislation enacted by Parliament.[59]

Before exploring the extent of the courts' interpretative powers under s. 3(1) HRA later in this chapter, it is helpful to analyse different possible interpretations of s. 3(1) HRA that are reconcilable with the doctrine of parliamentary sovereignty. It has been argued that s. 3(1) HRA would be rendered otiose if the courts were not empowered to go against the original

---

[55] CRAWFORD, above n. 29, pp. 41, 44–46. See also C. CHANDRACHUD, Reconfiguring the discourse on political responses to declarations of incompatibility, [2014] PL 624, 634.
[56] Even though Parliament can override a court's s. 3(1) HRA-interpretation by amending the legislation and reinstating the incompatibility, in contrast to declarations of incompatibility, s. 3(1) HRA rulings have not attracted as much public interest and have, thus, predominantly stayed under the political radar; see CRAWFORD, above n. 29, pp. 41, 44.
[57] KAVANAGH, above n. 51, p. 1025.
[58] R. (Hammond) v. Secretary of State for the Home Department [2005] UKHL 69, para. 17 (Lord Bingham); Secretary of State for the Home Department v. AF [2009] UKHL 28, para. 95 (Lord Scott).
[59] A. WAGNER and G. BARTH, Judicial interpretation or judicial vandalism? Section 3 of the Human Rights Act 1998, (2016) 21 JR 99, 101.

intention of the enacting parliament.[60] I will refute this thesis in the following. Multiple possible interpretations of s. 3(1) HRA exist that preserve parliamentary sovereignty. The starting point is that the wording of s. 3(1) HRA is vague. By using the word "possible", Parliament has intentionally delegated to the judges the power to determine the extent of permissible judicial law-making under s. 3(1) HRA. That means that different interpretations of s. 3(1) HRA are possible and permissible as long as they remain within the boundaries set by the doctrine of parliamentary sovereignty. First, equating the outer limits of the judicial function under s. 3(1) HRA with the judiciary's law-making powers according to conventional canons of construction is not convincing in the light of the provision's legislative history. Second, one possible interpretation of s. 3(1) HRA would be to equate the courts' powers under s. 3(1) with their powers under the principle of legality. That was the view of Lord Hoffmann in *Simms*.[61] It will be shown in Section 8 that the interpretative powers available to judges under the principle of legality extend beyond the limits of the judicial function according to conventional canons of construction.

Third, I have established in Chapter 2 that English courts have not yet drawn the full consequences of the purposive approach. That is because the doctrine of parliamentary sovereignty can also support a system of interpretation according to which judicial law-making is generally permissible in order to give effect to the intention of the enacting legislature if that intention is insufficiently expressed in the statutory words. A third possible reading of s. 3(1) HRA could endorse this system of interpretation. It would exceed judicial powers available under conventional canons, and it would not limit judicial powers to read in, out or down words in legislation to exceptional cases. For post-HRA statutes, the strength of rights-consistent judicial law-making would be bolstered by a powerful presumption that the enacting parliament intended to comply with Convention rights. This presumption would be based on s. 3(1), (2)(a) HRA. It would form part of the background against which post-HRA legislation is being enacted. It would inform what is plausible to think that the enacting legislature decided. The situation would be different for pre-HRA legislation because an enacting parliament could not have foreseen the forthcoming HRA. The presumption enshrined in s. 3(1), (2)(a) HRA would not form part of the original context of the legislation and the enacting parliament's presumed intentions.[62] Convention-compatible interpretation of pre-HRA legislation would therefore not go as far as Convention-compatible interpretation of post-HRA legislation.[63]

---

[60] For a different view, see KAVANAGH, above n. 50, pp. 81, 114, 331.
[61] *R. (Simms) v. Secretary of State for the Home Department* [2002] 2 AC 115 (HL), 131–132 (Lord Hoffmann).
[62] Neither the words of s. 3(1) HRA nor its legislative history require a more radical reading. For an apparently different view, see KAVANAGH, above n. 50, pp. 99–100.
[63] We will see later that this view has not prevailed in English courts.

Even for pre-HRA legislation, the doctrine of parliamentary sovereignty may not rule out the taking into account of objective factors of interpretation (in this case Convention rights) as long as the rights-consistent meaning is reconcilable with the enacting legislature's intent. Admittedly though, this would be a grey area of statutory interpretation. An "always speaking" statute allows for changes since the legislation was initially framed and allows for legislative intent to be evaluated at the time of adjudication. In the case of vague or ambiguous statutory words, s. 3(1) HRA could be decisive for tipping the balance in favour of a Convention-compatible meaning of a pre-HRA provision. Convention rights could inform the evaluative scope that is available to a judge in the reasoning process.

There is a fourth possible reading of s. 3(1) HRA. That reading is based on the thesis that in certain circumstances a court can depart from the intention of the enacting parliament without undermining the orthodox doctrine of parliamentary sovereignty. This thesis requires elaboration. A sovereign parliament has the power to repeal any Act of an earlier parliament. A sovereign parliament can also make any law with any content whatsoever. It follows that a sovereign parliament can enact a statute obliging courts to reinterpret legislation of earlier parliaments. If such reinterpretation is possible in an individual case, the doctrine of implied repeal does not apply. One example of such a law could be s. 3(1), (2)(a) HRA as the legislation refers to pre-HRA provisions even though a pre-HRA parliament could not have foreseen the coming into force of the HRA. A judge who reinterprets a pre-HRA statute in the light of the HRA may depart from the intention of the parliament enacting the challenged legislation by giving effect to the intention of the Parliament of 1998. Does this reading of s. 3(1) HRA involve a modification of the orthodox doctrine of parliamentary sovereignty? No, it does not. It is true that a court in this case would disconnect the meaning of the earlier legislation from the intention of the enacting legislature, but that does not mean that the judge ignores legislative supremacy. Instead, by giving effect to the later Act of Parliament, the judge acknowledges the continuing sovereignty of Parliament and the rule that a parliament cannot bind its successor. This reading of s. 3(1) HRA is reconcilable with an orthodox understanding of parliamentary sovereignty. The vague terms of s. 3(1) HRA ("possible") as such do not answer the question of whether the Parliament of 1998 actually intended to grant judges such wide-ranging powers to reinterpret existing legislation and to deviate from the intention of earlier parliaments when interpreting pre-HRA legislation. Neither does s. 3(1) HRA stipulate the limits of such reinterpretation. This fourth reading of s. 3(1) HRA is constitutionally significant as it alters the notion recognised under conventional canons of interpretation that a court cannot depart from the intention of the enacting parliament. The granting of such wide-ranging powers to judges under s. 3(1) HRA would entail a departure from the judicial role as traditionally understood and a reshaping of the judicial role vis-à-vis the legislature.

There is no actual indication that the 1998 Parliament intended this fourth reading of s. 3(1) HRA. Can the 1998 Parliament be presumed to have adopted this fourth reading? Since the fourth reading includes a constitutionally significant change in the separation of powers, the principle of legality[64] applies. The principle of legality will be analysed in detail in Section 8. According to this principle, fundamental constitutional principles recognised by the common law cannot be overridden by general or ambiguous statutory words. It was shown in Chapter 2 that a court cannot depart from the enacting parliament's intent under conventional canons of construction. This is a fundamental principle recognised by the common law. Applying the principle of legality, the general statutory language of s. 3(1) HRA ("possible") cannot override this fundamental principle. Parliament when enacting s. 3(1) HRA cannot be presumed to have intended such a fundamental change. Even if this fourth interpretation of s. 3(1) HRA were to be adopted, a court's power to deviate from the intention of the enacting legislature would not apply to post-HRA legislation. For post-HRA statutes, the strength of rights-consistent judicial law-making would be bolstered by a presumption that the enacting parliament intended to comply with Convention rights. Further than that a court could not go. A court that departed from the intention of a post-1998 parliament would prefer the intention of an earlier parliament over the intention of a later parliament. It would in effect bind the later post-HRA parliament and would thereby exceed its judicial function as that is something that a court cannot do according to constitutional orthodoxy.

This book demonstrates in Section 7.2 that English courts have adopted none of the above-mentioned possible interpretations of s. 3(1) HRA. Instead, they have ventured even further as they have empowered themselves not only to depart from the intention of a pre-HRA parliament but also from the intention of a post-HRA parliament.

2. AIM OF RIGHTS-CONSISTENT INTERPRETATION

When a German court engages in constitution-consistent interpretation, it aims to find a possible meaning of a provision that complies with the German Basic Law. It is the intention of the legislature that determines what meanings of a provision are possible. The intention of the legislature is a malleable concept that can, for example, refer to the actual intention of the enacting legislature (subjective concept) or to the presumed intention of a reasonable legislature at the time of interpretation (objective concept). Since the BVerfG has the power to

---

[64] Alternatively, the presumption that Parliament does intend to legislate in conformity with background constitutional principles.

invalidate unconstitutional legislation, a reasonable enacting legislature intends to comply with the German Basic Law. The aim of constitution-consistent interpretation can therefore be reconciled with the aim of statutory interpretation under conventional canons of construction, i.e. to ascertain the (objectivised) intention of the legislature. The strength of the objective approach to statutory interpretation is visible when the BVerfG interprets legislation pre-dating the German Basic Law in conformity with the German Basic Law. In these cases, the BVerfG objectifies the purpose of the legislation by reading it in the context of the German Basic Law as understood at the time of applying the legislation.[65]

The duty of an English court under s. 3(1) HRA is to find a meaning that best accords with Convention rights.[66] Convention rights are a standard external to the statute under consideration. When English courts interpret legislation according to conventional principles of construction, their primary task is to ascertain the intention of Parliament. Lord Woolf CJ has said that this traditional role of the courts has to be adjusted when s. 3(1) HRA applies.[67] "The role of the court is not (as in traditional statutory interpretation) to find the true meaning of the provision, but to find (if possible) the meaning which best accords with Convention rights".[68] Lord Cooke expressed the same view during the passage of the Human Rights Bill in Parliament.[69] In the words of Lord Hope in *R. v. A (No. 2)*, "[c]ompatibility with Convention rights is the sole guiding principle".[70] This guiding principle is limited because the compatibility can only be achieved so far as it is possible as a matter of interpretation. Lady Justice Arden has remarked extrajudicially that, in truth, interpretation according to s. 3(1) HRA "is no longer a matter of looking at Parliamentary intention" as expressed in the statutory words.[71] This adjustment of the traditional role of the

---

[65] In detail, Section 5 below.
[66] *Ghaidan v. Godin-Mendoza* [2004] UKHL 30, para. 46 (Lord Steyn).
[67] *Poplar Housing and Regeneration Community Association Ltd. v. Donaghue* [2001] EWCA Civ 595, para. 75 (Lord Woolf CJ). See also *S v. L* [2012] UKSC 30, para. 15 (Lord Reed, with whom all other members of the court agreed); *Wilson v. First County Trust Ltd. (No. 2)* [2003] UKHL 40, para. 61 (Lord Nicholls); A. KAVANAGH, The role of parliamentary intention in adjudication under the Human Rights Act 1998, (2006) 26 *OJLS* 179, 196; LORD JUSTICE LAWS, The impact of the Human Rights Act 1998 on the interpretation of enactments in the UK, in R. BIGWOOD (ed.), *The statute: making and meaning*, LexisNexis NZ, Wellington 2003, pp. 241, 248; R. MASTERMAN, *The separation of powers in the contemporary constitution*, CUP, Cambridge 2010, pp. 176–177.
[68] *R. (Wright) v. Secretary of State for Health* [2007] EWCA Civ 999, para. 112 (Dyson LJ).
[69] *Hansard*, HL Deb 3 November 1997, vol 582 col 1272 (Lord Cooke, "Traditionally, the search has been for the true meaning; now it will be for a possible meaning that would prevent the making of a declaration of incompatibility").
[70] *R. v. A (No. 2)* [2001] UKHL 25, para. 108 (Lord Hope).
[71] LADY JUSTICE ARDEN, The changing judicial role: human rights, Community law and the intention of Parliament, (2008) 67 *CLJ* 487, 496.

Chapter 3. Rights-Consistent Interpretation

courts is constitutionally significant because it alters the notion of discerning Parliament's intention as the aim of statutory interpretation.[72] The aim of statutory interpretation is linked to the function of the judge, the separation of powers and the doctrine of parliamentary sovereignty.

In order to reconcile the role of the court under s. 3(1) HRA with the doctrine of parliamentary sovereignty, judges distinguish between two different intentions of Parliament:[73] first, the intention of the parliament that enacted the challenged legislation and, second, the intention of the parliament that enacted the HRA. Ascribing a Convention-compatible interpretation to legislation fulfils the latter parliament's intention in enacting s. 3(1) HRA. Courts also use this reasoning when they depart from the intention of the parliament that enacted the challenged legislation.[74] In such a case, a court prefers and gives priority to the legislative intention of the parliament that enacted the HRA over the legislative intention of the parliament that enacted the other statute.[75] This applies even if the other statute post-dates the HRA, as was the case in *Attorney General's Reference (No. 4 of 2002)*.[76] Giving priority to the intention of an earlier parliament over the intention of a subsequent parliament involves a diminution of the orthodox doctrine of parliamentary sovereignty.[77] Whether this power of the courts is reconcilable with constitutional theory will be explored later in this book.[78]

The aim of constitution-consistent interpretation in Germany and of s. 3(1) HRA in England is primarily to avoid possible contradictions between the challenged legislation and the German Basic Law/Convention rights.

---

[72] Ibid., 497 ("revolutionised statutory interpretation"); cf. *R. (JS) v. Secretary of State for Work and Pensions* [2015] UKSC, para. 92 (Lord Reed).

[73] See *Ghaidan v. Godin-Mendoza* [2004] UKHL 30, paras. 26, 30 (Lord Nicholls); *Attorney General's Reference (No. 4 of 2002)* [2004] UKHL 43, para. 53 (Lord Bingham); *Ahmed and others v. HM Treasury* [2010] UKSC 2, para. 115 (Lord Phillips); *S v. L* [2012] UKSC 30, para. 15 (Lord Reed, with whom all other members of the court agreed); LADY JUSTICE ARDEN, The interpretation of UK domestic legislation in the light of European Convention on Human Rights jurisprudence, (2004) 25 *Statute Law Review* 165, 178; LAWS, above n. 67, pp. 241, 248; LORD PHILLIPS, The art of the possible: statutory interpretation and human rights, First Lord Alexander of Weedon lecture, April 2010, pp. 38–43, available online at https://www.supremecourt.uk/news/speeches.html; NEUBERGER, above n. 44, p. 6, para. 14; P. SALES, A comparison of the principle of legality and section 3 of the Human Rights Act 1998, (2009) 125 *LQR* 598, 608; cf. *R. v. A (No. 2)* [2001] UKHL 25, para. 44 (Lord Steyn); *Ghaidan v. Godin-Mendoza* [2004] UKHL 30, para. 106 (Lord Rodger).

[74] In detail, Section 7.2 below.

[75] LAWS, above n. 67, pp. 241, 248; PHILLIPS, above n. 73, p. 38; KAVANAGH, above n. 67, pp. 179, 187; cf. *Ghaidan v. Godin-Mendoza* [2004] UKHL 30, para. 30 (Lord Nicholls), para. 40 (Lord Steyn), para. 106 (Lord Rodger); *Attorney General's Reference (No. 4 of 2002)* [2004] UKHL 43, para. 53 (Lord Bingham).

[76] *Attorney General's Reference (No. 4 of 2002)* [2004] UKHL 43, paras. 28, 53 (Lord Bingham).

[77] PHILLIPS, above n. 73, p. 41.

[78] See Section 7.2 below.

Both interpretative doctrines aim to establish compatibility between legal norms at different normative levels. It is thus possible to characterise both doctrines as an attempt to avoid a contradiction between norms by means of statutory interpretation. Courts in both jurisdictions have combined this task with their traditional role in statutory interpretation to ascertain the intention of the legislature. Rights-consistent interpretation in English and German judicial practice is directed at identifying a possible meaning that complies with a standard external to the provision under consideration. The focus of the interpretative exercise is not, however, placed on the process of identifying possible meanings of a provision. That is because rights-consistent interpretation requires an interpretation of the German Basic Law or the Convention rights as a first step. Once this step is completed and the benchmark is set, it becomes clear what readings of the challenged legislation accord with Convention rights or the German Basic Law. The rights-consistent meaning is predetermined by an external standard rather than found by looking at the intention of the legislature. That explains why rights-consistent interpretation is more result driven compared with the process-driven approach of ascertaining legislative intent according to conventional canons of statutory interpretation. The focus of rights-consistent interpretation in judicial practice shifts towards the question of whether the desired reading of the challenged legislation can be squared with the intention of the legislature. This brings the limits of rights-consistent interpretation to the fore.

3. RELATIONSHIP WITH CONVENTIONAL CANONS OF INTERPRETATION

The relationship between conventional canons of construction and constitution-consistent interpretation is controversial in German scholarship.[79] Whereas some scholars contend that constitution-consistent interpretation is a separate canon of construction, others submit that it can be integrated into the systematic approach. Of those scholars who understand constitution-consistent interpretation as a separate canon, some split the process of interpretation into two stages.[80] As a first step, national law is interpreted solely using conventional canons of construction in order to ascertain the possible meanings of a provision. If after a weighing and balancing of the interpretative criteria the statutory words are capable of bearing more than one meaning and if at least one of the possible

---

[79] For an overview of the discussion, see CANARIS, above n. 11, pp. 141, 142, 154; G. HAGER, *Rechtsmethoden in Europa*, Mohr Siebeck, Tübingen 2009, pp. 230–231; IPSEN, above n. 24, pp. 169–170.

[80] C. HÖPFNER, *Die systemkonforme Auslegung*, Mohr Siebeck, Tübingen 2008, pp. 180–184.

meanings is compatible with the German Basic Law, constitution-consistent interpretation is applied as a second step. Constitution-consistent interpretation entails that the meaning that is consistent with the German Basic Law must be favoured over all other possible meanings. This two-step approach in its strict form limits the doctrine of constitution-consistent interpretation to a selection rule between several possible meanings.[81]

German courts have not yet decisively ruled on the theoretical relationship between constitution-consistent interpretation and conventional canons of construction. They do not follow a strict two-step approach.[82] First, constitution-consistent interpretation as applied by the BVerfG cannot be reduced to a selection rule. The BVerfG operates a strong presumption that the ordinary legislature intended to comply with the German Basic Law. Applying this presumption influences how a judge arrives at possible meanings of a provision and bears upon the range of possible meanings. Second, constitution-consistent interpretation in a narrow sense is often intertwined with a provision's interpretation according to conventional canons of construction in judicial practice.[83] In these instances, the provision is interpreted in the light of the German Basic Law according to conventional canons of interpretation. This is sometimes called constitution-oriented interpretation in legal scholarship,[84] but this terminology has not been adopted by German courts. An interpretation of a provision in the light of the German Basic Law illustrates that the boundaries between interpretation according to conventional canons of construction and constitution-consistent interpretation blur in judicial practice. It illustrates why constitution-consistent interpretation in a narrow sense can be entangled with and difficult to separate from the historical or purposive approach to construction in German case law.

Looking at English courts, the application of s. 3(1) HRA involves a two-step approach.[85] First, English judges interpret a provision according to conventional maxims of statutory construction without recourse to s. 3(1) HRA. These maxims include a presumption that Parliament intended the provision to comply with international treaty obligations (in this case the ECHR). Applying this presumption will often be sufficient to enable a court to interpret a provision in a way which is compatible with Convention rights.[86] It has also

---

[81] Ibid., pp. 183–184.
[82] See, e.g. BVerfG, *NJW* 1973, 1491, 1494.
[83] BVerfG, *NJW* 2015, 1359 paras. 131–138 – *Kopftuch*.
[84] See, e.g. HÖPFNER, above n. 80, pp. 178–183.
[85] See *R. v. A (No. 2)* [2001] UKHL 25, paras. 39, 43–44 (Lord Steyn), paras. 58, 68, 106 (Lord Hope), para. 136 (Lord Clyde), para. 155 (Lord Hutton); *Ghaidan v. Godin-Mendoza* [2004] UKHL 30, paras. 59, 60 (Lord Millett); *R. (Hurst) v. Commissioner of Police of the Metropolis* [2007] UKHL 13, para. 49 (Lord Brown); *Manchester City Council v. Pinnock* [2010] UKSC 45, paras. 68–70 (Lord Neuberger, giving the judgment of the court); *S v. L* [2012] UKSC 30, paras. 15–17 (Lord Reed, with whom all other members of the court agreed). See also SALES, above n. 73, pp. 598, 608.
[86] *Ghaidan v. Godin-Mendoza* [2004] UKHL 30, para. 60 (Lord Millett).

been argued that this first step encompasses the principle of legality,[87] which will be discussed in Section 8. If the challenged provision can be given a meaning that complies with Convention rights according to conventional canons, s. 3(1) HRA will not come into play.[88] If the ordinary interpretation of the provision produces a prima facie incompatibility with Convention rights, however, the court is obliged to construe the provision with reference to s. 3(1) HRA.[89] A typical case falling under this second stage of the interpretative process arises where a Convention-compatible meaning can only be achieved by expanding or narrowing the scope of application of the provision beyond the possible semantic meanings of the statutory words. These are cases that would be categorised as constitution-consistent judicial law-making in Germany. The second stage of the interpretative process lies at the heart of the analysis in this chapter. A court is not confined to ascertain the intention of Parliament from the words used or by having recourse to conventional canons of construction. The two-step approach shows that s. 3(1) HRA cannot be integrated into conventional canons of statutory interpretation. It is a separate canon of construction. We have already learned in the previous section that s. 3(1) HRA allows judges to give legislation a meaning that it could not be given under conventional canons of statutory interpretation.[90] Determining the border between the first and the second step can be quite difficult since the limits of judicial law-making under conventional canons of interpretation are to a large extent affected by the circumstances of the individual case. This border is not decisive for the purposes of this book, however, as the outer limits and techniques of Convention-compatible interpretation are those of the second, not the first step.

It is implicit in the two-step approach that the outer limits of Convention-compatible interpretation exceed those of conventional canons of construction. Convention-compatible interpretation shifts the boundary between statutory interpretation and legislation in favour of the judiciary. If a court has to rely on

---

[87] *A v. BBC* [2014] UKSC 25, para. 57 (Lord Reed).
[88] *R v. A (No. 2)* [2001] UKHL 25, paras. 58, 106 (Lord Hope); *Ghaidan v. Godin-Mendoza* [2004] UKHL 30, para. 60 (Lord Millett); *S v. L* [2012] UKSC 30, para. 15 (Lord Reed, with whom all other members of the court agreed); *Poplar Housing and Regeneration Community Association Ltd. v. Donaghue* [2001] EWCA Civ 595, para. 75 (Lord Woolf CJ).
[89] *Ghaidan v. Godin-Mendoza* [2004] UKHL 30, para. 30 (Lord Nicholls), para. 59 (Lord Millett). See also *In re S (Minors)* [2002] UKHL 10, para. 37 (Lord Nicholls, "This is a powerful tool whose use is obligatory. It is not an optional canon of construction"); *Poplar Housing and Regeneration Community Association Ltd. v. Donaghue* [2001] EWCA Civ 595, para. 75 (Lord Woolf CJ).
[90] *R. v. A (No. 2)* [2001] UKHL 25, para. 44 (Lord Steyn), paras. 58, 108 (Lord Hope); *Ghaidan v. Godin-Mendoza* [2004] UKHL 30, paras. 25, 29 (Lord Nicholls), para. 60 (Lord Millett); *S v. L* [2012] UKSC 30, paras. 15–17 (Lord Reed, with whom all other members of the court agreed); *Poplar Housing and Regeneration Community Association Ltd. v. Donaghue* [2001] EWCA Civ 595, para. 75 (Lord Woolf CJ); *Cachia v. Faluyi* [2001] EWCA Civ 998, para. 21 (Brooke LJ, with whom the other members of the court agreed); SALES, above n. 73, pp. 598, 609.

s. 3(1) HRA, it should also limit the extent of a provision's modified meaning to that which is necessary to achieve compatibility.[91] This guideline contains a form of judicial restraint. It respects and shows deference to the intention of the legislature that enacted the challenged legislation. I will show in the next section that a parallel guideline is applied in German judicial practice as a German court has to choose the constitution-consistent meaning that takes into account the enacting legislature's intention as far as possible. Despite this guideline, English scholars have criticised the courts for showing insufficient deference to the legislature by embracing wide limits of interpretation under s. 3(1) HRA and by undermining the intention of the parliament enacting the challenged legislation.[92] This criticism is justified since English courts have read s. 3(1) HRA as empowering them to depart from the intention of the enacting legislature. English courts can patronise the enacting legislature by declaring what the legislature ought to have intended. It thus appears questionable whether Convention-compatible interpretation affords Parliament a higher degree of deference than a declaration of incompatibility.

English and German courts follow a different interpretative structure when they apply constitution-consistent interpretation and s. 3(1) HRA. This difference exists because the relationships between the limits of conventional canons of interpretation and s. 3(1) HRA in England on the one hand and the limits of conventional canons of interpretation and constitution-consistent interpretation in Germany on the other hand are not the same. The interpretative powers available to English judges under s. 3(1) HRA extend beyond those under conventional maxims of construction. In Germany, the outer limits of constitution-consistent interpretation coincide with those of conventional canons of construction.[93] The distinction in the interpretative structure is only technical, however. It does not answer the question of whether and to what extent the outer limits and techniques of rights-consistent interpretation in both jurisdictions differ or overlap. Whereas a typical case decided under s. 3(1) HRA can be categorised as judicial law-making, most cases of constitution-consistent interpretation in Germany concern interpretation within the possible semantic meaning of the statutory words. For our purposes, this is a technical distinction due to the different relationships between both interpretative doctrines and conventional canons of construction. This distinction does not affect the outer limits and techniques of both doctrines.

---

[91] *Poplar Housing and Regeneration Community Association Ltd. v. Donaghue* [2001] EWCA Civ 595, para. 75 (Lord Woolf CJ).

[92] A.D.P. BRADY, *Proportionality and deference under the UK Human Rights Act*, CUP, Cambridge 2012, p. 190.

[93] In detail, Section 7.1 below.

4. INTERPRETATIVE PRIORITY

The next two sections will examine two characteristics of rights-consistent interpretation: the interpretative priority rule and the presumption of compliance. Interpretative priority rules create legal certainty. That is because an interpretative priority rule dictates which interpretative result, out of multiple possible meanings, a court must choose. The choice is not left to the discretion of the judge.

A key feature of constitution-consistent interpretation in Germany is that the constitution-consistent meaning enjoys interpretative priority. If according to the interpretative criteria a provision is capable of bearing more than one meaning and if one of those meanings is inconsistent with the German Basic Law, but at least another one complies with the German Basic Law, a court is obliged to give priority to the latter meaning over all other possible meanings.[94] The court effectively eliminates meanings of a provision that are possible according to the interpretative criteria, but unconstitutional.[95] When a court gives priority to a provision's constitution-consistent meaning, it shows respect to the ordinary legislature. The interpretative priority rule applies even if other persuasive arguments count in favour of a provision's inconsistent meaning, as long as the constitution-consistent meaning is a possible outcome of the interpretative process. This process comprises interpretation in a narrow sense and judicial law-making. If a provision can be given more than one meaning and out of those, multiple meanings comply with the German Basic Law, the respect for the ordinary legislature requires a court to uphold the maximum possible of what the enacting legislature intended. A court must choose the constitution-consistent meaning that takes into account the enacting legislature's intention as far as possible.[96] Whether or not a provision is capable of bearing more than one meaning is not governed by the interpretative priority rule, but by the interpretative criteria. The priority rule does not influence how a judge weighs conflicting interpretative criteria. It does not give precedence to a specific interpretative criterion and does not exclude a weighing of the interpretative criteria, but requires a judge to choose a possible interpretative result that complies with the German Basic Law. The interpretative priority rule only applies once a statutory provision is open to interpretation and can be given

---

[94] BVerfG, *NJW* 1965, 1427; BVerfG, *NJW* 1972, 1123, 1125; BVerfG, *NJW* 1973, 1491, 1494; BVerfG, *NJW* 1979, 151; BVerfG, *NJW* 1983, 2811, 2812; BVerfG, *NJW* 1993, 2861, 2863; BVerfG, *NVwZ* 1996, 574, 578; BVerfG, *NJW* 2005, 1923, 1927.
[95] BVerfG, *NJW* 1975, 1355, 1356; H. Bethge, §31 BVerfGG, in T. Maunz et al. (eds.), *Bundesverfassungsgerichtsgesetz: Kommentar*, Beck, Munich 2014, §31, para. 273.
[96] BVerfG, *NJW* 1958, 1227; BVerfG, *NJW* 1959, 1123; BVerfG, *NJW* 1979, 151; BVerfG, *NJW* 1992, 2947, 2950; BVerfG, *NJW* 2000, 347, 349; BVerfG, *NJW* 2015, 2949, para. 46. For criticism, see H.-J. Koch and H. Rüßmann, *Juristische Begründungslehre*, C.H. Beck, Munich 1982, p. 270.

more than one possible meaning, one of which fulfils the requirements of the German Basic Law. In sum, the interpretative priority rule governs the choice between different possible meanings of a provision.[97]

English courts have also applied an interpretative priority rule for Convention-compatible interpretation. If the application of s. 3(1) HRA allows an English court to construe a provision in conformity with Convention rights, the court is obliged to adopt this Convention-compatible meaning.[98] This meaning prevails over all other possible but incompatible meanings reached under conventional principles of interpretation. It is also irrelevant if the Convention-compatible meaning appears to be unreasonable or if the incompatible meaning appears to be more obvious, natural or reasonable than the Convention-compatible meaning.[99] Section 3(1) HRA thus incorporates an interpretative priority rule that operates as a selection rule between different possible interpretative results. This interpretative priority rule is very similar in operation and in its characteristics when compared to the interpretative priority rule for constitution-consistent interpretation in Germany.

5. PRESUMPTION OF COMPLIANCE

This section will analyse the strength and the limits of the presumption of compliance as applied in English and German courts. A German case that shows the presumption of compliance at work is *Geldwäsche durch Strafverteidiger*. The BVerfG interpreted s. 261 of the German Criminal Code (StGB). The claimants, criminal defence lawyers, were convicted under s. 261(2) StGB for money laundering by a German criminal court because they improperly accepted legal fees. The claimants' clients paid the legal fees with money that stemmed from a criminal offence. According to the wording of s. 261(5) StGB, it is sufficient if the offender recklessly fails to recognise that the asset (here the lawyers' fee) resulted from a criminal offence mentioned in s. 261(1) StGB. The claimants brought a constitutional complaint on the grounds that the interpretation of s. 261 StGB by the criminal court infringed their basic right freely to pursue a professional activity (art. 12(1) GG). The BVerfG held that (a) a wide interpretation of the *mens rea* requirement in s. 261(2), (5) StGB would indeed infringe the basic right of a criminal defence lawyer under art. 12(1) GG and (b) this infringement

---

[97] CANARIS, above n. 11, pp. 141, 154; HÖPFNER, above n. 80, pp. 176–177; VOSSKUHLE, above n. 14, pp. 177, 181.
[98] *Ghaidan v. Godin-Mendoza* [2004] UKHL 30, para. 60 (Lord Millett), para. 106 (Lord Rodger), para. 144 (Baroness Hale).
[99] See ibid., para. 44 (Lord Steyn, "Parliament specifically rejected the legislative model of requiring a reasonable interpretation"), para. 59 (Lord Millett, "There is no residual discretion to disobey the obligation which the section imposes"), para. 67 (Lord Millett, "It means only that the court must take the language of the statute as it finds it and give it a meaning which, however unnatural or unreasonable, is intellectually defensible").

would be disproportionate.¹⁰⁰ The BVerfG further argued that a complete exemption of criminal defence lawyers from the scope of s. 261(2) StGB is, however, not required by the German Basic Law. Instead, an infringement of art. 12(1) GG by s. 261 StGB is justified if a criminal defence lawyer, at the time of receipt of a fee, knows with certainty that the fee stems from a criminal offence mentioned in s. 261(1) StGB.

The BVerfG continued to interpret s. 261(2), (5) StGB in conformity with art. 12(1) GG.¹⁰¹ It pointed out that the enacting legislature deliberately chose a broad wording of s. 261(2) and (5) StGB in order to combat money laundering effectively. The court further explained that the enacting legislature insufficiently considered the constitutional implications of the statutory provision for criminal defence lawyers. The legislative materials contained no information about the alleged constitutionality of this provision with regard to criminal defence lawyers. Since the wording of s. 261(5) StGB clearly applied to criminal defence lawyers who recklessly failed to recognise that the lawyers' fees resulted from a criminal offence, the BVerfG reverted to constitution-consistent judicial law-making (in detail, Section 6.1 below).¹⁰² It declared that it cannot be assumed that the legislature would not have restricted s. 261(5) StGB for criminal defence lawyers had it been aware of the unconstitutionality of the provision. Therefore, a constitution-consistent interpretation of s. 261(5) StGB was deemed possible.¹⁰³ This reasoning of the BVerfG is based on the hypothetical intention of the enacting legislature.¹⁰⁴ It is equivalent to applying a presumption that the

---

¹⁰⁰ BVerfG, *NJW* 2004, 1305, 1310–1311 – *Geldwäsche durch Strafverteidiger*.
¹⁰¹ Ibid., 1311–1312. The BVerfG's methodological reasoning in its written judicial opinion focuses on s. 261(2) StGB, but the reasoning can be applied to s. 261(5) StGB as well. Here, the focus is on the constitution-consistent interpretation of s. 261(5) StGE, which is easier to present.
¹⁰² See ibid., 1310 ("constitution-consistent teleological reduction"). The terminology used by the BVerfG is, however, inconsistent; see ibid., 1310 ("constitution-consistent restrictive interpretation in a narrow sense"). Judicial law-making of criminal legislation that alleviates (instead of aggravates) the defendant's liability in criminal law is not barred by art. 103(2) German Basic Law.
¹⁰³ Confirmed in BVerfG, *NJW* 2015, 2949, para. 46. For criticism of the BVerfG's reasoning, see CANARIS, above n. 11, pp. 141, 151; L. KUHLEN, above n. 11, p. 58. These authors also classify the BVerfG's reasoning as constitution-consistent teleological reduction.
¹⁰⁴ See also BVerfG, *NJW* 1973, 1491, 1494 and BVerfG, *NJW* 1972, 25, 29, where the BVerfG argued that the enacting legislature did not foresee the constitutional implications of the challenged statutory provision and that the legislature would have created a different (constitution-consistent) statutory provision had it seen them. For criticism of a methodological reasoning that is based upon the hypothetical intention of the legislature, see G. RESS, Die richtlinienkonforme "Interpretation" innerstaatlichen Rechts, *DöV* 1994, 489, 491; J. SCHÜRNBRAND, Die Grenzen richtlinienkonformer Rechtsfortbildung im Privatrecht, *JZ* 2007, 910, 916; A. WEISS, Der mutmaßliche Gesetzgeberwille als Argumentationsfigur, *ZRP* 2013, 66–68; cf. LEMBKE, above n. 17, p. 131. For an argument in favour of relying on hypothetical legislative intent in statutory interpretation, see D. LOOSCHELDERS and W. ROTH, *Juristische Methodik im Prozeß der Rechsanwendung*, Duncker & Humblot, Berlin 1996, pp. 227, 298; H. SCHLEHOFER, Juristische Methodologie und Methodik der Fallbearbeitung, *JuS* 1992, 572, 576.

ordinary legislature intended to comply with the German Basic Law.[105] A court that applies the presumption shows respect for the ordinary legislature. Like the interpretative priority rule, the presumption can therefore be reconciled with the underlying reason for the doctrine of constitution-conforming interpretation. It is worth noting that the BVerfG relied on the presumption of compliance even though the wording of s. 261(5) was unambiguous. Furthermore, the BVerfG counted on the reasonably presumed intention of the enacting legislature even though, at the same time, it departed from an identifiable objective of the enacting legislature. In *Geldwäsche durch Strafverteidiger*, the presumption was not rebutted by the specific but inadvertently unconstitutional regulatory decision of the enacting legislature, which found expression in the wording and the legislative history. Presumed intent trumped actual intent. This illustrates the powerful operation of the presumption. Applying the presumption influences the purpose of a provision and how a judge arrives at possible meanings. The presumption is rebutted if a court exceeds an outer limit of interpretation, i.e. a *contra legem* limit. The strength of the presumption thus ultimately depends on how narrowly or widely these limits are drawn.

Even though the BVerfG has applied the principle of constitution-consistent interpretation to legislation pre-dating the German Basic Law, it has not openly argued with the presumed or hypothetical intention of the legislature to comply with the German Basic Law in these cases. That indicates that the presumption of compliance for constitution-conforming interpretation does not apply if the legislation pre-dates the German Basic Law. It does not follow, however, that constitution-conforming interpretation of legislation that pre-dates the German Basic Law is necessarily less far-reaching. The German Basic Law can affect the purpose of legislation that pre-dates it and can influence how a judge arrives at possible meanings of a provision. That is because the BVerfG has held that constitutional values enshrined in the German Basic Law influence the sense and purpose of legislation that also pre-dates it.[106] A provision's purpose is not limited to the purpose ascribed by the enacting legislature but includes "objectivised" elements when the provision is read in context with the whole of German law, which includes the German Basic Law as understood at the time of the provision's application.[107] This is not a surprising result, but flows from the aim of statutory interpretation to ascertain the "objectivised" intention of the legislature as expressed in the provision. The weighing of the interpretative criteria then determines how much weight judges give to the intention of the

---

[105] In favour of such a presumption: IPSEN, above n. 24, p. 156.
[106] Cf. BVerfG, *NJW* 1958, 257 – *Lüth*; BVerfG, *NJW* 1965, 1427, 1428; BVerfG, *NJW* 1979, 534, 536. See also BVerwG, *NVwZ* 1997, 384, 386. For criticism, see HÖPFNER, above n. 80, p. 197.
[107] See J. SCHMIDT-SALZER, Vorkonstitutionelle Gesetze, verfassungskonforme Auslegung und ungeschriebene unbestimmte Rechtsbegriffe, *DöV* 1969, 97, 99; cf. B. BENDER, Inhalt und Grenzen des Gebots der verfassungskonformen Gesetzesauslegung, *MDR* 1959, 441, 446.

enacting legislature compared to the provision's objectivised purpose. How far a judge is able to depart from the purpose ascribed to the legislation by the enacting legislature is a question that is addressed by the outer limits of constitution-consistent interpretation. This, in the end, is a very similar result compared to cases in which the presumption of compliance applies.

English courts have also relied on a presumption of compliance in the realm of Convention-compatible interpretation. Lord Hoffmann argued in *Wilkinson* that s. 3(1) HRA creates a strong presumption that Parliament did not intend to legislate contrary to Convention rights.[108] This "presumption of compliance" goes beyond resolving ambiguities in legislation. It applies even if the statutory language is unambiguous. The presumption of compliance is thus stronger than the presumption employed under conventional canons of interpretation that Parliament intends to give effect to the UK's international obligations fully and consistently. Lord Hoffmann combined the presumption with the notion of ascertaining Parliament's intention as expressed in the actual language of the statute in *Wilkinson*.[109] This understanding of the presumption is at odds with *Ghaidan*, which will be discussed in the next section. The majority of the House of Lords in *Ghaidan* concluded that statutory interpretation under s. 3(1) HRA may require a court to depart from Parliament's intention as expressed in the statutory language.[110] Furthermore, the view that the presumption of compliance "informs but does not displace what it is plausible to think that the enacting legislature decided"[111] cannot be reconciled with *Ghaidan*. That is because the majority in *Ghaidan* relied on s. 3(1) HRA in order to depart from the intention of the enacting legislature. Lord Steyn also pointed out that "Parliament specifically rejected the legislative model of requiring a reasonable interpretation".[112]

Even though criticism of Lord Hoffmann's reasoning is warranted, this does not mean that the presumption of compliance should be rejected as well. Lord Steyn said in *Ghaidan* that "[i]n practical effect there is a strong rebuttable presumption in favour of an interpretation consistent with Convention rights".[113] Lord Justice Sales has remarked extrajudicially that s. 3(1) introduces an interpretative presumption of particular force.[114] One argument in favour of this view is that the presumption of compliance stems from a constitutional statute. The presumption forms part of the context of the challenged legislation.

---

[108] *R. (Wilkinson) v. Inland Revenue Commissioners* [2005] UKHL 30, para. 17 (Lord Hoffmann).
[109] See Section 7.2.2 below.
[110] *Ghaidan v. Godin-Mendoza* [2004] UKHL 30, para. 30 (Lord Nicholls). In detail, see Section 7.2.2 below.
[111] SALES and EKINS, above n. 50, p. 232.
[112] *Ghaidan v. Godin-Mendoza* [2004] UKHL 30, para. 44 (Lord Steyn).
[113] Ibid., para. 50 (Lord Steyn). See also *Hansard*, HL Deb 3 November 1997, vol 582 col 1272 (Lord Cooke, "In effect, the courts are being asked to solve these problems by applying a rebuttable presumption in favour of the convention rights").
[114] SALES and EKINS, above n. 50, p. 232.

Chapter 3. Rights-Consistent Interpretation

It therefore influences the range of possible meanings of the challenged legislation and affects the legislation's purposive interpretation. The presumption of compliance is embodied in s. 3(1) HRA itself and is thus ascribed to the parliament that enacted the HRA. The strength of the presumption ultimately depends on the underlying issue of how the intention of the parliament that enacted the HRA and the intention of the parliament that enacted the challenged legislation can be reconciled. The answer to this issue is not to be found in the presumption itself, but in the outer limits of Convention-compatible interpretation. The presumption of compliance is rebuttable and is refuted if a court exceeds an outer limit of interpretation. In German terminology, the presumption is refuted if a court breaches the *contra legem* limit of interpretation.

Whereas the presumption of compliance in German law does not apply when a court construes legislation pre-dating the German Basic Law, an English court can rely on the presumption of compliance when it construes pre-HRA legislation. Section 3(2)(a) HRA stipulates that the obligation to interpret national legislation compatibly with Convention rights applies to legislation "whenever enacted". For legislation that post-dates the HRA, the presumption of compliance is supported by a statement of compatibility under s. 19(1)(a) HRA that a bill's provisions are compatible with Convention rights. According to Lord Hope in *R. v. A (No. 2)*, such a statement, which is given by a minister in Parliament, indicates that it was not Parliament's intention to infringe a Convention right.[115] Yet s. 19 HRA has not had a significant role in judicial decision-making under s. 3(1) HRA.[116] One reason is that such a statement reflects the will of the executive but cannot be equated with the will of Parliament.[117] Lord Nicholls clarified the role of ministerial statements in Parliament in the course of a debate on a bill for judicial decision-making. He said in *Wilson v. First Country Trust Ltd (No. 2)* that "the courts must be careful not to treat the ministerial or other statement as indicative of the objective intention of Parliament. Nor should the courts give a ministerial statement, whether made inside or outside Parliament, determinative weight".[118] If a statement of compatibility under s. 19(1)(a) HRA were analysed through a German legal lens, its weight in rights-consistent interpretation would

---

[115] *R v. A (No. 2)* [2001] UKHL 25, para. 69 (Lord Hope). Cf. *R. (Simms) v. Secretary of State for the Home Department* [2000] 2 AC 115 (HL), 132 (Lord Hoffmann). This seems to be the view of Lady Hale as well; see *R. (GC) v. Commissioner of Police of the Metropolis* [2011] UKSC 21, para. 70 (Lady Hale).
[116] M. AMOS, *Human rights law*, 2nd ed., Hart, Oxford 2014, p. 144; P. SALES, Partnership and challenge: the courts' role in managing the integration of rights and democracy, [2016] PL 456, 469; cf. *R v. A (No. 2)* [2001] UKHL 25, para. 69 (Lord Hope, "But they are no more than expressions of opinion by the minister. They are not binding on the court, nor do they have any persuasive authority").
[117] For further reasons, see SALES, above n. 116, p. 469.
[118] *Wilson v. First Country Trust Ltd. (No. 2)* [2003] UKHL 40, para. 66 (Lord Nicholls).

probably increase. That is because German courts use legislative materials drafted by the executive that remain unchallenged in the course of a bill's legislative processing as indications of the intention of the enacting legislature. Looked at through a German legal lens, strong weight could be attached to the presumed general intention of the legislature, as evidenced by a ministerial statement under s. 19(1)(a) HRA, to fully comply with Convention rights if a specific objective in the challenged legislation does not prima facie comply with Convention rights.

When comparing the operation of the presumption of compliance in English and German courts, we can see that the German Basic Law and the HRA both function as background constitutional principles when a legislature enacts legislation. That affects the interpretation of "ordinary" legislation via a presumption of compliance. The significant strength of the presumption in English and German courts can to a large extent be explained by its origin: it stems from a higher-order law in Germany and from a constitutional statute in England. The presumption of compliance applies to pre-HRA legislation in England. Therefore, it cannot be described as a presumption as to probable legislative intent of the enacting legislature. The BVerfG has not yet referred to the presumption of compliance when interpreting legislation that pre-dates the German Basic Law. This difference from English judicial practice is surprising because under conventional canons of construction, German courts have clearly and more openly than their English counterparts embraced the search for objective legislative intent. A reason that may explain the reluctance of the BVerfG could simply be that it does not appear convincing to presume that the ordinary legislature in 1922, for example, intended to comply with the German Basic Law. The 1922 legislature could not possibly have foreseen the coming into force of the German Basic Law. It thus appears that the English presumption of compliance is more powerful than its German equivalent. Nonetheless, I have shown that the BVerfG has in the past objectivised the interpretation of pre-GG legislation via a less transparent route. It has held that the German Basic Law can influence the purpose of pre-GG legislation as interpreted at the time of adjudication. In English law, the duty to interpret pre-HRA legislation in conformity with Convention rights is embodied in statute (s. 3(2)(a) HRA, "legislation whenever enacted"). English judges can therefore rely on a statutory base when they apply the presumption of compliance with pre-HRA legislation. German judges cannot rely on an equivalent statutory base. Despite this difference in English and German case law, the German presumption is not necessarily refuted if a German court departs from an identifiable objective of the enacting legislature. Courts in both jurisdictions thus operate a "presumption of objective purpose", which is not necessarily linked to the purpose that the enacting legislature envisioned.[119] The maximum strength of

---

[119] On presumptions of objective purpose, see A. BARAK, *Purposive interpretation in law*, Princeton University Press, Princeton 2005, pp. 170–176, 358–363.

the presumption is ultimately determined by the outer limits of interpretation. Relying on the presumption does not empower courts to surpass an outer limit of interpretation, but a strong presumption of compliance entails wide outer limits of interpretation.

The dogmatic bases for the presumption of compliance (as well as for the interpretative priority rule) are different in both jurisdictions. The presumption derives from s. 3(1) HRA in England, a statutory rule of construction. In German law, the presumption can be traced back to the interest in preserving a legal provision and respect for the ordinary legislature. Both these reasons underlying the presumption of compliance are also the normative reasons justifying the judge-made obligation of constitution-consistent interpretation. The different dogmatic bases for the presumption affect the style of judicial reasoning in both jurisdictions. Whereas the strength of the presumption in England can be seen when a court balances the intentions of two different parliaments, the strength of the presumption in Germany is visible when a court balances the identifiable and the presumed intention of the legislature. How the respective two intentions can be reconciled in individual cases is affected by the outer limits of rights-consistent interpretation.

6. TECHNIQUES OF JUDICIAL LAW-MAKING

6.1. GAP-FILLING

After examining two characteristics of rights-consistent interpretation in both jurisdictions, we will now turn to an analysis of the techniques of judicial law-making in Germany and England. The BVerfG applies the same interpretative techniques for constitution-consistent judicial law-making as for conventional judicial law-making.[120] These techniques have already been presented in Section 3.1 of Chapter 2. In *Geldwäsche durch Strafverteidiger*, the BVerfG used the technique of constitution-consistent teleological reduction. The court did not elaborate much on the details of how it established and filled the gap. Since the BVerfG argued with the hypothetical intention of the legislature, it can be assumed that the gap in the legislation did not simply arise because s. 261(5) StGB, as construed under conventional canons of statutory interpretation, infringed the German Basic Law. The infringement only established the incompleteness of the German legislation. The incompleteness was also unintended (*planwidrig*) since the BVerfG presumed that the ordinary German legislature intended to

---

[120] See, e.g. BVerfG, *NJW* 1993, 2861, 2863; BVerfG, *NJW* 2004, 1305, 1311–1312 – *Geldwäsche durch Strafverteidiger*; BVerfG, *NVwZ* 2015, 510, para. 86.

comply with the German Basic Law. According to this two-step reasoning, a covert gap existed in the legislation.

This reasoning brings to the fore another feature of constitution-consistent judicial law-making: the plan and purpose of the challenged provision, when read in the context of the German Basic Law, is affected by the presumption that the (reasonable) legislature intended to comply with the German Basic Law. I have shown in the preceding section that the presumption can interact with a provision's purpose. It is the purpose of the German Basic Law that requires that a certain case must be excluded from the scope of the provision in order for the provision to be constitutional. It is also recognised under conventional judicial law-making that a provision's sense and purpose can be affected by a provision's relationship with other statutory provisions. The strength of the presumption of compliance is illustrated by *Geldwäsche durch Strafverteidiger*, where the BVerfG relied on the reasonably presumed intention of the legislature in order to establish a gap in the legislation. The notion of gap is objectivised for constitution-consistent judicial law-making as it extends beyond the plan and purpose of the challenged provision as envisaged by the original legislature. In *Geldwäsche durch Strafverteidiger*, the BVerfG closed the gap by excluding the case that a criminal defence lawyer accepts a lawyer's fee from the scope of application of s. 261(5) StGB despite the provision's clear wording.

Cases of constitution-consistent gap-filling by analogy are possible but rare in judicial practice.[121] In these cases, the German Basic Law requires that a certain case must be covered by the scope of a statute. If this case cannot be brought under the terms of a statute by means of interpretation in a narrow sense, the statute prima facie infringes the German Basic Law. This infringement establishes the incompleteness of the legislation. This incompleteness will often be unintended since the BVerfG presumes that the ordinary German legislature intends to comply with the German Basic Law. Therefore, an open gap is established. It is only possible to close this gap via an argument by analogy if a statutory provision exists that governs a fundamentally similar case and whose purpose covers the new case. The gap can then be closed by extending the scope of this provision to cover the hitherto novel case.

6.2. READING IN, OUT OR DOWN OF WORDS IN LEGISLATION

The leading authority on the interpretative powers of the judiciary under s. 3(1) HRA is *Ghaidan*. The case was decided by the House of Lords in

---

[121] See, e.g. BVerfG, *NJW* 1966, 243, 245 and the discussion of this case in CANARIS, above n. 11, pp. 155–156. C. HERRESTHAL, Die richtlinienkonforme und die verfassungskonforme Auslegung im Privatrecht, *JuS* 2014, 289, 297 advocates for a limited admissibility of constitution-consistent gap-filling by analogy.

June 2004.¹²² *Ghaidan* dealt with the question of whether the homosexual partner of a deceased individual is entitled to succeed to a protected tenancy of which the deceased individual was the tenant. Paragraph 2(1) of Sch. 1 to the Rent Act 1977 conferred the right of succession on the surviving "spouse" of the original tenant, and para. 2(2) stipulated that the word spouse includes a person who was living with the tenant "as his or her wife or husband". The question arose whether the words "as his or her wife or husband" in para. 2(2) of Sch. 1 to the Rent Act 1977 could be interpreted so as to include cohabiting homosexual couples. The same question had arisen in *Fitzpatrick*, which was decided by the House of Lords in 1999.

Fitzpatrick also concerned a claim by the survivor of a stable and permanent homosexual relationship. The appellant wanted to be treated as "the surviving spouse" of the original tenant within the meaning of para. 2(1) of Sch. 1 to the Rent Act 1977. The appellant argued that he had lived with the original tenant "as his or her wife or husband". The House of Lords unanimously rejected that claim and ruled that para. 2(2) of Sch. 1 to the Rent Act 1977 did not include persons in a same-sex relationship. That is because Parliament used gender-specific words in para. 2(2), and this plainly indicates a relationship between two persons of opposite sexes.¹²³ Lord Hobhouse said to "accept the submission of the plaintiff would be an exercise of legislation, not interpretation".¹²⁴ Lord Slynn opined that it was Parliament's intention that the words "as his or her wife or husband" refer to partners of opposite sexes, not to homosexual partners.¹²⁵ Parliament would have used different statutory words when it introduced para. 2(2) of Sch. 1 into the Rent Act in 1988 if it had intended that a homosexual partner should have the same protection under the Rent Act as an unmarried heterosexual partner.¹²⁶ The House of Lords interpreted para. 2(2) of Sch. 1 based on conventional canons of statutory interpretation in *Fitzpatrick*. The HRA did not apply to the situation in *Fitzpatrick*, since the original tenant had died before its coming into force. Lord Slynn indicated, however, that this construction of para. 2(2) of Sch. 1 to the Rent Act 1977 might discriminate against same-sex couples and might have to be reconsidered when the HRA was in force.¹²⁷

---

¹²² Pre-*Ghaidan* case law on the scope and limits of s. 3(1) HRA, which was not explicitly approved of in *Ghaidan*, should be approached with caution. Lord Steyn pointed out that this case law may contain a misunderstanding of the proper functioning of s. 3(1) HRA; *Ghaidan v. Godin-Mendoza* [2004] UKHL 30, paras. 38–41 (Lord Steyn).
¹²³ *Fitzpatrick v. Sterling Housing Association Ltd.* [2001] 1 AC 27 (HL), 34 (Lord Slynn), 43 (Lord Nicholls), 47 (Lord Clyde), cf. 57 (Lord Hutton).
¹²⁴ Ibid., 69 (Lord Hobhouse).
¹²⁵ Ibid., 34 (Lord Slynn), cf. 58 (Lord Hutton), 69 (Lord Hobhouse, "Parliament did not go so far as to extend the provision to homosexual relationships akin to marriage …, however close or long lasting, not accompanied by the additional factor of living together as husband and wife").
¹²⁶ Ibid., 34 (Lord Slynn), 58 (Lord Hutton), 72 (Lord Hobhouse).
¹²⁷ Ibid., 34 (Lord Slynn).

In *Ghaidan*, the original tenant died after the HRA came into force. The House of Lords first held that para. 2 of Sch. 1 to the Rent Act 1977 as interpreted in *Fitzpatrick* violated the defendant's rights under art. 14 read in conjunction with art. 8 ECHR.[128] Second, the House of Lords had to decide whether s. 3(1) HRA allows the court to depart from the interpretation of para. 2 of Sch. 1 as declared in *Fitzpatrick* and extend para. 2's reach to the survivor of a couple of the same sex in order to abolish the difference of treatment between homosexual and heterosexual couples. Lord Nicholls, Lord Steyn, Lord Rodger and Lord Millett gave extensive guidance on the scope, limits and application of s. 3(1) HRA in *Ghaidan*.[129] Baroness Hale agreed with Lord Steyn and Lord Rodger on the interpretation of s. 3(1) HRA.[130] By a majority of 4:1, Lord Millett dissenting,[131] the House of Lords held that the term "as his or her wife or husband" applies to persons of the same sex living together in a marriage-like relationship.[132]

Ghaidan clarified that the interpretative techniques available under s. 3(1) HRA go beyond those of conventional principles of construction. Lord Nicholls stated, for example:

[Section 3] is also apt to require a court to read in words which change the meaning of the enacted legislation, so as to make it Convention-compliant. In other words, the intention of Parliament in enacting section 3 was that, to an extent bounded only by what is "possible", a court can modify the meaning, and hence the effect, of primary and secondary legislation.[133]

Lord Rodger opined that the application of s. 3(1) HRA "may involve a considerable departure from the actual words"[134] of the provision. Lord Millett used even stronger language when he stated that a court "can do considerable violence to the language and stretch it almost (but not quite) to breaking point".[135] Case law on s. 3(1) HRA has established that a court can go as far as

---

[128] *Ghaidan v. Godin-Mendoza* [2004] UKHL 30, paras. 5, 24 (Lord Nicholls), paras. 54–55 (Lord Millett), paras. 127–128 (Lord Rodger).

[129] Ibid., paras. 26–35 (Lord Nicholls), paras. 39–50 (Lord Steyn), paras. 59–77 (Lord Millett), paras. 104–124 (Lord Rodger).

[130] Ibid., para. 145 (Baroness Hale).

[131] Lord Millett's speech shows a considerable conformity with the majority's view about the extent and limits of ss. 3(1) and 4 HRA (cf. ibid., para. 69 (Lord Millett)). He mainly disagreed about the application of these principles to the particular facts in *Ghaidan*. For this assessment of Lord Millett's speech, see also A. KAVANAGH, Choosing between sections 3 and 4 of the Human Rights Act 1998: judicial reasoning after Ghaidan v. Mendoza, in H. FENWICK, G. PHILIPSON and R. MASTERMAN (eds.), *Judicial reasoning under the UK Human Rights Act*, CUP, Cambridge 2007, pp. 114, 126.

[132] *Ghaidan v. Godin-Mendoza* [2004] UKHL 30, para. 35 (Lord Nicholls), para. 51 (Lord Steyn), para. 129 (Lord Rodger), para. 144 (Baroness Hale).

[133] Ibid., para. 30 (Lord Nicholls).

[134] Ibid., para. 119 (Lord Rodger).

[135] Ibid., para. 67 (Lord Millett).

Chapter 3. Rights-Consistent Interpretation

reading in[136] additional words in legislation, reading out[137] words in legislation and reading down[138] general words in legislation.

Lord Rodger and Lord Nicholls emphasised in *Ghaidan* that if a court reads words into a provision, their number or precise form are insignificant; only their substantive effect matters.[139] Lord Rodger also pointed out that

> [t]he preferred technique will depend on the particular provision and also, in reality, on the person doing the interpreting. This does not matter since they are simply different means of achieving the same substantive result. … It is enough that the interpretation placed on the provision should be clear, however it may be expressed and whatever the precise means adopted to achieve it.[140]

The substance of the Convention-compatible interpretation must be clear. The clarity of the substantive result also presupposes that a court must identify clearly the particular provision or provisions that it interprets pursuant to its obligation under s. 3(1) HRA.[141] This requirement contains an interpretative limit for s. 3(1) HRA. It is a formal aspect of Convention-compatible interpretation that aims to achieve a higher degree of legal certainty.[142] Furthermore, Lord Rodger said that only the substantive result of the Convention-compatible interpretation as opposed to the language used or the interpretative technique employed matters. This is a clear deviation from conventional canons of construction. That does not mean that this deviation is incompatible with the absolute doctrine of parliamentary sovereignty. I have argued that the orthodox constitutional doctrine is capable of supporting a system of interpretation according to

---

[136] *R. v. A (No. 2)* [2001] UKHL 25, para. 44 (Lord Steyn); *Ghaidan v. Godin-Mendoza* [2004] UKHL 30, para. 32 (Lord Nicholls), para. 67 (Lord Millett), paras. 117, 121–124 (Lord Rodger). For examples, see *Principal Reporter v. K* [2010] UKSC 56, paras. 69–70 (Lord Hope and Lady Hale, giving the judgment of the court); *Goode v. Martin* [2001] EWCA Civ 1899, paras. 45–47 (Brooke LJ, with whom Latham LJ and Kay LJ agreed).

[137] *R. v. Holding* [2005] EWCA Crim 3185, para. 49 (Simon J, "we would read down the words of s. 75 by deleting the word 'or'").

[138] *R. v. A (No. 2)* [2001] UKHL 25, para. 44 (Lord Steyn); *Ghaidan v. Godin-Mendoza* [2004] UKHL 30, para. 67 (Lord Millett), para. 124 (Lord Rodger). For examples, see *Attorney General's Reference (No. 4 of 2002)* [2004] UKHL 43, para. 53 (Lord Bingham); *R. v. Waya* [2012] UKSC 51, paras. 14–16 (Lord Walker and Sir Anthony Hughes, with whom Lady Hale, Lord Judge, Lord Kerr, Lord Clarke and Lord Wilson agreed); *R. (M) v. Hackney London Borough Council* [2011] EWCA Civ 4, para. 66 (Toulson LJ).

[139] *Ghaidan v. Godin-Mendoza* [2004] UKHL 30, para. 35 (Lord Nicholls), paras. 122–123 (Lord Rodger). For a different view in pre-*Ghaidan* case law, see *R. v. Lambert* [2001] UKHL 37, para. 80 (Lord Hope).

[140] Ibid., para. 124 (Lord Rodger).

[141] *In re S (Minors)* [2002] UKHL 10, paras. 41, 43 (Lord Nicholls). Cf. *Ghaidan v. Godin-Mendoza* [2004] UKHL 30, para. 113 (Lord Rodger).

[142] ARDEN, above n. 73, pp. 165, 178.

Intersentia

which judicial law-making is generally permissible in order to give effect to the intention of the enacting legislature. Lord Rodger's focus on the substance rather than on the language of a provision is a theme that runs through the whole of his remarks on the characteristics and limits of Convention-compatible interpretation. It also lies at the heart of the majority's view in *Ghaidan*.

If the *substance* of the Convention-compatible interpretation must be clear, then a court must arguably be clear about whether it extends or limits the substantive scope of application of a provision. As in Germany, judicial law-making under s. 3(1) HRA concentrates on whether the field of application of a provision is widened or narrowed beyond its wording. It does not focus on which adjustments to the statutory language are necessary in order to achieve the substantive result. Distinguishing between substance and language when assessing techniques of interpretation was also undertaken by Lord Nicholls in *Inco Europe*. Yet *Ghaidan* went much further than applying *Inco Europe's* conditions.[143] Except for the limitation that the interpretative result must be clear, no further conditions regarding the language used or the interpretative technique employed are discernible. This illustrates the clear opposite of a restrictive approach to judicial law-making under s. 3(1) HRA. There is also no indication in the case law that the reading of additional words into a statute would be an exceptional use of judicial powers.[144] *Ghaidan* therefore liberates the interpretative role of judges under s. 3(1) HRA from the fetters of literalism. In the words of Lord Steyn: "Nowhere in our legal system is a literalistic approach more inappropriate than when considering whether a breach of a Convention right may be removed by interpretation under section 3".[145] When having recourse to s. 3(1) HRA, a court's interpretative role is not limited to seeking the intention reasonably to be attributed to Parliament in using the language in question.[146] Unlike conventional canons of construction, the default position is not that judicial law-making is generally impermissible under s. 3(1). It is rather that Convention-compatible judicial law-making is generally permissible. On the one hand, it has been shown that such a change in default position is not incompatible with the constitutional doctrine of parliamentary sovereignty as expressed in the Diceyan orthodoxy as long as courts do not depart from the intention of the enacting parliament.[147] On the other hand, if we take the orthodox doctrine of parliamentary sovereignty as it has developed in courts, with judges deriving legislative intent from the actual words used by Parliament,

---

[143] But see *Rowstock Ltd. v. Jessemey* [2014] EWCA Civ 185, paras. 38, 53 (Underhill LJ): "it seems that in the particular case of a frank drafting error ... there is no real difference between the Ghaidan approach and the approach based on purely domestic principles".
[144] SALES, above n. 73, p. 608 speaks of "considerable freedom" to read words into legislation.
[145] *Ghaidan v. Godin-Mendoza* [2004] UKHL 30, para. 41 (Lord Steyn).
[146] Ibid., para. 30 (Lord Nicholls).
[147] See Chapter 2, Section 5.

Chapter 3. Rights-Consistent Interpretation

then the courts' interpretation of s. 3(1) HRA signals a deviation from the doctrine as it has been traditionally understood. As S. Gardbaum has put it, s. 3(1) HRA "gives to the courts substantial scope to rewrite Acts of Parliament employing a broad, purposive method of interpretation that is once again alien to the British conception of judicial function under the separation of powers".[148]

In *Ghaidan*, the House of Lords applied s. 3(1) HRA and read para. 2 of Sch. 1 to the Rent Act 1977 as though the survivor of a homosexual couple living together in a close and stable relationship were the surviving spouse of the original tenant.[149] This meaning of the provision could not have been achieved by a reading down of the words "as his or her wife or husband". The House of Lords read additional words into para. 2 of Sch. 1 to the Rent Act 1977 in order to expand its field of application. Yet none of the judges in *Ghaidan* specified the precise form or number of words read into para. 2 of Sch. 1 to the Rent Act 1977 for this purpose.

Another case which illustrates that the interpretative techniques of s. 3(1) HRA go beyond conventional canons of construction is *R. v. A (No. 2)*. The case involved the interpretation of s. 41 of the Youth Justice and Criminal Evidence Act 1999. The provision applied to trials at which a person is charged with a sexual offence. Section 41 of the 1999 Act contained a general exclusion of evidence and questions about a complainant's prior sexual history except in certain circumstances with the leave of the court. The provision had been enacted just the year before the decision in *R. v. A*, and it severely curbed judicial discretion to admit sexual history evidence of the complainant in rape trials. Section 41 of the 1999 Act sought to protect the complainant from indignity and from humiliating questions about their sexual behaviour and history.[150] The provision read:

> If at a trial a person is charged with a sexual offence, then, except with the leave of the court – (a) no evidence may be adduced, and (b) no question may be asked in cross-examination, by or on behalf of any accused at the trial, about any sexual behaviour of the complainant.

According to s. 41(2) of the 1999 Act, a court may give leave if subsection (3) applies. Section 41(3)(c) permits evidence where

> it is an issue of consent and the sexual behaviour of the complainant to which the evidence or question relates is alleged to have been, in any respect, so similar – (i) to any sexual behaviour of the complainant which (according to evidence adduced or to

---

[148] S. Gardbaum, The new commonwealth model of constitutionalism, (2001) 49 *AJCL* 707, 738–739.
[149] Ibid., para. 35 (Lord Nicholls), para. 129 (Lord Rodger).
[150] *R. v. A (No. 2)* [2001] UKHL 25, para. 46 (Lord Steyn), paras. 142, 144 (Lord Hutton).

be adduced by or on behalf of the accused) took place as part of the event which is the subject matter of the charge against the accused ... that the similarity cannot reasonably be explained as a coincidence.

When *R. v. A (No. 2)* reached the House of Lords, the judges considered whether the exclusion of evidence about previous sexual experience between the complainant and the accused by s. 41 of the Youth Justice and Criminal Evidence Act 1999 was incompatible with the right to a fair trial under art. 6 ECHR. The majority, Lord Hope dissenting, agreed that s. 41 of the 1999 Act contained a prima facie excessive inroad on the right to a fair trial.[151] Lord Steyn opined that on traditional methods of purposive construction s. 41(3)(c) cannot be interpreted to cover cases similar to the one before the House of Lords, where it was alleged that there was a previous sexual experience between the complainant and the accused on several occasions during three weeks prior to the alleged rape. Hence, s. 41(3)(c) as interpreted under the ordinary method of purposive construction could not prevent the infringement of art. 6 ECHR in the case at issue.[152] Lord Steyn went on to consider s. 3(1) HRA. He regarded the detailed language of s. 41(3)(c) of the 1999 Act as unambiguous,[153] a view that was also shared by Lord Nicholls in *Ghaidan*.[154] Lord Steyn then relied on s. 3(1) HRA to interpret s. 41(3)(c) of the Youth Justice and Criminal Evidence Act 1999 "as subject to the implied provision that evidence or questioning which is required to ensure a fair trial under article 6 of the Convention should not be treated as inadmissible".[155] Lord Slynn and Lord Hutton agreed with this reasoning.[156] The House of Lords effectively extended the scope of application of s. 41(3)(c) in order to make it Convention compliant by reading additional words into the provision. None of the judges stipulated the number or precise form of those words.

An example of a reading down of statutory language is provided by *Attorney General's Reference (No. 4 of 2002)*. At issue was the interpretation of s. 11(2) of the Terrorism Act 2000, which unambiguously imposed a legal burden of proof on a defendant in criminal proceedings.[157] The majority held that this

---

[151] Ibid., para. 10 (Lord Slynn), para. 43 (Lord Steyn); see also para. 136 (Lord Clyde). Cf. Lord Hope's dissent at ibid., para. 106.
[152] Ibid., para. 43 (Lord Steyn). See also ibid., para. 161 (Lord Hutton).
[153] Ibid., para. 44 (Lord Steyn).
[154] *Ghaidan v. Godin-Mendoza* [2004] UKHL 30, para. 29 (Lord Nicholls).
[155] *R. v. A (No. 2)* [2001] UKHL 25, para. 45 (Lord Steyn).
[156] Ibid., para. 13 (Lord Slynn), para. 163 (Lord Hutton). Even though Lord Clyde also agreed with this interpretative outcome, he left open the question of whether it could be reached under conventional principles of statutory interpretation or by having recourse to s. 3(1) HRA; see ibid., paras. 137, 140.
[157] *Attorney General's Reference (No. 4 of 2002)* [2004] UKHL 43, paras. 7, 50 (Lord Bingham, with whom Lord Phillips and Lord Steyn agreed), para. 68 (Lord Rodger).

would infringe Convention rights. The majority of the House of Lords applied s. 3(1) HRA and read down s. 11(2) of the Terrorism Act 2000 so as to impose on the defendant an evidential and not a legal burden.[158] The House of Lords thus limited the provision's reach. This would not have been possible under conventional canons of construction.[159] In the spirit of *Ghaidan* and *R. v. A (No. 2)*, the House of Lords focused on the substantive change and did not elaborate on what alterations to the language of s. 11(2) of the 2000 Act are necessary in order to restrict its field of application.[160]

6.3. COMPARATIVE ANALYSIS

English and German courts can expand or restrict the scope of application of a provision beyond its wording under rights-consistent judicial law-making. The number or precise form of the words that are read into a provision are insignificant. A reluctance to read additional words into legislation cannot be detected in English courts. It is the substantive result of the rights-consistent interpretation that matters in both jurisdictions. There are, however, differences. The interpretative technique used to reach a Convention-compatible meaning does not matter in English courts. No German court has yet declared that the interpretative technique employed in order to reach a constitution-consistent meaning is insignificant. The opposite is true: interpretative technique matters. A German court must establish a gap. An argument by analogy and a teleological reduction require certain conditions to be fulfilled.[161] Yet, these differences between the two jurisdictions should not be overstated.

The concept of gap in German legal methodology requires that the legislation is incomplete and that this incompleteness is unintended. For constitution-consistent judicial law-making, the incompleteness arises out of

---

[158] Ibid., para. 53 (Lord Bingham, with whom Lord Phillips and Lord Steyn agreed).
[159] Ibid., para. 7 (Lord Bingham, with whom Lord Phillips and Lord Steyn agreed).
[160] This was different in the *pre-Ghaidan* case *R. v. Lambert* [2001] UKHL 37, where the majority of the House of Lords argued *obiter* that s. 28(2) and (3) of the Misuse of Drugs Act 1971 could be read down under s. 3(1) HRA so as to impose only an evidential burden. Lord Steyn, at para. 42, and Lord Hope, at para. 84 ("As it is a rule of construction, the exercise which section 3(1) prescribes makes it necessary to identify the words used by the legislature which would otherwise be incompatible with the Convention right and then to say how these words are to be construed according to the rule to make them compatible") and at para. 94, described how the existing statutory language in s. 28(2) and (3) had to be read in order to be rights consistent.
[161] Argument by analogy and teleological reduction are interpretative techniques *praeter legem*. If their conditions are not met, it does not follow automatically that judicial law-making is impermissible. A court may still engage in judicial law-making *extra legem* (for an overview see K. LARENZ and C.-W. CANARIS, *Methodenlehre der Rechtswissenschaft*, 3rd ed., Springer, Berlin 1995, pp. 245–252).

the prima facie unconstitutionality of a provision or statute as interpreted in a narrow sense. Similarly, s. 3(1) HRA only comes into play if Convention rights are infringed by the challenged legislation as interpreted under conventional canons of construction. The function of the unintendedness condition for gap-filling in German law is to separate permissible judicial interpretation from impermissible judicial legislation.[162] This function is fulfilled by the outer limits of Convention-compatible interpretation in English law. This brings us to the question of whether the concept of gap in German legal methodology fulfils a function that justifies its existence. Comparing judicial law-making in Germany with English case law on s. 3(1) HRA elucidates that the concept of a gap in the legislation as a requirement for legitimate judicial law-making can best be explained by historical context and tradition. One criticism of the concept of gap is that is does not capture the legal reality that gaps in the legislation are not an exception but the rule.[163] Notwithstanding this criticism, the concept of gap is dispensable.[164] The first function of this concept, to demarcate judicial law-making from interpretation in a narrow sense, is dispensable because both modes of interpretation constitute permissible judicial activity as long as they remain within the outer limits of interpretation.[165] The second role of the concept of gap is to demarcate judicial law-making from amendment of legislation. This objective is fully captured by the outer limits of statutory interpretation in Germany, which ultimately determine the constitutional issue of the limits of the judicial role. The congruence in the functions of the outer interpretative limits and the concept of gap explains why it sometimes appears random in judicial decision-making when a court either rejects a gap in the legislation or decides that the outer limits of judicial law-making are exceeded. The congruence also explains why the reasoning of a court in some decisions[166] as to why there is no gap in the legislation and as to why the outer limits of interpretation are breached is the same.

---

[162] C.-W. CANARIS, Die richtlinienkonforme Auslegung und Rechtsfortbildung im System der juristischen Methodenlehre, in H. KOZIOL et al. (eds.), *Festschrift für Franz Bydlinski*, Springer, Vienna 2002, pp. 47, 83; cf. K. LANGENBUCHER, Argument by analogy in European law, (1998) 57 *CLJ* 481, 485.

[163] RÜTHERS, FISCHER and BIRK, above n. 17, para. 822.

[164] For criticism of the concept of gap, see also C. HILLGRUBER, in T. MAUNZ and G. DÜRIG (founders), *Grundgesetz-Kommentar*, C.H. Beck, Munich 2017, Art. 97 GG, paras. 69–70; H. KELSEN, *Introduction to the problems of legal theory*, Clarendon Press, Oxford 1997, §§40–42; KOCH and RÜßMANN, above n. 96, p. 254; M. JESTAEDT, Richterliche Rechtsetzung statt richterliche Rechtsfortbildung, in C. BUMKE (ed.), *Richterrecht zwischen Gesetzesrecht und Rechtsgestaltung*, Mohr Siebeck, Tübingen 2012, pp. 49, 60–61.

[165] An exception applies to judicial law-making of criminal legislation to the detriment of the defendant, which is excluded in Germany due to art. 103(2) GG. Since judicial law-making is impermissible in such a case, the concept of gap is dispensable in this case as well.

[166] See, e.g. BAG, *NZA* 2010, 1020 paras. 30, 46 – *Urlaubsentgelt* (for the EU legal duty of conforming interpretation).

The third function of the concept of gap is transparency.[167] Since judicial law-making departs from the statutory words, it raises issues of the binding nature of the statute, the separation of powers and legal certainty to a significant degree. The concept of gap alerts a judge that he or she is active at the outer borders of the judicial role. It is submitted that the function of transparency does not justify a separate methodological criterion that is as indeterminate as the concept of gap in German judicial practice. The border between a wide or restrictive interpretation in a narrow sense and judicial law-making is not clear cut but fuzzy. The interpretative criteria are ultimately used by courts in order to establish and fill a gap in a provision or a statute. The weighing of these criteria depends on the circumstances of the individual case. In a similar vein, but without the concept of gap, English judges use the interpretative criteria when they decide whether or not a court can depart from the wording of the challenged legislation under s. 3(1) HRA. What should be necessary and sufficient is that a judge reveals in his or her reasoning if an interpretation goes beyond or against the possible semantic meanings of the statutory words. Once this has been done, judges are aware that they operate at the constitutional junction between interpretation and legislation. This is illustrated by English judicial practice. The comparison with English law thus shows that the concept of gap is superfluous for judicial law-making as applied in German judicial practice.

What is also interesting from a comparative perspective is that English judges have not limited their general power of judicial law-making under s. 3(1) HRA by adopting formal techniques such as argument by analogy or teleological reduction. That was a judicial choice. Even though no such technique can be deduced from the vague words of s. 3(1) HRA, the question remains why English judges have not adopted formal techniques of judicial law-making, which restrict judicial power. First, the absence of such a technical requirement appears to offer greater law-making powers to the judges. Second, we will see that a court's law-making power under s. 3(1) HRA is constrained by the outer limits of interpretation. It appears questionable whether a formal technical requirement such as argument by analogy adds any further constraint to current judicial practice. The third and arguably most significant reason is the historical context. Under the literal rule as it developed in England, informed by the constitutional doctrine of parliamentary sovereignty, gap-filling belonged to the realm of impermissible judicial amendment of legislation. English judges avoided using existing statutes as a source of analogy. Argument by analogy in the area of statutory interpretation carried the stigma of "a naked usurpation of the legislative function under the thin disguise of interpretation".[168] Adopting the terminology of argument by analogy as a technique of interpretation

---

[167] B. RÜTHERS, *Die unbegrenzte Auslegung*, 7th ed., Mohr Siebeck, Tübingen 2012, p. 515.
[168] *Magor and St Mellons Rural DC v. Newport Corp* [1952] AC 189 (HL), 191 (Lord Simonds).

for s. 3(1) HRA would bring this stigma into the area of rights-consistent interpretation.

English courts often use the terms "reading in" and "reading down" in the context of Convention-compatible interpretation.[169] These terms focus on the alteration of a provision's wording rather than a provision's scope of application. This terminology is also associated with an understanding of parliamentary sovereignty where legislative intent is taken to be derived from the actual language used by Parliament. The continuing use of this terminology is surprising because English courts have made the transition from language to substance when describing their interpretative powers under s. 3(1) HRA. Historical context and tradition can explain the continuing use of this terminology. It would be more appropriate if English courts simply adopted the terminology of extending or narrowing the scope of application of a provision. These latter terms are also applied by German courts and relate to an alteration of the substantive scope of application of a provision.

Even though English courts have not adopted formal techniques of judicial law-making, a comparison with German judicial practice shows that it does not necessarily follow from this that English judges have greater powers than German judges to make law. German courts engage in rights-consistent teleological reduction if the wording of a provision covers a certain case and if the German Basic Law requires that the case falls outside the provision's scope of application. If Convention rights require that a certain case falls outside a provision's scope of application, an English court can, depending on the provision's specific language, read in, out or down words in legislation in order to achieve this result. If a certain case must be covered by the scope of application of a statute in order for the legislation to be compatible with the German Basic Law, an argument by analogy can be used to achieve this result. If a certain case must be covered by the scope of application of a statute in order for the legislation to be compatible with Convention rights, an English court can read in, out or down words in legislation. An argument by analogy in German law requires that a statutory provision exists that governs a case that is fundamentally similar to the novel case. An argument by analogy will fail if an existing statute does not contain a provision that is fundamentally similar to the novel case.[170] The fundamental similarity criterion restricts judicial power to make law. No similar restriction seems to exist under s. 3(1) HRA, even though there are certainly English judgments[171] where a de facto reasoning by analogy appeared but without any such formal technical requirement. Despite this apparent difference between

---

[169] See, e.g. *Principal Reporter v. K* [2010] UKSC 56, paras. 69–70 (Lord Hope and Lady Hale, giving the judgment of the court).

[170] It is assumed here that a *Gesamtanalogie* (cf. Chapter 2, Section 3.1) is also not possible.

[171] See, e.g. *Manchester City Council v. Pinnock* [2010] UKSC 45, para. 77 (Lord Neuberger, giving the judgment of the court).

English and German judicial practice, an English court must identify clearly the particular provision or provisions that it interprets pursuant to its obligation under s. 3(1) HRA. A court "cannot construe something out of nothing".[172] It follows that a certain kind of link must exist between what is already stipulated in the statute and what can possibly be read into it by means of judicial interpretation. Furthermore, English courts recognise that they cannot create a different legislative scheme from the one enacted in the legislation by resorting to s. 3(1) HRA. These factors suggest that the difference in both jurisdictions with regard to analogical reasoning may be negligible in practice.

Whether this is actually the case is difficult to answer because argument by analogy has hardly been used by German courts for constitution-consistent judicial law-making. The parallel to argument by analogy under conventional judicial law-making shows that a "fundamental similarity" between the governed and the novel case is determined by a provision's intended plan and purpose. Whether or not a similarity is fundamental enough leaves ample scope for evaluative arguments and judicial discretion. The purpose of a provision can be expressed in narrow or wide terms, and case law is devoid of guidelines or factors determining the necessary level of specificity/generality of a provision's purpose. Furthermore, the plan and purpose of a provision that is read in the context of the German Basic Law is affected by the presumption that the legislature intended to comply with the German Basic Law. The presumption interacts with the provision's purpose, and this also influences how a gap can be filled. The impact of the presumption of compliance ultimately leads to a balancing exercise between the intention of the enacting parliament and the presumed intention of the reasonable legislature to comply with the German Basic Law. Similarly, s. 3(1) HRA ultimately requires a judge to balance the intention of the parliament that enacted the challenged legislation and the intention of the parliament that enacted s. 3(1) HRA. In neither jurisdiction is that balancing exercise governed by clear principled guidelines or an (exhaustive) list of factors.

In order to illustrate the abstract comparison of the techniques of judicial law-making in England and Germany, it seems helpful to create a hypothetical situation equivalent to *Ghaidan* under German law. In order to treat like with like, the national legislation would have pre-dated the German Basic Law, since the challenged legislation in *Ghaidan* pre-dated the HRA. Assuming that the legislation as interpreted in a narrow sense would have infringed fundamental rights protected by the German Basic Law, it is difficult to predict whether or not a German court would have been able to establish a gap in the legislation. It appears to be a borderline case. This may be contrasted with Baroness Hale's and

---

[172] See for conforming interpretation: *Fleming (t/a Bodycraft) v. Customs and Excise Commissioners* [2006] EWCA Civ 70, para. 80 (Ward LJ), para. 67 (Hallet LJ).

Lord Steyn's remarks that the Convention-compatible construction of para. 2 of Sch. 1 to the Rent Act 1977 was "well within" the bounds of what is possible under s. 3(1) HRA.[173] The difference in the strengths of the interpretative obligations exists because the context of the challenged legislation would not have included a presumption of compliance with the German Basic Law as the legislation pre-dated the German Basic Law. The hypothetical historical legislature could not have anticipated the German Basic Law. In comparison, s. 3(2)(a) HRA clearly empowers judges to interpret pre-HRA legislation in conformity with Convention rights. Despite this difference, we have seen that the constitutional values enshrined in the German Basic Law also influence the sense and purpose of legislation that precedes the German Basic Law. The intention of the legislature is "objectivised". Since the notion of gap for constitution-consistent judicial law-making is not only determined by the sense and purpose of the challenged provision but also by the context of the German Basic Law, a German court may been able to assume a gap in this hypothetical case.

The gap would have been open. The wording of the Rent Act did not cover the survivor of a homosexual couple living together in a close and stable relationship, but this case would have been covered by the purpose of the Act read in the light of the German Basic Law. The gap would have been closed by an argument by analogy because the survivor of a couple living together as husband and wife and the survivor of a homosexual couple living together in a close and stable relationship are in a fundamentally similar situation, judged by the underlying purpose of the Act. Lord Nicholls alluded to the fundamental similarity between both cases in *Ghaidan* when he said that "the social policy underlying the 1988 extension of security of tenure under paragraph 2 to the survivor of couples living together as husband and wife is equally applicable to the survivor of homosexual couples living together in a close and stable relationship".[174] Similarly, Baroness Hale stated in *Ghaidan* that a homosexual couple in a close and stable relationship are in an "analogous situation" to an unmarried heterosexual couple in such a relationship for the purposes of para. 2 of Sch. 1 to the Rent Act 1977.[175] A German court would have closed the gap by extending the scope of the Rent Act. The legal consequence (the right to succeed to a protected tenancy) would have been applied analogously to a survivor of a homosexual couple in a close and stable relationship.

All in all, the result of the comparison of the techniques of judicial law-making is that differences in terminology and classification, firmly anchored in historical context and in legal practice in both jurisdictions, are readily apparent.

---

[173] *Ghaidan v. Godin-Mendoza* [2004] UKHL 30, para. 51 (Lord Steyn), para. 144 (Baroness Hale).
[174] Ibid., para. 35 (Lord Nicholls).
[175] Ibid., paras. 138, 143 (Baroness Hale).

Chapter 3. Rights-Consistent Interpretation

If we turn the focus to substance, however, it becomes equally apparent that English and German courts proceed on converging lines. The extent of the commonalities is quite significant.

7. OUTER INTERPRETATIVE LIMITS

7.1. CONSTITUTION-CONSISTENT INTERPRETATION

This core section of the chapter will critically analyse the outer limits of rights-consistent judicial law-making as applied in German and English courts. The BVerfG applies the same interpretative limits for constitution-consistent judicial law-making as for conventional judicial law-making.[176] These limits have already been discussed in Chapter 2. This case law is justified as the constitutional doctrines of the separation of powers and the binding force of statute enshrined in art. 20(2), (3) GG do not differentiate between different modes of statutory interpretation within the national sphere. A provision cannot be given a certain constitution-consistent meaning if a court surpasses these limits by adopting that meaning. For example, a constitution-consistent meaning of a provision must be reached by applying recognised canons of statutory interpretation which include the recognised techniques of judicial law-making.[177] BVerfG case law further requires that a constitution-consistent interpretation must leave a provision with a reasonable meaning (*Sinn*) which does not contradict the provision's identifiable purpose.[178] This requirement implies that a teleological reduction with the effect of reducing the scope of application of a provision to zero, which amounts to a de facto repeal of the provision, cannot be reached by means of constitution-consistent interpretation.[179] The BVerfG has also clarified that a constitution-consistent interpretation is not permissible if the unconstitutionality of the provision or statute can be rectified in different ways by the legislature. That is because a court is not allowed to interfere with the freedom of the legislature.[180] In such a case, a regular court is required to initiate concrete judicial review of the challenged provision under the terms of art. 100 GG, and the BVerfG will declare invalid the unconstitutional provision.

---

[176] See, e.g. BVerfG, *NJW* 1993, 2861, 2863; BVerfG, *NJW* 2004, 1305, 1311–1312 – *Geldwäsche durch Strafverteidiger*; BVerfG, *NVwZ* 2015, 510, para. 86.
[177] BVerfG, *NJW* 1993, 2861, 2863; BVerfG, *NVwZ* 2015, 510, para. 86.
[178] See BVerfG, *NJW* 1959, 1123; BVerfG, *NJW* 1972, 1934, 1937; BVerfG, *NJW* 1982, 1375, 1378; BVerfG, *NJW* 2000, 347, 349.
[179] See also CANARIS, above n. 18, p. 57. Cf. BVerfG, *NJW* 2000, 347, 349.
[180] BVerfG, *NJW* 2000, 55, 67; BVerfG, *NJW* 2000, 1175, 1178–1179. See also BVerfG, *NJW* 1985, 2315, 2318 (dissenting opinion of Judge Steinberger).

Despite the commonalities between the limits and techniques of conventional and constitution-consistent judicial law-making, the latter exhibits certain features that merit closer examination. The BVerfG has clarified that a court is obliged to choose a possible constitution-consistent meaning of a provision even if strong arguments count in favour of a meaning that infringes the German Basic Law.[181] For example, it is immaterial whether a possible unconstitutional meaning would better correspond with the actual intention of the enacting legislature than a possible constitution-consistent meaning.[182] It is thus clear that a court can depart from the actual intention of the enacting legislature under constitution-consistent interpretation. A court can restrict or complement the enacting legislature's intention when interpreting national law in conformity with the German Basic Law as long as this interpretation stays within the framework set by the outer interpretative limits.[183] What the BVerfG has not specified is how far a court can go in restricting or complementing the intention of the legislature. This is governed by the outer limits of constitution-consistent interpretation, and this ultimately depends on the weighing of the interpretative criteria in an individual case. In *Geldwäsche durch Strafverteidiger*, for example, the BVerfG based its reasoning on the presumed intent of the enacting legislature and, at the same time, departed from an identifiable objective of the enacting legislature. It cannot be ruled out that a court would be able to fully depart from the intention of the enacting legislature under constitution-consistent judicial law-making in an individual case if a parallel is drawn to the BVerfG's *Soraya* decision. As in *Soraya*, a court could adopt an "objectivised" meaning of the challenged provision even if that meaning cannot reasonably be attributed to the enacting legislature. That this option exists is particularly relevant for those cases in which the contested legislation pre-dates the German Basic Law. I will show later in this section, however, that contemporary BVerfG case law places a significant role on the intention of the enacting legislature. It is thus doubtful whether a German court would nowadays fully depart from the intention of the enacting legislature in an individual case.

The BVerfG's *Eilversammlungen* ruling is an example of how far the BVerfG was willing to go in the past when complementing the legislature's intention.[184] The question arose whether express assemblies (*Eilversammlungen*) need to comply with s. 14(1) German Assembly Act (*Versammlungsgesetz*, VersG). Express assemblies are assemblies that are being planned and that have an organiser, but which cannot be registered with the responsible administrative authority within the registration period provided by s. 14(1) VersG without

---

[181] Cf. BVerfG, *NJW* 1982, 1509.
[182] BVerfG, *NJW* 1959, 1123; BVerfG, *NJW* 1979, 151; BVerfG, *NJW* 1982, 1375, 1378; BVerfG, *NJW* 1985, 1519, 1528; BVerfG, *NVwZ* 1996, 574, 578.
[183] BVerfG, *NJW* 1958, 1227; cf. BVerfG, *NJW* 1959, 1123–1124.
[184] BVerfG, *NJW* 1992, 890–891 – *Eilversammlungen*.

threatening the purpose of the assembly.[185] Section 14 VersG obliges anybody who intends to organise a public outdoor assembly to inform the responsible administrative authority of this intention "at least 48 hours before announcing" the decision to stage an assembly. The majority of judges in *Eilversammlungen* held that if the registration period provided by s. 14(1) VersG were to apply to express assemblies, express assemblies would be inadmissible from the outset. Section 14(1) VersG would thus be inconsistent with the freedom of assembly guaranteed under art. 8 GG. The majority avoided this result by arguing that s. 14(1) VersG can be interpreted in conformity with the German Basic Law by shortening the registration period for express assemblies.[186] Express assemblies must be registered as soon as registration is possible. The clear wording of s. 14(1) VersG ("at least 48 hours before announcing") did not bar this constitution-consistent interpretation according to the majority. The dissenting minority disagreed with this assessment.[187] The majority opinion in *Eilversammlungen* shows that the constitution-consistent interpretation went beyond the clear wording of s. 14(1) VersG. In contrast to the dissenting minority, the majority attached very little weight to the provision's clear wording. The term "at least" 48 hours excludes a shorter time period. Furthermore, the majority did not simply exclude express assemblies from the scope of s. 14(1) VersG, e.g. by giving a restrictive interpretation to the term "assembly". A teleological reduction or an argument by analogy could not have brought about the interpretative result reached by the BVerfG. Instead, the majority modified the meaning of s. 14(1) VersG for express assemblies. It effectively replaced the obligation to register an assembly "at least 48 hours before announcing" the decision to stage an assembly with the obligation to register an assembly "as soon as registration is possible". The dissenting minority rightly pointed out that this "interpretation" amounts to a judicial supplementing of the requirements of s. 14(1) VersG.[188]

The BVerfG's *Eilversammlungen* judgment illustrates that constitution-consistent interpretation can modify the meaning of a provision. That is also recognised under s. 3(1) HRA in England. Yet, Lord Nicholls expressed this judicial power in more transparent terms in *Ghaidan*[189] than the BVerfG has ever done for constitution-consistent interpretation. This difference in the level of transparency may be explained by s. 3(1) HRA being a statutory rule of construction. The modification of a provision's meaning is (allegedly) traceable to the will of the parliament that enacted the HRA. An equivalent explanation relating to the text of the German Basic Law and to the intention of

---

[185] Ibid., 890–891.
[186] Ibid., 891.
[187] Ibid., 891, dissenting opinion by Judges Seibert and Henschel.
[188] Ibid., 891.
[189] *Ghaidan v. Godin-Mendoza* [2004] UKHL 30, para. 30 (Lord Nicholls).

its authors is not possible for the judge-made doctrine of constitution-consistent interpretation. The BVerfG's *Eilversammlungen* ruling further shows that policy choices can be made by a court when interpreting a provision in conformity with the German Basic Law. If the BVerfG had declared s. 14(1) VersG void, the legislature could have achieved a result that complies with the German Basic Law in a variety of ways, e.g. by expressly excluding express assemblies from the scope of application of s. 14(1) VersG. The BVerfG pre-empted these choices in order to achieve a constitution-consistent result by means of statutory interpretation. Nonetheless, the court adopted a meaning that took into account the enacting legislature's intention as far as possible, i.e. the obligation to register an assembly within the 48-hour period, as far as possible. The BVerfG did not discuss how its decision is compatible with the outer interpretative limit that a constitution-consistent meaning cannot be adopted if the unconstitutionality of the provision can be rectified in different ways by the legislature. It would involve an over-interpretation of *Eilversammlungen* to discern from the judgment that the BVerfG intended to dismiss this outer limit of the judicial function. What *Eilversammlungen* does show is that this limit can be applied in a narrower or wider fashion depending on the circumstances of the individual case. The limit leaves ample scope for judicial discretion. Its inconsistent application in case law fails to provide for a high level of legal certainty.

German legal scholarship has been very critical of case law in which the BVerfG has restricted or complemented the legislature's intentions. This case law seems hardly compatible with the premise that constitution-conforming interpretation respects the legislature's authority and exhibits a form of judicial restraint towards the ordinary legislature.[190] A common criticism is that the BVerfG patronises the legislature when it replaces the latter's intention with what the legislature ought to have intended. We have already seen that a very similar criticism exists in England where scholars claim that English courts show insufficient judicial restraint when applying s. 3(1) HRA. German scholars have submitted that a clear invalidation of a provision due to its unconstitutionality may be better able to respect the legislature's authority than salvaging the provision in a version that the enacting legislature would not recognise.[191] It is possible to argue against this criticism that the case law of the BVerfG follows recognised patterns of conventional judicial law-making. The intention of the enacting legislature in itself does not function as an outer limit of interpretation for conventional judicial law-making. It can be complemented or restricted by other factors of interpretation. The interpretation is "objectivised". The identifiable intent of the enacting legislature is restricted or complemented by the presumption of compliance for constitution-consistent judicial law-making.

---

[190] See K.A. BETTERMANN, *Die verfassungskonforme Auslegung: Grenzen und Gefahren*, C.F. Müller, Heidelberg 1986, p. 22; LEMBKE, above n. 17, pp. 129–131.
[191] BETHGE, above n. 95, §31, para. 266.

The criticism that remains is that the BVerfG may have attached too much weight to the presumed intention of the legislature to comply with the German Basic Law in individual cases without attaching sufficient weight to the actual intention of the enacting legislature. It may have applied the outer limits of constitution-consistent interpretation in too loose a fashion.[192] A loose application is possible due to the indeterminate formulation of the limits of judicial law-making.[193] Critics add that constitution-consistent interpretation of legislation by the BVerfG should be particularly restrained because decisions of the BVerfG bind the legislature (s. 31(1) BVerfGG) and have the force of law if the conditions of s. 31(2) BVerfGG are fulfilled.[194] Decisions by the BVerfG affect the separation of powers between the legislature and the courts to a significant degree. One factor, however, that counts in favour of operating a powerful presumption of compliance is that the BVerfG has the power to invalidate an unconstitutional provision. This difference between conventional judicial law-making and constitution-consistent judicial law-making has the potential to affect the limits of the judicial function for constitution-consistent judicial law-making. Even though this difference from conventional judicial law-making is not visible in the abstract formulation of the outer limits of interpretation, a more liberal application of these limits seems warranted if the BVerfG engages in constitution-consistent interpretation.

In *Geldwäsche durch Strafverteidiger*, the BVerfG emphasised that a constitution-consistent interpretation is barred if it contradicts the wording *and* the clearly identifiable intention of the legislature (double criterion).[195] This limit was not breached in the case at issue. At other times, the BVerfG has formulated that a judge cannot attribute an opposite sense to a statute that is clear according to its wording and its purpose.[196] Whether this latter formulation is identical in meaning to the first expression of the double criterion is uncertain. What is

---

[192] For this criticism, see H. Bogs, *Die verfassungskonforme Auslegung von Gesetzen*, Kohlhammer Verlag, Mainz 1966, pp. 62–75; Korioth, above n. 22, para. 450; G.F. Schuppert, Funktionell-rechtliche Grenzen der Verfassungsinterpretation, Athenäum, Königstein/Ts. 1980, pp. 6–7. For a fundamental criticism of constitution-consistent interpretation which culminates in the thesis that constitution-consistent interpretation as practised in German courts (and mainstream legal scholarship) is inadmissible under the German Basic Law, see Lembke, above n. 17.

[193] The issue of the vagueness of the outer limits of the judicial function as expressed in judicial practice has already been critically evaluated in Chapter 2.

[194] M.-E. Geis, Die "Eilversammlung" als Bewährungsprobe verfassungskonformer Auslegung, *NVwZ* 1992, 1025, 1027.

[195] BVerfG, *NJW* 2004, 1305, 1311 – *Geldwäsche durch Strafverteidiger*. See also BVerfG, *NJW* 1964, 1563, 1564; BVerfG, *NJW* 1998, 3033, 3036; BVerfG, *NJW* 1999, 1853, 1855; BVerfG, *NJW* 2000, 347, 349; BVerfG, *NJW* 2007, 2977, para. 91; BVerfG, *NVwZ* 2015, 510, para. 86; BVerfG, *NJW* 2015, 1359, para. 132 – *Kopftuch*.

[196] BVerfG, *NJW* 1958, 2059, 2060–2061; BVerfG, *NJW* 1981, 39, 43; BVerfG, *NJW* 1985, 2315, 2318 (dissenting opinion of Judge Steinberger); BVerfG, *NJW* 1994, 2475, 2476; BVerfG, *NJW* 2007, 2977, para. 91; BVerfG, *NJW* 2015, 1359, para. 132 – *Kopftuch*.

implicit in both formulations of the double criterion is that a provision's clear wording does not in itself function as an outer limit of statutory interpretation. A constitution-consistent meaning may even contradict a provision's clear language in an individual case. The clear wording of s. 261(5) StGB was indeed surpassed in *Geldwäsche durch Strafverteidiger*. Yet, I have shown for conventional judicial law-making that the statutory wording is not at all meaningless for the limits of judicial law-making. A provision's unambiguous wording is not an outer limit of constitution-consistent judicial law-making in itself, but it can weigh heavily against the permissibility of constitution-consistent judicial law-making in an individual case.[197] The status of a provision's wording is not always consistent and at times confusing when the BVerfG expresses the outer limits of constitution-consistent judicial law-making.[198] For example, there is occasional case law stipulating that a judge cannot use constitution-consistent interpretation to give the opposite sense to a provision's clear wording.[199] This case law is difficult to reconcile with the above-mentioned expression of the double criterion. The apparently inconsistent case law may simply be due to a disagreement among the judges, given that dissenting opinions, albeit allowed (s. 30(2) BVerfGG), are uncommon in the BVerfG. If this hypothesis is true, it also illustrates the function of dissenting opinions to provide a higher degree of transparency in judicial reasoning.[200]

The double criterion is an abstract guideline. It hardly limits the power of a court to restrict or complement the intention of the legislature. The "identifiable intention of the legislature" as an element of the double criterion can refer to the intention of the enacting legislature or the underlying objective purpose and sense of the statutory provision. The BVerfG has not generally clarified what weight a judge has to give to the subjective and objective intention of the legislature. The court has not clarified how far a judge is able to depart from the purpose ascribed to the legislation by the enacting legislature. This is determined by the circumstances of the individual case. A judge who relies on the presumption of compliance for constitution-consistent interpretation also significantly stretches the *contra legem* limit. Applying the presumption entails that an intention of the legislature that militates against a constitution-consistent interpretation of the provision will regularly not be *clearly* discernible. It follows from this reasoning that the double criterion is heavily devalued since the wording of a provision can be surpassed for judicial law-making and since the legislature is assumed to have intended the creation of a provision that complies with the German Basic Law.[201]

---

[197] See, e.g. BVerfG, *NVwZ* 2015, 510 paras. 89–93 and the dissenting opinion of Judges Seibert and Henschel in BVerfG, *NJW* 1992, 890, 891 – *Eilversammlungen*.
[198] See with a discussion of case law, SAUER, above n. 14, pp. 3–6.
[199] BVerfG, *NJW* 1958, 1227. See also BVerwG, *NVwZ* 1998, 60, 61.
[200] See the aim of the German law introducing s. 30(2) BVerfGG to provide for a higher level of transparency in judicial reasoning (*Deutscher Bundestag*, Drucksache V/3816, p. 7).
[201] For a highly critical view of this case law of the BVerfG, see LEMBKE, above n. 17, pp. 125–126.

Relying on the presumption of compliance does not modify the double criterion; it does not shift the *contra legem* limit. However, it affects the double criterion as the element relating to the *clearly* identifiable intention of the legislature will regularly be absent. Applying a strong presumption of compliance therefore creates the danger that the ordinary legislation is simply used as a hollow that is filled with a constitution-consistent meaning by the courts, based on the interpretative tool of the presumed intention of the legislature.

A recent judgment illustrating that the BVerfG enjoys considerable flexibility when applying the outer limits of constitution-consistent interpretation is the court's *Kopftuch* ruling from 2015.[202] The decision concerned the constitution-consistent interpretation in a narrow sense (*Auslegung*) of s. 57(4) sentence 3 of the North Rhine-Westphalia Education Act (*Schulgesetz für das Land Nordrhein-Westfalen*, SchulG NW). Under s. 57(4) sentence 1 SchulG NW, at school, teachers may not publicly express views (*Bekundungen*) of a political, religious, ideological or similar nature which are likely to endanger or interfere with the neutrality of the *Land* with regard to pupils and parents, or disturb the political, religious and ideological peace at school. Pursuant to sentence 3 of s. 57(4) SchulG NW, carrying out the educational mandate in accordance with the constitution of the *Land* and accordingly presenting (*Darstellung*) Christian and occidental educational and cultural values or traditions does not contradict the prohibition set out in sentence 1 of s. 57(4) SchulG NW. The claimant was an employee at a state school and wore a *hijab* (Islamic headscarf) at school for religious reasons. The school authority requested that the claimant remove the headscarf while on duty. After the claimant had refused to remove the headscarf while on duty, her employer, the *Land* North Rhine-Westphalia, first issued a warning and then dismissed her. The claimant raised a constitutional complaint against s. 57(4) sentence 3 SchulG NW. The BVerfG held that this provision is intended to confer a privilege on presenting Christian and occidental educational and cultural values or traditions. The provision disadvantages followers of religions other than the Christian and Jewish faiths. The BVerfG concluded that the provision violates the right to equal treatment under the German Basic Law.[203] The BVerfG relied on the provision's legislative history in order to show that s. 57(4) sentence 3 was meant to bring about direct unequal treatment on religious grounds.[204]

The claimant's lawsuit had been unsuccessful in the labour courts before the claimant initiated the constitutional complaint to the BVerfG. The German Federal Labour Court (BAG) had interpreted s. 57(4) sentence 3 SchulG NW restrictively in order to reach a constitution-consistent meaning. The BAG had

---

[202] BVerfG, *NJW* 2015, 1359. For an English translation of the judgment, see http://www.bverfg.de/e/rs20150127_1bvr047110en.html.
[203] BVerfG, *NJW* 2015, 1359, para. 123 – *Kopftuch*.
[204] Ibid., paras. 127, 135.

held that "presenting" (*Darstellung*) Christian and occidental educational and cultural values sentence 3 of the provision cannot be considered identical with "expressing" (*Bekundungen*) an individual faith in sentence 1. Furthermore, the BAG had held that the word "Christian" refers to a set of values dissociated from Christian beliefs stemming from the tradition of Christian-occidental culture and upon which the Basic Law is also evidently based.[205] The BVerfG rejected such a restrictive interpretation in conformity with the German Basic Law as this would overstep the outer limits of constitution-consistent interpretation.[206] The court held that the BAG's restrictive interpretation of s. 57(4) sentence 3 SchulG NW does not coincide "with the legislative intent that became clearly evident in the legislative process".[207] The BVerfG referred to the provision's legislative history and showed that (a) the legislature was aware of a possible restrictive interpretation of the provision and (b) the government, as the drafter of the legislation, was of the opinion that the constitutionality of the provision was not in doubt if a constitution-consistent interpretation were adopted. Yet the intention to pass a law that would allow certain traditional clothing with religious connotations worn by adherents of Christian faiths and of Judaism, as opposed to the Islamic headscarf, was maintained in the further course of the legislative process.[208] Judges Schluckebier and Hermanns dissented. They argued first that the legislative history shows that (a) the original intentions of the government changed during the legislative process and (b) a constitution-consistent restrictive interpretation of s. 57(4) sentence 3 SchulG NW was intended by the legislature.[209] Second, they explained that during the course of the bill in Parliament, the wording in sentence 3 was altered from *Bekundung* to *Darstellung*. The effect of the change was a different wording in sentence 1 (*Bekundungen*) and sentence 3 (*Darstellung*) of s. 57(4), allowing for a different construction of both sentences. The difference in wording provided an objective factor of interpretation detached from the perceptions of the provision's drafters.[210] Both dissenting judges agreed with the BAG's constitution-consistent interpretation of sentence 3 of s. 57(4) SchulG NW.

The BVerfG's *Kopftuch* ruling in 2015 serves as an example of how different judges can give different weight to the interpretative criteria. Another example is the BVerfG's *Eilversammlungen* judgment discussed earlier in this section.

---

[205] BAG, NZA 2010, 227, para. 23. For criticism, see B. RUSTEBERG, Kopftuchverbote als Mittel zur Abwehr nicht existenter Gefahren, (2015) 70 JZ 637, 643; C. MÖLLERS, A tale of two courts, *Verfassungsblog*, 14.3.2015, available online at http://www.verfassungsblog.de/a-tale-of-two-courts/.
[206] BVerfG, NJW 2015, 1359 paras. 131–137 – *Kopftuch*.
[207] Ibid., para. 135.
[208] Ibid., paras. 134–135.
[209] BVerfG, NJW 2015, 1359, dissenting opinion by Judges Schluckebier and Hermanns, para. 23 – *Kopftuch*.
[210] Ibid., para. 22.

The majority of the judges in *Kopftuch* gave relatively little weight to the different wording in sentences 1 and 3 of s. 57(4) SchulG NW compared to the dissenting minority and the BAG. It is also clear that the difference in weight directly affected the outer limits of constitution-consistent interpretation. What is noticeable is that the majority of the BVerfG examined the provision's legislative history in detail and attached a significant role to the intention of the enacting legislature. That mirrors the strong weight that the BVerfG appears to attach to the historical criterion of interpretation since *Dreiteilungsmethode*.[211] The majority's decision in *Kopftuch* also illustrates a strict review of the constitutional limits of the judicial function.

The BVerfG did not argue with a presumed intention of the legislature to comply with the German Basic Law in *Kopftuch*. That was not necessary since the legislative history contained sufficient indications that the enacting legislature actually intended to comply with the German Basic Law. In *Geldwäsche durch Strafverteidiger*, the presumption of compliance was not rebutted by an inadvertently unconstitutional regulatory decision of the enacting legislature that was expressed in the unambiguous wording of s. 261(5) German Criminal Code and the legislative history. In *Kopftuch*, the reasoning of the minority shows that it would have been possible to reconcile the BAG's constitution-consistent meaning of s. 57(4) sentence 3 SchulG NW with the provision's wording and with the identifiable intention of the enacting legislature. The different application of the outer limits of constitution-consistent interpretation in both cases undermines legal certainty. The comparison between *Kopftuch* and *Geldwäsche durch Strafverteidiger* also shows that the outer limits of constitution-consistent interpretation were applied in an overly narrow fashion by the majority in *Kopftuch*. This cannot be explained by a greater judicial restraint towards the enacting legislature because the restrictive interpretation of s. 57(4) sentence 3 was actually intended by the enacting legislature. It may be argued that two intentions, both specifically expressed in the legislative materials, conflicted in *Kopftuch*: (a) the intention to grant a preferential treatment to followers of Christian faiths and of Judaism and (b) the intention to enact a constitution-consistent provision in s. 57(4) sentence 3 SchulG NW. In *Geldwäsche durch Strafverteidiger*, even a presumed intention prevailed over an inadvertently unconstitutional regulatory decision of the enacting legislature. It is thus unclear why the specifically expressed intention (b) was unable to prevail over intention (a) according to the majority in *Kopftuch*.

The grounds of the judgment may indicate a possible motivation for the majority.[212] The majority argued that the legislature was aware of the risk of the

---

[211] For discussion, see Section 3.3.4 of Chapter 2.
[212] Other authors point to a different motivation of the court. RUSTEBERG, above n. 205, p. 643 and MÖLLERS, above n. 205, argue that (a) the BVerfG, contrary to the BAG, was of the opinion that Christian values, as referred to in sentence 3 of s. 57(4) SchulG NW, cannot be independent of Christian beliefs and (b) the values underlying the German Basic Law are not specifically Christian.

provision's incompatibility with constitutional law. The majority also pointed out that a constitution-consistent interpretation of sentence 3 of s. 57(4) SchulG NW would allow a provision "to remain in force which, under a possible broad reading of its wording, could be understood as leaving an opening for discriminatory administrative practices, and whose vagueness in this regard was deliberately retained in the legislative process".[213] This reasoning of the majority should not be understood as meaning that a court cannot adopt a constitution-consistent meaning if a provision's wording is capable of bearing other unconstitutional meanings. Such a reading of the majority's reasoning would turn the interpretative priority rule upside down. Instead, this reasoning may be understood as criticising the drafters of the legislation for deliberately attempting to legislate at the thin border between constitutionality and unconstitutionality, in the hope that the courts will salvage the provision by (a) restricting its scope to what is constitutionally possible and (b) at the same time taking into account the enacting legislature's intention as far as possible. That the BVerfG does not want to be abused for ironing out the constitutional inadequacies of legislation can explain why the majority applied the outer limits of constitution-consistent interpretation narrowly in *Kopftuch*. The legislature deliberately used vague terms in the legislation, and the standard approach of a court in such a case would be to accept the delegation of law-making power.[214] Yet, the majority in *Kopftuch* declined. This is a new development. It remains to be seen (a) whether this development will be taken up in future decisions in order to re-determine the constitutional duties of the legislature and the courts and (b) whether this development is restricted to the realm of constitution-consistent interpretation.

7.2. SECTION 3(1) HUMAN RIGHTS ACT

Having examined the outer limits of constitution-consistent judicial law-making in Germany, this book will now critically analyse the outer limits of Convention-compatible judicial law-making in England. It is accepted in English courts that an interpretation under s. 3(1) HRA must not cross the boundary dividing permissible interpretation from impermissible judicial amendment of legislation.[215] Enacting and amending statutes is reserved to

---

[213] BVerfG, *NJW* 2015, 1359 paras. 135–136 – *Kopftuch*.
[214] See, e.g. BGH, *NJW* 2009, 1962, para. 13 – *Schiedsfähigkeit II*.
[215] *R. v. A (No. 2)* [2001] UKHL 25, para. 108 (Lord Hope); *In re S (Minors)* [2002] UKHL 10, paras. 38–39 (Lord Nicholls); *R. (Anderson) v. Secretary of State for the Home Department* [2002] UKHL 46, para. 81 (Lord Hutton); *Bellinger v. Bellinger* [2003] UKHL 21, para. 67 (Lord Hope); *Ghaidan v. Godin-Mendoza* [2004] UKHL 30, para. 63 (Lord Millett), paras. 113, 121 (Lord Rodger); *R. (GC) v. Commissioner of Police of the Metropolis* [2011] UKSC 21, para. 115 (Lord Rodger); *Poplar Housing and Regeneration Community Association Ltd. v. Donaghue* [2001] EWCA Civ 595, para. 75 (Lord Woolf CJ).

Parliament. Defining the outer limits of Convention-compatible statutory interpretation affects the relationship between the legislature and the judiciary. It is a task of constitutional significance. Even though s. 3(1) HRA is a statutory rule of interpretation, Parliament has not specified the standard by which possibility is to be judged.[216] Instead, judges have pronounced these outer limits of interpretation in case law. Lord Steyn argued in *Ghaidan* that a broad approach to interpretation is required under s. 3(1) HRA because s. 3(1) HRA is the principal remedial measure under the HRA.[217] This entails that the outer limits of Convention-compatible interpretation are not drawn too narrowly. Defining these limits is a decisive step for setting the remedial scope of s. 3(1) HRA. Unlike the outer limits of judicial law-making under conventional methods of interpretation, English judges have stipulated general interpretative limits that serve as the outer boundaries of the judicial function for all cases of judicial law-making under s. 3(1) HRA, irrespective of whether the legislation at issue is private, public or criminal legislation and irrespective of whether the parties to the case are public or private bodies.[218] That is to be welcomed from a perspective of legal certainty. If we reflect on the findings of Section 5 of Chapter 2, this change of judicial attitude was triggered by the change of the default position for judicial law-making from one of general impermissibility under conventional canons of interpretation to one of general permissibility under s. 3(1) HRA. Yet, despite the courts' endeavours to formulate abstract outer limits of the judicial function, the border between permissible interpretation under s. 3(1) HRA and impermissible amendment of legislation has been described as "highly elusive".[219] It is thus necessary to look at these limits in detail in the following sections.

7.2.1. Statutory Language

We have already seen that the interpretative obligation under s. 3(1) HRA goes beyond resolving ambiguities. It applies even if there is no ambiguity in

---

[216] *Ghaidan v. Godin-Mendoza* [2004] UKHL 30, para. 27 (Lord Nicholls).
[217] Ibid., para. 49 (Lord Steyn).
[218] Ibid., paras. 32–33 (Lord Nicholls), paras. 110–115, 121–122 (Lord Rodger), but see para. 50 (Lord Steyn, dissenting); *Vodafone 2 v. Revenue and Customs Commissioners* [2009] EWCA Civ 446, para. 38 (Sir Andrew Morritt C); *Churchill Insurance Co. Ltd. v. Fitzgerald & Wilkinson* [2012] EWCA Civ 1166, para. 50 (Aikens LJ, with whom Etherton and Maurice Kay LJJ agreed). In favour of a case-by-case approach that does not seek to define the boundary between the legitimate development of the law and impermissible judicial legislation under s. 3(1) HRA in abstract and general terms: *R. (Nicklinson) v. Ministry of Justice* [2014] UKSC 38, para. 101 (Lord Neuberger); T. BINGHAM, The Human Rights Act, [2010] *EHRLR* 568, 572.
[219] B. DICKSON, *Human rights and the United Kingdom Supreme Court*, OUP, Oxford 2013, p. 70.

the statutory language.[220] In the words of Lord Millett, it is possible under s. 3(1) HRA to "do considerable violence to the language", to "stretch it almost (but not quite) to breaking point" and to give the language an "abnormal meaning" which may even be "unnatural or unreasonable", as long as it is "intellectually defensible".[221] Section 3(1) HRA may require a court to attach a Convention-compatible meaning to a provision that "depart[s] from the unambiguous meaning the legislation would otherwise bear"[222] pursuant to conventional canons of interpretation. Unambiguous statutory language in itself does not function as an absolute limit of rights-conforming interpretation. What is striking is how openly English judges express the extent of their interpretative power under s. 3(1) HRA to depart from the actual words of the legislation. The traditional reluctance to engage in a strained construction or in gap-filling under conventional canons of construction is absent. This new judicial attitude even appears to surpass the German courts' willingness to speak of judicial law-making (*Rechtsfortbildung*) instead of disguising it as a restrictive or extensive interpretation in a narrow sense.

Judges attach different weight to the statutory language when they interpret a provision according to conventional canons of construction or under s. 3(1) HRA. This is illustrated if *Ghaidan* and *Fitzpatrick* are compared. In *Fitzpatrick*, the House of Lords focused on the gender-specific words Parliament had used in para. 2(2) of Sch. 1 to the Rent Act 1977. Had Parliament intended to include homosexual partners, their Lordships argued, it would have used different statutory words when it introduced para. 2(2) into the Rent Act in 1988.[223] In *Ghaidan*, on the other hand, neither of their Lordships nor her Ladyship dealt with the argument that Parliament would have used different statutory words had it intended to include homosexual partners in para. 2(2). It appears that the argument in *Fitzpatrick* loses its force entirely under s. 3(1) HRA and must be reversed: the wording of the provision could not bar a Convention-compatible interpretation because Parliament did not use words that exclude homosexual partners from para. 2(2) of Sch. 1 to the Rent Act 1977. The reason for this difference between the two cases may be due to the strong presumption of compliance that operates when s. 3(1) HRA is activated.

---

[220] *R. v. A (No. 2)* [2001] UKHL 25, para. 44 (Lord Steyn), para. 108 (Lord Hope); *Ghaidan v. Godin-Mendoza* [2004] UKHL 30, para. 29 (Lord Nicholls), para. 44 (Lord Steyn), para. 67 (Lord Millett); White Paper, Rights brought home: the Human Rights Bill, October 1997 (CM 3782), para. 2.7.

[221] *Ghaidan v. Godin-Mendoza* [2004] UKHL 30, para. 67 (Lord Millett).

[222] *Ghaidan v. Godin-Mendoza* [2004] UKHL 30, para. 30 (Lord Nicholls). See also ibid., para. 67 (Lord Millett); *R. (Hurst) v. Commissioner of Police of the Metropolis* [2007] UKHL 13, para. 49 (Lord Brown); *Ahmed and others v. HM Treasury* [2010] UKSC 2, para. 115 (Lord Phillips).

[223] *Fitzpatrick v. Sterling Housing Association Ltd.* [2001] 1 AC 27 (HL), 34 (Lord Slynn), 58 (Lord Hutton), 72 (Lord Hobhouse).

Lord Rodger clarified in *Ghaidan* that s. 3(1) HRA is not a limitless interpretative exercise. A change "as drastic as changing black into white" cannot be achieved under s. 3(1) HRA.[224] Yet contrary to Lord Millett's very similar viewpoint in *Ghaidan*,[225] he considered this example to express a substantive limit. The reason why such an interpretation lies outside a court's power under s. 3(1) HRA, Lord Rodger continued, is not because of "any linguistic changes, whether great or small", but because it "would remove the very core and essence, the 'pith and substance' of the measure that Parliament had enacted".[226] Lord Rodger differentiated between the language of a provision and the substance expressed in that language. He further opined in paras. 108 and 110 that s. 3(1) HRA "does not allow the courts … to change a provision from one where Parliament says that x is to happen into one saying that x is not to happen". Again, this quote could be traced back to the statutory language as an outer interpretative limit, but Lord Rodger did not follow that path. He combined this constraint with the substance of a provision as an outer interpretative limit: s. 3(1) HRA "does not allow the courts to change the substance of a provision completely". A complete change of substance occurs when the Convention-compatible meaning is the opposite of the substance of the provision.[227] Consequently, the statutory language in itself does not function as an outer interpretative limit for Convention-compatible statutory construction according to Lord Rodger.[228]

Similar to Lord Rodger's distinction between substance and language, Lord Nicholls distinguished between the actual language of a statute and the legislative concept expressed in that language.[229] He did not further explain what he meant by a provision's concept, but he focused on the social policy underlying the introduction of para. 2(2) into the Act in 1988 when he applied s. 3(1) HRA in *Ghaidan*. The social policy was the security of tenure for the survivor of a heterosexual couple in a stable relationship. This policy was, according to Lord Nicholls, equally applicable to the survivor of a homosexual couple living together in a stable relationship.[230] The reason underlying this social policy was that the survivors of couples that "share their lives and make their home together" shall be granted special protection. Lord Nicholls did not see

---

[224] *Ghaidan v. Godin-Mendoza* [2004] UKHL 30, para. 111 (Lord Rodger).
[225] Ibid., para. 70 (Lord Millett).
[226] *Ghaidan v. Godin-Mendoza* [2004] UKHL 30, para. 111 (Lord Rodger).
[227] *Birmingham City Council v. Doherty* [2008] UKHL 57, para. 49 (Lord Hope, "But it [s. 3(1) HRA] does not enable the court to change the substance of a provision from one where it says one thing into one that says the opposite").
[228] For an academic criticism of the role of the statutory language in determining the limits of a s. 3(1) HRA interpretation in English judicial practice, see KAVANAGH, above n. 131, pp. 114, 121.
[229] *Ghaidan v. Godin-Mendoza* [2004] UKHL 30, para. 31 (Lord Nicholls).
[230] Ibid., paras. 17, 35 (Lord Nicholls).

any rational or fair ground for distinguishing a homosexual from a heterosexual couple in this context.[231] It thus appears that the legislative concept, to which Lord Nicholls referred, coincides with the reasons underlying the specific purpose of the challenged provision.[232] These reasons are more abstract then the provision's specific purpose[233] since the specific purpose of para. 2(2) of Sch. 1 to the Rent Act 1977 was to grant special protection to the survivor of a heterosexual couple, and the underlying reasons for this social policy applied equally to homosexual couples. Lord Millett, on the other hand, was not prepared to go to a level as abstract as the reasons underlying the legislative purpose when determining the purpose of para. 2(2) of Sch. 1. If German terminology were adopted, one could say that Lord Nicholls favoured a more "objectivised" understanding of the challenged provision than did Lord Millett. The judges' reasoning in *Ghaidan* shows that whether or not an interpretative result is possible under s. 3(1) HRA can depend on whether a wide or narrow purpose is ascribed to the challenged legislation.

Lord Nicholls further argued that because a court may depart from a provision's unambiguous meaning, the operation of s. 3(1) HRA cannot

> depend critically upon the particular form of words adopted by the parliamentary draftsman in the statutory provision under consideration. ... If the draftsman chose to express the concept being enacted in one form of words, section 3 would be available to achieve Convention-compliance. If he chose a different form of words, section 3 would be impotent.[234]

He concluded that "the mere fact the language under consideration is inconsistent with a Convention-compliant meaning does not of itself make a Convention-compliant interpretation under section 3 impossible".[235] These statements by Lord Nicholls indicate that he agreed with Lord Rodger that the statutory language in itself is not a standard by which possibility is to be judged.

Neither Lord Rodger nor Lord Nicholls argued in *Ghaidan* that the statutory terms can be disregarded entirely. The statutory language is the primary way in which Parliament expresses its intention.[236] The language used by Parliament

---

[231] Ibid., para. 17 (Lord Nicholls).
[232] See also KAVANAGH, above n. 131, pp. 114, 120; J. VAN ZYL SMIT, The new purposive interpretation of statutes: HRA section 3 after *Ghaidan v. Godin-Mendoza*, (2007) 70 MLR 294, 299; cf. *Wilson v. First County Trust Ltd. (No. 2)* [2003] UKHL 40, paras. 61, 67 (Lord Nicholls, "the rationale underlying the legislation").
[233] VAN ZYL SMIT, above n. 232, p. 300 refers to Lord Nicholls's reasoning in *Ghaidan* as "abstract purposive interpretation".
[234] *Ghaidan v. Godin-Mendoza* [2004] UKHL 30, para. 31 (Lord Nicholls).
[235] Ibid., para. 32 (Lord Nicholls).
[236] KAVANAGH, above n. 131, pp. 114, 121; cf. *Wilson v. First County Trust Ltd. (No. 2)* [2003] UKHL 40, para. 67 (Lord Nicholls, "cardinal constitutional principle that the

will usually express, correspond with and determine the legislative concept, scheme and substance Parliament intends to enact. Yet the weight attached to the intention of the enacting Parliament and consequently to the statutory language is reduced when a court has recourse to s. 3(1) HRA. That is because the aim of statutory interpretation is modified under s. 3(1) HRA and a court has to reconcile the intention of the parliament that enacted the legislation under consideration with the intention of the parliament that enacted s. 3(1) HRA. According to both their Lordships, the statutory language is only one of the criteria, albeit an important one, to which a court has recourse in order to determine the legislative substance and concept. Other criteria include the overall scheme of the statute[237] and the provision's underlying purpose. These other criteria may point in a different direction and may allow a court to find a Convention-compliant meaning that is compatible with a provision's substance and concept but which is inconsistent with the statutory language. How much weight a judge must attach to the statutory language is not an entirely settled issue. It depends on the circumstances of the individual case in judicial practice. It allows for judicial discretion and may be answered differently by different judges, as evidenced by Lord Millett's dissent in *Ghaidan*. Whereas relatively little weight was attached to the statutory language by the majority in *Ghaidan*, other case law exists where judges have given considerable weight to the statutory language.[238] There are indications in case law that the more "flexibly" the statutory language is expressed and the more that language calls for (judicial) evaluation, the greater the scope for a Convention-compliant

---

will of Parliament is expressed in the language used by it in its enactments"); *Ghaidan v. Godin-Mendoza* [2004] UKHL 30, para. 31 (Lord Nicholls, "the concept expressed in that language"), para. 70 (Lord Millett, "the words of the statute … cannot be disregarded or given no weight, for they are the medium by which Parliament expresses its intention"), para. 123 (Lord Rodger, "What matters is not so much the particular phraseology chosen by the draftsman as the substance of the measure which Parliament *has enacted in those words*" – emphasis added); *R. (Countryside Alliance) v. Attorney General* [2005] EWHC 1677 (Admin), para. 267 (May LJ, "The policy and objects of a statute must be determined by interpreting its language, which alone represents Parliament's intention"); O. JONES and F.A.R. BENNION, *Bennion on Statutory Interpretation*, 6th ed., LexisNexis, London 2013, section 150.

[237] *Ghaidan v. Godin-Mendoza* [2004] UKHL 30, para. 110 (Lord Rodger).

[238] *R. (Wilkinson) v. Inland Revenue Commissioners* [2005] UKHL 30, para. 18 (Lord Hoffmann, "In the present case, there is no way in which any reasonable reader could understand the word 'widow' to refer to the more general concept of a surviving spouse. The contrary indications in the language of Part VII of the 1988 Act are too strong"); *AS (Somalia) v. Secretary of State for the Home Department* [2009] UKHL 32, para. 19 (Lord Hope, *obiter*); *Serious Organised Crime Agency v. Gale* [2010] EWCA Civ 759, paras. 41–42 (Carnwath LJ); *R. (Reilly) v. Secretary of State for Work and Pensions* [2016] EWCA Civ 413, para. 131 (Underhill LJ, giving the judgment of the Court; "We base that view principally on the phrase 'for all purposes' in section 1 (1) [of the Jobseekers (Back to Work Schemes) Act 2013] …. The effect of that phrase as a matter of ordinary domestic construction seems to us clear beyond argument; … its words seem to us incapable of being read down so as to have anything less than their plain literal meaning").

meaning that expands or restricts the statutory words.²³⁹ This connection between vague statutory words and greater judicial powers to go beyond the possible semantic meanings of those words was criticised in Chapter 1. Case law does not support the proposition, however, that (a) vague words are a precondition for a possible Convention-compatible interpretation under s. 3(1) HRA, and (b) s. 3(1) HRA is not available if precise statutory words are used by Parliament. In *Pomiechowski*, the Supreme Court used s. 3(1) HRA to read "absolute and inflexible" time limits for appeals in ss. 26(4), 103(9) and 108(4) of the Extradition Act 2003 "subject to the qualification that the court must have a discretion in exceptional circumstances to extend time for both filing and service, where such statutory provisions would otherwise operate to prevent an appeal in a manner conflicting with the right of access to an appeal process held to exist under article 6(1)" ECHR.²⁴⁰

Even though the statutory language does not function as an outer limit of Convention-compatible interpretation in itself, an exception can be made to this general rule. Resort to s. 3(1) HRA is not possible if the legislation contains express statutory language that contradicts the Convention-compliant meaning.²⁴¹ Before we explore this constraint for s. 3(1) HRA, it is important to realise that this "express terms limit" is not an exhaustive statement of the outer limits of the judicial function under s. 3(1) HRA. The boundary line between interpretation and legislation may be crossed even if a limitation on Convention rights is not stated in express terms,²⁴² but rather by the legislation's necessary implications.²⁴³ The outer limits of the judicial function can be exceeded and a Convention-compatible interpretation can be impossible even if there are insufficient indications that Parliament expressly intended to derogate from Convention rights.

---

[239] To that effect cf. *McDonald v. McDonald* [2016] UKSC 28, para. 68 (Lord Neuberger and Lady Hale, with whom Lord Kerr, Lord Reed and Lord Carnwath agreed; *obiter*); *R. (Wilkinson) v. Inland Revenue Commissioners* [2005] UKHL 30, paras. 18–19 (Lord Hoffmann) and see the comment by VAN ZYL SMIT, above n. 232, pp. 305–306.

[240] *Pomiechowski v. District Court of Legnica* [2012] UKSC 20, para. 39 (Lord Mance).

[241] *R. v. A (No. 2)* [2001] UKHL 25, para. 108 (Lord Hope); *R. v. Lambert* [2001] UKHL 37, para. 79 (Lord Hope); *R. (Anderson) v. Secretary of State for the Home Department* [2002] UKHL 46, para. 59 (Lord Steyn); *Ghaidan v. Godin-Mendoza* [2004] UKHL 30, paras. 75–76 (Lord Millett), para. 117 (Lord Rodger); cf. *In re S (Minors)* [2002] UKHL 10, para. 40 (Lord Nicholls); *Secretary of State for the Home Department v. AF* [2009] UKHL 28, para. 97 (Lord Scott). For a detailed discussion of the express terms limit of s. 3(1) HRA, see A. KAVANAGH, The elusive divide between interpretation and legislation under the Human Rights Act 1998, (2004) 24 *OJLS* 259, 275–279.

[242] *In re S (Minors)* [2002] UKHL 10, para. 40 (Lord Nicholls).

[243] *R. v. A (No. 2)* [2001] UKHL 25, para. 108 (Lord Hope); *R. v. Lambert* [2001] UKHL 37, para. 79 (Lord Hope); *R. (Anderson) v. Secretary of State for the Home Department* [2002] UKHL 46, para. 59 (Lord Steyn); *Ghaidan v. Godin-Mendoza* [2004] UKHL 30, paras. 75–76 (Lord Millett), para. 117 (Lord Rodger).

The scope of this express terms limit depends on how the term "express" is understood. The most direct way Parliament may declare an incompatibility with Convention rights is if the statutory language explicitly says that the provision infringes or may infringe Convention rights.[244] If the express terms limit has any scope of application, this case must fall under it. The full implications of the meaning of these words by Parliament and their political consequences would be obvious. A further question is whether statutory language that is less explicit than this case meets the express terms limit. Lord Millett opined in *Ghaidan* that the statutory language would have expressly contradicted the suggested Convention-compatible extension of para. 2(2) of Sch. 1 to the Rent Act 1977 to same-sex partners had Parliament explicitly used the words "of the opposite sex" in para. 2(2) of Sch. 1 to the Rent Act 1977.[245] Lord Millett's view suggest that the statutory language on its own renders recourse to s. 3(1) HRA unavailable where the language is contrary to the suggested compatible meaning, e.g. x is to happen *versus* x is not to happen or the same sex instead of the opposite sex. Under the express terms limit, however, express statutory language has to contradict the compatible meaning, i.e. the contradiction has to be explicit. It thus appears that this outer limit of interpretation is not met when the suggested compatible meaning simply contradicts the existing statutory language. The contradiction of the compatible meaning has to be qualified. Lord Millett's interpretation of the express terms limits is thus open to the criticism that (a) he seems to equate a contradiction, in other words the opposite,[246] with a contradiction by express statutory language or (b) he at least does not sufficiently clarify when a contradiction becomes explicit (express).

Lord Millett's interpretation of the express terms limit must be rejected on other grounds as well. Lord Rodger considered the case of opposites in *Ghaidan*. He analysed this scenario in the context of the change in a provision's substance, as we have seen above. The underlying notion of the majority's view in *Ghaidan* is that the substance of the legislation must always be taken into account when the outer limits of Convention-compliant interpretation are under consideration. It is not sufficient to take statutory language at face value. Instead, it is necessary to assess whether the language used enshrines a substantive principle that contradicts the Convention-compatible meaning. The conceptual difference between a provision's statutory language and its substance is significant. The difference in practice may not always be as significant since the statutory words are a key pointer when determining a provision's substance. Whether or not there

---

[244] The same applies if (fictitious) statutory words were to read that the statute "must be interpreted giving full weight to the language of the statute and the intention of Parliament even if such an interpretation infringes Convention rights".
[245] *Ghaidan v. Godin-Mendoza* [2004] UKHL 30, paras. 77, 82 (Lord Millett).
[246] See the definition of the term "contradiction" in the online *Oxford English Dictionary* (https://en.oxforddictionaries.com/definition/contradiction) and the online *Cambridge Dictionary* (http://dictionary.cambridge.org/dictionary/english/contradiction).

is a difference in practice will depend on the weight attached to the statutory words when assessing the provision's substance. The upshot is that it seems hardly possible that the standard of the express terms limit can be satisfied by anything other than an explicit stipulation in the legislation that the legislation contradicts or may contradict Convention rights. Even this interpretation of the express terms limit may be questioned since any attempt to define the limits of s. 3(1) HRA by reference to the statutory language alone seems to go against the substance-focused approach taken by the majority in *Ghaidan*. After *Ghaidan*, the scope of the express terms limit appears to be extremely narrow, and it is an open question as to whether the express terms limit has ceased to be a constraint for s. 3(1) HRA.[247] This discussion of the express terms limit also shows that the limit cannot be equated with unambiguous statutory language that contradicts the Convention-compatible meaning, even if a distinction is drawn between a mere departure from unambiguous words and a contradiction (the opposite) of those words.

The scope of the interpretative power under s. 3(1) HRA as expressed in *Ghaidan* is not something which all judges have wholeheartedly embraced.[248] In *MB*, the majority of the House of Lords applied s. 3(1) HRA and read a "fair trial" exception into paragraph 4(3)(d) of the Schedule to the Prevention of Terrorism Act 2005.[249] Even though Lord Bingham finally agreed with this application of s. 3(1) HRA, he questioned whether "section 3 should be relied on in these cases, first, because any weakening of the mandatory language used by Parliament would very clearly fly in the face of Parliament's intention …".[250] Lord Bingham's reasoning differs from the majority's reasoning in *Ghaidan* as he, like Lord Millett in *Ghaidan*, attached greater weight to the statutory words and the intention of the enacting parliament expressed in those words. In *AS (Somalia)*, Lord Hope argued *obiter* that s. 3(1) HRA cannot be used to read down the language of s. 85(5) of the Nationality, Immigration and Asylum Act 2002 because the statutory words are "unequivocal and unyielding".[251] Lord Hope did not rely on the fundamental features of the legislation as an outer limit of s. 3(1) HRA and he did not refer to the statutory words of s. 85(5) in order to determine those features. Neither did he refer to Lord Nicholls's speech in *Ghaidan*, nor did he

---

[247] The view that the fate of the express terms limit remains unclear after *Ghaidan* is shared by KAVANAGH, above n. 131, pp. 114, 121–124.
[248] See, e.g. *Secretary of State for the Home Department v. AF* [2009] UKHL 28, para. 95 (Lord Scott).
[249] *Secretary of State for the Home Department v. MB* [2007] UKHL 46, para. 72 (Lady Hale), para. 84 (Lord Carswell), para. 92 (Lord Brown).
[250] *Secretary of State for the Home Department v. MB* [2007] UKHL 46, para. 44 (Lord Bingham). See also the criticism of *MB* by the Joint Committee on Human Rights, Counter Terrorism Policy and Human Rights (HL 50/HC 199), 07.02.2008, para. 46.
[251] *AS (Somalia) v. Secretary of State for the Home Department* [2009] UKHL 32, para. 19 (Lord Hope, *obiter*).

explicitly argue that s. 85(5) contains express statutory language that contradicts the Convention-compliant meaning. Even though Lord Hope solely relied on the statutory language of the contested provision as an argument against using s. 3(1) HRA, it does not follow that his *obiter* remarks cannot be reconciled with the majority's view in *Ghaidan*. That is because Lord Hope cited with approval para. 121 of Lord Rodger's speech in *Ghaidan*, where Lord Rodger argued that s. 3(1) HRA cannot be used to read words into a statute that are inconsistent with the scheme of the legislation or with its essential principles.

7.2.2. Intention of Parliament and Purpose of the Legislation

It was shown that the term "intention of the legislature" is a highly ambiguous notion that is not used consistently in written judicial opinions.[252] This is true for both England and Germany. It can relate to the aim of statutory interpretation, the outer limits of statutory interpretation, the purpose of the legislation and the weighing of the interpretative criteria. Legislative intention permeates the whole of the interpretative process. As F.A.R. Bennion has said: "legislative intention is always the ultimate guide to legal meaning".[253] When a court interprets a provision under s. 3(1) HRA, its judicial role is not limited to ascertaining the intention of the parliament that enacted the challenged legislation but includes the obligation of a different parliament, i.e. the parliament that enacted s. 3(1) HRA, to read the challenged legislation compatibly with Convention rights.

English courts have argued that the Parliament of 1998 empowered the judiciary to depart from the intention of the parliament enacting the challenged legislation. This power was first explicitly expressed in *Ghaidan* by Lord Nicholls: "Section 3 [HRA] may require the court to depart ... from the intention of the Parliament which enacted the legislation".[254] Later case law has confirmed this position.[255] This construction of s. 3(1) HRA also applies if a statute post-dates

---

[252] See also Z. BANKOWSKI and N. MACCORMICK, Statutory interpretation in the United Kingdom, in N. MACCORMICK and R. SUMMERS (eds.), *Interpreting statutes: a comparative study*, Dartmouth, Aldershot 1991, pp. 359, 386–387; KAVANAGH, above n. 67, pp. 179, 181–186.

[253] JONES and BENNION, above n. 236, section 162. For the argument that relying on the "intention of Parliament" in statutory interpretation is misleading and unhelpful, see J. LAWS, Statutory interpretation – the myth of parliamentary intent, Renton Lecture, November 2017, available online at http://www.statutelawsociety.co.uk/wp-content/uploads/2017/11/The-Myth-of-Parliamentary-Intent-text.pdf.

[254] *Ghaidan v. Godin-Mendoza* [2004] UKHL 30, para. 30 (Lord Nicholls).

[255] *Attorney General's Reference (No. 4 of 2002)* [2004] UKHL 43, paras. 28, 53 (Lord Bingham); *Ahmed and others v. HM Treasury* [2010] UKSC 2, para. 115 (Lord Phillips); *S v. L* [2012] UKSC 30, para. 15 (Lord Reed, with whom all other members of the Court agreed); *Kennedy v. The Charity Commission* [2014] UKSC 20, para. 224 (Lord Carnwath); cf. *R. (Jackson) v. Attorney General* [2005] UKHL 56, para. 105 (Lord Hope). See also NEUBERGER, above n. 44, p. 6, para. 14; LADY HALE, Bryce Lecture 2015: The Supreme Court in the United Kingdom Constitution, 05.02.2015, p. 12, available online at https://www.supremecourt.uk/news/speeches.html.

the HRA, as was the case in *Attorney General's Reference (No. 4 of 2002)*.[256] It follows that the intention of the legislature that enacted the legislation under consideration does not in itself function as an absolute interpretative limit for s. 3(1) HRA. Even though the statutory language is the primary way in which Parliament expresses its intention, Lord Nicholls's statement cannot be read narrowly as simply meaning that a Convention-compatible interpretation can depart from the statutory words. The purposive approach to interpretation was well recognised when *Ghaidan* was decided in 2004. In *Spath Holme* in 2001, Lord Nicholls acknowledged that the intention of Parliament may be insufficiently expressed in the statutory words.[257]

In *Attorney General's Reference (No. 4 of 2002)*, the majority of the House of Lords read down s. 11(2) of the Terrorism Act 2000 so as to impose on the defendant an evidential and not a legal burden. Lord Bingham said that "[s]uch was not the intention of Parliament when enacting the 2000 Act, but it was the intention of Parliament when enacting section 3 of the 1998 Act".[258] In *Ghaidan* itself, the majority also applied an equivalent reasoning. Schedule 1 to the Rent Act 1977 was amended in 1988 when Parliament extended the concept of "spouse" to include cohabiting heterosexual couples. The underlying specific social policy and purpose of para. 2 of Sch. 1 to the Rent Act 1977 was to secure tenure for the survivor of a heterosexual couple in a stable relationship. The House of Lords extended the reach of para. 2(2) of Sch. 1 when it construed the words "as his or her wife or husband" so as to include cohabiting same-sex couples. The House of Lords deviated from the provision's specific purpose and thus departed from the intention of the enacting legislature.[259] It follows that a provision's underlying specific purpose, which is an aspect of the intention of the enacting parliament, does not in itself serve as an outer limit of interpretation for s. 3(1) HRA.[260] In the words of Lord Nicholls, "a court can modify the meaning, and hence the effect, of primary and secondary legislation".[261]

Lord Nicholls added in *Ghaidan* that "[t]he question of difficulty is how far, and in what circumstances, section 3 requires a court to depart from the

---

[256] *Attorney General's Reference (No. 4 of 2002)* [2004] UKHL 43, paras. 28, 53 (Lord Bingham).
[257] *R. (Spath Holme) v. Secretary of State for the Environment, Transport and the Regions* [2001] 2 AC 349 (HL), 397–398 (Lord Nicholls).
[258] *Attorney General's Reference (No. 4 of 2002)* [2004] UKHL 43, para. 53 (Lord Bingham).
[259] *Ghaidan v. Godin-Mendoza* [2004] UKHL 30, para. 128 (Lord Rodger); *R. (Wilkinson) v. Inland Revenue Commissioners* [2005] UKHL 30, para. 18 (Lord Hoffmann, "It may have come as a surprise to the members of the Parliament which in 1988 enacted the statute construed in the Ghaidan case that the relationship to which they were referring could include homosexual relationships. In that sense the construction may have been contrary to the 'intention of Parliament'").
[260] See also *Manchester City Council v. Pinnock* [2010] UKSC 45, paras. 69, 75, 77 (Lord Neuberger, giving the judgment of the court).
[261] *Ghaidan v. Godin-Mendoza* [2004] UKHL 30, para. 30 (Lord Nicholls).

Chapter 3. Rights-Consistent Interpretation

intention of the enacting Parliament. The answer to this question depends upon the intention reasonably to be attributed to Parliament in enacting section 3".[262] Lord Nicholls indicated that a reconciliatory balance needs to be found between the two potentially conflicting intentions of Parliament.[263] Using more constitutional language, P. Sales has described s. 3(1) HRA as "a mechanism through which the democratic tradition and the liberal human rights tradition are integrated into practice to produce determinate results in real cases. ... Thus both Parliament and the courts play active roles in creating and legitimising this sort of structured partnership in a joint constitutional endeavour".[264] The required reconciliatory balance shows that even though the intention of the parliament that enacted the contested legislation does not serve as an absolute interpretative limit for s. 3(1) HRA, it retains a certain limiting function as a judge cannot entirely disregard it either. The same applies to a provision's underlying specific purpose. P. Sales's reference to the partnership model captures the wide judicial law-making powers under s. 3(1) HRA and illustrates the change of judicial attitude compared to judicial law-making under conventional canons of interpretation. From a comparative perspective, such a partnership model between the judge and the legislature is also advocated by the BVerfG based on its understanding of art. 20(3) GG.

Lord Nicholls and Lord Rodger used the notion of substance/the "concept" of the legislation as a proxy for the intention of the enacting parliament. When a court determines the concept and substance of a provision, it ultimately gives effect to this intention. The remaining limiting function of the intention of the enacting parliament has to be derived from this legislative concept and substance. We have already seen that Lord Nicholls seemed to equate the notion of "concept" with the abstract reasons underlying the purpose of the contested provision in *Ghaidan*. One may thus infer that a Convention-compatible meaning must be consistent with and cannot depart from the more abstract reasons underlying the purpose of the challenged provision. In other words, a rights-consistent meaning is not possible if it departs from the abstract reasons underlying Parliament's specific intention as expressed in a specific provision. Yet the abstract method of purposive construction as employed by Lord Nicholls is difficult to undertake because he gave no guidance on where the necessary level of abstractness lies. What is more, Lord Nicholls did not consider this abstract purposive reasoning when he discussed the limits of Convention-compatible interpretation. He did not use the notion of concept as an interpretative limit itself. None of the

---

[262] Ibid., para. 30 (Lord Nicholls).
[263] See also *R. v. A (No. 2)* [2001] UKHL 25, para. 45 (Lord Steyn, "If this approach is adopted, section 41 will have achieved a major part of its objective but its excessive reach will have been attenuated in accordance with the will of Parliament as reflected in section 3 of the 1998 Act").
[264] SALES, above n. 116, p. 465.

other judges in *Ghaidan* attempted to reconcile the Convention-compatible meaning with the underlying reasons of the provision's purpose or drew on Lord Nicholls's notion of concept to develop limits of interpretation. This is to be welcomed, as the notion of concept as used by Lord Nicholls is too vague to be useful as a workable limit of interpretation. The notion of concept does not shed sufficient light on the question of how far a court can depart from the intention of the enacting parliament. I will demonstrate in the next section that both Lord Rodger and Lord Nicholls used the fundamental features of the legislation as a limit of interpretation and as a proxy for the (remaining) intention of the enacting parliament. The reconciliatory balance between the two intentions of Parliament is thus expressed in the outer interpretative limit that a court cannot depart from a fundamental feature of the challenged legislation.

Apart from the express terms of the legislation, another means of identifying the plain intention of Parliament is to determine what Parliament necessarily implied with the legislation.[265] If the legislation contains provisions that contradict the Convention-compatible meaning by necessary implication, it is not possible to achieve compatibility with Convention rights by using s. 3(1) HRA.[266] A further explanation of the necessary implication limit has not yet been given in a written judicial opinion in the context of s. 3(1) HRA. This limit remains highly vague in its unspecified form. An explanation of the necessary implication limit was provided by Lord Hobhouse in *R. (Morgan Grenfell)* in the context of the principle of legality. In that case, the question arose whether s. 20(1) of the Taxes Management Act 1970 abrogates the taxpayer's common law right to rely upon legal professional privilege. Lord Hobhouse remarked that a necessary implication is not the same as a reasonable implication. A necessary implication necessarily follows from the express provisions of a statute construed in their context.

> It distinguishes between what it would have been sensible or reasonable for Parliament to have included or what Parliament would, if it had thought about it, probably have included and what it is clear that the express language of the statute shows that the statute must have included. A necessary implication is a matter of express language and logic not interpretation.[267]

---

[265] *R. v. A (No. 2)* [2001] UKHL 25, para. 108 (Lord Hope); *Ghaidan v. Godin-Mendoza* [2004] UKHL 30, para. 75 (Lord Millett); cf. *R. (Anderson) v. Secretary of State for the Home Department* [2002] UKHL 46, para. 59 (Lord Steyn).

[266] *R. v. A (No. 2)* [2001] UKHL 25, para. 108 (Lord Hope); *R. v. Lambert* [2001] UKHL 37, para. 79 (Lord Hope); *R. (Anderson) v. Secretary of State for the Home Department* [2002] UKHL 46, para. 59 (Lord Steyn); *Ghaidan v. Godin-Mendoza* [2004] UKHL 30, paras. 75-76 (Lord Millett), para. 117 (Lord Rodger).

[267] *R. (Morgan Grenfell) v. Special Commissioners of Income Tax* [2002] UKHL 21, para. 45 (Lord Hobhouse). Confirmed in *B v. Auckland District Law Society* [2003] UKPC 38, para. 58.

Chapter 3. Rights-Consistent Interpretation

This explanation by Lord Hobhouse cannot be transferred to the necessary implication limit for s. 3(1) HRA since the outer limits of the principle of legality and of s. 3(1) HRA are not identical and since judges enjoy a greater degree of interpretative power under s. 3(1) HRA.[268] Lord Hobhouse's explanation also attaches too much weight to the statutory language when compared with *Ghaidan*. Under s. 3(1) HRA, a court may depart from unambiguous statutory language whereas the principle of legality does not allow a court to disregard an unambiguous expression of Parliament's intention.

In the light of *Ghaidan*, the necessary implication limit for s. 3(1) HRA should be clarified by looking at the substance of the legislation, which is itself determined by the statutory language, the overall scheme of the legislation and the provision's underlying purpose. Even if the question of what it is that Parliament implied with the legislation is based on the legislation's substance, it is not sufficient that the legislation's substance contradicts a Convention-compatible meaning. The implication must be necessary and that is a matter of the clearly expressed substance of the legislation. This condition is met if the legislation contains a substantive principle that contradicts the Convention-compatible meaning. It is submitted here that the necessary implication limit can be incorporated into the fundamental feature limit, which will be discussed in the next section. That is because the limiting function of the intention of the enacting parliament has to be derived from the substance of the legislation, and the fundamental feature limit serves as a proxy for the remaining limiting function of the intention of the enacting legislature. The necessary implication limit is thus a subset of the fundamental feature limit.[269] If this view is followed, the contested legislation contradicts the Convention-compatible meaning by necessary implication if it contains a fundamental feature that contradicts the Convention-compatible meaning. More recent case law expounding the limits of s. 3(1) HRA has not referred to the necessary implication limit and has instead focused on the fundamental feature limit.[270] This supports the view submitted here.

It is worth noting that the majority in *Ghaidan* did not argue that the compatible meaning of para. 2(2) of Sch. 1 to the Rent Act 1977 gave effect to

---

[268] *Ahmed and others v. HM Treasury* [2010] UKSC 2, paras. 115–117 (Lord Phillips); SALES, above n. 73, pp. 598, 611. See also R. CLAYTON, The empire strikes back: common law rights and the Human Rights Act, [2015] *PL* 1, 11–12; VAN ZYL SMIT, above n. 232, pp. 305. For a different view, see *R. (Simms) v. Secretary of State for the Home Department* [2002] 2 AC 115 (HL), 132 (Lord Hoffmann).

[269] We will see in the next subsection that the fundamental feature limit is wider than the necessary implication limit as it is not only activated when a Convention-compatible meaning contradicts a fundamental feature of the legislation but also when a Convention-compatible meaning is simply inconsistent with a fundamental feature of the legislation.

[270] Cf., e.g. *Vodafone 2 v. Revenue and Customs Commissioners* [2009] EWCA Civ 446, para. 38 (Sir Andrew Morritt C); *Churchill Insurance Co. Ltd. v. Fitzgerald & Wilkinson* [2012] EWCA Civ 1166, para. 50 (Aikens LJ, with whom Etherton and Maurice Kay LJJ agreed).

the presumed or hypothetical intention of the parliament that enacted the Rent Act 1977. The judges did not speculate as to what Parliament would have done had it been alerted to the (future) incompatibility at the time of the passing of the contested legislation.[271] They did not disguise their creative role by aligning the compatible meaning with the hypothetical intention of the enacting parliament. The judges also clearly stated that their new creative role in statutory interpretation under s. 3(1) HRA is based on the will of the parliament that enacted the HRA. The absence of an argument with the hypothetical or presumed intention of the parliament enacting the contested legislation illustrates a difference between conventional methods of interpretation and s. 3(1) HRA. This difference was already alluded to in the previous section where *Ghaidan* and *Fitzpatrick* were compared. Under conventional canons of interpretation, a court asks "positively" whether Parliament intended or could have reasonably intended to *include* the compatible meaning. Under s. 3(1) HRA, the reasoning of the majority in *Ghaidan* gives the impression that a court has to consider "negatively" whether there are sufficient indications, for example a contrary fundamental feature of the legislation, that Parliament intended to *exclude* the compatible meaning.[272] If such sufficient indications do not exist, the strong presumption of compliance is not rebutted and the compatible meaning is prima facie possible and can be chosen. Both approaches to ascertaining the intention of Parliament use a different standard of proof for reconciling the intention of the enacting parliament with the compatible meaning. The approach applied for s. 3(1) HRA enshrines the idea that a balance needs to be struck between the intention of the parliament that enacted the legislation under consideration and the intention of the parliament that created s. 3(1) HRA. The compatible meaning is prescribed by an external standard and the latter determines when the interpretation of the provision is Convention compliant. All that matters then is whether something bars a court from choosing the conforming meaning. This shifts the focus of statutory interpretation towards applying the interpretative limits of s. 3(1) HRA. Furthermore, the approach under s. 3(1) HRA also illustrates the working of the strong presumption of compliance. The interpretative approach that appears in some cases of Convention-compatible interpretation does not mean that judges no longer rely on presumed legislative intent when they use s. 3(1) HRA. *Ghaidan* concerned the interpretation of pre-HRA legislation. In cases where English courts interpret post-HRA

---

[271] For criticism of judicial reasoning that relies on a hypothetical intention of Parliament, see R. Ekins, A critique of radical approaches to rights consistent statutory interpretation, (2003) 6 *EHRLR* 641, 648.

[272] Cf. *Ghaidan v. Godin-Mendoza* [2004] UKHL 30, paras. 122, 128 (Lord Rodger). See also ibid., para. 86 (Lord Millett); *R. (GC) v. Commissioner of Police of the Metropolis* [2011] UKSC 21, para. 55 (Lord Phillips).

legislation compatibly with Convention rights, it is more common for them to argue with the presumed intention of the enacting parliament.[273] In these cases, the HRA forms part of the constitutional background against which the enacting parliament has legislated.

The most obvious indication that Parliament intended to exclude the Convention-compatible meaning occurs if the legislature uses express statutory language that contradicts the Convention-compliant meaning.[274] Furthermore, Parliament intends to exclude the compatible meaning if the *substance* of the challenged provision and the suggested Convention-compatible meaning are opposites.[275] We have already seen in the previous section that it is implicit in this outer limit of interpretation that Parliament's intention to exclude the Convention-compatible meaning is determined not only by the statutory language, but also by other criteria such as the overall scheme of the legislation and the purpose of the provision as understood by the enacting legislature. How these criteria have to be weighted in an individual case is not determined by methodological rules in judicial practice but depends on the circumstances of the individual case and grants scope for evaluative arguments and judicial discretion.

So far, I have not addressed the elephant in the room: can it be reconciled with constitutional theory that courts can depart from the intention of a post-HRA parliament?[276] English courts have argued that the orthodox doctrine that Parliament cannot bind its successor is indeed modified in the realm of the HRA. Laws LJ argued in *Thoburn* that the HRA is a "constitutional" statute that cannot be repealed by mere implication.[277] This common law constitutional development has found further judicial support since.[278] The judicial reading

---

[273] See, e.g. *R. v. A (No. 2)* [2001] UKHL 25, para. 45 (Lord Steyn, "After all, it is realistic to proceed on the basis that the legislature would not, if alerted to the problem, have wished to deny the right to an accused to put forward a full and complete defence by advancing truly probative material. It is therefore possible under section 3 to read section 41, and in particular section 41(3)(c), as subject to the implied provision that evidence or questioning which is required to ensure a fair trial under article 6 of the Convention should not be treated as inadmissible"); *R. (GC) v. Commissioner of Police of the Metropolis* [2011] UKSC 21, para. 28 (Lord Dyson).

[274] The express terms limit and the relationship between the statutory language and the intention of Parliament have already been discussed in the previous section.

[275] *Ghaidan v. Godin-Mendoza* [2004] UKHL 30, paras. 110–111, 122 (Lord Rodger).

[276] It was established in Section 1.2 above that a power of the courts to depart from the intention of a pre-HRA parliament can be reconciled with an orthodox understanding of parliamentary sovereignty. Yet, the correct interpretation of s. 3(1) HRA shows that the Parliament of 1998 did not grant this power to the courts.

[277] *Thoburn v. Sunderland City Council* [2002] EWHC 195 (Admin), paras. 60–63 (Laws LJ).

[278] *H. v. Lord Advocate* [2012] UKSC 24, para. 30 (Lord Hope); *R. (HS2 Action Alliance Ltd.) v. Secretary of State for Transport* [2014] UKSC 3, paras. 207, 208 (Lord Neuberger and Lord Mance (with whom Lady Hale, Lord Kerr, Lord Sumption, Lord Reed and Lord Carnwath agreed)); *R. (Miller) v. Secretary of State for Exiting the European Union* [2017] UKSC 51, para. 66 (Lord Neuberger, Lady Hale, Lord Mance, Lord Kerr, Lord Clarke,

of the HRA effects a limited form of entrenchment.[279] What this modification cannot explain, however, is why s. 3(1) HRA has "revolutionised statutory interpretation".[280] Even if the HRA is characterised as a constitutional statute that is not subject to implied repeal, it does not follow from this that s. 3(1) HRA empowers courts to depart from the intention of the enacting parliament. Whether or not s. 3(1) HRA is intended to convey that power on to courts is a question about the correct construction of s. 3(1) HRA. The doctrine of implied repeal refers to the relationship between a later parliament and an earlier parliament in the case of conflicting Acts of Parliament. Section 3(1) HRA deals with statutory interpretation: it refers to the relationship between the courts and Parliament and the limits of the judicial function.[281] Statutory interpretation (s. 3(1) HRA) and rules for resolving contradictions between different norms (e.g. the doctrine of implied repeal) are two different things.[282] If a Convention-compatible interpretation of a post-HRA statute fails, this simply means that conformity between a Convention right and domestic law cannot be reached by means of judicial interpretation as the limits of the judicial function are surpassed. It is clear from the terms of s. 3(1) HRA that a Convention-compatible

---

Lord Wilson, Lord Sumption, Lord Hodge); *R. (Miller) v. Secretary of State for Exiting the European Union* [2016] EWHC 2768 (Admin), paras. 43, 88 (Lord Thomas of Cwmgiedd CJ, Sir Terence Etherton MR, Sales LJ); cf. *Hansard*, HL Deb 18 November 1997, vol 583, col 509 (Lord Irvine, "That might give rise to the doctrine of implied repeal. That is a doctrine that can have no application because of the express terms of Clause 3").

[279] According to the "manner and form" theory of parliamentary sovereignty (see, e.g. M. GORDON, *Parliamentary sovereignty in the UK constitution*, Hart, Oxford 2015, chapters 2 and 4), Parliament is capable of laying down binding conditions concerning how and in what form legislation has to be enacted, but it cannot bind future Parliaments with regard to the substance of legislation. This theory allows for a limited form of entrenchment of legislation. Even though *obiter* comments in *R. (Jackson) v. Attorney General* [2005] UKHL 56 lend support to the "manner and form" theory, it is not currently supported by binding case law (see, e.g. *Ellen Street Estates v. Minister of Health* [1934] 1 KB 590 (CA), 597 (Maugham LJ, "The Legislature cannot, according to our constitution, bind itself as to the form of subsequent legislation"); *Thoburn v. Sunderland City Council* [2002] EWHC 195 (Admin), para. 59 (Laws LJ, "Parliament cannot bind its successors by stipulating against repeal, wholly or partly, of the ECA. It cannot stipulate as to the manner and form of any subsequent legislation. It cannot stipulate against implied repeal any more than it can stipulate against express repeal") whereas the orthodox view of parliamentary sovereignty is supported by precedent. For an alternative "third" account, see A. TUCKER, Uncertainty in the rule of recognition and in the doctrine of parliamentary sovereignty, (2011) 31 *OJLS* 61–83.

[280] ARDEN, above n. 71, pp. 487, 497; cf. *R. (JS) v. Secretary of State for Work and Pensions* [2015] UKSC, para. 92 (Lord Reed).

[281] This dimension of the limits of the judicial function vis-à-vis the legislature is not taken into account by A. YOUNG, Case comment: hunting sovereignty: Jackson v. Her Majesty's Attorney-General, [2006] *PL* 187, 189.

[282] BARAK, above n. 119, pp. 74–75. For a different view, see T.R.S. ALLAN, Parliamentary sovereignty: Lord Denning's dexterous revolution, (1983) 3 *OJLS* 22, 31; KAVANAGH, above n. 50, p. 297.

Chapter 3. Rights-Consistent Interpretation

interpretation can fail. In this case, a court gives effect to the intention of the 1998 Parliament by being unable to reach a Convention-compatible meaning. The consequence is that courts may make a declaration of incompatibility under s. 4 HRA. The matter of implied repeal does not arise in this context.[283]

The power of English courts to depart from the intention of a post-HRA parliament cannot be reconciled with the orthodox doctrine of parliamentary sovereignty. A court that deviates from the intention of a post-HRA parliament exceeds its judicial function as this is something that a court cannot do according to constitutional orthodoxy.[284] Such a power amounts to a fundamental constitutional change in the courts' law-making function. Therefore, it cannot be said that s. 3(1) merely expands or enhances methods of interpretation that the courts have traditionally used.[285] Such a view downplays the new constitutional role of the courts under s. 3(1) HRA. Section 3(1) HRA as applied in judicial practice extends beyond giving effect to presumed legislative intent. How did this constitutional change come about? It is controversial whether constitutional reform modifying the doctrine of parliamentary sovereignty can come about by Parliament enacting legislation, by the courts creating this change or by both developments together.[286] The answer to this controversy depends on who or what created the principle of parliamentary sovereignty. Despite scattered judicial *dicta* that parliamentary sovereignty is a construct of the judge-made common law,[287] the doctrine of parliamentary sovereignty cannot be ascribed to statute alone or to the common law alone.[288] Instead, the doctrine of parliamentary sovereignty has been recognised as the fundamental principle of the UK constitution because "it has for centuries been accepted as such by judges and others officially concerned in the operation of our constitutional system".[289] Even though judicial acceptance is a necessary condition for parliamentary sovereignty, judges alone cannot unilaterally modify the doctrine. Parliamentary sovereignty can evolve, but that requires a change in official consensus. It requires that judges and others officially concerned in the operation of the

---

[283] KAVANAGH, above n. 50, pp. 298–299, 301.
[284] See Section 1 above.
[285] For this view, see, however, KAVANAGH, above n. 50, pp. 108–109.
[286] For discussion, see J. GOLDSWORTHY, *Parliamentary sovereignty: contemporary debates*, CUP, Cambridge 2010, pp. 312–314.
[287] *R. (Jackson) v. Attorney General* [2005] UKHL 56, para. 102 (Lord Steyn), para. 126 (Lord Hope); *Thoburn v. Sunderland City Council* [2002] EWHC 195 (Admin), para. 60 (Laws LJ). See also T.R.S. ALLAN, *The sovereignty of law: freedom, constitution, and common law*, OUP, Oxford 2013, p. 135.
[288] Space constraints prevent a further elaboration of this controversial issue. Instead, the reader is guided to the following sources: T. BINGHAM, *The rule of law*, Penguin Books, London 2011, p. 167; GORDON, above n. 279, pp. 131–132; R. EKINS, Acts of Parliament and the Parliament Acts, (2007) 123 LQR 91, 103; GOLDSWORTHY, above n. 286, chapter 2; J. GOLDSWORTHY, *The sovereignty of Parliament: history and philosophy*, OUP, Oxford 2011, chapter 10.
[289] BINGHAM, above n. 288, p. 167; see also GOLDSWORTHY, above n. 286, pp. 54–56.

UK constitutional system, and that certainly includes Parliament, accept this evolution.[290] This evolution of official consensus is a result of legal deliberation and does not simply happen because public opinion or attitude changes. Has the doctrine of parliamentary sovereignty evolved in this way with regard to the power of the courts to depart from the intention of a post-HRA parliament? Has the general consensus changed? The correct answer to this question is no[291] for two reasons.

First, the legislative materials of the HRA discuss the impact of declarations of incompatibility on the principle of parliamentary sovereignty, but they do not specifically discuss the impact of s. 3(1) HRA on this principle. There are no indications that Parliament intended courts to be able to depart from the intention of a post-HRA parliament. The consensus was that the HRA is compatible with the doctrine of parliamentary sovereignty. Lord Millett rightly pointed out in *Ghaidan* that ss. 3 and 4 HRA were carefully crafted to preserve the doctrine of parliamentary sovereignty, "and any application of the ambit of section 3 beyond its proper scope subverts" the constitutional doctrine.[292] Second, applying the principle of legality[293] shows that Parliament when enacting s. 3(1) HRA cannot be presumed to have intended such a change.[294] The paramount fundamental constitutional principle in the UK that is recognised by the common law is the doctrine of parliamentary sovereignty. The general statutory language of s. 3(1) HRA ("possible") cannot override this doctrine. Lord Millett said in *Ghaidan* that any change in the fundamental constitutional doctrine of parliamentary sovereignty "should be the consequence of deliberate legislative action and not judicial activism".[295] Lord Thomas of Cwmgiedd CJ, Sir Terence Etherton MR and Sales LJ said in the High Court decision in *Miller* that

> the stronger the constitutional principle the stronger the presumption that Parliament did not intend to override it and the stronger the material required, in terms of express language or clear necessary implication, before the inference can properly be drawn that in fact it did so intend. Similarly, the stronger the constitutional principle, the more readily can it be inferred that words used by Parliament were intended to carry a meaning which reflects the principle.[296]

---

[290] GOLDSWORTHY, above n. 286, pp. 54–55.
[291] For a different view, see NEUBERGER, above n. 44, p. 7, para. 14.
[292] *Ghaidan v. Godin-Mendoza* [2004] UKHL 30, para. 27 (Lord Nicholls), para. 57 (Lord Millett).
[293] Alternatively: the presumption that Parliament does intend to legislate in conformity with background constitutional principles.
[294] Even if Parliament alone cannot bring about a change in the doctrine of parliamentary sovereignty, it can intend to initiate such a change. Parliament can intend to change the doctrine of parliamentary sovereignty, even though this intention is only a necessary but not a sufficient step to change the constitutional principle.
[295] *Ghaidan v. Godin-Mendoza* [2004] UKHL 30, para. 57 (Lord Millett).
[296] *R. (Miller) v. Secretary of State for Exiting the European Union* [2016] EWHC 2768 (Admin), paras. 82–83 (Lord Thomas of Cwmgiedd CJ, Sir Terence Etherton MR, Sales LJ).

Chapter 3. Rights-Consistent Interpretation

It can readily be inferred that the word "possible" in s. 3(1) HRA was intended to carry a meaning that reflects the doctrine of parliamentary sovereignty. No material exists that, in terms of express language or necessary implication, suggests that Parliament when enacting s. 3(1) HRA intended to confer on the courts a new constitutional role by empowering them to depart from the intention of the enacting parliament of challenged post-HRA legislation.[297]

It follows that the construction of s. 3(1) HRA by English courts and with it the fundamental constitutional change in the courts' law-making powers was not intended by the Parliament of 1998. Judges have attempted to initiate a modification to the doctrine of parliamentary sovereignty with their interpretation of s. 3(1) HRA, but this change was not and has not been supported by Parliament. The general consensus has not yet been altered. It follows that the courts have exceeded their constitutional role and the limits of their function by empowering themselves to depart from the intention of a post-HRA parliament when using s. 3(1) HRA.[298] This does not mean that the courts openly deny the sovereignty of Parliament. Their interpretation approach has not attracted much public criticism and has regularly stayed under the political radar. Ultimately, Parliament retains the power to reverse a Convention-compatible interpretation by amending the legislation and reinstating the incompatibility. The HRA preserves the doctrine of parliamentary sovereignty in formal terms, but judicial practice applying s. 3(1) HRA undermines the constitutional doctrine in substantive terms.[299] Even if one disagrees with the view that s. 3(1) HRA as interpreted in judicial practice involves a modification of the doctrine of parliamentary sovereignty, another alteration of the judicial role as traditionally understood remains. I have demonstrated in Chapter 2 that it is a fundamental constitutional principle, recognised by the common law, that a court cannot depart from the intention of the enacting parliament under conventional canons of construction. The judicial construction of s. 3(1) HRA empowers courts to deviate from the enacting parliament's intention and thus entails a modification of this fundamental principle. An application of the principle of legality leads to the result that the general statutory language of s. 3(1) HRA ("possible") cannot override this fundamental principle. Parliament when enacting s. 3(1) HRA cannot be presumed to have intended such a fundamental change. English courts have thus exceeded their judicial role when construing the terms of s. 3(1) HRA.

An alternative explanation for reconciling the wide interpretative powers under s. 3(1) HRA with the doctrine of parliamentary sovereignty was advanced

---

[297] Cf. Dickson, above n. 219, p. 63.
[298] For a different view, see P. Craig, Judicial power, the Judicial Power Project and the UK, December 2017, SSRN, p. 16, available online at http://www.ssrn.com.
[299] For a different view, see S. Gardbaum, *The new Commonwealth model of constitutionalism*, CUP, Cambridge 2013, p. 227.

by Lord Hoffmann in *Wilkinson*. He argued that Parliament's intention when enacting a statute is to be derived from the terms of the statute read in its context. Due to s. 3(1) HRA, this context now includes a strong presumption that Parliament did not intend to legislate contrary to Convention rights.[300] Lord Hoffmann further claimed that the aim of Convention-compatible interpretation still is, taking into account the presumption created by s. 3(1) HRA, to ascertain what "Parliament would reasonably be understood to have meant by using the actual language of the statute".[301] Lord Hoffmann's view shows that the obligation to interpret post-HRA legislation against the background of the earlier HRA can be reconciled with the maxim that a court cannot deviate from the intention of the enacting legislature under the doctrine of parliamentary sovereignty. Yet it is submitted here that this alternative explanation conflicts with *Ghaidan*, which established that a court may depart from the intention of the enacting parliament even if the legislation post-dates the HRA.[302]

7.2.3. Fundamental Features of the Legislation

Lord Nicholls and Lord Millett concurred in *Ghaidan* that a s. 3(1) HRA interpretation does not entitle the courts to adopt a meaning that is inconsistent with a fundamental feature of the legislation.[303] The first case that discussed the fundamental feature limit in the area of s. 3(1) HRA was *In re S (Minors)*. The case concerned appeals in two factually unrelated cases, both of which involved care orders issued by a judge in respect of two children under the Children Act 1989. Under the provisions of the Children Act 1989, a court may make a care order when the threshold conditions are met and when the court is satisfied that such an order would be in the best interest of the child. After the order has been made, the court has no continuing role with regard to the care order. Lord Nicholls gave the leading speech in *In re S (Minors)*. All the other members of the House of Lords agreed with him. He held that it is a cardinal principle of the Children Act that after a care order has been made, the local authority that has been ordered to receive the child into its care has parental responsibility for the child without the court retaining a supervisory role.[304] While a care order is in force, the court's powers to intervene are expressly excluded, with a few exceptions, according to the Children Act 1989.[305] Lord Nicholls reached this

---

[300] *R. (Wilkinson) v. Inland Revenue Commissioners* [2005] UKHL 30, paras. 17–18 (Lord Hoffmann).
[301] Ibid., para. 17 (Lord Hoffmann).
[302] Similarly, PHILLIPS, above n. 73, p. 40; NEUBERGER, above n. 44, p. 6, para. 13.
[303] *Ghaidan v. Godin-Mendoza* [2004] UKHL 30, para. 33 (Lord Nicholls), paras. 67–68, 73 (Lord Millett).
[304] *In re S (Minors)* [2002] UKHL 10, paras. 23, 25, 27–28 (Lord Nicholls).
[305] Ibid., paras. 23, 24, 42 (Lord Nicholls); cf. *Ghaidan v. Godin-Mendoza* [2004] UKHL 30, para. 113 (Lord Rodger).

interpretation by looking at the provisions of the Children Act 1989 and its legislative history.

Before *In re S (Minors)* was decided in the House of Lords, the Court of Appeal had made two major adjustments and innovations in the construction and application of the Children Act 1989 for cases in which an actual or prospective breach of arts. 6 or 8 ECHR by the local authority was demonstrated.[306] One of these innovations was a new procedure by which significant elements of a care plan would be identified and elevated to "starred status" at the trial. If a starred element was not achieved within a reasonable time of the date set at trial, either the guardian of the child or the local authority would have the right to apply to the court for directions.[307] The Court of Appeal's devised "starring system" thus conferred on the courts a power to supervise the way in which local authorities discharge their parental responsibilities under care orders. The local authority appealed to the House of Lords against this reasoning of the Court of Appeal in one of the cases in *In re S (Minors)*. In the other case, a mother appealed against the order made by the Court of Appeal. Lord Nicholls declared in the House of Lords that the introduction of a starring system into the Children Act 1989 by the Court of Appeal goes beyond legitimate interpretation under s. 3(1) HRA even if the Children Act 1989 is inconsistent with arts. 6 and 8 of the Convention.[308] He observed with regard to the outer limits of s. 3(1) HRA: "For present purposes it is sufficient to say that a meaning which departs substantially from a fundamental feature of an Act of Parliament is likely to have crossed the boundary between interpretation and amendment".[309] According to Lord Nicholls, a court "is empowered to impose an obligation on an authority concerning the future care of the child" and to "exercise a newly-created supervisory function" under the Court of Appeal's starring system.[310] Therefore, he stated, the starring system departs substantially from the Act's fundamental feature that while a care order is in force, the court has no supervisory role and no powers to intervene in the authority's discharge of its responsibilities. Consequently, the starring system could not be justified as a legitimate interpretation of the Children Act 1989 pursuant to s. 3(1) HRA.

Lord Nicholls's statement of the fundamental feature limit in *In re S (Minors)* is ambiguous due to the introductory words chosen ("[f]or present purposes it is sufficient") and due to the criterion of likelihood. In *Ghaidan*, Lord Nicholls removed this ambiguity and clearly stated that a court cannot adopt a meaning under s. 3(1) HRA that is inconsistent with a fundamental feature of the

---

[306] *In re S (Minors)* [2001] EWCA Civ 757, para. 32 (Thorpe LJ), paras. 71, 79 (Hale LJ).
[307] Ibid., para. 30 (Thorpe LJ), para. 79 (Hale LJ); cf. *In re S (Minors)* [2002] UKHL 10, para. 17 (Lord Nicholls).
[308] *In re S (Minors)* [2002] UKHL 10, para. 36 (Lord Nicholls).
[309] Ibid., para. 40 (Lord Nicholls).
[310] Ibid., para. 42 (Lord Nicholls).

legislation. His discussion of this outer limit of interpretation in *Ghaidan* suggests neither that the inconsistency must be substantial nor that an inconsistency *per definitionem* equals a substantial departure.[311] Lord Nicholls thus widened the fundamental feature limit of interpretation in *Ghaidan* compared to *In re S (Minors)*. Lord Rodger agreed in effect with this widening of the fundamental feature limit because he argued that a court cannot use s. 3(1) HRA to introduce into legislation "something which was actually inconsistent with one of its cardinal principles".[312] Since Lord Rodger also used the terms cardinal principle and fundamental feature without distinction,[313] this suggests that a simple inconsistency suffices for the fundamental feature limit. All the judges in *Ghaidan* who commented on the fundamental feature limit agreed that a court cannot adopt a meaning under s. 3(1) HRA that is inconsistent with a fundamental feature of the legislation. Later case law has confirmed this interpretative limit of s. 3(1) HRA.[314] For the majority in *Ghaidan*, the gender of the cohabitees was not a fundamental feature of the legislation. The phrase "living with the original tenant as his or her wife or husband" in para. 2(2) of Sch. 1 to the Rent Act 1977 could thus be interpreted to include same-sex couples.

When determining the fundamental features of the legislation, the speech of Lord Nicholls in *In re S (Minors)* and the speeches of Lord Nicholls and Lord Rodger in *Ghaidan* show that a court draws on the statutory text, the legislative history, the overall scheme of the legislation and the underlying purpose of the legislation. The wording[315] and the underlying purpose of the legislation therefore remain important elements when a judge analyses the limits of possible Convention-compatible interpretation. Recourse to the interpretative criteria[316] elucidates why the fundamental feature limit takes such a prominent role when judges discuss the outer limits of the judicial function for Convention-compatible interpretation. Judges give effect to the intention of the enacting parliament when they rely on the interpretative criteria. The intention of the enacting parliament thus retains a certain limiting function under s. 3(1) HRA. This limiting function is constrained, however, as it has to climb the threshold of being fundamental. The latter criterion incorporates the idea of a reconciliatory balance between the intention of the parliament enacting the challenged legislation and the intention of Parliament in enacting s. 3(1) HRA. The criterion answers the question of how far a court can depart from the

---

[311] *Ghaidan v. Godin-Mendoza* [2004] UKHL 30, paras. 30–32 (Lord Nicholls).
[312] Ibid., para. 114 (Lord Rodger).
[313] Ibid., paras. 113, 114 (Lord Rodger).
[314] *Kennedy v. The Charity Commission* [2014] UKSC 20, para. 224 (Lord Carnwath); *Hounslow London Borough Council v. Powell* [2011] UKSC 8, para. 62 (Lord Hope); *Benkharbouche and Janah v. Embassy of Sudan and others* [2015] EWCA Civ 33, para. 67 (Lord Dyson MR).
[315] See, e.g. *Hounslow London Borough Council v. Powell* [2011] UKSC 8, para. 62 (Lord Hope).
[316] For another example, see *R. (GC) v. Commissioner of Police of the Metropolis* [2011] UKSC 21, paras. 27, 24 (Lord Dyson).

Chapter 3. Rights-Consistent Interpretation

enacting parliament's intent, since it can only depart from this intention if the intention does not amount to a fundamental feature of the legislation. On a more critical note,[317] the same indeterminacy that surrounds the weighing of the interpretative criteria is present in the fundamental feature limit. Whether or not a certain feature of the legislation meets the threshold of being fundamental is dependent on the weight a judge attaches to the wording, history or purpose of the legislation. This weight is not determined by principled guidelines or a set of factors in case law on s. 3(1) HRA but instead depends on the circumstances of the individual case. The disagreement between Lord Millett and the majority in *Ghaidan* shows that attaching different weight to the interpretative criteria can lead to disagreement over whether a certain feature of the legislation is fundamental or not. For Lord Millett, both the language and the legislative history of para. 2(2) of Sch. 1 to the Rent Act 1977 indicated that a relationship between persons of the opposite sex is an essential feature of the statute.[318]

Another case illustrating the indeterminacy of the fundamental feature limit is *R. (GC) v. Commissioner of Police of the Metropolis*, which concerned the interpretation of s. 64(1A) of the Police and Criminal Evidence Act 1984 (PACE). Section 64(1A) PACE was enacted by s. 82 of the Criminal Justice and Police Act 2001. The provision confers a discretionary power on the police to retain the data obtained from a suspect in connection with the investigation of an offence.[319] The words of the provision do not specify any time limit for the retention of the data. The minority in the Supreme Court in *GC* contended that Parliament in 2001 intended that the data taken from suspects in connection with the investigation of an offence should be retained indefinitely.[320] In the light of ECtHR case law, it was common ground in the Supreme Court that an indefinite retention of data infringes art. 8 ECHR. The question arose whether s. 64(1A) PACE can be interpreted in conformity with art. 8 ECHR according to s. 3(1) HRA. It was uncontroversial among the Supreme Court judges that Parliament enacted s. 64(1A) PACE in order to reverse the requirement of the previous s. 64 PACE that data should be destroyed when a suspect was cleared of an offence. In contrast to the minority, the majority argued that even though Parliament intended to permit the retention of the data in order to fulfil the

---

[317] VAN ZYL SMIT, above n. 232 p. 303 criticises the fundamental feature limit as being "too unsettled to secure legal certainty".
[318] *Ghaidan v. Godin-Mendoza* [2004] UKHL 30, paras. 78, 81, 94 (Lord Millett).
[319] Section 64(1A) PACE reads as follows: "Where … fingerprints, impressions of footwear or samples are taken from a person in connection with the investigation of an offence [they] may be retained after they have fulfilled the purposes for which they were taken but shall not be used by any person except for purposes related to the prevention or detection of crime, the investigation of an offence, the conduct of a prosecution or the identification of a deceased person or of the person from whom a body part came".
[320] *R. (GC) v. Commissioner of Police of the Metropolis* [2011] UKSC 21, paras. 97, 106 (Lord Rodger), para. 147 (Lord Brown).

statutory purposes, it does not follow from the statutory purposes that the data should be retained indefinitely in all cases.[321] The minority asserted that an indefinite retention of data is a fundamental feature of the amending legislation that inserted s. 64(1A) into PACE.[322] Therefore, the minority concluded, s. 3(1) HRA cannot be used to reach a Convention-compliant meaning of s. 64(1A) PACE without crossing the line between interpretation and impermissible amendment of legislation. The majority disagreed and contended that it is not possible to "extract this fundamental feature from the statute".[323] The majority was thus able to read s. 64(1A) PACE compatibly with art. 8 ECHR. The disagreement about the correct purpose of the legislation between the majority and the minority in the Supreme Court directly affected the fundamental feature limit. If the 2001 Parliament did not intend to retain data indefinitely, it would go without saying that indefinite retention of data cannot constitute a fundamental feature of the legislation. What the minority failed to explain is the following: even if Parliament intended to retain data indefinitely in 2001, why would indefinite retention of data be a feature of the legislation that is fundamental to it? The Criminal Justice and Police Act 2001 concerns a huge variety of issues, reaching from police training to measures dealing with the consumption of alcohol in designated public places.[324] Even in Part 3 of this Act, which deals with amendments to PACE, the amendment relating to the retention of data is only one of many measures introduced by the new legislation.

Whether or not a feature of an Act of Parliament is fundamental or not cannot commonly be determined on the face of the statute. That is because it is uncommon for an Act of Parliament to differentiate expressly between fundamental and less fundamental provisions. Even if such qualifications were made, it would be an open question of whether courts would follow Parliament's assessment as it is the courts who determine whether a certain feature of a legislation is fundamental or not. The legislature is also unlikely to reflect about whether or not a certain feature of a statute is fundamental or not simply because a court may in the future depart from certain of the statute's features in order to render the statute compatible with Convention rights. The criterion of being fundamental is inherently evaluative and contains considerable scope for judicial discretion.[325] It has been shown that a very similar criticism applies for the outer interpretative limit of judicial law-making in Germany that a judge cannot distort or neglect a *fundamental* feature of a provision's objective.[326]

---

[321] Ibid., paras. 24–26 (Lord Dyson), para. 55 (Lord Phillips), para. 88 (Lord Kerr), cf. para. 72 (Lady Hale).
[322] Ibid., para. 114 (Lord Rodger).
[323] Ibid., para. 27 (Lord Dyson), para. 72 (Lady Hale).
[324] See the Criminal Justice and Police Act 2001, Explanatory Notes, paras. 3–4.
[325] Cf. SALES, above n. 73, pp. 598, 609 ("[t]he application of the relevant test calls for a value judgment on the part of the court").
[326] See Chapter 2, Section 3.3.1.

It is difficult to see how in a variety of cases the decision of whether or not a feature of the legislation is fundamental or not amounts to anything else but a policy decision. There is yet another reason that increases the indeterminacy of the fundamental feature limit: what limits the interpretative scope under s. 3(1) HRA is a fundamental feature of the legislation and not a fundamental feature of the particular provision that is being interpreted pursuant to s. 3(1) HRA. A feature has to be fundamental in the light of the overall statutory scheme. It follows that a court can depart from a certain feature of the challenged provision if the court does not consider this feature to be fundamental in the light of the whole of the Act of Parliament. Even though this understanding of the fundamental feature limit is compatible with *In re S (Minors)* and *Ghaidan*, there are indications in newer case law that at least some judges understand the fundamental feature limit as not referring to the level of the legislation but to the level of a provision or even of a subsection of a section in a statute.[327] This issue must thus be considered unresolved in current case law.

7.2.4. Scheme, Grain and Thrust of the Legislation

The fundamental feature limit does not comprehensively define the boundary between interpretation and legislation for the purposes of s. 3(1) HRA. Other limits of interpretation may bar a Convention-compatible interpretation.[328] In *Ghaidan*, the judges concurred that the scheme of the legislation functions as an outer limit for a s. 3(1) HRA interpretation. A Convention-compatible interpretation must not be inconsistent with the scheme of the legislation. Lord Nicholls and Lord Rodger referred to the House of Lords' decision in *In re S (Minors)*. They said that the Children Act 1989 could not be interpreted compatibly with the Convention because the starring system that conferred a supervisory function on the courts was "inconsistent in an important respect with the scheme"[329] of the Children Act 1989. Lord Steyn pointed out that interpretation under s. 3(1) HRA "could not provide a substitute scheme".[330] Lord Millett opined that a s. 3(1) HRA interpretation was not possible in *In re S (Minors)*, as "it would have been necessary to repeal the statutory scheme and substitute another".[331] Lord Rodger noted that a court cannot turn a legislative scheme inside out, that is to say, create a wholly different scheme from the one that was enacted by Parliament.[332] Consequently, there was agreement

---

[327] See, e.g. *R. (GC) v. Commissioner of Police of the Metropolis* [2011] UKSC 21, para. 27 (Lord Dyson, "the fundamental feature of section 64(1A)"), para. 115 (Lord Rodger).
[328] *Ghaidan v. Godin-Mendoza* [2004] UKHL 30, para. 115 (Lord Rodger).
[329] Ibid., para. 34 (Lord Nicholls), para. 113 (Lord Rodger).
[330] Ibid., para. 49 (Lord Steyn).
[331] Ibid., para. 65 (Lord Millett).
[332] Ibid., para. 110 (Lord Rodger).

in *Ghaidan* that a court cannot create a different legislative scheme from the one enacted in the legislation by resorting to s. 3(1) HRA.[333] When discussing *In re S (Minors)* in *Ghaidan*, Lord Nicholls and Lord Rodger did refer interchangeably to the scheme of the legislation as an outer interpretative limit and to the fundamental feature limit.[334] There are thus strong indications that both limits are in effect the same. There may be merit in the linguistic argument that the scheme of the legislation is a wider concept than a fundamental feature of the legislation. It may be argued that the fundamental features of the legislation taken together make up the scheme of the legislation. A suggested Convention-compatible meaning may be inconsistent with a fundamental feature of an Act of Parliament but may not be inconsistent with the scheme of the legislation as a whole. This reading of the scheme of the legislation limit is not supported by case law, however. Even if it is followed, the scheme of the legislation as an outer interpretative boundary would not add anything beyond the fundamental feature limit. If the former boundary were infringed, a fundamental feature of the legislation would always be infringed as well.

A court cannot create a different fundamental feature from the ones enacted in the legislation. Only Parliament can modify a fundamental feature of the legislation, as Lady Hale pointed out in *R. (GC) v. Commissioner of Police of the Metropolis*.[335] Lord Rodger considered the outer limits of the judicial function under s. 3(1) HRA in more abstract terms in *Ghaidan*. He said that implying words into legislation is not possible under s. 3(1) HRA if the implication contradicts an essential principle of the legislation. He continued: "Of course, the greater the extent of the proposed implication, the greater the need to make sure that the court is not going beyond the scheme of the legislation and embarking upon amendment".[336] Lord Rodger did not seem to differentiate between the "scheme of the legislation limit" and the "fundamental feature limit". The scheme of the legislation has to be ascertained, like the legislation's fundamental features, by having recourse to the interpretative criteria. In *McDonald v. McDonald*, a unanimous Supreme Court argued *obiter* that the scheme of the legislation has to be determined by the terms of the statute as opposed to the legislation's broader policy.[337] The Supreme Court did not consider how this *obiter* remark was in

---

[333] Arguably, this is why s. 3(1) HRA could not be used in *R. (Wright) v. Secretary of State for Health* [2009] UKHL 3, paras. 38–39 (Baroness Hale) to interpret the "provisional blacklisting" provisions for care workers in the Care Standards Act 2000 in a Convention-compliant manner. A Convention-compatible reading would have created a different legislative scheme from the one enacted in the Care Standards Act 2000.
[334] *Ghaidan v. Godin-Mendoza* [2004] UKHL 30, paras. 33–34 (Lord Nicholls), para. 113 (Lord Rodger).
[335] *R. (GC) v. Commissioner of Police of the Metropolis* [2011] UKSC 21, para. 72 (Lady Hale).
[336] *Ghaidan v. Godin-Mendoza* [2004] UKHL 30, para. 122 (Lord Rodger).
[337] *McDonald v. McDonald* [2016] UKSC 28, para. 69 (Lord Neuberger and Lady Hale, with whom Lord Kerr, Lord Reed and Lord Carnwath agreed).

Chapter 3. Rights-Consistent Interpretation

accord with Lord Nicholls's speech in *Ghaidan*, where Lord Nicholls relied on the reasons underlying the specific purpose of para. 2(2) of Sch. 1 to the Rent Act, i.e. the legislation's broader policy, when applying s. 3(1) HRA.

Like the fundamental feature limit, the scheme of the legislation as a boundary of Convention-compatible interpretation aims to flesh out the reconciliatory balance between the intention of the parliament enacting the challenged legislation and the intention of Parliament in enacting s. 3(1) HRA. That means that the intention of the parliament that enacted the legislation retains a limiting function. This function is constrained in the realm of s. 3(1) HRA as it has to cross the threshold of the scheme of the legislation for this particular interpretative limit. A recent dissenting opinion by Lord Carnwath in *Kennedy v. The Charity Commission* goes beyond this understanding of the scheme of the legislation limit. Lord Carnwath first accepted that a construction under s. 3(1) HRA must be possible, so that the scheme of the legislation remains workable. He then added that "that does not necessarily require a construction which would achieve ... the [scheme] which the legislature intended".[338] Lord Carnwath's understanding of the scheme of the legislation as a boundary of interpretation would significantly devalue that limit because a court would be able to deviate from the legislation's scheme as intended by the enacting parliament.

That the fundamental feature limit overlaps considerably with other outer limits of Convention-compatible interpretation can also be seen in relation to the following boundary: Lord Nicholls declared in *Ghaidan* that a Convention-compatible meaning must be compatible with "the underlying thrust of the legislation being construed" and must "go with the grain of the legislation".[339] Both limits have been applied in later case law.[340] Lord Nicholls did not specify any further what constitutes the grain and underlying thrust of the legislation, and these terms offer little guidance in themselves. What they do seem to indicate is that courts prefer to argue with a statute's general purposes rather than with its specific purposes when using s. 3(1) HRA. In *R. v. Waya*, the Supreme Court referred to the grain of the legislation as the essence of the legislation and described this essence with the purpose of the legislation as a whole, which was expressed in the explanatory notes at a relatively high level of abstraction.[341]

---

[338] *Kennedy v. The Charity Commission* [2014] UKSC 20, para. 224 (Lord Carnwath).
[339] *Ghaidan v. Godin-Mendoza* [2004] UKHL 30, para. 33 (Lord Nicholls).
[340] *Kennedy v. The Charity Commission* [2014] UKSC 20, para. 224 (Lord Carnwath, grain of the legislative scheme); *R. (GC) v. Commissioner of Police of the Metropolis* [2011] UKSC 21, para. 145 (Lord Brown); *Vodafone 2 v. Revenue and Customs Commissioners* [2009] EWCA Civ 446, para. 38 (Sir Andrew Morritt C); *Churchill Insurance Co. Ltd. v. Fitzgerald & Wilkinson* [2012] EWCA Civ 1166, para. 50 (Aikens LJ, with whom Etherton and Maurice Kay LJJ agreed); cf. *R. v. Waya* [2012] UKSC 51, para. 20 (Lord Walker and Sir Anthony Hughes, with whom Lady Hale, Lord Judge, Lord Kerr, Lord Clarke and Lord Wilson agreed).
[341] *R. v. Waya* [2012] UKSC 51, para. 21 (Lord Walker and Sir Anthony Hughes, with whom Lady Hale, Lord Judge, Lord Kerr, Lord Clarke and Lord Wilson agreed).

Like the notion of the concept of the legislation, the grain and underlying thrust of the legislation appear so vague that their function as limits of interpretation must be questioned. If the focus is put on the linguistic meaning of grain and thrust, it is possible to argue that both concepts are wider than a fundamental feature of the legislation. Yet, similarly to the relationship between the scheme of the legislation and a fundamental feature, the thrust and grain of the legislation as limits of interpretation do not express anything beyond the fundamental feature limit.[342] The significant overlap or even congruence between the scheme, grain, thrust and fundamental features of the legislation is mirrored in Lord Nicholls's speech in *Ghaidan*. He argued that *two* limits of Convention-compliant interpretation were present in *In re S (Minors)*: (a) the proposed starring system was inconsistent in an important respect with the scheme of the Children Act 1989 and (b) the proposed starring system had far-reaching practical ramifications for local authorities.[343] The first limit, the scheme of the legislation, was further explained by Lord Nicholls in the following way: courts cannot adopt a meaning that is inconsistent with a fundamental feature of the legislation under s. 3(1) HRA; the meaning adopted by application of s. 3(1) HRA must be compatible with the underlying thrust of the legislation and go with the grain of the legislation.[344]

7.2.5. Policy Choices and Issues Calling for Legislative Deliberation

Another limit of interpretation under s. 3(1) HRA is that a court cannot make decisions (a) for which it is not equipped or (b) that give rise to far-reaching practical repercussions that the court is not equipped to evaluate.[345] Lord Nicholls pointed out in *Ghaidan* that there may be several ways of making a provision Convention compliant, "and the choice may involve issues calling for legislative deliberation".[346] Lord Rodger clarified in *Ghaidan* that this boundary can render a suggested Convention-compatible interpretation impossible even if this interpretation does not run counter to any fundamental feature of the legislation.[347] Two things are implicit in Lord Nicholls's expression of this limit in *Ghaidan*. First, a court may have a choice between different possible

---

[342] This assessment is based on the premise that the fundamental feature limit refers to the fundamental features of the overall statutory scheme (the legislation) rather than a fundamental feature of the particular provision that is being interpreted pursuant to s. 3(1) HRA.
[343] *Ghaidan v. Godin-Mendoza* [2004] UKHL 30, para. 34 (Lord Nicholls).
[344] Ibid., para. 33 (Lord Nicholls).
[345] *Ghaidan v. Godin-Mendoza* [2004] UKHL 30, para. 33 (Lord Nicholls), para. 115 (Lord Rodger); *Vodafone 2 v. Revenue and Customs Commissioners* [2009] EWCA Civ 446, para. 38 (Sir Andrew Morritt C); *Churchill Insurance Co. Ltd. v. Fitzgerald & Wilkinson* [2012] EWCA Civ 1166, para. 50 (Aikens LJ, with whom Etherton and Maurice Kay LJJ agreed).
[346] *Ghaidan v. Godin-Mendoza* [2004] UKHL 30, para. 33 (Lord Nicholls).
[347] Ibid., para. 115 (Lord Rodger).

Convention-compliant meanings, i.e. there may be a number of ways in which a provision could be construed in order to make it compatible with requirements set by Convention rights. Second, the choice between these meanings may be taken by the court as long as it does not involve issues calling for legislative deliberation or give rise to far-reaching practical repercussions that the court is not equipped to evaluate. It follows that making policy decisions in itself is not a limit of interpretation under s. 3(1) HRA.[348] None of the judges of the majority in *Ghaidan* referred to the taking of a policy choice as a limit of interpretation. Only Lord Millett said in relation to *Bellinger v. Bellinger* that a question of social policy had arisen which ought properly to be left to Parliament and not decided by the judges.[349] In his dissent in *Ghaidan*, Lord Millett argued that the Civil Partnership Bill was currently being debated in Parliament and was going to amend para. 2 of Sch. 1 to the Rent Act 1977. The Bill would create a new legal partnership that persons of the same sex could enter into. Lord Millett criticised the interpretation of para. 2(2) of Sch. 1 to the Rent Act 1977 by the majority in *Ghaidan* as effectively foreclosing regulatory choices that Parliament could have debated and adopted. He concluded that these issues are "questions of social policy which should be left to Parliament".[350] It is not clear from Lord Millett's critique of the majority opinion whether he is of the opinion that (a) a court can never make a policy choice under s. 3(1) HRA or (b) a court can make a policy choice under s. 3(1) HRA unless that choice must be left to Parliament. If route (b) is taken, Lord Millett is in agreement with Lord Nicholls and Lord Rodger about the abstract limit of interpretation but in disagreement about its application to the specific facts in *Ghaidan*.

Convention-compatible interpretation under s. 3(1) HRA often involves the making of policy choices. In addition, Convention rights are broad and there are often a number of ways of construing a provision that is incompatible in order to make it compatible with Convention rights.[351] It is thus to be welcomed that the judges in *Ghaidan* did not argue that they cannot make policy choices. This is not the place to go into the elusive divide between legal and policy arguments.[352] After *Ghaidan*, the dividing line is between policy choices that

---

[348] Arden, above n. 73, pp. 165, 178; Arden, above n. 71, pp. 487, 497 ("the court may have in effect to make a selection from a number of possible ways in which the legislation could have been drafted on a Convention-compliant basis"); cf. *R. (Nicklinson) v. Ministry of Justice* [2014] UKSC 38, para. 230 (Lord Sumption).
[349] *Ghaidan v. Godin-Mendoza* [2004] UKHL 30, para. 65 (Lord Millett).
[350] Ibid., para. 101 (Lord Millett).
[351] Arden, above n. 73, pp. 178–179.
[352] See section 3 of Chapter 1 for a short discussion of this issue. There is a vast literature on this topic. See, e.g. M. Auer, *Materialisierung, Flexibilisierung, Richterfreiheit*, Mohr Siebeck, Tübingen 2005, pp. 81–83; J. Bell, *Policy arguments in judicial decisions*, Clarendon Press, Oxford 1983; J.A.G. Griffith, *The politics of the judiciary*, 5th ed., Fontana Press, London 1997, chapter 9; K. Mathis, Consequentialism in law, in K. Mathis (ed.), *Efficiency, sustainability, and justice to future generations*, Springer, Dordrecht 2011, pp. 3, 5–20.

judges are equipped to make and policy choices that are matters for Parliament, i.e. policy choices that involve issues calling for legislative deliberation or policy choices that give rise to important practical repercussions which the court is not equipped to evaluate. Making policy choices in areas of public controversy falls within the institutional competence of the legislature. In *In re S (Minors)* Lord Nicholls argued that the proposed starring system has far-reaching practical ramifications for local authorities and their care of children. It would increase administrative work and expense, and it would be likely to have a material effect on authorities' allocation of scarce financial resources. It would also affect the manner in which local authorities discharge their parental responsibilities. He concluded that these are matters to be decided by Parliament rather than the courts and said that it is impossible for a court to evaluate these ramifications or assess what would be the views of Parliament if changes were needed.[353] Lord Nicholls further opined that despite rejecting the starring system proposed by the Court of Appeal on legal grounds, a pressing need existed for the government to consider whether some degree of court supervision of local authorities' discharge of their parental responsibilities would bring about an overall improvement in the quality of child care provided by local authorities. "Answering this question calls for a wider examination than can be undertaken by a court".[354]

Another case in which a Convention-compliant interpretation failed because it would have entailed far-reaching ramifications, raising issues ill-suited for determination by the courts, is *Bellinger v. Bellinger*. At issue in that case was the interpretation of s. 11(c) of the Matrimonial Causes Act 1973, which provides that a marriage is void on the ground that "the parties are not respectively male and female". The appellant was male at birth and assigned the male gender in her birth certificate, but later underwent gender reassignment surgery and went through a marriage ceremony with a man. The ordinary meaning of the words "male" and "female" in s. 11(c) of the Matrimonial Causes Act 1973 failed to give legal recognition to the acquired gender of transsexual persons. These words could not be interpreted as including female-to-male and male-to-female transsexuals under ordinary methods of interpretation, which is why s. 11(c) of the Matrimonial Causes Act 1973 was prima facie incompatible with arts. 8 and 12 ECHR.[355] "Parliament regards gender as fixed and immutable" in relation to the validity of marriage.[356] The question arose in the House of Lords of whether s. 3(1) HRA can be used to read additional words into s. 11(c) of the

---

[353] *In re S (Minors)* [2002] UKHL 10, paras. 43–44 (Lord Nicholls).
[354] Ibid., para. 106 (Lord Nicholls).
[355] *Bellinger v. Bellinger* [2003] UKHL 21, para. 53 (Lord Nicholls), paras. 56, 58, 62, 64 (Lord Hope). For a different view, see HICKMAN, above n. 54, p. 330.
[356] *Bellinger v. Bellinger* [2003] UKHL 21, para. 83 (Lord Rodger).

Matrimonial Causes Act 1973 and thereby render that provision Convention compliant. No clear guidance was available to the judges regarding the criteria according to which a transsexual person's acquired gender should be recognised for the purposes of marriage. Lord Nicholls and Lord Hope concluded that the House of Lords is not in a position to decide where the demarcation line should be drawn.[357] Lord Nicholls further argued that the decision to recognise gender reassignment for the purposes of marriage cannot sensibly be made in isolation from a decision on similar issues in other areas like education, child care and birth certificates. Even in the context of marriage, Lord Nicholls continued, the question of gender reassignment raises wider issues since marriage is deeply embedded in UK culture and understood as a relationship between two persons of the opposite sex. The case raised a question which ought to be considered as part of an overall review of the most appropriate way to deal with the difficulties confronting transsexual people.[358] Such a review had been under way since the government had announced its intention to introduce a bill into Parliament dealing with various issues arising from the legal recognition of acquired gender, including the criteria according to which a transsexual person can marry in that gender. According to Lord Nicholls, recognising the appellant as female for the purposes of s. 11(c) of the Matrimonial Causes Act 1973 "would necessitate giving the expressions 'male' and 'female' in that Act a novel, extended meaning: that a person may be born with one sex but later become, or become regarded as, a person of the opposite sex".[359] He continued as follows:

> This would represent a major change in the law, having far reaching ramifications. It raises issues whose solution calls for extensive enquiry and the widest public consultation and discussion. Questions of social policy and administrative feasibility arise at several points, and their interaction has to be evaluated and balanced. The issues are altogether ill-suited for determination by courts and court procedures. They are preeminently a matter for Parliament, the more especially when the government, in unequivocal terms, has already announced its intention to introduce comprehensive primary legislation on this difficult and sensitive subject.[360]

Bellinger v. Bellinger involved, to paraphrase Lord Nicholls, issues whose solution calls for extensive enquiry and wide public consultation, in particular questions relating to social policy and administrative feasibility. The case raised a question that ought to be considered as part of an overall legislative review of the most appropriate way to deal with the difficulties confronting transsexual people. Lord Nicholls's reasoning also indicates that the outer limits

---

[357] Ibid., para. 43 (Lord Nicholls), para. 62 (Lord Hope).
[358] Ibid., paras. 46–48 (Lord Nicholls).
[359] Ibid., para. 36 (Lord Nicholls).
[360] Ibid., para. 37 (Lord Nicholls). For criticism of the court's reasoning, see HICKMAN, above n. 54, pp. 330–332.

of s. 3(1) HRA are surpassed if the Convention-compatible interpretation involves taking a decision which cannot sensibly be made in isolation from a decision on the like issue in other areas of law. Much of judicial law-making occurs by way of filling in gaps in the existing legislative framework. Judicial law-making is a piecemeal approach, and that approach is unsuitable, according to Lord Nicholls, if judicial law-making in one area of law would cause discordance, confusion or incoherence in the law as a whole. Furthermore, the government had announced its intention to introduce a bill into Parliament in unequivocal terms which would have addressed the issue of statutory interpretation that arose in *Bellinger v. Bellinger*.[361] These factors seem to speak against the feasibility of a Convention-compliant interpretation according to s. 3(1) HRA, and they seem to lead to the conclusion that the policy choice to be made is pre-eminently a question for Parliament. If this were correct, the dividing line between policy choices that judges are equipped to make and policy choices that involve issues calling for legislative deliberation would still not be determined by principled guidelines. However, the factors were known that need to be taken into account by a court when determining that border in an individual case.

Yet, a comparison with *Ghaidan* shows that this conclusion cannot be made.[362] A Convention-compatible interpretation of para. 2(2) of Sch. 1 to the Rent Act 1977 was possible in *Ghaidan* even though it involved a question of social policy. The Civil Partnership Bill was debated in Parliament at the time when *Ghaidan* was decided. It was preceded by a government consultation paper, which was followed by a wider public consultation. The purpose of the Bill was to enable same-sex couples to obtain legal recognition of their relationship. It also set out the legal consequences of forming a civil partnership, including the rights and responsibilities of civil partners. The Bill later became the Civil Partnership Act 2004, and the Act made amendments to a range of provisions relating to housing and tenancies (among them para. 2 of Sch. 1 to the Rent Act 1977), family homes, fatal accident claims, children, property and financial arrangements. The Bill addressed the issue of cohabiting same-sex couples, which arose in *Ghaidan*, and it addressed this issue as part of an overall legislative review of the most appropriate way to deal with relationships between same-sex couples. This indicates that the status of cohabiting same-sex couples cannot be clarified sensibly in isolation from decisions on similar issues in other areas of law.[363]

---

[361] It is contended in scholarship that a court is less likely to act under s. 3(1) HRA if there is evidence that Parliament intends to enact legislation which remedies the incompatibility with the Convention. See, e.g. J. WRIGHT, Interpreting section 2 of the Human Rights Act 1998: towards an indigenous jurisprudence of human rights, [2009] *PL* 595, 613.

[362] Regarding the function of the courts to protect minority interests (*R. (Nicklinson) v. Ministry of Justice* [2014] UKSC 38, para. 164 (Lord Mance)), both cases are comparable since they concern the protection of transsexual and homosexual people. In other words, the function of the courts to protect minority interests is not a factor that can be used to explain the difference in both cases.

[363] *Ghaidan v. Godin-Mendoza* [2004] UKHL 30, paras. 96–99 (Lord Millett).

Despite these parallels to *Bellinger v. Bellinger*, the majority in *Ghaidan* decided that a Convention-compatible interpretation was possible, i.e. that the question of the treatment of cohabiting same-sex couples for the purposes of the Rent Act 1977 did not call for legislative deliberation. The comparison between both cases shows that the dividing line that is operated in judicial practice between policy choices that judges are equipped to make and those that involve issues calling for legislative deliberation is elusive and disappoints from a viewpoint of legal certainty. The comparison also demonstrates that courts do not necessarily refuse to act under s. 3(1) HRA if the challenged legislation is the topic of current legislative activity.[364] Lord Rodger indicated in *Ghaidan* that this dividing line is not clear cut. Finding it will involve matters of degree which cannot be determined in the abstract but only by considering the particular legislation in issue.[365] Case law has not established factors that reliably specify this border and make it more predictable. Much seems to depend on the circumstances of the individual case, as indicated by Lord Rodger. In other words, it is to a large extent determined by evaluative arguments and judicial discretion on which side of the line an individual case falls. C. Gearty has pointed out that the difference in the judges' reasoning in *Ghaidan* and in *Bellinger v. Bellinger* can be explained by the facts of both cases: a "declaration of incompatibility would have been total defeat for Godin-Mendoza; for Bellinger it was a likely delayed victory".[366]

We saw in Section 7.2.3 above that the minority of the Supreme Court in *R. (GC) v. Commissioner of Police of the Metropolis* argued that s. 64(1A) PACE cannot be interpreted in conformity with art. 8 ECHR without infringing a fundamental feature of the legislation. The minority further contended that there is a range of possible ways to bring the regulation of retention of data in PACE into line with the requirements of art. 8 ECHR. The minority concluded that devising a Convention-compliant scheme for the retention of data is only for Parliament to do as it involves issues calling for legislative deliberation.[367] At the time of the Supreme Court judgment, there was already a proposal that s. 64 PACE would be amended by the Crime and Security Act 2010 in order to make that provision compatible with art. 8 ECHR. Following a change of government in May 2010, however, rather than bringing the Crime and Security Act into force, the incoming government announced its proposal for a new legislative scheme regarding the retention of data taken from suspects in connection with the investigation of an offence. The Protection of Freedoms Bill containing these proposals was before Parliament when the Supreme Court decided

---

[364] For the argument that judges should not act if the subject matter is of current legislative activity, see T. BINGHAM, The judge as lawmaker: an English perspective, in T. BINGHAM (ed.), *The business of judging*, OUP, Oxford 2000, pp. 31–32.
[365] *Ghaidan v. Godin-Mendoza* [2004] UKHL 30, para. 115 (Lord Rodger), paras. 146, 150 (Lord Brown).
[366] C. GEARTY, *On fantasy island*, OUP, Oxford 2016, p. 94.
[367] *R. (GC) v. Commissioner of Police of the Metropolis* [2011] UKSC 21, para. 115 (Lord Rodger).

R. (GC) v. Commissioner of Police of the Metropolis. The minority was thus right in pointing out that multiple ways existed for Parliament to devise a Convention-compliant regime. Yet, the making of a policy choice as such does not bar a Convention-compatible interpretation under s. 3(1) HRA. Did the current legislative activity signal that this policy choice falls inside the institutional competence of the legislature and involves issues calling for legislative deliberation? Such a formal understanding of this outer interpretative limit would insert an element of predictability and legal certainty into s. 3(1) HRA. What was the answer of the majority? It did not even discuss this outer interpretative limit of s. 3(1) HRA. It did not defer to the decisions of the democratic assembly. What this reasoning and the opinion of the minority in *R. (GC) v. Commissioner of Police of the Metropolis* does illustrate is that it is possible to specify the relatively abstract outer limits of Convention-compatible interpretation with clear guidelines or factors that "add" elements of legal certainty. Such steps have by and large not been taken by judges in the sphere of s. 3(1) HRA, which illustrates that the balance between formal justice and material justice is tilted towards the latter.

German case law also shows that forthcoming corrective legislation can but does not necessarily bar judicial law-making in courts.[368] Like their English counterparts, German judges have not established clear criteria that specify when judicial law-making is barred due to forthcoming corrective legislation. One possibility, which would increase the level of legal certainty provided, would be to adopt a formal criterion: judicial law-making is barred if a bill is debated in the German Bundestag and if that bill addresses the issue that is currently argued in court.

Benkharbouche is another example illustrating the indeterminate nature of the "legislative deliberation limit" as applied in the highest English courts. The case concerned employment claims of foreign nationals working in foreign embassies in London. Section 4(1) of the State Immunity Act 1978 (SIA) stipulates that a state is not immune as respects proceedings relating to contracts for employment with an individual where the contract is performed in the UK. Section 16(1)(a) SIA provides that s. 4 SIA does not apply to proceedings concerning the employment of embassy staff. Furthermore, one of the applicants was neither a UK national nor habitually resident in the UK when her contract of employment was made. This meant that s. 4(2)(b) SIA applied, granting immunity to the embassy from proceedings relating to the contract of employment. Due to these provisions of the State Immunity Act 1978, the employees' claims would

---

[368] See, e.g. BVerfG, *NJW* 1973, 1221, 1226 – *Soraya*; BGH, *NJW* 1969, 98, 100; BGH, *NJW* 1970, 2017, 2018. The issue is discussed in German legal scholarship under the topic "Sperrwirkung bevorstehender Gesetze". For a short overview of the discussion, see M. Franzen, *Privatrechtsangleichung durch die Europäische Gemeinschaft*, de Gruyter, Berlin 1999, pp. 401–402; R. Wank, *Grenzen richterlicher Rechtsfortbildung*, Duncker & Humblot, Berlin 1978, pp. 229–231.

have been unsuccessful under conventional canons of interpretation. The Court of Appeal decided, however, that s. 4(2)(b) and s. 16(1)(a) SIA infringe art. 6 ECHR.[369] The next question that arose was whether both provisions can be read down pursuant to the interpretative obligation imposed by s. 3(1) HRA. The appellants argued that both provisions can be read down by including an exception that restricts the scope of application of both provisions in cases where art. 6 ECHR is infringed. The appellants further contended that such a Convention-compatible interpretation would only restrict existing exceptions to the principle under s. 4(1) SIA that employment claims are not barred by a plea of immunity.[370] Section 4(1) SIA was, however, itself an exception to the general principle of immunity enshrined in s. 1(1) SIA.

The Court of Appeal held that the wording of s. 4(2)(b) and s. 16(1)(a) SIA cannot be read down under s. 3(1) HRA. Lord Dyson, who gave the judgment of the Court, argued that Parliament intended to confer immunity subject to specific exceptions when enacting the SIA. The Act was framed "so as to create a careful, detailed and clear pattern which balances considerations known to the legislature". A conforming interpretation that altered the width of one of these provisions would affect "the overall balance struck by the legislature whilst lacking Parliament's panoramic view across the whole of the landscape".[371] These, with respect, are overly generic arguments. Lord Dyson's two arguments, indicated as above in quotes, could be used to reject Convention-compatible judicial law-making in almost all cases. These arguments do, however, illustrate the indeterminate nature of the legislative deliberation limit. The application of this limit depends on the circumstances of the individual case, and these circumstances are not further structured in case law. Adopting a formal rule would bring more clarity and certainty into the case law.

7.3. COMPARATIVE ANALYSIS

J. Bell has rightly pointed out that (rights-based) constitutional review of legislation under the German Basic Law is very much a response to past experiences. It is an instrument that protects against the dangers of totalitarianism. In England, the absence of (rights-based) constitutional review may be explained by Parliament's role in establishing freedoms in the seventeenth-century revolutions.[372] These historical experiences can be

---

[369] *Benkharbouche v. Embassy of Sudan* [2015] EWCA Civ 33, para. 68 (Lord Dyson, giving the judgment of the court).
[370] Cf. *Benkharbouche v. Embassy of Sudan* [2014] ICR 169, para. 39 (Langstaff J).
[371] *Benkharbouche v. Embassy of Sudan* [2015] EWCA Civ 33, para. 67 (Lord Dyson, giving the judgment of the court).
[372] J. BELL, *Judiciaries within Europe: a comparative review*, CUP, Cambridge 2006, pp. 354–355.

superseded by other experiences in today's world, and the new experiences affect the development of constitutional law. Contemporary English judges are more concerned with the powers of Parliament to restrict freedoms and human rights. This is another factor that can explain why English judges have adopted wide outer limits of rights-consistent interpretation. The judicial role and the power of judicial law-making are not immutably fixed in time but variable concepts. They provide answers to current legal and political challenges. S. Vogenauer has similarly described the interpretative maxims in a legal order as a product of multiple factors of legal and societal culture.[373] Modern-day challenges influence statutory interpretation, judicial law-making and its limits within the parameters set by the constitutional framework.[374] The constitutional framework forms a bar for the adaptability of judicial power in rights-consistent interpretation. In Germany, this bar is the highly indeterminate art. 20(3) GG. In England, the doctrine of parliamentary sovereignty is the constitutional benchmark against which rights-consistent judicial law-making is judged. If judicial law-making exceeds the constitutional framework, it is unconstitutional unless it coincides with a change in the constitutional framework itself.

The outer limits of rights-consistent interpretation demarcate permissible interpretation from impermissible judicial legislation in both jurisdictions. These limits determine the constitutional relationship between the courts and the legislature in the area of statutory interpretation. Since the limits of rights-consistent construction are not clearly set by (constitutional) legislation in England and Germany, it is the courts who have worked out the demarcation line between interpretation and amendment of legislation. The vague statutory words of art. 20(3) GG and s. 3(1) HRA delegate to the judges, at least to some degree, the task of determining the extent of permissible rights-consistent judicial law-making. Both provisions can accommodate different interpretations. It is the task of the judges to devise a constitutionally appropriate division of labour between the courts and the legislature. This task involves evaluative arguments and judicial discretion. This institutional evaluation of the extent and limits of the judicial role within the constitutional framework is not specific to rights adjudication.[375] Courts in both jurisdictions make a very similar evaluation when they determine the outer limits of conventional judicial law-making. It is common ground that not all legislation can be interpreted in conformity with Convention rights or in conformity with the German Basic Law. For different normative reasons, a rights-consistent interpretation also has priority over a declaration of incompatibility (England) or the striking down of a statute as unconstitutional (Germany).

---

[373] S. VOGENAUER, *Die Auslegung von Gesetzen in England und auf dem Kontinent*, Mohr Siebeck, Tübingen 2001, pp. 1315, 1317.
[374] Ibid., 1314.
[375] For a seemingly different view, see A. KAVANAGH, Judge as partner, draft paper 2017 (on file with author).

7.3.1. Wide Powers of Rights-Consistent Judicial Law-Making

When English and German courts engage in rights-consistent judicial law-making, they start from the premise that judicial law-making is a permissible part of the judicial function. Both German and English courts are equally transparent about their possessing the power to engage in rights-consistent judicial law-making. For German law, the outer limits of constitution-consistent judicial law-making and the outer limits of conventional judicial law-making are the same according to the case law of the BVerfG. This result does not seem inevitable since the BVerfG can declare void unconstitutional legislation, and this power may have an impact on the outer limits of constitution-consistent interpretation. Yet, two reasons advocate for the same outer limits for both modes of judicial law-making. First, art. 20(2), (3) GG does not differentiate between different modes of statutory interpretation. Second, the BVerfG applies wide and flexible outer limits of interpretation under conventional judicial law-making. There is thus no need to set up even wider outer limits for constitution-consistent interpretation. In England, the outer limits of Convention-compatible interpretation exceed the law-making power available to courts under conventional canons of construction. This is due to s. 3(1) HRA, which specifically applies to rights-consistent interpretation. The change of the default position for judicial law-making in England and the consequential change in judicial attitudes has led to a converging judicial mindset about the judicial role in both jurisdictions in the area of rights-consistent interpretation. The difference in the interpretative powers of English and German courts that we encountered in Chapter 2 has ceased to exist. English and German courts enjoy wide powers under rights-consistent interpretation as they can modify the meaning of a provision. Courts may adopt a meaning which alters or supplements the statutory wording. For the most part, English courts do not give greater weight to a provision's wording in rights-consistent interpretation compared to German courts. In both jurisdictions, a court does not necessarily exceed the judicial function if it adopts a rights-consistent meaning that departs from a provision's unambiguous wording, a provision's underlying specific purpose and the intention of the enacting legislature. Rights-consistent interpretation cannot be described as "weak" in either England or Germany.[376] Scholars in both countries have criticised the courts for not respecting the authority of the legislature by ascribing to legislation strained meanings that the enacting legislature would never have intended. The comparison between rights-consistent judicial law-making in England and Germany also shows that s. 3(1) HRA should not be described as a "truly distinctive feature of the HRA"

---

[376] Rightly arguing against the characterisation of s. 3(1) HRA as "the weakest variant of weak-form review": KAVANAGH, above n. 51, p. 1032.

in contrast with an explicitly entrenched Bill of Rights combined with an explicit judicial "strike-down" power.[377]

The similar strength of rights-consistent interpretation in both countries also shows that the difference between a declaration of incompatibility (weak form of judicial review) and a strike-down power (strong form of judicial review) does not necessarily affect the interpretative power of the courts.[378] In both systems, factors exist that incentivise courts to adopt and apply wide outer limits of rights-consistent interpretation. These factors operate in the "open area" of adjudication, to use Richard Posner's words. In England, these factors relate to the legislative history of s. 3(1) HRA and the circumstances that a declaration of incompatibility offers litigants no remedy and puts political pressure on the government and Parliament. In Germany, the BVerfG has the power to invalidate unconstitutional legislation, and the exercise of this power offers litigants a remedy. Nonetheless, German courts also adopt and apply wide outer limits of rights-consistent interpretation. First, the possible invalidation of legislation puts political pressure on the government and on the legislature. Second, ensuring the validity of ordinary legislation through constitution-consistent interpretation respects and shows deference to the legislature's authority. Both factors work in the background and only affect the application of the limits of interpretation since the same outer limits apply for ordinary and for constitution-consistent judicial law-making in Germany.

Differences exist in how English and German courts justify their bold interpretative approach. In both countries, courts have used different arguments to justify the fact that objective factors of interpretation can be given considerable weight in rights-consistent judicial law-making. Section 3(1) HRA is claimed to have empowered the English judiciary to depart from the intention of the enacting parliament. English judges do not have to align and justify a Convention-compatible meaning with the enacting parliament's presumed intention. They can rely on the intention of the parliament that enacted s. 3(1) HRA. The German duty of constitution-consistent interpretation is not positively enacted but judge-made law. German judges cannot straightforwardly base their creative role in constitution-consistent interpretation on another will of a different parliament. It is art. 20(3) GG that, according to the BVerfG, allows for objective factors of interpretation to be taken into account because the content of a provision can evolve over time due to changes in social and political reality.[379] It is thus ultimately art. 20(3) GG that empowers German courts to

---

[377] For this view, see, however, KAVANAGH, above n. 50, p. 413.
[378] For an apparently different view, see CHANDRACHUD and KAVANAGH, above n. 48, pp. 63, 81–82; KAVANAGH, above n. 51, p. 1028. For an argument against the distinction between weak-form judicial review and strong-form judicial review as a way of conceptualising different systems of judicial review, see KAVANAGH, above n. 51, pp. 1030–1036.
[379] BVerfG, *NJW* 1990, 1593–1594.

depart from the intention of the enacting legislature. If an actual intention of the enacting legislature to comply with the German Basic Law is absent, the BVerfG argues with the presumed intention of the enacting legislature. This presumed intention can trump an identifiable objective of the enacting legislature. The BVerfG's reasoning can be traced back to the normative foundation of constitution-consistent interpretation, i.e. the interest in preserving a legal provision and the respect for the ordinary legislature. That is an objective factor of interpretation. This argument rests on the power of the BVerfG to invalidate unconstitutional ordinary legislation, a power that no English court currently enjoys. This line of argumentation also shows us that even in a system with strong-form judicial review, where constitutional law lies beyond the reach of ordinary statutes, the concept of presumed legislative intent is not necessarily discarded as a fiction, but can live on and flourish within constitution-consistent interpretation. The key question is how to reconcile the actual and reasonable intention, or in more abstract terms, subjective and objective factors of interpretation. This reconciliatory balance is expressed in the outer limits of constitution-consistent interpretation. In England, the key question for Convention-compatible interpretation is how a court balances the intentions of two different parliaments, i.e. how a court balances subjective and objective factors of interpretation. The reconciliatory balance is expressed by English judges in the outer limits of Convention-compatible interpretation. Despite the differences in both jurisdictions, the underlying main issue that determines the strength of rights-consistent interpretation is thus very similar. What is also very similar is that English and German courts trace their interpretative powers back to the intention of the legislature. That is a thinking that permeates the mindset of both English and German judges.

It does not follow from these commonalities that the outer limits of rights-consistent judicial law-making are the same in England and Germany. The question is how far courts can depart from the wording of a statute and the intention of the enacting legislature in order to justify a rights-consistent meaning. Different constitutional principles, namely art. 20(3) GG and the UK doctrine of parliamentary sovereignty, affect the balance between subjective and objective factors of interpretation in England and Germany. It thus appears reasonable to assume different outer limits of rights-consistent interpretation in both jurisdictions. Different constitutional settings ought to lead to different systems of interpretation. Lord Rodger described the difference between the UK constitution, in which the doctrine of parliamentary sovereignty is maintained by s. 3(1) HRA, and a constitutional system, in which the constitution is the supreme law to which other laws must conform on pain of invalidity, as important for determining the reach of rights-consistent interpretation in each system.[380]

---

[380] *Ghaidan v. Godin-Mendoza* [2004] UKHL 30, para. 120 (Lord Rodger).

I will show in the following, however, that a considerable congruence (as opposed to a considerable difference) can be determined when comparing the outer limits of rights-consistent judicial law-making in England and Germany.

7.3.2. High Level of Congruence

An English court cannot adopt a meaning under s. 3(1) HRA that is inconsistent with a fundamental feature of the legislation. A German judge has to respect the fundamental decision of the legislature and cannot distort or neglect a fundamental feature of a provision's objective. Despite the apparent similarity between both outer limits of interpretation, the juxtaposition reveals a noticeable difference. Whereas the "fundamental feature" relates to the level of legislation (statute) in England, it relates to the level of provision in Germany. It follows that an English court, but not a German court, could depart from a "fundamental" feature of a single provision if that feature did not amount to a fundamental feature of the whole of the statute. The analysis of English case law has also shown that an English court cannot go as far as adopting a Convention-compatible meaning that is the opposite of the substance of the challenged provision. A simple *departure* from a provision's fundamental feature is of a different quality than adopting the opposite of a provision's substance.[381] Despite this distinction, an English court's law-making powers under s. 3(1) go further than those of a German court under constitution-consistent interpretation in relation to the fundamental feature limits. This is quite a remarkable result when viewed against the history of literalism in England. This difference would cease to exist if English judges were to relate the fundamental feature limit to the level of provision. There are indeed indications in newer case law that this is happening, but the matter must currently be considered unresolved. Furthermore, a Convention-compatible meaning must be compatible with the thrust and grain of the legislation being construed. A German judge has to respect the fundamental decision of the legislature and cannot fundamentally redefine the normative content of a provision. Despite the apparent similarity between these outer limits of interpretation in both countries, there is a recognisable difference as these limits relate once to the level of legislation and once to the level of provision. A further commonality in the outer interpretative limits in both countries exists for the legislative scheme limit. A Convention-compatible interpretation must not be inconsistent with the scheme of the legislation, and an English court cannot create a different legislative scheme from the one enacted

---

[381] If the original legislature enacts and intends to enact "blue and green" and if the rights-consistent meaning is "blue, green and yellow", the rights-consistent meaning departs from the original legislature's intention, but it does not contradict it because the rights-consistent meaning is not the opposite of "blue and green". If the rights-consistent meaning is "not blue and green", however, this meaning contradicts the original legislature's intent.

in the legislation. Similarly, a German judge is not allowed to introduce a new scheme into the legislation under constitution-consistent interpretation.

German case law further demands that a teleological reduction cannot reduce the scope of application of a provision to zero, i.e. that a teleological reduction cannot affect a de facto repeal of a provision. In England, reducing the scope of application of a provision by means of s. 3(1) HRA must not remove the very core and essence, the "pith and substance" of the measure that Parliament had enacted.[382] Lord Rodger formulated this outer interpretative limit in *Ghaidan*. If this limit is applied at the level of provision, it would appear that an English court cannot adopt a Convention-compatible meaning that reduces the scope of application of a provision to zero. An English court could also not adopt a Convention-compatible meaning that leaves a provision without any substantial scope of application. A constitution-consistent interpretation in Germany must also ensure that a provision remains with a reasonable meaning that does not contradict the provision's identifiable purpose. It is more plausible, however, that Lord Rodger referred to the "pith and substance" of the statute as a whole. That is because Lord Rodger also mentioned the "grain of the legislation" and the fundamental features of an Act of Parliament as outer limits of interpretation for s. 3(1) HRA.[383] According to this reading of Lord Rodger's opinion, an English court's law-making powers under s. 3(1) go beyond the interpretative powers of German courts under constitution-consistent judicial law-making. Section 3(1) HRA could be used to reduce the scope of application of a provision to zero in order to safeguard the compatibility of the whole of the legislation with Convention rights. Whether an English court would actually go that far in its endeavour to find a compatible meaning must be regarded as unclear. UKSC case law on the EU legal duty of conforming judicial law-making indicates that disregarding a provision as a whole is not possible as a matter of statutory interpretation.[384]

A German judge surpasses the outer limits of the judicial function if the interpretative result contradicts the wording *and* the clearly identifiable intention of the legislature (double criterion). English courts do not explicitly operate an equivalent outer limit of rights-consistent interpretation. *Ghaidan* shows, however, that the statutory language and the substantive principles of the legislation must be taken into account when assessing whether a Convention-compatible meaning is possible. It was shown that the second element of the double criterion integrates all interpretative criteria in German judicial practice. Furthermore, the double criterion is devalued for rights-consistent judicial law-making since the wording of a provision can be surpassed and the legislature

---

[382] *Ghaidan v. Godin-Mendoza* [2004] UKHL 30, para. 111 (Lord Rodger).
[383] Ibid., paras. 115, 121 (Lord Rodger).
[384] This will be explored in Chapter 4, Section 7.2.

is assumed to have intended the creation of a provision that complies with the German Basic Law (presumption of compliance). The second element of the double criterion does not solely relate to the intention of the enacting legislature, but can also refer to the underlying objective purpose and sense of the statutory provision. The balance between the subjective and objective intention of the legislature depends on the circumstances of the particular case. The result is that the double criterion is an extremely malleable and nebulous concept. The way this concept is applied in judicial practice does not significantly deviate from the way English courts apply the outer limits of s. 3(1) HRA. If a Convention-compatible meaning is the opposite of the substance of the challenged provision, s. 3(1) HRA is also not available. A provision's substance is determined by the interpretative criteria. Similarly, German courts have held that a judge cannot attribute an opposite sense to a statute that is clear according to its wording and its purpose. Whereas German courts argue with the reasonably presumed intention of the enacting legislature to comply with the German Basic Law, English courts rely on the intention of the 1998 Parliament. How far a court can depart from an identifiable objective of the enacting legislature depends on the circumstances of the individual case in both jurisdictions.

There is very little case law in both countries that openly suggests that rights-consistent judicial law-making can go as far as contradicting the enacting Parliament's intent in an individual case.[385] Even though it is possible to distinguish between a "departure from" and a "contradiction of" the enacting legislature's intent, it is far less clear whether English and German courts actually use these terms in judgments with this distinction in mind. We have observed in our discussion of *Soraya* in Section 3.2 of Chapter 2 that judicial law-making in Germany can be permissible even if it departs from the statutory text and goes against the explicit and unambiguous intention of the enacting legislature. *Soraya* is certainly a borderline case and was decided in 1973. Statutory interpretation in German courts has moved on, and there is recent case law illustrating a tendency for the BVerfG to attach more weight to the intention of the enacting legislature in the interpretative process. It thus appears unlikely that the BVerfG would nowadays adopt a constitution-consistent meaning of legislation that contradicted (as opposed to simply departed from) the intention of the enacting legislature. The BGH has also declared in more recent decisions that a constitution-consistent interpretation "against the intention of the legislature" exceeds the judicial function.[386] In relation to the language of the statute as an

---

[385] BVerfG, *NJW* 2006, 3409, 3410 – *Marlene Dietrich*; *R. (Wilkinson) v. Inland Revenue Commissioners* [2005] UKHL 30, para. 18.

[386] BGH, *BeckRS* 2012, 16505, para. 50; BGH, *NJW* 2013, 2674, para. 38 – *Interprofessionelle Sozietät*. This statement of the BGH is ambiguous, however, as it does not explicitly relate to the intention of the enacting legislature.

interpretative criterion in itself, English judges have not yet explicitly said that a Convention-compatible meaning can contradict existing statutory words.[387] Yet the discussion of the express terms limit has shown that a Convention-compatible interpretation may go as far as contradicting unambiguous statutory language in an individual case. This is very similar in Germany. The BVerfG has held that (conventional) judicial law-making may be permissible even if it goes against the wording of a provision.[388] The analysis of the double criterion also suggests that a permissible constitution-consistent interpretation may contradict unambiguous statutory language in a particular case.

Even though courts in both jurisdictions can depart from unambiguous and specific statutory language, it does not follow that the statutory words are meaningless for the limits of judicial law-making. That is because the fundamental features of the legislation or of a provision, the thrust and grain of the legislation, a fundamental decision of the legislature, the fundamental normative content of a provision or the scheme of the legislation are all ultimately determined by a weighing of the interpretative criteria in both jurisdictions. Specific and clear statutory words can weigh heavily against the permissibility of judicial law-making in an individual case. It follows that the intention of the enacting legislature as manifested in the statutory wording can also weigh heavily against the permissibility of judicial law-making. The same applies to a provision's underlying specific purpose. Resort to s. 3(1) HRA is not possible if the legislation contains express statutory language that contradicts the Convention-compliant meaning. No similar outer limit of rights-consistent interpretation has been formulated by German courts. It has been argued that the express terms limit can only be satisfied by an explicit stipulation in the legislation that the legislation contradicts or may contradict Convention rights. Due to the power of the BVerfG to strike down unconstitutional legislation, it is very unlikely that the ordinary German legislature would explicitly stipulate that the statute contradicts fundamental rights protected under the German Basic Law. This may explain why no equivalent outer limit of interpretation has been expressed in German courts. If the German legislature were to use such express language, it seems highly unlikely that German courts would save the constitutionality of the provision by means of rights-consistent judicial law-making.

The judges' reasoning in England and Germany further shows that whether or not an interpretative result is possible under rights-consistent interpretation may depend on whether a wide or narrow purpose is ascribed to the

---

[387] For a case that came at the least very close to contradicting existing statutory words, see *R. (Hammond) v. Secretary of State for the Home Department* [2004] EWHC 2753 (Admin) and the discussion of this case in BEATSON et al. (eds.), above n. 34, paras. 5-109 and 5-118.
[388] BVerfG, *BeckRS* 2016, 47202, para. 7.

challenged legislation.[389] A popular route for courts in both jurisdictions to increase the scope of judicial law-making is to express a provision's or a statute's purpose in wide as opposed to specific terms. That is not peculiar to rights-consistent interpretation as the same issue arises also for conventional judicial law-making in both jurisdictions. The more widely the purpose is formulated, the more "objectivised" statutory interpretation becomes, and the more judicial discretion is inserted into statutory interpretation. Additionally, English and German judges do not offer generally applicable presumptions, rules, guidelines or criteria in order to establish at which level of generality a provision's purpose must be determined in an individual case. Stipulating such presumptions, rules, guidelines or criteria would be possible. For example, courts could always prefer a purpose at a lower level of abstraction to a purpose of a higher level of abstraction and at a given level of abstraction, a specific purpose could prevail over a general purpose. In judicial practice, the choice of the level of generality of the purpose is based on the exercise of judicial discretion.

If multiple Convention-compliant meanings exist, an English court may choose between these meanings as long as this choice does not involve issues calling for legislative deliberation or give rise to far-reaching practical repercussions which the court is not equipped to evaluate. In contrast, the BVerfG has held that a constitution-consistent interpretation is not possible if the unconstitutionality of the provision can be rectified in different ways by the legislature. German courts have also held that a judge cannot make a policy choice when interpreting legislation without surpassing the outer limits of the judicial function. A perfunctory comparison between these limits of interpretation seems to indicate a different institutional competence of the courts vis-à-vis the legislature in both jurisdictions. Whether the application of these interpretative limits amounts to a distinction in judicial practice in England and Germany must be doubted, however. We have seen in Chapter 1 that judges do make policy choices when interpreting legislation. German courts should therefore abandon the way they state the policy considerations limit. It is not surprising that this limit proves elusive when looking at German case law, for example *Fotokopie*.[390] In *Eilversammlungen*, the BVerfG did make a policy choice. It adopted a rights-consistent meaning of s. 14(1) VersG even though the legislature could have achieved a result that complies with the German Basic Law in a variety of ways. In England, a declaration of incompatibility puts considerable political pressure on the government and Parliament to change the law. If the BVerfG had declared void s. 14(1) VersG, the political pressure on the German government and legislature would have been similar. A similar incentive thus exists in both

---

[389] For a detailed discussion of the issue at which level the CJEU should determine the generality of the purpose of a statutory provision when interpreting EU law, see G. CONWAY, *The limits of legal reasoning and the European Court of Justice*, CUP, Cambridge 2012, pp. 225–246.
[390] For a discussion of *Fotokopie*, see Chapter 2, Section 3.3.

jurisdictions to adopt a rights-consistent meaning even if this interpretation pre-empts legislative choices. This pre-emption of legislative choices can be acute in the context of rights-consistent interpretation because of the open-textured formulation of fundamental rights in the German Basic Law and of Convention rights. When the BVerfG strikes down legislation as unconstitutional, the legislature often has considerable leeway to amend the legislation in a way which accommodates the BVerfG's constitutional pronouncements and still achieves the legislature's policy objectives.[391] A similar picture emerges in England when a court issues a declaration of incompatibility and when Parliament changes the law in order to make it Convention compliant.[392] The policy considerations limit as applied by English and German courts for rights-consistent interpretation takes away policy choices from the legislature. The objection that Parliament is able to change the legislation as long as the legislation remains constitutional/Convention compliant is no panacea in practice. Due to "burdens of inertia" and "legislative blind spots",[393] the judicial choice is sticky. Since statutory interpretation involves the making of policy choices, judges need to find a balance. Finding this balance answers the question of which institution (the legislature or the courts) is best placed to uphold rights. What must be kept in mind, however, is that (rights-consistent) judicial law-making provides a strong case for determinate limits of interpretation for reasons of legal certainty and the separation of powers. One may agree or disagree with where exactly the balance is to be found in an individual case, but at least one should know the criteria that determine how this balance can be found. Such criteria are provided by neither English nor German courts.

The outer limits of rights-consistent interpretation relating to courts making policy choices also leave ample scope for judicial discretion in both jurisdictions. The inconsistent application of these limits in case law fails to provide a high level of legal certainty. What is interesting is that English judges seem to be more transparent about their value-based considerations and their power to make policy choices when engaging in rights-consistent judicial law-making than their German counterparts. This difference in judicial attitude diverges from the finding in Chapter 2 of this book that a similar high level of non-transparency about their policy choices exists when courts apply the outer limits of statutory interpretation. The reason seems to be that the HRA has redefined the judicial role and has altered the balance of power between the judiciary and the

---

[391] For a general discussion of this point, see KAVANAGH, above n. 13.
[392] For discussion, see J. KING, Parliament's role following declarations of incompatibility, in M. HUNT, H. HOOPER and P. YOWELL (eds.), *Parliament and human rights*, Hart, Oxford 2015, pp. 165–188.
[393] For an explanation of these terms, see R. DIXON, Creating dialogue about socioeconomic rights: strong-form versus weak-form review revisited, (2007) 5 *I-CON* 391, 402–403.

legislature as it is traditionally understood.[394] Such a change in judicial attitudes did not occur in Germany, where the doctrine of rights-consistent interpretation is judge-made law as opposed to a statutory rule for which the legislative history contains indications that judges can go further than under conventional canons of construction.

7.3.3. The Constitutional Law Perspective

What is interesting from a comparative viewpoint is that the interpretative limits expressed in judgments are very similar despite different dogmatic foundations of rights-consistent interpretation in both jurisdictions. I have shown that different factors exist in both jurisdictions that push judges towards adopting wide outer limits of rights-consistent construction. The fact that they have adopted very similar outer limits may simply be a coincidence. If one agrees with this assessment, it does not follow that this result convinces at a normative level. The question is whether this similarity can also be explained from a constitutional law perspective. Very similar outer limits of rights-consistent interpretation in England and Germany could mean multiple things. First, it could mean that the constitutional settings presented in this book are in effect not relevant for the outer limits of the judicial function. It was shown in Chapter 2 that the opposite is correct. Second, it could mean that the constitutional settings underlying the outer limits of rights-consistent interpretation in England and Germany are not different. This explanation can be discarded due to English judges recognising the absolute doctrine of parliamentary sovereignty as a fundamental principle of the UK constitution. In England, Parliament is supreme and retains the right to enact legislation that is incompatible with Convention rights. In Germany, the power of the ordinary legislature is constrained by the German Basic Law. Third, it is possible to argue that someone has got it wrong. Either (a) English or German judges have overstepped the limits of their judicial function and trespassed into the realm of the legislature, or (b) English or German judges have not gone far enough when expressing the outer limits of rights-consistent interpretation. Fourth, I have already demonstrated that English courts have ventured outside their constitutional role for rights-consistent judicial law-making. Even though the highest English courts repeatedly emphasise that the HRA preserves parliamentary sovereignty, the use of s. 3(1) HRA in judicial practice undermines the doctrine. English courts have thus already made the transition from absolute parliamentary sovereignty to a qualified version of

---

[394] I. LEIGH and R. MASTERMAN, *Making rights real: the Human Rights Act in its first decade*, Hart, Oxford 2008, p. 129; R. STEVENS, *The English judges: their role in the changing constitution*, Hart, Oxford 2005, pp. 146, 150, 177.

parliamentary sovereignty in the sphere of rights-consistent interpretation. This affects the second and third points made above.

It can also be observed from a comparative angle that English judges have pushed their interpretative powers under s. 3(1) HRA beyond the doctrine of absolute parliamentary sovereignty. The outer limits of rights-consistent interpretation in England and Germany express a reconciliatory balance between subjective and objective factors of interpretation. The doctrine of parliamentary sovereignty is a factor in this balancing exercise as it flows from this doctrine that an English court cannot depart from the intention of the enacting parliament. If the outer limits of rights-consistent interpretation in both jurisdictions are very similar and if in some respects English courts' interpretative powers even exceed the powers of their German counterparts, then it appears that English judges have given insufficient weight to the doctrine of parliamentary sovereignty in the balancing exercise. This result is not a strict logical conclusion as it could also be that German courts have over-restricted judges' interpretative powers when determining the demarcation line between interpretation and amendment of legislation. In the light of *Soraya*, this possibility seems very unlikely. The comparison with German law thus shows that the way English courts have interpreted s. 3(1) HRA does not adhere to the constitutional doctrine of parliamentary sovereignty. What comparative constitutional law cannot answer is whether this deviation from the constitutional doctrine is legitimate or not. This question can only be answered from an internal UK constitutional law perspective, and it was demonstrated that English judges have exceeded their constitutional role.

I have shown in Chapter 2 that the doctrine of parliamentary sovereignty can support a system of interpretation according to which judicial law-making is generally permissible in order to give effect to the intention of the enacting legislature if that intention is insufficiently expressed in the statutory words. If English courts had adopted such a system of interpretation under s. 3(1) HRA, they would have retained the absolute constitutional doctrine, would have broadened the interpretative powers of judges in comparison to conventional canons of construction and would have fulfilled the intention of the 1998 Parliament that enacted s. 3(1) HRA. Such a system of interpretation would have recognised that a court cannot depart from the intention of the enacting parliament and would, thus, have stayed behind the interpretative powers of German judges. Such a system would have looked convincing from an internal UK constitutional viewpoint and from a comparative constitutional viewpoint. That is the system of rights-consistent interpretation that English courts did not, but should have adopted.

7.3.4. Formalism

English judges have also developed and stipulated general constraints for Convention-compatible interpretation that are intended to form outer limits of the judicial function for all cases that arise under s. 3(1) HRA. Conceptually, this is the same approach that German courts apply when they define the outer limits of constitution-consistent interpretation. The (ongoing) change in judicial attitude in England towards accepting generally applicable outer limits of interpretation can be explained by virtue of the change of the default position for Convention-compatible judicial law-making. Since judicial law-making is generally permissible under s. 3(1) HRA, the guiding function of a provision's wording is limited and the danger that judges may venture outside the legislature's intention seems higher than in a system where judges cannot add to, alter or ignore statutory words when interpreting legislation Furthermore, if neither the statutory words nor the intention of the enacting Parliament function as outer limits of interpretation of themselves, legal uncertainty reigns if courts are not to clarify the outer limits of the judicial function. In order to (a) increase the level of predictability of the outcome of a case and the level of legal certainty and (b) attenuate concerns of judges venturing into the sphere of the legislature, courts in both jurisdictions do not solely apply a case-by-case approach but have formulated general outer boundaries for rights-consistent judicial law-making that apply in every case. In this respect, the rule of law, the separation of powers and parliamentary sovereignty in England act in concert.

The change in judicial attitudes in England may also explain why some scholars[395] perceive an increase in formalism in Supreme Court judgments. This increase in formalism in itself is not due to judges attempting to conceal policy choices or to disguise their creative role. General outer boundaries of interpretation require a "formal" application of these limits in every case of judicial law-making. At least in theory, the outer limits of judicial law-making replace the guiding function of the wording of a statute from the viewpoint of legal certainty.[396] They aim to ensure that judges stay within the constraints of the judicial function and do not, without any democratic endorsement, rely on their own personal values and ideas about policy when interpreting legislation. Formalism in statutory interpretation is thus supported by constitutional law, in particular the rule of law and the separation of powers. The main issue is, however, that judges in both jurisdictions have deliberately embedded sufficient scope for evaluative arguments in the outer limits of rights-consistent interpretation. They have intentionally chosen to express the generally applicable outer limits of interpretation in vague terms, thus building an element of considerable judicial discretion into these limits. The "judicial formulas" chosen by judges contain a high amount of adaptive capacity. The effect is that judges (a) enjoy a considerable flexibility when applying these limits and (b) can to a large extent

---

[395] A. PATERSON, *Final judgment: the last Law Lords and the Supreme Court*, Hart, Oxford 2013, pp. 261–272.
[396] See Chapter 2, Section 5.

determine the effectiveness of these limits in an individual case. English and German courts prefer malleable over bright-line outer limits of rights-consistent interpretation. That is why the increase in formalism in English judgments does not coincide with judges' reasoning proceeding deductively according to clear interpretative rules. This judicial choice is not demanded by constitutional law or logic, but the vague words of s. 3(1) HRA and art. 20(3) GG do not rule out such a choice as they do not clearly set the outer limits of interpretation.

7.3.5. Evaluative Arguments

When the focus is turned to evaluative arguments in rights-consistent judicial law-making, the scope for these arguments is very similar in both jurisdictions when judges apply the outer limits of rights-consistent interpretation. Interpretation is value laden and involves issues of balancing values on which reasonable persons can and do differ.[397] Even though this issue was not at the core of the comparative analysis provided in this book, it should have become clear that neither English nor German courts have provided rules, principled guidelines or a set of consistent criteria or patterns that allow for a structuring of evaluative arguments.[398] The scope for evaluative arguments in the outer limits of rights-consistent interpretation allows for a contextualisation of these limits depending on the facts of the case, the area of legislation at issue, the age of the statute, the policy implications of the question of law to be answered etc. The room for this contextualisation is also the underlying reason why the border between permissible judicial law-making and impermissible judicial amendment of legislation is often described as unclear or elusive in both jurisdictions. As appears from judicial practice in both jurisdictions, it is mostly the weighing of the interpretative criteria in an individual case that ultimately determines whether or not the outer limits of interpretation are exceeded. The weighing process is not governed by a priority ordering, rules, clear principled guidelines or a clear set of factors. It leaves considerable scope for evaluative arguments and judicial discretion. Again, this is a judicial choice. How a court balances subjective and objective factors of interpretation is to a large extent governed by the circumstances of the individual case and pragmatic concerns in both jurisdictions. The indeterminacy inherent in the judicial balancing

---

[397] N. MACCORMICK and R. SUMMERS, Interpretation and justification, in N. MACCORMICK and R. SUMMERS (eds.), *Interpreting statutes: a comparative study*, Dartmouth, Aldershot 1991, pp. 511, 538–539.
[398] J. BELL, Policy arguments in statutory interpretation, in R.S. SUMMERS, N. MACCORMICK and J. BELL (eds.), *Legal reasoning and statutory interpretation: Rotterdam lectures in jurisprudence*, Gouda Quint, Arnhem 1989, pp. 55–79 provides a typology of policy arguments as applied in English judicial practice. This typology does not provide and is not aimed at providing rules, principled guidelines or a set of consistent criteria that reduces the level of judgement when courts apply policy arguments.

exercise of the interpretative criteria is transported into the limits of statutory interpretation. Judicial decisions on whether a rights-consistent meaning that surpasses the possible semantic meanings of the statutory words stays within the framework set by the outer limits of rights-consistent judicial law-making are neither sufficiently predictable nor "reckonable".[399] It does not appear to be possible to predict or reckon with a sufficient degree of accuracy how a court will exercise its discretion in an individual case of judicial law-making.

It was argued in Chapter 2 and in this chapter that judicial reasoning based on evaluative arguments and extra-legal arguments mainly appears ad hoc. These arguments cannot be described as steadying factors behind the courts' reasoning.[400] English and German courts do not use a single scale of measurable values but rather refer to an individual judge's conception of what is just, reasonable or fair. The indeterminacy of evaluative arguments in English and German judicial practice can be illustrated by the argument based on justice. Both English and German judges agree that a factor that co-determines the interpretation and application of legislation is the function of a judge to decide a particular case in a just and fair way.[401] It is therefore not surprising that judges refer to arguments based on justice when applying the outer limits of judicial law-making.[402] C. Gearty concluded that the "feel for individuated justice is one of the driving forces of the Human Rights Act" after considering the English courts' case law on s. 3(1) HRA.[403] This does not seem to be any different for rights-consistent interpretation in Germany. Courts in both jurisdictions claim that their function to decide a case in a just way has constitutional status, either via common law (constitutional) background assumptions or via art. 20(3) GG. But what does justice mean? Whose justice are the courts talking about? The justice of the enacting legislature, of the current legislature, of the majority opinion in the public or of the judge? What kind of justice are the courts talking

---

[399] The term "reckonability" is defined by G. BECK, *The legal reasoning of the Court of Justice of the EU*, Hart, Oxford 2012, p. 3 as meaning that judicial "outcomes may be correctly predicted in most but not all cases".

[400] BECK, ibid., spends considerable time on describing the steadying factors outside formal legal reasoning for the jurisprudence of the CJEU, but even he concludes that "this study does not maintain that the presence of certain steadying factors inevitably prompts the Court of Justice to decide in one way or the other, or even make it more likely than not that it will do so" (p. 11) and concedes that steadying factors "will vary ... from one case to another" (p. 42).

[401] BVerfG, *NJW* 1973, 1221, 1225 – *Soraya*; BVerfG, *NJW* 1990, 1593–1594; BVerfG, *NJW* 2006, 3409 – *Marlene Dietrich*; *Duport Steels Ltd. v. Sirs* [1980] 1 All ER 529 (HL), 551 (Lord Scarman); *R. (Nicklinson) v. Ministry of Justice* [2014] UKSC 38, paras. 164, 191 (Lord Mance). See also BARAK, above n. 119, p. 294; LORD NEUBERGER, Sausages and the judicial process: the limits of transparency, speech at the Annual Conference of the Supreme Court of New South Wales, August 2014, para. 39, available online at https://www.supremecourt.uk/docs/speech-140801.pdf. For discussion, see LARENZ and CANARIS, above n. 161, pp. 168–170.

[402] See, e.g. BVerfG, *NJW* 1973, 1221, 1225 – *Soraya*; BVerfG, *NJW* 2006, 3409 – *Marlene Dietrich*; BGH, *NJW* 2014, 2646, para. 28 – *Lebensversicherung II*; BGH, *NJW* 2017, 2842, para. 24.

[403] GEARTY, above n. 366, p. 95.

about? Formal justice (legal certainty), a form of generalised material justice (the greatest possible happiness for the greatest possible number of people?) or justice in an individual case?

The term justice can be used in a variety of ways with a variety of different meanings. A judge should thus be transparent[404] and coherent about whose justice and what kind of justice he or she refers to in a judgment. If justice only refers to the individual judge's idea of what justice requires,[405] justice is an inherently subjective and vague standard that cannot be further controlled or structured. Lord Mustill emphasised in *Doody* that the exercise of determining the requirements of fairness is "essentially an intuitive judgment", highly dependent on context and open to changes with the passage of time.[406] Such non-transparent standards of material justice and fairness as applied in English and German courts are inapt to reduce the subjective element in statutory interpretation. Such standards cannot be judged against an objective standard. They are case specific and unsystematic as no constant or coherent ruling practice has evolved in both jurisdictions. They can be filled with different contents and can be easily abused.[407] They cannot provide a high level of legal certainty. It is certainly not doubted here that legislation may contain provisions that are unable to deliver substantive justice in each individual case. Justice may thus provide a corrective to the binding force of statute within the framework set by constitutional law. It can also be that the legislature deliberately uses vague words in a provision in order to grant judges a certain evaluative scope. In that case, justice can be delivered within the four corners of the statute.

It does not follow from this, however, that an unstructured and uncontrollable concept must fill this evaluative scope for the outer limits of rights-consistent interpretation. This criticism applies even if one (a) argues that justice is not a simple and uniform standard of evaluation but has multiple aspects or (b) argues that the task to give a fair and just judgment entrusts judges with the resolution of fundamental and objective issues in philosophy of law and moral philosophy. Transparency about how judges resolve these issues is rarely provided in written judicial opinions. The bottom line then is that justice remains a black box, which can have a considerable impact on the outcome of a case. This criticism does not

---

[404] "The best response to the critique that judicial justification is but façade legitimation is to falsify it with unfailing candour in the statement of reasons for decisions": MacCormick and Summers, above n. 397, p. 543.

[405] *Duport Steels Ltd. v. Sirs* [1980] 1 All ER 529 (HL), 551 (Lord Scarman); cf. R. Zippelius, Rechtsnorm und richterliche Entscheidungsfreiheit, (1970) 25 *JZ* 241, 244.

[406] *R. (Doody) v. Secretary of State for the Home Department* [1994] 1 AC 531 (HL), 560 (Lord Mustill).

[407] German history provides sufficient illustrations for such abuses in the name of justice. See, e.g. K.-P. Sommermann, in: H. v. Mangoldt, F. Klein and C. Starck (eds.), *Kommentar zum Grundgesetz: Band 2, Artikel 20 bis 82*, 5th ed., Franz Vahlen, Munich 2005, Art. 20 Abs. 3, paras. 235–236.

mean that the concept of justice must be chiselled out into detailed elements before it can be applied via deduction in an individual case. Providing substantive individual justice is often based on induction. Inductive reasoning moves from specific instances to patterns and regularities, generalised conclusions and theories.[408] Yet, English and German courts have not provided such patterns, regularities or generalised conclusions for evaluative arguments when applying the outer limits of rights-consistent interpretation. That is of course difficult to achieve if justice and fairness have their basis in the judge's intuitive sense of what justice and fairness require. Here, a reference to psychological research may be warranted. A significant number of scholars in psychology distinguish between system 1 and system 2 of human decision-making.[409] System 1 of decision-making is fast, automatic and intuitive. System 2 of decision-making is slow, calculative and deliberative. System 1 of decision-making is distinctly associated with heuristics and behavioural biases. Behavioural research demonstrates that human decision-making is characterised by bounded rationality. A common observable pattern in decision-making is that individuals rely on rules of thumb (heuristics). Heuristics facilitate decision-making in a complex environment.[410] Their application can,[411] however, also be a source of errors (biases) and can cause errors of judgement.[412] There is sufficient research showing that judges are susceptible to behavioural biases as well.[413] Thus, intuition may not be a good guide for justice after all. If a judge interprets legislation based on his or her own ideas of what justice requires, which is necessarily influenced by biased personal experiences, scepticism is warranted.

G. Beck has categorised justice and fairness as essentially contestable concepts.[414] An essentially contestable concept is evaluative and subject to

---

[408] Cf. G. RADBRUCH, *Rechtsphilosophie: Studienausgabe*, 2nd ed., C.F. Müller, Heidelberg 1999, p. 37; R. ZIPPELIUS, *Das Wesen des Rechts: eine Einführung in die Rechtsphilosophie*, 5th ed., C.H. Beck, Munich 1997, pp. 112–113.

[409] E.g. D. KAHNEMAN, *Thinking, fast and slow*, Penguin, London 2011, pp. 20–21. See J. EVANS and K.E. STANOVICH, Dual-process theories of higher cognition: advancing the debate, (2013) 8 *Perspectives on Psychological Science* 223 for a review of the criticisms and a defence of a dual-process theory of human information-processing.

[410] C. ENGEL and G. GIGERENZER, Law and heuristics: an interdisciplinary venture, in G. GIGERENZER and C. ENGEL (eds.), *Heuristics and the law*, MIT Press, Cambridge, Mass. 2006, pp. 1, 2–4.

[411] Heuristics do not have to be a source of biases; see G. GIGERENZER and W. GAISSMAIER, Heuristic decision making, (2011) 62 *Annual Review of Psychology* 451, 456–458; P. SLOVIC et al., Rational actors or rational fools: implications of the affect heuristic for behavioral economics, (2002) 31 *Journal of Socio-Economics* 329, 337; A. TVERSKY and D. KAHNEMAN, Judgment under uncertainty: heuristics and biases, (1974) 185 *Science* 1124, 1130.

[412] C. JOLLS and C.R. SUNSTEIN, Debiasing through law, (2006) 35 *Journal of Legal Studies* 199, 204.

[413] For an overview, see A. WISTRICH, J. RACHLINSKI and C. GUTHRIE, Heart versus head: do judges follow the law or follow their feelings?, (2015) 93 *Texas Law Review* 855–923; A.J. WISTRICH and J. RACHLINSKI, Implicit bias in judicial decision making: how it affects judgment and what judges can do about it, in S.E. REDFIELD (ed.), *Enhancing justice: reducing bias*, ABA Book Publishing, Chicago 2018, pp. 87–130.

[414] BECK, above n. 399, pp. 61–71.

conflicts of ideas about the underlying value it expresses, which gives rise to continuing disputes over the most justifiable understanding of this value. These disputes cannot be resolved by clarifying the meaning of the concept or differentiating between its different meanings according to Beck.[415] In other words, Beck rejects the idea that justice or fairness are concepts that can be further controlled or structured. Other authors have argued that justice is ultimately a relative and subjective concept.[416] If one agrees with this viewpoint and if one takes into account the considerable scope for evaluative arguments in cases of rights-consistent judicial law-making, concepts like justice and fairness should have no role to play when judges apply the outer limits of rights-consistent judicial law-making. This follows from the need for determinate outer limits of judicial law-making as explained in Chapter 1. The viewpoint advocated here is that it is possible to reduce the subjective element inherent in evaluative arguments like justice and fairness if these arguments are controlled and structured and if common benchmarks for permissible evaluative arguments are provided. That is one way to make judicial reasoning more determinate and objective and one way to increase the level of legal certainty. A structuring of evaluative arguments includes a clearer boundary between permissible and impermissible evaluative arguments. For German law, this can be done in the following way: justice can be defined as exclusively governed by the requirements set by the German Basic Law. This constitutionalises justice exhaustively according to the terms of the German Basic Law. What justice requires in an individual case must be derived from the terms of the German Basic Law. The dominant opinion in legal scholarship in Germany argues that the German Basic Law and in particular its basic rights incorporate principles of justice, reasonableness and fairness, which is why the possible conflict between legislation and justice is ultimately resolved by examining whether a statute infringes the German Basic Law.[417] Hence, a judge sitting in a regular court cannot decide not to apply a statute because the statute allegedly infringes higher-order principles of justice. The judge can only (a) interpret the statute in a constitution-consistent way or

---

[415] Ibid., p. 70.
[416] H. KELSEN, *Was ist Gerechtigkeit?*, Reclam, Stuttgart 2016, p. 15; B. RÜTHERS, *Das Ungerechte an der Gerechtigkeit*, 3rd ed., Mohr Siebeck, Tübingen 2009, pp. 171–174.
[417] B. GRZESZICK, in T. MAUNZ and G. DÜRIG (founders), *Grundgesetz-Kommentar*, C.H. Beck, Munich 2016, Art. 20 Abs. 3 GG, paras. 67–70; M. JESTAEDT, Rechtsprechung und Rechtsetzung – eine deutsche Perspektive, in W. ERBGUTH and J. MASING (eds.), *Die Bedeutung der Rechtsprechung im System der Rechtsquellen*, Richard Boorberg Verlag, Stuttgart 2005, pp. 25, 33; E. SCHMIDT-AßMANN, Der Rechtsstaat, in J. ISENSEE and P. KIRCHHOF (eds.), *Handbuch des Staatsrecht der Bundesrepublik Deutschland, Band I*, 2nd ed., C.F. Müller, Heidelberg 1995, §24, paras. 42–45; M. SCHRÖDER, *Gesetzesbindung des Richters und Rechtsweggarantie im Mehrebenensystem*, Mohr Siebeck, Tübingen 2010, pp. 70–71; H. SCHULZE-FIELITZ, in H. DREIER (ed.), *Grundgesetz: Kommentar, Band II, Artikel 20–82*, Mohr Siebeck, Tübingen 2006, Art. 20 (Rechtsstaat), paras. 50–51, 94.

(b) refer a question about the unconstitutionality of the statute to the BVerfG under art. 100(1) GG. It is possible to adopt this reasoning for rights-consistent statutory interpretation as follows: justice is an evaluative argument that stands outside the specific statutory context; a judge who takes into account an argument based on justice when applying the outer limits of rights-consistent judicial law-making must trace back the specific justice argument to the values enshrined in the German Basic Law; structuring justice in this way reduces the subjective element in evaluative arguments and makes the application of the outer limits of judicial law-making more determinate.

An equivalent reasoning for English law would be to understand arguments based on justice in the sphere of Convention-compatible judicial law-making as exclusively governed by the HRA. What justice requires in an individual case must thus be derived exclusively from the terms of the HRA and Convention rights.

7.3.6. Legal (Un)certainty

Due to the considerable scope for evaluative arguments and their unstructured, ad hoc status in both jurisdictions, English and German judges possess an almost identical, considerable amount of judicial discretion when applying the outer limits of rights-consistent interpretation in an individual case. Discretion is inherent in values. Judges exercise discretion in relation to a particular set of circumstances. Judicial discretion is resistant to generally applicable categorisation, and an individual judge's personal values influence how judicial discretion is exercised.[418] The equally high level of judicial discretion in both countries demonstrates how similar judicial attitudes are in the realm of rights-consistent interpretation in England and Germany. It also shows (a) that English and German judges share a very similar understanding of the value of legal certainty in rights-consistent interpretation and (b) that English and German judges adopt the same balance between formal justice and material justice. Law is no more autonomous from values and policy arguments in German courts than in English courts when judges apply the outer limits of rights-consistent judicial law-making.[419]

The protection of human rights focuses on the concerns of the individual and the particularities of the individual case.[420] This impacts on the balance between formal justice and material justice. Judges may leave sufficient scope

---

[418] R.J. CAHILL-O'CALLAGHAN, The influence of personal values on legal judgments, (2013) 40 *Journal of Law and Society* 596, 620.
[419] For an apparently different view, see T. LUNDMARK, Legal science and European harmonisation, (2014) 130 *LQR* 68–82.
[420] G. KIRCHHOF, *Die Allgemeinheit des Gesetzes*, Mohr Siebeck, Tübingen 2009, p. 6.

for evaluative arguments and judicial discretion in the outer limits of rights-consistent interpretation in order to achieve substantive individual justice, e.g. by protecting the interests of minorities that are underrepresented in debates in Parliament. This may explain why it is in the area of human rights protection that English courts have stretched their interpretative powers quite far. This may also explain why, as some scholars claim, the BVerfG has applied the outer limits of judicial law-making in quite a lenient fashion in cases of rights-consistent judicial law-making. The downside is that vague outer limits of interpretation mask the application of values and trigger the impression of methodological arbitrariness.[421] Judicial choices are concealed in the shadow of formalism in order to preserve an image of neutrality and impartiality. That is one of the reasons why s. 3(1) HRA creates a far higher degree of uncertainty for citizens in knowing what the law is than conventional canons of interpretation.[422] I have also shown in Chapter 2 that concealing judicial choices in formalism is also one of the reasons why judicial law-making in Germany creates a higher degree of uncertainty in judicial practice when compared to English conventional canons of interpretation.

When the focus is drawn to the balance between providing legal certainty and giving effect to the intention of the legislature, rights-consistent judicial law-making may be seen as favouring the latter in both legal systems when compared to the English approach to judicial law-making under conventional canons of interpretation. Framing the balance in these terms seems dubious, on the one hand, because courts can depart from the intention of the enacting legislature under rights-consistent judicial law-making. On the other hand, it may be possible to conceptualise the "intention of the legislature" as the intention of a different parliament (s. 3(1) HRA) or the presumed intention of a reasonable legislature. Yet, relying on a different parliament or a reasonable legislature for rights-consistent interpretation moves the balance further away from legal certainty.

An apparently inconsistent application of the indeterminate limits of judicial law-making to the facts of the case by individual judges will often stem from judges disagreeing about the evaluative part of legal reasoning. This fails to provide a high level of legal certainty. Despite the very similar outer limits of interpretation in both jurisdictions, it thus does not follow that similar factual situations would be decided similarly in both jurisdictions. Very critical voices may add that it does not even follow that like situations would be treated in a like manner in the same jurisdiction due to the high level of indeterminacy of

---

[421] B. RÜTHERS, Methodenrealismus in Jurisprudenz und Justiz, JZ 2006, 53, 54; cf. GRIFFITH, above n. 352, p. 343.

[422] For this criticism, see SALES and EKINS, above n. 50, p. 223; cf. R. EKINS, Rights, interpretation and the rule of law, in R. EKINS (ed.), *Modern challenges to the rule of law*, LexisNexis, Wellington 2011, pp. 165, 181.

the outer limits of interpretation. Judicial disagreement about the evaluative part of legal reasoning would be a lesser concern if the outer limits of interpretation were more determinate and if the weighing of the interpretative maxims were guided by clear principles and criteria ("principled balancing") rather than being ad hoc. Both conditions would reduce the role of evaluative arguments and judicial discretion for the decision-making process. For example, A. Barak has proposed that judges should give priority to the purpose arising from the language of the statute itself when the purpose arising from statutory language contradicts the purpose arising from external sources like legislative history.[423] This book is mainly concerned with the maximum of what is possible as a matter of interpretation without the courts exceeding their constitutional role. That does not mean that courts will stretch the limits of the possible that far in every case. In England, for example, some scholars have argued that courts have recently demonstrated a reluctance to use their wide powers under s. 3(1) HRA.[424] In Germany, the BVerfG's *Kopftuch* decision may illustrate a similar development towards a stricter understanding of the binding force of statute. This development is not limited to constitution-consistent interpretation but appears in the sphere of conventional judicial law-making as well, as *Dreiteilungsmethode* demonstrates. Judges can show this reluctance due to the vague formulation of the outer limits of interpretation: a fertile soil for legal uncertainty.

It follows from all this that the outer limits of interpretation in both jurisdictions perform poorly when judged against their function to (a) limit the scope of possible meanings of a provision, (b) limit judicial power and thus address separation of powers concerns and (c) reduce the area of extra-legal considerations and subjective judicial evaluation in rights-consistent interpretation. The analysis of the outer boundaries of rights-consistent interpretation in England and Germany thus confirms the realist critique. The application of these limits is to a large extent governed by evaluative arguments and judicial discretion and to a lesser extent governed by formal legal reasoning. This finding is concerning because, as was shown in Chapter 1, judicial law-making demands determinate outer limits of interpretation. This finding is not inevitable,[425] however, because the "open area" can be reduced or at least

---

[423] BARAK, above n. 119, pp. 216, 179, 364 (e.g. a court should prefer a specific purpose to a general purpose; legal norms governing the choice between conflicting purposes; when purpose arising from statutory language contradicts the purpose arising from external sources like legislative history, judges should give priority to the purpose arising from the language of the statute itself).

[424] M. AMOS, Proposals for the reform of sections 3 and 4 of the Human Rights Act 1998, Queen Mary School of Law Legal Studies Research Paper No. 238/2016, 2016, p. 8, available online at https://papers.ssrn.com/sol3/papers.cfm?abstract_id=2814973; S. GARDBAUM, *The new Commonwealth model of constitutionalism*, CUP, Cambridge 2013, p. 192; WAGNER and BARTH, above n. 59, pp. 99, 102, 104.

[425] For a different view, see R. POSNER, *How judges think*, Harvard University Press, Cambridge, Mass. 2008, p. 249.

structured if judges were to formulate clearer outer limits of interpretation or were to control and structure permissible evaluative arguments. Courts could increase the level of specificity of interpretative maxims and of the outer limits of judicial law-making by including more formal elements. Examples of such formal elements were provided in this section. Increasing the level of formal elements in judicial reasoning reduces the area in which evaluative arguments can operate, and it reduces the level of judicial discretion.

7.3.7. Convergence of Judicial Reasoning

The comparative discussion so far has revealed how similar judicial reasoning operates in England and Germany in relation to the outer limits of rights-consistent interpretation. The extent to which the application of these limits is governed by formal legal reasoning, evaluative arguments and judicial discretion appears almost identical in both jurisdictions. This commonality is based on a common understanding of the (constitutional) function of the judge vis-à-vis the legislature. A large legal cultural distinction or distinction in the style of legal reasoning does not exist. There is no dichotomy between an allegedly systematic and deductive style in Germany and an inductive and facts-centred style that is driven by the circumstances of the individual case in England. The claim[426] that continental European judges are more legalistic, less pragmatic and less creative than English ones is not sufficiently specific and incorrect with regard to the formulation and application of outer limits of rights-consistent interpretation. In particular, the German style does not appear more legalistic and deductive than the English style of judicial reasoning when judges argue that a rights-consistent meaning is reconcilable with the outer limits of judicial law-making. The English style does not appear more discursive,[427] case specific and justice centred than the German style. Context is equally important in both jurisdictions. For the outer limits of rights-consistent interpretation, this book's findings validate S. Vogenauer's thesis[428] that statutory interpretation in England and Germany is fundamentally uniform. B. Markesinis has compared the judicial style and judicial reasoning in both jurisdictions and has claimed "that the style of one [an English judgment] is to say what it thinks while the style of the other [a German judgment] is to conceal it under a screen of apparently deductive reasoning".[429] Markesinis may be right so far as the transparency about judicial

---

[426] Ibid., p. 263.
[427] For the finding that the English style of statutory interpretation can be described as discursive, whereas the German style can be described as deductive, see R. SUMMERS and M. TARUFFO, Interpretation and comparative analysis, in N. MACCORMICK and R. SUMMERS (eds.), *Interpreting statutes: a comparative study*, Dartmouth, Aldershot 1991, pp. 461, 492–493, 498.
[428] VOGENAUER, above n. 373, pp. 1295–1308.
[429] B. MARKESINIS, Judicial style and judicial reasoning in England and Germany, (2000) 59 *CLJ* 294, 308.

discretion in statutory interpretation is concerned. Yet, this is only one part of the story. When an English court argues that a rights-consistent meaning is compatible with the thrust of the legislation, what else is it doing other than concealing a policy choice? The style of rights-consistent judicial law-making in both jurisdictions appears formal and deductive on paper. In reality, however, English and German courts are significantly influenced by the facts of a case and policy arguments to the same extent. On a spectrum of form and substance in legal reasoning,[430] rights-consistent judicial law-making can be described as considerably "substantive" in both jurisdictions.

One of the key factors that can explain this commonality is that courts in both jurisdictions claim that they can deviate from the intention of the enacting parliament. Neither s. 3(1) HRA nor art. 20(2), (3) GG demand that courts should be able to depart from an identifiable objective of the enacting legislature. Instead, both provisions are open for the interpretation that courts cannot derogate from this intention. It is submitted here that both English and German courts should provide a higher level of legal certainty by adopting and honouring such an outer limit of rights-consistent judicial law-making. This would remove some of the excesses of an overly objectivised approach to statutory interpretation. Judicial law-making would not be overly restrained and the legislature would not be overburdened if this outer limit were adopted in both jurisdictions. English judicial practice shows that updating construction is very much possible with such an outer limit of interpretation. I have argued in Chapter 2 that the BVerfG has recently moved towards restricting a court's power to depart from the intention of the enacting legislature. *Kopftuch* indicates that this development also appears for constitution-consistent interpretation. If one acquiesces with this observation as being the tendency in the newest German case law, then German case law is developing towards a position that shows more deference to the legislature than English courts show when they apply s. 3(1) HRA as interpreted in *Ghaidan*. Scholars who argue that English courts have recently demonstrated a reluctance to use their wide powers under s. 3(1) HRA would probably see a similar development towards showing more deference to the legislature.

8. A LOOK INTO THE FUTURE: A UK BILL OF RIGHTS?

Recent political developments indicate that the future of the HRA in the UK is uncertain. The comparison of constitution-consistent judicial law-making in German courts and of Convention-compatible judicial law-making in English

---

[430] P.S. Atiyah and R.S. Summers, *Form and substance in Anglo-American law*, Clarendon Press, Oxford 1987, chapter 1.

courts might henceforth need re-evaluation. Before the Brexit referendum on 23 June 2016, the Conservative Party in power had argued for a repeal of the HRA and the UK's withdrawal from the ECHR. The intention was to replace the current UK human rights framework with a UK Bill of Rights.[431] The motivation behind this intention was partly built upon (a) political and public resentment against decisions of the ECtHR, which are binding upon the UK as a matter of international law,[432] and (b) the use of the HRA in courts to grant protection to illegal immigrants, criminals, prisoners and suspected terrorists. For our purposes, it is relevant that criticism of the HRA has also targeted the role of courts in human rights protection. One aspect of this criticism is that judges have overstretched their interpretative powers under s. 3(1) HRA.[433] The Conservative Party proposed to "prevent our laws from being effectively re-written through 'interpretation'" and that the "courts will interpret legislation based upon its normal meaning and the clear intention of Parliament".[434] It is not clear, however, what an interpretation clause in a UK Bill of Rights would look like as the plans for a UK Bill of Rights still remain at a very early and very uncertain stage.[435] Some commentators have argued that the courts have recently demonstrated a reluctance to use s. 3(1) HRA due to the rise in criticism in the media and by politicians about activist judges and their wide powers under s. 3(1) HRA.[436] At least for the time being, plans to repeal the HRA and to withdraw from the ECHR have been dropped from the political agenda. The White Paper *Legislating for the United Kingdom's withdrawal from the European Union* stated that "there are no plans to withdraw from the ECHR".[437] The Conservative manifesto for the

---

[431] Conservative Party, Protecting human rights in the UK, London 2014. The debate about replacing the Human Rights Act 1998 with a British Bill of Rights is older; see, e.g. Joint Committee on Human Rights, A Bill of Rights for the UK?, 2007–08, HL 165-I, HC 150-I, 2008; Commission on a Bill of Rights, A UK Bill of Rights? The choice before us, Vol. 1, London 2012, available online at http://webarchive.nationalarchives.gov.uk/20130206021312tf_/ http://www.justice.gov.uk/about/cbr/. For an overview of the discussion, see ELLIOTT and THOMAS, above n. 48, pp. 806–809.

[432] Art. 46 ECHR.

[433] Cf. Conservative Party, Protecting human rights in the UK, London 2014, p. 6; D. MEAGHER, The scope of judicial rights interpretation under Bills of Rights (and its political consequences), (2009) *Public Law Review* 214, 222; EKINS, above n. 271, pp. 647–648; A. SPEAIGHT, Mechanisms of a UK Bill of Rights, in Commission on a Bill of Rights, above n. 431, pp. 257–261, available online at http://www.justice.gov.uk/about/cbr. There are certainly commentators who have criticised the House of Lords/Supreme Court for not using their powers under s. 3(1) HRA more vigorously; see, e.g. T. HICKMAN, *Public law after the Human Rights Act*, Hart, Oxford 2010, pp. 90–94.

[434] Conservative Party, Protecting human rights in the UK, London 2014, p. 6, available online at https://www.conservatives.com/~/media/files/downloadable%20files/human_rights.pdf.

[435] For a proposal for such an interpretation clause, see SPEAIGHT, above n. 433, p. 261.

[436] WAGNER and BARTH, above n. 59, pp. 99, 102, 104.

[437] Department for Exiting the European Union, Legislating for the United Kingdom's withdrawal from the European Union, March 2017, para. 2.22.

2017 general election declared that a Conservative government "will not repeal or replace the Human Rights Act while the process of Brexit is underway"; the UK "will remain [a] signator[y] to the European Convention on Human Rights for the duration of the next parliament".[438]

These current political developments indicate that the comparative findings of this chapter will not enter the realm of modern legal history any time soon. However, there is another principle of statutory interpretation employed in English courts that justifies a critical evaluation and a comparative analysis with constitution-consistent interpretation in Germany, not only due to the uncertain future of the HRA, but also due to the growing use of this principle in English courts. Since the debate about the UK's withdrawal from the ECHR is partly filled with a desire to regain lost sovereignty in respect of the level of human rights protection in the UK, it is plausible to assume that a future, post-HRA UK human rights framework will retain the doctrine of parliamentary sovereignty. Rather than granting the power to determine the level of human rights protection to English courts, politicians and the media have supported a UK Bill of Rights because decisions about human rights protection should be made in Parliament. The scepticism about the future role of the courts in human rights protection puts the principle of legality into the limelight. This principle has developed in the shadow of the doctrine of parliamentary sovereignty without pressure from an external source of law but with the protection of common law constitutional principles, including fundamental rights, in mind. The principle of legality can be described as a presumption of general application operating as a constitutional principle.[439] It obliges courts to interpret legislation in the light of fundamental constitutional principles. Before the coming into force of the HRA, the principle of legality was the closest English comparator to constitution-consistent interpretation in Germany. It is a presumption that is part of a statute's objective purpose, operating at a high level of abstraction. It means that fundamental human rights and other fundamental constitutional principles recognised by the common law cannot be overridden by general or ambiguous statutory words.[440]

> This is because there is too great a risk that the full implications of their unqualified meaning may have passed unnoticed in the democratic process. In the absence of

---

[438] The Conservative and Unionist Party manifesto 2017, p. 37, available online at https://www.conservatives.com/manifesto.

[439] *R. (Simms) v. Secretary of State for the Home Department* [2000] 2 AC 115 (HL), 130 (Lord Steyn) with reference to R. CROSS, Statutory interpretation, Butterworths, London 1995, pp. 165–166.

[440] *R. (Simms) v. Secretary of State for the Home Department* [2002] 2 AC 115 (HL), 131 (Lord Hoffmann); *McE v. Prison Service of Northern Ireland* [2009] UKHL 15, para. 62 (Lord Hope); *Ahmed and others v. HM Treasury* [2010] UKSC 2, para. 61 (Lord Hope); *AXA General Insurance Ltd. v. Lord Advocate* [2011] UKSC 46, para. 152 (Lord Reed); *R. (Evans) v. Attorney General* [2015] UKSC 21, paras. 57–58 (Lord Neuberger, with whom Lord Kerr and Lord Reed agreed); *Secretary of State for the Home Department v. GG* [2009] EWCA Civ 786, para. 29 (Dyson LJ).

express language or necessary implication to the contrary, the courts therefore presume that even the most general words were intended to be subject to the basic rights of the individual.[441]

Parliament must make clear its intention to legislate contrary to constitutional fundamentals; it must squarely confront what it is doing and accept the political cost. If Parliament's intention is expressed in clear and unambiguous terms, courts cannot intervene to protect the constitutional right or principle at issue.

When judges describe the principle of legality, they often refer to fundamental human rights, but the principle extends to other fundamental constitutional principles.[442] This is the view adopted here. Even if one does not share this view, the practical effect would be immaterial. That is because the principle of legality is a subset of the wider interpretative principle that there is a presumption that Parliament does intend to legislate in conformity with background constitutional principles.[443] The principle of legality has been applied in English courts for a long time[444] but it began to gain traction in the period leading up to the HRA.[445] This development seems to have accelerated in the wake of the uncertain future of the HRA,[446] and the new focus on the common law in rights adjudication may be the Supreme Court's response to prepare for a time after a repeal of the HRA. Interestingly, however, this development is difficult to square with the Conservative government's desire to make decisions about the level of human rights protection in Parliament rather than in the courts.

The interpretative powers that judges enjoy under the principle of legality could serve as a blueprint for an interpretation clause in a possible future UK Bill of Rights. It is thus necessary to scrutinise these powers and ascertain

---

[441] *R. (Simms) v. Secretary of State for the Home Department* [2002] 2 AC 115 (HL), 131 (Lord Hoffmann).

[442] *R. (Pierson) v. Secretary of State for the Home Department* [1998] AC 539 (HL), 588–589 (Lord Steyn); *R. (Morgan Grenfell) v. Special Commissioners of Income Tax* [2002] UKHL 21, para. 44 (Lord Hobhouse); *Watkins v. Secretary of State for the Home Department* [2006] UKHL 17, para. 61 (Lord Rodger); *R. (Privacy International) v. Investigatory Powers Tribunal* [2017] EWCA Civ 1868, para. 21 (Sales LJ); cf. *R. (Miller) v. Secretary of State for Exiting the European Union* [2017] UKSC 51, paras. 81–87, 108 (Lord Neuberger, Lady Hale, Lord Mance, Lord Kerr, Lord Clarke, Lord Wilson, Lord Sumption, Lord Hodge).

[443] *R. (Miller) v. Secretary of State for Exiting the European Union* [2016] EWHC 2768 (Admin), paras. 82–83 (Lord Thomas of Cwmgiedd CJ, Sir Terence Etherton MR, Sales LJ).

[444] See, e.g. *Nairn v. University of St Andrews* [1909] AC 147 (HL), 161 (Lord Loreburn LC), 163 (Lord Ashbourne).

[445] *R. (Nicklinson) v. Ministry of Justice* [2013] EWCA Civ 961, para. 64 (Lord Dyson MR and Elias LJ).

[446] Cf. *R. (Osborn) v. Parole Board* [2013] UKSC 61, paras. 57, 63 (Lord Reed); *Kennedy v. The Charity Commission* [2014] UKSC 20, para. 46 (Lord Mance). For discussion, see H. Fenwick and R. Masterman, The Conservative project to "break the link between British courts and Strasbourg": rhetoric or reality?, (2017) 80 *MLR* 1111, 1133–1135; Gearty, above n. 366, pp. 196–198.

how they fare in the light of parliamentary sovereignty.[447] Lord Phillips argued in *Ahmed* that the principle of legality does not permit a court to disregard an unambiguous expression of Parliament's intention.[448] Lord Bingham declared in *Gillan* that the principle of legality has no application where the infringement of a fundamental human right occurs as a result of "provisions of a detailed, specific and unambiguous character".[449] Lord Steyn said in *Anufrijeva* that Parliament can displace an applicable constitutional principle by "specific and unmistakeable terms".[450] Other case law indicates that the principle of legality only applies if the statutory language is ambiguous or cast in general terms.[451] Whereas the reading down of general language is an interpretative technique employed by courts in the past when the principle of legality applied, it is less clear to what extent the reading of additional words into a provision is permitted under that principle.[452] What is apparent is that a court's interpretative powers under the principle of legality fall short of the interpretative power available to judges under s. 3(1) HRA or under constitution-consistent judicial law-making in Germany.[453] From a comparative perspective, it is noteworthy that Lord Hoffmann opined in *Simms* that the courts

> presume that even the most general words were intended to be subject to the basic rights of the individual. In this way the courts of the United Kingdom, though acknowledging the sovereignty of Parliament, apply principles of constitutionality little different from those which exist in countries where the power of the legislature is expressly limited by a constitutional document.[454]

---

[447] Given that a repeal of the Human Rights Act is currently not on the political agenda, the discussion in this section will be limited to the principle of legality. Other questions of statutory interpretation related to a repeal of the Human Rights Act, e.g. how should legislation in a post-HRA era be interpreted if that legislation has already been subject to a Convention-compliant interpretation, will not be discussed; for discussion of this issue, see GEARTY, above n. 366, p. 192.

[448] *Ahmed and others v. HM Treasury* [2010] UKSC 2, para. 117 (Lord Phillips).

[449] *R. (Gillan) v. Commissioner of Police of the Metropolis* [2006] UKHL 12, para. 15 (Lord Bingham, with whom all other members of the court agreed).

[450] *R. (Anufrijeva) v. Secretary of State for the Home Department* [2003] UKHL 36, para. 31 (Lord Steyn).

[451] *R. (Nicklinson) v. Ministry of Justice* [2013] EWCA Civ 961, para. 66 (Lord Dyson MR and Elias LJ); cf. *R. (Roszkowski) v. Secretary of State for the Home Department* [2017] EWCA Civ 1893, para. 32 (McCombe LJ).

[452] Compare SALES, above n. 73, p. 610 and P. SALES, The judicial role in the interpretation of statutes, Presentation for the Netherlands Academy for Legislation, April 2011, p. 1, available online at http://www.statutelawsociety.co.uk/wp-content/uploads/2014/01/Judicialroleintheinterpretationofstatutes.pdf.

[453] For a different view, see VOGENAUER, above n. 373, p. 1258.

[454] *R. (Simms) v. Secretary of State for the Home Department* [2000] 2 AC 115 (HL), 132 (Lord Hoffmann).

Lord Hoffmann alluded to the similarities between the principle of legality and constitution-consistent interpretation in countries with a written constitution such as Germany.

It has been argued that the principle of legality deviates from conventional canons of construction.[455] This assessment may be questioned on the basis that courts take constitutional background assumptions (long-standing principles of the common law) into account when ascertaining the intention of Parliament because these assumptions are part of the context in which a provision was made.[456] In most cases the use of the presumptions will indeed be consistent with the reasonably presumed intention of the enacting parliament.[457] Furthermore, judges have not yet pronounced that the role of the court under the principle of legality is to find the meaning which best accords with constitutional principles rather than to find the true meaning of the provision. The view that the principle of legality departs from conventional canons of construction is nonetheless correct for two reasons. The first reason relates to the permissible scope of judicial law-making under the principle of legality. P. Sales has said that the principle of legality confers upon the courts greater "interpretative discretion" than do conventional canons of statutory interpretation.[458] Unless fundamental rights or other constitutional principles are excluded by express words or necessary implication, a court can read down general words in a statute[459] in order to ensure that the statute is applied in conformity with fundamental rights and constitutional principles. The reading down of general terms is generally possible under the principle of legality, even though it is a technique of judicial law-making. It cannot be characterised as a power that judges only resort to in exceptional circumstances. The default position for judicial law-making by means of reading down general terms is that it is a permissible function of the judge under the principle of legality. This is a deviation from conventional canons of interpretation. From the viewpoint of legal certainty, it is noticeable that the general permissibility of reading down general statutory words is not accompanied by general outer limits of judicial law-making for the principle of legality. The reason may be that if courts were to openly acknowledge these boundaries, they would openly acknowledge judicial

---

[455] SALES, above n. 116, p. 457. But see his more "conventional" understanding of the principle of legality in SALES, above n. 73, pp. 604–607.
[456] J. VAN ZYL SMIT, Statute law: interpretation and declarations of incompatibility, in D. HOFFMANN (ed.), *The impact of the UK Human Rights Act on private law*, CUP, Cambridge 2011, pp. 66, 82; cf. *R. (Gujra) v. Crown Prosecution Service* [2012] UKSC 52, para. 108 (Lord Mance).
[457] GOLDSWORTHY, above n. 286, p. 241; SALES, above n. 73, pp. 604–607.
[458] SALES, above n. 116, p. 457.
[459] *R. (Nicklinson) v. Ministry of Justice* [2013] EWCA Civ 961, para. 65 (Lord Dyson MR and Elias LJ). See, e.g., *Anisminic v. Foreign Compensation Commission* [1969] 2 AC 147 (HL), 170–171 (Lord Reid) and its assessment by GRIFFITH, above n. 352, pp. 106–107; *B (Algeria) v. Secretary of State for the Home Department* [2018] UKSC 5, paras. 29–31 (Lord Lloyd-Jones, with whom Lady Hale, Lord Mance, Lord Hughes and Lord Hodge agreed).

law-making. This would undermine the traditional approach to give effect to the doctrine of parliamentary sovereignty by following the enacted words. One consequence of the courts not formulating general limits of interpretation that apply in every case of judicial law-making is that the outer interpretative limits of permissible reading down under the principle of legality seem particularly unclear compared to conventional canons of interpretation, s. 3(1) HRA and, as we will see in Chapter 4, conforming interpretation. Under the principle of legality, courts aim to uphold mostly substantive aspects of the rule of law, but they seem to give insufficient weight to the circumstance that the principle of legal certainty is also one formal aspect of the rule of law.[460]

The default position for judicial law-making under the principle of legality is difficult to reconcile with the doctrine of parliamentary sovereignty and with its impact on the role of judges in statutory interpretation as traditionally understood by English judges. Furthermore, as opposed to s. 3(1) HRA or s. 2(4) ECA, there is no indication in legislation that the courts' interpretative powers under the principle of legality go further than under conventional canons of statutory interpretation. I have shown, however, that a system of interpretation according to which judicial law-making is generally permissible in order to give effect to the intention of the enacting legislature is compatible with the doctrine of parliamentary sovereignty.[461] The clash between the principle of legality and parliamentary sovereignty does not occur simply because courts have the general power to read down general statutory words. It occurs because courts have in the past substituted the presumed intention of the enacting legislature for what the legislature ought to have intended. That is the second reason that explains why the principle of legality departs from conventional canons of construction. Parliament can only squarely confront what it is doing if the constitutional fundamental at issue can be clearly identified as being applicable at the time the legislation is enacted.[462] If that is not the case, and if the right or principle is not so well established that Parliament must be taken to have legislated with it in mind, then reading down general words in legislation in order to protect that right or principle undermines Parliament's intention instead of honouring it.[463] The Supreme Court's inventive approach when identifying and concretising relevant but contested constitutional principles thus undermines the enacting

---

[460] For a discussion of formal and substantive conceptions of the rule of law, see P. CRAIG, Formal and substantive conceptions of the rule of law: an analytical framework, [1997] PL 467–487.
[461] See Chapter 2, Section 5.
[462] Lord Dyson MR and Elias LJ argued in *R. (Nicklinson) v. Ministry of Justice* [2013] EWCA Civ 961, para. 65 that the principle of legality has been adopted in cases where "precise and well established fundamental rights have been in issue".
[463] D. MEAGHER, The principle of legality and contemporanea exposition est optima et fortissima in lege, (2017) 38 *Statute Law Review* 98, 99, 109; SALES, above n. 73, p. 605.

legislature's intention.[464] The scope and substance of common law rights is often unclear in the absence of a fixed list of common law rights and of a written constitution.[465]

The underlying judicial attitude of this inventive approach is that of seeing "the courts and Parliament as being partners both engaged in a common enterprise involving the upholding of the rule of law".[466] That partnership model builds on a certain understanding of the relationship between two constitutional principles and the relative weight assigned to them: the rule of law and parliamentary sovereignty. It carries the risk that judges impose upon Parliament (a) their conception of the rule of law and (b), under the pretext of ascertaining the presumed legislative intent of Parliament, their view of what Parliament ought to have meant with the statutory words.[467] That leads to de facto substantive constraints on Parliament's law-making powers by means of statutory interpretation. The judicial thinking apparent in decisions discussing the principle of legality is that a reasonable parliament follows the rule of law and, thus, cherishes fundamental human rights. This statement correctly characterises the German doctrine of constitution-consistent interpretation, assuming that the fundamental right at issue is protected under the German Basic Law. Since the ordinary legislature is bound by the German Basic Law and since the BVerfG has the power to declare void unconstitutional legislation, it can be presumed that a reasonable legislature intends to comply with the German Basic Law. Reading down general words in legislation in order to safeguard a right protected under the German Basic Law ensures the validity of the legislation and, therefore, respects the ordinary legislature and shows deference to the legislature's authority.

In a constitutional system where Parliament is sovereign, however, Parliament is the ultimate guardian of constitutional principle as opposed to judges in courts.[468] This understanding of parliamentary sovereignty is still

---

[464] For discussion, see M. HAIN, Guardians of the constitution – the constitutional implications of a substantive rule of law, *UK Constitutional Law Blog*, 12.09.2017, available online at https://ukconstitutionallaw.org/2017/09/12/michal-hain-guardians-of-the-constitution-the-constitutional-implications-of-a-substantive-rule-of-law/; cf. J. SUMPTION, Judicial and political decision-making: the uncertain boundary, (2011) 16 *JR* 301, 305.

[465] P. BOWEN, Does the renaissance of common law rights mean that the Human Rights Act 1998 is now unnecessary?, [2016] *EHRLR* 361, 366; C. O'CINNEIDE, Human rights and the UK constitution, in J. JOWELL, D. OLIVER and C. O'CINNEIDE (eds.), *The changing constitution*, 5th ed., OUP, Oxford 2015, pp. 67, 81, with reference to case law.

[466] LORD WOOLF, Droit public – English style, [1995] *PL* 57, 69. See also *R. (Cart) v. Upper Tribunal* [2011] UKSC 28, para. 89 (Lord Phillips); SALES, above n. 116, 456.

[467] GOLDSWORTHY, above n. 286, pp. 308–309; MEAGHER, above n. 463, p. 106.

[468] C. FORSYTH, Who is the ultimate guardian of the constitution?, ALBA papers on judicial activism, 12.12.2016, para. 7, available online at https://judicialpowerproject.org.uk/; J.A.G. GRIFFITH, The common law and the political constitution, (2001) 117 *LQR* 42, 66–67.

formally intact. The Diceyan doctrine of absolute parliamentary sovereignty was recently referred to as a fundamental principle of the UK constitution in the High Court and in the Supreme Court in *Miller*.[469] Parliament can legislate against the rule of law. Yet, what rights and principles are recognised as fundamental at common law for the purposes of the principle of legality is ultimately a matter of judicial choice. Since no English court can invalidate or, outside the scope of EU law, disapply allegedly unconstitutional legislation, the argument relating to the reasonable legislature used by the BVerfG does not equally persuade in the UK legal sphere. Neither does the reading down of general words show deference to the legislature's authority. Due to these distinctions between both legal systems, there ought to be differences in statutory interpretation when German courts apply constitution-consistent interpretation and when English courts apply the principle of legality. One distinction should be that relying on presumed legislative intent, i.e. relying on constitutional background assumptions that Parliament must have had in mind when enacting the legislation at issue, should only be handled carefully for the principle of legality. For example, the presumption should be rebuttable by contrary indications in the text of the statute. Furthermore, the powers of English courts to read down general words in legislation should be framed in narrower terms than the corresponding powers of German courts under constitution-consistent judicial law-making. With these considerations in mind, Sales LJ's judgment in *Privacy International* is a step in the right direction.[470] Despite scholarly criticism that Sales LJ sidelined the rule of law,[471] he rightly focused on the statutory language and the immediate legislative context of the Regulation of Investigatory Powers Act 2000 (RIPA) when construing the ouster clause[472] in s. 67(8) RIPA. He brought the discussion of ouster clauses into the correct arena, which is the arena of statutory interpretation as opposed to the arena of underlying constitutional norms at play. Instead of speculative inferences about parliamentary intention

---

[469] *R. (Miller) v. Secretary of State for Exiting the European Union* [2017] UKSC 51, para. 43 (Lord Neuberger, Lady Hale, Lord Mance, Lord Kerr, Lord Clarke, Lord Wilson, Lord Sumption, Lord Hodge); *R. (Miller) v. Secretary of State for Exiting the European Union* [2016] EWHC 2768 (Admin), paras. 20–23 (Lord Thomas of Cwmgiedd CJ, Sir Terence Etherton MR, Sales LJ).

[470] *R. (Privacy International) v. Investigatory Powers Tribunal* [2017] EWCA Civ 1868, paras. 1–49 (Sales LJ).

[471] M. ELLIOTT, *Privacy International* in the Court of Appeal: *Anisminic* distinguished – again, 26.11.2017, available online at https://publiclawforeveryone.com/2017/11/26/privacy-international-in-the-court-of-appeal-anisminic-distinguished-again/; T. FAIRCLOUGH, Privacy International: Constitutional substance over semantics in reading ouster clauses, UK Constitutional Law Blog, 04.12.2017, available online at https://ukconstitutionallaw.org/2017/12/04/thomas-fairclough-privacy-international-constitutional-substance-over-semantics-in-reading-ouster-clauses/.

[472] An ouster clause is a statutory provision that precludes, or appears to preclude, judicial review of administrative action.

vis-à-vis the rule of law and instead of relying on what a reasonable legislature should have intended with the rule of law in mind, he relied on what Parliament did intend. He gave effect to parliamentary sovereignty.

There is a sufficient amount of case law where it cannot be said that English judges only gave effect to (presumed) legislative intention. Instead, the judges were more concerned with protecting constitutional fundamentals when interpreting legislation according to the principle of legality despite contrary indications in the text of the statute.[473] English judicial practice shows that there is a line that is too easily overstepped between using the principle of legality to ascertain the presumed intention of the enacting parliament and using the principle of legality to protect a right that Parliament ought to have had in mind. Clear outer limits of interpretation should guard this line. These limits do not exist in the case law.[474] English judges have overstepped the boundary between interpretation and impermissible amendment of legislation. They have undermined parliamentary sovereignty by means of adventurous reinterpretation of legislation. One example is *Anisminic*, where the words in s. 4(4) of the Foreign Compensation Act 1950 that the determination by the Foreign Compensation Commission of any application made to them under the Act "shall not be called in question in any court of law" were read down by the House of Lords. The statutory words did not succeed in excluding the jurisdiction of the courts.[475]

What can further elucidate this unsatisfactory state of the law is that the principle of legality is a favoured playground for common law constitutionalism, where the orthodox account of absolute parliamentary sovereignty, without openly refusing it or openly refusing the legislation as enacted, is put into doubt. Whereas the issue in *Anisminic* was framed in terms of statutory interpretation, recent UKSC case law on the principle of legality often leaves this arena and explicitly ventures into an open discussion of relevant constitutional principles.[476] Instead of limiting their discussion to questionable assumptions about what Parliament could not reasonably have intended, contemporary judges are

---

[473] See the discussion of case law in M. ELLIOTT, Judicial power and the United Kingdom's changing constitution, SSRN 2017, pp. 12–14, available online at http://www.ssrn.com; J. LAWS, Judicial activism, ALBA papers on judicial activism, 12.12.2016, paras. 16–22, available online at https://judicialpowerproject.org.uk/.

[474] Compare Lord Neuberger's (paras. 51–59) and Lord Hughes's (paras. 154–156) analyses in *R. (Evans) v. Attorney General* [2015] UKSC 21.

[475] *Anisminic v. Foreign Compensation Commission* [1969] 2 AC 147 (HL), 170–171 (Lord Reid); see the comments by GRIFFITH, above n. 352, pp. 106–107. For discussion, see also ELLIOTT and THOMAS, above n. 48, pp. 558–559. For a different assessment of this case, see GOLDSWORTHY, above n. 286, p. 286.

[476] For a discussion of the case law, see M. ELLIOTT, Through the looking-glass? Ouster clauses, statutory interpretation and the British Constitution, University of Cambridge Legal Studies Research Paper Series, Paper no. 04/2018, January 2018, pp. 13–17, available online at http://www.ssrn.com.

explicitly juggling with the idea that there may be constitutional fundamentals that Parliament is constitutionally incapable of abrogating. The principle of legality as applied in the highest English courts has thus caused cracks in the façade of the doctrine of parliamentary sovereignty. Lord Steyn's *dictum* in *Jackson* serves as an example: in exceptional circumstances, Lord Steyn opined, the Supreme Court "may have to consider" whether there are "constitutional fundamental[s] which even a sovereign Parliament … cannot abolish".[477] In a similar vein, Lord Hope said in *Axa* that "[t]he rule of law requires that the judges must retain the power to insist that legislation of that extreme kind is not law which the courts will recognise".[478] According to Lord Steyn and Lord Hope, there may be constitutional limits to Parliament's law-making authority, albeit it is not at all clear what those limits are. If the relationship between the rule of law and the principle of parliamentary sovereignty is unclear, there can be no clear limits that guard the line between relying on the principle of legality and honouring parliamentary sovereignty. That is the current state of the law when judges apply the principle of legality. M. Elliott has described this state of the law as "a form of constitutional discourse the conduct of which involves the testing and determination of the respective boundaries of judicial and legislative power".[479] It is clear that this state of affairs is unsatisfactory from the viewpoint of legal certainty, which is of course an element of the rule of law. The principle of legality as applied by contemporary judges thus demonstrates that common law constitutionalism is very much alive, yet disguised as statutory interpretation. M. Elliott and R. Thomas have rightly pointed out that giving legislation a meaning that is different from that which was intended by Parliament has "a similar effect to refusing to apply it at all", but "is less likely to attract the criticism that judges are overstepping the mark".[480] It is in the shadow of statutory interpretation where courts are developing the idea that there are substantive limits on Parliament's authority to make law, rather than merely ascertaining the meaning of parliamentary legislation.

This section has criticised how English judges apply the principle of legality in practice. It was shown that it is inconsistent to (a) formally preserve the doctrine of absolute parliamentary sovereignty and (b), at the same time, undermine the doctrine with tools of statutory interpretation. It was also shown that this inconsistency undermines legal certainty. This criticism of judicial practice stands regardless of whether Parliament should or should not lack the power to make laws that violate fundamental constitutional principles.

---

[477] *R. (Jackson) v. Attorney General* [2005] UKHL 56, para. 102 (Lord Steyn).
[478] *AXA General Insurance Ltd. v. Lord Advocate* [2011] UKSC 46, para. 51 (Lord Hope).
[479] Elliott, above n. 476, pp. 19.
[480] Elliott and Thomas, above n. 48, p. 247. See also Forsyth, above n. 468, para. 12.

CHAPTER 4
THE EUROPEAN LEGAL DUTY OF CONFORMING INTERPRETATION

> *When national courts apply domestic law, they are bound to interpret it, so far as possible, in the light of the wording and the purpose of the directive concerned in order to achieve the result sought by the directive.*[1]

This statement by the CJEU expresses the legal principle which is referred to as the European legal duty of conforming interpretation (or short: conforming interpretation) in this book.[2] Conforming interpretation of national legislation is the task of national courts, not the task of the CJEU.[3] Conforming interpretation lies at the core of the relationship between an EU directive and provisions of national law that fall within the directive's scope. Case law of English and German courts is regularly preoccupied with the question of how far a court can strain national legislation to achieve consistency with a directive. Chapter 4 thus compares the outer limits and techniques of conforming judicial law-making[4] as applied in English and German judicial practice. It has been suggested in scholarship that English courts may not show the same commitment to interpreting domestic law in conformity with directives after

---

[1] Case C-212/04, *Adeneler et al. v. Ellinikos Organismos Galaktos*, ECLI:EU:C:2006:443, para. 108. See also Case C-106/89, *Marleasing v. La Comercial Internacional de Alimentación*, ECLI:EU:C:1990:395, para. 8; Case C-397/01, *Pfeiffer v. Deutsches Rotes Kreuz*, ECLI:EU:C:2004:584, para. 113; Case C-371/02, *Björnekulla Fruktindustrier v. Procordia Food*, ECLI:EU:C:2004:275, para. 13; Case C-555/07, *Kücükdeveci v. Swedex*, ECLI:EU:C:2010:21, para. 48; Case C-12/08, *Mono Car Styling v. Dervis Odemis*, ECLI:EU:C:2009:466, para. 60; Case C-305/08, *CoNISMa v. Regione Marche*, ECLI:EU:2009:807, para. 50.

[2] The terminology varies in judgments and academic articles, and the following terms have been used to refer to this interpretative duty laid down by the CJEU: principle of compatible construction, *Marleasing* principle, principle of consistent interpretation, principle of indirect effect and principle of harmonious interpretation.

[3] Settled case law. See, e.g. Case C-414/07, *Magoora v. Dyrektor Izby Skarbowej w Krakowie*, ECLI:EU:C:2008:766, para. 32; Case C-7/11, *Criminal proceedings against Caronna*, ECLI:EU:C:2012:396, para. 54. See also BVerfG, *NJW* 2012, 669 paras. 47–48. That does not stop the CJEU from providing guidance in individual cases on how the national legislation ought to be interpreted; see, e.g. Case C-306/12, *Spedition Welter v. Avanssur*, ECLI:EU:C:2013:650, paras. 31–32.

[4] "Conforming judicial law-making" refers to conforming interpretation that goes beyond or against the possible semantic meanings of the statutory words.

the Brexit referendum of 23 June 2016. As post-referendum case law shows,[5] however, that has not happened. The EU legal duty of conforming interpretation will impact on the interpretation of English law as long as the European Communities Act 1972 (ECA) is in force and the UK is a member of the EU. The UK's obligations under the EU Treaties have been incorporated into English law by the ECA. I will demonstrate in Section 8 of this chapter that conforming interpretation will continue to apply after exit day to UK legislation enacted prior to exit day according to the European Union (Withdrawal) Act 2018. Conforming interpretation will thus retain an important role in statutory interpretation in the UK after Brexit. It will also be shown that the EU legal duty of conforming interpretation will continue to apply in the UK during the transition period as if the UK were still a Member State of the EU if the Withdrawal Agreement in its current draft form is finalised and incorporated into UK law.[6]

Beyond the questions set out in Chapter 1 of this book, Chapter 4 will address additional issues: how does the CJEU's case law influence the outer limits and techniques of conforming interpretation in England and Germany? Are these limits and techniques sufficiently adaptive to integrate European influences? Do these limits and techniques deviate from other modes of statutory interpretation? Do they surpass these modes and widen the scope of the judicial role? Do English and German courts go further than the CJEU requires?

Existing scholarship analysing approaches of national courts to conforming interpretation has produced inconsistent results. On the one hand, scholars have expressed concerns that judges' willingness to interpret national law in conformity with EU directives is potentially low.[7] On the other hand, scholars in England and Germany regularly accuse national courts of exceeding the limits of the judicial function when engaging in conforming judicial law-making.[8]

---

[5] See, e.g. *British Gas Trading Ltd. v. Lock* [2016] EWCA Civ 983; *Howe v. Motor Insurers' Bureau* [2017] EWCA Civ 932, paras. 27–37 (Lewison LJ).

[6] Draft agreement on the withdrawal of the United Kingdom of Great Britain and Northern Ireland from the European Union and the European Atomic Energy Community, 19.03.2018. The draft Withdrawal Agreement is available online at https://www.gov.uk/government/publications/draft-withdrawal-agreement-19-march-2018.

[7] Cf. S. DRAKE, Twenty years after Von Colson: the impact of "indirect effect" on the protection of the individual's community rights, (2005) 30 *ELR* 329, 348.

[8] G. AIRS, Conforming construction, (2008) 956 *Tax Journal* 15; N. BALDAUF, *Richtlinienverstoß und Verschiebung der Contra-legem-Grenze im Privatrechtsverhältnis*, Mohr Siebeck, Tübingen 2013, pp. 179, 185, 191, 196; T. HERVEY and N. SHELDON, Judicial method of English courts and tribunals in EU law cases: a case study in employment law, in U. NEERGAARD, R. NIELSEN and L. ROSEBERRY (eds.), *European Legal Method – Paradoxes and Revitalisation*, DJØF Publishing, Copenhagen 2011, pp. 327, 370–371; L. MICHAEL and M. PAYANDEH, Richtlinienkonforme Rechtsfortbildung zwischen Unionsrecht und Verfassungsrecht, *NJW* 2015, 2392.

I will argue that (a) the former concern is not warranted for English and German courts and (b) the latter criticism is warranted for English courts, but not for German courts. Chapter 4 will further contribute to the scholarly debate about whether differences exist in the outer limits of conforming interpretation in the Member States. Diverging outer limits could threaten the full effectiveness and uniform application of directives in the Union and ultimately deprive directives of their function as a harmonisation instrument.[9] I will explore why the outer limits and techniques of conforming interpretation as expressed and applied in English and German judicial practice do not give rise to such concerns. Chapter 4 will also tackle concerns that (a) national methods of statutory interpretation are inapt for the interpretative tasks of ordinary courts in a Europeanised environment[10] and (b) legal cultures and legal mentalities in Europe may not converge.[11]

Chapter 4 will be concerned with cases of unimplemented or incorrectly transposed directives since the outer limits and techniques of conforming judicial law-making usually remain unexplored in cases of adequately transposed directives. An incorrect transposition often occurs inadvertently. That is the case, for example, if the CJEU interprets the requirements of a directive after its implementation in national law, and if the national implementing legislature did not foresee this interpretation. In England, an EU directive can be implemented into national law by either primary legislation or delegated legislation. In contrast to the situation in Germany, the majority of implementation of directives takes place in delegated legislation. The volume of delegated legislation in the UK has increased over time and is increasing.[12]

---

[9] Expressing such concerns: U. BABUSIAUX, *Die richtlinienkonforme Auslegung im deutschen und französischen Zivilrecht*, Nomos, Baden-Baden 2007, p. 105; A. JOHNSTON and H. UNBERATH, European private law by directives: approach and challenges, in C. TWIGG-FLESNER (ed.), *The Cambridge Companion to European Union Private Law*, CUP, 2010, pp. 85, 96–97; S. PRECHAL, *Directives in EC law*, 2nd ed., OUP, Oxford 2005, p. 194; K. RIESENHUBER, Methodendivergenzen ertragen!, *GPR* 2016, 158, 159; cf. T. LUNDMARK, *Charting the divide between common and civil law*, OUP, Oxford 2012, pp. 426–427. Arguing against such concerns: G. HAGER, *Rechtsmethoden in Europa*, Mohr Siebeck, Tübingen 2009, pp. 279–280, 286; E.A. KRAMER, Duplik zu Riesenhuber, Methodendivergenzen ertragen, *GPR* 2016, 210–211.

[10] For this concern, see C. ECKES, European Union legal methods, in ULLA NEERGAARD and RUTH NIELSEN (eds.), *European legal method: towards a new European legal realism?*, DJØF Publishing, Copenhagen 2013, pp. 163, 188.

[11] P. LEGRAND, European legal systems are not converging, (1996) 45 *ICLQ* 52–81. See also C. HARLOW, Voices of difference in a plural community, (2002) 50 *ACJL* 339, 347–348; G. TEUBNER, Legal irritants: good faith in British law or how unifying law ends up in new divergencies, (1998) 61 *MLR* 11, 12.

[12] C. HARLOW and R. RAWLINGS, *Law and administration*, 3rd ed., CUP, Cambridge 2009, p. 165. For an overview of types of, and the making of, judicial review and parliamentary scrutiny of delegated legislation, see House of Commons Information Office, Statutory Instruments, Factsheet L7, May 2008, available online at https://www.parliament.uk/documents/commons-information-office/l07.pdf.

Section 2(2) ECA authorises the making of Orders in Council and ministerial regulations for the purpose of implementing directives in the UK. Since it may be necessary to amend Acts of Parliament in order to comply with a directive, such Orders in Council and ministerial regulations are expressly permitted to amend primary legislation, even primary legislation that is passed after the ECA, subject to compliance with Schedule 2 to the Act.[13]

Chapter 4 is structured as follows. Section 1 provides an introduction to the case law of the CJEU on the EU legal duty of conforming interpretation. It focuses on answering the question of what requirements this case law contains for national legal methodology on conforming interpretation. Section 2 discusses the aim of conforming interpretation, and Section 3 explores the relationship between conforming interpretation, conventional canons of construction and rights-consistent interpretation in England and Germany. The next two sections examine two characteristics of conforming interpretation: the interpretative priority rule and the presumption of compliance. Section 6 analyses the techniques of conforming judicial law-making, and Section 7 its outer limits in both jurisdictions. The last section examines the future of conforming interpretation in England after Brexit.

1. THE EUROPEAN DIMENSION[14]

The EU legal duty of conforming interpretation is not explicitly mentioned in the Treaty on the Functioning of the European Union (TFEU). It was developed by the CJEU in *von Colson and Kamann*[15] and specified in later case law. The CJEU derives the principle of conforming interpretation from art. 288(3) TFEU[16] and also draws on art. 4(3) Treaty on European Union (TEU)[17] to

---

[13] Section 2(4) ECA. It is controversial whether s. 2(2) read in conjunction with s. 2(4) ECA is a so-called (prospective) "Henry VIII clause". In favour: *Thoburn v. Sunderland City Council* [2002] EWHC 195 (Admin), para. 38 (Laws LJ); HARLOW and RAWLINGS, above n. 12, p. 180; D. FELDMAN, *English Public Law*, 2nd ed., OUP, Oxford 2009, para. 1.122; M. GORDON, *Parliamentary sovereignty in the UK constitution: process, politics and democracy*, Hart, Oxford 2015, p. 164. Against, and for a *sui-generis* status of s. 2(2), (4) ECA: *Oakley Inc. v. Animal Ltd.* [2005] EWCA Civ 1191, paras. 13, 18 (Waller LJ), para. 69 (Jacob LJ); *ITV Broadcasting Ltd. v. TV Catchup Ltd. (No. 2)* [2011] EWHC 1874 (Pat.), para. 66 (Floyd J). On "Henry VIII clauses", see N.W. BARBER and A. YOUNG, The rise of prospective Henry VIII clauses and their implications for sovereignty, [2003] *PL* 112.

[14] Sections 1.3–1.5 provide a summary of M. BRENNCKE, Hybrid methodology for the EU principle of consistent interpretation, (2018) 39 *Statute Law Review* 134–154.

[15] Case 14/83, *von Colson and Kamann v. Land Nordrhein-Westfalen*, ECLI:EU:C:1984:153, para. 26.

[16] Settled case law since Case 14/83, *von Colson and Kamann v. Land Nordrhein-Westfalen*, ECLI:EU:C:1984:153, para. 26.

[17] Case 14/83, *von Colson and Kamann v. Land Nordrhein-Westfalen*, ECLI:EU:C:1984:153, para. 26; Case C-111/97, *EvoBus Austria v. Niederösterreichische Verkehrsorganisations Gesellschaft mbH*, ECLI:EU:C:1998:434, para. 18.

justify it.[18] In addition, the court understands this principle as being inherent in the system of the Treaty, since the interpretative obligation permits the national courts to ensure the full effectiveness of EU directives.[19] German[20] and English[21] courts also refer to the European origin of this interpretative principle when they construe national law in the light of directives.

1.1. SCOPE OF THE EU LEGAL DUTY OF CONFORMING INTERPRETATION

The principle of conforming interpretation applies to national law that falls within the scope of application of an EU directive irrespective of whether the relevant national provisions were adopted before or after the passing of the directive[22] and irrespective of whether the directive was correctly transposed,[23] inadequately transposed or not transposed at all into national law.[24] The EU legal duty of conforming interpretation is not limited to national provisions enacted in order to implement the applicable directive, but applies to the whole body of rules of national law,[25] including provisions of national law adopted for reasons other than the implementation of a directive.

---

[18] Referring to art. 288(3) TFEU as well as art. 4(3) TEU as the legal basis of the doctrine: BGH, *NJW* 2009, 427, para. 19 – *Quelle II*; BGH, *NJW* 2012, 1073, para. 24 – *Weber II*; C. HERRESTHAL, Voraussetzungen und Grenzen der gemeinschaftsrechtskonformen Rechtsfortbildung, *EuZW* 2007, 396, 397; M. KLAMERT, *The principle of loyalty in EU law*, OUP, Oxford 2014, p. 78; F. MÜLLER and R. CHRISTENSEN, *Juristische Methodik, Band II: Europarecht*, 3rd ed. 2012, Duncker & Humblot, Berlin 2012, pp. 461–462; PRECHAL, above n. 9, p. 180.

[19] Case C-397/01, *Pfeiffer v. Deutsches Rotes Kreuz*, ECLI:EU:C:2004:584, para. 114; Case C-212/04, *Adeneler et al. v. Ellinikos Organismos Galaktos*, ECLI:EU:C:2006:443, para. 109.

[20] BVerfG, *NJW-RR* 2016, 1366, para. 41; BGH, *NJW* 2009, 427, para. 19 – *Quelle II*; BVerwG, judgment of 29.1.2004 – case number: 3 C 39.03, para. 31, available online at http://www.juris.de; BAG, *NZA* 2003, 742, 747.

[21] *Litster v. Forth Dry Dock & Engineering Co Ltd.* [1990] 1 AC 546 (HL), 558 (Lord Templeman); *Robertson v. Swift* [2014] UKSC 50, para. 20 (Lord Kerr); *Revenue and Customs Commissioners v. IDT Card Services Ireland Ltd.* [2006] EWCA Civ 29, paras. 68, 79 (Arden LJ); *British Gas Trading Ltd. v. Lock* [2016] EWCA Civ 983, paras. 31–32 (Sir Colin Rimer, with whom Gloster LJ and Sir Terence Etherton MR agreed).

[22] Case C-106/89, *Marleasing v. La Comercial Internacional de Alimentación*, ECLI:EU:C:1990:395, para. 8; Case C-91/92, *Paola Faccini Dori v. Recreb Srl.*, ECLI:EU:C:1994:292, para. 25; Case C-334/92, *Wagner Miret v. Fondo de Garantía Salarial*, ECLI:EU:C:1993:945, para. 20; Case C-456/98, *Centrosteel Srl v. Adipol GmbH*, ECLI:EU:C:2000:402, para. 16; Case C-371/02, *Björnekulla Fruktindustrier v. Procordia Food*, ECLI:EU:C:2004:275, para. 13; Case C-212/04, *Adeneler et al. v. Ellinikos Organismos Galaktos*, ECLI:EU:C:2006:443, para. 108; Case C-378/07, *Angelidaki and Others v. Organismos Nomarkhiaki Aftodiikisi Rethimnis*, ECLI:EU:C:2009:250, para. 197.

[23] Case C-62/00, *Marks & Spencer plc. v. Commissioners of Customs and Excise*, ECLI:EU:C:2002:435, paras. 24, 27.

[24] See Case C-240/98, *Océano Grupo Editorial v. Rocío Murciano Quintero*, ECLI:C:2000:346, para. 30; PRECHAL, above n. 9, pp. 187–188.

[25] Case C-397/01, *Pfeiffer v. Deutsches Rotes Kreuz*, ECLI:EU:C:2004:584, para. 115; Case C-212/04, *Adeneler et al. v. Ellinikos Organismos Galaktos*, ECLI:EU:C:2006:443,

The EU legal duty of conforming interpretation applies irrespective of whether a provision in a directive is capable of having direct effect or not.[26] It is settled CJEU case law that individuals are entitled, as against public bodies, to rely on the provisions of a directive which are unconditional and sufficiently precise if the directive was incorrectly implemented into national law or was not transposed within the implementation period.[27] If an individual can rely on such a provision in a directive, national courts must disapply the rules of national law that are incompatible with the directive. In proceedings between private individuals, however, the CJEU has consistently held that a directive cannot of itself impose obligations on an individual and cannot therefore be relied on as such against an individual.[28] The CJEU has ruled out horizontal direct effect of directives even if a provision in a directive is sufficiently precise and unconditional.[29] If a national court is unable to interpret the national legislation in conformity with the directive in a horizontal case, the non-conforming national legislation remains applicable in horizontal scenarios,[30] unless narrow exceptions apply.[31] Whether a strict order of precedence exists between direct effect and conforming interpretation for cases in which both are possible is not fully clear in CJEU case law even though most case law seems to

---

paras. 108, 111; Case C-268/06, *Impact v. Minister for Agriculture and Food and others*, ECLI:EU:C:2008:223, para. 101; Case C-12/08, *Mono Car Styling v. Dervis Odemis*, ECLI:EU:C:2009:466, para. 64.

[26] See, e.g. Case C-12/08, *Mono Car Styling v. Dervis Odemis*, ECLI:EU:C:2009:466, paras. 59–60.

[27] Case 148/78, *Ratti*, ECLI:EU:C:1979:110, paras. 20–23; Case 237/07, *Janecek v. Freistaat Bayern*, ECLI:EU:C:2008:447, para. 36; Case C-404/13, *ClientEarth v. Secretary of State for the Environment, Food and Rural Affairs*, ECLI:EU:C:2013:805, para. 54.

[28] Case 152/84, *Marshall v. Southampton and South-West Hampshire Area Health Authority*, EU:C:1986:84, para. 48; Case C-91/92, *Faccini Dori v. Recreb Srl*, ECLI:EU:C:1994:292, paras. 20, 24–25; Case C-397/01, *Pfeiffer v. Deutsches Rotes Kreuz*, ECLI:EU:C:2004:584, paras. 108–109; Case C-212/04, *Adeneler et al. v. Ellinikos Organismos Galaktos*, ECLI:EU:C:2006:443, para. 113.

[29] Case C-12/08, *Mono Car Styling v. Dervis Odemis*, ECLI:EU:C:2009:466, para. 59.

[30] BAG, *NZA* 2010, 1020, paras. 21–22; BAG, *EuZW* 2009, 465, paras. 55–56 – *Schultz-Hoff*; BAG, *NZA* 2009, 378, para. 52; BAG, *NZA* 2006, 862, para. 41. Cf. Case C-168/95, *Criminal proceedings against Arcaro*, ECLI:EU:C:1996:363, paras. 39–43; Case C-282/10, *Dominguez v. Centre informatique du Centre Ouest Atlantique*, ECLI:EU:C:2012:33, paras. 37, 41–44.

[31] These exceptions relate to (a) the doctrine of "incidental horizontal direct effect" of a directive in actions between private individuals (Case C-443/98, *Unilever Italia v. Central Food*, ECLI:EU:C:2000:496, para. 50; P. CRAIG, The legal effect of Directives: policy, rules and exceptions, *ELR* 2009, 349, 364–369) and (b) CJEU case law holding that general principles of EU law can have horizontal direct effect even where they cover the same terrain as a directive which would not have such effect between private parties (Case C-144/04, *Mangold v. Helm*, ECLI:EU:C:2005:709, paras. 74–77; Case C-555/07, *Kücükdeveci v. Swedex*, ECLI:EU:C:2010:21, paras. 50–51; Case C-411/14, *Dansk Industri (DI) v. Estate of Karsten Eigil Rasmussen*, ECLI:EU:C:2016:278, paras. 35–38).

indicate a preference for conforming interpretation.[32] It follows that the function of conforming interpretation cannot be limited to remedying the absence of a directly effective provision in a directive.[33] Despite the great majority of more recent case law suggesting that the duty of conforming interpretation does indeed function as the first port of call to ensure the effectiveness of a directive and to avoid contradictions between national legislation and a directive,[34] the case law is inconsistent.[35] The order between direct effect and conforming interpretation seems to depend on the individual case,[36] e.g. on the wording of the preliminary questions. Relying on the doctrine of conforming interpretation has the advantage of being less invasive and more consistent with the idea of subsidiarity.[37]

In horizontal scenarios, national courts are required to apply the EU legal duty of conforming interpretation even where it results in the imposition of civil liability or a civil obligation upon an individual which may not otherwise have resulted from national law alone.[38] This consequence can be distinguished conceptually from horizontal direct effect as the obligation is imposed on the basis of national law and not directly ("as such") on the basis of the directive.

---

[32] For a discussion of case law, see M.J.M. VERHOEVEN, *The Costanzo obligation: the obligations of national administrative authorities in the case of incompatibility between national law and European law*, Intersentia, Cambridge 2011, pp. 37–38.

[33] For this "origin" of the doctrine, see Case 14/83, *von Colson and Kamann v. Land Nordrhein-Westfalen*, ECLI:EU:C:1984:153 paras. 21–27; Case 79/83, *Harz v. Deutsche Tradax*, ECLI:EU:C:1984:155, paras. 21–27.

[34] Case C-282/10, *Dominguez v. Centre informatique du Centre Ouest Atlantique*, ECLI:EU:C:2012:33, paras. 23, 32; Case C-621/10, *Balkan and Sea Properties v. Direktor na Direktsia "Obzhalvane i upravlenie na izpalnenieto"*, ECLI:EU:C:2012:248, paras. 53–54, 62; Case C-97/11, *Amia v. Provincia Regionale di Palermo*, ECLI:EU:C:2012:306, paras. 30–32; Case C-124/12, *AES-3C Maritza East 1 EOOD v. Direktor na Direktsia "Obzhalvane i upravlenie na izpalnenieto" pri Tsentralno upravlenie na Natsionalnata agentsia za prihodite, Plovdiv*, ECLI:EU:C:2013:488, para. 54; Case C-142/12, *Marinov v. Direktor na Direktsia "Obzhalvane i upravlenie na izpalnenieto"*, ECLI:EU:C:2013:292, paras. 37–39; Case C-306/12, *Spedition Welter v. Avanssur*, ECLI:EU:C:2013:650, para. 28; cf. Case C-187/15, *Pöpperl v. Land Nordrhein-Westfalen*, ECLI:EU:C:2016:550, paras. 42–45.

[35] See, e.g. Case C-46/15, *Ambisig v. AICP*, ECLI:EU:C:2016:530, paras. 20–24 where the CJEU examined direct effect and only turned to conforming interpretation after holding that direct effect is not available in that case.

[36] Opinion of AG BOBEK in Case C-187/15, *Pöpperl v. Land Nordrhein-Westfalen*, ECLI:EU:C:2016:194, para. 62.

[37] J.H. JANS and M.J.M. VERHOEVEN, Europeanisation via consistent interpretation and direct effect, in J.H. JANS, S. PRECHAL and R.J.G.M. WIDDERSHOVEN (eds.), *Europeanisation of public law*, 2nd ed., Europa Law Publishing, Groningen 2015, pp. 71, 73.

[38] See, e.g. Case C-240/98, *Océano Grupo Editorial v. Roció Murciano Quintero*, ECLI:EU:C:2000:346; Case C-421/92, *Habermann-Beltermann v. Arbeiterwohlfahrt*, ECLI:EU:C:1994:187, paras. 8–9; Opinion of AG JACOBS in Case C-456/98, *Centrosteel Srl v. Adipol GmbH*, ECLI:EU:C:2000:137, para. 35; G. BETLEM, The doctrine of consistent interpretation – managing legal uncertainty, (2002) 22 *OJLS*, 397, 407; CRAIG, above n. 31, p. 363; DRAKE, above n. 7, pp. 337–338; C. TIMMERMANS, Community directives revisited, (1997) 17 *Yearbook of European Law* 1, 23.

The CJEU has not answered concerns voiced by scholars[39] that imposing obligations upon private persons by means of conforming interpretation of national law leads to an allegedly forbidden de facto horizontal direct effect of directives. We will see later in this chapter that the duty of conforming interpretation can fail due to limits imposed by national legal methodology. It is not a limitless obligation regardless of the terms of the domestic measure. The consequence is that there is also a de facto distinction between the interpretative obligation and horizontal direct effect of directives. In proceedings between individuals and public authorities, it is not only the individual who can rely on the principle of conforming interpretation, but also the public authority even if the construction is detrimental to the individual's interests.[40] A limitation exists in criminal cases, however:[41] conforming interpretation cannot have the effect, on the basis of the directive and independently of legislation adopted for its implementation, of determining or aggravating the liability in criminal law of persons who act in contravention of a directive's provisions.[42] More specifically, the EU legal duty of conforming interpretation cannot be used to interpret domestic criminal legislation extensively to the detriment of the defendant, for example by way of analogy, due to the principle of legal certainty.[43] The EU legal duty of conforming interpretation cannot be used to give national criminal legislation a meaning which the words of the legislation cannot possibly bear if this interpretation is detrimental to the defendant.

The question of whether directives may have an impact on the interpretation of national legislation before the directive's implementation period has passed falls outside the scope of this book. The EU legal duty of conforming interpretation applies without a doubt after the date for implementing the directive has expired. The CJEU has held that where a directive is transposed belatedly, the EU legal duty of conforming interpretation "exists only once the period for its [the directive's] transposition has expired".[44] It is also a

---

[39] For an overview of the academic discussion see Prechal, above n. 9, pp. 211–214; T. Tridimas, Black, white, and shades of grey: horizontality of directives revisited, (2001) 21 *Yearbook of European Law* 327, 346–353.

[40] Case C-321/05, *Kofoed v. Skatteministeriet*, ECLI:EU:C:2007:408, paras. 45–46; Case C-53/10, *Land Hessen v. Franz Mükcsh OHG*, ECLI:EU:C:2011:585, para. 34. For discussion, see Prechal, above n. 9, pp. 214–215. For criticism, see Betlem, above n. 39, p. 415.

[41] This limitation does not apply outside the context of criminal cases. See Opinion of AG Jacobs in Case C-456/98, *Centrosteel Srl v. Adipol GmbH*, ECLI:EU:C:2000:137, para. 34; Opinion of AG Bot in Case C-441/14, *Dansk Industri (DI) v. Estate of Karsten Eigil Rasmussen*, ECLI:EU:C:2015:776, para. 68; Prechal, above n. 9, p. 212; Tridimas, above n. 40, p. 349.

[42] Case C-74/95, *Criminal proceedings against X*, ECLI:EU:C:1996:491, para. 24; Case C-168/95, *Criminal proceedings against Arcaro*, ECLI:EU:C:1996:363, para. 42.

[43] Case C-74/95, *Criminal proceedings against X*, ECLI:EU:C:1996:491, para. 25.

[44] Case C-212/04, *Adeneler et al. v. Ellinikos Organismos Galaktos*, ECLI:EU:C:2006:443, para. 115; Case C-378/07, *Angelidaki and Others v. Organismos Nomarkhiaki Aftodiikisi Rethimnis*, ECLI:EU:C:2009:250, para. 201.

well-established principle in CJEU jurisprudence that Member States are obliged to refrain from taking measures liable seriously to compromise the attainment of the result prescribed by the directive during the period assigned for the transposition of a directive.[45] This obligation must be distinguished from the EU legal duty of conforming interpretation. What is less clear is (a) how far reaching this prohibition on frustrating the objectives of the directive during the implementation period actually is and (b) whether it demands a certain degree of harmonious interpretation.[46] Furthermore, the CJEU has not yet clearly answered the question whether the EU legal duty of conforming interpretation can apply during the transposition period if the directive is not transposed belatedly but if a Member State passes implementing legislation during the transposition period. The answer to this question is controversial in legal scholarship.[47] The court's reasoning in *Inter-Environnement Wallonie* seems to suggest that conforming interpretation does not apply in this scenario.[48] If a Member State transforms a directive into its national law before the expiry of the transposition deadline, a duty to interpret national law in conformity with the directive can also arise out of national law.[49] There is only a small amount of case law in the highest English and German courts that deals with the interpretation of domestic legislation in harmony with a directive during its implementation period. The BGH has taken the position that the EU legal duty of conforming interpretation does not apply during this period.[50] Underhill J argued in *Coleman* that the EU legal duty of conforming interpretation applies during this period.[51] Due to these uncertainties, it is assumed in this book that the temporal scope of the EU legal duty of conforming interpretation only starts to run after the expiry of the implementation period.

1.2. FUNCTIONS OF CONFORMING INTERPRETATION

The main function of the European duty of conforming interpretation is to safeguard the full effectiveness and uniform application of EU directives in

---

[45] Case C-144/04, *Mangold v. Helm*, ECLI:EU:C:2005:709, para. 67; Case C-212/04, *Adeneler et al. v. Ellinikos Organismos Galaktos*, ECLI:EU:C:2006:443, para. 121; Case C-378/07, *Angelidaki and Others v. Organismos Nomarkhiaki Aftodiikisi Rethimnis*, ECLI:EU:C:2009:250, para. 206.
[46] For a recent discussion of these issues, see M.P. KUBITZA, Die Vorwirkung von Richtlinien – die richtlinienbezogene Auslegung und ihre Grenzen, *EuZW* 2016, 691–696.
[47] For discussion, see ibid., pp. 696–697; PRECHAL, above n. 9, pp. 21–22.
[48] Case C-129/96, *Inter-Environnement Wallonie*, ECLI:EU:C:1997:628, paras. 45, 47–48.
[49] S. PERNER, *EU-Richtlinien und Privatrecht*, Manz, Vienna 2012, p. 124; W.-H. ROTH and C. JOPEN, §13 Die richtlinienkonforme Auslegung, in K. RIESENHUBER (ed.), *Europäische Methodenlehre*, 3rd ed., C.H. Beck, Munich 2015, §13, para. 40.
[50] BGH, *NJW* 2012, 2422, paras. 20, 22.
[51] *EBR Attridge Law LLP v. Coleman* [2010] ICR 242 (EAT), para. 22 (Underhill J).

the Member States.⁵² The duty mitigates the differences that may arise out of a different interpretation of national legislation within a directive's scope of application in different Member States.⁵³ The degree to which the duty of conforming interpretation is able to safeguard the effectiveness of directives is influenced by two main factors: (a) the limits of judicial interpretation and (b) the degree of variance between the terms of a directive and the terms of national legislation.⁵⁴ Both factors are connected. This connection can be seen when a national legislature decides against a simple copying-out⁵⁵ of the terms of the directive into national law. The national legislature may decide to use different words and terminology when implementing the directive,⁵⁶ and the legislature may inadvertently fail to transpose the directive adequately into national law. The more powerful the interpretative duty is, that is to say the wider the limits of the judicial function are, the less the intended uniform application of the directive is affected by shortcomings in transpositions into national law. A certain degree of variance may be compensated by wide outer limits of interpretation.

The EU legal duty of conforming interpretation also functions for the benefit of certain individuals and the effective protection of their EU rights. Conforming interpretation has a remedial function when direct effect is not available.⁵⁷ The full effect of directives and the protection of an individual's rights are often two sides of the same coin. They do not always coincide, however, for example when the tax administration relies on the principle of conforming interpretation, leading to an interpretation that is detrimental to the individual's interests. Where national implementing legislation fails to give full effect to a directive and where the directive enshrines a right in EU law but lacks the conditions of direct effect, individuals may still be able to derive

---

52   Cf. Case C-397/01, *Pfeiffer v. Deutsches Rotes Kreuz*, ECLI:EU:C:2004:584, para. 114; Case C-282/10, *Dominguez v. Centre informatique du Centre Ouest Atlantique*, ECLI:EU:C:2012:33, para. 29; Case C-97/11, *Amia v. Provincia Regionale di Palermo*, ECLI:EU:C:2012:306, para. 28; KLAMERT, above n. 18, p. 133; C. LANGENFELD, Zur Direktwirkung von EG-Richtlinien, *Die Öffentliche Verwaltung* 1992, 955, 964; D.-U. GALETTA, *Procedural autonomy of EU Member States: Paradise Lost?*, Springer, Heidelberg 2011, p. 22; W.-H. ROTH, The importance of the instruments provided for in the treaties for developing a European legal method, in U. NEERGAARD and R. NIELSEN (eds.), *European legal method: paradoxes and revitalisation*, DJØF Publishing, Copenhagen 2011, pp. 75, 88, 92.
53   S. VOGENAUER, Eine gemeineuropäische Methodenlehre des Rechts – Plädoyer und Programm, *ZEuP* 2005, 234, 238.
54   Cf. PRECHAL, above n. 9, pp. 192–193, who enumerates different types of inadequate transposition which affect the degree of variance.
55   Copy-out legislation refers to national implementing legislation which adopts the same wording as that of the directive.
56   For an assessment of different possible methods of transposition of directives, see R. KRÁL, On the choice of methods of transposition of EU Directives, (2016) 41 *ELR* 220–242.
57   Cf. Case C-212/04, *Adeneler et al. v. Ellinikos Organismos Galaktos*, ECLI:EU:C:2006:443, para. 113.

their EU rights "indirectly" by virtue of a conforming construction of national law.[58] Furthermore, in litigation between two private individuals, the duty of conforming interpretation also mitigates the lack of horizontal direct effect of EU directives.[59] In these cases, it is, apart from exceptional situations,[60] the sole instrument that can guarantee the full effectiveness of a directive for the aggrieved party.

If national law cannot be interpreted in conformity with a directive, the European Commission can initiate infringement proceedings under art. 258 TFEU against the Member State at fault. Furthermore, in the absence of direct effect, an aggrieved individual may be able to claim damages for the loss sustained as a result of the state's infringement of an EU directive based on the *Francovich* doctrine.[61] It has been argued that mechanisms that allow individuals to enforce their EU rights, such as the EU duty of conforming interpretation, are justified because the effectiveness of infringement proceedings by the European Commission is questionable.[62] Since the effectiveness of *Francovich* liability is also dubious,[63] conforming interpretation becomes an important remedial mechanism to safeguard the EU law rights of individuals. Irrespective of the shortcomings of infringement proceedings and *Francovich* liability, the duty of conforming interpretation has a different function from the perspective of the Member State: it prevents the Member State from being in breach of its duty to give effect to directives.[64] It protects the Member State from Member State liability.[65] Since the duty of conforming interpretation serves the

---

[58] DRAKE, above n. 7, p. 332.
[59] Opinion of AG COLOMER in Case C-397/01, *Pfeiffer v. Deutsches Rotes Kreuz*, ECLI:EU:C:2003:245, para. 24; V. SKOURIS, Effet utile versus legal certainty: the case-law of the Court of Justice on the direct effect of directives, [2006] *EBLR* 241, 255; S. WEATHERILL, *Law and values in the European Union*, OUP, Oxford 2016, p. 202; D. WYATT et al., *Wyatt and Dashwood's European Union Law*, 6th ed., Hart, Oxford 2011, p. 241.
[60] See n. 31 above.
[61] See, e.g. Case C-282/10, *Dominguez v. Centre informatique du Centre Ouest Atlantique*, ECLI:EU:C:2012:33, paras. 37, 41–43; Case C-46/15, *Ambisig v. AICP*, ECLI:EU:C:2016:530, para. 26.
[62] J. MARSON and K. FERRIS, The transposition and efficacy of EU rights: indirect effect and a coming-of-age of state liability?, (2015) 36 *Business Law Review* 158, 159–160.
[63] For discussion, see ibid., pp. 164–168.
[64] *R. (Nutricia Ltd.) v. Secretary of State for Health* [2015] EWHC 2285 (Admin), para. 133 (Green J).
[65] C. HÖPFNER, Voraussetzungen und Grenzen richtlinienkonformer Auslegung und Rechtsfortbildung, (2009) *Jahrbuch Junger Zivilrechtswissenschaftler* 73, 82; PERNER, above n. 49, p. 121. Member States are obliged to implement a directive with the specificity, precision and clarity required in order to satisfy the requirement of legal certainty (Case C-197/96, *Commission v. France*, ECLI:EU:C:1997:155, para. 15). There is thus a strong case that conforming judicial law-making cannot achieve the clarity and precision needed to meet the requirement of legal certainty (M. FRANZEN, "Heininger" und die Folgen: ein Lehrstück zum Gemeinschaftsprivatrecht, *JZ* 2003, 321, 327–328; cf. Case C-144/99, *Commission v. Netherlands*, ECLI:EU:C:2001:257, para. 21). If a conforming judicial law-making is adopted, the non-transparent implementation of the directive will not lead to *Francovich* liability of

interests of one party to the proceedings, the Member State and the EU, there exist considerable incentives for a national court to find a conforming meaning. One way to make sure that this is possible is to adopt wide outer limits and techniques of conforming interpretation.

Another function of the EU legal duty of conforming interpretation is its mediating function. Conforming interpretation avoids normative conflicts between a directive and national law by using interpretative techniques. It harmonises the application and the interplay of different legal rules stemming from different legal orders and different legislatures.[66] It is thus possible to say that the doctrine is a procedural mechanism that manages (but does not eliminate) legal pluralism.[67] Through its harmonising approach, the doctrine also has a reconciliatory impact on constitutional conflicts between EU and Member State law.[68] The doctrine of supremacy of EU law resolves the conflict between norms at these levels by setting aside national legislation and giving primacy to directly effective EU law. National courts are required to disapply the incompatible national law.[69] EU law prevails over conflicting national law. The disapplication of national legislation is separate from interpretation and falls outside the scope of the doctrine of conforming interpretation.[70] Conforming interpretation avoids the constitutional conflict by using techniques of interpretation.

---

the Member State for incorrect transposition of the directive. Infringement proceedings are, however, at least a theoretical consequence of a non-transparent implemention of a directive.

[66] M. AMSTUTZ, In-between worlds: Marleasing and the emergence of interlegality in legal reasoning, (2005) 11 *ELJ* 766, 769–770. See also J. BENGOETXEA, Rethinking EU law in the light of pluralism and practical reason, in M. MADURO, K. TUORI and S. SANKARI (eds.), *Transnational law: rethinking European law and legal thinking*, CUP, Cambridge 2014, pp. 145, 169; A. FURRER, *Zivilrecht im gemeinschaftsrechtlichen Kontext*, Stämpfli, Bern 2002, p. 150; C. HERRESTHAL, *Rechtsfortbildung im europarechtlichen Bezugsrahmen*, C.H. Beck, Munich 2006, pp. 56, 58.

[67] Cf. generally on procedural mechanisms and institutions that manage legal pluralism P.S. BERMAN, Global legal pluralism, (2007) 80 *Southern California Law Review* 1155, 1192–1196; P.S. BERMAN, The new legal pluralism, (2009) 5 *Annual Review of Law and Social Science* 225, 238.

[68] E. LAMARQUE, The Italian courts and interpretation in conformity with the constitution, EU law and the ECHR, (2012) 4 *Rivista AIC* 1, 13; G. MARTINICO, Is the European convention going to be "supreme"? A comparative-constitutional overview of ECHR and EU law before national courts, (2012) 23 *EJIL* 401, 409; cf. J. BENGOETXEA, Conform interpretation as a method for balancing autonomy and heteronomy: introduction, (2011) 1(9) *Oñati Socio-Legal Series* 1, 4; M. ROSS, Effectiveness in the European legal order(s): beyond supremacy to constitutional proportionality?, (2006) 31 *ELR* 476, 491.

[69] See, e.g. Case C-404/13, *ClientEarth v. Secretary of State for the Environment, Food and Rural Affairs*, ECLI:EU:C:2014:2382, para. 54; Case C-237/07, *Janecek v. Freistaat Bayern*, ECLI:EU:C:2008:447, para. 36.

[70] *Fleming (t/a Bodycraft) v. Customs and Excise Commissioners* [2008] UKHL 2, para. 25 (Lord Walker); BAG, *NZA* 2010, 1020, para. 23. This is not uncontroversial in legal scholarship; for discussion, see J. GOLDSWORTHY, *Parliamentary sovereignty: contemporary debates*, CUP, Cambridge 2010, p. 294.

Even though not all of these functions of conforming interpretation are relevant in every case, there are no resulting consequences for the interpretative maxims established by the CJEU for conforming interpretation. The book will also establish that neither English nor German courts formulate different outer limits and techniques of interpretation based on whether or not certain functions of the doctrine of conforming interpretation are satisfied in an individual case.

1.3. PRINCIPLE OF EQUIVALENCE

It is settled case law since the CJEU's Grand Chamber judgment in *Pfeiffer* that domestic courts can apply their "interpretative methods recognised by national law" when they interpret national law in conformity with a directive.[71] Yet, *Pfeiffer* did not leave national rules of construction untouched. Regarding the duty of conforming interpretation, the CJEU held that

> if the application of interpretative methods recognised by national law enables, in certain circumstances, a provision of domestic law to be construed in such a way as to avoid conflict with another rule of domestic law or the scope of that provision to be restricted to that end by applying it only in so far as it is compatible with the rule concerned, the national court is bound to use those methods in order to achieve the result sought by the directive.[72]

What the CJEU demands in this part of its ruling is that a national court must not fall short of applying the same range of interpretative maxims for conforming interpretation that is available to the court when it construes purely domestic law (principle of equivalence).[73] *Pfeiffer* clarified that a national court is required to fully exhaust its methodological latitude and to use every interpretative tool available in order to identify a conforming meaning.[74] It must do "whatever lies within its jurisdiction".[75] The principle of equivalence refers back to national legal methods. It rests on the principle that cases affected by EU law must not be treated less favourably than similar domestic cases without

---

[71] Case C-397/01, *Pfeiffer v. Deutsches Rotes Kreuz*, ECLI:EU:C:2004:584, para. 116.
[72] Ibid., para. 116. See also Case C-12/08, *Mono Car Styling v. Dervis Odemis*, ECLI:EU:C:2009:466, para. 62.
[73] PERNER, above n. 49, p. 82; J. SCHÜRNBRAND, Die Grenzen richtlinienkonformer Rechtsfortbildung im Privatrecht, *JZ* 2007, 910, 912–913.
[74] See also Case C-64/15, *BP Europa v. Hauptzollamt Hamburg-Stadt*, ECLI:EU:C:2016:62, para. 41 ("when national courts apply domestic law, they are bound to interpret it, *to the fullest extent possible*, in the light of the wording and the purpose of the directive concerned ..." – emphasis added).
[75] Case C-397/01, *Pfeiffer v. Deutsches Rotes Kreuz*, ECLI:EU:C:2004:584, para. 118.

an EU law element. What the CJEU expressed in rather cryptic terms in *Pfeiffer* goes even beyond the principle of equivalence. Paragraph 116 of the ruling cited above can be read in the following way: if the application of methods of interpretation recognised by national law leads to a possible conforming meaning of the legislation, the domestic court must apply these methods and choose the conforming meaning. Choosing this meaning becomes an obligation under the EU legal duty of conforming interpretation if this is necessary to reach the result sought by the directive.[76] This reading of *Pfeiffer* privileges EU law and goes beyond the non-discrimination rationale inherent in the principle of equivalence. It implies an interpretative priority rule which will be discussed in Section 1.4.1 below.

The principle of equivalence cannot prevent different limits for conforming interpretation in different Member States threatening the full effectiveness and uniform application of directives in the Union. What is possible as a matter of construction in one legal system may not be possible in another one.[77] This may be the reason why the CJEU does not restrict its case law on the methodology of conforming interpretation to a reference to national legal standards alone.

1.4. EUROPEAN METHODOLOGICAL RULES

Even though the CJEU does not make the case for a common European methodology for the interpretation of harmonised domestic legislation,[78] the court has developed European methodological rules which interact with national canons of statutory construction.[79] Lord Templeman's statement

---

[76] Cf. S. PRECHAL, Case note on Joined Cases C-397/01 to C-403/01, Bernhard Pfeiffer et al., judgment of the Court (Grand Chamber) of 5 October 2004, (2005) 42 *CMLR* 1445, 1458.

[77] Ibid., p. 1459; VOGENAUER, above n. 53, pp. 238, 242–243, 259 footnote 117. For a detailed discussion, see M. BRENNCKE, Europäisierung der Methodik richtlinienkonformer Rechtsfindung, (2015) 50 *Europarecht* 440, 443–444.

[78] I have argued against such a legal methodology: BRENNCKE, above n. 77, p. 445. In favour of such a legal methodology: BABUSIAUX, above n. 9, p. 131; T. HENNINGER, *Europäisches Privatrecht und Methode*, Mohr Siebeck, Tübingen 2009, p. 324; VOGENAUER, above n. 53, pp. 242–243, 259–260, 262. Against such a legal methodology: J. HELLERT, *Der Einfluss des EG-Rechts auf die Anwendung nationalen Rechts: eine rechtsvergleichende Studie zum Recht in der Bundesrepublik Deutschland und im Vereinigten Königreich von Großbritannien und Nordirland*, Lang, Frankfurt am Main 2001, pp. 251–253; HERRESTHAL, above n. 66, pp. 35–41, 63; K. KRIEGER, Die gemeinschaftsrechtskonforme Auslegung des deutschen Rechts, LIT, Münster 2005, pp. 327–333; M. WEBER, *Grenzen EU-rechtskonformer Auslegung und Rechtsfortbildung*, Nomos, Baden-Baden 2010, pp. 213, 215.

[79] For scholarship recognising a trend towards a Europeanisation of consistent interpretation, see BRENNCKE, above n. 77, pp. 446–451; O. MÖRSDORF, Unmittelbare Anwendung von EG-Richtlinien zwischen Privaten in der Rechtsprechung des EuGH, (2009) 44 *Europarecht* 219, 230; ROTH and JOPEN, above n. 49, §13, paras. 26, 28, 45.

Chapter 4. The European Legal Duty of Conforming Interpretation

in *Duke* that "[t]he E.E.C. Treaty does not interfere and the European Court of Justice in the von Colson case did not assert power to interfere with the method or result of the interpretation of national legislation by national courts"[80] has thus been overtaken by later judicial development at the European level. EU methodological rules set an EU-wide standard but they do not provide for a complete methodological order. Outside their limited scope, national interpretative maxims apply for conforming interpretation. The methodology for conforming interpretation is thus neither solely domestic nor European but bears elements of both legal orders. Therefore, the EU legal duty of conforming interpretation is, according to its methodological design, a hybrid legal instrument.[81] The European methodological rules are committed to the full effectiveness of directives and to improving the uniform application of directives in the EU. The Europeanisation of conforming interpretation also gives rise to a fragmentation of national legal methodology because European methodological rules do not apply outside the scope of directives. A fragmentation of legal methodology in the Member States is not necessarily a development that is uniquely European, however. A fragmentation also exists in English legal methodology between conventional canons of construction and the interpretative approach under s. 3(1) HRA.

It is highly controversial whether the development of European methodological rules by the CJEU falls within the Union competence and in particular the competence of the CJEU to develop the law, here art. 288(3) TFEU and art. 4(3) TEU, further. Numerous scholars reject a European intervention into the methodology of conforming interpretation due to a lack of EU competence.[82] This debate lies outside the scope of this book. What matters for us is that the highest English and German courts have recognised European methodological rules when applying the EU legal duty of conforming interpretation, as we will discover in Sections 4 and 5 below.

---

[80] *Duke v. Reliance Ltd.* [1988] AC 618 (HL), 641 (Lord Templeman).
[81] In detail BRENNCKE, above n. 14, pp. 152–153.
[82] BALDAUF, above n. 8, p. 104; C.-W. CANARIS, Die richtlinienkonforme Auslegung und Rechtsfortbildung im System der juristischen Methodenlehre, in H. KOZIOL et al. (eds.), *Festschrift für Franz Bydlinski*, Springer, Vienna 2002, pp. 47, 57, 61; W. DÄNZER-VANOTTI, Die richtlinienkonforme Auslegung deutschen Rechts hat keinen rechtlichen Vorrang, *RIW* 1991, 754, 755; B. GSELL, Zivilrechtsanwendung im Europäischen Mehrebenensystem, (2014) 214 *AcP* 99, 136–139; M. HERDEGEN, Richtlinienkonforme Auslegung im Bankrecht: Schranken nach Europa- und Verfassungsrecht, *WM* 2005, 1921, 1926–1927; HERRESTHAL, above n. 66, pp. 54–55, 63; SCHÜRNBRAND, above n. 73, p. 916; WEBER, above n. 78, pp. 106, 126, 213, 215; cf. PRECHAL, above n. 9, p. 203 ("highly disputable"). In favour of a Europeanisation of the methodology of conforming interpretation: R. CHRISTENSEN and M. BÖHME, Europas Auslegungsgrenzen: Das Zusammenspiel von Europarecht und nationalem Recht, (2009) 40 *Rechtstheorie* 285, 299.

1.4.1. Interpretative Priority of the Conforming Meaning

The CJEU has required in Chamber and Grand Chamber rulings that a domestic court must favour the interpretation of the national legislation which is the most consistent with the result sought by the directive in order thereby to achieve an outcome compatible with the provisions of the directive. The court has applied this methodological rule to legislation pre-dating or post-dating an applicable directive.[83] What the CJEU requires is in effect that the interpretative result which complies with a directive must be given priority over all other possible but non-conforming meanings. The reasoning of the CJEU does not indicate that the priority rule itself influences how a judge arrives at possible meanings of a provision. Whether or not a provision is capable of bearing more than one meaning is not governed by this rule, but by the interpretative criteria. Nor does the priority rule influence how a judge weighs conflicting interpretative criteria recognised by domestic law. It is implicit in the CJEU's reasoning that the interpretative priority rule only applies once a statutory provision is at all open to interpretation and can be given more than one possible meaning, one of which fulfils the requirements of a directive. Therefore, the priority rule is limited to a selection rule between different possible meanings of a provision.

1.4.2. Presumption of Compliance

A second European methodological rule is the presumption that the domestic legislature intended to transpose the directive fully and correctly into national law (presumption of compliance). The national court must "presume" that the Member State "had the intention of fulfilling entirely the obligations arising from the directive concerned".[84] Contrary to the interpretative priority rule, the presumption of compliance influences how a judge arrives at possible meanings of a provision and bears upon the range of possible meanings. It interacts with other (national) canons of statutory construction like the historical and purposive approach.[85] Applying the presumption of compliance

---

[83] Case C-240/98, *Océano Grupo Editorial v. Rocío Murciano Quintero*, ECLI:EU:C:2000:346, para. 32; Case C-212/04, *Adeneler et al. v. Ellinikos Organismos Galaktos*, ECLI:EU:C:2006:443, para. 124; Case C-414/07, *Magoora v. Dyrektor Izby Skarbowej w Krakowie*, ECLI:EU:C:2008:766, paras. 43–44; Case C-305/08, *CoNISMa v. Regione Marche*, ECLI:EU:C:2009:807, para. 50. See also Opinion of AG Mengozzi in Case C-12/08, *Mono Car Styling v. Dervis Odemis*, ECLI:EU:C:2009:24, para. 107.

[84] Case C-397/01, *Pfeiffer v. Deutsches Rotes Kreuz*, ECLI:EU:C:2004:584, para. 112. See also Case C-334/92, *Wagner Miret v. Fondo de Garantía Salarial*, ECLI:EU:C:1993:945, para. 20.

[85] See BGH, *NJW* 2014, 2646, para. 23 – *Lebensversicherung II* for the statement that the EU presumption of compliance needs to be taken into account when determining the purpose of an implementing provision.

can lead to the result that the national provision under consideration can only be given one meaning.⁸⁶

The CJEU has so far required national courts to employ the presumption of compliance in two situations. On the one hand, the Grand Chamber in *Pfeiffer* demonstrates that the presumption applies to the interpretation of legislation which is specifically enacted for the purpose of transposing a directive into domestic law.⁸⁷ On the other hand, the presumption applies to the interpretation of legislation pre-dating a directive if the Member State does not consider it necessary to amend its law in order to bring it into line with the applicable directive because it (mistakenly) considers the pre-existing legislation to already satisfy the requirements of the directive concerned, which was the case in the CJEU's Fifth Chamber ruling in *Wagner Miret*.⁸⁸ Both in *Pfeiffer* and in *Wagner Miret*, there were indications that the legislature intended to comply with the requirements of the directive with regard to the legislation under consideration. This book thus distinguishes between (a) situations where there is no indication of legislative intent to comply with the directive with regard to the legislation under consideration and the presumption does not apply and (b) situations where such intent is present and the presumption applies, but the presumption may be rebutted. For example, a domestic court is not obliged to apply the presumption for the interpretation of pre-existing national legislation if the legislature neither amended the pre-existing legislation in order to implement the directive nor considered the pre-existing legislation to already satisfy the requirements of the directive.⁸⁹

---

86 This can easily be conceived of when all canons of construction point in the direction of the conforming meaning. It is also presupposed here that whether or not a meaning is "possible" depends on a contextualised approach to statutory interpretation, i.e. an approach that is based on all the applicable methodological criteria and presumptions in context. It follows that a specific criterion or presumption cannot be isolated and singled out in order to render an interpretative result "possible" in a de-contextualised way and in order to artificially increase the number of "possible" meanings. For example, even though the word "bank" can refer to the bank of a river, this interpretation is not a possible meaning of the word bank in a Banking & Financial Services Act. A meaning must still be reasonably attributable to the legislature in order to be a possible meaning. Cf. *Kirkness (Inspector of Taxes) v. John Hudson & Co. Ltd.* [1955] AC 696 (HL), 735–736 (Lord Reid, "A provision is not ambiguous merely because it contains a word which in different contexts is capable of different meanings"); *Attorney-General v. Prince Ernest Augustus of Hanover* [1957] AC 436 (HL), 461 (Viscount Simonds, "words, and particularly general words, cannot be read in isolation: their colour and content are derived from their context"), 473 (Lord Somervell).
87 Case C-397/01, *Pfeiffer v. Deutsches Rotes Kreuz*, ECLI:EU:C:2004:584, para. 112.
88 Case C-334/92, *Wagner Miret v. Fondo de Garantía Salarial*, ECLI:EU:C:1993:945, paras. 4, 5, 21. Note that in para. 21 of the judgment in its English version, the words "a national court" should be read as meaning "a Member State". This reading is supported by the authentic Spanish version as well as the French and German language versions.
89 Such were the cases in BAG, *NZA* 2009, 1020 paras. 26–27, 30, 46 – *Urlaubsentgelt* and BGH, *NJW* 2013, 2674 paras. 36, 40, 42–43. Neither the BAG nor the BGH applied the presumption of compliance. In both cases, the German courts argued that the national law could not be

The key significance of the presumption of compliance is that a court must assume that the national legislature intended to comply *entirely* with the requirements of the directive.[90] The main case of the application of the presumption thus occurs when the legislature transposes a directive into domestic law without clarifying that specific substantive objectives in the implementing act comply with the directive. Since it must be assumed that the legislature intended to implement the directive entirely, a court that interprets a specific statutory provision of the implementing Act must assume that the legislature had the intention to *only* enact conforming objectives.

The question of whether or not the presumption applies must be differentiated from the rebuttal of the presumption.[91] The presumption can be negated by evidence to the contrary, for example, by showing that the national legislature intended to depart from specific provisions of the directive. Hence, the presumption is rebutted if the legislature implements the directive in general but deliberately decides to keep or enact a non-conforming specific objective. How, then, must the legislature express such an intention? In the absence of CJEU case law on the matter, this question is governed by national legal methods. It is submitted here that the presumption of compliance can only be rebutted if a national court surpasses an outer limit of conforming interpretation which bars the conforming meaning. That means that the ultimate answer to the question of how the presumption of compliance can be refuted is to be found in the *contra legem* limit of conforming interpretation.

The European presumption of compliance can have far-reaching consequences in the event that the legislative history of an implementing act contains inadvertent inconsistencies with EU law. This can occur if (a) a specific objective of a provision is expressed in the legislative history but contradicts the directive's requirements as subsequently interpreted by the CJEU and (b) there is no indication that the legislature realised the inconsistency. Whether or not the presumption of compliance is rebutted in this scenario would prima facie be determined by national law. Yet, the answer to this question is provided by EU law as the following discussion shows. The decisive case is *Björnekulla*.[92] The Sixth Chamber of the CJEU stipulated that a national court has to construe domestic law in conformity with an applicable directive "notwithstanding any contrary interpretation which may arise from the travaux préparatoires for the national rule".[93] Assuming that the Swedish law could have been given another

---

interpreted in conformity with the directive concerned since such an interpretation would have surpassed the *contra legem* limit.

[90] See, e.g. *British Gas Trading Ltd. v. Lock* [2016] EWCA Civ 983, para. 107 (Sir Colin Rimer, with whom Gloster LJ and Sir Terence Etherton MR agreed).

[91] It is implicit in the CJEU's case law that the presumption is rebuttable. See Case C-334/92, *Wagner Miret v. Fondo de Garantía Salarial*, ECLI:EU:C:1993:945, paras. 20, 22.

[92] Case C-371/02, *Björnekulla Fruktindustrier v. Procordia Food*, ECLI:EU:C:2004:275, para. 10.

[93] Ibid., para. 13.

(conforming) meaning according to national legal methods,[94] the reasoning of the Sixth Chamber in *Björnekulla* illustrates the European interpretative priority rule. The reasoning of the CJEU can also be used to elucidate the European presumption of compliance: possible non-conforming meanings of a provision which may arise from the *travaux préparatoires* generally do not rebut the presumption that the legislature intended to enact only conforming objectives. Hence, the presumption of compliance itself contains an element of priority: the presumed (or actual) general intention of the legislature to fully implement the directive prevails over a specific but inadvertently non-conforming objective of a particular provision which is expressed in the *travaux préparatoires*. Resolving the contradiction between the general and the specific intention is not left to national rules of construction or to the discretion of the domestic court, but prescribed by EU law. This provides legal certainty, and this is significant given that neither English nor German courts have established rules for resolving conflicts between inconsistent purposes within a statute.

What remains open is the demarcation line between an inadvertent inconsistency with EU law and a deliberate intention to contradict or refuse to implement a certain provision of a directive. As the EU presumption of compliance currently stands, Member State legal methodologies determine where this line is to be drawn. This distinction was not discussed in *Björnekulla* since the *travaux préparatoires* in that case did not suggest that the Swedish legislature specifically intended to contradict the directive. Therefore, the CJEU's reasoning in *Björnekulla* leaves open the possibility that the provision as interpreted in its context, which includes the *travaux préparatoires*, can only be given one meaning which does not comply with the directive since the legislature deliberately intended to depart from certain requirements of the directive. In this case, the *contra legem* limit of conforming interpretation is breached and the presumption of compliance is rebutted.

1.4.3. Relationship with National Legal Methodologies

The relationship between national legal methods and European methodological rules can be described with the following concepts: overlapping, intervention and "Europeanisation from the inside". These concepts are not mutually exclusive categories but can coexist in a domestic legal order as they can apply at the level of specific interpretative rules.

If judges achieve the result sought by the directive by using their national canons of statutory construction, they secure the full effectiveness of the directive and therefore do not need to use European methodological rules.

---

[94] Cf. ibid., para. 10.

National and European rules can overlap. Overlapping includes the situation where the substance of a European methodological rule is fully part of national maxims of construction. In other words, a twin exists in domestic law. European methodological rules can also intervene in national legal methodologies. A court must apply the European rules if they permit a conforming interpretation of legislation and if the court cannot reach the result sought by the directive by applying domestic standards alone. In this scenario, the European rules increase the scope for interpretation available to a judge. These rules do not simply add a separate and standalone layer to the interpretative process. The EU presumption of compliance interacts with the historical and purposive approach to statutory interpretation. Therefore, national canons of construction may need to adapt to the presumption rule in order to guarantee its effective operation. This adaptation is itself required by EU law as domestic law must be interpreted in accordance with primary EU law (EU methodological rules).

If a national court intends to achieve the full effectiveness of directives through an interpretation of domestic law, it may consider extending the scope of permissible judicial reasoning for conforming interpretation beyond existing national canons of construction and beyond the requirements of European methodological rules. Whether or not this is possible is determined by Member State law; it is referred to here as a "Europeanisation from the inside". For instance, courts could decide to apply the European presumption of compliance to cases which lie outside CJEU case law on its scope of application, e.g. to legislation pre-dating an applicable directive even if the *Wagner Miret* exception is not met.[95] Having said that, other limits of the EU legal duty of conforming interpretation arising from general principles of EU law, such as the principle of legal certainty, may bar such a "Europeanisation from the inside" in an individual case.[96] The notion of "Europeanisation from the inside" particularly captures the question of whether domestic courts have gone further than required by the

---

[95] In *EuZW* 2009, 465 paras. 58–59, 67 – *Schultz-Hoff*, the BAG applied the European presumption of compliance to legislation pre-dating an applicable directive even though the *Wagner Miret* exception was not met and the case fell outside the scope of application of the EU presumption as interpreted by the CJEU. In BAG, *NZA* 2010, 1020 – *Urlaubsentgelt*, however, the BAG did not apply the EU presumption of compliance in a similar scenario and thus seems to have departed from its earlier position in *Schultz-Hoff*.

[96] The CJEU distinguishes between (a) limits of conforming interpretation arising from legal certainty as a general principle of EU law and (b) the *contra legem* limit of interpretation, which concerns the question of what is methodologically possible under the canons of statutory interpretation. Cf. Case C-212/04, *Adeneler et al. v. Ellinikos Organismos Galaktos*, ECLI:EU:C:2006:443, para. 110; Case C-268/06, *Impact v. Minister for Agriculture and Food and others*, ECLI:EU:C:2008:223, para. 100; Case C-12/08, *Mono Car Styling v. Dervis Odemis*, ECLI:EU:C:2009:466, para. 61; Case C-378/07, *Angelidaki and Others v. Organismos Nomarkhiaki Aftodiikisi Rethimnis*, ECLI:EU:C:2009:250, para. 199.

CJEU for conforming interpretation.[97] The process of "Europeanisation from the inside" can also impact on the national separation of powers if a domestic court surpasses the existing limits of interpretation and thereby shifts the *contra legem* limit in favour of the judiciary specifically for conforming interpretation. Whether or not this widening of the judicial function is legitimate is for national constitutional law to decide.

1.5. THE *CONTRA LEGEM* LIMIT

The European duty of conforming interpretation does not oblige[98] a judge to construe national legislation *contra legem*.[99] The *contra legem* limit has a functional meaning. It enshrines the principle that a judge is bound by statute. It provides, it is submitted, that a barrier exists which separates permissible judicial interpretation from impermissible judicial legislation which lies outside of a court's jurisdiction.[100] A *contra legem* construction surpasses the outer limits of the judicial function. The *contra legem* limit has a constitutional dimension and presupposes a separation of powers between the judiciary and the legislature. The existence of the *contra legem* limit alone does not reveal where the boundary actually lies, i.e. under which circumstances interpretation crosses the threshold to impermissible judicial legislation. After *Marleasing*,[101] confusion arose about whether at all, and if so to what extent, the duty of conforming interpretation can be restricted by national methods of interpretation.[102] In later case law, the CJEU has recognised that a conforming interpretation of domestic legislation can fail due to limits imposed by national legal methodology.[103]

---

[97] LORD MANCE, The interface between national and European law, (2013) 38 *ELR* 437, 450 raises this question with regard to UK law.
[98] See, e.g. Case C-268/06, *Impact v. Minister for Agriculture and Food and others*, ECLI:EU:C:2008:223, para. 103 ("Community law ... cannot be interpreted *as requiring* the referring court ... to interpret national law *contra legem*". – emphasis added).
[99] Case C-212/04, *Adeneler et al. v. Ellinikos Organismos Galaktos*, ECLI:EU:C:2006:443, para. 110; Case C-268/06, *Impact v. Minister for Agriculture and Food and others*, ECLI:EU:C:2008:223, para. 100; Case C-12/08, *Mono Car Styling v. Dervis Odemis*, ECLI:EU:C:2009:466, para. 61; Case C-378/07, *Angelidaki and Others v. Organismos Nomarkhiaki Aftodiikisi Rethimnis*, ECLI:EU:C:2009:250, para. 199.
[100] Cf. Opinion of AG BOT in Case C-441/14, *Dansk Industri (DI) v. Estate of Karsten Eigil Rasmussen*, ECLI:EU:C:2015:776, paras. 76–77; A.I.L. CAMPBELL, National legislation and EC directives, (1992) 43 *Northern Ireland Law Quarterly* 330, 347; G. CONWAY, *The limits of legal reasoning and the European Court of Justice*, CUP, Cambridge 2012, p. 14.
[101] Case C-106/89, *Marleasing v. La Comercial Internacional de Alimentación*, ECLI:EU:C:1990:395, paras. 9, 13.
[102] For an overview of the discussion, see A.I.L. CAMPBELL, National legislation and EC directives, (1992) 43 *Northern Ireland Law Quarterly* 330, 346–352; PRECHAL, above n. 9, pp. 197–199.
[103] Case C-235/03, *QDQ Media v. Alejandro Omedas Lecha*, ECLI:EU:C:2005:147, paras. 14–15; Case C-268/06, *Impact v. Minister for Agriculture and Food and others*, ECLI:EU:C:2008:223,

Since national courts can principally apply their domestic canons of interpretation when they interpret domestic law in accordance with EU directives, the outer limits of conforming interpretation are principally determined by national (constitutional) law. In particular, the CJEU has not yet decided whether clear and unambiguous statutory language of national legislation marks or does not mark the *contra legem* limit as per European law.[104] This question is decided by domestic law, and national methodologies can differ between Member States. As I have shown elsewhere, the CJEU in *Spedition Welter*[105] has not "interfered" with the *contra legem* limit and has not extended the scope of the EU duty of conforming interpretation for copy-out legislation by requiring that such legislation must be interpreted in conformity with the applicable directive as construed by the CJEU regardless of whether it might be possible to do so or not under national law.[106]

The *contra legem* limit is principally but not fully determined by domestic law.[107] National autonomy is confined by European methodological rules. The presumption of compliance, in particular, has the ability to influence, to "stretch" or to shift the *contra legem* limit.[108] European methodological rules thus have the potential to carry judges beyond the judicial function as accepted under their domestic legal order and to intervene in the national separation of powers between the legislature and the judiciary.[109] Irrespective of the question of whether the CJEU possesses the competence to rule into the *contra legem* limit of conforming interpretation, this potential of a "Europeanisation" of the *contra legem* limit carries the risk of undermining legal certainty and of undermining the rule that directives do not possess horizontal direct effect.

---

paras. 95–104; Case C-176/12, *Association de médiation sociale v. Union locale des syndicats CGT*, ECLI:EU:C:2014:2, paras. 39–41.

[104] For a different view, see R. SCHÜTZE, Direct effects and indirect effects, in R. SCHÜTZE and T. TRIDIMAS (eds.), *Oxford principles of European Union law*, vol. 1, OUP, Oxford 2018, pp. 265, 292.

[105] Case C-306/12, *Spedition Welter v. Avanssur*, ECLI:EU:C:2013:650, paras. 31–32.

[106] BRENNCKE, above n. 14, pp. 145–148. For a different view, see C.N.K. FRANKLIN, Limits to the limits of the principle of consistent interpretation?, (2015) 40 *ELR* 910; ROTH and JOPEN, above n. 49, §13, para. 34.

[107] For the view that the *contra legem* limit is *solely* determined by national law, see CANARIS, above n. 82, p. 91; M. KLAMERT, Richtlinienkonforme Auslegung und unmittelbare Wirkung von EG-Richtlinien in der Rechtsprechung der österreichischen Höchstgerichte, *JBl* 2008, 158, 160; *cf. Revenue and Customs Commissioners v. IDT Card Services Ireland Ltd.* [2006] EWCA Civ 29, para. 81 (Arden LJ).

[108] In detail BRENNCKE, above n. 14, pp. 144–145.

[109] A Europeanisation of the *contra legem* limit does not have to lead to an enlargement of the judicial function in a Member State. For example, if judicial law-making were a permissible function of the judicial role in Member State A and if the CJEU were to hold that unambiguous statutory words mark an outer limit of conforming interpretation, such a Europeanisation of the *contra legem* limit would lead to a diminution of the judicial function in Member State A.

2. AIM OF CONFORMING INTERPRETATION

The EU legal duty of conforming interpretation obliges national courts to find a meaning of the national provision under consideration that is compatible with the directive. It will be explored in this section how English and German courts have aligned this aim of conforming interpretation with their constitutional role in statutory interpretation to ascertain the intention of the national legislature.

German courts must apply the EU legal duty of conforming interpretation due to legislation bringing this EU law obligation into force in Germany, namely the German Act approving the Treaty of Lisbon (cf. art. 23(1) sentence 2 GG). The BGH has held with reference to CJEU case law that a national court is bound to interpret domestic legislation, so far as possible, in the light of the wording and purpose of the directive concerned in order to achieve the result pursued by the directive.[110] It is the intention of the legislature that determines what meanings of a provision are possible. This intention can be "objectivised" under German legal methodology. For implementing legislation, the aim of conforming interpretation can be aligned with the presumed intention of the enacting legislature to fully and correctly implement the directive into national law.[111] Yet, conforming interpretation of implementing legislation possesses characteristics that deviate from conventional canons of statutory interpretation. When a judge applies conventional canons, he or she commonly aims to discern specific substantive objectives of a provision whereas the intention of the legislature to fully implement a directive into national law is a vehicle that incorporates specific aims. These aims originate from a legal source outside national legislation, i.e. the provisions of the directive. The national court is thus required to interpret the directive in the first place or is bound by the interpretation of the directive by the CJEU in a preliminary ruling procedure. Once the purpose and meaning of the directive are established, its specific substantive aims can be "transferred" to the implementing national legislation. The device that makes this transfer possible is the presumed or specifically expressed intention of the national legislature to fully implement the directive into national law. This approach has been criticised as it entails the danger that the national implementing legislation is reduced to an empty hollow that can be filled with the aims of the directive as interpreted by the CJEU.[112]

---

[110] BGH, *NJW* 2009, 427, para. 19 – *Quelle II*; BGH, *NJW* 2012, 1073, para. 24 – *Weber II*; BGH, *NJW* 2014, 2646, para. 20 – *Lebensversicherung II*.

[111] BGH, *NJW* 1975, 213, 214; BGH, *NJW* 2009, 427, paras. 24, 25 – *Quelle II*; BGH, *NJW* 2012, 1073, para. 34 – *Weber II*; cf. BAG, *EuZW* 2009, 465, para. 58.

[112] B. Gsell, Anmerkung, *JZ* 2009, 522, 524; Herdegen, above n. 82, p. 1929; D. Kaiser, EuGH zum Austausch mangelhafter eingebauter Verbrauchsgüter, *JZ* 2011, 978, 980; Schürnbrand, above n. 73, p. 913; cf. S. Hetmank, Im Korsett der UGP-Richtlinie, *GRUR* 2015, 323, 324.

The decisive question appears to be whether the transfer of aims from the directive to the national legislation is barred by limits of interpretation.

Despite this criticism, ascertaining the intention of the legislature is an inherent aim of conforming interpretation.[113] This can be seen most distinctly in cases that deal with the interpretation of non-implementing national legislation that precedes an applicable directive. In *Urlaubsentgelt*, for example, the BAG was unable to give s. 13(2) of the German Federal Law on Leave (Bundesurlaubsgesetz; BUrlG) a conforming meaning. The court applied the interpretative criteria in order to ascertain the intention of the legislature and concluded that adopting a conforming meaning would contradict a clear decision of the national legislature.[114] In *Interprofessionelle Sozietät*, the BGH argued that s. 59a(1) of the German Federal Regulations for Lawyers cannot be given a conforming meaning since such a meaning would contradict the intention of the national legislature which the court discerned from the interpretative criteria.[115] A conforming interpretation failed in both cases as the conforming meaning could not be aligned with the intention of the national legislature. In neither case did the German courts refer to the CJEU a question about the proper interpretation of the applicable directive.

English courts have also held with reference to CJEU case law that a national court must interpret domestic legislation, so far as possible, in the light of the wording and purpose of the directive concerned in order to achieve the result pursued by the directive.[116] Since the UK follows a dualist conception of international law, at least according to orthodox constitutional doctrine,[117]

---

[113] For a different view, see C. HÖPFNER, *Die systemkonforme Auslegung*, Mohr Siebeck, Tübingen 2008, pp. 157–159; C. HÖPFNER and B. RÜTHERS, Grundlagen einer europäischen Methodenlehre, (2009) 209 *AcP* 1, 21–22.

[114] BAG, *NZA* 2010, 1020, paras. 30, 46 – *Urlaubsentgelt*.

[115] BGH, *NJW* 2013, 2674, para. 36 – *Interprofessionelle Sozietät*. The case will be discussed in more detail in Section 6.1 below.

[116] *Litster v. Forth Dry Dock & Engineering Co Ltd.* [1990] 1 AC 546 (HL), 558 (Lord Templeman); *Robertson v. Swift* [2014] UKSC 50, para. 20 (Lord Kerr); *Revenue and Customs Commissioners v. IDT Card Services Ireland Ltd.* [2006] EWCA Civ 29, paras. 68, 79 (Arden LJ).

[117] See, e.g. *Pham v. Secretary of State for the Home Department* [2015] UKSC 19, para. 80 (Lord Mance); *R. (Miller) v. Secretary of State for Exiting the European Union* [2017] UKSC 51, paras. 55, 57 (Lord Neuberger, Lady Hale, Lord Mance, Lord Kerr, Lord Clarke, Lord Wilson, Lord Sumption, Lord Hodge); *Salomon v. Commissioners of Customs and Excise* [1967] 2 QB 116 (CA), 143 (Diplock LJ); *EN (Serbia) v. Secretary of State for the Home Department* [2009] EWCA Civ 630, para. 119 (Laws LJ); P. SALES and J. CLEMENT, International law in domestic courts: the developing framework, (2008) 124 *LQR* 388. For a judicial challenge of this orthodox position with regard to human rights-related treaties see Lord Kerr's dissenting speech in *R. (JS) v. Secretary of State for Work and Pensions* [2015] UKSC 16. For the (controversial) argument that the UK Supreme Court in *R. (Miller) v. Secretary of State for Exiting the European Union* [2017] UKSC 51 did not follow strict dualism by recognising EU law as an independent source of domestic law, see T. POOLE, Devotion to legalism: on the Brexit case, (2017) 80 *MLR* 696, 701–702.

English courts must apply the EU legal duty of conforming interpretation as a result of s. 2(1) ECA.[118] The EU legal duty of conforming interpretation is an obligation that arises under the Treaties in the sense of s. 2(1) ECA. Section 2(4) ECA envisages past and future legislation ("any enactment passed or to be passed") and establishes a rule of construction as legislation passed prior or subsequent to 1972 must be construed subject to s. 2(1) ECA. The scope of s. 2(4) ECA covers not only delegated legislation made in exercise of powers conferred by s. 2(2) ECA, but also primary legislation.[119] National legislation is construed in the light of s. 2(1) and (4) ECA. According to Lady Justice Arden, s. 2 ECA "contains the mandate for the English courts to interpret domestic legislation in accordance with applicable Union directives".[120] Even though it appears that Lady Justice Arden refers to a national (rather than a European) origin of the duty of conforming interpretation,[121] the relationship between s. 2(4) ECA and s. 2(1) ECA and the latter's incorporation of the EU legal duty of conforming interpretation into English law clarify that a national duty of conforming interpretation would not deviate from the European obligation.

Lady Justice Arden suggested in *IDT Card Services* that the aim of statutory interpretation under the EU legal duty of conforming interpretation departs from the conventional aim of statutory interpretation when courts construe domestic legislation. This is because English courts can adopt a construction which is not "the natural one" under conforming interpretation.[122] Arden LJ did not offer further explanation but did pronounce that the same applies for the interpretative duty under s. 3(1) HRA. With regard to s. 3(1) HRA, Lord Justice Dyson, as he then was, declared that the role of the court is not (as in traditional statutory interpretation) to find the true meaning

---

[118] *White v. White* [2001] UKHL 9, para. 32 (Lord Cooke); *Revenue and Customs Commissioners v. IDT Card Services Ireland Ltd.* [2006] EWCA Civ 29, paras. 73–74 (Arden LJ); cf. *Cartier International AG v. British Sky Broadcasting Ltd.* [2014] EWHC 3354 (Ch), para. 130 (Arnold J); European Union Act 2011, Explanatory notes para. 119.

[119] See with regard to primary legislation: *Garland v. British Rail Engineering Ltd.* [1983] 2 AC 751 (HL), 771 (Lord Diplock); *Prudential Assurance Co. Ltd. v. Revenue and Customs Commissioners* [2013] EWHC 3249 (Ch), para. 106 (Henderson J).

[120] *Revenue and Customs Commissioners v. IDT Card Services Ireland Ltd.* [2006] EWCA Civ 29, paras. 73–74 (Arden LJ).

[121] This is not clear because she also refers to the European origin of the duty of conforming interpretation in her judgment. See ibid., paras. 68, 79 (Arden LJ). For the argument that s. 2(4) ECA provides the legal basis for construing national law so as to conform with EU law, see, e.g. B. FITZPATRICK, The significance of EC Directives in UK sex discrimination law, (1989) 9 *OJLS* 336, 347–348. M. HUNT, *Using human rights law in English courts*, Hart, Oxford 1997, p. 122 argues that the origin of the duty of conforming interpretation in England is to be found in common law.

[122] *Revenue and Customs Commissioners v. IDT Card Services Ireland Ltd.* [2006] EWCA Civ 29, para. 82 (Arden LJ).

of the provision, but to find a possible meaning which is compatible with the ECHR.[123] Lord Justice Sales has adopted this statement extrajudicially *mutatis mutandis* for the EU legal duty of conforming interpretation.[124] Such an adjustment of the aim of statutory interpretation is constitutionally significant.[125] Despite this adjustment, English judges, like their German counterparts, generally aim to ascertain the intention of the parliament that enacted the legislation under consideration when they engage in conforming interpretation. When they interpret implementing legislation, they emphasise the enacting legislature's intention to fully implement the directive into national law.[126] When this intention to implement is given considerable weight in the interpretative process, the focus of statutory interpretation shifts more towards ascertaining what the legislature intended the language to mean than establishing what the statutory language means. It has already been established that this approach entails the danger that the national implementing legislation is reduced to an empty hollow that can be filled with the aims of the directive as interpreted by the CJEU.[127] This danger is manifest if the purpose of a national implementing provision is simply equated with the legislature's intention to fully implement the applicable directive into national law.[128] Lord Hope pointed out this danger in *Russell v. TransOcean International Resources Ltd*, when he said that under the EU legal duty of conforming interpretation the terms of the implementing legislation "are of secondary importance" to the terms of the directive.[129]

The litmus test for the relationship between conforming interpretation and a court's duty to ascertain the intention of Parliament is the interpretation of legislation that precedes an applicable directive. In *Duke v. GEC Reliance Ltd*,[130]

---

[123] *R. (Wright) v. Secretary of State for Health* [2007] EWCA Civ 999, para. 112 (Dyson LJ).
[124] P. SALES, A comparison of the principle of legality and section 3 of the Human Rights Act 1998, (2009) 125 *LQR* 598, 608.
[125] See Chapter 3, Section 2.
[126] See, e.g. *Pickstone v. Freemans Plc* [1989] AC 66 (HL), 112 (Lord Keith), 121–122 (Lord Templeman), 126–127 (Lord Oliver); *Litster v. Forth Dry Dock & Engineering Co Ltd.* [1990] 1 AC 546 (HL), 576–577 (Lord Oliver); *R. v. Johnstone* [2003] UKHL 28, para. 63 (Lord Walker); *Moreno v. The Motor Insurers' Bureau* [2016] UKSC 52, paras. 15, 28 (Lord Mance, with whom all other members of the court agreed); *Football Association Premier League Ltd. v. QC Leisure* [2012] EWCA Civ 1708, para. 50 (Etherton LJ); cf. *Duke v. GEC Reliance Ltd.* [1988] AC 618 (HL), 638 (Lord Templeman).
[127] Cf. MANCE, above n. 97, pp. 450–451.
[128] D. GREENBERG, The "copy-out" debate in the implementation of European Union law in the United Kingdom, (2012) 6 *Legisprudence* 243, 248. See, e.g. *Pickstone v. Freemans Plc* [1989] AC 66 (HL), 112 (Lord Keith), 121–122 (Lord Templeman), 126–127 (Lord Oliver).
[129] *Russell v. TransOcean International Resources Ltd.* [2011] UKSC 57, para. 22 (Lord Hope). In a similar vein, see *Unilin Beheer BV v. Berry Floor NV* [2004] EWCA Civ 1021, para. 39 (Jacob LJ). Judicial practice is not fully consistent, however; see *Airtours Holidays Transport v. Revenue and Customs Commissioners* [2016] UKSC 21, para. 17 (Lord Neuberger).
[130] *Duke v. GEC Reliance Ltd.* [1988] AC 618 (HL).

Chapter 4. The European Legal Duty of Conforming Interpretation

the Sex Discrimination Act 1975 pre-dated the Equal Treatment Directive (Directive 76/207/EEC). The House of Lords examined whether it is possible to interpret the old s. 6(4) Sex Discrimination Act 1975 in conformity with the Equal Treatment Directive. It concluded that Parliament's intention barred a conforming meaning of s. 6(4). Under s. 6(2) Sex Discrimination Act 1975, discriminatory dismissal of a woman is unlawful. The old s. 6(4) provided that s. 6(2) does "not apply to provision in relation to … retirement". The appellant was dismissed by her employer, a private company, shortly after reaching her retirement age. According to the employer's retirement policy, the retirement age for women was 60, whereas it was 65 for men. In an earlier 1986 decision in *Marshall v. Southampton and South West Hampshire AHA*, the CJEU had been concerned with a similar case which arose under s. 6(2) and (4) Sex Discrimination Act 1975. The court had held that the Equal Treatment Directive requires Member States to prohibit differential treatment of men and women in respect of the age of retirement based on an employer's policy.[131] The appellant's forced retirement in *Duke* was thus discrimination contrary to the requirements of the Equal Treatment Directive. In the House of Lords, Lord Templeman, with whom all other Lords agreed, found that s. 6(4) makes discriminatory retirement ages lawful. He noted that (a) the Sex Discrimination Act was not intended to give effect to the Equal Treatment Directive as subsequently construed by the CJEU, (b) Parliament intended to preserve discriminatory retirement ages and (c) the words of s. 6(4) were not reasonably capable of bearing a conforming meaning.[132] The House of Lords felt unable to "distort the meaning" of s. 6(4) Sex Discrimination Act 1975 in order to accommodate the Equal Treatment Directive.

Duke's precedential authority was, however, put into doubt by *Webb (No. 2)*.[133] *Webb (No. 2)* also concerned a case where the national law, *in concreto* s. 1(1) and 5(3) Sex Discrimination Act 1975, preceded the applicable Equal Treatment Directive. The appellant was hired by the respondents for an indefinite period in order to replace a pregnant employee during the latter's maternity leave. Shortly after starting her new job, the appellant realised that she was pregnant and informed her employer about this. The employer dismissed her on the ground that she would not be available during the period which she was hired for. Section 6(2) Sex Discrimination Act 1975, read in conjunction

---

[131] Case 152/84, *Marshall v. Southampton and South West Hampshire AHA*, ECLI:EU:C:1986:84, para. 38.
[132] *Duke v. GEC Reliance Ltd.* [1988] AC 618 (HL), 637–639 (Lord Templeman).
[133] It is controversial in legal scholarship whether the House of Lords in *Webb (No. 2)* departed from the outer limit of conforming interpretation established in *Duke* that a court cannot distort the meaning of a provision. For discussion, see BETLEM, above n. 39, p. 417; J. SUHR, *Richtlinienkonforme Auslegung im Privatrecht und nationale Auslegungsmethodik*, Nomos, Baden-Baden 2011, p. 141.

with ss. 1(1) and 5(3) of the Act, rendered it unlawful to discriminate against an employee on grounds of sex by dismissing the employee. When the case arrived at the Court of Appeal, the three Lord Justices argued *obiter* that even if the Equal Treatment Directive had to be interpreted in such a way that the dismissal of the appellant amounted to a contravention of its provisions, giving ss. 1(1) and 5(3) Sex Discrimination Act 1975 a conforming meaning would nevertheless not have been possible. Following *Duke*, adopting the conforming meaning would have amounted to a distortion of the meaning of that Act.[134]

On appeal (*Webb (No. 1)*), Lord Keith said in the House of Lords that the appellant's dismissal did not constitute unlawful discrimination on a "proper construction" of the Sex Discrimination Act 1975.[135] He added, however, that if the appellant's case were considered as unlawful discrimination under the Equal Treatment Directive, the House of Lords would need to assess whether the national law could be interpreted in conformity with the Equal Treatment Directive.[136] Lord Keith thus left it explicitly open whether a conforming interpretation was possible. The House of Lords then referred to the CJEU the question of the correct interpretation of the Equal Treatment Directive. The CJEU held that the Equal Treatment Directive precludes the dismissal of an employee "who is recruited for an unlimited term with a view, initially, to replacing another employee during the latter's maternity leave and who cannot do so because, shortly after recruitment, she is herself found to be pregnant".[137] The CJEU did not suggest that or how the national law is amenable to a conforming interpretation.

When the case returned to the House of Lords (*Webb (No. 2)*), Lord Keith construed ss. 1(1) and 5(3) of the 1975 Act in conformity with the Equal Treatment Directive. He held that the appellant's dismissal constituted unlawful discrimination.[138] Even though Lord Keith specified the interpretative result, he did not clarify how this result could be reached on grounds of statutory interpretation. Lord Keith did not elaborate on the interpretative technique employed. Moreover, Lord Keith did not refer to *Duke* in *Webb (No. 2)*, something he had done in his speech in *Webb (No. 1)*. His conforming interpretation of the 1975 Act departed substantially from its "proper construction" reached under conventional canons of interpretation. It appears that Lord Keith deviated

---

[134] *Webb v. EMO Air Cargo (UK) Ltd.* [1992] 2 All ER 43 (CA), 57 (Glidewell LJ), 60–61 (Balcombe LJ), 64 (Beldam LJ).
[135] *Webb v. EMO Air Cargo (UK) Ltd.* [1992] 4 All ER 929 (HL), 935 (Lord Keith, with whom all other Lords agreed).
[136] Ibid., 940 (Lord Keith).
[137] Case C-31/93, *Webb v. EMO Air Cargo (UK) Ltd*, ECLI:EU:C:1994:300, para. 29.
[138] *Webb v. EMO Air Cargo (UK) Ltd. (No. 2)* [1995] 4 All ER 577 (HL), 582 (Lord Keith, with whom all other member of the court agreed).

from conventional canons of statutory interpretation in order to reach the conforming meaning. This is what Lord Oliver had done in the earlier cases of *Pickstone* and *Litster*,[139] which were, however, not cited in *Webb (No. 2)*. Lord Keith himself had argued in *Pickstone* that if a court implies words into a provision, the precise terms of that implication are insignificant.[140] This may explain why Lord Keith did not explain his methodological reasoning in *Webb (No. 2)*. Furthermore, *Webb (No. 2)* was decided after the CJEU's ruling in *Marleasing*, at a time when it was still unclear to what extent the EU legal duty of conforming interpretation could be restricted by national methods of interpretation. *Duke*, however, was decided before the CJEU clarified in *Marleasing* that conforming interpretation applies to national legislation whenever enacted.[141] The powerful operation of conforming interpretation in *Marleasing* may have functioned as an incentive for the House of Lords to adopt a strained, but possible conforming interpretation of ss. 1(1) and 5(3) Sex Discrimination Act 1975. What *Webb (No. 2)* does not suggest is that courts are empowered to depart from the intention of the enacting legislature under the EU legal duty of conforming interpretation.[142] This follows neither from the non-existent methodological reasoning in *Webb (No. 2)* nor from a departure from conventional canons of construction per se.

Webb (No. 2) left a void in how conforming interpretation of non-implementing legislation that precedes an applicable directive can be reconciled with a court's task to ascertain Parliament's intention, i.e. the intention of the legislature that enacted the national legislation. One could think of an interpretative presumption created by the ECA that forms part of the background against which post-ECA legislation is being enacted. Yet, an enacting parliament cannot foresee post-ECA but future EU directives. It is thus not convincing to argue that a future directive forms part of the background against which national legislation is enacted. Rightly, this kind of reasoning did not feature in *Webb (No. 2)*. I will show in Section 7 below that the void was later filled by case law empowering courts to depart from the enacting legislature's intention.

---

[139] Both cases will be discussed in Section 3 below.
[140] *Pickstone v. Freemans Plc* [1989] AC 66 (HL), 112 (Lord Keith); *Lehman Brothers International (Europe) (In Administration), Re* [2012] UKSC 6, para. 131 (Lord Dyson); *Revenue and Customs Commissioners v. IDT Card Services Ireland Ltd.* [2006] EWCA Civ 29, para. 114 (Arden LJ); *Vodafone 2 v. Revenue and Customs Commissioners* [2009] EWCA Civ 446, para. 37 (Sir Andrew Morritt C); *Churchill Insurance Co. Ltd. v. Fitzgerald & Wilkinson* [2012] EWCA Civ 1166, para. 50 (Aikens LJ, with whom Etherton and Maurice Kay LJJ agreed); *Birmingham Hippodrome Theatre Trust Ltd. v. Revenue and Customs Commissioners* [2014] EWCA Civ 684, para. 38 (Lewison LJ, with whom Sharp LJ and Vos LJ agreed).
[141] Case C-106/89, *Marleasing v. La Comercial Internacional de Alimentación*, ECLI:EU:C:1990:395, paras. 9, 13.
[142] For a different view, see A. SCHAEFFER, Linking Marleasing and s. 3(1) of the Human Rights Act 1998, [2005] *JR* 72, 73–74.

When English courts derogate from the enacting legislature's intention, they modify the aim of statutory interpretation as traditionally understood. This is a constitutionally significant alteration of the judicial role. What guides judges when they depart from the intention of the enacting parliament? At an abstract level, it is possible to distinguish between two different intentions of Parliament:[143] first, the intention of the parliament that enacted the legislation under consideration and, second, the intention of the parliament that enacted the ECA. The latter parliament enacted s. 2 ECA and thereby absorbed the EU doctrines of direct effect, supremacy and conforming interpretation into UK law. Ascribing a conforming interpretation to legislation fulfils Parliament's intention in enacting s. 2(4) ECA, even if a court deviates from the intention of the parliament that enacted the legislation under consideration. In such a case, a court prefers the legislative intention enshrined in the ECA over the legislative intention manifested in the other Act of Parliament, even if the other statute post-dates and is not more general than the ECA. I will explore in Section 7 below whether this power of the courts is reconcilable with constitutional theory. Compared to case law on s. 3(1) HRA, it is barely visible in English case law on conforming interpretation that courts distinguish between the intentions of two different parliaments in order to justify a departure from the conventional aim of statutory interpretation. There may be multiple reasons for this difference. First, there are more indications in the wording of s. 3(1) HRA and in its legislative history that English courts can adopt a construction which is not "the natural one" under s. 3(1) HRA. Such indications are missing for s. 2(4) ECA.[144] Second, the duty of conforming interpretation ultimately has a European origin and s. 2 ECA incorporates this duty into UK law. Third, most of the English case law on conforming interpretation is concerned with implementing legislation. When a court construes implementing legislation, it can rely on the actual or presumed general intention of the enacting legislature to fully transpose the directive into national law. Even if a court deviates from a specific objective of the legislation, the conforming meaning may still be reconcilable with the reasonably presumed intention of the enacting legislature. Relying on a presumed general intention of the enacting legislature is in harmony with constitutional orthodoxy. Courts thus prefer this reasoning over an argument that objectifies statutory interpretation even further.

A comparison with German case law, in particular *Urlaubsentgelt* and *Interprofessionelle Sozietät*, demonstrates that courts in other Member States have shown restraint towards conforming interpretation when legislation is at

---

[143] *Pickstone v. Freemans Plc* [1989] AC 66 (HL), 125, 127, 128 (Lord Oliver, "This conclusion is justified, in my judgment, by the manifest purpose of the legislation, by its history, and by the compulsive provision of section 2(4) of the Act of 1972").

[144] See Section 3.2.2 below.

issue that does not implement and pre-dates an applicable directive. German courts have rejected a conforming interpretation in the past on the grounds that the conforming result could not be aligned with the intention of the national legislature. One difference between *Webb (No. 2)* and the two German cases is that the German courts did not refer to the CJEU the question of the correct interpretation of the applicable directive. *Webb (No. 2)* may thus serve as an example that a judgment of the CJEU can incentivise a national court to find a conforming meaning. This is only one relevant factor that influences judicial reasoning, however, and it can be outweighed by other factors.[145] The book has shown that English and German judges possess a considerable amount of judicial discretion when they apply the outer limits of rights-consistent interpretation in an individual case.[146] I will argue in Section 7 below that the same is true in the realm of conforming interpretation. That is why factors like a preliminary reference ruling from the CJEU can have a significant impact on the outcome of a case even though, from a viewpoint of formal legal reasoning, a CJEU ruling on a directive's correct construction should not affect whether the national law can or cannot be interpreted in conformity with an applicable directive according to national canons of construction.

To conclude, conforming interpretation in England and Germany is primarily aimed at avoiding possible contradictions between the challenged national legislation and an applicable directive. Courts in both jurisdictions have combined this task with their traditional role in statutory interpretation to ascertain the intention of Parliament. English and German courts emphasise the enacting legislature's intention to fully implement the directive into national law when construing implementing legislation. A heavy reliance on this intention entails the danger that the national implementing provision is reduced to an empty hollow. Compared with their German counterparts, English courts seem to have struggled more with the requirements of conforming interpretation in cases that are concerned with the interpretation of non-implementing national legislation that precedes an applicable directive. The two German cases discussed above, *Urlaubsentgelt* and *Interprofessionelle Sozietät*, illustrate a certain willingness of German courts to hold that a provision's conforming result cannot be aligned with the intention of the national legislature. Such judicial attitude is absent from *Webb (No. 2)*. Two reasons may explain this. First, *Webb (No. 2)* was decided shortly after *Marleasing*, whereas the two German judgments are more recent and were given at a time when the CJEU jurisprudence on the limits of conforming interpretation was much clearer and more developed. Second, only the English court in *Webb (No. 2)* was faced with

---

[145] I will show in the discussion of the German case *Gasversorgung II* in Sections 7.1 and 7.3 below that this factor can be outweighed by other factors.
[146] See Chapter 3, Section 7.3.6.

a preliminary reference ruling by the CJEU holding that the applicable national legislation infringed the requirements of the directive.

As with rights-consistent interpretation, conforming interpretation is directed at identifying a possible meaning that complies with a standard external to the provision under consideration. Conforming interpretation requires a construction of the applicable directive as a first step. Once this step is completed and the benchmark is set, it becomes clear which readings of the challenged legislation accord with the directive. The conforming meaning is predetermined by an external standard (the directive) rather than found by looking at the intention of the legislature. The focus of statutory interpretation in judicial practice thus shifts towards the question of whether the desired conforming reading of the challenged legislation can be squared with the intention of the legislature. This brings the limits of conforming interpretation to the fore.

3. RELATIONSHIP WITH OTHER NATIONAL CANONS OF INTERPRETATION

This section will analyse the relationship between the EU legal duty of conforming interpretation and other national canons of interpretation in England and Germany. First, the interpretative structure of conforming interpretation will be examined. Second, we will learn that conforming judicial law-making is permissible in both countries. That raises the question of which outer limits apply to conforming judicial law-making, and whether these limits extend beyond those of judicial law-making recognised under conventional canons of construction. Third, two developments in case law will be scrutinised: (a) English courts have drawn an analogy between conforming interpretation and s. 3(1) HRA and (b) German courts have drawn an analogy between conforming interpretation and constitution-consistent interpretation. It follows from the analogy that the outer interpretative limits and techniques of conforming interpretation ought to be the same as those under s. 3(1) HRA in England and those under constitution-consistent interpretation in Germany. From an EU law viewpoint, national courts have established equivalence between conforming interpretation and s. 3(1) HRA in England and between conforming interpretation and constitution-consistent interpretation in Germany.

3.1. INTERPRETATIVE STRUCTURE

The relationship between conventional canons of statutory interpretation and the principle of conforming interpretation is controversial in German legal theory.¹⁴⁷ The controversy is very similar to the controversy surrounding the relationship between constitution-consistent interpretation and conventional canons of construction that was described in Chapter 3. It is thus not necessary to go into the details again. Some scholars reduce the significance of conforming interpretation to a selection rule between different possible interpretative results. These scholars apply a two-stage process to conforming interpretation.¹⁴⁸ As we have noticed, however, this two-step approach and understanding of conforming interpretation does not accord with CJEU case law, in particular the EU presumption of compliance. German courts have not yet decisively ruled on the theoretical relationship between conforming interpretation and conventional canons of construction. A strict two-step approach for conforming interpretation can only sometimes be discerned in written judicial opinions.¹⁴⁹ More often, conforming interpretation in a narrow sense is intertwined with the interpretation of a provision according to conventional canons of construction.¹⁵⁰

A two-step approach can generally be discerned if English courts interpret a domestic provision in accordance with an applicable directive. First, an English court interprets a provision according to conventional canons of statutory interpretation. That includes a presumption that Parliament intended to legislate in full compliance with the UK's international obligations (here: EU obligations).¹⁵¹ If this interpretation renders the provision compatible with the relevant directive, recourse to the wider interpretative powers available under the EU legal duty of conforming interpretation is not necessary.¹⁵² If, however, an English court is unable to produce compatibility with an EU directive on the basis of conventional canons of interpretation alone, the court must, as a second step, resort to the "more flexible" purposive approach available under the principle of conforming interpretation.¹⁵³ The typical case falling under this

---

147 For an overview of the discussion, see S.A.E. MARTENS, *Methodenlehre des Unionsrechts*, Mohr Siebeck, Tübingen 2013, pp. 437–440.
148 HÖPFNER, above n. 113, pp. 272–275, 282–284; HÖPFNER and RÜTHERS, above n. 113, p. 22. Cf. CANARIS, above n. 82, pp. 80–81. For a criticism of such a two-step approach, see MARTENS, above n. 147, pp. 438–440.
149 That is particularly true for conforming interpretation of legislation that pre-dates an applicable directive as the European presumption of compliance generally does not apply in such a case. See, e.g. the court's reasoning in BGH, *NJW* 2013, 2674 – *Interprofessionelle Sozietät*.
150 See, e.g. BVerwG, judgment of 29.01.2004, no. 3 C 39.03, paras. 1.3–1.4, available online at http://www.bverwg.de; BAG, *NZA* 2006, 862 paras. 44–46; BAG, *EuZW* 2009, 465, para. 59 – *Schultz-Hoff*. In favour of such a "unifying" approach: DÄNZER-VANOTTI, above n. 82, pp. 754, 755; M. FRISCH, *Die richtlinienkonforme Auslegung nationalen Rechts*, Schüling, Münster 2000, pp. 78–83.
151 This presumption of compatibility is discussed in Chapter 2, Section 2.2.
152 C. MANCHESTER and D. SALTER, *Exploring the law: the dynamics of precedent and statutory interpretation*, Sweet & Maxwell, London 2006, para. 4-030.
153 For this two-stage interpretative approach, see *Clarke v. Kato* [1998] 1 WLR 1647 (HL), 1655–1656 (Lord Clyde); cf. *Litster v. Forth Dry Dock & Engineering Co Ltd.* [1990]

second step of the interpretative process arises where a conforming meaning can only be achieved by expanding or narrowing the scope of application of a provision beyond the possible semantic meanings of the statutory words. These are cases which would be categorised as conforming judicial law-making in Germany. The two-step approach contains the notion that conforming interpretation departs from the outer limits of conventional canons of construction. It also shows that the EU legal duty of conforming interpretation cannot be integrated into conventional canons of statutory construction. It is a separate canon of construction, as has been explicitly recognised in case law.[154] More recent English case law interpreting national implementing legislation does not always follow this two-step approach. Instead, if a court discerns that the literal meaning of the domestic provision does not comply with the requirements of a directive, it may immediately consider the case under the principle of conforming interpretation without first considering its interpretation according to purely conventional canons of construction.[155]

The English two-step approach for conforming interpretation deviates from the approach adopted by German courts. This difference exists because the relationships between the outer limits of conventional canons of interpretation and conforming interpretation in England and the outer limits of conventional canons of interpretation and conforming interpretation in Germany are not the same.[156] The difference in the interpretative structure of conforming interpretation is only technical, however, and does not answer the question of whether and to what extent the outer limits and techniques of conforming interpretation in Germany and England differ or overlap. Interestingly, neither English nor German courts adopt an approach that separates conforming interpretation according to domestic legal methods from conforming interpretation according to European methodological rules. If the latter are applied in English and German courts, they are integrated into the reasoning process together with domestic canons of construction.[157] European methodological rules interact with domestic legal methods.

[^] 1 AC 546 (HL), 576–577 (Lord Oliver); *R. (Hurst) v. Commissioner of Police of the Metropolis* [2007] UKHL 13, para. 52 (Lord Brown); *Blackwood v. Birmingham and Solihull Mental Health NHS Foundation Trust* [2016] EWCA Civ 607, para. 48 (Underhill LJ); *Cartier International AG v. British Sky Broadcasting Ltd.* [2016] EWCA Civ 658, para. 66 (Kitchin LJ).

[154] *Rowstock Ltd. v. Jessemey* [2014] EWCA Civ 185, para. 40 (Underhill LJ).

[155] *Rowstock Ltd. v. Jessemey* [2014] EWCA Civ 185, para. 39 (Underhill LJ); cf. *EN (Serbia) v. Secretary of State for the Home Department* [2009] EWCA Civ 630, para. 77 (Stanley Burnton LJ).

[156] This will be further explored in Section 3.2 below.

[157] See, e.g. BGH, *NJW* 2014, 2646, para. 23 – *Lebensversicherung II*; *British Gas Trading Ltd. v. Lock* [2016] EWCA Civ 983, para. 107 (Sir Colin Rimer, with whom Gloster LJ and Sir Terence Etherton MR agreed).

One commonality of conforming judicial law-making in both jurisdictions is that courts often focus on the "negative" question of whether there is a legislative intent that opposes the conforming meaning.[158] This is a change in interpretative approach compared to conventional canons of construction. English and German courts often analyse whether the conforming meaning is *excluded* by the interpretative criteria. In other words, a court typically focuses on the question of whether the conforming meaning lies within the framework set by the outer interpretative limits. The main reason for this "negative" test is that the conforming result is predetermined by the directive rather than found by looking at the intention of the domestic legislature. Furthermore, the "negative" test also indicates the working of a strong presumption of compliance.[159] The focus of the interpretative endeavour under this negative test is on (a) the correct meaning of the directive and (b) whether this meaning can be squared with national law.[160] This negative test applies irrespective of how the directive is transposed into national law, whether it is simply copied or reworded. The analogy to rights-consistent interpretation shows that the transposition method does not necessarily impact on the interpretative structure of conforming interpretation.[161] The issue of transposition method does not arise in the area of rights-consistent interpretation, and the structure of rights-consistent interpretation can also be described as a "negative" approach in both jurisdictions.

3.2. CONVENTIONAL LIMITS OF JUDICIAL LAW-MAKING

Since judicial law-making is permissible under conventional canons of interpretation in both England and Germany, two things follow from the EU principle of equivalence for conforming interpretation. First, conforming judicial law-making must be permissible in both jurisdictions and, second, it must not fall short of the outer limits of judicial law-making under conventional canons of statutory interpretation.[162] Case law in both jurisdictions has indeed clarified that judges may venture outside the constraints of the text if this is necessary to arrive at a meaning that complies with the requirements of a directive.

---

[158] See, e.g. *Revenue and Customs Commissioners v. IDT Card Services Ireland Ltd.* [2006] EWCA Civ 29, para. 113 (Arden LJ); BVerwG, judgment of 29.1.2004, case number: 3 C 39.03, paras. 28–31, available online at http://www.juris.de.
[159] The presumption of compliance will be explored in Section 5 below.
[160] Cf. LADY HALE, The United Kingdom Constitution on the move, The Canadian Institute for Advanced Legal Studies' Cambridge Lectures, July 2017, p. 12, available online at https://www.supremecourt.uk/news/speeches.html.
[161] This will be further explored in Section 3.3 below.
[162] Cf. BRENNCKE, above n. 14, p. 136.

3.2.1. Rejection of a "Europeanisation from the Inside" in Germany

The first German case that explicitly recognised conforming judicial law-making was the BGH's *Quelle II* judgment in 2008.[163] The EU legal duty of conforming interpretation can thus be divided into conforming interpretation in a narrow sense (conforming interpretation within the possible semantic meanings of the statutory words) and conforming judicial law-making.[164] If a German court is not able to align a national statutory provision with an applicable EU directive by means of interpretation in a narrow sense, it is obliged, as a second step,[165] to examine whether conforming judicial law-making is possible. In *Quelle II*, the mail-order company Quelle delivered a defective stove-set to one of its customers in August 2002 for the customer's private use. In January 2004, the customer noticed the defect in the appliance and returned it to Quelle, who replaced it with a new unit. Quelle then claimed compensation from the customer for the benefit which she had obtained from using the appliance for almost two years. The applicable German law recognised such a claim. Under s. 439(4) read in conjunction with s. 346(1) and (2)(Nr. 1) German Civil Code, the seller is entitled to receive compensation for the benefits which the buyer derived from the seller's delivery of the original, defective good if the seller replaces the defective good.

When the case first came to the BGH, it stated in its *Quelle I* ruling that the wording of these provisions read together was unambiguous and supported Quelle's claim.[166] The court saw no possibility to correct the "inappropriate national legislation" by way of interpretation in a narrow sense.[167] However, s. 439(4) German Civil Code was introduced into the German Civil Code when the German legislature transformed Directive 1999/44/EC on certain aspects of the sale of consumer goods and associated guarantees into national law. The German legislature asserted in the legislative materials that the seller's right to claim compensation from the consumer-buyer for the benefits derived from using the defective good complies with the underlying EC directive.[168]

---

[163] BGH, *NJW* 2009, 427, paras. 21–26 – *Quelle II*.
[164] BGH, *NJW* 2009, 427, paras. 20–21 – *Quelle II*; BGH, *ZUM* 2010, 429, para. 22 – *Bob Dylan (No. 2)*; BVerwG, *NVwZ* 2014, 1586, para. 54. The EU legal duty of conforming interpretation is commonly translated as *richtlinienkonforme Auslegung* in German legal practice, even if a court engages in conforming judicial law-making. Therefore, when courts apply conforming judicial law-making, they sometimes refer to the term *richtlinienkonforme Auslegung* as encompassing *richtlinienkonforme Rechtsfortbildung* (see, e.g. BAG, *EuZW* 2009, 465, para. 65 – *Schultz-Hoff*; BGH, *NJW* 2013, 2674, para. 43 – *Interprofessionelle Sozietät*; BGH, *NJW* 2014, 2646 paras. 18, 20–21 – *Lebensversicherung II*).
[165] Cf. BGH, *NJW* 2009, 427, paras. 20–21 – *Quelle II*; BAG, *EuZW* 2009, 465, paras. 64–66 – *Schultz-Hoff*; BGH, *NJW* 2012, 1073, paras. 28–30 – *Weber II*.
[166] BGH, *NJW* 2006, 3200 paras. 12, 14 – *Quelle I*.
[167] Ibid., para. 12.
[168] *Deutscher Bundestag*, Drucksache 14/6040, p. 233.

This was doubted by the BGH. The German court stayed proceedings and referred the matter to the CJEU. The European court ruled that art. 3(2)–(4) of Directive 1999/44/EC precludes the contested German legislation.[169] When the case returned to the BGH, it held in *Quelle II* that s. 439(4) German Civil Code cannot be interpreted in conformity with Directive 1999/44/EC by applying conventional canons of interpretation in a narrow sense since interpretation in a narrow sense cannot surpass the possible semantic meanings of the statutory words.[170] The BGH then decided that the EU legal duty of conforming interpretation demands that German courts engage in conforming judicial law-making where this is necessary and possible.[171] It proceeded to construe s. 439(4) German Civil Code under the principle of conforming judicial law-making.[172]

The next question to ask is whether the limits of conforming judicial law-making equal those of conventional judicial law-making in judicial practice. The EU principle of equivalence does not bar a "Europeanisation from the inside": it does not bar German courts from extending the outer limits of conforming judicial law-making beyond those of conventional judicial law-making. Yet, the BVerfG has dismissed such a "Europeanisation from the inside" in 2011 in a case that concerned the constitutional limits of conforming interpretation of national legislation. The BVerfG reviewed the interpretation of s. 5 of the Law on the Cancellation of Doorstep Transactions and Analogous Transactions (HWiG) by regular German courts. In the *Heininger* litigation,[173] the question had arisen in German courts whether a consumer could withdraw from a mortgage credit transaction that was negotiated at the doorstep. The majority opinion in Germany had answered that question in the negative, and that was before the CJEU interpreted the Doorstep Selling Directive 85/577/EEC. Section 1(1) HWiG granted a right of withdrawal to consumers but s. 5(2) HWiG established an exception by providing that for transactions that fall within the scope of the German consumer credit law (*Verbraucherkreditgesetz*), *only* the provisions of the latter law apply. The German consumer credit law applied to mortgage credit transactions but excluded in its s. 3(2) a right of withdrawal in these cases. In its first *Heininger* ruling, the BGH made a reference to the CJEU regarding the applicability of the Doorstep Selling Directive to consumer credit secured by a mortgage on

---

[169] Case C-404/06, *Quelle v. Bundesverband der Verbraucherzentralen und Verbraucherverbände*, ECLI:EU:C:2008:231, paras. 28–37, 43.
[170] BGH, *NJW* 2009, 427, para. 20 – *Quelle II*.
[171] Ibid., para. 21.
[172] Ibid., paras. 21–26. Cf. in detail Section 6.1 below.
[173] For a concise account of the facts of the case and the details of the litigation, see N. REICH, Balancing in private law and the imperatives of the public interest: national experiences and (missed?) European opportunities, in R. BROWNSWORD et al. (eds.), *The Foundations of European Private Law*, Hart, Oxford 2011, pp. 221, 230–232.

the property.¹⁷⁴ The CJEU decided that the Doorstep Selling Directive grants to consumers a right of withdrawal for mortgage credit transactions that were negotiated at the doorstep.¹⁷⁵ When the case returned to the BGH, the German court argued that s. 5(2) HWiG was open to an interpretation in conformity with the Doorstep Selling Directive. It construed s. 5(2) HWiG restrictively by holding that the provision does not apply where the German consumer credit law does not grant to the consumer a right of withdrawal equal in scope to that provided by the HWiG.¹⁷⁶ The consequence of this reading of s. 5(2) HWiG was that the consumer had a right of withdrawal under s. 1(1) HWiG. The BVerfG clarified in its 2011 judgment that this interpretation of s. 5(2) HWiG by the BGH was actually (permissible) gap-filling by teleological reduction and not restrictive interpretation in a narrow sense.¹⁷⁷

The BVerfG referred to art. 20(2), (3) GG, and it applied the same outer limits for conforming statutory interpretation that it uses to describe the limits of the judicial function for conventional methods of interpretation.¹⁷⁸ The court then clarified that it reviews the constitutional limits of permissible judicial law-making according to the same standard whether or not the applicable domestic law implements an EU directive.¹⁷⁹ It follows that the outer interpretative limits and techniques of conforming interpretation must not fall short of, and at the same time must not exceed, those of judicial law-making in a purely domestic context. The BVerfG further stated that the duty of conforming interpretation cannot go beyond the scope of permissible judicial reasoning according to national legal tradition.¹⁸⁰ Does this mean that the BVerfG rejects European methodological rules for the EU legal duty of conforming interpretation? The answer is No, because the BVerfG derives the interpretative priority rule for the EU legal duty of conforming interpretation from art. 4(3) TEU in the same judgment.¹⁸¹ An interpretative priority rule is also recognised for constitution-consistent interpretation in Germany. Such a rule is therefore a permissible interpretative instrument in the German legal tradition. The reference to national legal tradition by the BVerfG means that the scope of permissible judicial reasoning for conforming interpretation cannot go beyond the common constitutional limits of statutory interpretation. This case law of the BVerfG has an impact on the *contra legem* limit of conforming

---

[174] BGH, *NJW* 2000, 521 – *Heininger I*.
[175] Case C-481/99, *Heininger v. Bayerische Hypo- und Vereinsbank AG*, ECLI:EU:C:2001:684, para. 40.
[176] BGH, *NJW* 2002, 1881, 1882–1883 – *Heininger II*.
[177] BVerfG, *NJW* 2012, 669, paras. 58–59.
[178] Ibid., paras. 43–45.
[179] Ibid., para. 46. Confirmed in BVerfG, *NJW-RR* 2016, 1366, para. 41.
[180] BVerfG, *NJW* 2012, 669, para. 47. Confirmed in: BVerfG, *NZA* 2015, 375, para. 31; BVerfG, *NJW-RR* 2016, 1366, para. 41.
[181] BVerfG, *NJW* 2012, 669, para. 46.

interpretation. I have argued that the *contra legem* limit is partially determined by European methodological rules according to the jurisprudence of the CJEU.[182] That may have the effect of shifting the *contra legem* limit in a national legal order and of intervening in the national separation of powers. What the BVerfG is saying in its 2011 judgment is that this potential effect of the EU legal duty of conforming interpretation will not be recognised in Germany. The BVerfG did not raise the question of whether or not the case law of the CJEU on conforming interpretation actually shifts the *contra legem* limit in the German legal order.[183]

3.2.2. Endorsement of a "Europeanisation from the Inside" in England

English courts have, earlier than German courts, held that conforming interpretation can go beyond the statutory words. In *Pickstone*[184] the House of Lords interpreted s. 1(2)(c) Equal Pay Act 1970 in conformity with art. 119 of the Treaty establishing the European Economic Community (EEC) (now art. 157 TFEU) and the Equal Pay Directive. The case concerned a claim by Miss Pickstone against her employer for equal pay. The applicable s. 1(1) Equal Pay Act 1970 implied an equality clause into every contract of employment of a woman. Section 1(2) of the Act set out the effect of the equality clause. In an earlier case, the CJEU had held that the UK had failed to comply with the requirement of the Equal Pay Directive that entitles a woman to equal pay for work of equal value to that of a man in the same employment.[185] In order to remedy this deficiency and in response to the decision of the CJEU, s. 1(2)(c) was inserted into the Equal Pay Act 1970 by delegated legislation, the Equal Pay Regulations 1983. These Regulations were made in exercise of the powers conferred under s. 2(2) ECA. Section 1(2)(c) Equal Pay Act 1970 modified any term in a woman's contract which is less favourable than a term of a similar kind in the contract of a man "(c) where a woman is employed on work which, not being work in relation to which paragraph (a) or (b) above applies, is ... of equal value to that of a man in the same employment". According to s. 1(2)(a) Equal Pay Act 1970, any woman was entitled to claim

---

[182] See Section 1.5 above.
[183] Concerns that the European methodological rules, as they currently stand, may alter the separation of powers between the national legislature and the judiciary in Germany are addressed and refuted in M. BRENNCKE, Entwicklung der methodischen Grenzen richtlinienkonformer Rechtsfindung, (2014) *Jahrbuch Junger Zivilrechtswissenschaftler* 11, 17–35 and BRENNCKE, above n. 77, pp. 455–459. For a more critical view and the claim that the European presumption of compliance leads to a de facto and inadmissible shift of the national *contra legem* limit in Germany, see SCHÜRNBRAND, above n. 73, pp. 916–917 and WEBER, above n. 78, pp. 99–100.
[184] *Pickstone v. Freemans Plc* [1989] AC 66 (HL).
[185] Case 61/81, *Commission v. United Kingdom*, ECLI:EU:C:1982:258, para. 14.

equal pay where the woman was employed on like work with a man in the same employment. Miss Pickstone was employed as a warehouse operative and was paid the same salary as male warehouse operatives. She claimed that she was entitled to equal pay with male checker warehouse operatives in the employer's enterprise, who were paid more than she was, on the basis that her work was of equal value to that of male warehouse checkers.

The evident wide purpose of the Equal Pay Regulations was to produce full compliance with the UK's obligation under the EC Treaty and the Equal Pay Directive as interpreted by the CJEU.[186] The literal meaning of paragraph (c) of s. 1(2) Equal Pay Act 1970 fell short of this intention, however, since paragraph (a) of s. 1(2) Equal Pay Act 1970 applied to Miss Pickstone. On a literal reading, it was not possible to interpret s. 1(2)(c) in conformity with the requirements of the Equal Pay Directive even though it appeared perfectly plain to their Lordships that Parliament cannot possibly have intended such a shortcoming.[187] In order to give effect to the clear but inadequately expressed intention of Parliament, Lord Templeman read into s. 1(2)(c) by necessary implication after the word "applies" the words "as between the woman and the man with whom she claims equality"[188] even though the statutory words themselves were unambiguous.[189] This purposive interpretation of s. 1(2)(c) Equal Pay Act 1970 goes beyond the possible semantic meanings of the existing statutory words.

This purposive approach to conforming interpretation was confirmed shortly afterwards in *Litster*.[190] The legislation at issue was the Transfer of Undertakings Regulations 1981. The Regulations were expressly enacted for the purpose of complying with Directive 77/187/EEC and were made under the statutory powers of s. 2(2) ECA. In *Litster*, an undertaking's insolvent old owner dismissed his workforce at the behest of a solvent new owner one hour before the transfer of the undertaking took place. The purpose of this course of action was to circumvent the statutory scheme and effectively deprive the employees of their rights. According to CJEU case law, an employee is to be treated as still employed by the undertaking at the time of the transfer for the purposes of art. 3(1) Directive 77/187/EEC if the employee is dismissed by the transferor for a reason connected with the transfer at a time before the transfer takes effect.[191] Regulation 5 of the Transfer of Undertakings Regulations 1981 only

---

[186] *Pickstone v. Freemans Plc* [1989] AC 66 (HL), 112 (Lord Keith), 121–122 (Lord Templeman), 126–127 (Lord Oliver).
[187] Ibid., 112 (Lord Keith), 125–127 (Lord Oliver).
[188] Ibid., 120–121 (Lord Templeman), 126 (Lord Oliver).
[189] Ibid., 126, 128 (Lord Oliver); *Pickstone v. Freemans Plc* [1987] 3 WLR 811 (CA), 821–822 (Nicholls LJ), 826 (Purchas LJ), 834 (Sir Roualeyn Cumming-Bruce).
[190] *Litster v. Forth Dry Dock & Engineering Co Ltd.* [1990] 1 AC 546 (HL).
[191] Ibid., 554 (Lord Keith) and 569–573 (Lord Oliver) for a discussion of the relevant case law of the CJEU.

protected those workers who were employed "immediately before" the transfer of an undertaking, even though the provision was intended to correspond with art. 3 of the directive. Regulation 5 of the Transfer of Undertakings Regulations 1981 did not cover the situation in *Litster* on a purely literal reading even though the case clearly fell within the purpose of reg. 5 and the purpose of Directive 77/187/EEC as interpreted by the CJEU in earlier cases.[192] Lord Oliver opined that such a result could not possibly have been intended by the Secretary of State in framing the legislation.[193] In order to comply with the manifest purpose of the Regulations, the House of Lords "inserted" additional words into reg. 5(3) of the Transfer of Undertakings Regulations 1981.[194]

Until the coming into force of s. 3(1) HRA, the EU principle of equivalence did not require English courts to go beyond the outer limits of judicial law-making as accepted under conventional canons of statutory interpretation. I will demonstrate next (a) that English courts went beyond these limits in *Pickstone* and *Litster* and (b) why this was constitutionally possible.

In *Pickstone*, the House of Lords interpreted s. 1(2)(c) Equal Pay Act 1970 purposively by reading additional words into it. Lord Oliver said that "so to construe a provision which, on its face, is unambiguous involves a departure from a number of well-established rules of construction".[195] This implies that the purposive construction that was applied by Lord Oliver deviates from the ordinary purposive approach. Lord Oliver signalled that the departure arose because he filled in "a gap by an implication" despite the statutory words being unambiguous.[196] It was established in Chapter 2 that the reading in of words can be permissible under purposive interpretation in exceptional circumstances. Yet when *Pickstone* was decided, those circumstances were arguably very exceptional. For example, the power of courts to alter statutory language when updating the meaning of a statute was not yet explicitly recognised. *Fitzpatrick* and *Quintavalle* belonged to the future and Lord Wilberforce's guidance in *Royal College of Nursing of the United Kingdom* was "only" a dissenting opinion. *Pickstone* does not fall into the category of updating construction. Regarding the category of correcting obvious drafting errors, it is important to note that *Pickstone* was decided more than 10 years before *Inco Europe* at a time when the correction of drafting mistakes by altering the statutory language seems to have been less accepted in English courts. Earlier attempts by Lord Diplock in *Jones v. Wrotham Park Settled Estates* and *Kammins Ballrooms* to justify judicial law-making in cases where the literal

---

[192] Ibid., 575–576 (Lord Oliver), cf. 554 (Lord Keith).
[193] Ibid., 569, 576–577 (Lord Oliver).
[194] Ibid., 577 (Lord Oliver), cf. 554 (Lord Keith), 558 (Lord Templeman).
[195] *Pickstone v. Freemans Plc* [1989] AC 66 (HL), 126 (Lord Oliver).
[196] Ibid., 125 (Lord Oliver).

meaning of the language used leads to a result that clearly defeats the purpose of the statute were not supported by the majority of their Lordships in both cases. In sum, it seems likely that the reach of the purposive approach as applied to purely domestic legislation in the late 1980s would not have justified the conforming meaning in *Pickstone*.[197] Furthermore, when *Pickstone* was decided in the Court of Appeal, Lord Justice Nicholls (as he then was) applied the mischief approach to statutory interpretation but felt unable to attach a conforming meaning to s. 1(2)(c) Equal Pay Act 1970 due to the provision's unambiguous wording.[198] The Court of Appeal was nonetheless able to provide a remedy for Miss Pickstone as it relied on the directly effective art. 119 EEC (now art. 157 TFEU). Section 1(2)(c) did not encroach upon any directly effective rights under art. 119 EEC.[199]

Admittedly, one cannot rule out that it may have been possible for Lord Oliver to reach the conforming meaning in *Pickstone* by applying judicial law-making under conventional canons of interpretation. Yet this is not what actually happened in this case. Instead, Lord Oliver changed the default position for conforming judicial law-making, at least as far as implementing legislation is concerned, from judicial law-making generally being an impermissible function of the judge to judicial law-making being a permissible function of the judge. Therefore, Lord Oliver went beyond conventional canons of statutory interpretation and rightly referred to the purposive construction of s. 1(2)(c) Equal Pay Act 1970 as a departure from a number of well-established rules of construction. That is also why he said in *Litster* that *Pickstone* has established that the purposive approach to interpretation offers judges a "greater flexibility"[200] when they interpret legislation implementing EU law in conformity with an applicable directive. Such a change of the default position for permissible judicial law-making can be reconciled with the doctrine of parliamentary sovereignty.[201] In *Litster*, Lord Oliver applied a purposive construction to reg. 5(3) of the Transfer of Undertakings Regulations 1981. He also clarified that it would not have been possible to construe the Regulations in conformity with the applicable directive under conventional principles of construction without reference to Treaty obligations.[202] In *IDT Card Services*, Arden LJ said with regard to *Litster* that

---

[197] For a different view, see S. VOGENAUER, *Die Auslegung von Gesetzen in England und auf dem Kontinent*, Mohr Siebeck, Tübingen 2001, p. 1320.
[198] *Pickstone v. Freemans Plc* [1987] 3 WLR 811 (CA), 820–821 (Nicholls LJ).
[199] Ibid., 822–823 (Nicholls LJ).
[200] *Litster v. Forth Dry Dock and Engineering Co Ltd.* [1990] 1 AC 546 (HL), 576–577 (Lord Oliver). See also *Hemming (t/a Simply Pleasure Ltd) v. Westminster City Council* [2013] EWCA Civ 591, para. 72 (Beatson LJ).
[201] See Chapter 2, Section 5.
[202] *Litster v. Forth Dry Dock & Engineering Co Ltd.* [1990] 1 AC 546 (HL), 576–577 (Lord Oliver).

the House of Lords made a significant change to the wording of the legislation by adding words that were not there. This is not possible in statutory interpretation under purely domestic law. If the courts took the same approach to a purely domestic statute, it would probably be regarded as impermissible judicial legislation.[203]

Later case law has adopted Lord Oliver's reasoning[204] and has confirmed that the European legal duty of conforming interpretation empowers English judges to go beyond what can be done by way of statutory interpretation under conventional canons of construction.[205] Later case law has also established that the more flexible purposive approach applies not only to implementing legislation, but to all domestic legislation that is interpreted in conformity with an applicable EU directive.[206]

Did European law require the House of Lords in *Pickstone* or *Litster* to extend the permissibility of conforming judicial law-making beyond conventional canons of interpretation? It has been argued that the EU legal duty of conforming interpretation obliges national courts not just to look at the wording of the national legislation but also to consider its purpose when judges engage in

---

[203] *Revenue and Customs Commissioners v. IDT Card Services Ireland Ltd.* [2006] EWCA Civ 29, para. 76 (Arden LJ).

[204] *Ghaidan v. Godin-Mendoza* [2004] UKHL 30, para. 118 (Lord Rodger); *Assange v. Swedish Prosecution Authority* [2012] UKSC 22, para. 203 (Lord Mance); *Vodafone 2 v. Revenue and Customs Commissioners* [2009] EWCA Civ 446, para. 37 (Sir Andrew Morritt C); *Hemming (t/a Simply Pleasure Ltd) v. Westminster City Council* [2013] EWCA Civ 591, para. 72 (Beatson LJ). See also LORD PHILLIPS, The art of the possible: statutory interpretation and human rights, First Lord Alexander of Weedon lecture, April 2010. p. 17, available online at https://www.supremecourt.uk/news/speeches.html.

[205] *Rhys-Harper v. Relaxion* [2003] UKHL 33, para. 106 (Lord Hope); *Lehman Brothers International (Europe) (In Administration), Re* [2012] UKSC 6, para. 131 (Lord Dyson); *McCall v. Poulton* [2008] EWCA Civ 1313, para. 28 (Waller LJ); *Vodafone 2 v. Revenue and Customs Commissioners* [2009] EWCA Civ 446, para. 37 (Sir Andrew Morritt C); *Test Claimants in the FII Group Litigation v. Revenue and Customs Commissioners* [2010] EWCA Civ 103, para. 260 (Arden LJ); *Churchill Insurance Co. Ltd. v. Fitzgerald & Wilkinson* [2012] EWCA Civ 1166, para. 50 (Aikens LJ, with whom Etherton and Maurice Kay LJJ agreed); *Hemming (t/a Simply Pleasure Ltd) v. Westminster City Council* [2013] EWCA Civ 591, para. 72 (Beatson LJ); *Rowstock Ltd. v. Jessemey* [2014] EWCA Civ 185, para. 38 (Underhill LJ); *ITV Broadcasting Ltd. v. TV Catchup Ltd.* [2015] EWCA Civ 204, para. 86 (Kitchin LJ); *Cartier International AG v. British Sky Broadcasting Ltd.* [2016] EWCA Civ 658, para. 72 (Kitchin LJ); *Test Claimants in the FII Group Litigation v. Revenue and Customs Commissioners* [2016] EWCA Civ 1180, para. 106 (Underhill LJ, giving the judgment of the court); *ITV Broadcasting Ltd. v. TV Catchup Ltd. (No. 2)* [2011] EWHC 1874 (Pat.), para. 116 (Floyd J). See also *Assange v. Swedish Prosecution Authority* [2012] UKSC 22, para. 174 (Lady Hale), para. 203 (Lord Mance). See also MANCE, above n. 97, pp. 449–450; LORD PHILLIPS, above n. 204, p. 17.

[206] See, e.g. *Howe v. Motor Insurers' Bureau* [2017] EWCA Civ 932, paras. 27–32, 36–37 (Lewison LJ, with whom McFarlane LJ and Sir James Munby agreed); cf. A. ARNULL, The Law Lords and the European Union: swimming with the incoming tide, (2010) 35 *ELR*, 57, 73; A.W. BRADLEY, K.D. EWING and C.J.S. KNIGHT, *Constitutional and administrative law*, 16th ed., Pearson, Harlow 2015, p. 139.

conforming interpretation.[207] Others have argued that conforming interpretation requires national courts to adopt the teleological approach adopted by the CJEU.[208] Such an understanding of the EU legal duty of conforming interpretation goes beyond the principle of equivalence and is not supported by CJEU case law.[209] There is, however, support in English case law for the position that English judges are under a European obligation to give a purposive construction to domestic legislation when the EU legal duty of conforming interpretation is involved.[210] That, of course, does not render the statutory language for the process of conforming interpretation nugatory, as the reference to "the wording and the purpose"[211] of the directive in settled CJEU case law illustrates. Furthermore, at least in retrospect,[212] the principle of equivalence as expressed by the CJEU in *Pfeiffer* also required the House of Lords in *Pickstone* to give a purposive interpretation to s. 1(2)(c) Equal Pay Act 1970 because the purposive approach to statutory interpretation was already well established in English case law when *Pickstone* was decided. But be that as it may, the conventional English purposive approach does not include a general interpretative rule that a national court must give precedence to the purpose of a provision over its unambiguous wording.

Does the principle of equivalence go further than this? The reading in, out or down of words in legislation is possible under conventional canons of

---

[207] PRECHAL, above n. 9, p. 184; cf. M. KLAMERT, *Die richtlinienkonforme Auslegung*, Manz, Vienna 2001, pp. 177–179.
[208] ARNULL, above n. 206, p. 80.
[209] It is submitted here that a purposive interpretation of national law does not follow inevitably *qua* EU law from the duty of national courts to interpret national law, so far as possible, in the light of the wording and the purpose of the directive. The reference to the wording and the purpose of the directive signifies that both need to be considered when interpreting the directive. The interpretation of the directive must be separated from the interpretative criteria employed for the interpretation of national legislation. For England and Germany, purposive interpretation belongs to the accepted canons of interpretation of national law. The principle of equivalence requires that a German or English court has recourse to purposive interpretation when construing national law in conformity with a directive. For both countries, this duty arises from EU law (the principle of equivalence), but only because purposive interpretation is an accepted canon of construction according to national legal methods. This would be different if purposive interpretation were not a permissible canon of statutory interpretation in a Member State.
[210] *Litster v. Forth Dry Dock & Engineering Co Ltd.* [1990] 1 AC 546 (HL), 558 (Lord Templeman); *Robertson v. Swift* [2014] UKSC 50, para. 30 (Lord Kerr); *R. (Nutricia Ltd.) v. Secretary of State for Health* [2015] EWHC 2285 (Admin), para. 115 (Green J). It is widely recognised in English case law that the purposive approach applies to the interpretation of domestic legislation in conformity with an applicable directive; see, e.g., *Alderson v. Secretary of State for Trade and Industry* [2003] EWCA Civ 1767, paras. 25–26 (Lord Phillips MR).
[211] See, e.g. Case C-212/04, *Adeneler et al. v. Ellinikos Organismos Galaktos*, ECLI:EU:C:2006:443, para. 108.
[212] Case C-397/01, *Pfeiffer v. Deutsches Rotes Kreuz*, ECLI:EU:C:2004:584 was decided more than 15 years after *Pickstone*.

statutory interpretation "in certain circumstances",[213] such as saving statutes from absurdity or the correction of obvious drafting errors. Does the limited possibility to depart from the statutory words become a general obligation for all cases of conforming interpretation in all circumstances under equivalence reasoning? The answer is No as the principle of equivalence does not require national courts to go beyond the *contra legem* limit of interpretation. One underlying reason for the rule that judicial law-making is generally not possible under conventional canons of interpretation is the separation of powers between the legislature and the judiciary. Separation of powers concerns are also inherent in the *contra legem* limit of conforming interpretation. Even if *Pickstone* is considered in the light of the EU presumption of compliance,[214] applying the EU presumption to that case would not lead to a shift in the *contra legem* limit and would not carry English judges beyond the judicial function as accepted under their domestic legal order. In sum, EU law did not require Lord Oliver to (a) depart from well-established canons of interpretation and (b) extend the permissibility of conforming judicial law-making beyond conventional judicial law-making.[215]

The bottom line is that in *Pickstone*, Lord Oliver went further than what the CJEU requires for conforming interpretation. Lord Oliver indicated that the deviation from conventional canons of interpretation is warranted because domestic legislation that is passed in order to give effect to European Union obligations "falls into a special category" by virtue of s. 2(4) ECA.[216] Lord Oliver thus indicated that it was the Parliament of 1972, by using written legislation, and not the courts that demanded the change in canons of construction and judicial powers. A reasoning of this kind, which dodges an explicit analysis of constitutional principle, denies a judicial policy choice and attributes all responsibility to Parliament, can also be found in the later case of *Factortame (No. 2)*, where Lord Bridge declared that it was Parliament itself that voluntarily accepted a limitation of its sovereignty when it enacted the ECA.[217] Common law constitutionalism was still asleep. It may be possible to argue, as Lord Oliver

---

[213] This is the terminology used by the CJEU in *Pfeiffer*.
[214] At the time when *Pickstone* was decided, the CJEU had not yet expressed the EU presumption of compliance in its case law.
[215] Cf. Hervey and Sheldon, above n. 8, p. 371; N. Maltby, Case comment – Marleasing: what is all the fuss about?, (1993) 109 *LQR* 301, 303, 311. For the view that the EU legal duty of conforming interpretation requires English courts to depart from conventional canons of statutory interpretation, see G. de Burca, Giving effect to European Community Directives, (1992) 55 *MLR* 215, 221, 223, 228, 233–234; Klamert, above n. 207, pp. 177–178; F. Snyder, The effectiveness of European Community law: institutions, processes, tools and techniques, (1993) 56 *MLR* 19, 43.
[216] *Pickstone v. Freemans Plc* [1989] AC 66 (HL), 126, 128 (Lord Oliver).
[217] *R. (Factortame (No. 2)) v. Secretary of State for Transport* [1991] 1 AC 603 (HL), 658–659 (Lord Bridge).

did, that domestic implementing legislation must be interpreted purposively by virtue of s. 2(4) ECA, i.e. by virtue of domestic law. This reasoning does not explain, however, why the purposive approach for implementing legislation must go beyond the recognised purposive approach under conventional canons of statutory interpretation.[218] Moreover, Lord Oliver did not argue that s. 2 ECA serves as the legal basis for a national duty of conforming interpretation that goes beyond the requirements of the EU legal duty of conforming interpretation. Parliament intended to incorporate EU law obligations into national law in s. 2 ECA, but nothing in s. 2 ECA suggests that Parliament intended to provide for a "Europeanisation from the inside" with regard to the methods of conforming interpretation by virtue of national law, as was the effect of Lord Oliver's reasoning in *Pickstone*. In 1972, the CJEU had not even expressed the EU legal duty of conforming interpretation.

An analysis of the legislative history of s. 2(4) ECA also confirms that that provision was not intended to empower judges to deviate from well-established rules of construction. During the parliamentary debates of the ECA, Viscount Colville of Culross made the point that s. 2(4) ECA empowers judges to "look to the Statutes as well as to the directly applicable law, and they are to attempt if they possibly can to construe the former in conformity with the latter". Section 2(4) ECA grants them specific authority to use their interpretative powers and to "try as hard as possible to see if they could avoid a situation which would produce a conflict"[219] between an English statute and a directly applicable EU law, unless Parliament intentionally legislated contrary to Union obligations. Since the purpose of the Equal Pay Regulations was to produce full compliance with the requirements of art. 119 EEC and the Equal Pay Directive, the situation in *Pickstone* seems to be an obvious example of when a judge should try as hard as possible to interpret the statute in conformity with the directive. It does not follow, however, that s. 2(4) ECA empowers courts to depart from well-established canons of construction. First, to hide such a significant change in the sole word "construed" in s. 2(4) ECA would be quite a remarkable thing for a legislature to do.[220] There is a presumption against such a change unless that change is conveyed in express language or by necessary implication.[221] Second, the parliamentary debates also clarify that the power of the judge "to try as hard

---

[218] Cf. *Pickstone v. Freemans Plc* [1987] 3 WLR 811 (CA), 822 (Nicholls LJ) with regard to the effect of s. 2(4) ECA 1972 on conforming interpretation. European methodological rules had not been expressed by the CJEU at the time when *Pickstone* was decided.

[219] Hansard, HL Deb 8 August 1972, vol 334, cols 1023–1024, European Communities Bill (Viscount Colville of Culross).

[220] See O. JONES and F.A.R. BENNION, *Bennion on Statutory Interpretation*, 6th ed., LexisNexis, London 2013, section 269 for the presumption that statutes are not designed to effect substantial change in the law casually or coincidentally.

[221] For discussion, see Chapter 3, Section 8.

as possible" remains within the bounds of conventional rules of construction: "[O]n the present rules of construction if there was really no way of assimilating the directly applicable law or the Community obligation, or whatever it might be, and the English Statute which had been subsequently passed, then I think that the courts under present rules would be bound to prefer the English Statute and to give effect to that".[222]

Lord Diplock also stayed within the realm of conventional canons of construction when he added in the parliamentary debates that

> [t]his clause [s. 2(4) ECA] is designed to ensure that the courts ... will recognise that it was the intention of Parliament not to conflict with the Community law. It is in those cases where there is an ambiguity – and there are many of those – that this is a rule of construction which is laid down and which the courts will observe. ...[223]

Lord Diplock suggested that the scope for finding ambiguity is rather wide when he added that it is difficult to think of any section in an Act of Parliament that is not ambiguous. Viscount Colville of Culross went on to explain that in a case of complete conflict between domestic law and Union obligations, "at present" English courts would give precedence to the domestic law. He continued:

> The only possibility – and this is something which has nothing to do with this Bill at all – is that rules of interpretation do change over time and the courts are capable of changing their own rules of interpretation. Therefore in many, many years' time I do not know that it would be necessarily true that precisely the same rules would apply.[224]

This last point summarises, it is submitted here, what happened in *Pickstone*: Lord Oliver independently, and not Parliament in 1972, initiated a change in the maxims of interpretation for the EU legal duty of conforming interpretation.

Why did he do that? Since none of the reasons given in the written opinion in *Pickstone* provide a fully convincing answer, some deeper analysis is warranted. The House of Lords decided *Pickstone* in June 1988. That decision preceded the CJEU's judgment in *Marleasing*[225] by more than two years. It is thus not possible to conclude that the House of Lords was swayed by the confusion that arose after *Marleasing* about whether EU law prescribes the methods of

---

[222] Hansard, HL Deb 8 August 1972, vol 334, col 1024, European Communities Bill (Viscount Colville of Culross).
[223] Ibid., col 1029 (Lord Diplock).
[224] Ibid., col 1025 (Viscount Colville of Culross).
[225] Case C-106/89, *Marleasing v. La Comercial Internacional de Alimentación*, ECLI:EU:C:1990:395.

conforming interpretation or whether national courts can still use national canons of construction. At the time when *Pickstone* was decided, the leading CJEU case on conforming interpretation was *von Colson*. The CJEU held in this case that a national court is obliged to interpret national implementing legislation in conformity with the directive "in so far as it is given discretion to do so under national law",[226] a limitation which Lord Oliver expressly mentioned in *Pickstone*. The issues that arose in *Pickstone* were also not referred to the CJEU. A CJEU judgment which could have nudged the House of Lords to find a conforming meaning is thus absent. The earlier judgment by the House of Lords on conforming interpretation in *Duke*, decided a few months before *Pickstone*, can be better described as a restrictive approach to the limits of conforming interpretation. The same restrictive approach can be seen in *Finnegan*,[227] which was decided almost two years after *Pickstone*. *Duke* concerned legislation that preceded the applicable directive. In *Finnegan*, the national legislation had been enacted after the directive, but the legislation was not adopted with the intention of implementing the directive according to the House of Lords.[228] Lord Oliver sat on the bench in all three cases, but he only derogated from conventional canons of interpretation in *Pickstone*, which concerned implementing legislation. A case may thus be made that the House of Lords, at least initially, adopted a special approach to conforming interpretation of implementing legislation.[229] This is not an unreasonable assumption as the leading CJEU cases at that time for conforming interpretation, *von Colson* and *Harz*, both concerned legislation specifically introduced to implement the applicable directive.[230] It was controversial after *von Colson* whether the duty of conforming interpretation applied only to implementing legislation or more generally.[231] It was only in *Marleasing*, another half a year after *Finnegan*, that the CJEU clarified that the duty of conforming interpretation applies to all provisions of national law, whether they were adopted before or after the directive.[232] A reason for the different treatment of implementing

---

[226] Case 14/83, *von Colson and Kamann v. Land Nordrhein-Westfalen*, ECLI:EU:C:1984:153, para. 26.
[227] *Finnegan v. Clowney Youth Training Programme Ltd.* [1990] 2 AC 407 (HL).
[228] Ibid., at 416 (Lord Bridge).
[229] DE BURCA, above n. 215, p. 234; S. DRAKE, Legislation and the role of the judiciary: the EU principle of consistent interpretation in UK courts, SLS 2016 Annual Conference, manuscript (on file with author) pp. 4–5; cf. *Finnegan v. Clowney Youth Training Programme Ltd.* [1990] 2 AC 407 (HL), 416 (Lord Bridge).
[230] Case 14/83, *von Colson and Kamann v. Land Nordrhein-Westfalen*, ECLI:EU:C:1984:153, paras. 4, 26, 28; Case 79/83, *Harz v. Deutsche Tradax*, ECLI:EU:C:1984:155, paras. 4, 26, 28. See also WYATT et al., above n. 59, p. 240.
[231] For discussion, see C. DOCKSEY and B. FITZPATRICK, The duty of national courts to interpret provisions of national law in accordance with Community law, (1991) 20 *Industrial Law Journal* 113, 118.
[232] Case C-106/89, *Marleasing v. La Comercial Internacional de Alimentación*, ECLI:EU:C:1990:395, para. 8.

legislation in *Pickstone* was most likely the circumstance that the enacting parliament intended to implement the directive in general. Yet this is not a sufficient explanation that justifies a departure from well-established canons of interpretation.

Could it be that Lord Oliver extended the courts' interpretative powers out of a motivation to dodge (a) the question of direct effect of art. 119 EEC (now art. 157 TFEU), the preferred solution of the Court of Appeal, and (b) ultimately the question of the relationship between the supremacy of EU law and the doctrine of parliamentary sovereignty?[233] The latter relationship was only clarified more than two years after *Pickstone* in *Factortame (No. 2)*.[234] Yet this viewpoint does not seem convincing either. The Court of Appeal had already decided in *Macarthys* in 1980 that the directly effective art. 119 EEC takes priority over inconsistent English law.[235] Lord Oliver indicated that he would have referred to the CJEU the question whether art. 119 EEC is directly enforceable in the circumstances of the instant case if it had not been possible to interpret the Equal Pay Act 1970 in compliance with the Equal Pay Directive.[236] Lord Templeman referred in his speech in *Pickstone* to *Defrenne v. Sabena*,[237] in which the CJEU had established the (horizontal) direct effect of art. 119 EEC.[238]

We are thus left with one final point of discussion. Lord Oliver's departure from conventional canons of construction may have been motivated by constitutional developments. It is submitted here that changes in the doctrine of parliamentary sovereignty provide a pointer and the most convincing explanation for why Lord Oliver felt able to extend the interpretative power of courts for conforming interpretation. This also shows that changes in constitutional settings can entail changes in the outer limits of statutory interpretation. Before we can assess the merits of the submission, we must first deal with the objection that the House of Lords construed the Equal Pay Regulations 1983 in *Pickstone*. The Equal Pay Regulations are delegated legislation. Parliamentary scrutiny of delegated legislation is less intensive than its scrutiny of primary legislation as Parliament can only accept or reject a statutory instrument, but cannot amend it.[239]

---

[233] See D. NICOL, *EC membership and the judicialization of British politics*, OUP, Oxford 2001, chapter 7 for the argument that before the House of Lords's decision in *Factortame (No. 2)* the courts avoided a showdown between parliamentary sovereignty and the supremacy of EU law.

[234] *R. (Factortame (No. 2)) v. Secretary of State for Transport* [1991] 1 AC 603 (HL), 658–659 (Lord Bridge).

[235] *Macarthys Ltd. v. Smith* [1981] QB 180 (CA), 200 (Lord Denning MR), 201 (Cumming-Bruce LJ).

[236] *Pickstone v. Freemans Plc* [1989] AC 66 (HL), 124 (Lord Oliver).

[237] Case 43/75, *Defrenne v. Sabena*, ECLI:EU:C:1976:56.

[238] *Pickstone v. Freemans Plc* [1989] AC 66 (HL), 115 (Lord Templeman).

[239] Ibid., para. 36. See also *R. (Public Law Project) v. Lord Chancellor* [2016] UKSC 39, para. 22 (Lord Neuberger, with whom all other members of the court agreed). Criticising the

The lawfulness of delegated legislation can be challenged in court, and a court will hold delegated legislation "to be invalid if it has an effect, or is made for a purpose, which is *ultra vires*, that is, outside the scope of the statutory power pursuant to which it was purportedly made".[240] If delegated legislation is *ultra vires*, a court upholds the supremacy of Parliament over the executive by declaring the delegated legislation invalid.[241] Delegated legislation does not enjoy legislative supremacy even if it is subject to the affirmative or negative resolution procedure.[242] Since delegated legislation does not "benefit" from the sovereignty of Parliament, changes in the latter doctrine may not affect the former's interpretation. Yet, multiple arguments point in the direction that Lord Oliver did not restrict his reasoning in *Pickstone* to the interpretation of delegated legislation but understood it as applying to the interpretation of all (implementing) legislation, including primary legislation. First, there are no indications in *Pickstone* that limit Lord Oliver's analysis of the courts' powers under conforming interpretation to delegated legislation. Second, English courts generally apply the same interpretative criteria and limits of interpretation for primary and delegated legislation. Third, Lord Oliver declared in *Litster* that *Pickstone* has established the approach to the construction of "primary and subordinate legislation" enacted to give effect to the UK's obligations under the EU Treaties.[243]

The orthodox doctrine of parliamentary sovereignty was the decisive reason why domestic courts adopted a narrow understanding of the scope of the judicial function when interpreting statutes. It will be shown in Section 7 below that the supremacy of EU law has modified the orthodox doctrine of parliamentary sovereignty in two ways: (a) it has modified the principle of implied repeal and (b) the second limb of the orthodox doctrine is qualified due to the English courts' power to disapply domestic legislation that is incompatible with directly effective EU law. Particularly the latter modification increases the constitutional powers of the judiciary vis-à-vis the legislature. It is not far-fetched to assume that the increase in judicial powers due to qualifications to the doctrine of parliamentary sovereignty may also widen what is possible as a

---

parliamentary scrutiny procedures of delegated legislation as unsatisfactory: Hansard Society, The devil is in the detail: Parliament and delegated legislation, Executive summary, 2014, pp. 5–7.

[240] R. (Public Law Project) v. Lord Chancellor [2016] UKSC 39, para. 22 (Lord Neuberger, with whom all other members of the court agreed).

[241] Ibid., para. 23 (Lord Neuberger, with whom all other members of the court agreed).

[242] F Hoffmann-La Roche & Co. v. Secretary of State for Trade and Industry [1975] AC 295 (HL), 365 (Lord Diplock); R. (Public Law Project) v. Lord Chancellor [2016] UKSC 39, paras. 21–23 (Lord Neuberger, with whom all other members of the court agreed); BRADLEY, EWING and KNIGHT, above n. 206, p. 50.

[243] Litster v. Forth Dry Dock & Engineering Co Ltd. [1990] 1 AC 546 (HL), 559 (Lord Oliver).

matter of interpretation when judges construe national legislation in conformity with EU law. To take the matter further: wide limits of interpretation seem prima facie less intrusive into the doctrine of parliamentary sovereignty and the intention of the enacting parliament than a disapplication of a statutory provision. Since a national court has the power to disapply non-conforming legislation, ensuring the application of ordinary legislation through a powerful application of the EU legal duty of conforming interpretation respects and shows deference to the legislature's authority. There is a parallel here to how the BVerfG has justified its broad interpretative powers for rights-consistent interpretation with the notions of respect for the ordinary legislature and judicial restraint. Even though this line of reasoning applies with regard to directives where a provision in a directive is directly effective, it does not apply in disputes between private individuals. Incompatible national legislation remains applicable and does not have to be disapplied in such horizontal cases. This distinction between directly effective and not directly effective EU law and its impact on the limits of conforming interpretation was made by Lord Templeman in *Duke*.[244] Even though *Pickstone* and *Litster* concerned horizontal disputes, Lord Oliver did not rely on Lord Templeman's distinction. Contemporary English courts apply the same wide limits and techniques of conforming interpretation for vertical and horizontal cases.[245] Yet, the qualification of the second limb of the doctrine of parliamentary sovereignty cannot justify this parallel between vertical and horizontal cases.[246] This remains a blind spot in the case law.

A further argument militates in favour of the view that the change in default position for conforming judicial law-making in England may have been motivated by modifications in the doctrine of parliamentary sovereignty due to the supremacy of EU law. The wider interpretative powers available to judges under conforming judicial law-making have not yet spilled over to the interpretation of legislation in a purely national context according to conventional canons of interpretation. That is because the modifications in the orthodox doctrine of parliamentary sovereignty due to the supremacy of EU law do not apply outside the scope of EU law.

The preceding constitutional reasons aimed to shed some light on Lord Oliver's motivation to depart from conventional canons of construction. These reasons can be reconciled with the argumentation further above that the Parliament of 1972 did not intend to empower judges to deviate

---

[244] *Duke v. Reliance Ltd.* [1988] AC 618 (HL), 639–640 (Lord Templeman).
[245] See Section 7.3 below.
[246] For the argument that courts should apply the outer limits of conforming interpretation in a narrower fashion in horizontal scenarios and a wider fashion in vertical scenarios, see Section 7.3 below.

from well-established canons of construction. The conventional canons of interpretation are the product of the common law. They are judge-made law. The courts are capable of changing these interpretative maxims as long as they stay within the framework set by the constitutional legal order. The Parliament of 1972 did not take away from the courts the power to decide about the appropriate interpretative tools for conforming interpretation. The framework set by constitutional law refers to the doctrine of parliamentary sovereignty. What is important to realise is that Lord Oliver's reasoning in *Pickstone* is, in contrast to the reasoning of the House of Lords in *Ghaidan*, reconcilable with an orthodox understanding of how the powers of interpreting and amending legislation are distributed between the courts and the legislature. Lord Oliver did not diverge from the intention of the enacting law-maker in *Pickstone*. Nor does it follow from his departure from a number of well-established rules of construction that he intended to empower courts to deviate from the enacting legislature's intent. The House of Lords in *Pickstone* argued that the Equal Pay Regulations were intended to *fully* comply with the Equal Pay Directive. I have demonstrated in Chapter 2 that the orthodox doctrine of parliamentary sovereignty can support a system of interpretation according to which judicial law-making is generally permissible in order to give effect to the intention of the enacting legislature. Adopting such a system for conforming interpretation entails a deviation from a number of well-established conventional rules of construction. That may be what Lord Oliver had in mind in *Pickstone*. The significant modification of conventional interpretative techniques by Lord Oliver amounted to a (common law) evolution of statutory interpretation. This evolution is consistent with constitutional doctrine and reconcilable with the vague statutory word "construed" in s. 2(4) ECA. In the light of the changes in the doctrine of parliamentary sovereignty, Lord Oliver redefined the constitutional role of the judiciary vis-à-vis the legislature in the field of statutory interpretation.

To conclude, *Pickstone* and *Litster* have established that a court can exceed the outer limits of conventional canons of statutory interpretation for the EU legal duty of conforming interpretation. The House of Lords did not elaborate in *Pickstone* or in *Litster* on how much further a court can go. Neither judgment clarifies the question of what outer limits apply for conforming interpretation. This situation did not change much in the following decade. Lord Clyde said in *Clarke v. Kato* in 1998 that conforming interpretation "should not exceed the limits of what is reasonable".[247] He did not elaborate any further on what he considered reasonable. *Pickstone* and *Litster* certainly do not suggest that interpreting national legislation by adding words to the

---

[247] *Clarke v. Kato* [1998] 1 WLR 1647 (HL), 1656 (Lord Clyde).

statutory language is only feasible under limited circumstances similar to those under conventional canons of statutory construction. A cautiousness to avoid an over-purposive construction or to remain, as far as possible, loyal to the language chosen by the legislature cannot be detected. This is another argument that advocates for the view that Lord Oliver modified the default position for conforming judicial law-making to the effect that it is generally possible for a court to read additional words into the statutory language under the guise of purposive construction if this is necessary to fulfil the legislation's purpose of giving effect to the provisions of a directive.

3.2.3. Comparative Analysis

Judges in England and Germany have recognised that the EU legal duty of conforming interpretation obliges them to engage in conforming judicial law-making if this is necessary to achieve the result sought by the directive. Whereas the BVerfG has clarified that the outer limits and techniques of conforming judicial law-making equal and may not exceed those of judicial law-making in a purely national context, the situation is different in England. The House of Lords has established that domestic courts can depart from and surpass the limits and techniques of conventional judicial law-making for the EU legal duty of conforming interpretation. Whereas the BVerfG has rejected a "Europeanisation from the inside" for German law, Lord Oliver's speech in *Pickstone* had the effect of establishing it for English law. This difference between both jurisdictions cannot simply be explained by asserting that the outer limits of permissible statutory interpretation in England are more flexible due to the absence of a codified constitution. The outer limits of permissible judicial law-making are not clearly set by art. 20(3) GG and leave sufficient room for multiple possible interpretations of the extent of judicial law-making powers.[248] Furthermore, what is interesting from a comparative viewpoint is that the BVerfG could have followed a similar route to the one taken by Lord Oliver in *Pickstone* and could have widened a court's interpretative powers under the EU legal duty of conforming interpretation. It has been argued in German legal scholarship that (a) art. 23(1) GG serves as the legal basis for the (national) legal duty of conforming interpretation[249] and that (b) this provision has the effect of extending the judicial function in a European context beyond conventional

---

[248] See Chapter 3, Section 3 above.
[249] It is not uncommon that scholars or courts in the Member States assert that national constitutional law includes and thus functions as a legal base for a national constitutional obligation to interpret all national law consistently with EU law. For England, see the discussion above (Section 2) of Lady Justice Arden's opinion in *Revenue and Customs Commissioners v. IDT Card Services Ireland Ltd.* [2006] EWCA Civ 29 and Fitzpatrick, above n. 121, pp. 347–348. For Greece, see P. Kapotas. Case note on Greek Council of State, Judgment 3470/2011, (2014) 10 *European Constitutional Law Review* 162, 170–171.

national legal methods.[250] In contrast to the BGH in two earlier decisions,[251] however, the BVerfG did not engage with this scholarly viewpoint at all in its 2011 judgment.

The different approaches to extending judges' interpretative powers beyond those available under conventional canons of interpretation must be seen in the light that the default positions for judicial law-making differ considerably in England and Germany.[252] In contrast to conventional English methods, judicial law-making in Germany is generally a permissible judicial activity and is not limited to certain exceptions. The outer limits of judicial law-making in Germany are expressed in vague terms and can accommodate extensive judicial powers to extend or narrow the scope of application of a provision. Adopting these limits for conforming judicial law-making provides judges with sufficient leeway to align national legislation with the result sought by the directive, particularly if implementing legislation is under consideration. Judged from a European point of view, an alleged need or pressure to extend these limits in order to increase the effectiveness of directives is less prominent in Germany than it was in England. Judged from a national constitutional viewpoint, it was argued that the "Europeanisation from the inside" in Lord Oliver's reasoning in *Pickstone* may have been motivated by modifications in the orthodox doctrine of parliamentary sovereignty due to the supremacy of EU law. The doctrine of parliamentary sovereignty is the constitutional origin of the narrow approach to judicial law-making under conventional canons of interpretation in English judicial practice. An equivalent doctrine does not exist in German constitutional law.

---

[250] C. HERRESTHAL argues that the legal basis of the duty to interpret national law in conformity with EU directives is (also) enshrined in German law, i.e. art. 23(1) first sentence GG (this view is also shared by: H.D. JARASS and S. BELJIN, Unmittelbare Anwendung des EG-Rechts und EG-rechtskonforme Auslegung, *JZ* 2003, 768, 774; ROTH and JOPEN, above n. 49, §13, para. 39; WEBER, above n. 78, p. 120). That provision lays down a binding structure for Germany's participation in the development of the European Union. According to art. 23(1) second sentence GG, sovereign powers may only be transferred to the EU by a law and with the approval of the Bundesrat. C. HERRESTHAL then asserts that art. 23(1) GG incorporates a modification of the separation of powers between the national legislature and judiciary in the European legal context and, therefore, mandates a "Europeanisation" of the EU legal duty of conforming interpretation by virtue of German law ("from the inside"). He claims that the outer methodological limits of permissible conforming interpretation surpass those limits that judges apply when they interpret national law in a purely domestic context. See in detail HERRESTHAL, above n. 66, §5 and §6. For a convincing criticism of Herrestahl's view, see BALDAUF, above n. 3, pp. 222–225; SCHÜRNBRAND, above n. 73, p. 917; M. WEBER, above n. 78, pp. 107–122.

[251] BGH, *NJW* 2009, 427, para. 29 – *Quelle II*; BGH, *NJW* 2012, 1073, para. 45 – *Weber II*.

[252] The courts' powers to engage in judicial law-making under conventional canons of construction were more limited at the time when *Pickstone* was decided in the House of Lords compared to nowadays.

3.3. ANALOGY TO RIGHTS-CONSISTENT INTERPRETATION

It will be established in this subsection that English and German courts have objectively and in the abstract drawn an analogy between the EU legal duty of conforming interpretation and rights-consistent interpretation. In other words, the courts have established equivalence between conforming interpretation and rights-consistent interpretation. The CJEU has not specified in its case law on conforming interpretation how equivalence ought to be determined. What is helpful is the case law of the CJEU on the principle of equivalence in the context of national procedures and remedies for the enforcement of European rights. The principle of equivalence demands in this context that these procedures and remedies "cannot be less favourable than those relating to similar actions of a domestic nature".[253] In order to establish the necessary degree of similarity, national courts must consider "objectively, in the abstract" "whether the actions concerned are similar as regards their purpose, cause of action and essential characteristics".[254] It is not the CJEU that establishes equivalence but national courts as they alone have "direct knowledge of the procedural rules governing actions in the field of domestic law".[255] Likewise, national courts alone have direct knowledge of the rules of legal methodology governing the interpretation of provisions in the field of domestic law.

3.3.1. Constitution-Consistent Interpretation in Germany

The German Federal Labour Court has declared in a number of judgments that the same interpretative limits apply to conforming statutory interpretation and constitution-consistent interpretation.[256] The BAG did not explicitly refer to the principle of equivalence in order to establish this analogy, and it did not explain why such a parallel exists. The BAG has not yet drawn an analogy between conforming interpretation and constitution-consistent interpretation. The BVerfG seems to endorse the analogy implicitly. In its 2011 ruling on the constitutional limits of conforming interpretation, the BVerfG described the outer limits of conforming judicial law-making and referred to its case law on constitution-consistent judicial law-making.[257] The analogy is endorsed in

---

[253] Case 33/76, *Rewe-Zentralfinanz eG and Rewe-Zentral AG v. Landwirtschaftskammer für das Saarland*, ECLI:EU:C:1976:188, para. 5.
[254] Case C-79/98, *Preston v. Wolverhampton Healthcare NHS Trust*, ECLI:EU:C:2000:247, paras. 57, 63; Case C-63/08, *Pontin v. T-Comalux*, ECLI:EU:C:2009:666, paras. 45, 46.
[255] Case C-78/98, *Preston v. Wolverhampton Healthcare NHS Trust*, ECLI:EU:C:2000:247, para. 49; Case C-63/08, *Pontin v. T-Comalux*, ECLI:EU:C:2009:666, paras. 45, 49.
[256] BAG, *NZA* 2003, 742, 747; BAG, *NZA* 2006, 862, para. 43; BAG, *EuZW* 2009, 465, para. 65 – Schultz-Hoff.
[257] BVerfG, *NJW* 2012, 669 paras. 55–57.

German legal scholarship,[258] but has not remained without criticism.[259] From a European perspective, it is for national courts to declare objectively and in the abstract that such an analogy exists. That is what the BAG has done and what the BVerfG has alluded to. An argument can thus be made that German courts have established equivalence between the EU legal duty of conforming interpretation and the doctrine of constitution-consistent interpretation. It follows that a national court that construes legislation in conformity with directives must not fall short of the outer interpretative limits and techniques available under constitution-consistent interpretation. The European principle of equivalence does not stop a German court from going beyond the outer limits of constitution-consistent interpretation for conforming interpretation. Yet it follows from the analogy between both interpretative doctrines as established by German courts that conforming interpretation cannot exceed the outer limits of constitution-consistent interpretation without breaching the analogy.

It has been argued in legal scholarship that conforming interpretation and constitution-consistent interpretation exhibit an essential difference since the former serves to enforce a legal provision (*Normdurchsetzung*), whereas the latter serves to preserve a legal provision (*Normerhaltung*).[260] A national provision that cannot be interpreted in conformity with a directive and thus infringes the latter remains applicable in proceedings between private parties, whereas a national provision that cannot be interpreted in conformity with the German Basic Law is invalidated by the BVerfG. This difference between both interpretative obligations is significant for horizontal scenarios as directives do not possess horizontal direct effect. In a vertical scenario, however, when an individual relies on an unconditional and sufficiently precise provision in a directive against the state, a national provision that infringes the requirements of the directive has to be disapplied.[261] Even though disapplication does not touch on the validity of the national law, its effect in an individual case is similar to invalidation insofar as the national legislation under consideration is not applied in either case. The difference in function between both interpretative obligations thus seems negligible in vertical scenarios.

---

[258] C.-W. CANARIS, Gemeinsamkeiten zwischen verfassungs- und richtlinienkonformer Rechtsfindung, in H. BAUER et al. (eds.), *Festschrift für Reiner Schmidt*, C.H. Beck, Munich 2006, pp. 41, 58; HERDEGEN, above n. 82, p. 1928; Y. SCHNORBUS, Die richtlinienkonforme Rechtsfortbildung im nationalen Privatrecht, (2001) 201 *AcP* 860, 884–886.

[259] HÖPFNER, above n. 65, p. 99.

[260] CANARIS, above n. 258, p. 44. See MÜLLER and CHRISTENSEN, above n. 18, pp. 162–165 for a discussion of various differences between conforming interpretation and constitution-consistent interpretation.

[261] Case C-429/09, *Fuß v. Stadt Halle*, ECLI:EU:C:2010:717, paras. 35, 40; Case C-61/11 PPU, *Hassen El Dridi*, ECLI:EU:C:2011:268, paras. 46, 61.

Yet, the difference persists if a Member State intends to rely on a provision of a directive against an individual. The direct effect of a directive cannot be pleaded against an individual,[262] even if the national legislation cannot be interpreted in conformity with the directive. The incompatible national legislation continues to apply. Regardless of this distinction between horizontal and vertical scenarios, German courts apply the same outer limits of conforming interpretation for both horizontal and vertical cases.

Despite these differences between conforming interpretation and constitution-consistent interpretation, both doctrines are characterised by an interpretative priority rule and a presumption of compliance. We have also seen that (a) both doctrines are directed at identifying a possible meaning that complies with a standard external to the provision under consideration and (b) the relationship between each of the two interpretative obligations and conventional methods of construction is similar. Structurally, constitution-consistent interpretation has more in common with conforming interpretation than with conventional canons of interpretation. Constitution-consistent interpretation is the closest comparator to conforming interpretation in German legal methodology, both for horizontal and vertical scenarios, despite any remaining differences.

3.3.2. Section 3(1) Human Rights Act in England

The first English judgment addressing the relationship between conforming interpretation and s. 3(1) HRA was *Ghaidan*. Lord Steyn highlighted that s. 3(1) HRA was modelled on the EU legal duty of conforming interpretation.[263] He concluded that the strength of the interpretative obligation under EU law can serve as a signpost to the meaning of s. 3(1) HRA. Lord Rodger agreed with that assessment and also concurred with Lord Steyn that *Pickstone* and *Litster* reinforce the approach taken by the House of Lords in interpreting s. 3(1) HRA, which eschews linguistic arguments in favour of a broad purposive approach.[264] These signs of a close analogy between conforming interpretation and Convention-compatible interpretation were picked up by Lady Justice Arden in *IDT Card Services*. The case concerned the conforming interpretation of provisions in the Value Added Tax Act 1994. When Lady Justice Arden considered the outer limits of the EU legal duty of conforming interpretation, she drew guidance from the House of Lords' decision in *Ghaidan*.

---

[262] Case 152/84, *Marshall v. Southampton and South-West Hampshire Area Health Authority*, ECLI:EU:C:1986:84, para. 48; Case C-91/92, *Faccini Dori v. Recreb Srl*, ECLI:EU:C:1994:292, para. 20.
[263] *Ghaidan v. Godin-Mendoza* [2004] UKHL 30, paras. 45, 46 (Lord Steyn).
[264] Ibid., para. 48 (Lord Steyn), paras. 118, 121 (Lord Rodger).

Her Ladyship regarded *Ghaidan* as "authority as to what is 'possible' as a matter of statutory interpretation" for conforming interpretation.[265] She opined that the guidance given by the House of Lords in that case regarding the interpretative limits and techniques can also in general equally apply when the limits and techniques of interpretation under the *Marleasing* principle arise for consideration.[266] Latham and Pill LJJ agreed with Arden LJ's reasoning.[267]

The analogy between both interpretative obligations was consolidated in *Vodafone 2*[268] and has received widespread judicial support since.[269] In *British Gas Trading Ltd. v. Lock*, Sir Colin Rimer said that the principles applicable to s. 3(1) HRA and to the EU legal duty of conforming interpretation "are the same".[270] The consequence of the analogy is that English courts have established equivalence between both interpretative duties. It follows that English judges would infringe their obligations under the EU legal duty of conforming interpretation if they fell short of applying the outer limits and techniques for conforming interpretation that they use for Convention-compatible interpretation.[271] The claim that "[n]othing in EU law ... requires national courts to depart from the ordinary canons of statutory interpretation"[272] is therefore wrong. Since the coming into force of the Human Rights Act 1998 and in particular after *Ghaidan*, the "Europeanisation from the inside" established by Lord Oliver in *Pickstone* has ceased to exist. When an English court interprets legislation in accordance with a directive and follows the analogy to s. 3(1) HRA,

---

[265] *Revenue and Customs Commissioners v. IDT Card Services Ireland Ltd.* [2006] EWCA Civ 29, para. 85 (Arden LJ).
[266] Ibid., paras. 85, 92 (Arden LJ).
[267] Ibid., para. 119 (Latham LJ), para. 141 (Pill LJ).
[268] *Vodafone 2 v. Revenue and Customs Commissioners* [2009] EWCA Civ 446, paras. 37–38, 44, 57 (Sir Andrew Morritt C), paras. 68–69 (Longmore LJ).
[269] *Dabas v. High Court of Justice in Madrid* [2007] UKHL 6, para. 76 (Lord Brown); *R. (Hurst) v. Commissioner of Police of the Metropolis* [2007] UKHL 13, para. 52 (Lord Brown); *Assange v. Swedish Prosecution Authority* [2012] UKSC 22, para. 203 (Lord Mance); *Robertson v. Swift* [2014] UKSC 50, para. 21 (Lord Kerr); *Digital Satellite Warranty Cover Ltd. v. The Financial Services Authority* [2011] EWCA Civ 1413, para. 42 (Patten LJ); *Churchill Insurance Co. Ltd. v. Fitzgerald & Wilkinson* [2012] EWCA Civ 1166, para. 49 (Aikens LJ, with whom Etherton and Maurice Kay LJJ agreed); *Google Inc. v. Vidal-Hall* [2015] EWCA Civ 311, para. 88 (Lord Dyson MR and Sharp LJ, with whom McFarlane LJ agreed); *British Gas Trading Ltd. v. Lock* [2016] EWCA Civ 983, para. 32 (Sir Colin Rimer, with whom Gloster LJ and Sir Terence Etherton MR agreed). See also MANCE, above n. 97, p. 449; SALES, above n. 124, p. 608.
[270] *British Gas Trading Ltd. v. Lock* [2016] EWCA Civ 983, para. 32 (Sir Colin Rimer, with whom Gloster LJ and Sir Terence Etherton MR agreed).
[271] For a different view, see K. SAWYER, The principle of "interpretation conforme": how far can or should national courts go when interpreting national legislation consistently with European Community law?, (2007) 28 *Statute Law Review* 165, 181.
[272] HERVEY and SHELDON, above n. 8, p. 371.

the court does not go beyond the interpretive requirements set up by the CJEU for the EU legal duty of conforming interpretation. It also follows from the analogy to s. 3(1) HRA that conforming interpretation cannot exceed the outer limits of Convention-compatible interpretation without breaching the analogy.

Arden LJ claimed in *IDT Card Services* that "the differences in concept between s 3 [HRA] interpretation and interpretation under the *Marleasing* principle are more apparent than real".[273] This claim is debatable. The ECHR contains no principle of direct effect or supremacy.[274] Convention rights can be overridden by national legislation.[275] Incompatible legislation must be applied as it stands by the courts, and they may make a declaration of incompatibility. This position is reinforced by s. 2(1) HRA, which does not bind courts to follow decisions of the ECtHR,[276] but obliges them to take the latter into account. These features of the ECHR and the HRA stand in contrast to legislation that infringes directly effective EU law as this legislation has to be disapplied by English courts. I have argued in section 3.2.2 above that the inroad created by the supremacy of EU law into the second limb of the doctrine of parliamentary sovereignty contributes to a widening of the outer limits of conforming interpretation. An equivalent argument cannot be made for s. 3(1) HRA. This is why Lord Rodger was arguably mistaken when he said in *Ghaidan* that Parliament, when enacting s. 3(1) HRA, referred "at the least" to the wide interpretative powers available to the courts under the EU principle of conforming interpretation. Neither s. 3(1) HRA nor s. 4 HRA creates an inroad into the second limb of the doctrine of parliamentary sovereignty. Therefore, it seems more convincing to argue that Parliament referred "at the most" to the wide interpretative powers under conforming interpretation when enacting s. 3(1) HRA. It follows from that reasoning that different outer limits of interpretation could apply to both interpretative doctrines. Yet, the distinction drawn here is only justified for vertical and not for horizontal scenarios as EU law does not oblige national courts to disapply national legislation that infringes the requirements of a directive in horizontal situations. As we have already discovered, however, English courts do not differentiate between vertical and horizontal scenarios when setting the outer limits of conforming interpretation.

---

[273] Ibid., para. 92 (Arden LJ).
[274] For a discussion of national case law that extends the EU principles of direct effect and supremacy to the ECHR, see MARTINICO, above n. 68, pp. 401–424. The author notices a trend of approximation in how national judges treat EU law and the ECHR, but such approximation is not uniform across the Member States.
[275] *R. (Simms) v. Secretary of State for the Home Department* [2000] 2 AC 115 (HL), 131 (Lord Hoffmann).
[276] *R. v. Horncastle* [2009] UKSC 14, para. 11 (Lord Phillips); *Manchester City Council v. Pinnock* [2010] UKSC 45, para. 48 (Lord Neuberger).

Despite these differences between conforming interpretation and s. 3(1) HRA, both doctrines are characterised by an interpretative priority rule and a presumption of compliance. The function of s. 3(1) HRA to effectively bring rights home is comparable to the remedial function of the doctrine of conforming interpretation. The application of s. 3(1) HRA involves a two-step approach, which is very similar to the two-step approach that English courts operate under conforming interpretation. Judicial law-making is a permissible judicial activity in general in the sphere of conforming interpretation and s. 3(1) HRA; it is not limited to certain exceptions. Both interpretative obligations are not directed at discerning the true meaning of the provision, but at identifying an interpretation that complies with a standard external to the provision at issue. The terms of both interpretative duties "are in substance the same" according to Sir Andrew Morritt in *Vodafone 2*.[277] For these reasons, s. 3(1) HRA has more in common with conforming interpretation than with conventional canons of construction. Convention-compatible interpretation is therefore the closest comparator to conforming interpretation in English legal methodology.

Moreover, Lord Steyn traced the origin of s. 3(1) HRA to the EU duty of conforming interpretation in *Ghaidan*. This is a strong argument in favour of the analogy. A paradox remains, however. It follows from the origin of Convention-compatible interpretation under s. 3(1) HRA that its limits should also be drawn along the lines of those contained in the duty of conforming interpretation. This is a convincing argument from the perspective of s. 3(1) HRA. From the perspective of EU law and in particular the principle of equivalence, however, the argument is circular. If equivalence between s. 3(1) HRA and conforming interpretation is assumed, the interpretative limits of s. 3(1) HRA should apply to conforming interpretation – not the other way around. Pre-*Ghaidan* English case law on the EU legal duty of conforming interpretation, particularly *Pickstone* and *Litster*, hardly established abstract outer limits for conforming interpretation. The House of Lords solved the paradox in *Ghaidan* by going beyond existing English case law on conforming interpretation when stipulating the outer interpretative limits for s. 3(1) HRA.

3.3.3. Comparative Analysis

Courts in both countries have drawn an analogy between conforming interpretation and rights-consistent interpretation.[278] Rights-consistent

---

[277] *Vodafone 2 v. Revenue and Customs Commissioners* [2009] EWCA Civ 446, para. 41 (Sir Andrew Morritt C).
[278] Rights-consistent interpretation is a significant subgroup of constitution-consistent interpretation in Germany.

interpretation is the closest comparator to conforming interpretation in both jurisdictions. It follows from this analogy that the outer limits and techniques that apply to s. 3(1) HRA in England and constitution-consistent interpretation in Germany ought to apply to conforming interpretation in both jurisdictions. Furthermore, English and German judges would infringe their obligations under the EU legal duty of conforming interpretation if they fell short of using the outer limits and techniques for conforming interpretation that they apply for rights-consistent interpretation. I have also argued that the analogy between conforming and rights-consistent interpretation is more compelling for horizontal than for vertical scenarios in England. In Germany, however, the analogy between conforming and rights-consistent interpretation appears more compelling for vertical than for horizontal scenarios. This difference can be traced back to different powers of the courts in both legal orders. Whereas the BVerfG possesses the power to invalidate legislation that infringes rights protected under the German Basic Law, no English court possesses the power to invalidate or disapply a statutory provision that infringes rights protected under the Human Rights Act. Either way, English and German courts do not differentiate between horizontal and vertical scenarios when they set the outer limits for conforming interpretation. One reason for this may be that such a distinction would make the law very complex. A second reason may be that it is difficult to see how this distinction can be "translated" into different outer limits of interpretation.

Whereas the analogy plays a significant role in English judgments, reliance on the analogy in German judgments is far less prominent. The reason for this difference is that the outer limits and techniques of constitution-consistent judicial law-making equal those of conventional judicial law-making according to the case law of the BVerfG. The BVerfG has held that the outer limits and techniques of conforming interpretation must not fall short of and at the same time must not exceed those of judicial law-making in a purely domestic context in Germany. It follows that the perceived need to draw a parallel to constitution-consistent interpretation in order to show that conforming interpretation does not surpass the limits of the judicial role as recognised in the national sphere is relatively low. This is different in England, where *Pickstone* established that conforming interpretation can exceed conventional limits of statutory interpretation. After *Pickstone* and pre-*Ghaidan*, the outer limits and techniques of conforming interpretation were mostly left in the dark. It was clear that *Pickstone* had established that a court can exceed the outer limits of conventional canons of statutory interpretation for the EU legal duty of conforming interpretation, but it was less clear to what extent that is possible. This development was not required by European law. Furthermore, neither the wording nor the legislative history of s. 2(4) ECA provide a clear expression of Parliament's will to empower the judiciary to extend their interpretative powers beyond those available to the courts under conventional canons of construction. The analogy with s. 3(1) HRA thus added legitimacy to the courts' wide interpretative powers under conforming judicial law-making. With s. 3(1) HRA in force, the "Europeanisation from the inside" established by Lord Oliver in *Pickstone* ceased to exist.

4. INTERPRETATIVE PRIORITY IN NATIONAL COURTS

The next two sections will examine two characteristics of conforming interpretation as applied in English and German courts: the interpretative priority rule and the presumption of compliance. It is recognised in German case law that if a provision is capable of bearing more than one meaning, the meaning that is consistent with a directive must be favoured over all other possible but non-conforming meanings.[279] The conforming meaning has interpretative priority. The BVerfG refers to art. 4(3) TEU as the legal basis for this priority rule.[280] The BAG does not derive this interpretative rule from EU law in its jurisprudence but refers to national legal methods as its legal basis by asserting an analogy to constitution-consistent interpretation.[281] Some scholars derive a (national) interpretative priority rule for conforming interpretation directly from art. 23(1) GG.[282] These explanations can coexist from the point of view of EU law, as the relationship between national legal methods and European methodological rules shows.

Similarly, it is recognised in English case law that if a provision can be given a certain meaning that complies with an applicable directive, the national court is obliged to apply that meaning.[283] As in Germany, the conforming meaning has interpretative priority. It prevails over all other possible but non-conforming interpretative results of a provision.[284] English courts have not yet explicitly relied on an EU legal base like art. 4(3) TEU as the legal origin for this interpretative priority rule. Due to the analogy between the EU legal duty of conforming interpretation and s. 3(1) HRA, a "twin" exists for the EU interpretative priority rule under English law. The national explanation for

---

[279] BAG, *NZA* 2003, 742, 747; BAG, *NZA* 2006, 862 paras. 36, 43; BVerwG, judgment of 29.1.2004, case number: 3 C 39.03, para. 31, available online at http://www.juris.de. See also BVerwG, *NVwZ* 2002, 858, 861.
[280] BVerfG, *NJW* 2012, 669, para. 46; BVerfG, *BeckRS* 2017, 136546, para. 37.
[281] BAG, *NZA* 2003, 742, 747; BAG, *NZA* 2006, 862, para. 43.
[282] U. EHRICKE, Die richtlinienkonforme und die gemeinschaftsrechtskonforme Auslegung nationalen Rechts, (1995) 59 *RabelsZ* 598, 616; ROTH and JOPEN, above n. 49, §13, paras. 42–45.
[283] *Alderson v. Secretary of State for Trade and Industry* [2003] EWCA Civ 1767, para. 27 (Lord Phillips MR).
[284] The priority rule is often only implicit in the reasoning of English courts.

the priority rule, which is based on this analogy, can coexist with the European methodological rule, and a national judge can rely on either rule.

It was argued in Chapter 3 that an interpretative priority rule creates legal certainty. Since the interpretative priority of the conforming meaning is prescribed by an EU methodological rule, we can also see that the hybridity of conforming interpretation does not necessarily lead to legal uncertainty.[285]

5. PRESUMPTION OF COMPLIANCE IN NATIONAL COURTS

5.1. THE PRESUMPTION RULE IN GERMAN COURTS

Another methodological characteristic of conforming interpretation that requires further investigation is the presumption of compliance. Its strength and limits as applied in English and German courts will be analysed in this section. The BGH and the BAG presume that the national legislature intended to fully comply with the requirements of the directive when they interpret implementing legislation.[286] This presumption derives from art. 288(3) TFEU according to the BAG.[287] The BVerfG has also recognised that a national court can, in case of doubt, presume that the national legislature did not intend to infringe its European duty enshrined in art. 288(3) TFEU, but the BVerfG has not yet clarified the presumption's legal basis.[288]

The highest German courts have not yet established the presumption of compliance for the EU legal duty of conforming interpretation by means of an analogy to the doctrine of constitution-consistent interpretation. The presumption of compliance for constitution-consistent interpretation applies in all cases where the challenged legislation post-dates the German Basic Law. It is reasonable to assume in these cases that the ordinary legislature intends that its legislation persists under the rule of the German Basic Law. If the analogy between constitution-consistent and conforming interpretation were applied to the presumption of compliance, the national presumption of compliance for conforming interpretation would go beyond the scope of application of the

---

[285] For the argument that a hybrid conception of conforming interpretation leads to legal uncertainty, see D. CHALMERS, G. DAVIES and G. MONTI, *European Union Law*, 3rd ed., CUP, Cambridge 2014, p. 320.
[286] BGH, *NJW* 1975, 213, 214; BGH, *NJW* 2009, 427, para. 25 – *Quelle II*; BGH, *NJW* 2012, 1073 para. 34 – *Weber II*; BGH, *NJW* 2017, 1093, paras. 45, 51; cf. BAG, *EuZW* 2009, 465, para. 58 – *Schultz-Hoff*.
[287] BAG, *EuZW* 2009, 465, para. 58 – *Schultz-Hoff*.
[288] BVerfG, *NJW* 2012, 669, para. 51; BVerfG, *NJW-RR* 2016, 1366, para. 44.

EU presumption of compliance. That is because such a national presumption would apply in all cases in which the challenged legislation post-dates the applicable directive[289] even if there are no discernible indications that the legislature intended to comply with the requirements of the directive.[290] The CJEU has so far only relied on the EU presumption of compliance in cases where there is an indication that the legislature intended to comply with the requirements of the directive with regard to the legislation under consideration.[291] Even though the scope of application of the national presumption of compliance would extend beyond the scope of application of the EU methodological rule, this extension would not be a "Europeanisation from the inside" as it would be required by the EU principle of equivalence. Furthermore, the analogy to constitution-consistent interpretation does not demand a national presumption of compliance for legislation that precedes an applicable directive. Yet, in analogy to constitution-consistent interpretation of legislation that precedes the German Basic Law, a court ought to take the directive into account when determining the (objectivised) sense and purpose of the legislation. If one applied the analogy, the directive could affect the (objectivised) purpose of the legislation and could influence how a judge arrives at possible meanings of a provision even if the legislation pre-dates the directive. This also goes beyond the current scope of the EU presumption of compliance.

A case that illustrates the strong operation of the presumption of compliance in German courts is the BGH's decision in *Lebensversicherung II* in 2014. The case concerned the conforming interpretation of s. 5a of the German Law on Insurance Contracts (*Versicherungsvertragsgesetz*, VVG[292]). Section 5a(1) VVG granted a policy holder a right to object within 14 days of receiving the contractual insurance documents. The right to object expired in any case one year after payment of the first premium even if the policy holder had

---

[289] The argument from equivalence does not lead to the conclusion that the presumption ought to apply in all cases where the challenged legislation post-dates the German legislation bringing the Treaties into force in Germany (as opposed to post-dating the applicable directive). If this were the case, the presumption would apply to cases in which the enacting national legislature could not possibly have foreseen a future directive. The equivalent scenario for constitution-consistent interpretation would refer to the interpretation of legislation that precedes the German Basic Law as the enacting legislature could not have foreseen the future German Basic Law. Yet, the presumption of compliance for constitution-consistent interpretation does not apply in this latter case. For legislation that was enacted after the coming into force of the German Basic Law, however, the enacting legislature was aware of the provisions of the German Basic Law.

[290] For a different view and for general criticism of a (national) presumption of compliance for conforming interpretation, see HERDEGEN, above n. 82, p. 1929; C. HERRESTHAL, Die richtlinienkonforme und die verfassungskonforme Auslegung im Privatrecht, *JuS* 2014, 289, 293.

[291] See Section 1.4.2 above.

[292] Section 5a(1) VVG was repealed with effect from 1.1.2008, but the old version was applicable to the facts of the case in the main proceedings.

never been informed about the right to object (s. 5a(2) sentence 4 VVG). On a reference from the BGH, the CJEU ruled that s. 5a(2) sentence 4 VVG is precluded by the second and third Life Assurance Directives (Directive 90/619/EEC and Directive 92/96/EEC).²⁹³ On return of the case, the BGH stipulated that s. 5a(2) sentence 4 VVG cannot be construed in conformity with EU law by using interpretation in a narrow sense due to the provision's unambiguous wording. The court then engaged in judicial law-making by means of teleological reduction.²⁹⁴

The BGH referred to the legislative materials and showed that s. 5a VVG, including the fourth sentence of s. 5a(2) VVG, was specifically enacted by the German legislature to implement the second and third Life Assurance Directives into German law. The fourth sentence of s. 5a(2) VVG, however, contradicted this intention. The limitation period in the fourth sentence of s. 5a VVG was warranted by legal certainty according to the legislative materials. The BGH then stated, for the first time explicitly, that if the legislature intends to transpose a directive with a body of provisions, this purpose has to be granted priority over a contradicting purpose of one of the specific provisions.²⁹⁵ The BGH thus gave priority to the legislature's general intention to correctly implement the directives over an inadvertently non-conforming purpose of a specific provision. The BGH also stated in its reasoning that it can be excluded that the legislature would have enacted s. 5a(2) sentence 4 VVG in the same way if it had been aware that the provision in its current form does not comply with the directives. This argument is premised on presumed intent. It goes back to national legal methodology and demonstrates the working of a strong (national) presumption of compliance. A very similar argument relating to the legislature's presumed intention to fully and correctly comply with the terms of the directive had been used before by the BGH in *Weber II*.²⁹⁶ This case will be discussed in the next section, and it illustrates that the presumed general intention of the enacting legislature to fully and correctly implement the directive can trump an identifiable objective of the enacting legislature. The comparison of *Lebensversicherung II* with the BVerfG's reasoning in *Geldwäsche durch Strafverteidiger* for constitution-consistent interpretation further demonstrates that the BGH's reasoning does not breach the outer interpretative limits set by art. 20(2) and (3) GG.²⁹⁷

---

[293] Case C-209/12, *Endress v. Allianz*, ECLI:EU:C:2013:864, para. 32.
[294] BGH, *NJW* 2014, 2646 paras. 21–34 – *Lebensversicherung II*.
[295] BGH, *NJW* 2014, 2646, para. 26 – *Lebensversicherung II*. This priority of the general over the specific intention was already implicit in BGH, *NJW* 2012, 1073 para. 34 – *Weber II*. For criticism, see O. Brand, Ausschluss des Ausschlusses? – Zur Europarechtswidrigkeit des §5a Abs. 2 S. 4 VVG a.F. nach der Entscheidung des EuGH vom 19.12.2013 (VersR 2014, 225) in der Rechtssache Endress/Allianz, *VersR* 2014, 269, 274.
[296] See BGH, *NJW* 2012, 1073 para. 34 – *Weber II*.
[297] For a detailed analysis, see Brenncke, above n. 183, pp. 29–34.

Where the remit of a *national* presumption of compliance overlaps with the EU presumption, a court can apply the national presumption without having recourse to the EU rule.[298] The significance of *Lebensversicherung II* is that the BGH applied the European presumtion of compliance for the first time in this decision. The court not only relied on the national presumption, but also referred to the European presumption of compliance in order to justify the priority of the legislature's presumed general intention to correctly and fully transpose a directive into national law over the legislature's specific, but inadvertently non-conforming regulatory decision. The BGH thus correctly applied the priority element of the EU presumption of compliance. The court declared that due to the European presumption as laid down by the CJEU in *Pfeiffer*, the purpose of national legislation that is specifically enacted for the purpose of transposing a directive has to be determined by considering the legislature's intention to correctly implement a directive, except when the legislature expressly refuses to implement a directive's provision.[299] The latter limitation of the presumption of compliance will be explored in Section 7 below. It refers to an outer limit of conforming interpretation that negates the presumption. In other words, the presumption is rebutted if an outer limit of conforming interpretation is breached.

5.2. THE PRESUMPTION RULE IN ENGLISH COURTS

When English courts apply the EU legal duty of conforming interpretation, they presume that Parliament intended to fully comply with an applicable directive when it enacts implementing legislation (presumption *a*).[300] This presumption of compliance is given great weight in conforming interpretation.[301] That in itself is no surprise as English courts operate a common law presumption that Parliament intends to give effect to the UK's international obligations fully and consistently (presumption *b*). It was shown in Chapter 2 that presumption *b* only applies when the statutory language is ambiguous. This limitation

---

[298] See Section 1 above.
[299] BGH, *NJW* 2014, 2646, para. 23 – *Lebensversicherung II*. See also BVerwG, *BeckRS* 2017, 103948, para. 29.
[300] *EB Central Services v. Revenue and Customs Commissioners* [2008] EWCA Civ 486, para. 19 (Mummery LJ); *Bear Scotland Ltd. v. Fulton* [2015] ICR 221 (EAT), paras. 46, 64 (Langstaff J); cf. *Axa UK Plc. v. Revenue and Customs Commissioners* [2011] EWCA Civ 1607, para. 49 (Arden LJ).
[301] See, e.g. *Pickstone v. Freemans Plc* [1989] AC 66 (HL), 112 (Lord Keith), 121 (Lord Templeman); *Litster v. Forth Dry Dock & Engineering Co Ltd.* [1990] 1 AC 546 (HL), 554 (Lord Keith), 559 (Lord Oliver); *R. v. Johnstone* [2003] UKHL 28, para. 63 (Lord Walker); *EB Central Services v. Revenue and Customs Commissioners* [2008] EWCA Civ 486, paras. 36, 40 (Mummery LJ).

of presumption *b* led Nicholls LJ, as he then was, in the Court of Appeal in *Pickstone* to conclude that s. 1(2)(c) Equal Pay Act 1970 cannot be given a conforming meaning.[302] Lord Oliver did not rely on presumption *b* when he departed from the unambiguous statutory words of s. 1(2)(c) Equal Pay Act 1970 in *Pickstone* by reading additional words into the legislation. *Pickstone* thus emancipated the EU legal duty of conforming interpretation from the common law presumption *b*. The EU legal duty of conforming interpretation "imposes a stronger requirement than" presumption *b*.[303] As in German judgments, the legal basis of the presumption of compliance is not necessarily seen in EU law. Even though there are English judgments that refer to the *European* presumption as articulated by the CJEU in *Pfeiffer*,[304] other judgments mention s. 2(4) ECA as the origin of a strong (*national*) presumption of compliance for conforming interpretation.[305] I have argued elsewhere that both explanations can coexist.[306]

The presumption of compliance appears particularly strong in two situations: (a) for copy-out legislation and (b) when English courts interpret delegated legislation made under the powers granted by s. 2(2) ECA. Regarding (a), adopting the same language as that of the directive serves as a strong indication that the national legislature intended to adopt the same meaning that is given to the directive by the CJEU.[307] The suggestion that the implementing law bears a different meaning from that of the directive to which it gives effect faces the obstacle that the legislature would have used different language if the same meaning had not been intended.[308] Regarding (b), the "primary objective" of delegated legislation under s. 2(2) ECA must be to bring into force EU obligations in the UK.[309] It follows that the underlying purpose of

---

[302] *Pickstone v. Freemans Plc* [1987] 3 WLR 811 (CA), 822 (Nicholls LJ).
[303] *EN (Serbia) v. Secretary of State for the Home Department* [2009] EWCA Civ 630, para. 77 (Stanley Burnton LJ). Cf. *Assange v. Swedish Prosecution Authority* [2012] UKSC 22, para. 203 (Lord Mance) where the strong *Pupino* interpretative obligation (conforming interpretation) was contrasted with the "weaker" English common law presumption that Parliament does not intend to legislate contrary to the UK's international obligations.
[304] *Churchill Insurance Co. Ltd. v. Fitzgerald & Wilkinson* [2012] EWCA Civ 1166, para. 47 (Aikens LJ, with whom Etherton and Maurice Kay LJJ agreed); *British Gas Trading Ltd. v. Lock* [2016] EWCA Civ 983, para. 107 (Sir Colin Rimer, with whom Gloster LJ and Sir Terence Etherton MR agreed).
[305] Cf. *Pickstone v. Freemans Plc* [1989] AC 66 (HL), 126, 128 (Lord Oliver). For an argument that the presumption is based in common law, see HUNT, above n. 121, p. 97.
[306] BRENNCKE, above n. 14, pp. 148–150.
[307] *British Airways plc. v. Williams* [2012] UKSC 43, para. 21 (Lord Mance, with whom Lord Hope, Lord Walker, Lord Clarke and Lord Sumption agreed).
[308] Cf. for the English common law presumption that Parliament intends to legislate in compliance with its international obligations, *Assange v. Swedish Prosecution Authority* [2012] UKSC 22, para. 161 (Lord Dyson).
[309] *Brent LBC v. Risk Management Partners Ltd.* [2011] UKSC 7, para. 24 (Lord Hope); *Oakley Inc. v. Animal Ltd.* [2005] EWCA Civ 1191, para. 38 (Waller LJ); *ITV Broadcasting Ltd. v. TV Catchup Ltd. (No. 2)* [2011] EWHC 1874 (Pat.), para. 66 (Floyd J).

delegated legislation made under s. 2(2) ECA that implements a directive into UK law is to give effect to the directive.[310] These arguments can explain why it may appear "easier"[311] to interpret delegated legislation in conformity with EU directives than primary legislation. Allocating different strengths to the presumption for delegated and for primary legislation appears counter-intuitive at first sight. That is because the presumption of compliance is rebutted if an outer limit of interpretation is breached, and English courts apply the same outer limits for delegated and primary legislation. It will be shown in Section 7 below, however, that the outer limits of conforming interpretation are formulated in sufficiently wide terms. They leave considerable scope for judicial discretion and can be handled restrictively or widely in individual cases. A conforming interpretation of delegated legislation made under s. 2(2) ECA thus calls for a wide application of the outer limits of interpretation. Similarly, we have seen in Chapter 2 that the *Inco Europe* conditions can be applied widely for the interpretation of delegated legislation.[312]

Due to the analogy between s. 3(1) HRA and conforming interpretation, the presumption of compliance for Convention-compatible interpretation ought to apply *mutatis mutandis* to the EU legal duty of conforming interpretation. This is required by EU law based on equivalence reasoning. That means that courts must presume that Parliament did not intend to legislate contrary to directives. The presumption of compliance for Convention-compatible interpretation also applies to legislation pre-dating the HRA, even though Parliament could not have known or foreseen this presumption when it enacted the original legislation. *Wilkinson* and *Ghaidan*, for example, concerned the interpretation of legislation that pre-dated the HRA. If the analogy between s. 3(1) HRA and Convention-compatible interpretation is followed, English courts ought to apply a presumption of compliance even in cases where there are no indications that the enacting legislature intended to comply with the requirements of an applicable directive, e.g. where relevant national legislation precedes an applicable directive. This has not yet been confirmed by case law, however, and it also goes beyond the current scope of application of the EU presumption of compliance. It is not a "Europeanisation from the inside", but an application of the EU principle of equivalence. One argument in favour of

---

[310] Cf. the wording of s. 2(2)(a) ECA, "for the purpose of implementing". For examples, see *R. (Risk Management Partners Ltd.) v. Brent London Borough Council and Harrow London Borough Council* [2011] UKSC 7, paras. 22, 24 (Lord Hope, with whom Lord Walker, Lord Brown and Lord Dyson agreed); *ITV Broadcasting Ltd. v. TV Catchup Ltd.* [2015] EWCA Civ 204, para. 105 (Arden LJ). Cf. *Moreno v. The Motor Insurers' Bureau* [2016] UKSC 52, para. 27 (Lord Mance, with whom all other members of the Court agreed).

[311] Cf. Lady Hale, Bryce Lecture 2015: The Supreme Court in the United Kingdom Constitution, February 2015, p. 13, available at https://www.supremecourt.uk/news/speeches.html.

[312] See Chapter 2, Section 4.4.

this equivalence reasoning is that the *national* presumptions of compliance for Convention-compatible interpretation and for conforming interpretation have an equivalent origin in constitutional statutes (s. 3(1) HRA and s. 2(1), (4) ECA). If this equivalence reasoning were adopted, a difference would exist between the (national) presumption of compliance for conforming interpretation in England and the presumption of compliance in Germany. Based on equivalence reasoning to constitution-consistent interpretation, the German presumption of compliance for conforming interpretation does not apply when a court construes legislation that pre-dates an applicable directive. This difference is, however, attenuated by the fact that a German court ought nonetheless to take the directive into account when determining the (objectivised) purpose of pre-dating legislation.[313] In other words, the directive forms part of the context of the provision. It is ultimately the outer interpretative limits that determine how far a court can diverge from the purpose ascribed to the pre-dating legislation by the enacting legislature. The same is true for the English presumption of compliance even if it is applied to legislation that precedes an applicable directive.

A case that illustrates the application of the EU presumption of compliance in English courts is *British Gas Trading Ltd v. Lock*. The question arose whether a commission element must be included in the calculation of the holiday pay to which an employee is entitled if the employee's salary consists of a results-based commission and a basic salary. It was undisputed in the Court of Appeal that holiday pay is confined to basic pay without any commission element if the employee's entitlement to holiday pay is judged through a domestic lens only, i.e. reg. 16 of the Working Time Regulations 1998 read in accordance with s. 221(2) Employment Rights Act 1996 under conventional domestic canons of construction. The Working Time Regulations 1998 were, however, enacted "solely and deliberately for the purpose of implementing the requirements of" Directive 2003/88/EC concerning certain aspects of the organisation of working time.[314] They were made under s. 2(2) ECA. On a reference for a preliminary ruling from the Employment Tribunal, the CJEU had held that art. 7 of Directive 2003/88/EC must be interpreted as precluding national legislation under which a worker whose remuneration consists of a basic salary and results-based commission is entitled to holiday pay composed exclusively of his basic pay.[315] When the case reached the Court of Appeal, the key

---

[313] This is due to the analogy to constitution-consistent interpretation. As was shown in Section 5 of Chapter 3, the German Basic Law can influence the purpose of legislation that precedes the German Basic Law and can influence how a judge arrives at possible meanings of a provision.
[314] *British Gas Trading Ltd. v. Lock* [2016] EWCA Civ 983, para. 107 (Sir Colin Rimer, with whom Gloster LJ and Sir Terence Etherton MR agreed).
[315] Case C-539/12, *Lock v. British Gas Trading Ltd.*, ECLI:EU:C:2014:351, para. 24.

question was whether the Working Time Regulations 1998 can be interpreted as including the results-based commission element in calculating holiday pay. The Court of Appeal applied the EU presumption of compliance which requires "the court to presume that the United Kingdom government intended by the WTR [Working Time Regulations 1998] to fulfil *entirely* the obligations arising under the Directive".[316] We have seen in the previous subsection that the BGH expressed the impact of the EU presumption of compliance on the purpose of national implementing legislation in a very similar vein in *Lebensversicherung II*. The Court of Appeal explained that the presumption of compliance is rebutted if "a legislative choice has been made that is directly at odds with the requirements of the Directive".[317] The Court of Appeal thus recognised, as did the BGH in *Lebensversicherung II*, that the presumption is constrained by outer limits of interpretation as determined by national legal methodology.[318] An outer limit of interpretation was not breached in *British Gas Trading v. Lock*. The Court of Appeal argued that the UK government simply did not foresee the interpretation given to art. 7 Directive 2003/88/EC by the CJEU in 2014 when it enacted the Working Time Regulations in 1998.[319] This was the decisive argument given in the written judicial opinion in favour of why the Working Time Regulations could be given a conforming meaning. The other side of this argument is that the court applied the EU presumption of compliance and placed decisive weight on the reasonably presumed intention of the enacting legislature. *British Gas Trading v. Lock* therefore illustrates a strong operation of the EU presumption of compliance.

The strength of the presumption of compliance is, however, not settled in English case law, as can be seen in *Football Association Premier League Ltd. v. QC Leisure*. In that case, a football association was the owner of film copyright contained in broadcasts of live Premier League matches. It claimed that the defendant publicans, by using foreign decoder cards to access and show foreign transmissions of live Premier League football matches on television screens to customers in their public houses, had communicated its copyright works to the public contrary to s. 20 of the Copyright, Designs and Patents Act 1988 (CDPA). According to s. 20(1)(b) CDPA, the communication to the public of the work is an act restricted by the copyright in a film. Section 20 CDPA, as

---

[316] *British Gas Trading Ltd. v. Lock* [2016] EWCA Civ 983, para. 107 (Sir Colin Rimer, with whom Gloster LJ and Sir Terence Etherton MR agreed).
[317] Ibid., para. 109 (Sir Colin Rimer, with whom Gloster LJ and Sir Terence Etherton MR agreed).
[318] See also *R. (Chester) v. Secretary of State for Justice* [2013] UKSC 63, para. 74 (Lord Mance); *Test Claimants in the FII Group Litigation v. Revenue and Customs Commissioners* [2010] EWCA Civ 103, para. 108 (Arden LJ).
[319] *British Gas Trading Ltd. v. Lock* [2016] EWCA Civ 983, paras. 107, 110–111 (Sir Colin Rimer, with whom Gloster LJ and Sir Terence Etherton MR agreed).

substituted by reg. 6(1) of the Copyright and Related Rights Regulations 2003 (2003 Regulations), purports to implement art. 3 of the Information Society Directive (Directive 2001/29/EC).[320] The 2003 Regulations were made under the powers granted by s. 2(2) ECA. In the High Court, Kitchin J, as he then was, was unsure whether the publicans have communicated the copyright works to the public within the meaning of art. 3 of the Information Society Directive. He referred the matter to the CJEU, and the CJEU held that the concept "communication to the public" in art. 3 of the Information Society Directive must be interpreted as covering transmission of the broadcast works, via a television screen and speakers, to the customers present in a public house.[321]

When the case returned to the High Court, Kitchin LJ argued that the publicans' acts fell under s. 20 CDPA as interpreted in conformity with art. 3 of the Information Society Directive. He then considered whether s. 72(1) CDPA provided the publicans with a defence to the alleged infringement of the claimant's film copyright under s. 20 CDPA. Section 72 CDPA stems from national law and its old subsection (1)(c) provided that the showing in public of a broadcast to an audience who have not paid for admission to the place where the broadcast is to be seen or heard "does not infringe any copyright in (a) the broadcast; … or (c) any film included in it". Article 5 of the Information Society Directive provides for an exhaustive enumeration of exceptions and limitations to the right of communication to the public provided for in art. 3 of the directive.[322] Kitchin LJ recognised that the Information Society Directive does not permit a defence in the terms of s. 72(1)(c) CDPA. Yet, he felt unable to ascribe to s. 72(1)(c) CDPA a conforming meaning as this would exceed the limits of the doctrine of conforming interpretation.[323] Kitchin LJ thus dismissed the football association's claim against the defendant publicans for infringement of copyright under s. 20 CDPA. The football association subsequently appealed and the Court of Appeal also held that a conforming interpretation of s. 72(1)(c) CDPA would go beyond the principles of legitimate statutory interpretation.

Etherton LJ's reasoning in the Court of Appeal, with which Munby and Lewison LJJ agreed, can be summarised as follows:[324] Etherton LJ

---

[320] *Football Association Premier League Ltd. v. QC Leisure* [2012] EWCA Civ 1708, para. 28 (Etherton LJ, with whom Munby and Lewison LJJ agreed); see The Copyright and Related Rights Regulations 2003, explanatory note.
[321] Joined Cases C-403/08 and C-429/08, *Football Association Premier League Ltd. et al. v. QC Leisure et al.*, ECLI:EU:C:2011:631, paras. 195–207.
[322] Cf. recital 32 of the directive.
[323] *Football Association Premier League Ltd. v. QC Leisure* [2012] EWHC 108 (Ch), paras. 71–78 (Kitchin LJ).
[324] *Football Association Premier League Ltd. v. QC Leisure* [2012] EWCA Civ 1708, paras. 50–62 (Etherton LJ).

acknowledged, based on the legislative history of the 2003 Regulations, that the government had clearly intended to fully implement the Information Society Directive with the 2003 Regulations. The problem was that the government had erred about the correct scope of the communication to the public right enshrined in art. 3 of the Information Society Directive. The government had not appreciated that the communication to the public right in the amended s. 20 CDPA included the "showing or playing in public of a broadcast" within s. 72(1) CDPA. "[T]he corollary of the Government's mistake as to the ambit of section 72(1) is that the Government did not intend to introduce a specific new limitation to its ambit …".[325] The wording of s. 72(1) is clear and unambiguous in embracing within its ambit any "showing or playing in public of a broadcast". Etherton LJ then argued that a limit to conforming interpretation was exceeded in the case on the basis of reading the statutory language in the context of the government's clear intention, apparent from the legislative history, to maintain to the fullest extent possible the UK's existing exceptions to copyright infringement.

At the core of Etherton LJ's main argument are two contradictory intentions of the government as revealed by the legislative history of the Copyright and Related Rights Regulations 2003:[326] (a) the specific intention not to alter the ambit of s. 72(1) CDPA and to maintain to the fullest extent possible the existing exceptions to copyright infringement and (b) the general intention to fully implement the Information Society Directive with the 2003 Regulations. Etherton LJ gave precedence to the former over the latter. We have already seen that the BGH in *Lebensversicherung II* applied a strong presumption of compliance and arrived at the opposite conclusion in a very similar scenario. Etherton LJ did not refer to a presumption of compliance. One reason may be that s. 72(1) CDPA was not specifically enacted to transpose the Information Society Directive. Section 72(1) stems from national law as enacted by Parliament in 1988, and the statutory language of s. 72(1) that was at issue in *Football Association Premier League Ltd. v. QC Leisure* had not been amended by the 2003 Regulations. The 2003 Regulations only introduced a limitation to the provision's ambit relating to sound recording.

To describe s. 72(1) CDPA simply as pre-dating legislation would be inaccurate, however, since the amending law-maker in 2003 had the intention not to alter the ambit of s. 72(1) any further and to maintain the existing exceptions to copyright infringement. Therefore, the exceptions to copyright infringement enshrined in s. 72(1) formed part of the intention of

---

[325] Ibid., para. 52 (Etherton LJ).
[326] Ibid., paras. 50–52 (Etherton LJ).

the government when making the 2003 Regulations. The 2003 Regulations amended the CDPA "insofar as its provisions do not conform or comply with the Directive".[327] Nothing in the 2003 Regulations or their legislative history indicates that the government considered that the unaltered s. 72(1) CDPA could be incompatible with the requirements of the Information Society Directive. The government must have assumed that the existing s. 72(1) complied with the directive, which is why it did not amend the statutory language at issue. Yet, the government erred in its assessment at the time of making the 2003 Regulations. It did not foresee the interpretation given to art. 3 of the Information Society Directive by the CJEU in 2011. We have observed that the Court of Appeal used a very similar argument in *British Gas Trading v. Lock* in order to defend the conforming interpretation of the Working Time Regulations 1998. For the reasons given it appears justified to apply a strong presumption of compliance in *Football Association Premier League Ltd. v. QC Leisure*. Applying a strong presumption would have entailed the assumption that the government did not intend to infringe the Information Society Directive as it did not positively consider the consequences of maintaining a non-conforming objective in s. 72(1) CDPA. It is also possible to adopt the reasoning of the BGH in *Lebensversicherung II*: it can be ruled out that the law-maker would have enacted (here: maintained) s. 72(1) in the same way if it had been aware that the provision in its current form did not comply with the directive. Etherton LJ should have given precedence to the general intention to fully implement the Information Society Directive over the inadvertently non-conforming objective of s. 72(1) CDPA.

This analysis corresponds with case law on the interpretative power of judges under s. 3(1) HRA. It was argued, based on a comparison between *Ghaidan* and *Fitzpatrick* in Chapter 3, that a court does not ask whether the legislature positively intended to include the compatible meaning but whether there are sufficient indications that the legislature intended to exclude the compatible meaning. This reasoning illustrates the strong presumption of compliance that operates in the field of s. 3(1) HRA. An equivalent interpretative structure is often followed by courts for conforming interpretation.[328] It follows that Etherton LJ should have asked whether there were sufficient indications that the government intended to exclude the compatible meaning. Was the retention of the introductory language of s. 72(1) CDPA when making the 2003 Regulations such a sufficient indication? Like Kitchin LJ in the High Court, Etherton LJ gave strong weight to the statutory language as an indication of the government's intention to make no alteration to the ambit of s. 72(1) CDPA.

---

[327] *Football Association Premier League Ltd. v. QC Leisure* [2012] EWHC 108 (Ch), paras. 43–44 (Kitchin LJ); Copyright and Related Rights Regulations 2003, explanatory note.

[328] See Section 3.1 above.

Yet, the answer to the question must be No, since the government erred about the ambit of s. 72(1) and intended to fully implement the Information Society Directive. Furthermore, the explanatory note to the 2003 Regulations shows that the government intended to comply with the regime of defences to copyright infringement contained in art. 5 of the Information Society Directive. Etherton LJ gave too strong a weight to the statutory language which cannot be reconciled with a strong presumption of compliance.

Another question is whether Etherton LJ's reasoning is compatible with the EU presumption of compliance. The CJEU established in *Wagner Miret* that the EU presumption applies to the interpretation of legislation preceding a directive if the Member State does not consider it necessary to amend its law in order to bring it into line with the applicable directive because it (mistakenly) considers the pre-existing legislation to already satisfy the requirements of the directive concerned.[329] These conditions are met by s. 72(1) CDPA, so that the EU presumption of compliance impacts on its conforming interpretation. Furthermore, the legislative history of the 2003 Regulations contains an inadvertent inconsistency with the Information Society Directive regarding the ambit of s. 72(1) CDPA. The EU presumption of compliance encompasses a priority element. Its application to the case at issue leads to the result that the possible inconsistent meaning of s. 72(1) CDPA does not rebut the presumption that the government intended to enact only consistent objectives when making the 2003 Regulations. The general intention of the law-maker to fully implement the directive prevails over the specific but inadvertently inconsistent objective of s. 72(1) CDPA, as expressed in the legislative history, to maintain to the fullest extent the existing exceptions to copyright infringement. The Court of Appeal's omission to apply the priority element of the EU presumption of compliance was not, however, material to the outcome of the case. Utilising the EU presumption of compliance in *Football Association Premier League Ltd. v. QC Leisure* would not have led to s. 72(1) CDPA being amenable to a conforming interpretation because an outer interpretative limit was surpassed.[330] Applying the priority element of the EU presumption only means that the presumption cannot simply be trumped by the specific non-conforming objective of s. 72(1) CDPA as expressed in the legislative history. Yet, the EU presumption of compliance is rebutted if a court for some other reason infringes a *contra legem* limit of interpretation, i.e. an outer limit of the judicial function. The same is true if, as was argued above, applying a national presumption of compliance would have led to the result that precedence must be given to the government's general intention to fully implement the Information Society Directive.

---

[329] Case C-334/92, *Wagner Miret v. Fondo de Garantía Salarial*, ECLI:EU:C:1993:945, paras. 4, 5, 21.
[330] See in detail Section 7.2 below.

5.3. COMPARATIVE ANALYSIS

English and German courts operate a strong presumption of compliance when they interpret implementing legislation. The strength of the presumption is visible when a court balances the intention of the enacting legislature to achieve a specific objective and the presumed intention of the legislature to comply fully and correctly with the directive. The presumption may even empower an English or a German court to depart from an identifiable objective of the enacting legislature. The legal basis of the presumption is not necessarily seen in EU law in both jurisdictions, but is often seen in national law. Courts in both jurisdictions have nonetheless also referred to and applied the EU presumption of compliance. The priority element of the EU presumption was correctly applied by the BGH in *Lebensversicherung II*, but not by the Court of Appeal in *Football Association Premier League Ltd. v. QC Leisure*. It is recognised in both jurisdictions that the presumption of compliance is rebutted if a court exceeds an outer limit of interpretation. The maximum strength of the presumption is thus ultimately determined by the *contra legem* limit of conforming interpretation.

Neither English nor German courts have yet derived the full implications for the presumption of compliance for conforming interpretation from an analogy with the presumption of compliance in the realm of rights-consistent interpretation. The BGH in *Lebensversicherung II* and the Court of Appeal in *British Gas Trading v. Lock* have recognised that the EU presumption of compliance bears upon the range of possible meanings and interacts with national canons of construction. This illustrates the harmonising influence of European methodological rules on national legal methodologies. The integration of the EU presumption into the judicial reasoning process based on national canons of interpretation further demonstrates how adaptable these canons are for, to use Lord Denning's famous words, the incoming tide of EU law. This example strengthens the position of those who argue that legal cultures in Member States are not static and may evolve based on a European harmonisation programme.[331] Conversely, the example weakens the position of those who suggest that legal cultures in Europe may not converge.[332]

---

[331] L.-P. Brandt, Die Chancen für eine einheitliche Auslegung eines Europäischen Zivilgesetzbuches, V&R unipress, Osnabrück 2009, pp. 93, 145; M. Gisewski, *Methodik der Auslegung im kontinentaleuropäischen und angelsächsischen Recht: Vergleich und Synthese juristischer Denkweisen vor dem Hintergrund der europäischen Privatrechtsvergleichung*, Kovač, Hamburg 2008, p. 278; J. Hage, Legal reasoning and legal integration, (2010) 10 *MJ* 67, 95; C. Lyons, Perspectives on convergence within the theatre of European integration, in P. Beaumont, C. Lyons and N. Walker (eds.), *Convergence and divergence in European public law*, Hart, Oxford 2002, pp. 79, 84–85.

[332] Legrand, above n. 11, pp. 52–81. See also Harlow, above n. 11, pp. 347–348; Teubner, above n. 11, p. 12.

6. TECHNIQUES OF JUDICIAL LAW-MAKING

6.1. GAP-FILLING

Section 6 of this chapter will compare the techniques of conforming judicial law-making employed by English and German courts. German courts apply the same interpretative techniques for conforming judicial law-making that they use for conventional judicial law-making and constitution-consistent judicial law-making. These techniques have already been presented in Chapters 2 and 3. It is thus sufficient to focus here on the characteristic features of *conforming* judicial law-making.

6.1.1. Legislation Adopted for the Purpose of Transposing a Directive

The leading case in Germany on the outer limits and techniques of conforming judicial law-making is the BGH's ruling in *Quelle II*.[333] When the BGH engaged in conforming judicial law-making of s. 439(4) German Civil Code in *Quelle II*, the court applied the traditional concept of gap as used in a purely national context.[334] The question of how a gap is established for conforming judicial law-making is one of the most controversial questions of conforming interpretation in German legal scholarship.[335] Two things stand out from the BGH's reasoning.[336] First, a gap in the legislation did not simply arise because s. 439(4) German Civil Code as interpreted in a narrow sense infringed Directive 1999/44/EC. The infringement only established the incompleteness of the German legislation. Second, the BGH argued that this incompleteness is unintended because it can be ruled out that the legislature would have enacted s. 439(4) in the same way if it had been aware that the provision in its current form does not comply with the directive. This reasoning of the BGH is based on the presumed intention of the enacting legislature and informed by the presumption of compliance. The BGH effectively gave priority to the legislature's specific intention to enact s. 439(4) German Civil Code in conformity with the

---

[333] *Quelle II* was discussed in Section 3.2.1 above.
[334] Some scholars argue that the national legal system (*nationale Gesamtrechtsordnung*) is composed of purely national legislation, directly applicable EU law and Member States' duties to transpose EU directives, without there being a common plan (*Gesamtplan*) for the whole of the national legal system. Therefore, they contend that the traditional concept of gap as used in a purely national context is inadequate for conforming judicial law-making. See A. FLESSNER, Juristische Methode und europäisches Privatrecht, *JZ* 2002, 14, 16; HERRESTHAL, above n. 66, pp. 221–224.
[335] For an overview of the discussion, see B. RÜTHERS, C. FISCHER and A. BIRK, *Rechtstheorie*, 7th ed., C.H. Beck, Munich 2013, paras. 912a–912e; SCHÜRNBRAND, above n. 73, p. 913.
[336] BGH, *NJW* 2009, 427, paras. 21–26 – *Quelle II*.

directive over the likewise specifically expressed intention to grant the seller a right to claim compensation.[337] Both conflicting intentions were expressed in the explanatory memorandum of the bill.

The BGH established the gap by looking at the intended plan and purpose of s. 439(4) German Civil Code which, when read in the context of the applicable directive, included an assumption that the German legislature did not intend to infringe the directive.[338] This illustrates that (a) the court gave considerable weight to the presumed intention of the legislature and (b) the court determined the gap by looking at the "objectivised" plan and purpose of the provision. The BGH's reasoning also shows how adaptable the techniques of judicial law-making, and in particular the concept of gap, are for the effects of directives in national law. The BVerfG has resorted to similar reasoning in the context of constitution-consistent interpretation in *Geldwäsche durch Strafverteidiger*.[339] The BVerfG did not simply rely on the German Basic Law as a benchmark for establishing the unintendedness criterion in that case. Instead, the BVerfG relied on the presumed intention of the enacting legislature in order to establish a gap in the legislation. The BGH in *Quelle II* determined the gap by looking at the intended plan and purpose of s. 439(4) German Civil Code itself. Hence, the court did not have to answer the controversial question of whether a gap can also be determined by (a) qualifying the directive itself or at least its duty to transpose, after the expiry of its transposition deadline, as part of the plan of the whole of the (German) law and by (b) using the directive as a benchmark for establishing the unintendedness criterion (*die Planwidrigkeit*) of the legislation.[340] The upshot of accepting this reasoning would be that an infringement of a directive due to an incorrect transposition would almost always establish a gap in the law except when the legislature expressly refuses to implement a directive's provision. The answer to this controversial question depends on two other controversial issues in German legal methodology: (a) how narrowly or widely the term gap can be defined[341]

---

[337] Some scholars argue in favour of giving priority to the inadvertently non-conforming specific purpose of a provision over the contradicting legislature's specific intention to create a conforming statutory provision. See R. FREITAG, Privatrechtsangleichung auf Kosten Privater, *Europarecht* 2009, 796, 799; SCHÜRNBRAND, above n. 73, p. 917.

[338] For criticism of this reasoning, see GSELL, above n. 112, pp. 522, 525; HERDEGEN, above n. 82, p. 1929; C. HÖPFNER, Das deutsche Urlaubsrecht in Europa – Zwischen Vollharmonisierung und Koexistenz – Teil 1, *RdA* 2013, 16, 22; KAISER, above n. 112, pp. 978, 980; SCHÜRNBRAND, above n. 73, pp. 913–914. These scholars contend that a gap must be determined solely by looking at national law without having recourse to the directive or an assumption that the legislature intended to fully implement the directive into national law. For further criticism of the BGH's reasoning, see HERRESTHAL, above n. 290, p. 293.

[339] See Chapter 3, Section 6.

[340] For this view, see CANARIS, above n. 82, pp. 85–88; MÖRSDORF, above n. 79, p. 229. For criticism of this view, see FRANZEN, above n. 65, pp. 327–328; RÜTHERS, FISCHER and BIRK, above n. 335, para. 912d; SCHÜRNBRAND, above n. 73, pp. 913–914.

[341] For discussion, see CANARIS, above n. 82, pp. 84–85.

and (b) whether a directive can be considered legislation or law under art. 20(3) GG.[342] Even though the BGH was criticised for its reasoning in *Quelle II* because it leads to a dynamic reference to the aims of the directive in its interpretation by the CJEU, the BVerfG's reasoning in *Geldwäsche durch Strafverteidiger* has a similar effect: the presumption that the ordinary legislature intended to comply with the German Basic Law de facto leads to a dynamic reference to the purposes of the German Basic Law as interpreted by the BVerfG. After establishing the covert gap in the legislation, the BGH closed the gap with a teleological reduction in *Quelle II*.[343] Directive 1999/44/EC in its interpretation by the CJEU informed the BGH's decision on how to close the gap. It could be discerned from the directive which case[344] had to be excluded from the scope of s. 439(4) German Civil Code in order for the German legislation to comply with the directive.

The BGH's methodological reasoning in *Quelle II* was followed and extended in later cases. *Weber II* concerned the interpretation of s. 439(3) German Civil Code.[345] The provision was intended to transpose Directive 1999/44/EC on certain aspects of the sale of consumer goods and associated guarantees into national law. The unambiguous wording of s. 439(3) grants the seller a right to refuse the only possible method of subsequent performance due to an absolute lack of proportionality. On a reference from the BGH, the CJEU had confirmed that art. 3 of Directive 1999/44/EC precludes a national provision such as s. 439(3) German Civil Code.[346] Since the unambiguous wording of s. 439(3) barred a conforming interpretation in a narrow sense, the BGH applied conforming judicial law-making by means of teleological reduction in order to exclude from the scope of application of s. 439(3) the case that infringed the requirements of art. 3 of Directive 1999/44/EC. As in *Quelle II*, the court faced the problem of two conflicting intentions expressed in the explanatory memorandum of the bill. In contrast to the situation in *Quelle II*, however, the explanatory memorandum did not contain a (mistaken) specific statement regarding the conformity of the specific regulatory decision in the challenged provision (s. 439(3) German Civil Code) with Directive 1999/44/EC. Instead, it contained a statement that the whole Act was intended to implement Directive 1999/44/EC into national law. The BGH effectively gave priority to the presumed general intention of the enacting legislature to fully and correctly implement the directive over the specifically expressed purpose

---

[342] For an overview of the discussion, see HÖPFNER, above n. 65, pp. 96–100; ROTH and JOPEN, above n. 49, §13, para. 39; WEBER, above n. 78, pp. 121–122.
[343] BGH, *NJW* 2009, 427, para. 26 – *Quelle II*.
[344] The seller's right to claim compensation from the consumer-buyer for the benefits derived from using the defective good.
[345] BGH, *NJW* 2012, 1073 – *Weber II*.
[346] Case C-65/09, *Gebr. Weber GmbH v. Wittmer*, ECLI:EU:C:2011:396, para. 78.

of s. 439(3) German Civil Code.³⁴⁷ The court assumed in effect that the national legislature misunderstood the content of the directive and that the specific purpose of s. 439(3) was inadvertently non-conforming. The German Basic Law does not require that priority is given to the legislature's specific intention. This latter point is illustrated if a parallel is drawn to the BVerfG's reasoning in *Geldwäsche durch Strafverteidiger*, where the BVerfG de facto gave precedence to the legislature's presumed general intention to comply with the German Basic Law over a specific but inadvertently unconstitutional purpose of s. 261(5) German Criminal Code. Article 20(2), (3) GG do not determine whether a court ought to give preference to a presumed intention to fully comply with a directive over an inadvertently non-conforming specific purpose of a provision or vice versa.

The BGH's judgment in *Lebensversicherung II* further consolidates the case law. The BGH engaged in judicial law-making via teleological reduction in this case, and the court explicitly granted priority to the legislature's intention to transpose the directive with a body of provisions over a conflicting purpose of one of the specific provisions.³⁴⁸ The BGH also explicitly stated that an applicable directive serves as a benchmark for both establishing and filling a gap.³⁴⁹ Yet, the court did not solely use the directive as a benchmark for establishing the unintendedness criterion. To the contrary, the BGH established the unintendedness criterion by relying on the intended plan and purpose of s. 5a(2) sentence 4 VVG itself which, when read in the context of the applicable directives, included a (European) presumption that the German legislature intended to correctly implement the directives. This reasoning of the BGH, which focuses on the intention of the enacting legislature,³⁵⁰ may be explained by recent BVerfG case law on the limits of the judicial function. It was established in Chapter 2 that the BVerfG urges courts to give sufficient consideration to the intention of the enacting legislature and the legislative materials when interpreting legislation in order to comply with art. 20(2), (3) GG.

The BGH closed the gap in *Lebensversicherung II* via a teleological reduction by excluding from the scope of application of s. 5a(2) sentence 4 VVG, and against the provision's wording, cases that fall within the scope of the second and

---

[347] BGH, *NJW* 2012, 1073 para. 34 – *Weber II*. Some scholars argue in favour of giving priority to the inadvertently non-conforming specific purpose of a provision over the contradicting (presumed) general intention of the legislature to fully and correctly implement the directive. See FRANZEN, above n. 65, pp. 324, 328; C. HÖPFNER, Anmerkung, *JZ* 2012, 473, 475–476; S. LORENZ, Ein- und Ausbauverpflichtung des Verkäufers bei der kaufrechtlichen Nacherfüllung, *NJW* 2011, 2241, 2244; SCHÜRNBRAND, above n. 73, p. 917.
[348] BGH, *NJW* 2014, 2646 paras. 21–34 – *Lebensversicherung II*. See Section 5.1 above.
[349] Ibid., para. 23. See also BVerwG, *BeckRS* 2017, 103948, para. 29.
[350] BGH, *NJW* 2014, 2646 paras. 23–26 – *Lebensversicherung II*.

third Life Assurance Directives.[351] Since the directive functions as a benchmark for filling the gap, it followed from the second and third Life Assurance Directives which cases had to be excluded from the scope of s. 5a(2) sentence 4 VVG in order for the German legislation to comply with the directives. As for establishing the gap, the filling of the gap in *Lebensversicherung II* can be reconciled with the aim of a teleological reduction to accomplish the plan and purpose of a statute because the plan and purpose of s. 5a(2) sentence 4 VVG included the presumed intention of the legislature to fully and correctly implement the directive. For all other types of insurance falling outside the scope of the second and third Life Assurance Directives, s. 5a(2) sentence 4 VVG remained applicable according to the BGH since a gap in the legislation did not exist. The second and third Life Assurance Directives do not guide the interpretation of s. 5a(2) sentence 4 VVG in these cases, and the provision's specific purpose to ensure legal certainty must be honoured. The court declared that neither EU law nor national law demand a uniform interpretation of a national provision that can be separated into a part that is determined by EU law and interpreted in conformity with an applicable directive and another part that is solely determined by national law and national legal methods.[352]

In a 2016 decision, the BVerfG confirmed that the BGH followed recognised methods of statutory interpretation when it established and filled a gap in *Lebensversicherung II*.[353] Despite the BVerfG's claim that conforming interpretation cannot go beyond the scope of permissible judicial reasoning according to national legal tradition, the BVerfG implicitly recognised that a regular court does not necessarily infringe this interpretative limit by relying on a European methodological rule. The BVerfG also implicitly recognised that the BGH did not breach art. 20(2), (3) GG by (a) relying on

---

[351] Ibid., para. 27.
[352] BGH, *NJW* 2014, 2646, para. 28 – *Lebensversicherung II*. Outside the scope of a directive, the EU legal duty of conforming interpretation does not apply. What is controversial in German legal scholarship is how national law has to be interpreted that gold-plates a directive (*überschießende Richtlinienumsetzung*). The gold-plated part of the national legislation could be interpreted in the light of the requirements of the directive (conforming-oriented interpretation; *richtlinienorientierte Auslegung*) or it could be interpreted solely based on national legal methods (diverging interpretation; *gespaltene Auslegung*). For an overview of the discussion, see M. HABERSACK and C. MAYER, Gold-plating: the implementation of directives through national provisions with a wider scope of application, in K. RIESENHUBER (ed.), *European legal methodology*, Intersentia, Cambridge 2017, §14, paras. 17–28; A.-C. MITTWOCH, Richtlinienkonforme Auslegung bei überschießender Umsetzung, *JuS* 2017, 296–301. This issue has occurred in English case law as well; see, e.g., *The United States of America v. Nolan* [2015] UKSC 63, paras. 14, 71–72 (Lord Mance, with whom Lord Neuberger, Lady Hale and Lord Reed agreed); *The United States of America v. Nolan* [2014] EWCA Civ 71, paras. 23–25 (Underhill LJ).
[353] BVerfG, *NJW-RR* 2016, 1366, para. 42.

the European presumption of compliance in order to establish a gap in the German legislation and (b) giving priority to the legislature's general intention to correctly transpose a directive into national law over the legislature's specific, but inadvertently non-conforming regulatory decision.

The BGH's methodological reasoning in *Quelle II*, *Weber II* and *Lebensversicherung II* has been adopted by the BVerwG in a case of conforming judicial law-making by means of argument by analogy.[354] Section 13(1) sentence 1 of the German law on Telecommunications (*Telekommunikationsgesetz*, TKG) exhaustively[355] enumerates measures taken by the German Federal Network Agency for which the consultation and consolidation procedure (s. 12 TKG) applies *mutatis mutandis*. The provisions regulating the issue of an authorisation of fees by the German Federal Network Agency, in particular s. 35(3) TKG, are not mentioned in s. 13(1) sentence 1 TKG. Based on the wording of s. 13(1) alone, the consultation and consolidation procedure did not apply to the issue of an authorisation of fees. The BVerwG then made a reference to the CJEU, and the CJEU decided that the applicable directives regulating electronic communications networks and services require a national regulatory authority to carry out a consolidation procedure before issuing an authorisation of fees.[356] When the case returned to the BVerwG, the German court argued that a gap in the legislation exists. That is because the legislative materials of the TKG expressed the aim of implementing the applicable directives in s. 13(1) TKG. An interpretation of s. 13(1) TKG in a narrow sense was not, however, able to achieve this aim. According to the BVerwG, it can be excluded that the legislature would have enacted s. 13(1) TKG in the same way if it had been aware that the provision in its current form does not comply with the applicable directives.[357] The BVerwG closed the gap by extending the scope of application of s. 13(1) sentence 1 TKG to cover decisions by the German Federal Network Authority about the issue of an authorisation of fees. The BVerwG effectively relied on and gave priority to the legislature's reasonably presumed intention to correctly and fully implement the directives over an inadvertently non-conforming objective of a specific provision, i.e. the objective to exclude authorisations of fees from the scope of application of the consultation and consolidation procedure. When closing the gap, the BVerwG did not explain why the novel case and the cases captured by the wording of s. 13(1) TKG are fundamentally similar from the perspective of the intended plan and purpose of s. 13(1) TKG. Such a cursory examination of the

---

[354] BVerwG, *BeckRS* 2017, 103948.
[355] BVerwG, *NVwZ* 2014, 1586, paras. 53–54.
[356] This is a simplified overview of the decision. See Case C-395/14, *Vodafone GmbH v. Bundesrepublik Deutschland*, ECLI:EU:C:2016:9, para. 58.
[357] BVerwG, *BeckRS* 2017, 103948 paras. 29, 30.

"fundamental similarity" condition of gap-filling by means of argument by analogy can be seen in other cases of conforming judicial law-making as well.[358] The BVerwG emphasised that the national legislature intended to correctly implement the applicable directives regulating electronic communications networks and services with s. 13(1) TKG.[359] This rationale extends to the new case and can thus explain the fundamental similarity.

6.1.2. Non-Implementing Legislation that Precedes a Directive

We have already briefly encountered the BGH's judgment in *Interprofessionelle Sozietät* in Section 2 above. This case serves as an example of how German courts interpret non-implementing national legislation that precedes an applicable directive. The case concerned the interpretation of the old s. 59a(1) of the German Federal Regulations for Lawyers (BRAO). The provision allows lawyers to cooperate with members of certain other professions on the basis of a joint exercise of the profession. The claimant, a lawyer, wanted to pursue his professional activities in cooperation with a medical doctor in the form of a professional partnership. Yet, medical doctor is a profession not mentioned by s. 59a(1) BRAO, which is why the registry court denied the entry of the professional partnership into the register. When the case arrived at the BGH, the court construed s. 59a(1) BRAO according to its wording, the intention of the enacting legislature as evidenced by legislative materials and its sense and purpose. The court concluded that the enumeration of certain other professions in the section is exhaustive.[360] The claimant further argued that (a) this interpretation of s. 59a(1) BRAO is incompatible with art. 25(1) of the Services Directive (Directive 2006/123/EC) and that (b) s. 59a(1) BRAO must be interpreted broadly in order to comply with the Services Directive. Article 25(1) of the Services Directive governs multidisciplinary activities between service providers.

The BGH explicitly left open the question to what extent art. 25(1) of the Services Directive applies to lawyers. There was no CJEU case law on that question either at the time of the BGH's ruling. Instead, the BGH argued that s. 59a(1) BRAO cannot in any case be interpreted in conformity with art. 25(1) of the Services Directive, even assuming that the latter applied to lawyers, since such an interpretation would exceed the limits of the judicial function.[361] The BGH explained that s. 59a(1) BRAO pre-dates the

---

[358] See BGH, *ZUM* 2010, 429, para. 22 – *Bob Dylan (No. 2)*; BGH, *NJW* 2015, 3511, para. 31 – *Elektronische Leseplätze II*.
[359] BVerwG, *BeckRS* 2017, 103948, para. 30.
[360] BGH, *NJW* 2013, 2674, paras. 6, 28–36 – *Interprofessionelle Sozietät*.
[361] Ibid., paras. 39, 42–43. The BGH further argued that art. 25(1) of the Services Directive lacks direct effect; see ibid., paras. 48–49.

Services Directive and is not intended to implement art. 25(1) of that directive. An identifiable intention of the German legislature that s. 59a(1) BRAO complies with the Services Directive does not exist. Moreover, the German legislature had considered an extension of the right of lawyers to jointly exercise the profession with members of certain other professions such as medical doctors. This proposed amendment of s. 59a BRAO was unaffected by the Services Directive. According to the legislative materials, the proposal was rejected during the passage of the bill through Parliament on the grounds of considerable differences of opinion within the legal profession, which is why the legislature decided to address the issue separately in a later bill.[362] This argument by the BGH may indicate that the issue requires legislative deliberation and that, therefore, the outer limits of judicial law-making were exceeded in *Interprofessionelle Sozietät*. For these reasons, the BGH concluded that s. 59a(1) BRAO does not contain a gap, which would be required for a conforming judicial law-making by means of a teleological reduction.[363]

In contrast to *Quelle II*, *Weber II* and *Lebensversicherung II*, where the BGH interpreted national implementing legislation, *Interprofessionelle Sozietät* shows considerable restraint towards conforming judicial law-making when non-implementing legislation that precedes an applicable directive is at issue. This is not an isolated case.[364] Yet in all these four cases, the BGH focused on the legislative materials of the provision under consideration and gave significant weight to the intention of the enacting legislature. In other words, there is no difference in the overall interpretative approach in these four cases. Yes, the BGH did not argue with a presumed intention of the enacting legislature to comply with the applicable directive in *Interprofessionalle Sozietät*.[365] That is because there were no indications that the German legislature intended to create a conforming provision with s. 59a(1) BRAO. The EU presumption of compliance does not apply in such a case. Hence, *Interprofessionelle Sozität* read in comparison with *Quelle II*, *Weber II* and

---

[362] Ibid., para. 34.
[363] Ibid., para. 43.
[364] See BAG, NZA 2010, 1020 – *Urlaubsentgelt*. The claimant in that case asserted that s. 13(2) BUrlG is incompatible with art. 7(1) of Directive 2003/88/EC. Assuming that the claimant's interpretation of art. 7(1) of Directive 2003/88/EC is correct, the BAG held that s. 13(2) BUrlG cannot be interpreted in conformity with the directive by means of conforming judicial law-making. The BAG argued that, taking into account the four interpretative criteria, s. 13(2) BUrlG does not contain a gap (ibid., paras. 30, 37). The BAG did not consider art. 7(1) of Directive 2003/88/EC when ascertaining the meaning of s. 13(2) BUrlG, which pre-dated Directive 2003/88/EC and was not intended to implement this directive.
[365] For arguments against the application of a national presumption of compliance based on national legal methodology for the interpretation of pre-dating domestic legislation, see CANARIS, above n. 82, pp. 47, 50–51; PERNER, above n. 49, p. 93.

Lebensversicherung II also shows that applying the EU or national presumption of compliance can have a significant effect for the outcome of a case of conforming judicial law-making.

Even though the BGH did not apply a presumption of compliance in *Interprofessionelle Sozietät*, it was argued above that a court ought to take the directive into account when determining the (objectivised) sense and purpose of domestic legislation that precedes a directive if the analogy to constitution-consistent interpretation is fully followed. The BGH did not do this as it did not consider the aim of art. 25(1) of the Services Directive when determining the true meaning of s. 59a(1) BRAO and when determining whether the latter provision contained a gap.[366] Taking the directive into account when determining the meaning of non-implementing, pre-dating legislation would imply a highly objectivised understanding of the aim of conforming interpretation. Such an objectivised interpretation would certainly not be common in contemporary German judicial practice, but it would not be unheard of either. It may involve a deviation from the intention of the enacting legislature, but we have discovered in Chapter 2 that such a departure does not necessarily exceed the outer limits of the judicial role. What may explain the reluctance of the BGH to venture down this path may be recent BVerfG case law on the limits of the judicial function. It was shown in Chapter 2 that the BVerfG urges courts to give sufficient consideration to the intention of the enacting legislature and the legislative materials when interpreting legislation in order to comply with art. 20(2), (3) GG. A highly objectivised interpretation of s. 59a(1) BRAO would have been incompatible with this guideline. Furthermore, determining a gap by relying on such a highly objectivised plan and purpose of non-implementing, pre-dating legislation comes close to using the directive itself as a benchmark for establishing the unintendedness criterion of the legislation. The BGH has so far avoided the issue of whether the directive itself can be used as a benchmark for establishing the unintendedness criterion, which gives rise to further controversial questions as noted in the previous subsection. One of these questions is whether a directive

---

[366] See, however, BAG, *EuZW* 2009, 465, paras. 58–59, 66–67 – *Schultz-Hoff*, where the BAG interpreted s. 7(3) and (4) BUrlG in conformity with the applicable Directive 2003/88/EC. The German legislation was not enacted in order to implement Directive 2003/88/EC, but pre-dated this directive. Furthermore, the German legislature did not indicate in the legislative materials that s. 7(3) and (4) comply with the directive's requirements. Yet, the BAG argued that the conforming meaning complies with the wording, the context and the purpose of the national provisions when the aims of art. 7(1) and (2) of Directive 2003/88/EC and the presumed intention of the national legislature to fully implement directives into national law are taken into account. The BAG seems, however, to have backtracked from this reasoning in BAG, *NZA* 2010, 1020 – *Urlaubsentgelt* (see discussion in note 364 above).

can be considered legislation or law under art. 20(3) GG and can thus be part of the binding force of a statute. If the BGH were to rely on the directive in order to argue that the directive affects the purpose of the contested national provision even if a presumed intention of the enacting legislature to comply with the directive's requirements is absent, this would come very close to categorising the directive as legislation or law under art. 20(3) GG.

Another difference between the four cases discussed here,[367] which may affect the possibility of conforming judicial law-making, is that the CJEU had not decided on the conformity of s. 59a(1) BRAO with EU law in *Interprofessionelle Sozietät*. *Quelle II*, *Weber II* and *Lebensversicherung II* were all preceded by a CJEU judgment ruling that the applicable directives precluded the challenged national legislation as interpreted in a narrow sense. None of the CJEU judgments gave guidance on the issue of whether a conforming interpretation of the national legislation is possible or not. From a purely methodological viewpoint, this difference between *Interprofessionelle Sozietät* and the other three cases should be immaterial. That is because it falls exclusively to the referring national court to determine whether a conforming interpretation is possible or not. Having said that, a judgment by the CJEU may de facto increase the willingness of a national court to find a conforming meaning.[368] It has already been discovered that the concept of gap as applied in judicial practice is significantly malleable, and it will later be established in this chapter that the outer limits of conforming judicial law-making leave considerable scope for judicial discretion to include extra-legal factors such as the authority exerted by a CJEU judgment. The *Heininger* and *Quelle* litigation illustrate how a CJEU judgment can nudge the BGH to make interpretative U-turns. In both cases, the referring BGH felt first unable to ascribe to the national law at issue a meaning that, as it appeared after the decision of the CJEU, complied with the applicable directive. In neither case did the CJEU suggest to the BGH that or how the national law is amenable to a conforming interpretation. Yet, when both cases returned to the BGH, it reached a conforming reading using national methods of interpretation.[369]

A worrying development is that the highest German courts are using a new "strategy" to dodge the preliminary reference procedure. This is not the place to

---

[367] *Quelle II*, *Weber II*, *Lebensversicherung II* and *Interprofessionelle Sozietät*.
[368] This factor may explain the venturous reasoning of the BAG in *EuZW* 2009, 465, paras. 58–59, 66–67 – *Schultz-Hoff* (see discussion in note 366 above). Before the BAG's judgment in *Schultz-Hoff*, the CJEU had effectively ruled that the BAG's settled interpretation of s. 7(3) and (4) BUrlG did not comply with Directive 2003/88/EC (see Case C-350/06, *Schultz-Hoff v. Deutsche Rentenversicherung Bund*. ECLI:EU:C:2009:18, paras. 52, 62).
[369] For *Heininger*, see: BGH, *NJW* 2000, 521 – *Heininger I*; Case C-481/99, *Heininger v. Bayerische Hypo- und Vereinsbank AG*, ECLI:EU:C:2001:684; BGH, *NJW* 2002, 1881 – *Heininger II*. For *Quelle*, see: BGH, *NJW* 2006, 3200 – *Quelle I*; Case C-404/06, *Quelle v. Bundesverband der*

go into the details of other key strategies of national courts to avoid preliminary references such as the *acte clair* doctrine or the art of distinguishing precedents. A sufficient amount of ink has been spilled on these strategies and also on the reasons why English courts appear to refer fewer questions to the CJEU than, for example, their German counterparts.[370] There is also a considerable amount of academic criticism and case law[371] on the topic that German judges avoid preliminary references to the CJEU.[372] One possible motivation for a national court not to involve the CJEU seems to be that a domestic court intends to avoid the pressure that a CJEU judgment can exert. Having said that, the CJEU rarely suggests an adventurous conforming interpretation of the national law in its preliminary reference rulings. The pressure thus seems to arise from the circumstance that the national law as interpreted by a national court infringes the requirements of a directive as construed by the CJEU. This situation creates incentives for a national court to reach a conforming meaning of the challenged legislation.[373] In *Interprofessionalle Sozietät*, the BGH refused to refer to the CJEU the question about the directive's interpretation even though the German court admitted that it was unsure about the correct interpretation of the directive.[374] The pattern in this and other cases[375] is similar: the national court does not refer because it (a) claims that the national law cannot be interpreted in conformity with the alleged meaning of a directive as suggested by one of the parties to the proceedings because such an interpretation would be *contra legem* and at the same time (b) asserts, and rightly so for proceedings exclusively between private parties, that the provision of the directive at issue does not have direct effect. In this scenario, the correct interpretation of the directive will often not have any bearing on the decision of the dispute. This "strategy" of dodging the preliminary reference procedure has featured more in German than in English cases. It goes without saying that a refusal of national

---

Verbraucherzentralen und Verbraucherverbände, ECLI:EU:C:2008:231; BGH, *NJW* 2009, 427 – *Quelle II*.

[370] A. ARNULL, The UK Supreme Court and references to the CJEU, (2017) 36 *Yearbook of European Law* 314–357; M. BROBERG and N. FENGER, *Preliminary references to the European Court of Justice*, 2nd ed., OUP, Oxford 2014, pp. 37–58; H. RÖSLER, *Europäische Gerichtsbarkeit auf dem Gebiet des Zivilrechts*, Mohr Siebeck, Tübingen 2012, §4; T. TRIDIMAS, Knocking on heaven's door: fragmentation, efficiency and defiance in the preliminary reference procedure, (2003) 40 *CMLR* 9, 38.

[371] See, e.g. BVerfG, *NJW* 2015, 1294 (the opinion of the BGH that s. 5a(1), (2) sentence 1 VVG complies with the applicable EU directive is "objectively untenable and arbitrary").

[372] For recent discussion, see M. EBERS, Krise des Vorabentscheidungsverfahrens im Versicherungsrecht?, *VuR* 2017, 47–51.

[373] In detail, Section 1.2 above.

[374] BGH, *NJW* 2013, 2674, paras. 36, 39–43, 44–51 – *Interprofessionelle Sozietät*.

[375] See also BGH, *NJW* 2017, 3387, paras. 23–26; BAG, *NZA* 2010, 1020 paras. 16, 26–27 – *Urlaubsentgelt*; BAG, *NZA* 2004, 375, 382; OLG München, *Neue Juristische Online Zeitschrift* 2014, 204, 207.

Chapter 4. The European Legal Duty of Conforming Interpretation

courts to cooperate with the CJEU by dodging the preliminary reference procedure seriously threatens the uniform interpretation and application of directives in the Member States.

6.2. READING IN, OUT OR DOWN OF WORDS IN LEGISLATION

English courts apply the "the same robust techniques"[376] for conforming interpretation that are available under s. 3(1) HRA. That is a result of the analogy between s. 3(1) HRA and conforming interpretation. Since these techniques have already been presented in Section 6.2 of Chapter 3, it is sufficient to provide a short account of how these techniques work in the sphere of conforming judicial law-making. It also follows from the analogy to s. 3(1) HRA that the techniques of conforming judicial law-making go beyond those of conventional canons of construction. English courts have held that the interpretative technique that a court needs to employ in order to reach the conforming meaning does not matter.[377] There is agreement that a court can read words (imply words)[378] into a provision or read down a provision. Whereas in some judgments[379] this terminology refers to the change of the statutory language, in other judgments[380] the terminology refers to the change of the scope of application of the provision. I have argued in Section 6 of Chapter 3 that it would be more appropriate for English courts to adopt the terminology of extending or narrowing the scope of application of a provision for rights-consistent judicial law-making. The same is true with regard to conforming judicial law-making.[381] Despite the terminological confusion, what is clear

---

[376] *Revenue and Customs Commissioners v. IDT Card Services Ireland Ltd.* [2006] EWCA Civ 29, para. 92 (Arden LJ).
[377] *Google Inc. v. Vidal-Hall* [2015] EWCA Civ 311, para. 90 (Lord Dyson MR and Sharp LJ, with whom McFarlane LJ agreed); *ITV Broadcasting Ltd. v. TV Catchup Ltd. (No. 2)* [2011] EWHC 1874 (Pat.), para. 121 (Floyd J).
[378] "Reading" and "implying" words into a statute are mostly used interchangeably by the courts. See, e.g. *Fleming (t/a Bodycraft) v. Customs and Excise Commissioners* [2006] EWCA Civ 70, para. 44 (Arden LJ); *Ghaidan v. Godin-Mendoza* [2004] UKHL 30, para. 121 (Lord Rodger).
[379] *Lehman Brothers International (Europe) (In Administration), Re* [2012] UKSC 6, para. 131 (Lord Dyson, "[conforming interpretation] permits the implication of words necessary to comply with Community law"); *Revenue and Customs Commissioners v. IDT Card Services Ireland Ltd.* [2006] EWCA Civ 29, para. 114 (Arden LJ); *EB Central Services Ltd. v. Revenue and Customs Commissioners* [2008] EWCA Civ 486, para. 49 (Mummery LJ), para. 87 (Dyson LJ); *NHS Leeds v. Larner* [2012] EWCA Civ 1034, paras. 89–90 (Mummery LJ, *obiter*, with whom Tomlinson and Henderson LJJ agreed).
[380] *ITV Broadcasting Ltd. v. TV Catchup Ltd.* [2015] EWCA Civ 204, paras. 105–106 (Arden LJ, *obiter*); *Google Inc. v. Vidal-Hall* [2015] EWCA Civ 311, para. 89 (Lord Dyson MR and Sharp LJ, with whom McFarlane LJ agreed).
[381] This is, for example, argued by Underhill J in: *EBR Attridge Law LLP v. Coleman* [2010] ICR 242 (EAT), para. 14 (Underhill J, "an extension of the scope of the legislation as enacted").

is that a court can (a) expand a provision's scope of application, (b) narrow a provision's scope of application, (c) read additional words into a provision and (d) read down general words in a provision in order to achieve a conforming meaning. It is therefore negligible that the use of terminology regarding the interpretative techniques is not uniform in English judgments.

In *Pickstone*, for example, the House of Lords extended the scope of application of s. 1(2)(c) Equal Pay Act 1970 by reading into s. 1(2)(c) after the word "applies" the words "as between the woman and the man with whom she claims equality".[382] In *Litster*, the House of Lords extended the scope of reg. 5 of the Transfer of Undertakings Regulations 1981 by reading the provision "as if there were inserted after the words 'immediately before the transfer' the words 'or would have been so employed if he had not been unfairly dismissed in the circumstances described in regulation 8(1)'".[383] In *IDT Card Services*, the Court of Appeal interpreted Sch. 10A of the Value Added Tax Act 1994 (VATA 1994) in the light of the Sixth EC VAT Directive (77/388/EEC). VATA 1994 implemented the Sixth EC VAT Directive into national law and contained provisions designed to avoid double taxation and non-taxation. The court extended the scope of para. 3(3) of Sch. 10A VATA 1994 by reading into it a further disapplication of para. 3(2) of Sch. 10A in order to avoid the non-taxation in the case at hand.[384] This meant in effect that a duty to pay VAT was imposed upon an individual as a result of the conforming reading of the legislation even though no such liability to tax existed if the legislation was construed in accordance with conventional canons of statutory interpretation.[385] In *British Gas Trading v. Lock*, the Court of Appeal interpreted the Working Time Regulations 1998 as including the results-based commission element in calculating holiday pay by reading additional words into reg. 16 of the Working Time Regulations 1998.[386]

If a court reads words into a provision, their number or precise form is insignificant.[387] Even though English judges sometimes use terms in written judicial opinions that would indicate a specific condition for a technique

---

[382] *Pickstone v. Freemans Plc* [1989] AC 66 (HL), 120–121 (Lord Templeman), 126 (Lord Oliver).
[383] *Litster v. Forth Dry Dock & Engineering Co Ltd.* [1990] 1 AC 546 (HL), 577 (Lord Oliver), cf. 554 (Lord Keith), 558 (Lord Templeman).
[384] *Revenue and Customs Commissioners v. IDT Card Services Ireland Ltd.* [2006] EWCA Civ 29, paras. 113–114 (Arden LJ).
[385] Cf. *Revenue and Customs Commissioners v. IDT Card Services Ireland Ltd.* [2006] EWCA Civ 29, paras. 113–114 (Arden LJ), paras. 133, 135 (Pill LJ); *Vodafone 2 v. Revenue and Customs Commissioners* [2009] EWCA Civ 446, para. 43 (Sir Andrew Morritt C). The state thus relied on the principle of conforming interpretation and its application gave rise to a liability to tax upon a private individual.
[386] *British Gas Trading Ltd. v. Lock* [2016] EWCA Civ 983, paras. 26, 112–114 (Sir Colin Rimer, with whom Gloster LJ and Sir Terence Etherton MR agreed).
[387] *Pickstone v. Freemans Plc* [1989] AC 66 (HL), 112 (Lord Keith); *Lehman Brothers International (Europe) (In Administration), Re* [2012] UKSC 6, para. 131 (Lord Dyson); *Revenue and*

of judicial law-making in a German legal context, i.e. the term "gap",[388] English judges have used these terms in an untechnical way. Applying the guidance given in *Ghaidan*, only the substantive effect of the conforming interpretation matters as opposed to the language used or the interpretative technique employed. As for s. 3(1) HRA, a court must identify clearly the particular provision or provisions to which it applies a specific conforming interpretation.[389] If this cannot be done, a limit of conforming interpretation is breached. Ward LJ said in *Fleming*, for example, that it is not possible to construe "something out of nothing".[390] Hallett LJ added that reading an adequate transitional period into the amended reg. 29(1A) of the Value Added Tax Regulations 1995 in order to make it compatible with primary EU law is not possible as "there is nothing to extend. ... [T]here is no provision to be given a purposive construction, even if there is little if any disagreement between the parties on what would have been an appropriate transitional period".[391]

6.3. COMPARATIVE ANALYSIS

In judicial practice, English and German courts follow the analogy between conforming interpretation and rights-consistent interpretation when dealing with techniques of judicial law-making. Therefore, the comparative discussion provided in Section 6.3 of Chapter 3 for rights-consistent interpretation applies *mutatis mutandis* for the comparison of the techniques of conforming judicial law-making in England and Germany.[392] Building on the discussion in Section 6.3 of Chapter 3, for example, English judges do not necessarily have greater powers than German judges to make law in the sphere of conforming judicial law-making even though English judges, in contrast

---

Customs Commissioners v. IDT Card Services Ireland Ltd. [2006] EWCA Civ 29, para. 114 (Arden LJ); *Vodafone 2 v. Revenue and Customs Commissioners* [2009] EWCA Civ 446, para. 37 (Sir Andrew Morritt C); *Churchill Insurance Co. Ltd. v. Fitzgerald & Wilkinson* [2012] EWCA Civ 1166, para. 50 (Aikens LJ, with whom Etherton and Maurice Kay LJJ agreed); *Birmingham Hippodrome Theatre Trust Ltd. v. Revenue and Customs Commissioners* [2014] EWCA Civ 684, para. 38 (Lewison LJ, with whom Sharp LJ and Vos LJ agreed).

388 *Pickstone v. Freemans Plc* [1989] AC 66 (HL), 124–125 (Lord Oliver, "filling a gap"); *Revenue and Customs Commissioners v. IDT Card Services Ireland Ltd.* [2006] EWCA Civ 29, para. 113 (Arden LJ, "not dissimilar situation"); *Fleming (t/a Bodycraft) v. Customs and Excise Commissioners* [2006] EWCA Civ 70, para. 67 (Hallett LJ, "fill the lacuna").

389 *Prudential Assurance Co. Ltd. v. Revenue and Customs Commissioners* [2016] EWCA Civ 376, para. 111 (Lewison LJ); cf. *Fleming (t/a Bodycraft) v. Customs and Excise Commissioners* [2006] EWCA Civ 70, para. 67 (Hallett LJ).

390 *Fleming (t/a Bodycraft) v. Customs and Excise Commissioners* [2006] EWCA Civ 70, para. 80 (Ward LJ).

391 Ibid., para. 67 (Hallett LJ).

392 This comparative analysis is thus not repeated here.

to their German counterparts, do not adopt formal techniques of conforming judicial law-making. Furthermore, a methodological criterion like the concept of gap as applied in German judicial practice hardly constrains judicial law-making. A comparison with English case law shows that it is dispensable.

I have already shown in the previous section how adaptable domestic canons of interpretation are for incorporating the effects of the EU legal duty of conforming interpretation in national law. Another example for this flexibility is provided by the techniques of conforming judicial law-making when implementing legislation is at issue. These techniques as applied in German courts, in particular the concept of gap, prove highly adaptable and malleable, and this safeguards the effectiveness of directives in the national legal sphere. This high level of adaptability is correlated with the high level of indeterminacy of these techniques. For example, German courts can rely on the European presumption of compliance when establishing a gap in the German legislation. This flexibility devalues the limiting function of the techniques of judicial law-making. A very similar picture exists in England, where the more flexible purposive approach as established in *Pickstone* illustrates that English legal methodology has adapted in order to incorporate the effects of directives in national law. In the light of the analogy to s. 3(1) HRA, the techniques of conforming judicial law-making used by English courts are highly adaptable, too. Only the substantive result of the conforming judicial law-making as opposed to the language used or the interpretative technique employed matters.

Compared to implementing legislation, the case law of the highest German courts on conforming judicial law-making of non-implementing legislation that pre-dates an applicable directive can be characterised by judicial restraint and a narrow application of the techniques of judicial law-making. As regards English case law, we have seen in Section 2 above that the House of Lords first adopted a rather restrictive approach to conforming interpretation of non-implementing legislation that precedes an applicable directive in *Duke*. After *Webb (No. 2)*, this restrictive approach no longer appears to be followed in English courts.[393] Whether that is actually the case is difficult to assess as there is an insufficient amount of case law coming from the highest English courts that construes this kind of legislation. An explanation for the different judicial attitudes visible in *Webb (No. 2)* and the German cases was provided in Section 2 above. I have argued that the presence or absence of a preliminary reference ruling by the CJEU and the pressure that such a ruling can exert on a

---

[393] ARNULL, above n. 206, p. 73; BRADLEY, EWING and KNIGHT, above n. 206, p. 139.

national court to find a conforming meaning is one factor that may explain this difference.[394]

7. OUTER INTERPRETATIVE LIMITS

This core section of Chapter 4 will critically analyse the outer limits of conforming judicial law-making as applied in English and German courts. English and German courts have held, in line with CJEU case law, that the outer limits of conforming interpretation are determined by national legal methodology.[395] Arden LJ expressed this credo particularly forcefully when she said that

> the national court is not concerned to ask what interpretative approach is adopted by the courts of the other member states of the European Union. The question of how far it can go under the guise of interpretation, and whether it can for instance adopt what would otherwise be regarded as a strained construction, is a matter for domestic law.[396]

It is recognised in English and German courts that there may be circumstances where it is not possible to interpret domestic legislation compatibly with the corresponding directive even though the legislature intended to correctly implement the directive.[397]

English and German courts have drawn the boundary between possible and impossible conforming interpretation at the constitutional junction between permissible judicial interpretation and impermissible judicial amendment of legislation, the latter remaining the exclusive task of the legislature.[398] This boundary is determined by national constitutional law, which explains why

---

[394] I will explore in the discussion of the German case *Gasversorgung II* in Sections 7.1 and 7.3 below that this factor may be outweighed by other factors.
[395] BVerfG, *NJW* 2012, 669, para. 47; BVerfG, *NJW-RR* 2016, 1366, para. 42; BGH, *NJW* 2009, 427, para. 21 – *Quelle II*; BAG, *NZA* 2003, 747; *Duke v Reliance Ltd.* [1988] AC 618 (HL), 641 (Lord Templeman); *Revenue and Customs Commissioners v. IDT Card Services Ireland Ltd.* [2006] EWCA Civ 29, para. 81 (Arden LJ); cf. *Cooper v. HM Attorney General* [2010] EWCA Civ 464, para. 79 (Arden LJ).
[396] *Revenue and Customs Commissioners v. IDT Card Services Ireland Ltd.* [2006] EWCA Civ 29, para. 81 (Arden LJ).
[397] BAG, *NZA* 2003, 742, 748; *Google Inc. v. Vidal-Hall* [2015] EWCA Civ 311, para. 86 (Lord Dyson MR and Sharp LJ, with whom McFarlane LJ agreed).
[398] BVerfG, *NJW* 2012, 669, paras. 44–47; BGH, *NJW* 2009, 427, paras. 30–31 – *Quelle II*; *Revenue and Customs Commissioners v. IDT Card Services Ireland Ltd.* [2006] EWCA Civ 29, paras. 82, 90 (Arden LJ); *O'Brien v. Ministry of Justice* [2015] EWCA Civ 1000, para. 48 (Lewison LJ); cf. *ITV Broadcasting Ltd. v. TV Catchup Ltd.* [2015] EWCA Civ 204, para. 86 (Kitchin LJ).

English and German courts refer to national legal tradition when establishing the outer limits of conforming interpretation. A court that surpasses this boundary exceeds its judicial function. This functional understanding of the outer limits of conforming interpretation is in accordance with CJEU case law. When expressing this boundary in case law, English courts often refer to the "as far as possible" limit[399] and German courts predominantly use the term *contra legem* limit.[400] The preference of the courts to use different terminology in both jurisdictions is probably due to the analogy to s. 3(1) HRA in England and to the common judicial use of the *contra legem* limit of interpretation according to conventional canons in Germany.

Neither English nor German courts have explicitly recognised the potential of European methodological rules to confine national autonomy and to shift the outer limits of conforming interpretation. One reason for this is that it is controversial whether the EU possesses the competence to intervene in the national separation of powers between the legislature and the judiciary. Neither the UK Supreme Court nor the BVerfG have yet explicitly accepted such a power of the EU. It will be demonstrated in this section that a second reason is that the domestic outer limits of conforming judicial law-making are expressed in vague terms in both Member States. These limits are sufficiently adaptive to be applied in a European-friendly manner, and they can assimilate the effects of the European presumption of compliance.

7.1. LIMITS OF CONFORMING JUDICIAL LAW-MAKING IN GERMANY

The BVerfG applies the same outer limits for conforming judicial law-making that it uses for conventional judicial law-making and for constitution-consistent judicial law-making.[401] The underlying reason for this is art. 20(2), (3) GG, which does not differentiate between different modes of statutory interpretation. German courts also use the same outer limits of conforming interpretation in cases where the national legislation pre-dates or post-dates, implements or does

---

[399] See, e.g. *Revenue and Customs Commissioners v. IDT Card Services Ireland Ltd.* [2006] EWCA Civ 29, paras. 82, 91 (Arden LJ); *Airtours Holidays Transport v. Revenue and Customs Commissioners* [2016] UKSC 21, para. 17 (Lord Neuberger). For a recent use of the term *contra legem* limit, see *British Gas Trading Ltd. v. Lock* [2016] EWCA Civ 983, paras. 100–104 (Sir Colin Rimer, with whom Gloster LJ and Sir Terence Etherton MR agreed).
[400] BGH, *NJW* 2009, 427, para. 21 – *Quelle II*; BAG, *EuZW* 2009, 465, para. 65 – *Schultz-Hoff*.
[401] BVerfG, *NJW* 2012, 669, paras. 43–46, 55–57 (conforming judicial law-making); BVerfG, *NJW* 1999, 1853, 1855 (constitution-consistent judicial law-making); BVerfG, *NJW* 2011, 842, paras. 51–55 – *Dreiteilungsmethode* (conventional judicial law-making); BVerfG, *NJW* 2012, 3081, paras. 74–77 – *Delisting* (conventional judicial law-making).

not implement an applicable directive.⁴⁰² Since the outer limits of conventional and constitution-consistent judicial law-making have already been presented in Chapters 2 and 3, it is not necessary to provide a complete account here. For example, a conforming meaning cannot be adopted if it alters a clear legislative decision based on a judge's own policy considerations.⁴⁰³ A court would exceed the limits of the possible if it were to give a contrary meaning to a provision that is clear according to its wording, scheme and purpose.⁴⁰⁴ According to the BAG, a conforming interpretation is barred if the national legislature deliberately refuses to transform a directive into national law at all.⁴⁰⁵ In line with case law on conventional and constitution-consistent judicial law-making, German courts have clarified that a provision's wording does not in itself function as an outer limit of conforming judicial law-making. A conforming judicial law-making may be possible even against a provision's clear wording.⁴⁰⁶

The BGH held in a 2017 judgment that a conforming interpretation is only possible if it (still) corresponds with and does not change the identifiable intention of the legislature.⁴⁰⁷ This outer limit of interpretation can be applied more narrowly or more widely, depending on how much correspondence is needed and how objectivised the notion of "intention of the legislature" is understood. It is clear from the context that this outer limit of interpretation is neither intended to signal a departure from the BGH's earlier case law on conforming judicial law-making, which the BGH cites with approval, nor intended to signal a narrower application of the outer limits of conforming interpretation. For example, the BGH referred to *Quelle II*, where the court denied the seller a right to claim compensation from the consumer-buyer for the benefits derived from using the defective good. It was, however, the intention of the enacting legislature to grant the seller such a right. The BGH thus interpreted s. 439(4) German Civil Code contrary to this identifiable objective of the enacting legislature. Yet, the conforming interpretation still corresponded with the specifically expressed intention of the enacting legislature to correctly implement the directive in s. 439(4) German Civil Code. In *Weber II*, the identifiable intention of the enacting legislature was altered as well, but the conforming interpretation still corresponded with the reasonably presumed

---

[402] Cf. BVerfG, *NJW* 2012, 669, paras. 42–47; BAG, *EuZW* 2009, 465, paras. 58, 65 – *Schultz-Hoff*; BGH, *NJW* 2016, 1718, paras. 40–43 – *Gasversorgung II*.
[403] BGH, *NJW* 2009, 427, para. 31 – *Quelle II*.
[404] BAG, *NZA* 2006, 862, para. 43.
[405] BAG, *NJW* 2006, 3161, para. 25. See also OLG Stuttgart, *WM* 2009, 1416, para. 193.
[406] BGH, *NJW* 2009, 427, para. 20 – *Quelle II*; BGH, *ZUM* 2010, 429, para. 22 – *Bob Dylan (No. 2)* ("irrespective of the provision's opposing wording"); BGH, *NJW* 2012, 1073, para. 28 – *Weber II*; BGH, *NJW* 2014, 2646, para. 21 – *Lebensversicherung II*.
[407] BGH, *NJW* 2017, 1093, para. 38. See also BGH, *NJW* 2016, 1718, para. 43 – *Gasversorgung II*.

general intention of the enacting legislature to fully and correctly implement the directive. This illustrates that even if a court derogates from a specific objective of the implementing legislation, the conforming meaning may still be reconcilable with what can reasonably be supposed to have been the intention of the enacting legislature. Compared to the level of "objectivised" legislative intent that the German courts have adopted in *Soraya* and *Fotokopie*, for example, judicial law-making of implementing legislation appears less controversial. In *Soraya* and *Fotokopie*, the German courts departed from an identifiable objective of the enacting legislature, and the meaning that was eventually adopted by the courts via judicial law-making could not reasonably be attributed to the enacting legislature. In its 2017 ruling itself, the BGH engaged in conforming interpretation in a narrow sense. It emphasised that despite the legislative materials being unclear, they did not contain indications that the enacting legislature intended to oppose the interpretation of the applicable directive that it was later given by the CJEU. The BGH then relied on the presumed general intention of the enacting legislature to fully implement the directive. It held that s. 476 German Civil Code could be interpreted in conformity with art. 5(3) of Directive 1999/44/EC on certain aspects of the sale of consumer goods and associated guarantees into national law as interpreted by the CJEU.[408]

In an *obiter* statement in *Quelle II* and in *Weber II*, the BGH explicitly left open whether a conforming judicial law-making can have the effect of a complete disapplication of a provision.[409] If this were possible, it would have the effect of a widening of the judicial function compared with conventional judicial law-making and constitution-consistent judicial law-making. The reason for this is that a court cannot reduce the scope of application of a provision to zero by means of interpretation under the latter two modes of judicial law-making. The BVerfG, however, rejected such a "Europeanisation from the inside" in a ruling in 2011, when it held that the outer boundaries of permissible conforming judicial law-making are governed by the same outer limits of interpretation that apply for the other two modes of judicial law-making.[410] Despite the BVerfG's clarification, the BGH interpreted sentence 4 of s. 8(5) VVG[411] in the case *Lebensversicherung im Antragsmodell* in conformity with the second and third Life Assurance Directives[412] by means of

---

[408] BGH, *NJW* 2017, 1093, paras. 44–45, 51.
[409] BGH, *NJW* 2009, 427, para. 29 – *Quelle II*; BGH, *NJW* 2012, 1073, para. 45 – *Weber II*.
[410] BVerfG, *NJW* 2012, 669, paras. 43–46. Confirmed in BVerfG, *NJW-RR* 2016, 1366, para. 41. For a different view, see HERRESTHAL, above n. 18, p. 400.
[411] Section 8(5) VVG was repealed with effect from 1.1.2008, but the old version was applicable to the facts of the case in the main proceedings.
[412] Directive 90/619/EEC and Directive 92/96/EEC.

teleological reduction.⁴¹³ Section 8(5) VVG granted a policy holder a right to cancel the life assurance contract within 30 days after concluding the contract. The period of 30 days only started to run when the insurer informed the rights holder about the right of cancellation. In the case at issue, the insurer's information about the right of cancellation failed to meet the necessary formal requirements. The consequence was that the cancellation period of 30 days had never started to run. Sentence 4 of s. 8(5) VVG stipulated, however, that in the event of a lack of information the right of cancellation expires one month after payment of the first premium. The claimant in *Lebensversicherung im Antragsmodell* had already paid insurance premiums and the period of one month after payment of the first premium had long passed.

It was clear that an interpretation of sentence 4 of s. 8(5) VVG according to conventional canons of construction infringed the applicable directives. That is because the CJEU had interpreted the second and third Life Assurance Directives in an earlier reference from the BGH. The European court had held that these directives preclude a national provision that provides for the expiry of the policy holder's right to cancel the contract at a time when the policy holder has not been informed about that right.⁴¹⁴ Therefore, in *Lebensversicherung im Antragsmodell*, the BGH decided to apply the same principles that led to a conforming judicial law-making of s. 5a(2) sentence 4 VVG in the case *Lebensversicherung II* to sentence 4 of s. 8(5) VVG.⁴¹⁵ In contrast to *Lebensversicherung II*, the conforming teleological reduction of sentence 4 of s. 8(5) VVG had the effect of a complete disapplication of the regulatory decision contained in this sentence.⁴¹⁶ In other words, the BGH reduced the scope of application of sentence 4 of this provision to zero. The BGH argued, however, that sentence 4 of s. 8(5) VVG is only one part of the wider principle that applies to all insurance contracts that the right of cancellation or the right to object expires one month after payment of the first premium. Sentence 4 of s. 8(4) VVG stipulated that for insurance contracts other than life assurance contracts, in case of a lack of information the right to object expires one month after payment of the first premium. The BGH referred to the legislative materials and asserted that sentence 4 of s. 8(5) VVG and sentence 4 of s. 8(4) VVG must be seen as one "unitary complex" (*einheitliche Regelung*). Therefore, the BGH concluded that a conforming teleological reduction of sentence 4 of s. 8(5) VVG is permissible because the unitary complex remains applicable for cases that do not fall under the second and third Life Assurance Directives.⁴¹⁷

---

[413] BGH, *NJW* 2015, 1023, para. 24 – *Lebensversicherung im Antragsmodell*.
[414] Case C-209/12, *Endress v. Allianz*, ECLI:EU:C:2013:864, paras. 26, 32.
[415] BGH, *NJW* 2015, 1023 paras. 20–23 – *Lebensversicherung im Antragsmodell*.
[416] Ibid., para. 23.
[417] Ibid., paras. 23–27.

This reasoning of the BGH has rightly been criticised in the literature.[418] The BGH's reasoning is, however, not necessarily incompatible with the BVerfG's case law on the outer limits of judicial law-making. That is because the outer limit of interpretation that a teleological reduction cannot reduce the scope of application of a provision to zero is itself expressed in unclear terms. What is clear is that this constraint applies at the level of provision. The BVerfG has not yet provided a clear answer to the question of whether this outer limit also bars judicial law-making that reduces the scope of application of a subsection of a section or of a whole sentence in a subsection of a section of a statute to zero. *Lebensversicherung im Antragsmodell* dealt only with the latter scenario. Framing the issue in these terms presupposes a formal understanding of this outer limit of interpretation. The BGH went beyond this formal understanding and instead applied a substantive understanding. The court attempted to frame the outer interpretative limit as being infringed only if the scope of application of a "unitary complex" enshrined in a provision[419] is reduced to zero. Compared to the formal understanding of this limit, the substantive understanding increases the scope of judicial discretion to define when such a unitary complex of different sentences and subsections in a provision occurs or even to define when a unitary complex of different sections in a statute occurs. Expressing the outer limit of interpretation in substantive as opposed to formal terms further reduces the level of legal certainty.

Another outer limit of conforming judicial law-making that warrants scrutiny is the double criterion: a conforming interpretation must not disregard the wording *and* the clearly identifiable intention of the legislature.[420] A court significantly devalues the double criterion when it relies on the presumption of compliance for constitution-consistent judicial law-making.[421] A very similar stretching of the *contra legem* limit occurs for conforming judicial law-making when a court, as in *Weber II* and *Lebensversicherung II*, uses the presumption of compliance for conforming judicial law-making. Relying on the presumed general intention of the legislature to fully and correctly implement the directive has the effect that an intention of the legislature that militates against a conforming meaning is regularly *not clearly* identifiable. Therefore, the double criterion is not activated. This reasoning extends the scope for judicial law-making considerably. Relying on the presumed intention of the legislature

---

[418] E. FROHNECKE, Unbegrenzter Widerspruch gleich unbegrenzter Rücktritt vom Lebensversicherungsvertrag?, *NJW* 2015, 985, 986–987; L. MICHAEL, Verfassungsrechtliche Grenzen richtlinienkonformer Rechtsfortbildung, (2015) 54 *Der Staat* 349, 357–368.

[419] The BGH actually left open whether the "unitary complex" must be enshrined in a provision or in the statute as a whole.

[420] BGH, *NJW* 2013, 2674, para. 42 – *Interprofessionelle Sozietät*; BAG, *NZA* 2003, 747; BAG, *NZA* 2006, 867, para. 43; BAG, *NJW* 2010, 557, para. 38; cf. BGH, *NJW* 2006, 3200, para. 15.

[421] See Chapter 3, Section 7.1.

to fully implement the directive also has the effect that the purpose of the domestic legislation is equated with the aims of the directive as interpreted by the CJEU. The function of the national implementing legislation is thus reduced to an empty hollow. Even though this reasoning by German courts has been criticised,[422] the comparison with constitution-consistent interpretation shows that it does not go beyond the scope of permissible judicial reasoning according to national legal tradition. To the contrary, the analogy between conforming interpretation and constitution-consistent interpretation requires that a German court adopts this reasoning in order to honour the EU principle of equivalence. The diminishing role of the national implementing legislation in statutory interpretation has also been recognised by English courts.[423] What is also clear is that the presumption of compliance exerts a significant effect on the double criterion. That is illuminated by case law interpreting national law that gold-plates (over-implements) a directive (*überschießende Richtlinienumsetzung*). Both in *Quelle II* and in *Lebensversicherung II*, the BGH rejected an extension of the conforming judicial law-making to cases that fell outside the scope of application of the directives at issue. In *Quelle II*, the BGH emphasised that extending the teleological reduction of s. 439(4) German Civil Code to the gold-plated part of the provision would infringe the double criterion.[424]

The BGH further clarified in an *obiter* statement in *Lebensversicherung II* that the purpose of a national provision cannot be determined by reference to the legislature's presumed intention to correctly and fully implement a directive when the legislature expressly refuses to implement a directive's provision (*ausdrückliche Umsetzungsverweigerung*).[425] Such an express refusal bars a conforming interpretation. *Lebensversicherung II* concerned the conforming interpretation of sentence 4 of s. 5a(2) VVG, and s. 5a VVG was specifically enacted to implement the second and third Life Assurance Directives. It is thus possible that this outer limit is surpassed even if the legislature implements the directive in general, but intends to deviate from a certain requirement of the directive. The BAG has similarly recognised that a conforming interpretation is not possible if the national legislature deliberately departs from a specific requirement of the directive.[426] If the express refusal limit is breached, a gap in the legislation is missing and judicial law-making is not possible. That is

---

[422] W. Durner, Verfassungsrechtliche Grenzen richtlinienkonformer Rechtsfortbildung, *Schriftenreihe des Zentrums für Europäisches Wirtschaftsrecht* Nr. 180, Bonn 2010, p. 34; Michael and Payandeh, above n. 8, pp. 2392, 2395; Schürnbrand, above n. 73, pp. 916–917.
[423] See Section 2 above.
[424] BGH, *NJW* 2009, 427, para. 28 – *Quelle II*.
[425] BGH, *NJW* 2014, 2646, para. 23 – *Lebensversicherung II*. See also BVerwG, BeckRS 2017, 103948, para. 29.
[426] BAG, *NJW* 2006, 3161, para. 25.

because an express refusal to implement a directive's provision is intended by the legislature and falls within the plan and purpose of the domestic legislation. A non-conforming specific objective in the legislation cannot be outweighed or trumped by presumed legislative intent when this limit is exceeded.[427] The BGH did not further specify when a refusal to implement a directive's provision is express as opposed to implied. It is clear from the case law that an inadvertent inconsistency with the requirements of the directive does not meet the express refusal limit even if a provision's clear wording appears to oppose the requirements of the directive. The most explicit way for the legislature to declare an incompatibility with a directive's provision occurs if the statutory language explicitly says that the provision infringes or may infringe an applicable directive. This case must fall under the express refusal limit. Further than that, the reach of the limit has not yet been clarified. The BGH has also left it open whether the refusal is only express if it is plain from the wording of the provision[428] or whether a refusal can also be express if the legislature's non-conforming intention is sufficiently clear according to the whole range of conventional canons of interpretation.[429]

Another outer limit of conforming interpretation that merits discussion is the policy considerations limit. The BAG stipulated in a 2013 decision that the choice of effective, proportionate and dissuasive penalties for infringements of the German law (*Arbeitnehmerüberlassungsgesetz*) implementing Directive 2008/104/EC on temporary agency work is not the task of the labour courts but of the legislature. This choice exceeds the outer limits of conforming judicial law-making, "unless it clearly follows from the national legal order that only one specific legal consequence can be chosen in order to implement the EU legal duty [enshrined in Directive 2008/104/EC] to stipulate effective penalties".[430] The BAG was alluding to the outer interpretative limit that judges are not allowed to base their legal reasoning on their own policy considerations. We discovered in Chapter 3 that the BVerfG has expressed the view that a constitution-consistent interpretation is not possible if the unconstitutionality of the provision or statute can be rectified in different ways. I have also established in Chapter 3 that this outer interpretative limit mostly exists on paper and is often infringed in judicial practice by the highest German courts. This is no different for conforming judicial law-making, which clarifies once more that German courts should abandon the way they state the policy considerations limit.

---

[427] I have shown in Section 1.4.2 above that the express refusal limit is compatible with the CJEU's *Björnekulla* judgment.
[428] For this view, see M. FRANZEN, *Privatrechtsangleichung durch die Europäische Gemeinschaft*, de Gruyter, Berlin 1999, p. 399.
[429] For this view, see CANARIS, above n. 82, pp. 85–86.
[430] BAG, *NJW* 2014, 956, para. 34.

An illustration of a judicial policy choice can be seen in a 2012 BAG judgment that dealt with the interpretation of sentence 3 of s. 7(3) BUrlG. Section 7(3) BurlG provides:

> Leave must be authorised and taken in the course of the current calendar year. The carrying-over of leave to the next calendar year shall be permitted only if justified on compelling operational grounds or by compelling reasons relating to the worker himself. If leave is carried over it must be authorised and taken during the first three months of the following calendar year.

In a preliminary reference ruling relating to a different German case, the CJEU had held in *KHS* that in respect of a worker who is unfit for work for several consecutive reference periods, the worker's right to paid annual leave acquired during that period can lapse with the expiry of a carry-over period. Any carry-over period for annual leave not taken by the end of the reference period must be substantially longer than the reference period in respect of which it is granted.[431] That followed from the interpretation of art. 7(1) of Directive 2003/88/EC. In *KHS*, the reference period was one calendar year and the carry-over period of 15 months satisfied this requirement in the case at issue. The reference period under the BUrlG is one calendar year. It was thus clear that the carry-over period of three months stipulated in sentence 3 of s. 7(3) BUrlG infringes EU law for workers who are unfit for work for several consecutive reference periods. The BAG was concerned with a claim for payment in lieu of unused leave by such a worker in its 2012 judgment. The German court therefore engaged in a conforming interpretation of s. 7(3) BUrlG. It held that an entitlement to paid annual leave granted by statute does not lapse before a carry-over period of 15 months after the end of the reference period has expired if the worker had been prevented from working for health-related reasons during the whole of the reference period and the three months following it.[432] The BAG admitted that EU law does not prescribe that the length of the carry-over period must always be 15 months. The court also mentioned that the German legislature is free to enact a different carry-over period, as long as this period is substantially longer than the reference period.[433] It is thus clear that the BAG made a policy choice when reading the 15-month carry-over period into s. 7(3) BUrlG by means of conforming interpretation.

---

[431] Case C-214/10, *KHS AG v. Schulte*, ECLI:EU:C:2011:761, para. 38.
[432] BAG, *NJW* 2012, 3529, paras. 32–33, 41. In an earlier decision (BAG, *NZA* 2012, 514, para. 37), the BAG raised the question but deliberately left it undecided whether stipulating the specific length of the carry-over period falls into the jurisdiction of the labour courts or the legislature.
[433] Ibid.

We will now look at the question of whether German courts use different interpretative approaches for implementing legislation and for non-implementing legislation that precedes an applicable directive. In *Gasversorgung II*, a gas supply undertaking claimed payment of the sums due between 2005 and 2007 from its customer. The sums due resulted partly from a unilateral increase of the price of gas by the undertaking. A right for the gas supplier to adjust the price of gas unilaterally was not explicitly mentioned in s. 4(1) and (2) of the Regulation on General Terms and Conditions for the Supply of Gas to Standard Rate Customers of 21 June 1979 (*Verordnung über Allgemeine Bedingungen für die Gasversorgung von Tarifkunden*; AVBGasV). That had not stopped the BGH from holding in its earlier jurisprudence that these provisions grant such a right to a gas supply undertaking based on their wording, legislative history and purpose.[434] The legislation as interpreted by the BGH allowed a gas supply undertaking to adjust the price of gas unilaterally without indicating the reasons and preconditions for that adjustment or its scope. Section 4(2) AVBGasV only obliged gas supply undertakings to publish price adjustments. After a preliminary reference from the BGH, the CJEU held that the transparency requirements in Directive 2003/55/EC preclude national legislation that allows the price of supplied gas to be adjusted unilaterally, "but which does not ensure that customers are to be given adequate notice, before that adjustment comes into effect, of the reasons and preconditions for the adjustment, and its scope".[435] When the case returned to the BGH, the court decided that s. 4(1) and (2) AVBGasV cannot be interpreted in conformity with the transparency requirements enshrined in Directive 2003/55/EC since such an interpretation would deviate from the identifiable intention of the maker of the delegated legislation.[436] The main arguments relied on by the BGH were that (a) the German legislature and the delegated law-maker in the relevant period for the case at issue did not transpose the transparency requirements in Directive 2003/55/EC into national law and that (b) the legislative materials did not contain any indication that the existing national law complies with these requirements.[437] The AVBGasV did not and was not intended to implement the European transparency requirements, even though there were no indications either that the national law-maker deliberately intended to go against the requirements of the directive. The AVBGasV was replaced by another Regulation (GasGVV[438]) in 2006, which

---

[434] BGH, *NJW* 2016, 1718, paras. 20–24 – *Gasversorgung II*.
[435] Joined Cases C-359/11 and C-400/11, *Schulz and Egbringhoff*, ECLI:EU:C:2014:2317, para. 53.
[436] BGH, *NJW* 2016, 1718, para. 14 – *Gasversorgung II*.
[437] Ibid., paras. 44, 46, 48.
[438] Regulation on the Standard Terms and Conditions for the Basic Supply of Household Customers and the Alternative Supply of Gas from the Low Pressure Network (Verordnung über Allgemeine Bedingungen für die Grundversorgung von Haushaltskunden und die Ersatzversorgung mit Gas aus dem Niederdrucknetz).

was amended in 2014. The BGH argued based on the legislative materials of the GasGVV that the intention of the delegated law-maker to implement the European transparency requirements only existed in 2014. For the question of whether s. 4(1) and (2) AVBGasV can be interpreted in conformity with Directive 2003/55/EC, however, "the *original* intention of the delegated law-maker" is decisive.[439] After examining the legislative materials of the GasGVV, the BGH concluded that the German delegated law-maker intentionally recognised only a limited level of transparency of price adjustments before 2014, which did not meet the transparency requirements enshrined in Directive 2003/55/EC.[440]

Gasversorgung II fits well with other cases in which the BGH interpreted non-implementing legislation that precedes an applicable directive such as *Urlaubsentgelt* and *Interprofessionelle Sozietät*. Like the last two cases, *Gasversorgung II* shows a restraint towards conforming interpretation that is absent in cases of implementing legislation such as *Quelle II*, *Weber II* or *Lebensversicherung II*. The BGH left open throughout the judgment whether it examined a conforming interpretation in a narrow sense or a conforming judicial law-making of s. 4(1) and (2) AVBGasV. That indicates that it was not the (sufficiently wide) wording of s. 4(2) AVBGasV ("publish") that was the decisive interpretative criterion that barred a conforming interpretation. Instead, it was the original intention of the delegated law-maker. When the AVBGasV was made in 1979, the national law-maker could not have foreseen the future European transparency requirements. The legislative materials of the 1979 Regulation only indicated that price adjustments can become effective after they have been published. There were no indications whatsoever that other transparency conditions were required in order for price adjustments to take effect. That situation did not change in the relevant period for the case at issue. The restraint towards conforming interpretation in *Gasversorgung II* can be explained on the ground that the BGH primarily relied on the legislative materials and gave significant weight to the intention of the original law-maker. This restraint is thus the result of an interpretative approach that the BGH follows in cases of implementing legislation as well. *Gasversorgung II* reinforces the result from Section 6 above that there is no difference in the general interpretative approach between cases where non-implementing legislation pre-dates an applicable directive and cases where implementing legislation post-dates an applicable directive.[441] In both situations, the reluctance of the BGH to adopt a highly objectivised

---

[439] BGH, *NJW* 2016, 1718, para. 61 – *Gasversorgung II* – emphasis added.
[440] Ibid., paras. 55, 59–61.
[441] The BGH also concluded that as a result of the incompatibility of s. 4(1) and (2) AVBGasV with the transparency requirements of Directive 2003/55/EC, the right of the gas supplier to adjust the price of gas unilaterally can no longer be derived from s. 4(1) and (2) AVBGasV (ibid., para. 66). The BGH failed to provide any legal reasoning for this conclusion. For a critical discussion of this aspect of the judgment, see K. RIESENHUBER, BGH: Grenzen der richtlinienkonformen Auslegung, *beck-fachdienst Zivilrecht – LMK* 2016, 375867;

interpretation of the legislation at issue fits in seamlessly with the emerging trend, driven by the BVerfG, towards a more subjective understanding of the intention of the legislature that we have discovered in Chapters 2 and 3. *Gasversorgung II* also illustrates that German courts apply the same limits of conforming interpretation when construing delegated and primary legislation.

Even though *Gasversorgung II* does not deviate from the interpretative approach used in other cases of conforming interpretation, it is possible to argue that the BGH fell short of interpreting s. 4(1) and (2) AVBGasV to the fullest extent possible in the light of the wording and the purpose of Directive 2003/55/EC.[442] First, the intention of the enacting law-maker is not an insurmountable outer limit of interpretation in itself. The intention of the original law-maker can be complemented or restricted by other factors of interpretation in German judicial practice. Second, in analogy to constitution-consistent interpretation of legislation that pre-dates the German Basic Law, Directive 2003/55/EC could affect the (objectivised) purpose of s. 4(1) and (2) AVBGasV and could influence how a judge arrives at possible meanings of s. 4(1) and (2) AVBGasV. I have discussed in Section 6.1 above, however, why the BGH has so far shied away from directly relying on the directive, without the intermediating step of the (presumed) intention of the enacting legislature, when the court determines the purpose of non-implementing, pre-dating legislation. In contrast to *Interprofessionelle Sozietät*, *Gasversorgung II* was even preceded by a CJEU judgment holding that the applicable directive precludes the challenged legislation in its interpretation by the German courts. Such a judgment puts pressure on the referring court to find a conforming meaning. In *Gasversorgung II*, however, and in contrast to *Quelle II*, *Weber II* and *Lebensversicherung II*, the BGH did not change the interpretation of the domestic legislation. A key factor, which in the end had a stronger pull than the CJEU's preliminary reference ruling, seems to be that the contested legislation in *Gasversorgung II* was non-implementing and preceded the applicable directive.

7.2. LIMITS OF CONFORMING JUDICIAL LAW-MAKING IN ENGLAND

Having examined the outer limits of conforming judicial law-making in Germany, I will now critically analyse the outer limits of conforming judicial

---

[442] K. UFFMANN, Das "vertragliche" Preisanpassungsrecht im Tarifkundenbereich der Energieversorger, *NJW* 2016, 1696–1698.
Case C-64/15, *BP Europa v. Hauptzollamt Hamburg-Stadt*, ECLI:EU:C:2016:62, para. 41 ("… when national courts apply domestic law, they are bound to interpret it, *to the fullest extent possible*, in the light of the wording and the purpose of the directive concerned …" – emphasis added).

law-making in England. Due to the analogy between s. 3(1) HRA and conforming interpretation, the outer interpretative limits of s. 3(1) HRA apply *mutatis mutandis* to conforming interpretation.[443] Since these limits have already been presented in Chapter 3, it suffices here to focus on the characteristic features of conforming judicial law-making. English courts apply the same outer limits when they interpret primary or delegated legislation in conformity with an applicable directive.

It is sometimes said that it is "easier" to interpret implementing legislation than legislation that precedes an applicable directive under the EU legal duty of conforming interpretation.[444] This is correct because the purpose of implementing legislation, at a general level, is to transpose the directive into national law and because the EU presumption of compliance applies. It does not follow from this, however, that narrower outer limits or techniques of conforming interpretation are used in judicial practice when courts construe legislation preceding an applicable directive. At least since English courts have established the analogy between s. 3(1) HRA and the EU legal duty of conforming interpretation, the same outer limits and techniques apply to conforming interpretation of legislation that pre-dates, post-dates, is intended to implement or is not intended to implement an applicable directive.[445] The *Ghaidan*-approach to Convention-compatible interpretation applies to conforming interpretation, and *Ghaidan* itself concerned the interpretation of legislation that preceded the Human Rights Act 1998. Be that as it may, the outer limits of conforming interpretation are sufficiently indeterminate and allow judges to handle them in a narrower or wider fashion.

7.2.1. Intention of the Enacting Parliament

In accordance with the analogy to s. 3(1) HRA, case law has established that the EU legal duty of conforming interpretation may require a court to depart from the intention of the parliament that enacted the challenged legislation.[446] The issue of how far a court can deviate from the intention of the enacting parliament

---

[443] *Revenue and Customs Commissioners v. IDT Card Services Ireland Ltd.* [2006] EWCA Civ 29, para. 89 (Arden LJ).
[444] *R. (Irving) v. Secretary of State for Transport* [2008] EWHC 1200 (Admin), para. 34 (Saunders J); *Vodafone 2 v. Revenue and Customs Commissioners* [2008] EWHC 1569 (Ch), para. 70 (Evans-Lombe J); cf. *Littlewoods Retail Ltd. v. Revenue and Customs Commissioners* [2010] EWHC 1071 (Ch), para. 74 (Vos J).
[445] Cf. *R. (Irving) v. Secretary of State for Transport* [2008] EWHC 1200 (Admin), paras. 32–35 (Saunders J).
[446] *Revenue and Customs Commissioners v. IDT Card Services Ireland Ltd.* [2006] EWCA Civ 29, para. 113 (Arden LJ), para. 133 (Pill LJ); *Blackwood v. Birmingham and Solihull Mental Health NHS Foundation Trust* [2016] EWCA Civ 607, para. 55 (Underhill LJ, with whom Lewison and Patten LJJ agreed). See also HALE, above n. 311, p. 12.

is clarified by the outer limits of conforming interpretation. This issue can also be expressed as a reconciliatory balance between the intention of the enacting parliament and the intention of the parliament that enacted s. 2(4) ECA. In common with the outer limits of Convention-compatible interpretation, this balance is de facto determined by a weighing of the interpretative criteria in an individual case and leaves considerable scope for judicial discretion.

Applying the analogy to Convention-compatible interpretation means that a court can not only depart from an identifiable objective of the enacting legislature but also from what can reasonably be presumed to be the intention of the enacting parliament. This is illustrated by Arden LJ's reasoning in *IDT Card Services*. Even though Arden LJ interpreted implementing legislation, she did not base her reasoning on the presumed general intention of the enacting parliament to comply with the requirements of the directive. After stating that Parliament did not specifically intend to deviate from the Sixth EC VAT Directive, she focused on the "negative test" of whether the conforming meaning would be inconsistent with an outer interpretative limit like a fundamental feature of the Value Added Tax Act 1994. If that is not the case, she continued, the conforming meaning of the legislation can be adopted by a court even if "Parliament did not intend" it.[447] Arden LJ thus adopted a highly objectivised approach to conforming interpretation. This approach entails that a court can diverge from the enacting legislature's intent as long as this is reconcilable with Parliament's intention in enacting s. 2(4) ECA. This highly objectivised approach seems particularly relevant when an English court interprets non-implementing legislation that precedes an applicable directive.[448] It was argued in the previous section that German courts are reluctant to adopt a highly objectivised approach to conforming interpretation in these cases. When interpreting implementing legislation, the comparison with German case law highlights that it is generally not necessary for a court to depart from the reasonably presumed intention of the enacting legislature in cases of conforming judicial law-making. German courts rely on a powerful presumption of compliance. That kind of reasoning has also been used by English courts, for example in *British Gas Trading v. Lock*. Even though the Court of Appeal deviated from an identifiable objective of the Working Time Regulations 1998 in that case, it relied on the enacting legislature's reasonably presumed intention to comply *entirely* with the terms of Directive 2003/88/EC.

If a conforming meaning can be reconciled with the reasonably presumed intention of the enacting parliament, the doctrine of parliamentary sovereignty

---

[447] *Revenue and Customs Commissioners v. IDT Card Services Ireland Ltd.* [2006] EWCA Civ 29, para. 113 (Arden LJ).
[448] Whether contemporary highest English courts would adopt such an approach when they interpret this kind of legislation is, however, open to speculation since there is an insufficient amount of case law as regards non-implementing legislation.

is not infringed even if a court diverges from a specific identifiable objective of the contested legislation. That is because it cannot be deduced from the doctrine of parliamentary sovereignty whether a court ought to prefer the specific over the reasonably presumed and general purpose of the enacting legislature or vice versa. The constitutional doctrine is indeterminate in this respect. This grants considerable discretion to judges, particularly because it is the judge who decides what is reasonable. The analogy to Convention-compatible interpretation goes even further as it empowers English courts to depart from what can reasonably be presumed to be the intention of the enacting parliament. This brings us to the questions of whether this power was granted to the judiciary by Parliament and whether this power can be reconciled with the limits of the judicial function. The starting point is the language of s. 2(4) ECA: "[A]ny enactment passed or to be passed … shall be construed and have effect subject to the foregoing provisions of this section". One of the foregoing provisions is s. 2(1) ECA, which makes directly effective EU law domestically effective. The phrase "shall be construed" amounts to a rule of interpretation. The phrase "have effect subject to" implies a rule of priority. If domestic law infringes directly effective EU law, national courts must disapply incompatible national law according to the doctrine of the supremacy of EU law.[449] To the extent that an Act of Parliament is inconsistent with EU law, it is ineffective. EU law takes precedence over inconsistent domestic law in the event of conflict.[450] Since the supremacy of EU law was well recognised when the UK joined the EU, this reading of s. 2(4) ECA is plausible. The 1967 Command Paper, Legal and Constitutional Implications of United Kingdom Membership of the European Communities, accepted the need for giving EU law precedence over domestic law.[451] That s. 2(4) ECA includes not only a rule of interpretation, but also a rule of priority is the intention which the reasonable reader would give to the statute read against its background.[452] This is the reading of s. 2(4) ECA that prevailed in *Factortame (No. 2)*[453] when the

---

[449] Case 106/77, *Amministrazione delle Finanze dello State v. Simmenthal*, ECLI:EU:C:1978:49, para. 21.

[450] For exceptions to this general rule, according to English courts, see *R. (Miller) v. Secretary of State for Exiting the European Union* [2017] UKSC 51, para. 67 (Lord Neuberger, Lady Hale, Lord Mance, Lord Kerr, Lord Clarke, Lord Wilson, Lord Sumption, Lord Hodge). In *Miller*, the majority clarified that legislation "which alters the domestic constitutional status of EU institutions or of EU law is not constrained by the need to be consistent with EU law". This is consistent with and develops similar views expressed in the *HS2* case (*R. (HS2 Action Alliance Ltd) v. Secretary of State for Transport* [2014] UKSC 3, paras. 207, 208 (Lord Neuberger and Lord Mance, with whom Lady Hale, Lord Kerr, Lord Sumption, Lord Reed and Lord Carnwath agreed). According to the CJEU, however, EU law overrides even the constitutional law of Member States; Case 11/70, *Internationale Handelsgesellschaft*, ECLI:EU:C:1970:114, para. 3.

[451] Cmnd. 3301, para. 23.

[452] For a different view, see NICOL, above n. 233, pp. 115–116.

[453] *R. (Factortame (No. 2)) v. Secretary of State for Transport* [1991] 1 AC 603 (HL).

House of Lords issued an injunction disapplying the relevant parts of the Merchant Shipping Act 1998. Disapplication of legislation is separate from interpretation. It is something that a court cannot lawfully do under the orthodox understanding of the doctrine of parliamentary sovereignty. According to A.V. Dicey, "[t]here is no person or body of persons who can ... make rules which override or derogate from an Act of Parliament, or which ... will be enforced by the courts in contravention of an Act of Parliament".[454] The second limb of the doctrine of parliamentary sovereignty, which according to Diceyan orthodoxy provides that no body or person can set aside the legislation of Parliament, is qualified by the supremacy of EU law.[455] Since the second limb of the doctrine is only modified within the scope of EU law, parliamentary sovereignty is not a uniform doctrine.

It is controversial whether the supremacy of EU law also qualifies the first limb of the orthodox doctrine of parliamentary sovereignty, namely that Parliament may make or unmake any law whatsoever.[456] Lord Hope went as far in *Jackson* and said that the "doctrine of the supremacy of [EU] law restricts the absolute authority of Parliament to legislate as it wants".[457] The formal position adopted by a majority of judges is that Parliament intended to limit its own powers when adopting the ECA.[458] EU law has supremacy as a matter

---

[454] A.V. Dicey, *Introduction to the study of the law of the constitution*, 10th ed., Macmillan, Basingstoke 1967, p. 40.

[455] N.W. Barber, The afterlife of parliamentary sovereignty, (2011) 9 *I-CON* 144, 151; V. Bogdanor, *The new British constitution*, Hart, Oxford 2009, p. 80; Hunt, above n. 121, p. 90; Lord Irvine, The influence of Europe on public law in the United Kingdom, in B.S. Markesinis (ed.), *The coming together of the common law and the civil law*, Hart, Oxford 2000, pp. 11, 12. Others contend that the disapplication approach is formally reconcilable with legislative supremacy because it does not involve the court in any invalidation of Acts of Parliament (A. Le Suer, M. Sunkin and J.E.K. Murkens, *Public law: text, cases, and materials*, 3rd ed., OUP, Oxford 2016, p. 852). Yet, according to Dicey, no person or body is recognised by the law of England as having a right to override or "set aside" the legislation of Parliament (Dicey, above n. 454, pp. 39–40).

[456] Against this view, see *R. (Miller) v. Secretary of State for Exiting the European Union* [2016] EWHC 2768 (Admin), paras. 20–22 (Lord Thomas of Cwmgiedd CJ, Sir Terence Etherton MR, Sales LJ); R. Ekins, Legislative freedom in the United Kingdom, (2017) 133 *LQR* 582, 585. For a short overview of the discussion, see C. Turpin and A. Tomkins, *British government and the constitution*, 7th ed., CUP, Cambridge 2011, pp. 351–356.

[457] *R. (Jackson) v. Attorney General* [2005] UKHL 56, para. 105 (Lord Hope).

[458] *R. (Factortame (No. 2)) v. Secretary of State for Transport* [1991] 1 AC 603 (HL), 658 (Lord Bridge); *R. (Jackson) v. Attorney General* [2005] UKHL 56, para. 159 (Baroness Hale); *R. (Miller) v. Secretary of State for Exiting the European Union* [2017] UKSC 51, paras. 67–68 (Lord Neuberger, Lady Hale, Lord Mance, Lord Kerr, Lord Clarke, Lord Wilson, Lord Sumption, Lord Hodge); *R. (Miller) v. Secretary of State for Exiting the European Union* [2016] EWHC 2768 (Admin), paras. 43, 53 (Lord Thomas of Cwmgiedd CJ, Sir Terence Etherton MR, Sales LJ).

of domestic law.⁴⁵⁹ Yet, Parliament retains the power to repeal or amend the ECA.⁴⁶⁰ In that way, Parliament remains sovereign. This formal position has been attacked by scholars claiming that the UK Parliament is no longer effectively sovereign because for all practical purposes it is most unlikely that Parliament will ever seek to withdraw the UK from the EU.⁴⁶¹ History has proven the formalists right. Parliament also retains the power to deliberately and expressly legislate in contradiction of a rule of EU law,⁴⁶² even though this point has never been explicitly confirmed by a Supreme Court ruling. For example, a conforming interpretation is not possible if express statutory language contradicts the requirements of a directive.⁴⁶³ This outer limit of conforming interpretation is recognised in German judicial practice as well. The express terms limit was discussed in Section 7 of Chapter 3 for s. 3(1) HRA, and the discussion applies *mutatis mutandis* for the EU legal duty of conforming interpretation.

If Parliament positively and deliberately chooses to enact an objective that is directly at odds with the requirements of a directive, the EU presumption of compliance, if applicable, is rebutted. In other words, a non-conforming specific objective in the legislation cannot be outweighed or trumped by the legislature's presumed general intention to fully implement the directive when this limit

---

⁴⁵⁹ R. *(Miller) v. Secretary of State for Exiting the European Union* [2017] UKSC 51, para. 67 (Lord Neuberger, Lady Hale, Lord Mance, Lord Kerr, Lord Clarke, Lord Wilson, Lord Sumption, Lord Hodge); cf. *R. (HS2 Action Alliance Ltd) v. Secretary of State for Transport* [2014] UKSC 3, para. 79 (Lord Reed, with whom Lord Neuberger, Lady Hale, Lord Mance, Lord Kerr, Lord Sumption and Lord Carnwath agreed).

⁴⁶⁰ R. *(Miller) v. Secretary of State for Exiting the European Union* [2017] UKSC 51, paras. 60–61, 67 (Lord Neuberger, Lady Hale, Lord Mance, Lord Kerr, Lord Clarke, Lord Wilson, Lord Sumption, Lord Hodge); *R. (Equal Opportunities) v. Secretary of State for Employment* [1992] ICR 341 (CA), 358 (Nolan LJ); *R. (Miller) v. Secretary of State for Exiting the European Union* [2016] EWHC 2768 (Admin), para. 21 (Lord Thomas of Cwmgiedd CJ, Sir Terence Etherton MR, Sales LJ); J. LAWS, Law and democracy, [1995] PL 72, 89.

⁴⁶¹ A. KING, *The British constitution*, OUP, Oxford 2007, p. 99.

⁴⁶² *Macarthys Ltd. v. Smith* [1979] ICR 785 (CA), 789 (Lord Denning MR); *Revenue and Customs Commissioners v. IDT Card Services Ireland Ltd.* [2006] EWCA Civ 29, para. 90 (Arden LJ); *British Gas Trading Ltd. v. Lock* [2016] EWCA Civ 983, paras. 109, 111 (Sir Colin Rimer, with whom Gloster LJ and Sir Terence Etherton MR agreed); *Thoburn v. Sunderland City Council* [2002] EWHC 195 (Admin), para. 63 (Laws LJ). See also LORD IRVINE, above n. 455, pp. 11, 13. P. CRAIG, The European Union Act 2011: locks, limits and legality, (2011) 48 *CMLR* 1881, 1905 and HUNT, above n. 121, p. 124 consider the possibility that the Supreme Court might not give effect to such a domestic statute. At the moment, the issue must be considered unresolved even though there is no case law suggesting that the courts would not give effect to such a statute. *R. (Miller) v. Secretary of State for Exiting the European Union* [2017] UKSC 51, para. 67 (Lord Neuberger, Lady Hale, Lord Mance, Lord Kerr, Lord Clarke, Lord Wilson, Lord Sumption, Lord Hodge) leaves open the question of what the courts will do when Parliament deliberately and expressly legislates in contradiction of a rule of EU law.

⁴⁶³ *Revenue and Customs Commissioners v. IDT Card Services Ireland Ltd.* [2006] EWCA Civ 29, para. 90 (Arden LJ). See, e.g., the Food Supplements (European Communities Act 1972 Disapplication) Bill 2005; for discussion, see TURPIN and TOMKINS, above n. 456, p. 355.

is breached. An inadvertent inconsistency with a directive, that is to say an inconsistency that Parliament did not foresee when it enacted the statute, fell short of reaching this limit in *British Gas Trading Ltd v. Lock*.[464] How narrowly this particular outer limit of conforming interpretation is understood by some English judges can be seen in *IDT Card Services*.[465] The case illustrates that a conforming interpretation may not be barred if Parliament made a conscious legislative choice and used clear words to express that legislative decision, but did not contemplate or foresee the inconsistency of that decision with the applicable directive.[466] The narrow scope of this outer limit[467] mirrors the narrow scope of the express terms limit under s. 3(1) HRA. The express terms limit is also related to the outer limit of conforming interpretation expressed by the BGH in *Lebensversicherung II* that conforming interpretation is barred when the legislature expressly refuses to implement a directive's provision despite implementing the directive in general.[468]

It was argued above that s. 2(4) ECA also includes a rule of priority. This reading of the provision comes into conflict with another element of the orthodox doctrine of parliamentary sovereignty: the principle of implied repeal. As a matter of statutory interpretation, a later Act of Parliament can be interpreted in accordance with orthodox constitutional doctrine against the background of an earlier Act of Parliament. If an inconsistency between both statutes cannot be avoided by means of statutory interpretation because a court would exceed an outer limit of interpretation, the later statute takes precedence. It follows that if post-ECA domestic legislation cannot be reconciled with directly effective EU law by way of interpretation, courts will not be able to disapply the legislation due to the doctrine of implied repeal. The principle of implied repeal would require a judge to hold that the later legislation impliedly repealed s. 2(4) ECA, which obliges courts to disapply inconsistent domestic law to the extent of the inconsistency. That is why the principle of implied repeal clashes with the supremacy of EU law. Even though this point was not argued in *Factortame (No. 2)*, the House of Lords solved the conflict between the earlier ECA and the later Merchant Shipping Act 1988 in

---

[464] *British Gas Trading Ltd. v. Lock* [2016] EWCA Civ 983, paras. 109–111 (Sir Colin Rimer, with whom Gloster LJ and Sir Terence Etherton MR agreed).
[465] For a justification of such a narrow understanding of this outer interpretative limit, see EKINS, above n. 456, p. 588 with reference to *R. (Factortame (No. 1)) v. Secretary of State for Transport* [1990] 2 AC 85 (HL), 140 (Lord Bridge).
[466] *Revenue and Customs Commissioners v. IDT Card Services Ireland Ltd.* [2006] EWCA Civ 29, para. 113 (Arden LJ), paras. 126, 134–135 (Pill LJ).
[467] Parliament positively and deliberately chooses to enact an objective that is directly at odds with the requirements of a directive.
[468] A more detailed comparison with *Lebensversicherung II* does not seem justified as the express refusal limit has not yet been further specified in German case law.

favour of the former, i.e. the Merchant Shipping Act 1988 did not impliedly repeal the ECA to the extent of the inconsistency.[469] The point was discussed by Laws LJ in *Thoburn*, where he argued that the ECA is a constitutional statute which cannot be repealed by mere implication.[470]

The interpretation of s. 2(4) ECA so far illustrates that English courts have recognised that the orthodox doctrine of parliamentary sovereignty is modified when EU law applies.[471] Different theories have been advanced as an explanation of how this is possible under the UK constitution.[472] It is controversial whether the constitutional change came about by Parliament enacting the ECA, by the courts creating this change or by both developments together. A very similar controversy exists for the Human Rights Act 1998.[473] In *Miller*, the majority of the Supreme Court argued that

> [t]he primacy of EU law means that, unlike other rules of domestic law, EU law cannot be implicitly displaced by the mere enactment of legislation which is inconsistent with it. That is clear from the second part of section 2(4) of the 1972 Act and *Factortame Ltd (No. 2)* [1991] 1 AC 603. The issue was informatively discussed by Laws LJ in *Thoburn*. ... The 1972 Act accordingly has a constitutional character, as discussed by Laws LJ in *Thoburn*.[474]

The reference to statute and *Factortame (No. 2)* indicates that according to the majority in *Miller*, the modifications to the orthodox doctrine of parliamentary sovereignty came about neither by the Parliament of 1972 alone[475] nor by the

---

[469] It is controversial in legal scholarship whether the decision in *Factortame (No. 2)* is inconsistent with the doctrine of implied repeal. That depends on what definition of implied repeal one adopts, in particular whether implied repeal is triggered by any conflict between two statutory norms or only if the inconsistency arises between two norms that deal with the same subject matter. The first alternative is adopted here (see Chapter 1, Section 1) and this is also the view adopted in *R. (Miller) v. Secretary of State for Exiting the European Union* [2017] UKSC 51, paras. 66–67 (Lord Neuberger, Lady Hale, Lord Mance, Lord Kerr, Lord Clarke, Lord Wilson, Lord Sumption, Lord Hodge) and in *Thoburn v. Sunderland City Council* [2002] EWHC 195 (Admin), para. 61 (Laws LJ). For discussion, see GORDON, above n. 13, pp. 169–177; GOLDSWORTHY, above n. 70, pp. 289–293; A. YOUNG, *Parliamentary sovereignty and the Human Rights Act 1998*, Hart, Oxford 2009, pp. 35–54.

[470] *Thoburn v. Sunderland City Council* [2002] EWHC 195 (Admin), paras. 60–63 (Laws LJ).

[471] For an argument to the effect that the doctrine of parliamentary sovereignty, including the doctrine of implied repeal, is not modified when EU law applies, see EKINS, above n. 456, pp. 587–590.

[472] For an overview, see G. MARSHALL, Metric measures and martyrdom by Henry VIII clauses, (2002) 118 *LQR* 493, 500 and M. ELLIOTT and R. THOMAS, *Public law*, 3rd ed., OUP, Oxford 2017, pp. 365–370.

[473] See Chapter 3, Section 2.

[474] *R. (Miller) v. Secretary of State for Exiting the European Union* [2017] UKSC 51, paras. 66–67 (Lord Neuberger, Lady Hale, Lord Mance, Lord Kerr, Lord Clarke, Lord Wilson, Lord Sumption, Lord Hodge).

[475] Lord Bridge appears to have argued in *R. (Factortame (No. 2)) v. Secretary of State for Transport* [1991] 1 AC 603 (HL), 658–659 that the modifications to the orthodox doctrine

common law alone,[476] but by Parliament intending it and by the common law accepting it. The upshot of this reasoning is that the second limb of the doctrine of parliamentary sovereignty and the doctrine of implied repeal are modified as the general consensus underlying the doctrine of parliamentary sovereignty has evolved.[477] Another controversy surrounding *Miller* relates to the majority's argument that the effect of the ECA is to "constitute EU law an independent and overriding source of domestic law".[478] It is controversial in the literature how the introduction of an independent source of law by an Act of Parliament can be reconciled with the doctrine of parliamentary sovereignty.[479] The majority of the Supreme Court in *Miller* argued that this status of EU law is compatible with parliamentary sovereignty.[480] Therefore, the majority did not seem to have consciously or deliberately intended to challenge the doctrine in this respect.

What the reasoning in *Miller* cannot explain is Lady Justice Arden's claim that the EU legal duty of conforming interpretation as operated by English courts has the effect that the "traditional doctrine of parliamentary sovereignty took on a new meaning".[481] Lord Mance has also recognised that the English courts' powerful application of conforming interpretation has shifted the constitutional boundary between interpretation and impermissible judicial legislation in favour of the judiciary.[482] Section 2(4) ECA incorporates a rule of interpretation. According to one view, s. 2(4) ECA operates as a strong presumption of compliance that forms part of the context of future legislation.

---

of parliamentary sovereignty came about solely by Parliament enacting the ECA. For this view, see also G. PHILLIPSON, EU law as an agent of national constitutional change: Miller v. Secretary of State for Exiting the European Union, (2017) 36 *YEL* 46, 92. For criticism of this view, see M. ELLIOTT, Sovereignty, primacy and the common law constitution: what has EU membership taught us?, University of Cambridge Legal Studies Research Paper Series No. 24/2018, March 2018, pp.13–15, available online at http://www.ssrn.com.

[476] For this view, see *Thoburn v. Sunderland City Council* [2002] EWHC 195 (Admin), paras. 59–60 (Laws LJ); HUNT, above n. 121, pp. 125–126.

[477] For a more detailed explanation of how the doctrine of parliamentary sovereignty can evolve, see Chapter 3, Section 7.2.2.

[478] *R. (Miller) v. Secretary of State for Exiting the European Union* [2017] UKSC 51, para. 65 (Lord Neuberger, Lady Hale, Lord Mance, Lord Kerr, Lord Clarke, Lord Wilson, Lord Sumption, Lord Hodge). For criticism of this argument, see M. ELLIOTT, The Supreme Court's judgment in *Miller*: in search of constitutional principle, (2017) 76 *CLJ* 271–273.

[479] For discussion, see P. ELEFTHERIADIS, Two doctrines of the unwritten constitution, (2017) 13 *European Constitutional Law Review* 525, 541.

[480] *R. (Miller) v. Secretary of State for Exiting the European Union* [2017] UKSC 51, para. 67 (Lord Neuberger, Lady Hale, Lord Mance, Lord Kerr, Lord Clarke, Lord Wilson, Lord Sumption, Lord Hodge). Agreeing with the majority in *Miller*: A. YOUNG, Case comment: R. (Miller) v. Secretary of State for Exiting the European Union: thriller or vanilla?, (2017) 42 *European Law Review* 280, 290–291.

[481] M. ARDEN, The changing judicial role: human rights, Community law and the intention of Parliament, (2008) 67 *CLJ* 487, 499.

[482] MANCE, above n. 97, p. 450.

Courts are thus justified in presuming that Parliament intended the legislation to take effect subject to applicable EU laws.[483] This understanding of the rule of interpretation enshrined in s. 2(4) ECA is consistent with orthodox constitutional doctrine. This understanding has not prevailed in judicial practice, however. Section 2(4) ECA as applied in judicial practice extends beyond giving effect to presumed legislative intent because courts have interpreted s. 2(4) ECA as empowering them to deviate from the intention of the enacting parliament even if the challenged legislation post-dates the ECA. Even though the doctrine of parliamentary sovereignty is modified when EU law applies, it does not follow from this modification that courts must be able to diverge from the enacting Parliament's intent. The supremacy of EU law does not require that English courts must be able to exceed the outer limits of conventional canons of construction for conforming interpretation. If a conforming interpretation of the challenged legislation fails, this simply means that conformity between EU law and domestic law cannot be achieved via judicial interpretation due to the national limits of the judicial function being exceeded. The challenged legislation does not impliedly repeal the ECA in such a case, and disapplying the incompatible domestic legislation ensures the supremacy of directly effective EU law.

I have argued in Section 7 of Chapter 3 that a rule of construction according to which courts can depart from the intention of the enacting parliament even if the challenged legislation post-dates the HRA (for the purposes of Chapter 4, the ECA) modifies the doctrine of parliamentary sovereignty. Did the Parliament of 1972 intend to effect such a change? The ambiguous words of s. 2(4) ECA are certainly open to multiple possible interpretations.[484] Yet, there are no indications that Parliament intended such a fundamental constitutional change. Furthermore, applying the reasons given in Sections 1.2 and 7.2.2 of Chapter 3 for the interpretation of s. 3(1) HRA *mutatis mutandis* also shows that Parliament when enacting the 1972 Act cannot be presumed to have intended to confer on the courts such a new constitutional role. The doctrine of parliamentary sovereignty can evolve but this requires that Parliament also accept this evolution. Judges alone cannot (lawfully) change the doctrine of parliamentary sovereignty.[485] It follows that the interpretation of s. 2(4) ECA by English courts that empowers them to depart from what can reasonably be presumed to be the

---

[483] EKINS, above n. 456, pp. 587–589. Cf. P. CRAIG, Sovereignty of the United Kingdom Parliament after Factortame, (1991) 11 *Yearbook of European Law* 221, 251; *R. (Factortame (No. 1)) v. Secretary of State for Transport* [1990] 2 AC 85 (HL), 140 (Lord Bridge).
[484] See, e.g., the different interpretations adopted in: *Garland v. British Rail Engineering Ltd.* [1983] 2 AC 751 (HL), 771 (Lord Diplock); *Duke v. GEC Reliance Ltd.* [1988] AC 618 (HL), 639–640 (Lord Templeman); *Pickstone v. Freemans Plc* [1987] 3 WLR 811 (CA), 822 (Nicholls LJ).
[485] See Chapter 3, Section 7.2.2.

enacting parliament's intent was a judicial choice that exceeded their judicial function. As for Convention-compatible interpretation, English courts have thus already made the transition from absolute parliamentary sovereignty to a qualified version of parliamentary sovereignty in the sphere of conforming interpretation. Even though English courts formally uphold the doctrine of parliamentary sovereignty, they have undermined it substantively with the EU legal duty of conforming interpretation.

7.2.2. Statutory Language

We have already seen that conforming interpretation goes beyond resolving ambiguities. Conforming interpretation can involve a substantial departure from the statutory language.[486] *Pickstone* established that conforming interpretation may require a court to deviate from an unambiguous wording of the statute.[487] Clear statutory language in itself is not an outer limit of conforming judicial law-making, but it is still a very influential factor when a court ascertains whether Parliament specifically intended to deviate from the requirements of a directive.[488] *IDT Card Services* and *Football Association Premier League Ltd. v. QC Leisure* are two cases illustrating that judges disagree over how much weight ought to be ascribed to the statutory language when conforming interpretation is at issue. In *IDT Card Services*, a conforming interpretation of para. 3 of Sch. 10A VATA 1994 was possible even though it derogated from the unambiguous wording of that provision and the intention of the enacting legislature. As in *IDT Card Services*, the Court of Appeal pointed out in *Football Association Premier League Ltd. v. QC Leisure* that the legislature did not contemplate the inconsistency of the challenged national provision (s. 72(1) CDPA) with the applicable directive (Information Society Directive).[489] As in *IDT Card Services*, (a) the wording of the challenged provision and the policy behind it was clear, and (b) the provision was inadvertently inconsistent with the applicable directive. Yet, the Court of Appeal was able to read another exemption into para. 3 of Sch. 10A VATA 1994 in *IDT Card Services*, whereas Etherton LJ rejected

---

[486] *Test Claimants in the FII Group Litigation v. Revenue and Customs Commissioners* [2016] EWCA Civ 1180, para. 106 (Underhill LJ, giving the judgment of the court).

[487] See also *Lehman Brothers International (Europe) (In Administration), Re* [2012] UKSC 6, para. 131 (Lord Dyson); *Vodafone 2 v. Revenue and Customs Commissioners* [2009] EWCA Civ 446, para. 37 (Sir Andrew Morritt C); *Churchill Insurance Co. Ltd. v. Fitzgerald & Wilkinson* [2012] EWCA Civ 1166, para. 50 (Aikens LJ, with whom Etherton and Maurice Kay LJJ agreed); *Revenue and Customs Commissioners v. IDT Card Services Ireland Ltd.* [2006] EWCA Civ 29, para. 89 (Arden LJ).

[488] See, e.g. *Revenue and Customs Commissioners v. IDT Card Services Ireland Ltd.* [2006] EWCA Civ 29, para. 90 (Arden LJ); *O'Brien v. Ministry of Justice* [2015] EWCA Civ 1000, para. 58 (Underhill LJ).

[489] For discussion, see Section 5.2 above.

a reading down of s. 72(1) CDPA in *Football Association Premier League Ltd. v. QC Leisure*. The comparison with *IDT Card Services* does not suggest that the alleged conforming reading of s. 72(1) CDPA, as proposed by the appellant, should have been possible. That is because other limits of conforming interpretation barred such a reading, as will be shown in the next paragraph. What it does suggest is that Etherton LJ's principal reliance on (a) the unambiguous wording of s. 72(1) CDPA and (b) the intention of the government not to alter the ambit of that provision in order to reject a conforming reading cannot be reconciled with the muscular approach to conforming interpretation adopted in *IDT Card Services*. It has to be said that Arden LJ, who gave the lead judgment in *IDT Card Services*, supports a particularly powerful doctrine of conforming interpretation, a view with which not all judges agree.[490] Additionally, however, Etherton LJ's analysis is also incompatible with the muscular approach to Convention-compatible interpretation taken by the House of Lords in *Ghaidan*, where the House of Lords departed from the unambiguous words of para. 2(2) of Sch. 1 to the Rent Act 1977, the provision's specific purpose and the intention of the enacting parliament.

Despite this criticism, Etherton LJ was right to conclude that ascribing to s. 72(1) CDPA the alleged conforming meaning would have gone beyond legitimate interpretation and would have encroached on Parliament's legislative role. His supporting considerations[491] reveal why an outer limit of conforming interpretation was surpassed. Etherton LJ stated that interpreting s. 72(1)(c) CDPA as applying only to the restricted act specified in s. 19(3) CDPA, as was argued by the appellant, would have been a major change from the previous statutory regime with significant practical implications. That is because s. 72(1) CDPA as originally enacted allowed public places to which entry is free like shops, hotel lobbies, restaurants and pubs to show television broadcasts without infringing the film copyright contained in the broadcast and, thus, without the need to obtain permission from the owner of the film copyright. Etherton LJ regarded it as impossible to say precisely what steps the government might have taken to address the practical consequences. He added that there was no certainty as to how the legislature would have addressed the significant practical implications of the conforming reading suggested by the appellant if it had appreciated them. Etherton LJ's supporting considerations reveal that adopting the alleged conforming reading of s. 72(1) CDPA would have required the court to make a policy decision (a) for which the court is

---

[490] See, in particular, Arden LJ's speech in *Fleming (t/a Bodycraft) v. Customs and Excise Commissioners* [2006] EWCA Civ 70, paras. 44, 57 (Arden LJ), dissenting on the issue of whether the court had the power to read into the legislation an adequate transitional period.

[491] *Football Association Premier League Ltd. v. QC Leisure* [2012] EWCA Civ 1708, paras. 53–57 (Etherton LJ).

not equipped or (b) that gives rise to important practical repercussions that the court is not equipped to evaluate. A court cannot make such a decision without exceeding an outer limit of conforming interpretation.[492] It was impossible to say precisely how the government or Parliament would have resolved the inconsistency of s. 72(1) CDPA with the Information Society Directive. Yet, the substance of any conforming interpretation must be clear. Subsequent developments support Etherton LJ's reasoning in this respect. The Intellectual Property Office published a consultation in 2015 on changes to s. 72 CDPA with the aim of complying with the Information Society Directive. The government's proposal to amend s. 72(1) CDPA and to bring the provision into consonance with the Information Society Directive was different from the two conforming readings of s. 72(1) CDPA proposed by the appellant in *Football Association Premier League Ltd. v. QC Leisure*.[493]

It has been argued in the past that judges do not make policy choices when they interpret implementing legislation, but simply give effect to the will of the EU legislature and ensure compliance with a judgment of the CJEU.[494] It has further been claimed that operating conforming interpretation in a powerful way when courts construe implementing legislation is less concerning from a separation of powers perspective as English judges do not make contested decisions over controversial substantive policy issues.[495] However, even a conforming interpretation of implementing legislation may be barred due to

---

[492] *Revenue and Customs Commissioners v. IDT Card Services Ireland Ltd.* [2006] EWCA Civ 29, paras. 89, 113 (Arden LJ); *Vodafone 2 v. Revenue and Customs Commissioners* [2009] EWCA Civ 446, para. 38 (Sir Andrew Morritt C); *Churchill Insurance Co. Ltd. v. Fitzgerald & Wilkinson* [2012] EWCA Civ 1166, para. 50 (Aikens LJ, with whom Etherton and Maurice Kay LJJ agreed).

[493] See Intellectual Property Office, A consultation on changes to Section 72 of the Copyright, Designs and Patents Act 1988 (which permits the free public showing or playing of a film contained in a broadcast), July 2015, p. 7, available online at https://www.gov.uk/government/uploads/system/uploads/attachment_data/file/443680/Section_72_CDPA_Consultation.pdf. After the consultation, the proposed change to s. 72(1) was abandoned by the government and, instead, the government proposed to remove "film" completely from s. 72(1); see Intellectual Property Office, Government Response to the further consultation and technical review on changes to Section 72 of the Copyright, Designs and Patents Act 1988 (which permits the free public showing or playing of a film contained in a broadcast), May 2016, p. 1 and Annex B, available online at https://www.gov.uk/government/uploads/system/uploads/attachment_data/file/521199/Gov-response-to-s72-technical-review.pdf. The latter proposal was adopted in reg. 3 of the Copyright (Free Public Showing or Playing) (Amendment) Regulations 2016. Whether the deletion of "film" from the statutory provision could have been reached by a conforming interpretation depends on the controversial issue of whether disregarding a certain part of a provision by means of conforming interpretation is permissible; for discussion, see Section 7.2.4 below.

[494] Cf. *Prudential Assurance Co Ltd. v. Revenue and Customs Commissioners* [2013] EWHC 3249 (Ch), para. 103 (Henderson J).

[495] G. DE BÚRCA, Giving effect to European Community Directives, (1992) 55 *MLR* 215, 240; cf. HAGER, above n. 9, p. 323.

issues calling for legislative deliberation or policy choices which give rise to important practical repercussions that the court is not equipped to evaluate. First, there may not be a CJEU judgment guiding the national court if the national court does not activate the preliminary reference procedure. Second, even if the CJEU gives a preliminary ruling, the CJEU may only hold that a certain interpretation of the national legislation is incompatible with EU law and is therefore precluded. If the directive contains general clauses, vague terms or legislative discretion for national legislators, there may still be multiple substantive ways to correctly implement the directive into national law. That also means that there may be a number of possible ways of construing a prima facie non-conforming provision in order to make it comply with a directive.[496] Choosing between these possible meanings does not necessarily, but may, involve issues calling for legislative deliberation. Furthermore, the aim of statutory interpretation is not to ascertain what the national legislature ought to have enacted judged against the standard of EU law, but what it intended to enact. Conforming interpretation must observe this distinction, which builds upon the separation of powers between the judiciary and the legislature.

If *Football Association Premier League Ltd. v. QC Leisure* is compared with German case law on conforming interpretation, two parallels come into sight. First, Etherton LJ's reasoning can be described as predominantly informed by a subjective theory of interpretation. That is because he focused on the actual intention of the historical law-maker, the legislative history of the 2003 Regulations and the purpose of the Regulations as pursued and understood by the historical law-maker at the time when the law was made. This style of judicial analysis also characterises the BGH's reasoning in *Weber II*, *Quelle II* and *Lebensversicherung II*. Ultimately, Etherton LJ relied strongly on the fact that the government retained the same clear and unambiguous statutory language in s. 72(1) CDPA when implementing the Information Society Directive. It is clear that the BGH attached less weight to the statutory language in *Quelle II*, *Weber II* and *Lebensversicherung II*. Second, a parallel can be drawn to the outer limit of conforming interpretation under German law that a court cannot disregard the wording and the clearly identifiable intention of the legislature (double criterion). Etherton LJ seemed to have had a very similar outer limit of conforming interpretation in mind in *Football Association Premier League Ltd. v. QC Leisure*. His main argument was that the alleged conforming meaning of s. 72(1) CDPA was not possible as it disregarded the provision's clear and unambiguous wording and the government's clear intention not to alter the ambit of s. 72(1) CDPA.

If we were to apply the double criterion as understood by recent German judgments on conforming judicial law-making to *Football Association Premier*

---

[496] *Vodafone 2 v. Revenue and Customs Commissioners* [2009] EWCA Civ 446, para. 59 (Sir Andrew Morritt C).

League Ltd. v. QC Leisure, the double criterion would not be infringed. *Weber II* and *Lebensversicherung II* show that the double criterion is not breached in a case where a specific but inadvertently non-conforming objective of a provision contravenes the legislature's presumed general intention to fully implement the directive. Due to the contradiction between these two purposes, the legislature's intention is not *clearly* identifiable. Similarly, Etherton LJ could have argued in *Football Association Premier League Ltd. v. QC Leisure* that the intention of the government when making the 2003 Regulations lacked the necessary clarity since two intentions contradicted each other. Furthermore, one may question whether the intention not to alter the ambit of s. 72(1) CDPA was as clear as claimed by Etherton LJ since the government unknowingly altered the ambit of s. 72(1) CDPA with the 2003 Regulations. It also seems questionable to characterise as clear the government's intention to maintain to the fullest extent possible the UK's existing exceptions to copyright infringement. That is because the explanatory note to the 2003 Regulations shows that the government intended to comply with the regime of defences to copyright infringement contained in art. 5 of the Information Society Directive.

7.2.3. Scheme and Fundamental Features of the Legislation

Another outer limit of conforming judicial law-making relied on in English courts is that a judge cannot use the EU legal duty of conforming interpretation to adopt a meaning that is inconsistent with a fundamental feature of the legislation.[497] A court cannot distort or undermine a fundamental feature of the legislation.[498] As for s. 3(1) HRA, this outer interpretative limit plays a significant role in case law.[499] Whether or not an element of the legislation is fundamental is determined by the interpretative criteria, including the provision's wording.[500] English case

---

[497] *Assange v. Swedish Prosecution Authority* [2012] UKSC 22, para. 203 (Lord Mance); *Revenue and Customs Commissioners v. IDT Card Services Ireland Ltd.* [2006] EWCA Civ 29, paras. 89–90 (Arden LJ); *Vodafone 2 v. Revenue and Customs Commissioners* [2009] EWCA Civ 446, para. 38 (Sir Andrew Morritt C); *Churchill Insurance Co. Ltd. v. Fitzgerald & Wilkinson* [2012] EWCA Civ 1166, para. 50 (Aikens LJ, with whom Etherton and Maurice Kay LJJ agreed); *ITV Broadcasting Ltd. v. TV Catchup Ltd.* [2015] EWCA Civ 204, para. 86 (Kitchin LJ); *Prudential Assurance Co. Ltd. v. Revenue and Customs Commissioners* [2016] EWCA Civ 376, para. 111 (Lewison LJ); *Hampshire v. Board of the Pension Protection Fund* [2016] EWCA Civ 786, para. 48 (Patten LJ).

[498] *Google Inc. v. Vidal-Hall* [2015] EWCA Civ 311, para. 90 (Lord Dyson MR and Sharp LJ, with whom McFarlane LJ agreed).

[499] *Revenue and Customs Commissioners v. IDT Card Services Ireland Ltd.* [2006] EWCA Civ 29, para. 90 (Arden LJ); *Google Inc. v. Vidal-Hall* [2015] EWCA Civ 311, para. 90 (Lord Dyson MR and Sharp LJ, with whom McFarlane LJ agreed).

[500] An argument based on the CJEU's ruling in *Björnekulla* that a court cannot have recourse to a provision's legislative history when establishing a fundamental feature of the legislation would overstretch the CJEU's judgment.

law on conforming interpretation shows that the fundamental criterion leaves sufficient scope for evaluative arguments and judicial discretion.[501] It is clear that a conscious legislative choice by Parliament does not in itself amount to a fundamental feature of the legislation.[502] Case law appears to suggest that where certain conditions have to be met before a right exists or where certain exceptions are granted from a statutory rule, reading in a further condition or another exception by means of conforming interpretation will often be possible.[503] This can only serve as a very rough guideline, however, and it certainly does not amount to a formal element that delivers a sufficient level of legal certainty. The discussion of *Benkharbouche* in Section 7.2 of Chapter 3 in the realm of Convention-compatible judicial law-making illustrates that even if exceptions to a general rule are provided for in the statutory scheme, extending an exception via judicial law-making may be barred by a fundamental feature of the legislation.[504]

More controversial is Pill LJ's reasoning in *IDT Card Services*. He argued that the scheme of the national legislation, as an outer limit of conforming interpretation,[505] "includes the fundamental duty arising from EU directives to impose VAT on the supply of services".[506] This suggests that the objectives of the directive directly co-determine the scheme of the national legislation and its fundamental features. Defining the fundamental features or the scheme of the national legislation directly with the objectives of the directive would render these outer limits of interpretation meaningless for the EU legal duty

---

[501] See, e.g. *Blackwood v. Birmingham and Solihull Mental Health NHS Foundation Trust* [2016] EWCA Civ 607, para. 57 (Underhill LJ): "To insist on such a characterisation in every case, as a means of achieving compliance with the requirements of the EU Directives, would be *unacceptably artificial*. It would also produce *unfair results*. ... In my view the scheme under sections 109 and 110 of the 2010 Act depends on the concept of agency being applied in accordance with the ordinary understanding, and a departure from that approach would be inconsistent with a fundamental feature of the legislation" – emphasis added.

[502] See, e.g. *Revenue and Customs Commissioners v. IDT Card Services Ireland Ltd.* [2006] EWCA Civ 29, para. 113 (Arden LJ); *Blackwood v. Birmingham and Solihull Mental Health NHS Foundation Trust* [2016] EWCA Civ 607, para. 55 (Underhill LJ).

[503] *Revenue and Customs Commissioners v. IDT Card Services Ireland Ltd.* [2006] EWCA Civ 29, para. 113 (Arden LJ), para. 133 (Pill LJ); *Vodafone 2 v. Revenue and Customs Commissioners* [2009] EWCA Civ 446, para. 44 (Sir Andrew Morritt C); *Churchill Insurance Co. Ltd. v. Fitzgerald & Wilkinson* [2012] EWCA Civ 1166, para. 75 (Aikens LJ, with whom Etherton and Maurice Kay LJJ agreed).

[504] Cf. *Benkharbouche v. Embassy of Sudan* [2015] EWCA Civ 33, para. 67 (Lord Dyson, giving the judgment of the court; "Any attempt to read down these provisions so as to remove immunity would be to adopt meanings inconsistent with fundamental features of the legislative scheme").

[505] A conforming interpretation (a) cannot be inconsistent with the scheme of the legislation and (b) cannot create a new and different scheme: *Revenue and Customs Commissioners v. IDT Card Services Ireland Ltd.* [2006] EWCA Civ 29, para. 142 (Pill LJ); *EB Central Services Ltd. v. Revenue and Customs Commissioners* [2008] EWCA Civ 486, para. 81 (Dyson LJ).

[506] *Revenue and Customs Commissioners v. IDT Card Services Ireland Ltd.* [2006] EWCA Civ 29, paras. 142–143 (Pill LJ).

of conforming interpretation. Yet, Pill LJ's view carries force in cases where Parliament enacted legislation designed to implement a directive as the court "will have guidance as to the purpose which that legislation was designed to achieve from the Directive itself".[507] It is important to note that the stretching of the outer limits of conforming interpretation by Pill LJ is possible and does not infringe the analogy to s. 3(1) HRA. This is because the fundamental features of the legislation or the scheme of the legislation are highly indeterminate concepts, as I have shown in Chapter 3.

7.2.4. Unsettled Outer Limits of Conforming Interpretation

The outer limits of conforming interpretation are not settled in English judicial practice, and this mirrors the finding in Section 5 above that the strength of the presumption of compliance is not settled in English case law. A case that illustrates this is *British Gas Trading Ltd v. Lock*. The case features the outer interpretative limit that a conforming meaning must not go against the grain of the legislation[508] and be compatible with the "underlying thrust of the legislation".[509] In the realm of s. 3(1) HRA, the Supreme Court in *R. v. Waya* has referred to the grain of the legislation as the essence of the legislation and described this essence with the purpose of the legislation as a whole as expressed in the explanatory notes at a relatively high level of abstraction.[510]

---

[507] *Vodafone 2 v. Revenue and Customs Commissioners* [2008] EWHC 1569 (Ch), para. 70 (Evans-Lombe J).

[508] *The United States of America v. Nolan* [2015] UKSC 63, para. 14 (Lord Mance, with whom Lord Neuberger, Lady Hale and Lord Reed agreed); *Assange v. Swedish Prosecution Authority* [2012] UKSC 22, para. 203 (Lord Mance); *English v. Thomas Sanderson Blinds Ltd.* [2008] EWCA Civ 1421, para. 32 (Laws LJ); *Vodafone 2 v. Revenue and Customs Commissioners* [2009] EWCA Civ 446, para. 38 (Sir Andrew Morritt C); *Churchill Insurance Co. Ltd. v. Fitzgerald & Wilkinson* [2012] EWCA Civ 1166, para. 50 (Aikens LJ, with whom Etherton and Maurice Kay LJJ agreed); *ITV Broadcasting Ltd. v. TV Catchup Ltd.* [2015] EWCA Civ 204, para. 86 (Kitchin LJ); *O'Brien v. Ministry of Justice* [2015] EWCA Civ 1000, para. 48 (Lewison LJ); *Prudential Assurance Co. Ltd. v. Revenue and Customs Commissioners* [2016] EWCA Civ 376, para. 111 (Lewison LJ); *British Gas Trading Ltd. v. Lock* [2016] EWCA Civ 983, para. 104 (Sir Colin Rimer, with whom Gloster LJ and Sir Terence Etherton MR agreed); *Howe v. Motor Insurers' Bureau* [2017] EWCA Civ 932, para. 37 (Lewison LJ, with whom McFarlane LJ and Sir James Munby agreed); cf. *Littlewoods Ltd. v. Revenue and Customs Commissioners* [2015] EWCA Civ 515, para. 118 (Arden LJ).

[509] *Assange v. Swedish Prosecution Authority* [2012] UKSC 22, para. 203 (Lord Mance); *Vodafone 2 v. Revenue and Customs Commissioners* [2009] EWCA Civ 446, para. 38 (Sir Andrew Morritt C); *Churchill Insurance Co. Ltd. v. Fitzgerald & Wilkinson* [2012] EWCA Civ 1166, para. 50 (Aikens LJ, with whom Etherton and Maurice Kay LJJ agreed); *British Gas Trading Ltd. v. Lock* [2016] EWCA Civ 983, para. 104 (Sir Colin Rimer, with whom Gloster LJ and Sir Terence Etherton MR agreed).

[510] *R. v. Waya* [2012] UKSC 51, para. 21 (Lord Walker and Sir Anthony Hughes, with whom Lady Hale, Lord Judge, Lord Kerr, Lord Clarke and Lord Wilson agreed).

Chapter 4. The European Legal Duty of Conforming Interpretation

In *British Gas Trading Ltd v. Lock*, however, the Court of Appeal concluded that the grain or thrust of "the WTR [Working Time Regulations 1998] can fairly be identified as directed at providing holiday pay for workers measured by reference to criteria required by article 7 [of Directive 2003/88/EC] as since explained by the CJEU".[511] The Court of Appeal referred to the applicable directive in order to co-determine the grain and thrust of the national implementing legislation. Furthermore, the Working Time Regulations 1998 deal with the maximum average weekly working time of workers, the average normal hours of night workers, rest breaks to be given to workers, the period of paid annual leave, etc. It is not clear either from the explanatory note or from the terms of the Regulations why the specific issue of the correct calculation of holiday pay for workers should be part of the grain or thrust of the Working Time Regulations 1998. Whereas in *R. v. Waya*, the Supreme Court determined the grain of the legislation by looking at the purpose of the legislation as a whole, the Court of Appeal in *British Gas Trading Ltd v. Lock* seemed to have relied on the grain of the challenged provision (reg. 16 Working Time Regulations 1998). Relying on the grain of the provision under consideration as an outer limit of interpretation compared to the grain of the legislation as a whole narrows the possible conforming readings of a provision. It reduces judicial discretion and increases legal certainty. Yet, it appears to be inconsistent with case law on s. 3(1) HRA.

Another case illustrating the unsettled state of the outer limits of conforming judicial law-making is *Google Inc v. Vidal-Hall*. It deals with the construction of s. 13(2) of the Data Protection Act 1998 (DPA). Section 13(2) DPA was intended to implement art. 23 of Directive 95/46/EC, but failed to do so on a literal interpretation.[512] The claimants demanded compensation for distress for breaches of data protection principles. According to s. 13(2) DPA, an individual who suffers distress by reason of a contravention by a data controller of any of the requirements of the DPA is entitled to compensation only if (i) the individual also suffers damage (pecuniary or material loss) by reason of the contravention or (ii) the contravention relates to the processing of personal data for the special purposes enumerated in s. 3 DPA. The claimants did not satisfy the conditions of s. 13(2) DPA. Article 23 of Directive 95/46/EC required Member States to provide an individual, who suffers damage as a result of a contravention by a data controller of any of the requirements of national law adopted pursuant to this directive, with a claim to receive compensation from the controller for the damage suffered. The Court of Appeal did not refer the question of the correct

---

[511] *British Gas Trading Ltd. v. Lock* [2016] EWCA Civ 983, para. 112 (Sir Colin Rimer, with whom Gloster LJ and Sir Terence Etherton MR agreed).
[512] *Google Inc. v. Vidal-Hall* [2015] EWCA Civ 311, para. 84 (Lord Dyson MR and Sharp LJ, with whom McFarlane LJ agreed).

interpretation of art. 23 of Directive 95/46/EC to the CJEU. It interpreted the term "damage" in art. 23 and concluded that it includes non-pecuniary loss including distress.[513] The next question that arose was whether s. 13 DPA can be rendered compatible with art. 23 of the directive by applying the EU duty of conforming interpretation. The Court of Appeal held that Parliament deliberately chose to restrict the right to compensation for distress to certain tightly defined circumstances, and that there is no evidence that indicates what Parliament had in mind when it created the limitation. The court then argued that the EU legal duty of conforming interpretation cannot be invoked to disapply the two conditions of s. 13(2) DPA because s. 13 is a central feature of the DPA, s. 13 is important to the DPA scheme as a whole and s. 13(2) is an important element of s. 13. The judges concluded that the limits set by Parliament to the right to compensation are a fundamental feature of the legislation. A conforming interpretation was not possible,[514] and the Court of Appeal disapplied s. 13(2) DPA.[515]

This reasoning of the Court of Appeal is lopsided. There is no mention of the presumption of compliance and of a presumed general intention to fully implement the directive. The judges did not mention that under conforming interpretation a court can depart from the intention of the enacting parliament. The reasoning of the Court of Appeal relating to Parliament's deliberate legislative choice fails to convince as well. This is not a constraint in itself that automatically bars a conforming meaning. *Google Inc v. Vidal-Hall* is difficult to reconcile with *IDT Card Services*, where a conforming interpretation was possible despite Parliament making a deliberate legislative choice, using clear wording to express that legislative decision, but not foreseeing the inconsistency of that choice with the applicable directive. The Court of Appeal in *Google Inc v. Vidal-Hall* did not address the possibility that s. 13(2) DPA may contain an inadvertent inconsistency with Directive 95/46/EC. Notwithstanding this criticism, a key question for the Court of Appeal was whether the exclusion of the right to compensation for distress, in the event the conditions stated in s. 13(2) DPA are not met, is a fundamental feature of the DPA.[516] The court answered in the affirmative, and this seems possible. This must not, however, disguise the fact that the reasoning of the Court of Appeal in this respect can be characterised as a purely evaluative argument.[517] It would have been equally possible to argue consequentially that it can be excluded that Parliament intended to restrict the right to compensation for distress to the cases mentioned in s. 13(2) DPA had it known of the incompatibility of such a legislative choice with the directive.

---

[513] Ibid., paras. 79–82.
[514] Ibid., paras. 91–94.
[515] Ibid., para. 95, 104.
[516] Ibid., para. 91.
[517] See ibid., para. 92.

Chapter 4. The European Legal Duty of Conforming Interpretation

There is no reason to assume that Parliament would have willingly run into a *Factortame* liability. No reason was given by the judges for why the provisions for compensation are a central feature of the DPA scheme as a whole. The indeterminacy of the fundamental feature limit is evident.

In an *obiter* statement, the Court of Appeal also reflected further on the outer limits of conforming interpretation. Lord Dyson MR and Sharp LJ said:

> [I]t does not follow that it is never possible to interpret a measure by disapplying or striking down part of it in order to make it compatible with the Convention or a directive. Various interpretative techniques may be deployed in order to eliminate an incompatibility. … [W]e do not see why, as a matter of principle, it is impermissible to disapply or strike down, say, a relatively minor incompatible provision in order to make the measure compatible. The question must always be whether the change that would result from the proposed interpretation (whichever interpretative technique is adopted) would alter a fundamental feature of the legislation.[518]

This statement indicates that it was not necessarily the wording of s. 13(2) DPA that was the determinative factor for the Court of Appeal's decision that a conforming interpretation of s. 13(2) DPA is inconsistent with a fundamental feature of the legislation. What is clear from this statement is that the fundamental feature limit relates to the legislation as a whole as opposed to the fundamental features of a specific provision. This is in line with case law on s. 3(1) HRA such as *In re S (Minors)* and *Ghaidan*. It was shown, however, that other case law on s. 3(1) HRA suggests that the fundamental feature limit can also relate to the level of provision. Similarly, *British Gas Trading Ltd v. Lock* and other case law[519] show that it is not settled for conforming interpretation whether the fundamental features, "the grain" or "the thrust" are determined by looking at the challenged provision or at the purpose of the legislation as a whole. More controversially, the Court of Appeal qualified the *disapplication* of a provision as a possible technique of interpretation for s. 3(1) HRA and for the EU legal duty of conforming *interpretation*. According to the judges, there may be cases where disapplying a provision in order to render it in conformity with an applicable directive will not exceed the outer limits of conforming interpretation. The Court of Appeal in *Google Inc v. Vidal-Hall* preferred flexibility over a rigid limit of interpretation and over legal certainty. The Court of Appeal's judgment in *British Gas Trading Ltd v. Lock*, in contrast, can be characterised by giving more weight to legal certainty. The case law is thus inconsistent and in need of clarification.

---

[518] Ibid., para. 90.
[519] *EB Central Services Ltd. v. Revenue and Customs Commissioners* [2008] EWCA Civ 486, para. 83 (Dyson LJ, "That would not involve a fundamental departure from item 6 [of Group 8, Schedule 8 to the Value Added Tax Act 1994] or the domestic legislation as a whole").

What is doubtful is whether the Court of Appeal's *obiter* statement in *Google Inc v. Vidal-Hall* complies with UKSC case law. In *Fleming*, Lord Walker clearly distinguished between disapplication and interpretation.[520] In *O'Brien*, the Supreme Court implicitly rejected a conforming interpretation by means of disapplication of a provision. The Supreme Court expressed

> no concluded view, as to whether judges (as a general class) would qualify as "workers" under the Regulations [the Part-time Workers (Prevention of Less Favourable Treatment) Regulations 2000], and as to whether Mr O'Brien would qualify as a worker if regulation 17 were to be disregarded (in the same way as part of a domestic measure was disregarded in Perceval-Price v. Department of Economic Development).[521]

Regulation 17 treats as inapplicable the Part-time Workers (Prevention of Less Favourable Treatment) Regulations 2000 in relation to fee-paid part-time judges.[522] The second part of the quote from the Supreme Court's judgment refers to the disapplication of reg. 17. It implies the understanding that disregarding a provision by means of conforming interpretation is not possible. That is because in *Perceval-Price*, the Court of Appeal of Northern Ireland held that the phrase "other than service of a person holding a statutory office" in s. 1(9) of the Equal Pay Act (Northern Ireland) 1970 and in art. 82(2) of the Sex Discrimination (Northern Ireland) Order 1976 was inconsistent with the terms of the Equal Treatment Directive 76/207/EC. The phrase therefore had to be "disapplied, that is to say, the courts should in applying the provisions of the Act and Order disregard the phrase".[523] The plain meaning of this phrase was that persons holding statutory offices are excluded from the application of the legislation. The House of Lords had recognised in another judgment that removing the express exclusion of statutory office-holders in *Perceval-Price* would have been amendment and not conforming interpretation, which is why the Northern Irish court did not employ the EU duty of conforming interpretation.[524] It was common ground in the Northern Irish case that the applicable terms of the Equal Treatment Directive had direct effect and that the departments responsible were emanations of the state. The Court of Appeal of Northern Ireland further stated that a judicial activity that amounts to a "deletion of portions of the legislation" is not possible under

---

[520] *Fleming (trading as Bodycraft) v. HM Revenue & Customs* [2008] UKHL 2, para. 62 (Lord Walker).
[521] *O'Brien v. Ministry of Justice* [2010] UKSC 34, para. 27 (Lord Walker, delivering the judgment of the court).
[522] Regulation 17 reads: "These Regulations do not apply to any individual in his capacity as the holder of a judicial office if he is remunerated on a daily fee-paid basis".
[523] *Perceval-Price v. Department of Economic Development* [2000] IRLR 380 (Carswell LCJ).
[524] *Percy v. Church of Scotland Board of National Mission* [2005] UKHL 73, para. 149 (Baroness Hale).

conforming interpretation.⁵²⁵ It is thus clear that the words "disapplied" and "disregarded" as used by the Court of Appeal of Northern Ireland in *Perceval-Price* refer to the effect of the supremacy of EU law on incompatible national legislation and not to conforming interpretation.

A reading out of words in legislation, that is to say disregarding those words, is possible in certain circumstances under conventional canons of construction.⁵²⁶ It follows that disregarding a certain part of a provision by means of conforming interpretation, as suggested *obiter* by the Court of Appeal in *Google Inc v. Vidal-Hall*, does not appear to exceed the outer limits of the judicial function. In this sense, a deletion of portions of the legislation would be possible under conforming judicial law-making. This, however, is a grey area of conforming interpretation at the moment. It would certainly benefit from a clarifying judgment by the Supreme Court. A reading of a provision that has the effect of disapplying the provision as a whole and leaving the provision with no scope of application appears to be of a different quality than the reading out of certain words or phrases in legislation.⁵²⁷ On the one hand, it is at least possible to make a formal distinction between both cases. On the other hand, it is unclear whether s. 3(1) HRA can be used to reduce the scope of application of a provision as a whole to zero in order to safeguard the compatibility of the whole of the legislation with Convention rights.⁵²⁸ This further illustrates that the case law is in need of clarification.

What the Court of Appeal suggested *obiter* in *Google Inc v. Vidal-Hall* is something that the BGH had already alluded to in *Quelle II* and in *Lebensversicherung II*, when the German court left open the issue whether a conforming judicial law-making can have the effect of a complete disapplication of a provision. Yet, the BGH was reminded by the BVerfG that such a "Europeanisation from the inside" would exceed the limits of the judicial function. The issue only seemed resolved. In *Lebensversicherung im Antragsmodell*,⁵²⁹ the BGH's conforming teleological reduction of sentence 4 of s. 8(5) VVG had the effect of a complete disapplication of the regulatory decision contained in this sentence. We have already seen how the BGH attempted to reconcile its testing of new heights of conforming judicial law-making with the case law of the BVerfG. A similar reasoning could be adopted by an English

---

⁵²⁵ *Perceval-Price v. Department of Economic Development* [2000] IRLR 380 (Carswell LCJ). Admittedly, the Supreme Court in *O'Brien* did not make explicit reference to this part of the Northern Irish judgment.
⁵²⁶ See Chapter 2, Section 4.
⁵²⁷ For a different view and the argument that the disapplication of a provision is a point along an interpretative spectrum, see HUNT, above n. 121, p. 79; cf. T.R.S. ALLAN, Parliamentary sovereignty: Lord Denning's dexterous revolution, (1983) 3 *OJLS* 22, 31; J. GOLDSWORTHY, Parliamentary sovereignty and statutory interpretation, in R. BIGWOOD (ed.), *The statute: making and meaning*, LexisNexis, Wellington 2004, pp. 187, 200–201.
⁵²⁸ See Chapter 3, Section 7.3.2.
⁵²⁹ Discussed in Section 7.1 above.

court, and this would arguably not exceed the analogy to the outer limits of s. 3(1) HRA due to their formulation in vague terms. What is clear in current BVerfG case law is that a teleological reduction cannot reduce the scope of application of a provision as a whole to zero. The Supreme Court seems to go in the same direction in *O'Brien*.

7.3. COMPARATIVE ANALYSIS

When the outer limits of conforming judicial law-making in English and German courts are compared, an obvious finding is that the strength of the EU legal duty of conforming interpretation has increased over time in both jurisdictions. This development also concurred with a widening of the outer limits of conforming interpretation over time. In Germany, *Quelle II* is a decisive case since the BGH explicitly recognised that conforming judicial law-making is part of the judicial function. In England, the conforming interpretation has evolved from *Duke* over *Pickstone* and *Webb (No. 2)* to the current approach, which is sometimes referred to as the *Ghaidan* approach to conforming interpretation. Whereas the rising strength of conforming interpretation corresponded with a changing understanding of parliamentary sovereignty in England, a similar constitutional development did not occur in Germany.

English and German courts apply the same outer limits in horizontal cases and in vertical cases, irrespective of whether an individual or the state relies on conforming interpretation. An argument can, however, be made that English and German courts should differentiate between horizontal and vertical scenarios. I have shown that different incentives exist in these cases.[530] A court could take these incentives into account and apply the outer limits of conforming interpretation in a narrower fashion in horizontal scenarios and in a wider fashion in vertical scenarios. Applying wide outer limits of interpretation in vertical cases, where an individual relies on the directive and where a provision in a directive fulfils the conditions of direct effect, is not only justified for remedial reasons. That is because relying on the direct effect of the directive combined with the disapplication of incompatible national legislation would fulfil the remedial function as well. The difference from horizontal cases exists because applying wide outer limits of interpretation shows respect to the legislature whose legislation could otherwise be disapplied in a vertical case. The BVerfG uses a similar argument to justify a powerful operation of the doctrine of rights-consistent interpretation in Germany. In England, the notion of respect for the legislature can also be used as a justification for applying wide outer limits of conforming interpretation in vertical scenarios.

---

[530] See Section 3 above.

That is different in horizontal cases. In horizontal cases, the remedial effect of disapplying incompatible national legislation is not available. This, one may think, seems to create an incentive for a court to apply the outer limits of conforming judicial law-making in a robust manner as well. Conforming interpretation is an important remedial mechanism in horizontal cases.[531] The argument is lopsided, however, as a generous application of the outer limits of conforming interpretation in horizontal cases would come at the expense of the other private party to the proceedings. That is why a court should not take this incentive into account. If one agrees with this differentiation between horizontal and vertical scenarios, a differentiated application of the outer limits of conforming interpretation seems appropriate. The outer limits of conforming judicial law-making contain sufficient scope for evaluative arguments and judicial discretion that would allow for this differentiation. Yet, neither English nor German courts appear to make this distinction as they apply the duty of conforming interpretation with equal force in vertical and horizontal cases.

7.3.1. Development Towards Converging Outer Limits of Conforming Judicial Law-Making

German courts trace the outer limits of conforming judicial law-making to art. 20(2), (3) GG. In England, these limits stem from s. 2(4) ECA, a specific provision for the European context. One of the questions for this chapter was whether conforming interpretation widens the limits of the judicial function in the national legal order when compared to other modes of interpretation. That is not the case in Germany and England. When English courts apply conforming judicial law-making, they generally follow the analogy to s. 3(1) HRA. They neither fall short of nor exceed the outer limits recognised for Convention-compatible interpretation. When German courts engage in conforming judicial law-making, they generally apply the same outer limits that are recognised for conventional judicial law-making and for constitution-consistent judicial law-making. Yet, a stretching of the outer limits of conforming interpretation has occurred in both jurisdictions. It follows that judges' willingness to interpret national law in conformity with EU directives cannot be said to be low in England or Germany. This stretching devalues the outer limits to a certain extent. That is, however, not an issue that is peculiar to conforming interpretation as a similar stretching of the outer limits of judicial law-making appears in the realm of rights-consistent interpretation in both jurisdictions. This stretching of the outer limits of conforming interpretation does not therefore infringe the analogy to s. 3(1) HRA in England or the analogy

---

[531] See Section 1.2 above.

to constitution-consistent interpretation in Germany. Moreover, courts in both jurisdictions do not show "greater prudence" towards conforming judicial law-making than towards rights-consistent judicial law-making or vice versa. Due to these findings, the comparative discussion provided in Section 7 of Chapter 3 for rights-consistent interpretation applies *mutatis mutandis* for the comparison of the outer limits of conforming judicial law-making in England and Germany.

The stretching of the judicial function is possible due to the indeterminacy of the outer limits of interpretation in both jurisdictions. This "stretching" must be distinguished from "exceeding" these limits and the judicial function. That the boundary between both is so difficult to establish is, of course, a consequence of the indeterminacy of these limits as expressed in written judicial opinions. German scholars,[532] for example, attempt to square the circle when they endorse an objectivised approach to interpretation, advocate for indeterminate outer limits of interpretation, assess the possibility of conforming judicial law-making via a holistic view of different arguments, but at the same time vigorously argue that German courts have overstepped the outer limits of conforming judicial law-making. The indeterminacy of the outer limits of statutory interpretation is prevalent for other modes of interpretation as well, as I have explored in Chapters 2 and 3. Indeterminate limits lead to incoherent case law, and that leads to a further undermining of legal certainty.

When English and German courts engage in conforming judicial law-making, they start from the premise that judicial law-making is a permissible part of the judicial function. The change of the default position for conforming judicial law-making in England and the consequential change in judicial attitudes has led to a converging judicial mindset about the judicial role in both jurisdictions. The difference in the interpretative powers of English and German courts that we encountered in Chapter 2 does not exist for conforming judicial law-making. Instead, a significant congruence is determinable. There are no significant divergences in the way the highest English and German courts express the outer limits of conforming interpretation. Any remaining differences do not appear to have the potential to threaten the uniform effectiveness of directives in both countries. In both jurisdictions, a court does not necessarily exceed the judicial function if it adopts a conforming meaning that departs from a provision's unambiguous wording, a provision's underlying specific purpose and the intention of the enacting legislature. I have demonstrated that courts in both countries adopt the same general interpretative approach and the same outer interpretative limits when they interpret implementing or non-implementing legislation and when they interpret legislation that

---

[532] MICHAEL, above n. 418, pp. 349–373.

pre- or post-dates an applicable directive. For the outer limits of conforming interpretation, this book's findings validate S. Vogenauer's thesis[533] that statutory interpretation in England and Germany is fundamentally uniform. In the following, the comparative discussion will only focus on issues that were not covered in Section 7 of Chapter 3 and that are peculiar to conforming interpretation.

One of these issues is the drafting style of directives. The interrelationship between the drafting style of legislation and maxims of statutory interpretation was explored in Chapter 2. It is often said that the drafting style of directives is generally less precise than the drafting style of domestic English legislation as it is often the product of compromise.[534] That may be true to some extent, but certainly does not characterise all directives. Directives can contain a very detailed and highly specific programme, particularly if they are delegated legislation made under art. 290 TFEU. If a directive contains general terms or deliberately ambiguous or vague language, its implementing legislation in England and Germany will often contain the same terms or at least equivalent terms with a similar level of generality or vagueness. That is because Germany often adopts a one-to-one transposition method,[535] and the UK favours a copy-out approach to implementation.[536] The implementing style is often similar in both jurisdictions.[537] This style of implementing legislation favours a purposive approach of interpretation rather than a literal approach if the directive contains general or vague terms. It also favours the role of judges as a driver of legal development. This explains why the BVerfG has claimed that an open formulation of statutory words justifies a court's power to engage in judicial law-making.[538] I have argued in Chapter 2, however, that it does not follow from general, ambiguous or vague statutory words that judges should be empowered to go beyond the possible semantic meanings of the statutory language. All in all, the variations in the drafting style of directives make it appear questionable to derive reliable conclusions for the interpretative approach of conforming judicial law-making. The variations in the level of precision and vagueness that appear in the text of different directives will often be mirrored in national implementing legislation in both jurisdictions.

---

[533] VOGENAUER, above no. 197, pp. 1295–1308.
[534] D. GREENBERG (ed.), *Craies on legislation*, Sweet & Maxwell, London 2017, paras. 3.10.6–3.10.7; *Johnson v. Medical Defence Union Ltd.* [2007] EWCA Civ 262, para. 89 (Arden LJ).
[535] Unlike in the UK, however, there is no government guidance to always use one-to-one transposition where it is available.
[536] Department for Business, Innovation and Skills, Transposition Guidance: How to Implement European Directives Effectively, April 2013. For discussion, see GREENBERG, above n. 534, para. 3.10.8.1; GREENBERG, above n. 128, pp. 243–256.
[537] See, e.g. KRÁL, above n. 56, p. 221 note 7, who uses copy-out and on-to-one transposition as synonyms.
[538] BVerfG, *NJW* 1998, 519, 520 – *Kind als Schaden*.

The transposition style of directives does, however, influence conforming interpretation in at least one way. If the national legislation uses the same language as the directive, the statutory language should prima facie bear the same meaning it has in EU law.[539] If a Member State adopts a one-to-one transposition method or a copy-out approach, using the same language as the directive is a very strong factor for the presumption that the enacting legislature intended to fully comply with the requirements of the directive.

CJEU case law on conforming interpretation like the EU principle of equivalence or European methodological rules is one factor that has influenced the development towards converging outer limits of conforming interpretation in England and Germany. It is important to point out that neither the European interpretative priority rule nor the European presumption of compliance have shifted the *contra legem* limit in England and Germany in favour of the judiciary. A second factor was CJEU case law that had an impact on UK constitutional law: CJEU case law on the supremacy of EU law led to modifications in the doctrine of parliamentary sovereignty. These modifications were arguably one reason that motivated Lord Oliver in *Pickstone* to depart from a number of well-established canons of construction. He thereby extended the interpretative powers of English judges and this in turn brought these powers closer to the recognised interpretative powers of German judges. This was a major converging move because Lord Oliver changed the default position for permissible conforming judicial law-making. A third factor is associated with constitutional developments in English law that happened outside the realm of EU law. That relates to the way English courts have interpreted their powers under s. 3(1) HRA. "Transferring" the outer limits of Convention-compatible interpretation to conforming interpretation further widened judicial powers, and this coincided with a further converging push towards the wide interpretative powers available to German judges. I have demonstrated in Section 7.3 of Chapter 3 that a comparison of rights-consistent judicial law-making in England and in Germany shows that the way English courts have interpreted s. 3(1) HRA does not adhere to the constitutional doctrine of parliamentary sovereignty. An equivalent reasoning applies to how English judges have interpreted s. 2(4) ECA when we compare the outer limits of conforming judicial law-making in both countries. From a UK constitutional viewpoint, this widening of the outer limits of conforming judicial law-making exceeds the judicial function and cannot be reconciled with the doctrine of parliamentary sovereignty. One reason for the convergence in the outer limits in England and Germany is thus that English judges have ventured outside their constitutional role. For the comparison of English and German law specifically, it is not incorrect to say that legal methodology

---

[539] See *ITV Broadcasting Ltd. v. TV Catchup Ltd.* [2015] EWCA Civ 204, paras. 106–108 (Arden LJ), cf. para. 86 (Kitchin LJ).

in the Member States converges because of an increasing Europeanisation of the national legal orders.[540] Yet, the picture that emerges here is more nuanced. First, compared to the "high jumps" by English legal methodology, German legal methodology on conforming judicial law-making hardly deviated from what is otherwise accepted under conventional canons of statutory interpretation in Germany. German courts have not ventured outside their judicial role when engaging in conforming judicial law-making. Second, the converging trend also occurs because of national legal developments in England outside the realm of EU law.

Scholars who advocate in favour of a common European standard of conforming interpretation could build on the findings of this book. The highly congruent outer limits of conforming judicial law-making in England and Germany could provide a starting point towards developing common European limits for conforming interpretation.[541] It should have become clear, however, that this is not the position taken in this book. That is because these limits are determined by the relationship between the judiciary and the legislature at national level, which is governed by constitutional law in each Member State. This relationship does differ in the Member States as the comparison between England and Germany shows. It is partly because English courts have ventured outside their constitutional role that this difference does not translate into divergences in the outer limits of conforming interpretation in England and Germany. As in England and in Germany, constitutional law in other Member States will most likely set an indeterminate framework for the outer limits of the judicial function. This will probably mean that courts in these Member States apply indeterminate outer limits of conforming interpretation. With the necessary caveat in mind, the results of this comparative study may thus be carefully used to gauge whether courts in other Member States "do whatever lies in their jurisdiction", fall short of going to the outer limits of the judicial function or exceed their judicial powers when interpreting national law in conformity with directives.

7.3.2. Evaluative Arguments and Judicial Discretion

It is one thing to have an abstract knowledge of what is the maximum possible as a matter of interpretation according to the outer limits and techniques of conforming judicial law-making. It is another thing to stretch these limits and techniques almost to breaking point in an individual case. Due to the indeterminacy of the limits and techniques of conforming judicial law-making, English and German judges enjoy a considerable scope for evaluative

---

[540]   E.A. KRAMER, *Juristische Methodenlehre*, 4th ed., Stämpfli, Bern 2013, p. 45.
[541]   In favour of developing such limits: VOGENAUER, above n. 53, pp. 242–243, 259–260.

arguments and a considerable degree of discretion when they engage in conforming judicial law-making. I have explored this in detail in relation to rights-consistent judicial law-making.[542] The scope for evaluative arguments and judicial discretion is almost identical in both jurisdictions when judges apply the outer limits of conforming interpretation in an individual case. It has been suggested in legal scholarship, based on art. 4(3) TEU, that national courts must exercise their interpretative discretion in a "euro-friendly" way. Article 4(3) TEU is part of the legal basis of the EU legal duty of conforming interpretation. The duty of sincere cooperation enshrined in art. 4(3) TEU requires national courts to take "any appropriate measure" within their competence to ensure the full application of EU law.[543] A wide understanding of this duty would entail that if a court is given interpretative discretion under national law, it is obliged to exercise this discretion (= appropriate measure) in a way that observes the full application of EU law.[544] There is currently, apart from the European presumption of compliance, no CJEU case law that explicitly requires national courts to use their interpretative discretion in a euro-friendly way when a court decides about whether a provision is capable of bearing a certain meaning according to the interpretative criteria. The interpretative priority rule is limited to a selection rule between different possible meanings of a provision. The reality is more nuanced, however, since the CJEU requires national courts "to do whatever lies in their jurisdiction"[545] and to interpret national law in conformity with directives "to the fullest extent possible".[546] Yet, the CJEU does not appear to comprehensively review the interpretative space available to national courts but instead focuses on the plausibility of the conforming or non-conforming meaning of national legislation.

The considerable scope for evaluative arguments and considerable degree of judicial discretion can count as the underlying reason why commentators have said that whether a conforming interpretation is possible or not is rather a subjective concept.[547] That is also why L. Niglia has noted that evaluative arguments, in particular reasons of substantive fairness in the circumstances, rather than formal arguments have been determinative for the position of

---

[542] See Chapter 3, Section 7.
[543] Opinion 1/09 of the CJEU (full court) of 8 March 2011, *European Patent Court*, ECLI:EU:C:2011:123, paras. 68–69.
[544] See A. WALLERMAN, Towards an EU law doctrine of the exercise of discretion in national courts? The Member States' self-imposed limits on national procedural autonomy, (2016) 53 *CMLR* 339, 343, 353, 359 on the implications of such a wide understanding of the duty.
[545] Case C-397/01, *Pfeiffer v. Deutsches Rotes Kreuz*, ECLI:EU:C:2004:584, para. 118.
[546] Case C-64/15, *BP Europa v. Hauptzollamt Hamburg-Stadt*, ECLI:EU:C:2016:62, para. 41.
[547] Sweet and Maxwell's Encyclopedia of Employment Law, Looseleaf, Vol. 2, chapter 8A, para. 1.12.

domestic courts in cases of conforming interpretation.⁵⁴⁸ L. Niglia provides the example of *Litster*, where Lord Oliver pointed out that if a conforming interpretation of reg. 5 of the Transfer of Undertakings Regulations 1981 had not been possible, the parties to the transfer would have been "at liberty to avoid the manifest purpose of the Directive by the simple expedient of wrongfully dismissing the workforce a few minutes before the completion of the transfer".⁵⁴⁹ Niglia's almost exclusive focus on substantive arguments underplays the role that formal arguments can play in conforming interpretation in judicial practice.⁵⁵⁰ This can be seen, for example, when the BAG departed from its settled case law in *Schultz-Hoff*.⁵⁵¹ According to the BAG's settled case law, a worker's right to paid annual leave is extinguished if the employer cannot authorise the leave during the leave year and during the carry-over period because the worker is unfit for work due to illness until the end of the carry-over period. The BAG stipulated in *Schultz-Hoff* that this "old" interpretation of s. 7(3) and (4) BUrlG contradicts the interpretation of art. 7 of Directive 2003/88/EC given by CJEU.⁵⁵² Even though the BAG indicated that it does not agree with the CJEU's interpretation of the directive, it considered itself bound by the CJEU's decision and changed the interpretation of s. 7(3) and (4) BUrlG by way of conforming judicial law-making.⁵⁵³ In these circumstances, it cannot be said that considerations of substantive fairness were determinative for the BAG's conforming judicial law-making.

7.3.3. Judicial Attitudes and the Stretching of the Outer Interpretative Limits

What is clear from the discussion so far is that judicial attitudes of national judges are a crucial element for the effective application of the EU legal duty of conforming interpretation. English and German judges can to a large extent determine the effectiveness of these limits in an individual case. Differences in judicial attitudes can have an impact on whether or not a conforming interpretation is possible in an individual case. That is obvious if one compares Etherton LJ's judgment in *Football Association Premier League Ltd. v. QC Leisure* with Arden LJ's judgment in *IDT Card Services*. Since judges most often work in senates in the highest German courts, or smaller groups like chambers in the BVerfG, when deciding a case, the panel composition matters. The latter is

---

[548] L. NIGLIA, Form and substance in European constitutional law: the "social" character of indirect effect, (2010) 16 *ELJ* 439, 452, 455.
[549] *Litster v. Forth Dry Dock & Engineering Co Ltd.* [1990] 1 AC 546 (HL), 563 (Lord Oliver).
[550] NIGLIA, above n. 548, p. 454.
[551] BAG, *EuZW* 2009, 465, paras. 45–47 – *Schultz-Hoff*.
[552] The CJEU later changed its interpretation of the directive in *KHS*, discussed in Section 7.1 above.
[553] BAG, *EuZW* 2009, 465, paras. 57–59, 64 – *Schultz-Hoff*.

true for England as well, particularly for the Court of Appeal where decisions are often made by a panel of three judges. A three-judge panel is common in the highest German courts as well. The latitude available to judges when they engage in conforming judicial law-making also explains why the cooperative relationship between the CJEU and national courts is a key element for the effectiveness of the EU legal duty of conforming interpretation. If we recall the discussion of contemporary English and German judgments in this section and in Section 6 above, a narrow judicial attitude towards EU law cannot generally be detected when judges engage in conforming interpretation. Generally speaking, a friendliness towards European law (*Europarechtsfreundlichkeit*) appears to be discernible when contemporary English and German courts engage in judicial law-making for implementing legislation.[554] This view competes with other possible explanations of why English and German courts have stretched the outer limits and techniques of conforming interpretation when interpreting implementing legislation. It may be argued that courts pay heed to legislative intention when they give considerable weight to the general intention of the legislature to comply with the requirements of the directive. Yet paying heed to legislative intention does not explain why in cases of implementing legislation the *presumed* general intention to fully implement the directive is given more weight than or priority over a specific and inadvertently non-conforming objective of a provision. I have argued that constitutional factors, s. 2(4) ECA and art. 20(2), (3) GG, cannot convincingly explain why courts give preference to the presumed general intention. However, a plausible explanatory factor is the European presumption of compliance, which interacts with national interpretative criteria. Even though the CJEU has not expressly fleshed out the *contra legem* limit, the presumption of compliance significantly impacts on the outer limits of conforming judicial law-making in English and German judicial practice. That is because the weighing of the interpretative criteria mostly determines whether or not an outer interpretative limit is exceeded. The European presumption that the national legislature intends to fully and correctly implement the directive into national law is thus a major factor that can explain the powerful operation of the doctrine of conforming judicial law-making in English and German courts for implementing legislation. Establishing this presumption was, at least in hindsight, a cunning move by the CJEU that comes close to harmonising the *contra legem* limit for conforming interpretation by stealth and without the likely backlash from national courts that an open and explicit harmonisation of the *contra legem* limit would have caused.

---

[554] The most senior English judges do not appear to show the high levels of EU-scepticism that may be prevalent in British politics and large parts of the British public. For this view, see Arnull, above n. 206, p. 81; Rösler, above n. 370, p. 200.

Chapter 4. The European Legal Duty of Conforming Interpretation

Relying on a presumed general intention to fully implement a directive also illustrates what was established in Chapter 3: ascribing a wide purpose to a provision increases the scope of judicial law-making. According to the European presumption of compliance, the *presumed* general intention of the legislature to fully implement the directive must be given priority over a specific and inadvertently non-conforming purpose of a provision that is expressed in the legislative materials. Scholars have criticised this priority element of the presumption due to concerns of legal certainty. It can indeed be argued that a higher level of legal certainty would be reached if priority were given to a provision's specific purpose. A possible objection against giving precedence to a provision's specific objective that is inadvertently inconsistent with the directive as interpreted by the CJEU might be that the legislature would be overburdened with legislative amendments. This objection must be rejected, however, due to the interrelationship between the interpretative maxims employed in courts and the legislative drafting style. If judges were to always give precedence to a non-conforming, specifically expressed legislative objective over a presumed general intention of the legislature, the legislature could simply say in either the statutory text or the legislative materials that the purpose of the statute is to fully and entirely implement an EU directive. In that case, two identifiable objectives, one specific and one general, would contradict. It seems warranted to give precedence to the specifically expressed general intention to fully comply with an EU directive because of (a) a Member State's European obligation to correctly implement directives and (b) the various incentives for a court to find a conforming meaning.

National judges who interpret implementing legislation cannot give priority to a specific legislative purpose explicitly mentioned in a statute's legislative history over a presumed general intention of the legislature to fully comply with a directive. It is, however, important to realise that the priority element of the European presumption also increases the level of legal certainty compared to the default position in judicial practice. This default position is that no generally applicable presumptions, rules, guidelines or criteria exist that decide at which level of generality a provision's purpose must be determined in an individual case. It follows that the priority element incorporated in the European presumption of compliance improves legal certainty as judicial discretion is diminished. Conversely, however, a danger exists that the implementing measure is reduced to an empty hollow that can be filled with the aims of the directive. This reduces legal certainty as the national legislation loses its guiding function for the citizen. One solution to minimise this danger would be to adopt determinate outer limits for conforming judicial law-making. That this has not been done in English and German judicial practice is one factor that can explain the powerful operation of the EU presumption of compliance.

Another explanation for why national courts stretch the outer limits and techniques of conforming interpretation relates to the fact that considerable incentives exist for national courts to find a conforming meaning. That is because the duty of conforming interpretation serves the interests of one party to the proceedings, the Member State and the EU. These incentives do not lead to a modification of the outer limits of interpretation, but to their application in a loose fashion. This strength of conforming interpretation in national courts mirrors the doctrine's functions. These functions are fulfilled best if the outer limits of conforming interpretation are applied in a loose fashion. One consequence of combining (a) wide and indeterminate outer limits of judicial law-making with (b) a stretching of these limits in individual cases is that the distinction between the EU legal duty of conforming interpretation and horizontal direct effect of directives appears blurred in horizontal cases. Yet, it is not only CJEU case law establishing the requirements of conforming interpretation that is to blame for this result. A key reason for this finding can be traced back to national courts and their application of national legal methodology.

The pressure to find a conforming meaning is, however, only one extra-legal factor that influences English and German courts. It can be outweighed by other factors. That is exemplified by German case law interpreting legislation that precedes and does not implement a directive. Here, German courts show more restraint towards conforming judicial law-making. Furthermore, a significant number of cases of conforming judicial law-making of implementing legislation discussed in this chapter were preceded by a CJEU judgment ruling that the applicable directive precluded the challenged national legislation as interpreted by the referring national court. Such a judgment by the CJEU is another factor that generally appears to increase the willingness of English and German courts to find a conforming meaning by means of judicial law-making. All in all, sufficient incentives exist for English and German courts to adopt contrived conforming interpretations of domestic legislation. These incentives are also factors that can explain why not only the general formulation, but also the application of the outer limits of conforming judicial law-making converge in both jurisdictions even if a considerable amount of judicial discretion is taken into account. Judges in both jurisdictions use this discretion similarly to respond to these incentives. P. Legrand's claim that the deep structures of law, legal cultures and legal mentalities remain historically unique and cannot be bridged has been disproved in this chapter.[555]

What has to be considered as well is that national courts that are willing to refer questions about the correct interpretation of a directive to the CJEU may also be more willing to comply with the CJEU's demand that national courts must do whatever lies in their jurisdiction and must interpret national

---

[555] LEGRAND, above n. 11, pp. 52–81.

law in conformity with directives to the fullest extent possible. These domestic courts may thus be more willing than non-referring courts to stretch the outer limits of conforming judicial law-making. This is supported by German (*Urlaubsentgelt, Interprofessionelle Sozietät*) and English (*Google Inc v. Vidal-Hall, Football Association Premier League Ltd. v. QC Leisure*) cases that were not preceded by a preliminary ruling from the CJEU. In these four cases, the national courts felt unable to interpret domestic legislation in conformity with the applicable directive due to the *contra legem* limit being breached. The national judges appeared to show more restraint towards a powerful application of conforming interpretation in all four cases. In *Gasversorgung II*, however, the BGH referred questions about the correct interpretation of the applicable directive to the CJEU but nonetheless felt unable to achieve a conforming meaning after the case returned to the BGH. As in *Urlaubsentgelt* and *Interprofessionelle Sozietät*, the German court in *Gasversorgung II* had to interpret non-implementing legislation that pre-dated the applicable directive. This thus seems to be a decisive factor for gauging whether a conforming judicial law-making is possible or not. The three German cases and *Google Inc v. Vidal-Hall*, for example, also show that the intention of the enacting legislature can still play an important limiting role for conforming judicial law-making without being an outer limit in itself. The comparator to *Gasversorgung II* in England is *Webb (No. 2)*, where the House of Lords made a reference to the CJEU and interpreted non-implementing legislation that preceded the applicable directive. When the case returned from the CJEU to the House of Lords, the judges held that a conforming meaning of ss. 1(1) and 5(3) Sex Discrimination Act 1975 can be adopted. It may be argued that the difference from *Gasversorgung II* shows that the most senior English judges are, or at least have been, loyal and uncritical towards CJEU rulings, and that this is informed by s. 3 ECA and the *stare decisis* tradition.[556] Yet, in *Webb (No. 1)* the House of Lords signalled that a conforming interpretation of ss. 1(1) and 5(3) Sex Discrimination Act 1975 may be possible. Furthermore, the decision in *Webb (No. 2)* has to be seen against the background of the CJEU's then recent *Marleasing* decision. After *Marleasing* and before further clarifying CJEU judgments in the 2000s, uncertainty existed about whether and to what extent the EU legal duty of conforming interpretation can be restricted by national methods of interpretation.

Other cases like *Pickstone*, *IDT Card Services* and *Lebensversicherung im Antragsmodell* illustrate that a preceding CJEU ruling is certainly not necessary for incentivising national courts to operate conforming interpretation in a very powerful way. It can thus be concluded that whether or not English and German

---

[556] Cf. for this argument Rösler, above n. 370, p. 195.

courts narrowly apply, liberally apply or stretch the outer limits of conforming judicial law-making depends on a multitude of legal and extra-legal factors that are weighed in an individual case. That brings us back to the indeterminate state of the outer limits of conforming interpretation and illustrates once more that judicial attitudes can have a decisive influence when courts apply the outer limits of conforming interpretation. A strong case for conforming interpretation in general and judicial law-making in particular exists when (a) a national court is willing to refer a question about the correct interpretation of EU law to the CJEU and (b) the national law at issue is implementing legislation. A strong case against conforming judicial law-making exists if a German court interprets non-implementing legislation that pre-dates an applicable directive and if a conforming meaning cannot be given to the legislation by means of interpretation in a narrow sense. These two scenarios may be described as "steadying factors" in the case law.

7.3.4. Adaptability of the Outer Interpretative Limits

The indeterminacy of the outer interpretative limits can in large part explain why these limits are malleable and highly adaptable to integrate European influences and to safeguard the effectiveness of directives in the national legal sphere. Examples of such adaptability include the application of the double criterion or the notion of gap in Germany, the integration of the EU presumption of compliance into the judicial reasoning process in both jurisdictions and the change of the rules of interpretation for the EU legal duty of conforming interpretation in *Pickstone* in England. The evaluative scope and judicial discretion that is available to a court under indeterminate outer limits of interpretation has been used by the courts in the past to adapt the law to changing political realities. EU membership is one of these realities. English and German methods of statutory interpretation thus appear sufficiently apt for the interpretative tasks of regular courts in a Europeanised environment.

Applying national interpretative maxims and outer interpretative limits does not pose a considerable limitation upon the harmonising effect of the doctrine of conforming interpretation in England and Germany. The disclaimer is that this adaptability must be paired with a judicial attitude to do whatever lies in the courts' jurisdiction in an individual case. Yet, this would not be any different if conforming interpretation were governed by uniform but equally indeterminate European interpretative maxims and European outer limits and techniques of interpretation. If the amount of academic criticism of contrived conforming interpretations is taken as a benchmark, contemporary highest English and German courts generally interpret national implementing legislation in conformity with directives "to the fullest extent possible". This result is not immutable, however, as early case law on conforming interpretation of non-implementing in England shows and as BAG case law in the early 2000s illustrates. The BAG interpreted national legislation without giving significant weight to the enacting legislature's general intention to correctly implement the applicable directive in the early 2000s.[557] If the required judicial attitude were missing in national courts, the CJEU could adopt a more hands-on approach for conforming interpretation. Occasional CJEU case law shows that the CJEU is not unwilling to do this.[558] English and German judges took time to grow into their roles as European judges and to apply conforming interpretation in a powerful way. CJEU case law, in particular *Marleasing* and *Pfeiffer*, certainly created nudges in this process.

7.3.5. Legal (Un)certainty

I have further evidenced in Chapter 4 that indeterminate outer limits of conforming judicial law-making combined with incentives to find a conforming meaning can lead to an unsettled status of these limits in both jurisdictions.[559] *Google Inc v. Vidal-Hall* and *Lebensversicherung im Antragsmodell* are cases in point. The underlying problem is that the outer limits of conforming interpretation as formulated in judicial practice fail to fulfil their functions to (a) limit the scope of possible meanings of a provision, (b) limit judicial power and thus address separation of powers concerns, (c) reduce the area of evaluative arguments and extra-legal considerations in statutory interpretation and (d) provide legal certainty. These findings are not specific to conforming interpretation as was demonstrated in Chapter 3. These findings also indicate a tension between giving full effectiveness to directives by conforming judicial law-making and the concern that "judicial re-writing of national law ... generates uncertainty and unpredictability in the law".[560] This tension requires further elaboration as the issue of legal certainty has specific characteristics in the sphere of conforming interpretation. It has been argued by claimants in English and German cases in the past that a conforming meaning of a provision should not be adopted because this would infringe the principle of legal certainty. One of the objections has been that the person affected by legislation must be able to foresee the manner in which it is to be applied by a court, and that the conforming judicial law-making envisaged by the court has not been foreseeable.[561] This objection has so far not

---

[557] BAG, *NZA* 2003, 742, 745, 748; BAG, *NZA* 2004, 375, 381–382.
[558] Case C-306/12, *Spedition Welter v. Avanssur*, ECLI:EU:C:2013:650, paras. 31–32.
[559] For a different view, claiming that UK courts "are clear as to the boundaries between interpretation and amendment of the law" when applying the EU legal duty of conforming interpretation, see DRAKE, above n. 229, p. 27.
[560] S. WEATHERILL, *Cases & Materials on EU law*, 12th ed., OUP, Oxford 2016, p. 139.
[561] For Germany: BVerfG, *NJW* 2012, 669, paras. 61–63; BVerfG, *NJW-RR* 2016, 1366, paras. 57–58; BGH, *NJW* 2009, 427, para. 33 – *Quelle II*; BGH, *NJW* 2012, 1073, para. 47 – *Weber II*. For England: *Revenue and Customs Commissioners v. IDT Card Services Ireland Ltd.* [2006] EWCA Civ 29, para. 110 (Arden LJ).

been crowned with success in the highest English and German courts. When dealing with this objection,[562] it is important to distinguish between the national principle of legal certainty and the EU principle of legal certainty.

This objection is indeed futile from a national law perspective. It was established in Chapter 1 of this book that interpretative maxims express the degree to which a (constitutional) legal order values legal certainty. The outer limits and techniques of conforming interpretation incorporate a balance between legal certainty and material justice. Concerns about the separation of powers and about legal certainty have led English and German courts to limit judicial law-making powers by stipulating and applying general outer limits and techniques of conforming judicial law-making. These limits and techniques exhaustively incorporate abstract concerns about legal certainty that relate to the foreseeability of judicial reasoning. Furthermore, concerns about legal certainty that relate to the predictability of judicial reasoning in an individual case are also exhaustively incorporated in the application of the outer techniques and limits of judicial law-making. That is because these techniques and limits leave sufficient room for judicial discretion and grant judges sufficient leeway to take the circumstances of the individual case into account. It follows that if a conforming judicial law-making is possible in an individual case according to English or German legal methodology, the national principle of legal certainty relating to the predictability of judicial reasoning does not function as another, separate hurdle for conforming interpretation. The principle of legal certainty does not further limit the possible meanings of a provision. The correct forum to discuss these concerns of legal certainty is the forum of determinate outer limits and techniques of judicial law-making that are sufficiently predictable in their application.

From an EU law perspective, the EU principle of legal certainty is a recognised general principle of law. The EU legal duty of conforming interpretation is limited by this general principle.[563] The principle "requires that legal rules be clear and precise, and aims to ensure that situations and legal relationships governed by [EU] law remain foreseeable".[564] The application of rules of law must be foreseeable by those subject to them.[565] The EU principle of legal

---

[562] I will only deal with the aspect of legal certainty relating to the foreseeability of judicial reasoning and not with the principle of legitimate expectations.
[563] Case C-268/06, *Impact v. Minister for Agriculture and Food and others*, ECLI:EU:C:2008:223, para. 100; Case C-12/08, *Mono Car Styling v. Dervis Odemis*, ECLI:EU:C:2009:466, para. 61.
[564] Case C-63/93, *Duff v. Minister for Agriculture and Food and Attorney General* ECLI:EU:C:1996:51, para. 20; cf. Case C-308/06, *Intertanko v. Secretary of State for Transport*, ECLI:EU:C:2008:312, para. 69; Case C-231/15, *Prezes Urzędu Komunikacji Elektronicznej and Petrotel v. Polkomtel*, ECLI:EU:C:2016:769, para. 29.
[565] Case C-201/08, *Planatol v. Hauptzollamt Darmstadt*, ECLI:EU:C:2009:539, para. 46; Case C-231/15, *Prezes Urzędu Komunikacji Elektronicznej and Petrotel v. Polkomtel*, ECLI:EU:C:2016:769, para. 29.

certainty binds Member States when they act within the scope of application of EU law. For example, the principle binds Member States when they implement a directive. The CJEU has held that national legislation implementing a directive should be worded unequivocally so as to give the persons concerned a clear and precise understanding of their rights and obligations.[566] The principle of legal certainty thus imposes certain constraints on the freedom of national authorities to choose the "form and methods" (art. 288 TFEU) when implementing directives. Since national courts are also "national authorities" in the sense of art. 288 TFEU, similar constraints exist for national courts when they interpret national legislation within the scope of an EU directive. That has implications for the methods of conforming interpretation employed in national courts. They must be sufficiently coherent and sufficiently determinate so that the interpretation and application of national legislation in conformity with an applicable directive is foreseeable by those subject to it.[567] It follows that the EU principle of legal certainty has the potential to bar and intervene in the techniques and limits of conforming judicial law-making as applied in national courts. Even though these techniques and limits are predominantly governed by national law, the EU principle of legal certainty acts as a safeguard.

A powerful application of this safeguard has the potential to (a) demand narrow and highly determinate outer limits of conforming judicial law-making and (b) intervene in the national separation of powers. There are multiple reasons why this potential has not been unlocked and is unlikely to be unlocked. First, a powerful application of the EU principle of legal certainty relating to the foreseeability of judicial reasoning in national courts would weaken the functions of conforming interpretation and would undermine the effectiveness of EU directives. Second, if the CJEU used the same standard of legal certainty that it employs for its own formulation and application of interpretative maxims when construing EU legislation, applying the EU principle of legal certainty as a safeguard would not be powerful.[568] Third, the CJEU's competence to develop European methodological rules is highly controversial in legal scholarship. This is all the more true if these European rules also intervene in the national separation of powers. This may be a key reason why the CJEU has not further harmonised the methods of conforming interpretation beyond the existing European methodological rules. A powerful application of the EU principle of legal certainty as a free-standing limit to conforming interpretation would,

---

[566] Case 143/83, *European Commission v. Denmark* [1985] ECR 427, para. 10.
[567] Admittedly, the CJEU has not yet expressed such a requirement for the methods of conforming interpretation used in national courts.
[568] Cf. the study by G. BECK, *The legal reasoning of the Court of Justice of the EU*, Hart, Oxford 2012, and in particular pp. 9–12.

however, further harmonise the methods of conforming interpretation in national courts via the back door. Fourth, the correct forum to increase the foreseeability of judicial reasoning in the sphere of conforming interpretation is the arena of interpretative maxims for conforming interpretation, which the CJEU has partly harmonised via European methodological rules. The priority element of the EU presumption of compliance illustrates that the CJEU generally values the effectiveness of directives more highly than the principle of legal certainty. An exception exists in the field of criminal law, where the CJEU has indicated that the EU principle of legal certainty impacts on and can limit the methods of conforming interpretation. The court has held that the EU legal duty of conforming interpretation cannot be used to interpret criminal legislation extensively to the detriment of the defendant,[569] for example by way of analogy, due to the principle of legal certainty.

All in all, conforming interpretation as operated in English and German judicial practice safeguards the full effectiveness and uniform application of EU directives in England and Germany. The EU legal duty of conforming interpretation fulfils its mitigating function. The aptitude of directives as an instrument of European legal harmonisation is not questioned by national methods of conforming interpretation in England and Germany.

8. A LOOK INTO THE FUTURE: BREXIT

The UK is preparing to leave the EU. Leaving the EU will have implications for the topics covered in and the comparative findings of this chapter. Yet, we will learn in this section that conforming interpretation will not enter the domain of modern British legal history any time soon. I will demonstrate that conforming interpretation will retain an important role in statutory interpretation in English courts after Brexit. I will also evidence why the key comparative findings of this chapter will continue to hold true after Brexit for a comparison between (a) the EU legal duty of conforming interpretation as applied in German courts and (b) the "new" duty of conforming interpretation under s. 5(2) European Union (Withdrawal) Act 2018 (EU(W) Act) as applied in English courts.

On 23 June 2016, the UK held a referendum on EU membership and a majority of people voted in favour of the UK's withdrawal from the EU. This is not the place to discuss the reasons for the referendum's outcome. The tension that lay at the heart of the debate that took place in the UK prior to the Brexit referendum was between the benefits of EU membership and the loss of a degree of national independence. "Vote leave, take back control" was an often-heard

---

[569] Case C-74/95, *Criminal proceedings against X*, EU:C:1996:491, paras. 24–25, 31; cf. Case C-168/95, *Criminal proceedings against Arcaro*, EU:C:1996:363, paras. 37, 42.

slogan of the Leave campaign and Boris Johnson claimed that the British people will remember the 23 June 2016 as the UK's independence day. The European Union (Notification of Withdrawal) Act 2017 was passed on 16 March 2017 and gave the Prime Minister the power to notify, under art. 50(2) TEU, the European Council of the UK's intention to withdraw from the EU. This notification was given on 29 March 2017. Once a withdrawal agreement between the UK and the EU has been negotiated and agreed and has entered into force, the EU Treaties cease to apply to and in the UK (art. 50(3) TEU). If an agreement cannot be reached, the EU Treaties will cease to apply to and in the UK two years after the notification, i.e. on 29 March 2019, unless an extension is granted to the two-year period under the terms of art. 50(3) TEU.

For this book's purposes, the key question is what will happen to the EU legal duty of conforming interpretation in the UK following the UK's exit from the EU? Once the ECA is repealed, the *EU* legal duty of conforming interpretation will cease to have effect in the UK. Will there be an equivalent or a similar interpretative obligation that will take its place? Primary legislation that was enacted in order to implement a directive will continue to have legal effect, unless it is amended, replaced or repealed. Questions arise about its interpretation, however. Will a directive continue to influence the interpretation of this legislation post-Brexit, and if so in what way? If the CJEU interprets the directive after Brexit in a way that the UK implementing legislature did not foresee, will that have any effect on the implementing legislation's interpretation? Delegated legislation that was enacted in order to implement a directive also stays in force, unless it is amended or repealed or the primary legislation under which it was made is removed. Since the UK is en route to repealing the ECA, all of the delegated legislation which has been made under s. 2(2) ECA would lapse and cease to be part of the UK statute book, unless saved expressly.

On 13 July 2017, the UK government introduced the European Union (Withdrawal) Bill into the House of Commons. The Bill received Royal Assent on 26 June 2018. Section 1 EU(W) Act repeals the ECA on exit day.[570] One general purpose of the 2018 Act is to ensure legal continuity after exit day and to avoid gaps on the statute book, which is why the Act converts EU law as it stands at the moment of exit into domestic law and preserves domestic legislation that has been made with the purpose of implementing EU obligations.[571] To do this,

---

[570] Section 20(1) EU(W) Act defines "exit day" as meaning 29 March 2019 at 11 pm. The 2018 Act, in s. 20(3), (4), grants government ministers the power to amend that definition of exit day in order to ensure that the day and time specified in the definition are the day and time that the Treaties are to cease to apply to the UK.

[571] European Union (Withdrawal) Act 2018, Explanatory notes, paras. 10–11, 23–24. See also White Paper, Legislating for the United Kingdom's withdrawal from the European Union, Cm 9446, March 2017, paras. 1.12–1.13.

the Act's ss. 2, 3 and 4 create a new body of law known as "retained EU law".[572] The questions thus arise how, after exit, English courts will interpret retained EU law that was implementing legislation before exit day and how they will interpret legislation that otherwise fell within the scope of application of a directive before exit day. How will English courts interpret retained EU law if it is amended after exit day? To answer these questions, it is necessary to analyse the EU(W) Act in detail.

8.1. RETAINED EU LAW

Section 2(1) EU(W) Act stipulates that "EU-derived domestic legislation, as it has effect in domestic law immediately before exit day, continues to have effect in domestic law on and after exit day". EU-derived domestic legislation includes delegated legislation made under s. 2(2) ECA.[573] Section 2(1) of the 2018 Act ensures that such legislation remains in force when the ECA, the current legal basis for such legislation, is repealed. EU-derived domestic legislation also includes any enactment "so far as" (i) made, passed or operating "for a purpose mentioned in" s. 2(2)(a) or (b) ECA, (ii) "relating to anything" which falls within s. 2(2)(a) or (b) ECA and (iii) "relating otherwise to the EU or the EEA".[574]

Section 2(2)(a) ECA clearly mentions the purpose of implementing any EU obligation of the UK. Since s. 2(2)(a) EU(W) Act refers to delegated legislation made under s. 2(2) ECA and since s. 2(2)(b) of the 2018 Act refers to any enactment made for a purpose mentioned in s. 2(2)(a) or (b) ECA, it follows that s. 2(2) EU(W) Act covers primary legislation passed to implement a directive into UK law. Section 2(2)(b) of the 2018 Act also applies to delegated legislation made for the purpose of implementing a directive into UK law that has been created under powers in another (other than the ECA) Act of Parliament. Due to the term "operating", s. 2(2)(b) EU(W) Act further encompasses primary and delegated legislation that was not passed with the intention of implementing a directive into UK law but that nonetheless demonstrates the UK's compliance with the requirements of EU directives.[575] The ambit of s. 2 EU(W) Act is thus very broad.[576] Furthermore, gold-plated provisions are included in the scope of EU-derived domestic legislation under s. 2(2)(c) of the Act.[577] Domestic legislation is only retained under s. 2(2) EU(W) Act

---

[572] Cf. s. 6(7) EU(W) Act.
[573] Section 2(2)(a) EU(W) Act.
[574] Section 2(2)(b)–(d) EU(W) Act.
[575] European Union (Withdrawal) Act 2018, Explanatory notes, para. 77.
[576] Ibid., para. 78. For criticism, see House of Lords Select Committee on the Constitution, European Union (Withdrawal) Bill, HL Paper 69, 29.01.2018, para. 21.
[577] European Union (Withdrawal) Act 2018, Explanatory notes, para. 77.

"so far as" the legislation fulfils the conditions stipulated in s. 2(2)(a)–(d). For example, if an implementing Act of Parliament also includes provisions with a purely domestic background, those provision will not fall within the ambit of s. 2(2).[578] Hence, some parts of this statute will constitute EU-derived domestic legislation, while other parts of the same statute will not. The importance of s. 2(2) of the Act in relation to primary legislation is not to keep it on the statute book.[579] For this category of legislation, s. 2 EU(W) Act operates rather so as to enable the powers in the Act to be used to modify it.[580] Furthermore, the EU legal duty of conforming interpretation will continue to apply to the interpretation of EU-derived domestic legislation according to s. 5(2) EU(W) Act. The wide drafting of s. 2 EU(W) Act is designed to achieve the outcome that EU-derived domestic legislation operates and is interpreted in precisely the same way as before Brexit in order to prevent legal uncertainty.[581] What is not clear on the face of the statute is whether a provision that falls within the scope of application of an EU directive, but does not and is not intended to demonstrate compliance with the requirements of the directive, will also become EU-derived domestic legislation under s. 2(2)(d) of the Act.[582] The wide wording of the section, "relating otherwise to the EU", is capable of covering such a provision. The explanatory notes remark that domestic legislation is only preserved under s. 2 EU(W) Act "so far as it is operating for any of the purposes set out at subsections 2(a) to (d). If it is not operating for those purposes, it will not fall within the ambit of this clause".[583] A provision that falls within the scope of application of an EU directive, but does not and is not intended to comply with the directive, cannot be said to be operating for the purpose of "relating otherwise to the EU". Furthermore, such a provision often conflicts with or is at least difficult to reconcile with implementing legislation, which is why it should not become EU-derived domestic legislation after exit. Preserving legal continuity after exit day only requires that the EU legal duty of conforming interpretation continues to apply to such a provision, and this is the case as I shall show later in this section.

Section 3(1) EU(W) Act converts "direct EU legislation",[584] so far as operative immediately before exit day, into domestic law. The category of

---

[578] Ibid., para. 78.
[579] The same applies to delegated legislation enacted under primary legislation other than the ECA.
[580] European Union (Withdrawal) Act 2018, Explanatory notes, para. 23, note 6.
[581] *Hansard*, HC Deb 15 November 2017, vol 631, col 412, European Union (Withdrawal) Bill (Solicitor General).
[582] Such a provision does not fall under s. 2(2)(c) EU(W) Act as it is not, to use the words of the explanatory notes, "tied in some way to EU law, or to domestic law which implements EU law"; cf. European Union (Withdrawal) Act 2013, Explanatory notes, para. 77.
[583] Ibid., para. 78.
[584] As defined in s. 3(2) EU(W) Act.

retained "direct EU legislation" includes EU regulations. Section 4(1) of the Act retains "any rights, power, liabilities, obligations, restrictions, remedies and procedures which, immediately before exit day (a) are recognised and available in domestic law by virtue of section 2(1) of the European Communities Act 1972". The purpose of s. 4 is to recognise and make available in domestic law after exit day any remaining EU rights and obligations which do not fall within ss. 2 and 3 of the Act.[585] Section 4(1) EU(W) Act appears to domesticate the EU legal duty of conforming interpretation because this obligation arises under the EU Treaties and is thus recognised and available in domestic law by virtue of s. 2(1) ECA. This is, however, not the case due to s. 5(2) of the 2018 Act, which directly domesticates the EU legal duty of conforming interpretation. Section 5(2) is *lex specialis* to s. 4(1) with regard to this interpretative duty.[586] The heading of s. 5 reads "Exceptions to savings and incorporation". Section 5 sets out two exceptions to the saving and incorporation of EU law provided for under ss. 2, 3 and 4 EU(W) Act.[587] One of these exceptions is the principle of supremacy of EU law, which also includes the EU legal duty of conforming interpretation according to the drafters of the Act.[588]

Section 4(1) EU(W) Act also domesticates directly effective rights arising under an EU directive, but only insofar as such rights have been recognised by an EU or UK court[589] in a case decided before exit day (cf. s. 4(2)(b)).[590] Rights in directives are capable of having vertical direct effect, but it is settled CJEU case law that directives are not capable of having horizontal direct effect. The wording of s. 4(1) does not clarify whether an individual can only directly rely on domesticated rights arising under an EU directive in vertical scenarios. This is indeed the case, and the section is not ambiguous in this respect.[591] Section 4(1) EU(W) Act reads that the relevant rights which "are recognised and available in domestic law by virtue of section 2(1) of the European Communities Act 1972" "continue on and after exit day to be recognised and available in domestic law". This aim of s. 4(1) of the Act is in harmony with the general purpose of the Act to provide legal continuity after Brexit. Before exit day, an individual could only directly rely on an EU right arising from a directive in domestic courts in a vertical scenario. This situation will "continue" after exit day according to s. 4 of the Act. Furthermore, it is not clear on the face of the

---

[585] European Union (Withdrawal) Act 2018, Explanatory notes, para. 92.
[586] For the maxim *generalibus specialia derogant*, see JONES and BENNION, above n. 220, p. 1038.
[587] European Union (Withdrawal) Act 2018, Explanatory notes, para. 100.
[588] This will be discussed in Section 8.3 below.
[589] Section 4(2)(b) EU(W) Act refers to "any court or tribunal in the United Kingdom". The term UK courts refers to the courts of the UK's distinct legal orders: England and Wales, Scotland and Northern Ireland.
[590] European Union (Withdrawal) Act 2018, Explanatory notes, para. 97.
[591] For other ambiguities in the drafting of this provision, see House of Lords Select Committee on the Constitution, above n. 576, paras. 33–35.

Act how ss. 2 and 4 will work together. The wording of s. 4 does not make an exception with regard to provisions of directives that have been implemented in domestic law by means of EU-derived legislation, which will (where necessary) be saved by s. 2 of the Act. Does that mean that the working of ss. 2 and 4 of the Act together can result in two versions of an EU-derived norm within the domestic legal system, i.e. the version contained in EU-derived domestic legislation and the version domesticated by s. 4? If the purpose of s. 4 is taken into account, it becomes clear that s. 4 does not operate when a directly effective right in a directive has already been domesticated through the medium of EU-derived domestic legislation. Section 4 is, however, significant if a right enshrined in a directive has not been or has only been incorrectly implemented in the UK, and if a conforming interpretation of EU-derived domestic legislation is not possible.

8.2. THE PRINCIPLE OF THE SUPREMACY OF EU LAW

Section 5(1) EU(W) Act provides that the principle of the supremacy of EU law does not apply to legislation passed or made on or after exit day. The drafting of s. 5(1) is misleading because the provision does not actually envisage a conflict between UK law and EU law and does not directly refer to the principle of the supremacy of EU law as established and applied by the CJEU. Neither EU law nor the *EU* principle of the supremacy of EU law will apply in the UK post exit. The explanatory notes of the EU(W) Act clarify that s. 5(1) and (2) apply when a conflict between retained EU law and other domestic legislation arises,[592] i.e. a conflict between two or more national enactments. It follows that in the event of conflict between an Act of Parliament passed on or after exit day and retained EU law, the Act of Parliament passed on or after exit day prevails.[593] That is the meaning of s. 5(1) of the Act. In compliance with constitutional orthodoxy, a later Act of Parliament will take precedence

---

[592] European Union (Withdrawal) Act 2018, Explanatory notes, para. 103. For this understanding of s. 5(1) and (2) EU(W) Act, see also House of Lords Select Committee on the Constitution, above n. 576, para. 78; Bingham Centre for the Rule of Law, The EU (Withdrawal) Bill: A rule of law analysis of clauses 1–6, 21.02.2018, paras. 87–88, available online at https://binghamcentre.biicl.org/publications/reports; T. HORLEY, In (domestic) courts we trust: the European Union (Withdrawal) Bill and the interpretation of retained EU law, *UK Constitutional Law Blog*, 27.11.2017, available online at https://ukconstitutionallaw.org/2017/11/27/thomas-horsley-in-domestic-courts-we-trust-the-european-union-withdrawal-bill-and-the-interpretation-of-retained-eu-law/; A. YOUNG, Benkharbouche and the future of disapplication, *UK Constitutional Law Blog*, 24.10.2017, available online at https://ukconstitutionallaw.org/2017/10/24/alison-young-benkharbouche-and-the-future-of-disapplication/.

[593] European Union (Withdrawal) Act 2018, Explanatory notes, para. 102; White Paper, above n. 571, para. 2.19.

over an earlier Act of Parliament based on the doctrine of implied repeal.[594] Section 5(1) does not specify whether delegated legislation passed on or after exit day will also prevail over retained EU law that is primary legislation in the event of an inconsistency. EU-derived domestic legislation, for example, continues to have the same status as either delegated or primary legislation before and after exit day.[595] The explanatory notes only give an example relating to later primary legislation made after exit day,[596] but the wording of s. 5(1) speaks of "any enactment". This also includes delegated legislation according to s. 20(1) EU(W) Act. However, s. 5(1) only answers the question of whether or not the principle of the supremacy of EU law applies. The provision does not govern the question which constitutional principle solves an inconsistency between different legal provisions if the principle of the supremacy of EU law does not apply. The purpose of s. 5(1) is to take "the principle of the supremacy of EU law" out of the equation, but not otherwise to break with recognised constitutional principles. It follows that a conflict between post-exit delegated legislation and retained EU law that is primary legislation is solved in the same way as such a conflict would be solved outside the scope of EU law or retained EU law. Since primary legislation is higher in the legal hierarchy than delegated legislation, the retained primary law prevails in this scenario. In legal practice, such inconsistencies should mostly be ruled out by amendment according to s. 8(1) EU(W) Act. Section 8 is a Henry VIII clause (cf. s. 8(5)). It empowers the government to modify retained EU law with delegated legislation under certain circumstances. This allows the government to remove an incompatibility between retained EU law and delegated legislation made on or after exit day by modifying the retained EU law.

The "principle of the supremacy of EU law" will continue to apply on or after exit day so far as relevant to the interpretation, disapplication or quashing of legislation made before exit day according to s. 5(2) EU(W) Act. This seems perplexing at first sight because once the UK leaves the EU, EU law will not apply in the UK and there will simply be no EU law to which the supremacy principle can attach. The explanatory notes of the EU(W) Act help to clarify the ambiguity in s. 5(2) and help to overcome the conceptual difficulty. Section 5(2) envisages a conflict between pre-exit[597] domestic legislation and

---

[594] A further issue arises, however, if retained EU legislation is regarded as a constitutional statute, which is not subject to the doctrine of implied repeal; see A. YOUNG, Status of EU law post Brexit: part one, *UK Constitutional Law Blog*, 02.05.2018, available online at https://ukconstitutionallaw.org/2018/05/02/alison-young-status-of-eu-law-post-brexit-part-one/.
[595] Section 7(1) EU(W) Act.
[596] European Union (Withdrawal) Act 2018, Explanatory notes, para. 102.
[597] In the following, I will use the shorter form "pre-exit" legislation as meaning "pre-exit day" legislation. Likewise, I will use the shorter form "post-exit" legislation to refer to "post-exit day" legislation.

retained EU law.⁵⁹⁸ The "supremacy of EU law" thus applies to retained EU law after exit day, but only in relation to legislation enacted before exit day. It is clear from the words of s. 5(2), "disapplication", that Parliament intended to empower courts to disapply pre-exit primary or delegated domestic legislation if that legislation is in conflict with retained EU law.⁵⁹⁹ The doctrine of implied repeal does not apply. Retained EU law in whatever form⁶⁰⁰ will take precedence over inconsistent pre-exit primary or delegated domestic legislation. One of the effects of s. 5(2) is that it creates a hierarchy of domestic laws. Retained EU law that is delegated legislation is higher in the hierarchy of norms than a pre-exit Act of Parliament. That is the consequence of domesticating "the supremacy of EU law" since EU law, in whatever form, would have taken precedence over an earlier or a later Act of Parliament before exit. Another intended effect of s. 5(2) is that the inroads into the orthodox doctrine of parliamentary sovereignty that the supremacy of EU law entails continue to exist after exit. These inroads relate to a modification of the doctrine of implied repeal and to a modification of the second limb of the orthodox doctrine of parliamentary sovereignty according to which no body or person can set aside the legislation of Parliament. Both elements of the doctrine of parliamentary sovereignty are qualified in relation to retained EU law according to s. 5(2) EU(W) Act. Parliament could have decided to terminate (a) giving supremacy to a specific body of law and (b) the power of courts to disapply legislation after Brexit. Parliament could have decided to eliminate an existing and controversial fragmentation of the doctrine of parliamentary sovereignty, but it chose not to. P. Craig has further shown that the intended outcome of s. 5(2) could have been achieved without reference to

---

⁵⁹⁸ European Union (Withdrawal) Act 2018, Explanatory notes, para. 103 ("Where, however, a conflict arises between pre-exit domestic legislation and retained EU law, …").

⁵⁹⁹ What remains unclear is whether a court has the power to disapply pre-exit primary legislation in the event of conflict with retained EU law if the pre-exit primary legislation is a constitutional statute. This issue relates to the controversy about the proper scope of the supremacy of EU law, which is not interpreted in the same way by the CJEU and the UK Supreme Court. In other words, the term "the supremacy of EU law" in s. 5(2) EU(W) Act is ambiguous as it is not clear whether it refers to the conception of EU supremacy by the CJEU or by the UK Supreme Court; see A. YOUNG, Status of EU law post Brexit: Part Two, *UK Constitutional Law Blog*, 04.05.2018, available online at https://ukconstitutionallaw.org/2018/05/04/alison-young-status-of-eu-law-post-brexit-part-two/.

⁶⁰⁰ Section 7 EU(W) Act specifies the legal status of retained EU law. The provision does not classify retained EU law under s. 3 or s. 4 of the Act as either primary or delegated legislation. Instead, it introduces the categories of "retained direct principal EU legislation" and "retained direct minor EU legislation" for retained EU law under s. 3. With regard to retained EU law under s. 3 and s. 4, s. 7 only governs how this law can be modified. The provision therefore fails to provide clarity about the legal status of retained EU law under s. 3 and s. 4; for discussion, see YOUNG, above n. 594. Section 23ZA(1)(b) of the Interpretation Act 1978 (see para. 20 of Schedule 8 to the 2018 Act) presupposes that retained direct EU law under s. 3 EU(W) Act can have the status of either primary or delegated legislation.

the principle of the supremacy of EU law.[601] The purpose of the Act, to achieve legal continuity after exit day, would not have necessitated that the principle of the supremacy of EU law continues to apply after exit day.

The explanatory notes of the EU(W) Act further clarify that the principle of the supremacy of EU law is not "relevant to provisions made by or under this Act or to other legislation which is made in preparation for the UK's exit from the EU".[602] This restriction of s. 5(2) is not expressly spelled out in the statutory text. It does not require a reading down of s. 5(2), however, because the supremacy of EU law only continues to apply "so far as relevant". That means, for example, that the principle of the supremacy of EU law will not be "relevant" for and will thus not apply to a conflict between retained EU law and the pre-exit EU(W) Act itself or a provision in other pre-exit legislation made in preparation for the UK's exit from the EU. Section 5(2) also implies that retained EU law will prevail over conflicting pre-exit legislation if the pre-exit legislation is enacted between the EU(W) Act and exit day, unless this legislation is made in order to prepare for Brexit. The phrase "so far as relevant" in s. 5(2) is not further specified in the Act. This adds unnecessary legal uncertainty. What is worse, the explanatory notes show that the phrase "so far as relevant" is not only determined by the scope of the principle of the supremacy of EU law before exit day. Instead, the phrase is also used to exclude certain legislation from the ambit of s. 5(2). Time will tell whether this vague phrase will incentivise courts to exclude other legislation (constitutional statutes?) from the ambit of the supremacy principle. Moreover, s. 5(3) of the 2018 Act clarifies that the supremacy of EU law continues to apply to pre-exit legislation that is modified on or after exit day if the application of the supremacy principle "is consistent with the intention of the modification". Section 5(3) clarifies that pre-exit legislation does not lose its "pre-exit" status merely because it has been modified post-exit. What the Act and the explanatory notes leave open is how courts have to determine whether applying the supremacy principle is consistent with what the law-maker intended when it enacted the amendment. That intention has to be discerned based on conventional canons of statutory interpretation. Section 5(3) does not answer the question whether retained EU law that is modified on or after exit day continues to benefit from the supremacy of EU law.[603] The wording of the provision and its relationship with s. 5(1) show that s. 5(3) only governs the application of the supremacy principle to pre-exit domestic legislation that is modified on or after exit day. The definition of retained EU law in s. 6(7) EU(W) Act suggests, however, that

---

[601] P. CRAIG, The Withdrawal Bill, status and supremacy, *UK Constitutional Law Blog*, 19.02.2018, available online at https://ukconstitutionallaw.org/2018/02/19/paul-craig-the-withdrawal-bill-status-and-supremacy/.

[602] European Union (Withdrawal) Act 2018, Explanatory notes, para. 103.

[603] Incorrect: Bingham Centre for the Rule of Law, above n. 592, paras. 110–111.

"the supremacy of EU law" continues to attach to retained EU law even if it is modified post-exit.[604]

An important limitation of the supremacy principle in s. 5(2) EU(W) Act relates to EU-derived domestic legislation under s. 2 EU(W) Act. In the pre-Brexit world, this legislation is not EU law but domestic legislation, and it does not enjoy supremacy over other national legislation. The underlying EU directive is supreme, but not the domestic (implementing) legislation. Therefore, EU-derived domestic legislation should not prevail over all other pre-exit legislation in the event of conflict based on the supremacy principle.[605] If all EU-derived domestic legislation were to benefit from the supremacy of EU law, this could have unintended consequences when EU-derived domestic legislation incorrectly implements a directive and cannot be interpreted in conformity with this directive. Granting supremacy to such non-conforming legislation over all other pre-exit legislation has no equivalent in EU or UK law in the pre-Brexit sphere and cannot be presumed to be intended by the Parliament of 2018. What is more, retained EU law should only benefit from the supremacy of EU law so far as it corresponds to EU law that itself benefited from the supremacy of EU law before exit. The purpose of the Act, to ensure legal continuity after exit day, does not justify the granting of supremacy to EU-derived domestic legislation. This interpretation of s. 5(2) EU(W) Act does not require a reading down of the term "the supremacy of EU law" for EU-derived domestic legislation due to the words "as far as relevant" in s. 5(2). There is also no need for granting supremacy to EU-derived domestic legislation in order to maintain the status quo in a post-Brexit world. The EU legal duty of conforming interpretation applies to EU-derived domestic legislation and other pre-exit domestic legislation, as I will show in the next section. If domestic legislation cannot be interpreted in conformity with a directive as construed by the CJEU prior to exit day, a directly effective right arising from a directive is domesticated by s. 4 EU(W) Act. It then follows from s. 5(2) that this s. 4-retained EU law prevails over inconsistent pre-exit primary or delegated domestic legislation.

It is the intention of Parliament that "retained EU law" inherits the supremacy of EU law. It is controversial in scholarship whether this is constitutionally possible. The doctrine of parliamentary sovereignty is not a uniform doctrine. It is fragmented as a national court's power to disapply an Act of Parliament only exists if EU law applies. This modification of the doctrine

---

[604] See s. 6(7) EU(W) Act, "as that body of law is added to or otherwise modified by or under this Act or by other domestic law from time to time".
[605] For this understanding of s. 5(2) EU(W) Act, see also House of Lords Select Committee on the Constitution, above n. 576, para. 82; Bingham Centre for the Rule of Law, above n. 592, paras. 106–107.

in the sphere of EU law goes back to an evolution of the doctrine based on a change in official consensus, which included Parliament (ECA) and the courts (*Factortame (No. 2)*). We will recall that according to the majority in *Miller*,[606] the qualifications of the orthodox doctrine of parliamentary sovereignty, which the supremacy of EU law entails, came about by Parliament intending it and by the common law accepting it. Since EU law does not apply in the UK post exit, the underlying reason for the modifications of the doctrine of parliamentary sovereignty disappears. Although the EU(W) Act intends to transfer the principle of the supremacy of EU law to a body of domestic law (retained EU law) in s. 5 EU(W) Act, this is not the same as the situation in relation to EU law before exit. Even if one agrees with the majority in *Miller* that the ECA constitutes EU law as an "independent and overriding source of domestic law",[607] the EU(W) Act intends a transfer of the qualifications of the doctrine of parliamentary sovereignty to a different body of domestic law. The supremacy of directly effective provisions of EU law is unique in the UK constitution and creates an inroad into the second limb of the doctrine. Unlike the phenomenon of constitutional statutes, which is not limited to the ECA but recognised for other statutes as well,[608] the power of UK courts to disapply an Act of Parliament is limited to the sphere of EU law prior to exit day. What is intended with s. 5(2) EU(W) Act is therefore a further development of this existing modification of the doctrine.[609] For the first time, Parliament intends to grant domestic courts the power to disapply an Act of Parliament outside the sphere of EU law. Parliament alone can only initiate such an evolution of the doctrine with the passing of the European Union (Withdrawal) Act 2018. Parliament alone cannot unilaterally change the official consensus. This also depends on the actions of the courts and other officials in the legal system. Time will tell whether the official consensus will change.

8.3. THE NEW LEGAL DUTY OF CONFORMING INTERPRETATION

The EU(W) Act contains two types of "conforming" interpretation. The first type is the interpretation of pre-exit domestic law in conformity with retained

---

[606] See Section 7.2.1 above.
[607] *R. (Miller) v. Secretary of State for Exiting the European Union* [2017] UKSC 51, para. 65 (Lord Neuberger, Lady Hale, Lord Mance, Lord Kerr, Lord Clarke, Lord Wilson, Lord Sumption, Lord Hodge).
[608] For the argument that it is unlikely that Brexit will cause a reversal in the UK case law on "constitutional statutes", see P. ELEFTHERIADIS, The coming constitutional instability, [2017] *PL* 347, 348; A. YOUNG, The constitutional implications of Brexit, (2017) 23 *European Public Law* 757, 776.
[609] For an apparently different view, see YOUNG, above n. 592.

EU law. This interpretative obligation is enshrined in s. 5(2). The second type is the interpretation of retained EU law in accordance with relevant pre-exit CJEU case law construing the "underlying" EU law. This interpretative obligation is governed by s. 6(3) EU(W) Act. This dual system of interpretation intends to mirror the pre-exit situation. It applies to EU regulations retained under s. 3, to Treaty rights retained under s. 4 and to s. 4-retained directly effective rights arising under an EU directive. In the case of a domesticated Treaty right, for example, s. 6(3) governs the interpretation of the domesticated Treaty right according to EU legal methods, and s. 5(2) applies to the interpretation of pre-exit domestic law in conformity with the domesticated Treaty right.[610] The problem is that this system does not work for EU directives and EU-derived domestic legislation, as I will show in this and the next section. The main reason for this finding is that the EU(W) Act does not domesticate EU directives themselves as they have already been implemented in domestic law.

According to the explanatory notes of the EU(W) Act,

> [t]he principle of supremacy also means that domestic law must be interpreted, as far as possible, in accordance with EU law. So, for example, domestic law must be interpreted, as far as possible, in light of the wording and purpose of relevant directives. Whilst this duty will not apply to domestic legislation passed or made on or after exit day, subsection (2) [of s. 5] preserves this duty in relation to domestic legislation passed or made before exit.[611]

This part of the explanatory notes refers to the EU legal duty of conforming interpretation. What the explanatory notes are saying is that the EU legal duty of conforming interpretation will not apply to domestic legislation enacted on or after exit day. That is the effect of s. 5(1) EU(W) Act. The interpretation of domestic legislation enacted on or after exit day ought to be governed in English courts according to English conventional canons of construction. The EU legal duty of conforming interpretation will, however, continue to apply after exit day to domestic legislation enacted prior to exit day at least for as long as that law remains unmodified after exit day. This meaning of s. 5(2) of the Act is not obvious on the face of the provision, but it becomes clear if the explanatory notes are taken into account as an aid to construction. Section 5(2) says that "the supremacy of EU law" continues to apply to the interpretation of legislation passed before exit day. The trouble is that the EU legal duty of conforming interpretation does not derive from the principle of the supremacy of EU law.

---

[610] This interpretative obligation mirrors the pre-exit interpretative duty of domestic courts to construe national law in conformity with EU Treaty provisions.

[611] European Union (Withdrawal) Act 2018, Explanatory notes, para. 104.

There are different possible readings of the term "interpretation" in s. 5(2) due to the ambiguous notion of "the supremacy of EU law". The term "supremacy of EU law" in s. 5(2) envisages a conflict between pre-exit domestic legislation and retained EU law. If "the supremacy of EU law" is understood as also referring to the EU legal duty of conforming interpretation, the supremacy of EU law generally governs the relationship between pre-exit domestic legislation and retained EU law. Does that mean that pre-exit domestic legislation has to be interpreted, as far as possible, in the light of the wording and the purpose of EU-derived domestic legislation? A first reading of s. 5(2) answers this question in the affirmative,[612] but this reading of the provision must be rejected for the following three reasons. The first reason is a textual argument. Section 5(2) says that the principle of the supremacy of EU law, in its shape of the EU legal duty of conforming interpretation, continues to apply so far as relevant to the interpretation of "any" enactment passed or made before exit day. Any enactment also includes EU-derived domestic legislation, which is passed or made before exit day. Taking the explanatory notes into account, that would mean that the EU legal duty of conforming interpretation also applies to EU-derived domestic legislation.

The second reason is a purposive argument. The first reading of s. 5(2) does not convince because such an interpretative obligation does not mirror a pre-exit interpretative obligation and thus does not achieve legal continuity. EU-derived domestic legislation will have been domestic legislation before exit day. The equivalent interpretative obligation to the first reading of s. 5(2) in a pre-Brexit world would include an obligation to interpret all other domestic legislation falling within the scope of application of a directive in the light of the purpose and the wording of domestic implementing legislation. Such an interpretative obligation, which relates to implementing legislation rather than its underlying EU directive, does not exist. It is not required by EU law, and English law does not know it. The CJEU held in *Pfeiffer* that a national court must choose a possible conforming meaning in case two provisions of domestic law appear to clash with each other but can be construed in such a way as to avoid conflict if the conforming reading can be reached by applying interpretative methods recognised by national law. There is also a general duty in English law to interpret different provisions in a statute in harmony with each other so as to avoid conflict.[613] There is, however, no duty recognised under English legal methods to always prioritise the implementing provision over all other provisions that fall within the scope of a directive by interpreting the latter

---

[612] In favour of this reading of s. 5(2) EU(W) Act: Bingham Centre for the Rule of Law, above n. 592, para. 89.

[613] JONES and BENNION, above n. 220, pp. 1037, 1053. Cf. *Marr (a bankrupt)* [1990] Ch. 773, 784 (Lloyd LJ).

provisions in the light of the implementing provision. The other provisions that fall within the scope of application of a directive also have to be interpreted in the light of the directive, but not in the light of domestic implementing legislation, which could itself suffer from an incorrect implementation of the directive's requirements. If implementing legislation contained inaccuracies in transposition and if this legislation could not be construed in conformity with the underlying directive, the effect of the first reading of s. 5(2) would be to perpetuate this incorrect transposition in domestic law. Such an outcome is not intended by the EU(W) Act.

The third reason against the first reading of s. 5(2) is also a purposive argument. Arguably, the construction of EU-derived domestic legislation in the light of an EU directive is a key case of application of the interpretative obligation enshrined in s. 5(2) that Parliament had in mind. Taking the explanatory notes into account, the purpose of s. 5(2) is clear: the subsection aims to incorporate the EU legal duty of conforming interpretation. As long as the UK is a Member State of the EU, the duty refers, for example, to the interpretation of implementing legislation in conformity with an applicable directive. After exit day, the meaning of the provision must mirror this original situation as the EU(W) Act does not domesticate directives themselves. That means that the interpretative duty in s. 5(2) also refers to the interpretation of EU-derived domestic implementing legislation in conformity with a directive.[614] The proper reading of s. 5(2) of the Act is therefore that (unmodified) pre-exit domestic legislation, including EU-derived domestic legislation, has to be interpreted, as far as possible, in the light of the wording and the purpose of an EU directive that was applicable prior to exit day. An exception applies to the EU(W) Act itself and to other pre-exit legislation that is made in preparation for the UK's exit from the EU. The new legal duty of conforming interpretation in s. 5(2) does not apply to this legislation.[615]

The reading of the interpretative obligation enshrined in s. 5(2) adopted in the paragraph above has the added advantage that the situation after exit day mirrors as closely as possible the situation before exit day. It follows that this understanding of s. 5(2) is in harmony with the general purpose of the Act to ensure legal continuity after Brexit. The circumstance that EU-derived domestic legislation does not prevail over all other pre-exit legislation in the event of conflict based on the supremacy principle does not contradict this reading of s. 5(2). That is because the phrase "so far as relevant" allows for a differentiation of the "the supremacy of EU law", which only applies to EU-derived domestic

---

[614] For this view, see also J. SIMSON CAIRD, V. MILLER and A. LANG, House of Commons Library: Briefing Paper No. 8079, European Union (Withdrawal) Bill, 01.09.2017, p. 30, available online at https://researchbriefings.parliament.uk/ResearchBriefing/Summary/CBP-8079.

[615] See the discussion of this exception to "the principle of the supremacy of EU law" in s. 5(2) EU(W) Act in Section 8.2 above.

legislation in its shape of the EU legal duty of conforming interpretation. Section 5(2) EU(W) Act is also a good example illustrating a very concise drafting style that favours general and vague terms over detailed and precise statutory language and that favours a purposive over a literal approach to statutory interpretation. The term "the principle of the supremacy of EU law" in s. 5(2) combines different elements of the supremacy principle. Not all of these elements apply to all categories of retained EU law. The phrase "so far as relevant" in s. 5(2) indicates that such a fragmented reading of the provision is indeed intended by the draftsmen. The Act would have benefited from a more detailed drafting, in particular a separate subsection for the EU legal duty of conforming interpretation and its continued application to EU-derived domestic legislation. That would have increased the level of legal certainty of s. 5 EU(W) Act.

The explanatory notes state that s. 5(2) "preserves this duty" (the EU legal duty of conforming interpretation) in relation to domestic legislation passed or made before exit.[616] These notes use the term "preserved legislation" with regard to EU-derived domestic legislation. The EU(W) Act preserves this legislation "as it exists immediately before exit day".[617] The explanatory notes thus envisage that the EU legal duty of conforming interpretation continues to apply, as it exists immediately before exit day, to the interpretation of pre-exit domestic legislation. In short, s. 5(2) domesticates the EU legal duty of conforming interpretation. It follows from this reading of the provision that European methodological rules will continue to apply to conforming interpretation after exit. It is further clear from this reading that conforming interpretation is modified insofar as it refers to the meaning of this interpretative obligation as specified by CJEU jurisprudence prior to exit day. This is also the effect of s. 6(1) EU(W) Act according to which post-exit CJEU case law does not bind UK courts. Hence, the EU legal duty of conforming interpretation, in its shape prior to exit day as construed by the CJEU in cases like *Marleasing* and *Pfeiffer*, applies in the UK on and after exit day to pre-exit domestic legislation including EU-derived domestic legislation. It also follows from s. 6(1) that post-exit, the domesticated new legal duty of conforming interpretation refers to EU directives in their interpretation by EU courts prior to exit day. A "snapshot" is taken before exit day. There is thus scope for divergence between EU and UK legal principles after exit day.

Even though interpretations of EU directives by the CJEU on or after exit day are not binding on UK courts, a domestic court may take such interpretations into account "so far as it is relevant to any matter before the court" according to s. 6(2) of the 2018 Act.[618] UK courts can but are not obliged to consider

---

[616] European Union (Withdrawal) Act 2018, Explanatory notes, para. 104.
[617] Ibid., para. 23.
[618] It is important to note that the scope of s. 6(2) is not limited to "retained EU law". See *Hansard*, HL Deb 23 April 2018, vol 790 col 1403 (Lord Keen).

post-exit CJEU case law as a persuasive authority. Section 6(2) was changed during the parliamentary process. Its first version read that a domestic court can take post-exit CJEU case law into account if the court "considers it appropriate to do so". This version of s. 6(2) was rightly criticised as giving courts "a wholly open-ended discretion as to whether to have regard to future CJEU case-law".[619] The provision's changed wording is intended to give greater guidance to UK courts as to when they can refer to CJEU judgments made after exit day. Whether the change from "appropriate" to "relevant" has achieved this aim must be doubted. The Oxford Online Dictionary, for example, defines "relevant" as "closely connected or appropriate to what is being done or considered".[620] Even though "relevant" is a standard that appears more objective or more difficult to satisfy than appropriate, it does not eliminate policy choices. Section 6(2) does not specify what factors a court must take into account when determining whether post-exit CJEU case law is relevant. The Act fails to give guidance about what might be considered "relevant".

Section 6(2) EU(W) Act does not apply to the principle of the supremacy of EU law itself, including the new legal duty of conforming interpretation. That means that UK courts cannot consider post-exit interpretations of the principle of the supremacy of EU law and of the EU legal duty of conforming interpretation by the CJEU. The meaning of "the supremacy of EU law"[621] is fixed in time. This exception to the general rule in s. 6(2) follows from para. 5 of Schedule 1 to the 2018 Act. The explanatory notes clarify that the term "the supremacy of EU law" refers to that principle as it stands on exit day, not as it will operate in EU law in the future.[622]

We have already seen that the principle of the supremacy of EU law can continue to apply to "a modification" made on or after exit day of pre-exit legislation if the application of the principle is "consistent with the intention of the modification" (s. 5(3) EU(W) Act). Since the term "the supremacy of EU law" incorporates the EU legal duty of conforming interpretation, this interpretative duty also applies to pre-exit legislation that is modified post-exit if this is consistent with the modification. If post-exit primary or delegated legislation amends one provision in a pre-exit statute, for example, s. 5(3) applies to the interpretation of that amended provision. The construction of all other unmodified provisions of the pre-exit statute continues to be governed

---

[619] Bingham Centre for the Rule of Law, above n. 592, para. 145. For discussion, see House of Lords Select Committee on the Constitution, above n. 576, paras. 132–142; HORLEY, above n. 592.
[620] Oxford Online Dictionary, available online at https://en.oxforddictionaries.com/definition/relevant.
[621] Section 5(2) EU(W) Act.
[622] European Union (Withdrawal) Act 2018, Explanatory notes, para. 216.

by s. 5(2) and the EU legal duty of conforming interpretation. This reading of s. 5(3) is consistent with its wording, which speaks of "a" modification. This also makes sense, for example, if an implementing statute is modified only by changing a reference in the legislation from an EU authority to a UK authority. In that case, the unmodified part of the statute should continue to be interpreted as before exit day. If the application of the EU legal duty of conforming interpretation is not consistent with the intention of the modification, the interpretation of the modified part of the legislation is governed by conventional canons of statutory construction. This creates complexity in statutory interpretation of modified pre-exit legislation. The complex situation can be avoided if pre-exit domestic legislation is not amended but repealed and replaced with a new piece of legislation.

One consequence of the construction of s. 5(2) adopted here is that English courts can apply their "interpretative methods recognised by national law"[623] according to the CJEU in *Pfeiffer* when they interpret national law in conformity with a directive. A key question is thus whether English courts will continue to apply the same outer limits and techniques to the EU legal duty of conforming interpretation before and after exit day. It is submitted that English courts should indeed apply the same limits and techniques of conforming judicial law-making before and after exit day.[624] Conforming interpretation will therefore remain a very powerful tool in the hands of the judges after exit day. First, s. 3(1) HRA still remains the closest comparator to the EU legal duty of conforming interpretation in its shape after exit day. Second, the aim of the EU(W) Act is to ensure legal continuity after Brexit. Legal continuity is preserved because pre-exit day legislation that has been interpreted prior to exit day by means of conforming judicial law-making in domestic courts does not have to be reinterpreted post exit day according to different interpretative maxims. This result also follows from s. 6(3) EU(W) Act, as we will learn in the next section. Third, I have argued in Section 3.2.2 above that modifications of the doctrine of parliamentary sovereignty motivated Lord Oliver in *Pickstone* to depart from a number of well-established conventional canons of construction. These modifications of the doctrine of parliamentary sovereignty will not disappear after Brexit.

Lady Hale has revealed that when the Supreme Court interprets implementing legislation, "our practice has been to go straight to the Directive and ask what it, rather than the Regulations [UK regulations implementing an

---

[623] Case C-397/01, *Pfeiffer v. Deutsches Rotes Kreuz*, ECLI:EU:C:2004:584, para. 116.
[624] A qualification to this finding is that English courts should not depart from what can reasonably be presumed to be the enacting parliament's intent under the new legal duty of conforming interpretation. Such a departure exceeds the judicial function, as I have shown in Section 7.2.1 above.

EU directive], means".⁶²⁵ She has also asked whether this practice can continue to apply after Brexit if existing UK regulations imperfectly implement an EU directive. Based on my previous analysis of s. 5(2), this question can be answered in the affirmative, at least when the relevant EU-derived domestic legislation remains unmodified.

8.4. INTERPRETATION OF RETAINED EU LAW

Section 6 EU(W) Act governs the interpretation of retained EU law on and after exit day and deals with the jurisprudence of the CJEU. Section 6(3) provides that retained EU law should be interpreted and given effect in accordance with any "retained case law" and any "retained general principles of EU law" on or after exit day so far as the retained EU law has not been modified by legislation such as regulations made under s. 8(1) EU(W) Act. The terms "retained case law" and "retained general principles of EU law" are further defined in s. 6(7). Retained case law includes pre-exit CJEU judgments that post-exit relate to retained EU law.⁶²⁶ One effect of s. 6(3) is that unmodified retained EU law should be interpreted in line with pre-exit CJEU jurisprudence. The aim of the provision is to provide continuity in statutory interpretation. The law that becomes retained EU law after exit should be interpreted in the same way before and after exit day.⁶²⁷ A typical case of application of s. 6(3) is the interpretation of a domesticated EU regulation under s. 3(1) EU(W) Act. The explanatory notes of the Act explain that the interpretative obligation enshrined in s. 6(3) means that a UK court should take a purposive approach to interpretation where the meaning of a retained measure is unclear.⁶²⁸ This is not the purposive approach according to conventional English canons of construction, but rather the approach to judicial reasoning employed by the CJEU, as the explanatory notes clarify: "the meaning of unmodified retained EU law will be determined in UK courts in accordance with pre-exit CJEU case law and general principles".⁶²⁹ Pre-exit CJEU judgments laying down interpretative maxims for EU primary and secondary law are capable of falling under the category of "retained EU case law" in s. 6(7) EU(W) Act. If they relate to retained EU law under ss. 3 or 4 of the Act, this retained EU law has to be interpreted in accordance with this CJEU case law owing to s. 6(3).

---

625   LADY HALE, The United Kingdom Constitution on the move, The Canadian Institute for Advanced Legal Studies' Cambridge Lectures, July 2017, p. 12, available online at https://www.supremecourt.uk/news/speeches.html.
626   Section 6(7) EU(W) Act.
627   Cf. White paper, above n. 571, para. 2.14.
628   European Union (Withdrawal) Act 2018, Explanatory notes, para. 111.
629   Ibid.

This reading of s. 6(3) provides continuity after exit day but it also leads to the incorporation of EU maxims of statutory construction into UK law. One of the effects of s. 6(3) is that retained EU law cannot simply be interpreted in English courts according to English conventional canons of statutory interpretation. This increases the complexity of statutory interpretation in the UK as, for example, English conventional methods of statutory interpretation and CJEU methods of statutory interpretation are not the same.[630] Section 6(3) therefore adds another fragmentation of statutory interpretation into English legal methods. This fragmentation of statutory interpretation does, of course, exist in similar form before exit day whenever an English court interprets EU legislation based on EU methods of interpretation. Where the meaning of EU legislation is unclear, the domestic court can refer a question about the correct interpretation of this legislation to the CJEU. Where the meaning of retained EU law is unclear after exit day, however, an English court cannot refer a question about the correct interpretation of the underlying EU law to the CJEU.[631] This will increase the interpretative workload of English courts. It follows that English courts are likely to use CJEU methods of statutory interpretation more often after Brexit than before Brexit.

In the light of how s. 6(3) EU(W) Act works for retained direct EU legislation and for s. 4-retained EU law, it seems plausible to assume that s. 6(3) also governs the interpretation of EU-derived domestic legislation in accordance with CJEU case law interpreting directives. Section 6(3) has the effect that retained direct EU legislation and s. 4-retained EU law have to be interpreted according to EU maxims of statutory construction after exit day. The parallel scenario in relation to EU-derived domestic legislation would mean that this legislation would have to be interpreted in the same way as an underlying EU directive based on methods of interpretation employed by the CJEU. This requirement would be inconsistent with the pre-exit EU legal duty of conforming interpretation, which allows national courts to apply their own domestic canons of construction. One aim of s. 6(3) EU(W) Act is to provide continuity in how retained EU law is interpreted before and after exit day. That means, for example, that a UK court can continue to apply domestic canons of construction when construing implementing legislation. This argument itself does not, however, take the EU legal duty of conforming interpretation outside the ambit of s. 6(3). That is due to the phrase "so far as they are relevant to it" in this provision. CJEU case law laying down interpretative maxims for EU directives

---

[630] F.A.R. BENNION, *Understanding common law legislation*, OUP, Oxford 2001, pp. 144–149. This issue falls outside the scope of this book and cannot be explored further due to space constraints. In contrast to English conventional canons of construction, for example, the default position for judicial law-making in EU courts interpreting EU legislation is that it is generally a permissible function of the judge.

[631] Section 6(1)(b) EU(W) Act.

could be said to be irrelevant for the way EU-derived domestic legislation has to be interpreted. Nonetheless, s. 6(3) does not govern the application of the EU legal duty of conforming interpretation to domestic law on and after exit day.[632] The provision does not govern the interpretation of EU-derived domestic legislation in accordance with the requirements of a directive for the following reasons.

First, it is the intention of Parliament that s. 5(2) EU(W) Act covers the conforming interpretation of EU-derived domestic legislation. Section 5(2) requires that (unmodified) pre-exit domestic legislation, including EU-derived domestic legislation, has to be interpreted, as far as possible, in the light of the wording and the purpose of an EU directive that was applicable prior to exit day. Second, the meaning of (unmodified) retained EU law has to be decided "in accordance with any retained case law" according to s. 6(3)(a) EU(W) Act. A pre-exit decision by the CJEU interpreting a directive would only qualify as "retained EU case law" under s. 6(7) if this decision "relate[d] to anything to which section 2, 3 or 4 applies". Section 2 of the 2018 Act applies to legislation that was domestic legislation before exit day, like national legislation implementing a directive into UK law. Section 2 does not domesticate EU directives themselves and does not apply to EU directives themselves. CJEU case law interpreting a directive does not therefore relate to anything to which s. 2 applies because the CJEU has no competence to interpret national legislation. In other words, the term "retained case law" in s. 6(3) does not incorporate CJEU case law construing directives if the interpretation of EU-derived domestic legislation is at issue.

This interpretation of s. 6(3) EU(W) Act does not imply that the provision has no meaning for the construction of EU-derived domestic legislation. What s. 6(3) does stipulate is that unmodified EU-derived domestic legislation that was interpreted by a domestic court before exit day in conformity with a directive has to be interpreted in the same way after exit.[633] The meaning of this EU-derived domestic legislation has to be decided "in accordance with any retained case law", and "retained case law" also refers to retained domestic case law according to s. 6(7). A decision by an English court construing implementing legislation before exit day is a decision that relates to this EU-derived domestic legislation after exit day, which is why it is "retained domestic case law". This reading of s. 6(3) achieves the provision's aim to provide continuity in how

---

[632] For a different view, see M. FORD and P. SYRPIS, Retained EU law in the EU (Withdrawal) Bill: a reaction to the House of Lords Constitution Committee Report, *UK Constitutional Law Blog*, 14.02.2018, available online at https://ukconstitutionallaw.org/2018/02/14/michael-ford-and-phil-syrpis-retained-eu-law-in-the-eu-withdrawal-bill-a-reaction-to-the-house-of-lords-constitution-committee-report/.

[633] This is subject to s. 6(4)(c) EU(W) Act, which clarifies that a court is not bound by "any retained domestic case law that it would not otherwise be bound by". For example, the Supreme Court would not be bound by a pre-exit decision of the Court of Appeal interpreting implementing legislation.

retained EU law is interpreted before and after exit day. Section 6(3) clarifies that the EU(W) Act does not tamper with the precedential value of pre-exit domestic case law relating to the interpretation of EU-derived domestic legislation. Distinguishing between the relevance of retained domestic case law and retained EU case law for construing EU-derived domestic legislation does not require a reading down of s. 6(3) of the Act due to the statutory words "so far as they are relevant to it". Pre-exit English case law interpreting domestic legislation by means of conforming judicial law-making thus continues to be relevant after exit day, and this provides a strong argument in favour of maintaining the same outer limits and techniques of conforming interpretation before and after exit day.

There is one scenario in which s. 6(3) does govern the interpretation of retained EU law in accordance with an EU directive. That is the case where a directly effective right arising under an EU directive is domesticated by s. 4(1), (2)(b) EU(W) Act. That occurs if a right enshrined in a directive has not been or has only been incorrectly implemented in the UK, and if a conforming interpretation of EU-derived domestic legislation fails. In this scenario, it is possible to distinguish between the interpretation of (a) the retained EU law that is domesticated by s. 4(1), (2)(b) EU(W) Act and (b) pre-exit domestic law. The interpretation of (a) follows EU methods of interpretation and is governed by s. 6(3), whereas the interpretation of (b) in conformity with (a) is governed by s. 5(2). Since a conforming interpretation of EU-derived domestic legislation and other pre-exit domestic law fails in this scenario, an interpretation of pre-exit domestic law in conformity with s. 4-retained EU law will also fail. It then follows from the principle of the supremacy of EU law that the s. 4-retained EU law, formerly a directly effective provision in a directive, takes precedence over all other inconsistent pre-exit domestic law.[634] This result is, however, limited to vertical situations where an individual relies on s. 4-retained EU law against the state. That is because s. 4-retained directly effective rights arising under an EU directive have effect only vertically, as I have explained in Section 8.1 above. In horizontal scenarios, the inconsistent pre-exit domestic law will continue to apply. The inconsistent pre-exit domestic law also includes EU-derived domestic legislation, which is itself retained EU law. In a vertical scenario, this leads to the peculiarity that s. 4-retained EU law takes precedence over other retained EU law. This mirrors the pre-exit situation and provides legal continuity, which is why this case is covered by a purposive reading of s. 5(2) EU(W) Act.

Section 6(4) EU(W) Act clarifies that the Supreme Court is not bound by any "retained EU case law". The Supreme Court can depart from this case

---

[634] Section 5(2) EU(W) Act.

law, following established domestic rules on judicial precedent (s. 6(5)). Section 6(5) relates to a Practice Statement made by the House of Lords in 1966, which has been adopted by the Supreme Court.[635] Other domestic courts cannot depart from and are bound by retained EU case law even if the CJEU has departed from its own case law after exit day.[636] The practical effect of s. 6(1)–(5) is that they confer the same binding (precedent) status as Supreme Court decisions on retained CJEU case law.[637] However, neither s. 6(4) nor s. 6(5) of the 2018 Act appear to govern the power of the Supreme Court to depart from an interpretation given to a directive by a European court if the retained EU law at issue is EU-derived domestic legislation. The reason for this finding is that a pre-exit decision by the CJEU interpreting a directive is not "retained EU case law" relating to EU-derived domestic legislation, as explained above. This construction of s. 6(4) and (5) means that there currently is no provision in the EU(W) Act governing the power of the Supreme Court to depart from an EU court's interpretation of a directive when construing EU-derived domestic legislation in conformity with an applicable directive. This differential treatment of EU directives compared to EU regulations or Treaty rights is unlikely to be intended by the Act. The solution to this issue is not to claim that since s. 6(3) does not govern the application of the EU legal duty of conforming interpretation, the Supreme Court is not bound by an EU court's interpretation of directives anyway. The new legal duty of conforming interpretation enshrined in s. 5(2) refers to EU directives in their interpretation by EU courts prior to exit day. It thus incorporates pre-exit CJEU case law construing directives. It also follows from s. 6(1) and (2), whose ambit is not limited to retained EU law, that pre-exit CJEU judgments construing directives are binding on UK courts. It also makes sense to recognise a power of the Supreme Court to depart from pre-exit EU court judgments interpreting directives in the same way that the Supreme Court is empowered to depart from pre-exit EU court judgments construing Treaty rights or EU regulations under s. 6(4) and (5) EU(W) Act. Yet, the way to reach this result by means of statutory interpretation is unclear due to a gap in the legislation.

The interpretation of retained EU law which has been modified on or after exit day is governed by s. 6(6) EU(W) Act. Section 6(6) sets out that modified retained EU law can be interpreted and given effect in accordance with any

---

[635] White Paper, above n. 571, paras. 2.16–2.17. See *Austin v. Mayor and Burgesses of the London Borough of Southwark* [2010] UKSC 28, para. 25 (Lord Hope, with whom Lord Brown and Lord Kerr agreed).

[636] That is the effect of s. 6(1)–(5) read together. See also European Union (Withdrawal) Act 2018, Explanatory notes, para. 113 ("unlike other courts"), paras. 110, 114.

[637] European Union (Withdrawal) Act 2018, Explanatory notes, paras. 24, 113; White paper above n. 571, para. 2.16.

retained case law and any retained general principles of EU law on or after exit day "if doing so is consistent with the intention of the modifications". Section 6(6) clarifies, as does the definition of "retained EU law" in s. 6(7) EU(W) Act, that retained EU law does not lose its status merely because it has been modified. It is important to realise that s. 6(6) does not govern the application of the EU legal duty of conforming interpretation to modified EU-derived domestic legislation. Section 5(3) of the Act is applicable in this case. If EU-derived domestic legislation is modified on or after exit day, s. 6(6) governs the question whether a pre-exit interpretation of this legislation by UK courts continues to apply. Section 6(6) only applies to the modified parts, but not to the remaining unmodified parts of the retained EU legislation at issue. The remaining unmodified part continues to fall under s. 6(3). This is the effect of the phrase "so far as that law is unmodified" in s. 6(3) of the 2018 Act. A fragmentation of statutory interpretation of retained EU law can occur if the interpretation of the modification in accordance with retained case law is not consistent with the intention of the modification. In such a case, the interpretation of the modified part of the legislation is governed by domestic conventional canons of statutory construction. Neither the Act itself not the explanatory notes clarify the phrase "consistent with the intention of the modifications". Discerning the intention of the law-maker is within the remit of the courts. That intention has to be discerned based on conventional canons of statutory interpretation. For statutory instruments made by ministers under the powers in the EU(W) Act, the government has committed to set out in the explanatory notes accompanying the delegated legislation "what is being changed or done and why".[638] The relevant minister must also make a statement explaining the purpose of the statutory instrument, the law before exit day which is relevant to it and the instrument's effect (if any) on retained EU law.[639] These statements should clarify the purpose of the modification and also give an indication as to whether its interpretation in accordance with retained case law is consistent with the modification's purpose.[640] In order to reduce legal uncertainty and costs, the explanatory notes of amending legislation should state expressly whether or not an interpretation in accordance with retained case law continues to be appropriate.

Section 6(3)–(6) EU(W) Act do not apply to the interpretation of the EU legal duty of conforming interpretation itself. That is because the interpretative obligation does not fall under the definition of "retained EU law"

---

[638] Department for Exiting the EU, European Union (Withdrawal) Bill: Memorandum concerning the delegated powers in the Bill for the Delegated Powers and Regulatory Reform Committee, para. 49, available online at https://publications.parliament.uk/pa/bills/cbill/2017-2019/0005/delegated%20powers%20memorandum%20for%20European%20Union%20(Withdrawal)%20Bill.pdf.
[639] Paragraph 28(6) of Schedule 7 to the EU(W) Act.
[640] Cf. *Hansard*, HL Deb 8 May 2018, vol 791 cols 123–124 (Baroness Goldie).

in s. 6(7). The EU legal duty of conforming interpretation is domesticated by s. 5(2), but the category of "retained EU law" does not refer to s. 5. It follows from s. 5(2) that the new legal duty of conforming interpretation has the same meaning as the EU legal duty of conforming interpretation as specified by CJEU jurisprudence prior to exit day. In contrast to s. 6(3)–(6), s. 6(1) applies to the new legal duty of conforming interpretation. Even though the heading of s. 6 reads "Interpretation of retained EU law", the wording of s. 6(1) is not limited to retained EU law, whereas the wording of s. 6(3)–(6) refers to retained EU law. A consequence of this reading of s. 6 is that the Supreme Court cannot decide to depart from the pre-exit meaning of the EU legal duty of conforming interpretation as laid down in CJEU case law by relying on s. 6(4)(a). Since s. 6(2) does also not apply to the principle of the supremacy of EU law and the new legal duty of conforming interpretation due to para. 5 of Schedule 1 to the 2018 Act, the meaning of both doctrines is fixed in time immediately before exit day. The meaning of both domesticated doctrines under s. 5(2) can only be changed by amending the EU(W) Act.

Admittedly, the interpretation of ss. 5 and 6 EU(W) Act adopted here in relation to directives, EU-derived domestic legislation and the new legal duty of conforming interpretation is not straightforward. The main purpose of the EU(W) Act is to ensure legal continuity. That means that the legislation that becomes EU-derived domestic legislation after exit day should be interpreted just as before exit day. That requires that, first, EU-derived domestic legislation must continue to be interpreted in conformity with EU directives, which the 2018 Act does not domesticate. Second, this conforming interpretation must continue to be governed by national canons of statutory interpretation. If there is agreement about this result, any purposive interpretation of ss. 5 and 6 that achieves this result will appear at least slightly contrived. The meaning of ss. 5 and 6 of the 2018 Act adopted here appears preferable to a contrived interpretation of s. 6(3) EU(W) Act according to which s. 6(3) covers the interpretation of EU-derived domestic legislation in conformity with EU directives. That is because the explanatory notes are clear about s. 5(2) incorporating the EU legal duty of conforming interpretation.

Overall, I have shown that the drafting of ss. 2–6 EU(W) Act is riddled with ambiguity and vagueness. A purposive interpretation of the Act is, however, capable of solving these riddles. It also achieves the general purpose of the Act to provide legal continuity after Brexit. The ECA significantly enhanced the institutional powers of the courts vis-à-vis the legislature, and the repeal of the ECA has the potential to significantly reduce these powers. That this potential will only slowly materialise is one of the key constitutional ramifications of the EU(W) Act. The courts' exceptional power to disapply Acts of Parliament will not end with exit day. The institutionally powerful role of the courts will reduce over time, however, because the power to disapply domestic legislation and to interpret legislation in conformity with directives only applies to law passed or made before exit day. With the passing of time, the distinctive features in the institutional relationship between the judiciary and the legislature established under the ECA and maintained in relation to pre-exit legislation under the EU(W) Act will become less and less relevant in legal practice. This should not deflect from the significant policy choices that the 2018 Act delegates to the judiciary. The Act puts important questions about the scope of the supremacy principle, the interpretation of (modified) retained EU law and the relevance of post-exit CJEU jurisprudence in the hands of domestic judges.

To conclude, conforming interpretation will retain an important role in statutory interpretation in English courts after Brexit. Hence, the key comparative findings of this chapter will continue to hold true after exit day for a comparison between (a) the EU legal duty of conforming interpretation as applied in German courts and (b) the new legal duty of conforming interpretation under s. 5(2) EU(W) Act as applied in English courts.

8.5. TRANSITION PERIOD

The previous discussion of the EU(W) Act does not take account of possible arrangements for a proposed transition period (implementation period) after the UK formally leaves the EU. The EU(W) Act is not designed with a transition period in mind. The Withdrawal Agreement in its current draft form[641] contains a transition period in its arts. 121–126.[642] The government intends to bring forward a separate European Union (Withdrawal Agreement) Bill, which will aim to implement the Withdrawal Agreement and thus to incorporate this transition period into UK law.[643] The forthcoming Bill will amend the EU(W) Act and the ECA in order to take account of the transition period.[644] It would be possible to set the term "exit day" in the EU(W) Act to 31 December 2020 or 1 January 2021

---

[641] Draft agreement on the withdrawal of the United Kingdom of Great Britain and Northern Ireland from the European Union and the European Atomic Energy Community, 19 March 2018. The draft withdrawal agreement is available online at https://www.gov.uk/government/publications/draft-withdrawal-agreement-19-march-2018.

[642] It is controversial whether a transition period can be settled as part of the Withdrawal Agreement concluded under art. 50(2) TEU. For discussion, see K. ARMSTRONG et al., Implementing transition: How would it work?, CELS/CPL Working Paper, October 2017, pp. 7–9, available online at http://www.ssrn.com; M. DOUGAN, An airbag for the crash test dummies? EU-UK negotiations for a post-withdrawal "status quo" transitional regime under Article 50 TEU, (2018) 55 *CMLR* 83–95; T. LOCK, Lost in transition?, Edinburgh School of Law Research Paper Series No. 2018/20, May 2018, pp. 1–2, available online at http://www.ssrn.com.

[643] White Paper, Legislating for the Withdrawal Agreement between the United Kingdom and the European Union, Cm 9674, July 2018, paras. 148–149.

[644] For discussion, see also ARMSTRONG et al., above n. 642, pp. 13–19.

by delegated legislation,[645] but the government does not intend to take this obvious path for political reasons. Instead, exit day will remain 29 March 2019 and the EU(W) Act will repeal the ECA on this day.[646] The European Union (Withdrawal Agreement) Bill will, however, include a transitional provision, in which the Bill will amend the EU(W) Act so that the effect of the ECA is saved for the time-limited transition period.[647] In other words, the (amended) ECA will remain legally effective during the transition period. The Bill will also ensure that the domestication of EU law by the EU(W) Act will only take place at the end of the transition period.[648]

According to art. 121 of the draft Withdrawal Agreement, the transition period will start on the day of entry into force of the Withdrawal Agreement and will end on 31 December 2020. The key provision is art. 122(1), which stipulates that "Union law shall be applicable to and in the United Kingdom during the transition period". Article 122(3) of the draft Agreement clarifies that Union law applicable to and in the UK during the transition period "shall produce in respect of and in the United Kingdom the same legal effects as those which it produces within the Union and its Member States and shall be interpreted and applied in accordance with the same methods and general principles as those applicable within the Union". Article 122(6) of the draft Agreement stipulates that any reference to Member States in the Union law applicable to and in the UK during the transition period shall be understood as including the UK. New EU law that becomes applicable during the transition period will also apply in the UK (cf. art. 123(7) draft Withdrawal Agreement). Moreover, the CJEU will have jurisdiction as provided for in the Treaties in relation to the UK during the transition period (art. 126 of the draft Agreement). In short, the UK will be legally obliged to continue applying the overwhelming majority[649] of EU law as if it were still a Member State under the terms of the current draft Withdrawal Agreement.

It follows from these provisions of the draft Withdrawal Agreement that, once they are given domestic legal effect through the European Union (Withdrawal Agreement) Act, the doctrine of the supremacy of EU law, the doctrine of direct effect and the EU legal duty of conforming interpretation will continue to apply in the UK during the transition period as if the UK were still a Member State of the EU.[650] Hence, the findings in this chapter will continue to apply during the transition period.

---

[645] Cf. s. 20(3), (4) EU(W) Act.
[646] White Paper, above n. 643, para. 60.
[647] Ibid.
[648] Ibid., para. 69.
[649] The draft Withdrawal Agreement also includes exceptions, i.e. provisions of EU law which will not be applicable to and in the UK during the transition period. These exceptions are immaterial for the purposes of this book.
[650] White Paper, above n. 643, paras. 56, 65.

CHAPTER 5
CONCLUSION

In this Chapter, I will first tie together key developments of conventional, rights-consistent and conforming judicial law-making in each jurisdiction and then draw comparative conclusions.

For German judicial practice, I have demonstrated in Chapters 2, 3 and 4 that the modern-day highest courts in Germany attach an increased weight to the intention of the enacting legislature in cases of judicial law-making, compared with case law in the second half of the 20th century. This change goes hand in hand with German courts giving an increased weight to the legislative history of a provision in recent times. It is unclear what has caused this change in judicial attitudes but one explanation seems to be a change in judicial mindset in contemporary judges in the BVerfG about the separation of powers between the legislature and the judiciary. This development certainly deviates from cases like *Soraya*. It also affects the outer limits of judicial law-making as it is mostly the weighing of the interpretative criteria in an individual case that ultimately determines whether or not these limits are exceeded. This development in newer German case law brings the interpretative powers of German judges closer to the powers of English judges recognised under conventional judicial law-making.

Time will tell whether these signs of a change in judicial attitudes indicate a return from the jurisprudence of values (*Wertungsjurisprudenz*), the predominant legal theory in Germany in the second half of the 20th century, back to the jurisprudence of interests (*Interessenjurisprudenz*), the predominant legal theory in Germany at the beginning of the 20th century. Both legal theories recognise that judicial law-making is a necessary and permissible function of the judge. They recognise that statutory interpretation contains not only formal legal reasoning, but also evaluative arguments and discretion. Both theories disagree about where the values that influence judicial decision-making ought to stem from. The theory of *Interessenjurisprudenz* is positivistic. It aims to restrict the evaluative scope available to the judge by binding the judge to the aims and interests of the enacting legislature.[1] *Wertungsjurisprudenz* creates

---

[1] For an introduction to this legal theory in Germany, see J. SCHRÖDER, Richter, Gesetz und juristische Methode in der Zweck- und Interessenjurisprudenz, *ZfPW* 2016, 307–318.

evaluative scope for the judge in order to enable the judge to take into account values that the enacting legislature did not contemplate when creating the statute or values that are external to the legislation at issue, such as values stemming from the German Basic Law.[2] *Wertungsjurisprudenz* thus decouples judicial decision-making more from the enacting legislature and the wording of the statute than does *Interessenjurisprudenz*. *Wertungsjurisprudenz* objectivises statutory interpretation to a higher degree. Despite scholarly attempts to create an objective value system that ought to inform judicial decision-making, scholarship in the 20th century has failed to create a consensus. It has failed to exert disciplining pressure on judicial law-making. If one agrees with the view that judicial attitudes in contemporary judges in the BVerfG have changed, one underlying reason for this change could be the failure of *Wertungsjurisprudenz*. *Wertungsjurisprudenz* creates evaluative scope for judges but it lacks structure, which is why it fails to provide a high level of predictability of judicial decision-making and legal certainty.[3] The rise of *Wertungsjurisprudenz* in the 20th century was also accelerated by an anti-positivistic attitude and a distrust of the legislature in German judicial practice and legal scholarship. The loss of faith in "statute" originated before the Second World War but was certainly accelerated by the injustices enacted by the legislature during the Nazi era.[4] Whether the signs indicating a change of judicial attitudes in the highest German courts also indicate that trust in the legislature has returned to the most senior German judges requires further analysis.

English statutory interpretation has seen a similar development towards an increased use of legislative history in statutory interpretation. This was motivated by the decision in *Pepper v. Hart* and the use of explanatory notes accompanying bills in Parliament since 1998. The increase in the weight given to legislative history in English and German courts is to be welcomed. It increases the level of legal certainty provided in statutory interpretation as it reduces judicial reliance on a "reasonable" legislature and on presumed legislative intent. The latter two concepts have been criticised in scholarship for leaving the determination of individual cases to judicial discretion. Despite this similarity to German case law, English law has seen an opposite trend away from adhering to the intention of the enacting parliament and towards a more objectivised understanding of legislative intent. This development has certainly occurred in the spheres of the EU legal duty

---

[2] For an introduction to this legal theory in Germany, see H.-P. HAFERKAMP, Richter, Gesetz und juristische Methode in der Wertungsjurisprudenz, *ZfPW* 2016, 319–334.

[3] K. RÖHL, Grundlagen der Methodenlehre II: Rechtspraxis, Auslegungsmethoden, Kontext des Rechts, in Enzyklopädie zur Rechtsphilosophie, February 2013, para. 46, available online at http://www.enzyklopaedie-rechtsphilosophie.net/neue-beitraege/19-beitraege/77-methodenlehre2#subsid. I have explored this failure of *Wertungsjurisprudenz* in relation to the argument based on justice in Chapter 3, Section 7.3.

[4] HAFERKAMP, above n. 2, pp. 322, 325.

of conforming interpretation and Convention-compatible interpretation.[5] There are early signs that this development may spill over into the sphere of conventional canons of construction as well. The key factor that drove this development was a weakening of the doctrine of parliamentary sovereignty. The way English judges have understood their interpretative role under s. 3(1) HRA has redefined the judicial role and has altered the balance of power between the judiciary and the legislature as traditionally understood. A distrust of the legislature is also one of the reasons underlying the development from literalism to purposivism in England according to S. Vogenauer.[6] Purposivism allows judges to take values into account when they argue with the reasonably presumed intention of Parliament. A return of trust in Parliament has certainly not occurred in the highest English courts. This is due to multiple factors such as (a) the rise of executive powers due to Henry VIII clauses in legislation, (b) the willingness of Parliament to restrict freedoms and human rights and (c) the ongoing controversy about the proper relationship between the rule of law and parliamentary sovereignty. These factors encourage judges to adopt a more objectivised understanding of legislative intention, which grants them more latitude when they decide what can reasonably be presumed to be the intention of Parliament.

Even though it is possible to discern contrasting trends in statutory interpretation in both jurisdictions, both trends appear to bring the outer limits of judicial law-making in England and Germany closer to one another. The picture that emerged in this book was, however, nuanced. I have established that different default positions exist in England and Germany when judges assess the permissibility of judicial law-making according to conventional canons of construction. The different default positions correspond with different judicial mentalities regarding judicial law-making in both countries. Judicial law-making under conventional canons of statutory interpretation is not fundamentally uniform in both jurisdictions, and judicial attitudes in English and German courts are not congruent. Even though the underlying reason for this incongruence relates back to differences in the constitutional framework in both jurisdictions, I have also demonstrated that this incongruence can to a considerable extent be explained by how judges understand and interpret the constitutional context. It was shown that the judges' understanding is to a considerable extent affected by tradition and historical context as opposed to precise and determinate constitutional requirements as such. Although there are a number of dynamic factors that affect patterns of judicial creativity in

---

[5] Claims by legal scholars that English courts have recently demonstrated a reluctance to use their wide powers under s. 3(1) HRA appear too early to assess and do not yet suggest a significant trend.

[6] S. VOGENAUER, *Die Auslegung von Gesetzen in England und auf dem Kontinent*, Mohr Siebeck, Tübingen 2001, pp. 1178–1197.

any specific period,[7] path dependence, historical factors and tradition can to a considerable degree explain the differences in judicial attitudes towards judicial law-making in both countries under conventional canons of construction. I have further shown in Chapter 2 that the indeterminate UK constitutional framework would allow a system of interpretation under which judicial law-making is generally a permissible function of an English judge. This would bring the English system much closer to the German model without any change in the doctrine of parliamentary sovereignty, but based on a (common law) evolution of statutory interpretation. It remains to be seen whether judicial law-making in English courts according to conventional canons of statutory interpretation heads in this direction. There are signs that the growing use of legislative history in courts and spillover effects from (a) interpreting EU legislation based on EU legal methods employed by the CJEU, (b) Convention-compatible judicial law-making and (c) conforming judicial law-making may indeed sway English judges to this end.

In contrast to conventional canons of construction, a comparison of the outer limits of rights-consistent judicial law-making in English and German courts and of conforming judicial law-making in both jurisdictions has unveiled a considerable congruence not only in the abstract expression of these limits, but also in their application in individual cases. English and German judges enjoy considerable powers of rights-consistent and conforming judicial law-making. The scope of these powers and the limits of the judicial role are fundamentally similar in both countries. Starting with *Pickstone*, English judges have changed their default position towards judicial law-making. They now accept that Convention-compatible and conforming judicial law-making is generally a permissible function of the judge. This change in default position is a key reason for the high level of congruence of the outer limits of rights-consistent and conforming judicial law-making in England and Germany. The extent to which the application of these limits is governed by formal legal reasoning, evaluative arguments and judicial discretion appears almost identical in both jurisdictions. This commonality is based on a common understanding of the constitutional function of the judge vis-à-vis the legislature. A distinctive mode of legal thinking in England and Germany could not be discerned for Chapters 3 and 4. Instead, judicial attitudes in both jurisdictions are converging and fundamentally similar. A fundamental unity of statutory interpretation therefore exists in English and German judicial practice in the sphere of rights-consistent and conforming judicial law-making.

The finding of a fundamental unity of statutory interpretation may surprise from a constitutional perspective, given the different constitutional settings in both jurisdictions that were presented in Chapter 1. If a legalist position

---

[7] J. BELL, *Judiciaries within Europe: a comparative review*, CUP, Cambridge 2006, pp. 372, 374, 382.

were adopted, different outer limits of interpretation should mirror the underlying constitutional differences. Yet, the legalist position is sustainable for two reasons. First, I have established that the constitutional settings have also converged. The UK constitutional framework has changed, mainly due to modifications in the orthodox doctrine of parliamentary sovereignty. This change has been triggered by both domestic influences, in particular the introduction of the HRA, and European influences. For example, the change in the default position for conforming judicial law-making was triggered by modifications to the doctrine of parliamentary sovereignty, which were themselves prompted by EU law requirements. The evolving UK constitutional framework brings UK constitutional law closer to the German constitutional framework. This is also a clear sign that developments in constitutional law can impact on the outer limits of statutory interpretation. Constitutional and international factors have affected English legal methodology. These factors have triggered changes in judicial attitudes towards judicial law-making and in the institutional relationship between the judiciary and the legislature. These factors can explain to a considerable extent the converging outer limits and techniques of rights-consistent and conforming judicial law-making in both jurisdictions. A. Young has argued that the UK constitution is becoming more judicialised and that abstract and deductive judicial reasoning from broad constitutional principles is growing in English courts.[8] This book's findings support her thesis The constitutional settings in both jurisdictions will continue to converge after Brexit. That is because the EU(W) Act intends to "transfer" the modifications of the orthodox doctrine of parliamentary sovereignty, which the supremacy of EU law entails, to the body of retained EU law after Brexit.

A second reason why the legalist position is sustainable is that English courts have exceeded their judicial powers and stepped outside their constitutional role. This is another reason for the high level of convergence in the sphere of rights-consistent and conforming judicial law-making in both jurisdictions. Even though English courts formally preserve the absolute doctrine of parliamentary sovereignty, they undermine the doctrine with tools of statutory interpretation, while avoiding openly declaring that they are refusing to apply a statute. This phenomenon has appeared in cases of Convention-compatible interpretation, of conforming interpretation and when judges apply the principle of legality. English courts have held that they have the power to depart from the intention of the enacting legislature even when they interpret legislation that post-dates the HRA or the ECA. This jurisprudence cannot be reconciled with the doctrine of parliamentary sovereignty. It was also argued that this jurisprudence undermines legal certainty.

---

[8] A. YOUNG, The constitutional implications of Brexit, (2017) 23 *European Public Law* 757, 780–785.

Why did these constitutional developments appear in the UK but not in Germany? One reason is that the powers of judicial law-making under conventional canons of construction are already quite extensive in Germany. A second reason is that the supremacy of EU law did not fundamentally alter the relationship between the judiciary and the legislature in Germany. German constitutional law does not endorse the doctrine of parliamentary sovereignty. Even though the supremacy of EU law also empowers judges in regular courts, the BVerfG already possessed the power to invalidate unconstitutional legislation. A third reason is the introduction of s. 3(1) HRA in England. This relates to a fourth reason, which is that constitutional change is easier in the UK. It is not subject to specific formal requirements as in Germany.[9] An English parliament can repeal a constitutional statute with a simple majority.

Compared to the significant changes in English legal methodology, the BVerfG applies the same methodological limits and techniques to all modes of judicial law-making. EU law has not caused a fundamental change of the methods of statutory interpretation or of the limits of the judicial function in Germany. One of the reasons for this is that the judicial law-making powers under conventional statutory interpretation are already extensive and highly malleable. These powers have proven flexible enough to accommodate the requirements of EU law and the German Basic Law. Despite scholarly criticism that German judges have exceeded the limits of their judicial function in the sphere of conforming judicial law-making and constitution-consistent judicial law-making, this has not happened. It does not follow from this finding that English judges apply a more powerful doctrine of rights-consistent or conforming judicial law-making than German judges. Like their English counterparts, German judges have stretched the highly adaptable outer limits and techniques of conforming and rights-consistent judicial law-making in individual cases. This entails an increase in judicial powers at the expense of the legislature. The extent of this shift of power in Germany is less than the shift of power that has occurred and is occurring in England.

It was argued in Chapter 1 that determinate interpretative limits and techniques are particularly important for judicial law-making for reasons of legal certainty and the separation of powers. I have also demonstrated in Chapters 3 and 4 that English and German judges share a very similar understanding of the value of legal certainty in rights-consistent and in conforming interpretation. They adopt the same balance between formal justice and material justice when expressing the outer limits of judicial law-making. It has been established throughout the book that the outer limits of judicial law-making are expressed in indeterminate terms in judgments in both jurisdictions. These limits can be

---

[9] Cf. art. 79(2) GG.

applied in a narrow or wide fashion. They leave sufficient room for evaluative arguments and judicial discretion. English and German judges possess a considerable amount of judicial discretion when applying the outer limits of rights-consistent and conforming judicial law-making in an individual case. This finding indicates that formal legal reasoning does not significantly guide the interpretative process in cases of judicial law-making when compared with other factors. Judicial attitudes matter, and these attitudes can and do change over time as they are affected by a multitude of dynamic factors.

Due to their indeterminate state, the outer limits of judicial law-making perform poorly in their functions to (a) restrict the scope of possible meanings of a provision, (b) limit judicial power and thus address separation of powers concerns, (c) reduce the area of evaluative arguments and extra-legal considerations in statutory interpretation and (d) provide legal certainty. This finding validates the core of the realist critique that judicial practice shows that the function of interpretative maxims to limit judicial power fails as these maxims are expressed in vague terms. The one exception to this assessment may be judicial law-making under conventional canons of interpretation in England. The reason for this is that the default position is that judicial law-making is generally impermissible and only available in exceptional cases, i.e. that the possible semantic meanings of the statutory words generally demarcate the outer limit of statutory interpretation. The level of legal certainty and predictability provided in the area of judicial law-making according to conventional canons of construction in England has historically outweighed the level of legal certainty provided when German courts engage in judicial law-making. This difference is diminishing, however, as there are considerable incentives for the English judiciary to alter the default position for conventional judicial law-making. Furthermore, I have also shown that the outer interpretative limits for correcting obvious drafting mistakes, updating construction and saving statutes from absurdity incorporate a considerable degree of judicial discretion.

It would be a mistake to conclude from this book that determinate outer limits of judicial law-making cannot be derived from constitutional doctrine or from constitutional statutes. The constitutional requirements limiting judicial law-making are vague in both jurisdictions. The statutory words "possible" in s. 3(1) HRA, "construed" in s. 2(4) ECA and "legislation and law" in art. 20(3) GG can accommodate multiple possible interpretations. These provisions do not set an exact border between permissible judicial law-making and impermissible judicial amendment of legislation. They delegate to the judiciary the task of working out a constitutionally appropriate division of labour between the courts and the legislature. These provisions leave the limits of judicial power in the hands of the empowered. At least in England and Germany, history shows that vague statutory provisions governing statutory interpretation and its limits have not led judges to adopt determinate outer limits and techniques of construction in the past. Vague statutes setting laws of interpretation have not had sufficient impact on how judges actually interpret statutes.[10] The realist critique is not inevitable, however. One way to improve the situation would be to codify the outer limits and techniques of statutory interpretation with a higher degree of exactitude.[11] For example, the evaluative scope left by art. 20(3) GG could be filled by the ordinary legislature in Germany, setting clearer maxims for permissible judicial interpretation and its outer limits and techniques. Since statute law is inherently more formal than case law,[12] this would achieve a higher level of legal certainty than a clearer expounding of the outer limits of judicial law-making in case law. Legislation governing the outer methodological limits of the judicial function could provide the following, for example: under no circumstances can a judge depart from the possible semantic meanings of the statutory words. Such a strict rule against the permissibility of judicial law-making would provide a much higher level of legal certainty than the current approach by English and German courts. Such a strict rule is, of course, unrealistic. Furthermore, it is certainly not disputed in this book that judicial law-making is a permissible and necessary function of the judge. The question is rather about the appropriate scope and the limits of judicial law-making. Another clear rule that would allow and at the same time constrain judicial law-making would be the following: under no circumstances can a judge depart from the intention of the enacting legislature. The hope that the legislature will set determinate outer limits of judicial law-making will probably remain a hope for the foreseeable future. An example is the EU(W) Act, which governs how English judges should interpret retained EU law in its s. 6. Section 6(2) is an example of an interpretation clause that is riddled with vagueness.[13] This section does not specify the methodological maxims or limits that apply to the interpretation of retained EU law. It leaves this decision to judges.

This failure of the English and German legislature to specify the outer limits and techniques of judicial law-making in legislation brings us back to these limits and techniques as expressed and applied in judicial practice. The development in contemporary German courts towards placing more emphasis on legislative

---

[10] A. BARAK, *Purposive interpretation in law*, Princeton University Press, Princeton 2005, p. 50; C. WENDEHORST, Methodennormen in kontinenataleuropäischen Kodifikationen, (2011) 75 *RabelsZ* 730, 732, 750–751.

[11] Cf. J.F. MANNING, Without the pretense of legislative intent, (2017) 130 *Harvard Law Review* 2397, 2432. It is controversial in legal scholarship whether a codification of legal methodology is desirable or possible. For an overview of the discussion, see WENDEHORST, above n. 10, pp. 732–734.

[12] P.S. ATIYAH and R.S. SUMMERS, *Form and substance in Anglo-American law*, Clarendon Press, Oxford 1987, pp. 96–98.

[13] Section 6(2) EU(W) Act: "Subject to this and subsections (3) to (6), a court or tribunal may have regard to anything done on or after exit day by the European Court, another EU entity or the EU so far as it is relevant to any matter before the court or tribunal".

materials and on the identifiable intention of the enacting legislature is a move in the right direction. This development also entails that legal certainty is increased and that a stricter separation of powers is adhered to in courts because the role of the legislature vis-à-vis the judiciary is strengthened. Legal certainty and the separation of powers are also the underlying reasons that call for determinate outer limits of judicial law-making. For that reason, the proposals made in this book to increase the level of determinacy of the outer interpretative limits of judicial law-making may fall on fertile ground, at least in German courts. I have explored two main pathways for making judicial reasoning more determinate and objective and for increasing the level of legal certainty provided in the area of judicial law-making. One way is to minimise the subjective element in statutory interpretation by increasing the level of specificity of the interpretative maxims and of the outer limits of judicial law-making. This can be done by including more formal elements in judicial reasoning. Formal elements reduce the area in which evaluative arguments can operate. Examples of such formal elements are priority rules and priority elements. Formal priority rules and elements are generally more determinate and more predictable than a weighing and balancing of conflicting arguments.[14] It was also argued that a formal understanding of the legislative deliberation limit under s. 3(1) HRA would insert an element of predictability and legal certainty: current legislative activity should signal that a policy choice falls inside the institutional competence of the legislature and involves issues calling for legislative deliberation. It was established that a formal, as opposed to a substantive, understanding of the outer limit of judicial law-making that a German court cannot reduce the scope of application of a provision to zero by means of a teleological reduction raises the level of legal certainty. Other formal rules of precedence could also be adopted. First, specifically expressed legislative intent should always prevail over presumed legislative intent.[15] Second, courts should prefer a purpose at a lower level of abstraction to a purpose at a higher level of abstraction and at a given level of abstraction, a specific purpose should prevail over a general purpose.[16]

A second way to minimise the subjective element in statutory interpretation is to control and structure evaluative arguments. This can be done by providing common benchmarks for permissible evaluative arguments. Judicial discretion

---

[14] R.S. SUMMERS, *Form and function in a legal system – a general study*, CUP, New York 2006, p. 265.

[15] In the sphere of the EU legal duty of conforming interpretation, however, the European presumption of compliance requires that a national court must give precedence to the presumed general intention of the legislature to fully implement the directive over a specific and inadvertently non-conforming purpose of a provision that is expressed in the legislative materials.

[16] I have argued for an exception to this formal rule of precedence in Chapter 4, Section 7.3.3, when a specifically expressed general intention to fully comply with an EU directive clashes with a specifically expressed legislative objective of a particular provision.

is constrained, and value pluralism is reduced. A controlling and structuring of the argument based on justice in the sphere of rights-consistent judicial law-making was proposed in Chapter 3 of this book. It was argued that justice can be constitutionalised exhaustively under the terms of the German Basic Law. An equivalent reasoning for English law would be to understand arguments based on justice in the sphere of Convention-compatible judicial law-making as exclusively governed by the HRA. What justice requires in an individual case must thus be derived exclusively from the terms of the HRA and Convention rights.

Looking into the future, the EU(W) Act envisages changes in constitutional law and a further fragmentation of statutory interpretation in the UK after Brexit. Despite these changes, my analysis of the EU(W) Act shows that the comparative findings for the EU legal duty of conforming interpretation as applied in English and German judicial practice will "survive" Brexit. Conforming interpretation and conforming judicial law-making will retain an important role in statutory interpretation in the UK because they will continue to apply after exit day to UK legislation enacted prior to exit day at least for as long as that legislation remains unmodified after exit day. After Brexit, considerable incentives will continue to exist for the English judiciary to adopt the default position that conventional judicial law-making is a generally permissible function of the court. First, there will be spillover effects from the new legal duty of conforming interpretation. These effects will be very similar to currently existing spillover effects created by the EU legal duty of conforming interpretation. Second, spillover effects from employing EU legal methods will not only remain but most likely increase. That is because s. 6(3) EU(W) Act requires English courts to use the EU methods of statutory interpretation when construing retained direct EU legislation and s. 4-retained EU law. One practical effect of s. 6(3) of the Act is that English courts are likely to employ maxims of statutory interpretation used by the CJEU more often after exit than before exit. It is an irony of Brexit that it has the potential to lead to a higher level of convergence between EU and English methods of statutory interpretation than before Brexit.

Lastly, the techniques and limits of judicial law-making are in a state of flux in England, and so is UK constitutional law. This state will continue after Brexit. In Germany, the powers of judicial law-making are not steady either. Judicial attitudes are changing. The question of whether and how far judicial law-making can depart from the intention of the enacting legislature is in a state of flux in German courts. I have also shown that the outer limits of conforming judicial law-making are unsettled in both jurisdictions. These are exciting times for scholars of legal methodology. In this book, I have argued in favour of less exciting, but more certain times.

INDEX

A

absurdity   59, 108, 114–115
argument by analogy   75–76, 115, 131–132, 166, 175–177
Auslegung   54–55, 68, 142

B

Bill of Rights   246–259
Brexit   9, 396–421, 427, 432

C

canons of construction, *see* interpretative criteria
civil law   10
common law   10, 105, 125, 248, 251, 254, 308
common law constitutionalism   111, 125, 203, 255–256, 301
conforming judicial law-making
   adaptable outer limits   392–393
   after Brexit   407–413
   aim   279–288
   analogy to rights-consistent judicial law-making   311–318
   default position   298, 382
   interpretative priority rule   318–319
   outer limits, *see* outer limits
   presumption of compliance   319–331, 388
   techniques   294, 332–347
   unsettled outer limits   374–380
constitution-consistent interpretation   139, 142–144, 179
   outer limits, *see* outer limits
constitutional review, *see* judicial review
constitutional statutes   5, 110–111, 203
contra legem limit   86, 99, 161, 163, 184–185, 277–278, 348, 388
Convention-compatible interpretation, *see* rights-consistent judicial law-making
conventional judicial law-making, *see* judicial law-making
convergence   7, 9, 108, 225, 245–246, 381–385, 390, 426–427, 432
copy-out legislation   323, 383
criminal legislation   44, 88, 115, 264, 396

D

declaration of incompatibility   144–148
delegated legislation   86, 119, 259, 305, 323–324, 359
direct effect   262–264, 267, 307, 312–313, 380
disapplication   268, 307, 312, 350–351, 362, 377–379, 419

double criterion   99–100, 183–184, 229, 352
drafting errors   115–119
drafting style of legislation   40, 67, 104, 108, 383, 410

E

EU-conforming judicial law-making, *see* conforming judicial law-making
Euro-friendliness   386, 388, 391
European legal duty of conforming interpretation
   after Brexit   397, 407–413
   contra legem limit   277–278, 295
   European methodological rules   270–277, 290
   functions   265–269
   hybrid legal instrument   271, 319
   interpretative priority rule   272
   presumption of compliance   272–275, 388
   principle of equivalence   269–270, 288, 291, 311, 320
   scope   261–265
European methodological rules, *see* European legal duty of conforming interpretation
Europeanisation from the inside   292–309, 314
evaluative arguments   30–32, 38–39, 60–61, 67, 75, 224, 236, 245, 373, 385–387, 390, 431
extra-legal arguments   32, 41, 102, 390

F

formal legal reasoning   30, 32–35, 40, 130, 235–242, 244–245, 431
   functions   34, 36
   increase   38, 127, 245, 431
fundamental feature limit, *see* outer limits
fundamental unity thesis   7–8, 129, 245, 383, 426

G

gap-filling   68–102, 106–107, 112–113, 119–121, 123, 165–166, 175, 332–343
   concept of gap   71
   covert gap   73
   criticism of concept of gap   173–175
   definition of gap   71, 92, 123
   open gap   72
   subsequent gap   73
Ghaidan   166–173, 177–178, 190, 197, 201, 203, 213, 216, 220, 229, 313–314

Index

I

implied repeal   5, 204, 364
indirect effect, *see* European legal duty of conforming interpretation
intention of the legislature, *see* legislative intention
Interessenjurisprudenz   423–424
interpretative criteria   54–68, 73, 90, 100, 108, 126
   adaptability   276, 331, 333, 346, 348
   weighing   54, 56–57, 61, 66, 161, 186, 231, 237

J

judicial attitudes   67, 106, 129, 133, 190, 199, 233, 236, 242, 253, 387–393, 423, 425–427, 429, 432
judicial deference   105, 107, 126, 137, 143, 157, 246
judicial discretion   33, 38–39, 84, 90, 102, 114, 117–118, 122, 124, 182, 212, 221, 224, 232–233, 242, 361, 373, 385–387, 424, 429
judicial function   53, 71, 86, 123, 129, 151, 225, 233
   limits   9, 41, 46, 89, 96, 104, 112, 125, 140, 187, 207, 224, 234, 340, 361, 368, 381, 385–387
judicial law-making
   conforming, *see* conforming judicial law-making
   default position   118, 127, 129–130, 135–136, 251–252
   definition   1, 41
   determinate limits and techniques   40
   extra legem   78–86
   outer limits, *see* outer limits
   praeter legem   72–78
   rights-consistent, *see* rights-consistent judicial law-making
judicial power   9, 39, 41, 71, 81, 83, 86, 102, 112, 170, 175, 194, 306, 419, 427, 429
judicial reasoning, *see* legal reasoning
judicial review   94–97, 105, 141, 147, 223, 226–227
justice   31–32, 36–40, 57, 70–71, 84–85, 98, 135–136, 238–246
   formal   36, 113, 134–135, 222, 242, 428
   material   37, 113, 134–135, 222, 242, 428

L

legal certainty   35–37, 39–41, 62, 100, 107, 127, 130, 133–135, 236, 242–245, 252, 256, 319, 352, 389, 393–396, 424, 428, 430
legal culture   7, 10, 40, 259, 331, 390
legal methodology   28–41, 91, 94
legal realism   28–41, 244, 429–430
legal reasoning
   style   11, 34, 130, 245–246
   transparency   126–127, 181, 239

legislation and law (art. 20(3) GG)   6, 31–32, 69, 74, 83, 87, 124, 137, 226, 334, 429–430
legislative history   57, 63–67, 97, 136, 164, 187, 274, 423–424
legislative intention   50–55, 68, 99, 101–102, 151, 197
   departure from   74, 124, 129, 162, 180, 197, 203–208, 211, 230, 246, 253, 279, 285, 308, 331, 359–360, 367, 427
   enacting legislature   51, 57–58, 67, 74, 78, 80, 100–101, 104, 122, 124, 132, 136, 210, 215, 225, 335, 357, 391
   objectivised   51, 53, 57–59, 125, 161–162, 178, 192, 246, 340, 350, 360, 424–425
   reasonable legislature   50, 59, 81, 100, 161, 180, 253, 337
literal rule   59, 62, 67, 103–106, 109, 116, 133–134

O

outer limits   39, 71, 79, 82, 86–87, 90, 92–94, 112, 117, 123, 129, 133–134, 145
   conforming judicial law-making   294, 347–396
   constitution-consistent interpretation   179–188
   definition   1
   express terms limit   194, 363–364
   functions   39, 41, 102, 236, 244, 393, 429
   fundamental feature limit   87, 90, 208–213, 216, 228, 372–374
   (in)determinacy   41, 85, 90, 108, 211, 213, 222, 233, 236, 243, 377, 382, 428–429
   legislative deliberation limit   216–223, 232, 339, 371
   policy considerations   82–84, 93, 232, 354–355
   relevance   28–41
   rights-consistent judicial law-making   179–246
   scheme of the legislation   98, 213–216, 228, 373
   statutory language   18, 184, 189–197, 230–231, 255, 368–372

P

parliamentary sovereignty   4, 103–107, 110, 112, 124–125, 131–133, 150, 153, 170, 235, 252, 360, 362, 368, 425
   Diceyan orthodoxy   111, 132, 170, 205, 254, 362–364
   evolution   206, 366–367, 406
   limits   111, 256
   modifications   203–208, 305, 307, 365–367, 403, 406, 427
partnership model   74, 199, 253
path dependence   133, 426
Pickstone   295–310, 317, 323, 344, 368, 384, 391
policy arguments, *see* evaluative arguments

policy choice   30, 109, 126–127, 182, 213, 216–223, 232–233, 355, 370–371
predictability   35–37, 38, 62, 127, 134–136, 394, 424
preliminary reference procedure   341
presumptions   58–59, 251
   against implicit alteration of the common law   31, 105
   of compatibility with international law   65, 155, 322
principle of legality   110, 151, 207, 248–256
purposive approach   60, 62, 64, 102, 106–109, 117, 133, 135, 276, 289, 296–302, 383, 414

Q

Quelle II   45, 292–293, 332–339, 349–350, 353, 379

R

reading in, out or down   102–125, 128–129, 131–132, 168–169, 172, 176, 250–251, 343–345, 379
Rechtsfortbildung   54–55, 68, 72, 142
Rechtsstaatsprinzip   35
retained EU law   398–401, 413–420
rights-consistent judicial law-making
   aim   151–154
   default position   170, 189, 236
   interpretative priority   158–159
   outer limits, *see* outer limits

presumption of compliance   159–165, 184, 202
techniques   165–179
rule of law   35, 37–40, 62, 66, 89, 132, 135, 236, 252–256

S

separation of powers   6, 40–41, 86, 96, 102, 104, 129, 135, 236, 278, 301, 395, 431
Soraya   79–86, 101, 126, 137, 180, 230, 350
spillover effects   136, 307, 426, 432
statutory language   40, 53–54, 62, 98, 109, 132, 134, 162, 170, 184
   unambiguous   98, 162, 190, 192, 368
strained interpretation   102, 145–148, 148, 190
supremacy of EU law   306–307, 361–362, 364, 367, 384, 427–428
   under the EU(W) Act   401–411

T

teleological extension   76
teleological reduction   75, 87, 131–132, 165, 176, 179, 229, 352
tradition   133, 176, 425–426
transition period   420–421

U

updating interpretation   119–125

W

Wertungsjurisprudenz   423–424

ABOUT THE AUTHOR

Martin Brenncke is Lecturer in Law at Aston Law School. Before joining Aston, he was Erich Brost Career Development Fellow in German and European Union Law at the University of Oxford and Lecturer in Commercial and Business Law at the University of Zurich, Switzerland. He has lived, studied and taught law in three countries (Germany, Switzerland and England), leading to a profound interest in how the law is interpreted and applied in different jurisdictions.

Lightning Source UK Ltd.
Milton Keynes UK
UKHW030614131118
332219UK00001B/1/P